ERNST KRENEK

Ernst Krenek. Photo by Alex Schlee.

ERNST KRENEK

A Bio-Bibliography

Compiled by Garrett H. Bowles

Bio-Bibliographies in Music, Number 22
Donald L. Hixon, Series Adviser

Greenwood Press
New York • Westport, Connecticut • London

Library of Congress Cataloging-in-Publication Data

Bowles, Garrett H., 1938-
  Ernst Krenek : a bio-bibliography / compiled by Garrett H. Bowles.
    p. cm. — (Bio-bibliographies in music, ISSN 0742-6968 ; no.
22)
  Bibliography: p.
  Includes index.
  ISBN 0-313-25250-5 (lib. bdg. : alk. paper)
  1. Krenek, Ernst, 1900-   —Bibliography. I. Title. II. Series.
ML134.K79B7 1989
780'.92'4—dc19   89-1883

British Library Cataloguing in Publication Data is available.

Library of Congress Catalog Card Number: 89-1883
ISBN: 0-313-25250-5
ISSN: 0742-6968

First published in 1989

Greenwood Press, Inc.
88 Post Road West, Westport, Connecticut 06881

Printed in the United States of America

The paper used in this book complies with the
Permanent Paper Standard issued by the National
Information Standards Organization (Z39.48-1984).

10 9 8 7 6 5 4 3 2 1

To Margaret, John, and Megan
for their forbearance.

Contents

Preface

Like many aspiring composers, I first encountered the work of Ernst Krenek through his textbook *Studies in counterpoint based on the twelve-tone technique*. In subsequent years I met his music many times, but each piece that I heard failed to conform to the image of his music which I had formed in my mind. The problem of grasping the character of Krenek's music finally came to a head when I accepted the position of Music Librarian at the San Diego campus of the University of California, where my responsibilites included the Ernst Krenek Archive. For my own benefit, I began to compile a list of compositions and of writings by the composer. The initial list has grown to become this book, which I hope will clarify for others the relationships among Krenek's prodigious musical and literary work.

This book is divided into four chapters: a biography, a list of compositions, a bibliography of Krenek's writings, and a bibliography of writings about the composer.

The biography highlights the major events of Krenek's life in the context of his musical and literary works. It is intended only as an outline. The "Writings" and "Bibliography" chapters contain references to many articles and books which discuss specific aspects of his life in detail. In addition, John L. Stewart is completing a definitive biography soon to be published by the University of California Press.

The comprehensive catalog of musical compositions is organized according to Krenek's own opus numbers in generally chronological order. An additional 105 compositions without opus numbers are included at the end of the chapter listed in chronological order. No thematic incipits are necessary because the identity of Krenek's works is clear. All information appears under the entry for a composition; publication, manuscript, recording, and performance data are gathered together under the entry. The title of each composition is given as Krenek first named it, followed in many instances with a translated title assigned by the composer. An abbreviation for publisher follows the title (see the "List of Publishers" at the end of this "Preface"), and the duration of the work is also noted. Instrumentation is given, including cast lists for the operas, and, where appropriate, the author of the text. Instrumentation for orchestral forces is given in a manner similar to the scheme used in *The Fleisher Library Catalog* (see "Instrumentation" below). The titles of specific movements are given, and in the case of vocal works, the first line of the text is also given along with English translations. The date of composition is specified with as much precision as possible in a paragraph labeled "Composed"; if only one date appears, it is usually the date the composition was finished. In some instances, the date range indicates both when the composition was begun and finished. In other instances, the date range only indicates the times the earliest and latest movement of the work were completed. To help clarify the date of composition, date and place of composition are noted by movement when available. Commissions and dedications are noted. Manuscripts are briefly described and their locations are noted by RISM siglum (see the "List of Libraries"). Complete or partial compositions published in collections or by other than the primary publisher are specified under the heading "Publication"; facsimiles are also noted under this heading. Most of Krenek's works have been performed many times; in the interest of space, only the first American and first European performances are detailed. Performances of revisions are also noted. The final element of the entry for a composition consists of discographic information about commercial recordings.

All references to compositions mentioned in the "Writings" and "Bibliography" chapters are cited in the entry for the appropriate composition. General information about a composition and reviews of its publication are cited following the title. References to performances follow the citation to the appropriate performance, and references to recordings follow the citation to the recording.

The "Writings" chapter is a comprehensive bibliography of the writings by Krenek, including both manuscript and published writings. It is arranged in chronological order according to date of writing. In those instances in which the date of writing is unavailable, the first ascertainable date is used; that date may be the date of a lecture or a publication date. Because many of Krenek's writings appear as portions of books, the bibliography format for books closely approximates the format used for journal articles. As much publication information as possible is given; the title is transcribed exactly as it appears on the manuscript or in the publication. As far as possible, volume and issue number, date, and pagination are given. Many of Krenek's articles have been reprinted; all known reprints and translations are included as sub-headings under the entry for the original article. I have constructed annotations for each entry after examining the publication or manuscript, and annotations for articles in English often include quotations. Annotations of articles in a language other than English are generally paraphrases; if there is a quotation, it was usually derived from a reprint in English translation. Manuscripts are briefly described and their locations are noted using RISM siglum.

"Bibliography," the fourth and final chapter, is a selective bibliography of writings about Krenek. It is arranged in alphabetic order by author, and multiple entries by an author are subarranged by date. With this scheme, the reader can follow a critic's evolving viewpoint on Krenek in a logical fashion. Authors whose names are represented by initials or abbreviations are filed under the first letter in direct order (e.g., o.st.; O.v.P.; etc.). Generally, I have tried to include reviews which appeared in close chronological and geographic proximity to a performance, excluding those further removed in time and space. As I compiled this bibliography I sometimes mused that the audiences of some of Krenek's concerts must have consisted entirely of reviewers because there are so many reviews for some concerts. Reviews in newspapers are most useful in documenting a performance; for concerts which occured in Europe before World War II, one can expect to find reviews in many of the major and minor papers. I have excluded reviews which do not refer to one of the performances given in the list of compositions. One other selective criterion was applied to reviews; those which I found in clipping files without significant bibliographic information were generally excluded.

Two appendices and a general index complete this volume. Appendix A, "Compositions : Titles and Genera," is an alphabetic listing of Krenek's musical compositions. All titles, translated titles, titles of movements, excluding those consisting solely of a tempo indication, and first lines are included. A genera classification to the compositions is also included. Appendix B, "Writings : Titles," is an alphabetic listing of the essays and books by Krenek, including the variant titles of reprints and translations. The "General Index" is an alphabetic listing of all names and subjects in the "Compositions," "Writings," and "Bibliography" chapters. All performers, performing organizations, individuals to whom a composition is dedicated, commissioners, joint authors, and others mentioned throughout these chapters are included in the index. Only the primary authors in the "Bibliography" chapter are excluded.

Sources

The largest collection of sources for the "Composition" chapter of this book are the collections of Krenek's music manuscripts on deposit from his first publisher Universal Edition at the Wiener Stadt- und Landesbibliothek and in the Oesterreichische Nationalbibliothek, additional music manuscripts owned by the Wiener Stadt- und Landesbibliothek, manuscripts owned by the publisher Bärenreiter Verlag, manuscripts in the Music Division of the Library of Congress in Washington, DC, manuscripts in the Hanns Moldenhauer Collection in the Harry Elkins Widener Library at Harvard University, and manuscripts in the possession of the composer. An important group of manuscripts consisting mostly of juvenalia turned up in the Gesellschaft der Musikfreund in Wien. Manuscripts housed in other libraries were also consulted and are listed.

Most performances listed in this book are documented with reviews, and many are also documented by programs which can be found in the two Ernst Krenek Archives at the Wiener Stadt- und Landesbibliothek and the Central University Library, University of California, San Diego, and in the composer's possession. The primary sources for discographic information included in the "Compositions" chapter are the *Rigler & Deutsch index of pre-LP commercial discs held by the Associated Audio Archives (AAA), The World's encyclpoaedia of recorded music* by Francis F. Clough and G. J. Cuming, and the Music Collection Department, Central University Library, University of California, San Diego. In addition, I received significant assistance from the noted discographer, J. F. Weber.

The primary sources for the "Writings" chapter of this book are the collections of Krenek's literary manuscripts spanning the period up to his emigration to America held by the Wiener Stadt- und Landesbibliothek in Vienna and his manuscripts covering the period following his emigration to America in the Ernst Krenek Archive at the University of California, San Diego.

The primary sources for the "Bibliography" chapter, in addition to the standard music periodical indexes and the extensive German bibliography index *Internationale Bibliographie der Zeitschriftenliteratur aus alles Gebieten des Wissens*, are the periodical indexes on cards at the Library of Congress and the index created by the WPA and now housed in the Music Library at Northwestern University. In addition, the clipping files kept by Krenek's major publishers, Universal Edition and Bärenreiter Verlag, the Ernst Krenek Archives at the Wiener Stadt- und Landesbibliothek and the University of California, San Diego, the New York Public Library, the Boston Public Library, the San Francisco Public Library, and by the composer, were invaluable resources.

While this bio-bibliography documents the significant accomplishments of Ernst Krenek, there are still many gaps in the information. First performances have been especially difficult to adequately document, and there must be many music and literary manuscripts which I have not found. I would appreciate any information which supplements or corrects that presented here; please send it to me at the Music Collection Department, Central University Library, University of California, San Diego, La Jolla, CA 92093.

Acknowledgements

The creation of a bibliography requires the assistance of many people. I owe a deep debt of gratitude to Ernst Krenek and his wife, Gladys Nordenstrom, for their continued enthusiasm and assistance throughout the compilation of this book. Without their help, I could not have finished this work. I also must thank Dr. John Stewart and Dr. Will Ogdon, University of California, San Diego; Dr. Claudia Mauer Zenck, Bornheim, Germany; and J. F. Weber, Utica, New York for their assistance in looking over working drafts and freely giving me many helpful comments. I also owe thanks to Michael Staehle, who helped me extensively with the finer points of translating German to English. This book would not have been possible without substantial support from the University of California, San Diego, the administrative assistance of Dorothy Gregor, University Librarian and Cecil Lytle, Chair, Department of Music, the financial assistance of two grants from the Librarians Association of the University of California San Diego, and the computing environment provided by the Center for Music Experiment.

In addition to the staff of the many libraries cited in this book, I especially want to thank Mary Ashe, Art and Music Department, San Francisco Public Library; Dr. Wolfgang Biba, Bibliothek, Gesellschaft der

Musikfreunde in Wien, Vienna; Robert C. Delvin, Illinois Wesleyan University, Bloomington, Illinois; Dr. Mary Kay Duggan and Ruth Tucker, University of California, Berkeley; Elizabeth A. Falsey, Houghton Library, Harvard University; Steven Fry and Marsha Berman, University of California, Los Angeles; Gerald Gibson and Samuel Brylawski, Motion Picture, Broadcasting, and Recorded Sound Division, Library of Congress; Louise Goldberg, Sibley Music Library, Eastman School of Music; Dr. Elena Hift, Universal Edition A.G., Vienna; Dr. Ernst Hilmar, Musiksammlung, Vienna, Wiener Stadt- und Landesbibliothek; Dr. Rosemary Hilmar, Musiksammlung, Oesterreichische Nationalbibliothek, Vienna; Dr. Harry Joelson-Strihbach, Stadtbibliothek, Winterthur, Switzerland; Kären Nagy and Elisabeth Rebman, Music Library, Stanford University; Dr. Michael Ochs, Music Librarian, Harvard University; John Newsome and Geraldine Ostrove, Music Division, Library of Congress; Barbara and Martin Silver, University of California, Santa Barbara. Dr. Amelie Sztatecsny, ORF Historical Archive, Vienna; and Dr. Wolfgang Timaeus, Bärenteiter Verlag, Kassel.

Instrumentation

Names of individual instruments and voices are written out fully in English; however, the instrumentation specification for groups is coded. Voices in a chorus are represented by:

S	Soprano
Mz	Mezzosoprano
A	Alto
T	Tenor
Bar	Baritone
B	Bass

The instruments of the orchestra are divided into groups in score order: *woodwinds; brass; plucked, keyboard and percussion instruments; and strings.* The groups of instruments are separated by slashes; numbers indicate the number of players needed for performance. The order of instruments for the *Woodwinds* is flute, oboe, clarinet, and bassoon. The order of instruments for the *Brasses* is horn, trumpet, trombone, and tuba. The names of plucked and keyboard instruments are fully spelled out and separated by slashes; percussion instruments are not specified beyond the general designation "percussion." The term "strings" means the normal orchestral complement of Violin I, Violin II, Viola, Cello, and Double bass. 2.2.2.2 / 1.1.1.0 / banjo / mandolin / percussion / strings.

List of Libraries

Austria

A-Sfest	Salzburg, Festspiele
A-Wn	Vienna, Oesterreichische Nationalbibliothek
A-Wgm	Vienna, Gesellschaft der Musikfreunde in Wien
A-Wst	Vienna, Wiener Stadt- und Landesbibliothek, Musiksammlung

Switzerland

| CH-B | Basle, Paul Sacher Stiftung |

CH-W   Winterthur, Stadtbibliothek, Rychenberg-Stiftung

West Germany

D-brd Erdman Estate   Estate of Eduard Erdmann
D-brd-Bhm   Berlin, Staatliche Hochschule für Musik und
                        Darstellende Kunst
D-brd-BNba   Bonn, Wissenschaftliches Beethovenarchiv
D-brd-DSim   Darmstadt, Internationales Musikinstitut,
                        Informationszentrum fur Zeitgenössische Musik
D-brd-Fassman   Frankfurt am Main, Assmann Verlag
D-brd-Kbärenreiter   Kassel, Bärenreiter Verlag
D-brd-KNwdr   Cologne, Westdeutscher Rundfunk

United States

US composer   Palm Springs, CA, Composer's collection
US-AUS   Austin, University of Texas, Humanities Research
                        Center
US-CA   Cambridge, MA, Harvard University, Harry
                        Elkins Widener Library
US-LJ   La Jolla, CA, University of California, San Diego,
                        Central University Library
US-PHf   Philadelphia, PA, Free Library of Philadelphia,
                        Edwin A. Fleischer Music Collection
US-R   Rochester, NY, Sibley Library, Eastman School of
                        Music
US-Wc   Washington, DC, Library of Congress

List of Publishers

AM   Los Angeles, CA, Affiliated Musicians
AMP   New York, NY, Associated Music Publishers
Ars Nova   San Diego, CA, Ars Nova
Assman   Frankfurt am Main, West Germany, Assmann
                        Verlag
BA   Kassel, West Germany, Bärenreiter Verlag
Belwin   Melville, NY, Belwin Mills
Bomart   Hillsdale, NY, Boelke-Bomart
Broude   New York, NY, Broude Brothers
Doblinger   Vienna, Austria, Verlag Doblinger
Elkan-Vogel   Philadelphia, PA, Elkan-Vogel
Gray   New York, NY, H. W. Gray
Hansen   Copenhagen, Denmark, Wilhelm Hansen
Marks   New York, NY, E. B. Marks
Mercury   New York, NY, Mercury Music Company
Mobart   Hillsdale, NY, Mobart Music Publications
Pagani   New York, NY, O. Pagani & Brothers Inc.
Rongwen   New York, NY, Rongwen Music
Schirmer   New York, NY, G. Schirmer
Schott   Mainz, West Germany, B. Schott's Söhne
Southern   New York, NY, Southern Music Publishing Co.
UE   Vienna, Austria, Universal Edition

ERNST KRENEK

Biography

Ernst Krenek is a complex composer and writer who has lived through a turbulent time during which musical styles and political entities have radically changed. Krenek's creative life, consequently, has reflected the turmoil of the times in which he has lived. As a composer, his musical style has changed from the post-impressionism of his teacher Franz Schreker, to a dissonant, motoric style influenced by Béla Bartók, to neo-classicism, to Schubertian neo-romanticism, to a dissonant style based upon the twelve tone technique in which he has employed integrated serialist and electronic mediums. His present style of composition incorporates elements of serialism in free twelve-tone technique. But even within this progression of styles, Krenek has alternated from strict adherence to a style to a more relaxed use of it. These changes of style have often confused the listener, and he has recognized the problem himself. "Looking back over the evolution of my musical style, I am not astonished that even benevolent observers became confused and vacillating in their faith. Whenever they thought I had comfortably settled down in some stylistic district, I was not at the expected place the next time, and the business of classifying had to start all over again... I have been striving for an ever-freer and more incisive articulation of musical thought."[1]

Krenek is not only a prolific composer, but he is an even more prolific writer musing about music in society, music's construction and aesthetics, and about society in general. He has written extensive series of essays in *Anbruch*, *Dreiundzwangzig*, *Frankfurter Zeitung*, *Wiener Zeitung*, and *Forum*. He has also written most of his own song and opera texts, and he has even written a short story, "The overcoat of Anton K."[2] Although Krenek spent his

---

[1] Krenek, "The composer speaks." (K514) Note, "K" and "B" numbers refer to the Bibliography of writings by and writings about Krenek where full bibliographic information can be found.

[2] K468, published in the *New Mexico Quarterly*.

early years in Vienna and returned there from 1928 to 1938, during which time he was an active Austrian nationalist, the major part of his life has been lived in the United States where Krenek became an American citizen in 1945.

Youth

Krenek was born in Vienna on August 23, 1900, to Emannuela Čížek and Ernst Křenek.[3] His parents, of predominately Austrian stock from Czechoslovakia, were born in Časlav, a small town south of Prague, his father in 1866 and his mother in 1880. His maternal grandfather was the town's postmaster. His father was an officer in the Quartermaster Corps of the Austro-Hungarian army stationed in Vienna, and his mother came from a military family.[4]

His early years included attendance at the Institut der Christlichen Schulbrüder beginning in 1906, the same year he began piano studies with Brother Wilfried.[5] His interest in music was encouraged by his mother, and during these early years he wrote short piano pieces. Some, dating from 1907, have been preserved in his mother's hand in the collection of the Vienna Gesellschaft der Musikfreund. In 1911, he matriculated at the Gymnasium Wien-Währing, and he began private music lessons in 1915 with Fridolin Balluff which included playing four-hand arrangements of Mahler symphonies and taking composition lessons.

In 1916, when Krenek began to take composition seriously, he entered the Wiener Musikakademie. Thus began six years of studies with Franz Schreker, a successful and popular composer of lushly romantic operas who, during Krenek's first year of study, emphasized the study of counterpoint.[6] In 1918, Krenek's music studies were minimally interrupted by service in the army; he was first posted to the "Kaserne von Kaiser-Ebersdorf," and later to the Arsenal. At this time, he encountered the *Lineare Kontrapunkt* of Ernst Kurth which "turned my entire musical orientation inside out. I was fascinated by the notion that music was not just a vague symbolization of *Gefuehl* instinctively conjured up into pleasant sounding matter, but a precisely planned reflection of an autonomous system of streams of energy materialized in carefully controlled tonal patterns."[7]

The first documented public performance of a composition by Krenek occurred on May 14, 1918 at the Vienna Staatsakademie für Musik und Darstellende Kunst when his life-long friend, the pianist and composer, Felix Petyrek played the *Doppelfuge* op.1a. After Krenek's separation from the army following the end of the First World War, he entered the Wiener Universität to study philosophy for two terms. During his army service and

---

[3] The family name was originally spelled with a haček over the "r" in the Czech style and was pronounced "Kschrenek." After Krenek's emigration to America, he dropped the haček; I have omitted it from his name throughout this book.

[4] Schöny, "Ernst Kreneks Vorfahren." (B1166)

[5] Saathen, "Im Endlichen nach allen Seiten," (B1121), 322-323.

[6] See the exercises written in 1917 (W33 -- W39) which led to *Doppelfuge* op.1a.

[7] Krenek, "A composer's influences." (K799)

his attendance at the University, he continued his weekly lessons with Schreker. In 1920, Schreker accepted a new teaching position at the Staatliche Hochschule für Musik und Darstellende Kunst in Berlin, and as a result of the financial sacrifices of his parents, Krenek was able to follow him.

Berlin during the years immediately following the First World War was in artistic ferment and economic chaos. During these early years in Berlin, Krenek met Ferruccio Busoni, a rival of Schreker and proponent of neo-classicism, the conductor Hermann Scherchen, the pianist and composer Eduard Erdmann, the pianist and composer Artur Schnabel,[8] and others. These friendships provided him with stimulation and encouragement throughout his career. Schreker's popularity during this period considerably reduced the time he was able to spend with his students; as a result, Krenek independently began to develop his own style.

Atonal Style

As a result of the various influences he experienced in Berlin, Krenek's compositional aesthetic, exemplified in his music through opus five, swerved away from Schreker's tonally extended style to free atonality. In early 1921, and with the encouragement of others (not Schreker), Krenek wrote and had performed his first substantial compositions. The *First string quartet* op.6, performed in June 1921 at the prestigious Deutsches Tonkünstlerfest in Nürnberg, and the *First symphony* op.7, performed in March 1922 by the Berlin Philharmonic under the direction of Hermann Scherchen, created sensations because of their stark dissonances and vigorous rhythms influenced by Bartók. The characteristics of this style are rhythmic uniformity and polyphonic technique in a dissonant chromatic idiom.

Notoriety brought him to the attention of Emil Hertzka, the enterprising general manager of Universal Edition, who was building the catalog by contracting new young composers. Universal Edition remained Krenek's sole publisher starting with the *First piano sonata* op.2, which was published in 1921, and continuing until the advent of the Second World War. Until his success in 1927, the advance on royalties from Universal Edition provided him a modest income amounting to a subsidy.[9]

In February 1922, Krenek met Anna Mahler, the painter daughter of Alma and Gustav Mahler, and they soon began living together. During that summer, Ernst and Anna stayed with the pianist Eduard Erdmann and his wife Irene, first in Neverstoff, then during August and September at the Mahler summer home in Breitenstein. This was a remarkably productive June and July, for Krenek completed the orchestration of his massive *Second symphony* op.12, composed the *Toccata und Chaconne über Ja ich glaub an Jesum Christum* op.13 and *Eine kleine suite von Stücken über den selbigen Choral* op.13a,[10] and began work on his first extended vocal work with orchestra,

---

[8] Krenek, "From a composer, reminiscing about Artur Schnabel." (K857)

[9] Heinsheimer, "Giselda is a bad girl." (B509)

[10] Krenek dedicated *Toccata und Chaconne über den Choral Ja ich glaub an Jesum Christum* op.13, *Eine kleine Suite von Stücken über denselbigen Choral*, verschiedenen

Die Zwingburg (The Tyrant's Castle) op.14, a scenic cantata on a text by his friend Fritz Demuth, which was edited by Franz Werfel. During August and September, he composed the five songs of his op.15 *Lieder*, and began the *Third symphony* op.16. His comic opera, *Der Sprung über den Schatten* (The leap over the shadow) op.17 to his own text was written in early 1923 and integrated jazz elements into his atonal style. The theme of both these works, and of all his operas, is centered around the idea of freedom and responsibility.[11] The theme of the opera *Orpheus and Eurydike* op.21, composed between April and July 1923 to a text by Oskar Kokoschka, is also concerned with sexual jealousy. The performance of his *Second symphony* op.12, dedicated to Anna Mahler, in June 1923 at the Allgemeines Deutsches Tonkünstlefest in Kassel, was received with widely mixed reactions. When Krenek heard it for the second time at its first American performance twenty years later, he described the work as "a terrific elemental force raging against stifling confinement."[12]

Through the encouragement of Hermann Scherchen, Krenek received a grant from the Swiss businessman Werner Reinhart at Christmas 1923 which enabled him to live in Winterthur, near Zürich, Switzerland for two years. Not only did Reinhart's grant allow Krenek to compose music without financial worries, but it provided him an opportunity to meet Friedrich T. Gubler, who later became chief editor of the "Feuilleton" section of the *Frankfurter Zeitung*, the poet Rainer Marie Rilke, and the composer and theorist Ernst Georg Wolff.[13] Each of these men was important to Krenek in his later life.[14] In January 1924, Krenek and Anna Mahler were married, only to become divorced by the end of the year.

Neo-Classic Style

At the end of 1924, Krenek traveled to Paris where he was so impressed by the neo-classical French musical style of Stravinsky and "Les Six" that he altered his own musical style. The "move was touched off by the exhilarating experience of Igor Stravinsky's *Pulcinella* and by my contacts with the seemingly carefree, unspeculative, straightforward music of my French contemporaries."[15] He immediately abandoned his Bartókian atonal style for a neo-classical style in which he composed the *Second concerto grosso* op.25 and the *Concertino for flute, violin, harpsichord and orchestra* op.27. "I decided that the tenets which I had followed so far in writing

---

Charakters op.13a, and *Zwei Lieder* op.13b which he composed during June 1922 in Neverstoff, to the Erdmanns. See "Erinnerungen an einen Freund" (K818) for more information about Krenek's relationshipt with the Erdmanns.

[11] Krenek, "Freiheit und Rechtfertigung." (K595)

[12] Krenek, "On meaning in music" (K588) and "Self-analysis" (K569-a), 12.

[13] See Krenek's reviews of Wolff's theories in "Beiträge zu Fragen der Musikästhetik" (K374) and "Neue Beiträge zur Musikästhetik." (K382) Wolff's theories were incorporated in Krenek's "Grundideen einer neuen Musikästhetik." (K403)

[14] Sulzer, *Zehn Komponisten um Werner Reinhart*, Vol.1. (B1323) and "Ernst Krenek in Winterthur, eine langjährige Freundschaft" (B1324), and Krenek, "Der Komponist Ernst Krenek erinnert sich" (K899) discuss his Winterthur years.

[15] Krenek, "A composer's influences" (K799)

'modern' music were totally wrong. Music, according to my new philosophy, had to fit the well-defined demands of the community for which it was written; it had to be useful, entertaining, practical."[16] In 1928, he married the well-known actress Berta Haas. In early June 1925, Paul Bekker, the Frankfurt music critic who had written one of the few positive reviews of *Sprung über den Schatten* op.17 and who had just assumed directorship of the Opera house in Kassel, invited Krenek to be his assistant at the conclusion of his grant in the Fall. Krenek's duties during the two years he spent in Kassel included writing program notes, appearing on the radio, providing incidental music for plays, and conducting. In November 1926, his opera *Orpheus und Eurydike* op.21 was produced by Bekker.

Neo-Romantic Style

As a result of his duties and because the Kassel Opera was one of the most technically modern houses, Krenek became thoroughly immersed in opera production. Between February and June of 1926, he wrote the first work in his new neo-romantic style, the opera *Jonny spielt auf* op.45. This new style developed as a result of Krenek's growing interest in the music of Franz Schubert to which he had been introduced several years earlier by Eduard Erdmann. At this time, Krenek's first significant essays appeared, reflecting his strong interest in opera.[17]

Jonny spielt auf op.45 received its premiere at the Leipzig Opera in January 1927 and was an immediate success. During its first season, it was produced in three houses for twenty-six performances; during the 1927/28 season it was produced in forty-five German opera houses for 421 performances. Its success was short-lived, however, for during the 1930/31 season it was only performed in two German opera houses for four performances and dropped out of the repertoire thereafter.[18] Though it was translated into many languages and presented all over the world, it was not always successfully received; performances in 1928 in Paris and at the Metropolitan Opera in New York in 1929, for example, were not successful. The theme of *Jonny spielt auf* continued Krenek's concept of freedom; the black Jonny represented the world of jazz and America, symbols which "stood for the fullness of life, optimistic affirmation, freedom from futile speculation, and devotion to the happiness of the moment." In contrast, the composer Max represented "the self-conscious, brooding, introspective, Central European intellectual."[19] The novel combination of jazz with a neo-romantic style, the inclusion of telephone, radio, and train as symbols of modern life, and the use of the most up-to-date theatrical effects captured

---

[16] Krenek, "Self-analysis" (K569-a), 14.

[17] "Zum Problem der Oper" (K9), "Musik in der Gegenwart" (K12), "Ein Ideologe über das Theater" (K32), "Ueber Ziel und Zweck des Theaters" (K36), and "'Materialbestimmtheit' der Oper." (K45)

[18] Wilhelm Altman "Opernstatistik 1926/27," *Anbruch* 9 (Dec.1927): 424-431. W. Altman "Opernstatistik 1927/28," *Anbruch* 10 (Nov/Dec.1928): 429-434. W. Altman "Opernstatistik von August 1930 bis Juli 1932," *Zeitschrift für Musik* 98 (1931): 948-968.

[19] Krenek, "Self-analysis" (K569-a), 16.

the German public and made the opera successful. In the Fall of 1927, Bekker and Krenek moved to the Wiesbaden Opera House where they continued their roles as director and assistant.

In the period 1926 to 1928, Krenek composed almost fifteen works in his neo-romantic style, many of which, when combined with the success of *Jonny spielt auf*, made him financially secure. During 1926 and 1927, Krenek composed three one-act operas *Der Diktator* (The dictator) op.49, *Das geheime Königreich* (The secret kingdom) op.50, and *Schwergewicht* (Heavyweight) op.55; these were successfully produced by Bekker in Wiesbaden on May 6th, 1928. For the next two seasons, the three one-act operas were often performed in Germany.

With the advent of financial security in 1928, he returned to Vienna, where he was able to devote himself to the creation of his musical and literary works. The move to Vienna, however, was more a retreat from active musical life than a direct confrontation with it; Vienna during this century has been an artistically conservative city, and it did not provide Krenek with many opportunities. Most of the music he wrote during this period received its first performance outside Vienna. The neo-romantic style of *Jonny spielt auf* continued with the opera *Leben des Orest* (The life of Orestes) op.60 (written between August 1928 and May 1929) which was produced in Leipzig on January 19th, 1930. The nationalistic song cycle influenced by Schubert, *Reisebuch aus den österreichischen Alpen* (Journey through the Austrian Alps) op.62, was composed almost a song a day between July 5th and 26th, 1929; he continued his exploration of tonality in the song cycles *Fiedellieder* (Fiddle songs) op.64 (February 5-6, 1930) and *Durch die Nacht* (Through the night) op.67 (Dec.31, 1930 to January 19, 1931). The three sets of songs also received their first performances outside Vienna; the first in Leipzig and the others in Dresden.

Krenek became seriously interested at this time in writing, first with articles about music in *Anbruch* (volumes 11 through 19, 1929-37), and then, starting in 1930, for the newspaper *Frankfurter Zeitung*. With Alban Berg, Rudolf Ploderer, and Willi Reich, Krenek founded the music journal 23 in 1932, and wrote for it until 1937. The title of the periodical referred to the number of the Austrian press law which provided for the correction of inaccurate information, and the policy of the magazine was to comment on and to correct reviews of contemporary music in Vienna.[20] During the 1934/35 season, Krenek presented a series of five concerts of new music to fill the void caused by the suspension of concerts by the Internationale Gesellschaft für Neue Musik (International Society for Contemporary Music.) He intended the concerts to present a balanced view of new music, and they were not dominated by any one group.[21] He was active in the Austrian chapter of the International Society for Contemporary Music, often serving as a delegate to the international festivals. In 1933, he was also elected chairman of the Austrian Association of Playwrights and Stage Composers (Genossernschaft dramatischer Schriftsteller und Komponisten.)[22]

---

[20] The editorial aims were laid out in the first issue in "Rechtfertigung." (K164)

[21] Krenek, "Zeitgenössische Musik im österreichischen Studio." (K272)

[22] His inaugural address appears in "Die Bedeutung unserer Genossenschaft."

As a young student in Vienna, Krenek had read the writings of the poet and satirist Karl Kraus with admiration, and Krenek at that time composed four songs to Kraus's texts.[23] Soon after Krenek's return to Vienna, he met Kraus and was admitted into his circle. Krenek has expressed his strong admiration of the poet, stating that "I have remained fascinated by the unique independence of his spirit and the intransigence of his ethical convictions."[24] In 1930 and 1931, Krenek composed two sets of songs to Kraus texts: *Durch die nacht* op.67, a set of seven songs, and *Die Nachtigall* op.68. These songs strongly influenced Krenek's own texts to the cycle *Gesänge des späten Jahres* (Songs of the late years) op.71 (composed from September 29th to December 27th, 1931). For the first time, Krenek experimented with using harmonic clusters of twelve-notes, an experiment which led him to adopt the twelve-tone technique.

Twelve-tone Technique

By this time, Krenek felt that he had thoroughly explored the resources of tonality. Through his friendship with the writer Karl Kraus, whom Krenek says "exercised the strongest influence upon me"[25] by providing a moral framework within which he could develop an independent aesthetic, he became more and more interested in twelve-tone music and experimented with it. Although he was a good friend to Alban Berg and Anton Webern at this time, he never discussed the twelve-tone technique with them; instead, he learned about it through studying their works. "Liberation of [my] thought from harmonic conventions and rhythmic patterns, and preparation of a new, genuinely polyphonic way of thinking which makes full and conscious use of the tremendous experience of tonality" became guiding factors.[26] In addition, his taking up the twelve-tone technique can also be seen as the "adoption of the musical technique that the tyrants hated most of all [and] may be interpreted as an expression of protest."[27] As the result of a commission by Clemens Krauss, the director of the Vienna Opera, Krenek began work on his twelve-tone opera, *Karl V* op.73, which he completed in May 1933. The commission was considered by Krenek to be long-overdue recognition by his home-land, and his choice of the Renaissance emperor and first king of Austria seemed to insure the opera's success in Vienna. However, the strongly Austrian nationalistic, Catholic, anti-Nazi subject matter which dealt with the conflict of free will versus determined circumstances resulted in the cancellation of the premiere by Clemens Krauss after rehearsals had already begun. This opera, which is undeniably Krenek's masterpiece, received only one performance before the onset of the Second World War when it was premiered in Prague in 1938; it was not performed in Vienna until 1984, fifty years following the cancellation of its premiere. Krenek was placed on a list

(K259)

[23] *Vor dem Schlafe* (W53), *Die Büsserin* (W63), and *Zwei Lieder* op.13b.
[24] Krenek, "Self-analysis" (K569-a), 11.
[25] Krenek, "Self-analysis" (K569-a), 22.
[26] Krenek, "The composer speaks" (K514)
[27] Krenek, "A composer's influences" (K799)

of degenerates when the Nazis assumed power in Germany in March 1933, and as a result he stopped writing for the *Frankfurter Zeitung* and became a regular free contributer to the *Wiener Zeitung* until his emigration to America in 1938.

During the ensuing years until his emigration, Krenek continued to compose with the twelve-tone technique; he considers the *Sixth string quartet* op.78 and the *Twelve variations for piano* op.79 to be his most important works. During this time, however, most of his energies were concentrated on his literary career. From October 23 through December 18, 1936, Krenek gave a series of lectures in Vienna which were published in 1937 under the title *Ueber neue Musik*; in 1939 the collection was translated into English and substantially re-written as *Music here and now*. In these lectures, Krenek propounded his view that a musical aesthetic must be general enough to encompass tonality and atonality; the musical idea is the basis of music and from its transformation and relationships emerges tonality and/or atonality. When combined, these musical thoughts become the form of a composition which in turn provides its outline. This aesthetic was derived from concepts presented by the theorist Ernst Georg Wolff and the philosopher Julius Bahle which Krenek had been considering for some time.[28] He has restated these views many times: "The creative process is essentially one of selection and elimination, no matter to what extent its different phases are conscious and possibly protracted labor, or quick, seemingly inspired decisions. The criteria applied in the selective processes are inner logic and originality."[29]

In late 1936, the Salzburg International Opera Guild asked him to prepare an arrangement of Monteverdi's *L'incoronazione di Poppea* which they presented in September 1937 and then, with Krenek, took on tour to America. While Krenek occasionally conducted the between-acts music, he was free to roam America, where he gave lectures and recitals of his music, and his reports to the *Wiener Zeitung* reflect those experiences. Aware of the worsening political climate in Europe and the need to augment his financial resources, he wrote in the Spring of 1937 his *Second piano concerto* op.81 as a solo vehicle for himself. In the Spring of 1938, Krenek was in Amsterdam to premiere the concerto with the Concertgebouw Orchestra under the direction of Bruno Walter when the Nazis annexed Austria; Krenek knew that he could not return to Vienna. He immediately began to seek the necessary papers to emigrate to America, and while waiting traveled to London, Brussels, Zurich, and Scandinavia, where he lectured and gave concerts.[30] His travels included a disappointing trip to Prague for the premiere of his opera *Karl V.* op.73, for he was informed when he arrived that the premiere had been postponed a week, and his itinerary prohibited his attending.

---

[28] Krenek discusses Bahle's philosophies in "Zur Psychologie des musikalischen Schaffens" (K300) and "*Der musikalische Schaffensprozess*" (K383).

[29] Krenek, "The role of inspiration in music" (K513)

[30] See Zenck, *Ernst Krenek, ein Komponist im Exil* (B1502) pp.107-110 for a detailed listing of his travels during this time.

Emigration to America

Krenek's arrival in America began a very different kind of existence for him; he had arrived at a time when many American musicians were becoming hostile to the seemingly innumerable European musicians who were taking jobs away from them and his options for supporting himself were very sparse. The only jobs available to him were in teaching, so he set about finding himself an appropriate position. By the end of 1938, Krenek was employed at the Malkin Conservatory in Boston, where Schoenberg had taught five years earlier upon his emigration to America.[31] In December 1938, Krenek composed *Twelve short piano pieces written in the twelve-tone technique* op.83; he premiered them in a National Broadcasting Company radio performance on January 3, 1939, just two weeks after completing the composition. During the first half of 1939, Krenek traveled around the United States giving lecture recitals; during the summer he taught at the University of Michigan; and in the Fall he began teaching at Vassar College. In 1940, his *Studies in counterpoint based on the twelve-tone technique*, a text book on the use of the twelve-tone technique, was published. As a consequence of his studies of early music, which he began as a result of his teaching experiences and the opportunities presented by the Vassar College library, Krenek began work in November 1941 on a composition for a cappella chorus based upon the Latin text of the Tenebrae services of Holy Week, *Lamentatio Jeremiae prophetae* op.93.[32] This difficult work was begun as an experiment to explore the manipulation of the twelve-tone row through the rotation of hexachordal scalar segments,[33] and was not completed until May 1942. Although excerpts were performed in 1943 at Hamline University in St. Paul, the *Lamentations* did not receive a complete performance until 1958. Krenek used the principles developed in this work in several other compositions written in the early nineteen forties, culminating in the *Seventh string quartet* op.96. He continued to experiment with the potentials of the twelve-tone technique, even writing compositions outside it. The *Trio for violin, clarinet, and piano* op.108 is an example of this experimentation; the movement written in the twelve-tone technique is very melodic sounding, while the freely written movement sounds dry and strongly chromatic.

In 1942, he was appointed head of the Music Department and Dean of the School of Fine Arts at Hamline University in St.Paul, Minnesota. As a result of his interest in musicological matters, and specifically in the music of Josquin des Prez and Johannes Ockeghem, he gathered together the papers of several of his graduate students and published them in the two volumes of *Hamline studies in musicology*, which he edited. During his years at Hamline University and after, he enjoyed the friendship of the Minneapolis Symphony Orchestra conductor Dimitri Mitropoulos, who participated in the premieres of several works, and commissioned the

---

[31] His "Teaching composition in America: reminiscences" (K868) covers his teaching experiences in America.

[32] His "*Lamentatio Jeremiae prophetae*" (K774) discusses this work in detail.

[33] His "New developments of the twelve-tone technique" (K520) includes a discussion of his experiments.

Fourth symphony op.113. He, Mitropoulos, and Louis Krasnar organized the local chapter of the International Society for Contemporary Music (ISCM) under whose auspices they presented a distinguished series of performances of new music for several years.[34]

Krenek's fascination with the railroad goes back to his childhood; he often composed during train trips and one of the major symbols in *Jonny spielt auf* was a locomotive. During the early nineteen forties, this fascination expressed itself in two important vocal works, *The Ballad of the railroads* op.98 and *Santa Fe timetable* op.102. Krenek wrote the text to his song cycle *The Ballad of the railroads* between March and May 1944 and completed the composition while on a train trip from Colorado to Hollywood in July and August. His a cappella choral work, *Santa Fe timetable*, was composed early in 1945 to a text consisting of the names which appeared in the Atcheson, Topeka, and Santa Fe railroad's timetable.

In the Spring and Summer of 1947, he was a guest lecturer at the University of New Mexico. Complaining about the cold weather in the Midwest, he moved to Los Angeles, where he received several commissions for chamber works within the next few years resulting in sonatas for solo piano, solo violin, and for viola and piano, as well as two string trios. In 1948, his autobiography was published in German under the title *Selbstdarstellung* (K569); it was translated into English and up-dated as "Self-analysis" (K569-a) in 1953. In 1949, Krenek wrote a brief history of American music published in German under the title *Musik im Goldenen Westen*, taught returning American soldiers under government support at the Southern California School of Art and Music,[35] briefly accepted a teaching position at the Chicago Musical College, and divorced his second wife.

In 1950, he settled permanently in the Los Angeles area, married his student from Hamline University days, the composer Gladys Nordenstrom, and resumed contacts with Europe after an absence of thirteen years. While he had continued to write twelve-tone music and had explored methods of extending its technique, he believed that the artistic isolation he felt in America hampered his growth as a composer. Ever since his first trip to America, Krenek had expressed the belief that American opera needed to utilize the restricted resources that were available.[36] He had written the chamber opera *Tarquin* op.90 to an English text by Emmet Lavery as a result of this view in 1940; during the fifties he composed two more chamber operas to his own English texts, *Dark waters* op.125, presented by the University of Southern California opera workshop in 1952, and *The bell tower* op.153, presented at the University of Illinois in 1953.

Krenek received many commissions and composed prolifically during the fifties. His return to Europe in 1950, the first performance since the

---

[34] Bailey, "The influence of Ernst Krenek on the musical culture of the Twin Cities" (B61) contains a detailed accounting of the St. Paul years.

[35] For a description of his experiences see "Komponist im Exil." (K703)

[36] For Krenek's view of an appropriate opera style see his "Plea for modern opera: A way out of the stagnation of present times" (K486), "New opera style" (K508), and "Where to begin? Operatic production or produce." (K516)

premiere of his opera *Karl V.* in Essen, which was well received, and his participation in the Summer Schools for New Music at Darmstadt excited him and encouraged him. He wrote sixty works between opus 120 in 1950 and opus 159 in 1956 including concertos for piano, violin, harp, cello, violin and piano, and two pianos. In addition to the two chamber operas, he composed the three-act opera *Pallas Athene weint* (Pallas Athene weeps) op.144 to his own German text. The opera's subject could be termed a parable on democracy, and the opera was considered the high point of the festival celebrating the opening of the new Hamburg State Opera in 1955.

Krenek's literary career continued to flourish during the fifties. In 1952, Krenek deposited the memoirs (K609) of his life before emigrating to America, on which he had been writing since 1942, in the Library of Congress to be sealed until fifteen years after his death.[37] In 1953, he published the book *Johannes Ockeghem*, the culmination of his studies on the renaissance composer's life and works. In 1955, Vienna recognized him with the Preis der Stadt Wien (City of Vienna Prize). In addition, the Ernst Krenek Archive was established at the Wiener Stadt- und Landesbibliothek, containing his papers covering the years up to his emigration to America.[38]

Integrated Serialism

Krenek's experiments with row rotation in the 1940s, his studies of Ockeghem and medieval contrapuntal technique, and his work with electronic music, led him to adopt the integrated serial technique in 1956 at a time when most of its early practitioners had moved on to other styles of composition.[39] Integrated serialism results from applying the same twelve-tone operation techniques used on pitch to all other elements of music, including dynamics and rhythm. In 1956, he moved to Tujunga, a suburb of Los Angeles; published the book *De rebus prius factis*, an examination of the connections between medieval contrapuntal and modern serial techniques and electronic music; and composed his first electronic work, *Spiritus intelligentiae, Sanctus* op.152 at the studios of Cologne Radio. A commission by the Fromm Foundation in 1957 resulted in the composition of *Sestina* op.161 for soprano and instrumental ensemble, his most significant serial composition, which was based upon the rotations found in the poetic sestina form. Reflecting his life-long interest in counterpoint, he published his two text-books in 1958 and 1959, *Tonal counterpoint in the style of the 18th century* and *Modal counterpoint in the style of the 16th century*. 1958 was also the year in which *Zur Sprache gebracht*, a collection of his essays, appeared. The next year he published *Gedanken unterwegs*, a collection of travel essays, most of which he had written for the *Frankfurter Zeitung* and the *Wiener Zeitung*. The fifties concluded with the strict serial works *Quaestio temporis* (A question of time) for orchestra op.170,[40] which was commissioned by the

---

[37] See his "On writing my memoirs." (K605)

[38] Hilmar, "Krenek-Bestände in Wien" (B549) and Hilmar, "Eine Ernst Krenek Ausstellung im Historischen Museum der Stadt Wien." (B551)

[39] See his "Vom Verfall des Einfalls." (K719)

[40] See Krenek's description of this work in "*Quaestio temporis*." (K742)

Fromm Foundation, and *Flötenstück neunphasig* (Flute piece in nine phases) op.171;[41] both works received their premieres in 1960. In a lecture given to a meeting of the Los Angeles chapter of the American Musicology Society in 1960, Krenek characterized the serial procedure by noting that "the more parameters are regulated by serial premeditation, the less predictable is the result in all its details. Thus the element of improvisation is built into the process of strict prearrangement, and the unexpected occurs by necessity."[42]

Honors

Krenek received many honors in recognition of his sixtieth year, including Ausserordentliches Mitglied des Akademie der Künste Berlin (Extraordinary membership in the Berlin Academy of Art), Goldenes Ehrenzeichnen der Stadt Wien (Gold Medal of the City of Vienna), and Grosses Silbernes Ehrenzeichnen für Verdienste um die Republik Oesterreich (Great Silver Medal for Service to the Austrian Republic). He also was elected to membership in the National Institute of Arts and Letters, and received an Honorary doctorate from the University of New Mexico. He received many other honors during the sixties including the Grosser Oesterreichischer Staatspreis (Grand Austrian State Prize) in 1963, the Grosses Verdienstkreuz der Bundesrepublik Deutschland (Grand Medallion of Merit, German Federal Republic) in 1965, the Hamburger Bachpreis in 1966, and the Music Prize from Brandeis University in 1969. In addition, many festivals were held in his honor in Europe and America including Raleigh, North Carolina (1963); Minneapolis and St. Paul, Minnesota (1965 and 1975); and, starting in 1969 and continuing almost annually, the "Steirischer Herbst," in Graz, Austria. Krenek also served as visiting professor at Brandeis University in 1965, the Peabody Institute in 1967, and the University of Hawaii in 1967.

Later Style

Krenek's prodigious composing and writing continued in the sixties, and though many of the works of this period use serial processes, he gradually relaxed his style. This gradual relaxation is clearly evident in the seven orchestral works from the sixties; *From three make seven* op.177, composed in 1960, is strongly influenced by procedures of integrated serialism while *Fivefold enfoldment* op.205, written in 1968, is more loosely constructed. This period saw his continued interest in electronic music with the composition of the *San Fernando sequence* op.185, *Quintona* op.190, *Doppelt beflüfeltes Band* (Tape and double) op.207, and the inclusion of electronic music in many other works. Continuing his interest in opera plots from mythology, *Der goldene Bock* (The golden ram) op.186 received its premiere during the International Congress of Contemporary Music in the Fall of 1964 in Hamburg, where his comic opera *Sardakai* op.206 later

---

[41] Opus 171 was the last composition to be fully composed using integrated serialism; henceforth, he used selected elements of serialism. See his "Ueber eigene Werke." (K793)

[42] Krenek "Serial music." (K735)

received its premiere in 1970. Krenek's interest in alternative forms of staging opera also resulted in two operas written specifically for television: *Ausgerechnet und verspielt* op.179, whose plot revolves around the relationship of chance, represented by the roulette table, and determinism, represented by the computer, and *Zauberspiegel* (The magic mirror) op.192.[43] In addition, Krenek composed two pieces of incidental music for plays presented at the Salzburg Festival; *Jedermann* op.176, which was re-worked as op.178 to accompany the film of the same name, and *König Oedipus* op.188.[44]

His writings during the sixties exhibit the wide range of his interests; "Extents and limits of serial technique," written in 1960, defended serial procedures while "Tradition in perspective," written in 1962, discusses the composer's dilemma in being presented with two very divergent compositional styles. In 1965, a collection of his writings including stories, librettos, and song texts, was published under the title *Prosa, Dramen, Verse*. In 1966, he moved to Palm Springs, and in the same year a collection of his essays in English was published as *Exploring music*. Krenek was awarded an appointment as Honorary Fellow of John Muir College at the University of California, San Diego, where *Exercises of a late hour* op.200 for orchestra, which was commissioned by the University, received its first performance in January 1968.

Krenek continued to receive many honors during the seventies, including the Ehrenring der Stadt Wien (Ring of Honor, City of Vienna) in 1970 and the Ehrenzeichen für Kunst und Wissenschaft der Republik Oesterreich (Honorary citation for arts and science, Republic of Austria) in 1975. Festivals were held at the California State University, Northridge in 1974 and at the University of California at Santa Barbara in 1979. In 1977, he was awarded an honorary doctorate from the Philadelphia Musical Academy.

The seventies began with Krenek's appointment as Regent's Lecturer at the San Diego campus of the University of California where he gave a series of four lectures reflecting upon his music and his life; the lectures were published in 1974 as *Horizons circled*. In 1974, his collected correspondence with Theodor W. Adorno, whom he had known since 1924 when they had met during rehearsals of *Sprung über den Schatten* op.17, was published under the title *Briefwechsel*; it also included reprints of the essays the two had written about each other. 1974 also saw the publication under the title *Das musikdramatische Werk* of the first of a projected three volume collection of all the texts Krenek had written for musical works; the second volume was published in 1977 and the third remains unpublished. In January 1978, Krenek established an "American" Archive to complement the one in Vienna when he deposited his post-emigration correspondence and writings at the University of California, San Diego.[45]

---

[43] Krenek views television as a very favorable medium for opera because camera techniques add new dimensions and clarify the drama. However, there is an added problem of synchronization between audio and video. See his "Persönliches zur Oper." (K902)

[44] See Krenek's "Musik im Schauspiel" (K812) for a discussion of the several works which he wrote to accompany plays.

[45] "Krenek Archiv in USA eroeffnet" (B703) and Arthur, "Krenek assists at UCSD

Krenek's music during the seventies continued to reflect his wide interests and it appeared in a wide variety of forms. In 1971, Krenek was commissioned by the oboist Heinz Holliger to compose a work for his wife and himself; the result was *Kitharaulos* op.213 for oboe and harp solo with ensemble. Reflecting his continuing interest in conceiving ensemble music in terms of electronic music, Krenek arranged the work for oboe and harp with electronic tape accompaniment as *Aulokitharos* op.213a. In 1972, Krenek wrote a television play, *Flaschenpost vom Paradies* (Bottled message from paradise) op.217, which was produced by the Oesterreichischer Rundfunk in 1974. Although he wrote in many diverse forms, for example *Dream sequence* op.224 for band and *Acco-music* op.225 for accordion, the 1970s are best characterized as a period of vocal music. His sacred music is represented by the *Messe "Gib uns den Frieden"* op.208 which was premiered in Hamburg in 1971. His most important vocal works during this period, however, are *Spätlese* (Late harvest) op.218 and *The Dissembler* op.229. Both were written for baritone to his own autobiographical texts, and are important not only for their music but also for their candid texts.

Krenek has continued to work through the 1980s: to compose important music, to write, and to lecture. Commissions from around the world have stimulated him to compose an *Eighth string quartet* op.232, *Concertos* for organ (op.235) and cello (op.236), and *Streichtrio in zwölf Stationen* op.237. The *Arc of life* op.234 for chamber orchestra, composed in a loose twelve-tone style with serial elements, amply demonstrates his musical fecundity. In 1988, he completed *Opus sine nomine* op.238, a large oratorio using Latin texts from Genesis combined with his own German text, on which he had worked throughout the decade. His literary writings have continued major themes: composing opera, music of the Second Viennese School, and explanations of his own works. In 1982, Krenek was awarded Ehrenbürgerschaft der Stadt Wien (Honorary citizenship, City of Vienna) and as a result, his European *pied à terre* became the house in which Arnold Schoenberg had lived in the 1920s in the Vienna suburb of Mölding. In 1984, another collection of essays was published; *Im Zweifelsfalle* included his writing about the possibilities of opera, reflections about composers, discussions on the rules of music, and reflections on the place of music in society. In 1985, the University of California at San Diego honored him with a festival during which twenty-two small compositions were offered by composer friends, students, and admirers from throughout the United States.[46]

As of this writing (1988), Krenek is at work on new commissions, and he recently completed an extensive three-part lecture on the vocal music of Schubert which was broadcast by the Westdeutscher Rundfunk in Cologne. He remains very active, returning to Europe each summer to attend festivals and performances of his music.

concert" (B45)
[46] "A Krenek Festschrift" (B707) and Pasler, "Ernst Krenek - In retrospect" (B964)

Compositions

Compositions are listed in chronological order in two sections. The first section is organized by the opus number assigned by the composer. The second section is a listing of compositions lacking opus numbers, and each entry is assigned a number preceded with the letter "W." Entries for each composition also include relevant discographic information. *"See"* references identify citations in the "Bibliography" sections; "K" for writings by Krenek and "B" for writings about him. The instrumentation of a given work follows the customary pattern of listing woodwinds first, followed by brasses, percussion and other instruments, and strings. Other abbreviations are explained in the Preface.

1a. *Doppelfuge* = *Double fugue.* (unpublished; dur: 3 min.)
   For piano.
   Composed: August 23 - September 1917.
   Dedication: Felix Petyrek.

   Manuscripts: **A-Wst:** MH 10289/c. 7 p. **A-Wst:** MH 10368/c. 5 p.

   Premiere: May 14, 1918, Vienna, Staatsakademie für Musik und Darstellende Kunst; Felix Petyrek, piano.

   Other Performances: B1330

   Published (Facsimile p.1): In *Ernst Krenek, eine Studie,* von Lothar Knessl. Oesterreichische Komponisten des 20. Jahrhunderts, 12. (Wien: Elisabeth Lafite, 1967): 22.

1b. *Tanzstudie.* (UE; dur: 1 min.)
   For piano.
   Composed: December 17, 1920.
   Dedication: Frau Malla Kochmann in Berlin.

   Manuscripts: **A-Wn:** L1 UE 664. 4 p.

   Published: In *Grotesken-Album,* edited by Carl Seelig. U.E. 6567. (Vienna: Universal Edition, 1922): 20.

2. *Sonata, piano, no.1, E-flat major.* (UE) *See:* B588, B1322, K803
   Composed: May 23 - July 7, 1919.

1: *Allegro moderato* (May 23 - June 26, 1919) **2:** *Adagio* (June 23 - July 7, 1919) **3:** *Rondo* (May 23, 1919)

Manuscripts: **A-Wn:** L1 UE 813. 36 p. **A-Wst:** MH 10290/c. 32 p.

Premiere: May 3, 1920, Salzburg; Felix Petyrek, piano.

Publications: B319

3. **Sonata, violin & piano, F-sharp minor.** (unpublished)
   Composed: 1919 - August 23, 1920.

   Manuscripts: **A-Wgm.** Assorted sketches & fair copies. **D-brd-Bhm.** Violin part. **D-brd-Bhm.** Non-autograph.

   Premiere: June 21, 1921, Berlin, Staatliche Akademische Hochschule für Musik, Konzertsaal, concert of Franz Schreker's students; Gustav Havemann, violin; composer, piano. *See:* B557, B1031, B1179

4. **Serenade.** (Assman; dur: 20 min.) *See:* B691, B1282, K3
   For clarinet, violin, viola & cello.
   Composed: June 18, 1919.

   1: *Moderato.* **2:** *Adagio, ma non troppo.* **3:** *Allegro molto.* **4:** *Langsamer.* **5:** *Allegretto grazioso.* **6:** *Allegro vivace.*

   Manuscripts: **A-Wst:** MH 10291. Sketch(16 p.) **US** composer Non-autograph score(29 p.) **US** composer Non-autograph parts(8, 13, 16, 10 p.) **US** composer Non-autograph parts(10 p. each) **D-brd-Fassman.**

   Premiere: February 8, 1921, Berlin, 4. Kammermusikabend des Anbruch; Boris Kront, clarinet; Erna Schulz, violin; Alfred Richter, viola; Ewel Stegman, cello. *See:* B693, B1010

   First U.S. Performance: May 4, 1984, Pasadena, CA, Pasadena Conservatory of Music; Almont Ensemble. *See:* B176

   Other Performances: B557, B1179, B1264

   Publications: B191

5. **Sonatinas, piano.** (unpublished; dur: 6 min. each.)
   No.1. Composed: June 26 - July 5, 1920.

   1: *Allegretto* (June 26, 1920) **2:** *Andante molto* (July 2, 1920) **3:** *Vivace* (July 5, 1920)
   No.2. Composed: July 6 - 15, 1920.

   1: *Andante con modo* (July 6, 1920) **2:** *Tema con variazioni: Andante molto* (July 16, 1920) **3:** *Gavotte en Rondeau: Allegro grazioso* (July 15, 1920)
   No.3. Composed: August 9 - 12, 1920.

   1: *Allegro moderato* (August 9 - 10, 1920) **2:** *Scherzettino, Tempo giusto* (August 10, 1920) **3:** *Lento - Allegro con modo* (August 11 - 12, 1920)
   Dedication: Frau Staatssekretär Dr. Reisch gewidmet.
   No.4. Composed: November 10 - 12, 1920.

   1: *Allegro capriccioso* (November 10 - 11, 1920) **2:** *Andante* (November 12, 1920)
   Dedication: Frau Erna Brilles in Berlin gewidmet.

   Manuscripts: **A-Wst:** MH 10292. No.1 - 3(26 p.) **A-Wst:** MH 10293. No.1(9 p.) **A-Wst:** MH 10294. No.2(12 p.) **A-Wst:** MH 10295. No.3(10 p.) **A-Wst:** MH 10296. No.4(4 p.)

6. **Quartet, strings, no.1.** (UE; dur: 30 min.) *See:* B73, B341, B372, B1116, B1282, B1368, B1519
   Composed: 1921.

1: *Lento.* 2: *Allegro, ma non troppo.* 3: *Adagio molto.* 4: *Presto.* 5: *Andante, quasi adagio.* 6: *Allegro vivace.* 7: *Fuga.* 8: *Lento come prima.*
Dedication: Lambinon-Quartett, Berlin.

Manuscripts: **A-Wn:** L1 UE 647. Score(35 p.)

Premiere: June 16, 1921, Nürnberg, 51. Deutsches Tonkünstlerfest; Lambinon Quartett. *See:* B260, B1202

Other Performances: B479, B526, B937, B1508

Published (Facsimile page): In *Allgemeine Musikzeitung* 48:23/24 (June 10, 1921): 405-407.

Publications: B319

Recording: Musikproduktion Dabringhaus und Grimm L 3280. compact disc. p1987. *See:* B1178
Sonare Quartett.
Duration: 32 min., 29 sec.
With his Quartet, strings, no.2, op.8.

7. **Symphony, no.1** (UE; dur: 30 min.) *See:* B78, B417, B752, B1282, K574, K838
For orchestra: 2.2.4.3 / 4.2.3.1 / timpani / percussion / strings.
Composed: 1921, Vienna.
1: *Vivace.* 2: *Nach und nach fliessender* (Andante con moto). 3: *Larghetto.* 4: *Subito molto piu mosso.* 5: *Presto.* 6: *A tempo.* 7: *Adagio.* 8: *Fuge.* 9: *Presto.*
Premiere: March 17, 1922, Berlin; Berliner Philharmonischen Orchester; Hermann Scherchen, conductor. *See:* B24, B749, B750, B1180, B1203, B1204, B1440
Recording: Amadeo 415 825-1. (415 826-1--415 827-1) 2 discs. 33 1/3 rpm. stereo. p1985. Oesterreichische Musik der Gegenwart, v.5. *See:* B154, B927, B1201, B1338
ORF-Symphonieorchester; Lothar Zagrosek, conductor.
Duration: 31 min.
Recorded June 3 - 5, 1985; Grosser Sendesaal des ORF-Funkhauses, Wien.
With his *Symphony, no.2, op.12* and *Symphony, no.3, op.16.*

8. **Quartet, strings, no.2.** (Assmann; dur: 30 min.) *See:* B372, B1282, B1519
Composed: 1921.
1: *Andante sostenuto; Allegretto moderato.* 2: *Allegro molto.* 3: *Adagio; Allegro moderato.*
Dedication: Havemann-Quartett, Berlin.
Manuscripts: **D-brd-**Fassman. Score(75 p.)
Premiere: April 24, 1922, Berlin, Singakademie; Havemann Quartett. *See:* B967, B1455
Other Performances: B937, B1508
Publications: B191
Recording: Musikproduktion Dabringhaus und Grimm L 3280. compact disc. p1987. *See:* B1178
Sonare Quartett.
Duration: 36 min.
With his Quartet, strings, no.1, op.6.

9. **Lieder.** (UE) *See:* B1041, B1168
For voice and piano. German texts by Gerd Hans Goering.
Composed: September 19, 1921 - February 5, 1922.

1: *Im Spiegel* (September 19, 1921, Vienna) "Wir sind nicht droben" **2:** *Räume* (October 19, 1921, Berlin) "Gross wuchsen alle Räume" **3:** *Das Bild* (November 30, 1921, Berlin) "Tag um Tag begeht mein Schritt" **4:** *Erinnerungen* (February 2, 1922, Berlin; 2d version February 5) "Und oft war's nur ein Hauch" **5:** *Sonne und Erde* (February 2, 1922, Berlin) "Wintersonne!" **6:** *Rätselspiel* (February 2, 1922, Berlin) "Du ewig Wandelbare" **7:** *Die Ballade vom König Lobesam* (January 3, 1922, Berlin) "Es war ein König Lobesam" **8:** *Das Lied* (October 28, 1921, Berlin) "Tänzeln mich des Tags"
Dedication: Gerd Hans Goering.

Other Performances: B18

Manuscripts: **A-Wn:** L1 UE 712. No.1(2 p.) **A-Wst:** MH 10297. No.2(1 p.) **A-Wst:** MH 10346. No.2(2 p.) **A-Wn:** L1 UE 713. No.2 - 6 & 8(8 p.; nos.3, 5 & 8 crossed out). **A-Wst:** MH 10309. No.3 & 7(6 p.) **A-Wst:** MH 10298. No.4, version 2(2 p.) **A-Wn:** L1 UE 679. No.7(6 p.)

Published: No.1 In *Musikblätter des Anbruch* 3:15/16 (October 1921)

Published: Nos.1, 2, 4 & 6 In his *Neun Lieder für Gesang und Klavier.* (Wien: Universal Edition, 1927): 3-12. U.E. 6005.

Published: No.7 (Wien: Universal Edidion, 1924) 9 p. U.E. 7573.

10. *Concerto grosso, no.1.* (withdrawn) *See:* B1282, K838
For flute, clarinet, bassoon, violin, viola, cello & string orchestra.
Composed: 1921 - 1922.

Premiere: August 19, 1922, Weimar, Weimarer Staatskapelle; Hermann Scherchen, conductor. *See:* B1144

11. *Symphonische Musik* = *Symphonic music.* (UE; dur: 35 min.) *See:* B417, B752, B1282, K4, K592
For chamber orchestra: 1.1.1.1 / 0.0.0.0 / string quintet.
Composed: 1922.
1: *Allegro deciso, ma non troppo.* **2:** *Adagio.*
Dedication: Hermann Scherchen.

Manuscripts: **CH-W:** Dep RS 35/5.

Premiere: July 30, 1922, Donaueschingen, 2. Donaueschinger Kammermusikfest zur Förderung zeitgenössischer Tonkunst; Hermann Scherchen, conductor. *See:* B798, B1147, B1268

First U.S. Performance: November 16, 1952, New York, Town Hall, New Friends of Music; New York Philharmonic-Symphony; Dimitri Mitropoulos, conductor. *See:* B958, B971, B1417

Other Performances: B479

12. *Symphony, no.2.* (UE; dur: 50 min.) *See:* B33, B72, B78, B336, B354, B417, B662, B752, B1282, B1326, B1369, B1447, B1498, K5, K574, K838, K908
For orchestra: 3.2.5.3 / 6.4.4.1 / timpani / celesta / percussion / strings.
Composed: March 27 - May 23, 1922.
1: *Andante sostenuto* (March 27 - April 17, 1922, Wien-Linz (Westbahnhof) - Berlin; Instr. April 18 - May 19, 1922, Berlin) **2:** *Allegro deciso, ma non troppo* (May 3 - 8, 1922, Berlin - Scharumselsee (Diensdorf); Instr. May 10 - 21, 1922, Berlin) **3:** *Adagio* (May 13 - 23, 1922, Berlin; Instr. May 23 - June 8, 1922, Berlin - Neverstoff)
Dedication: Anna Mahler.

Manuscripts: **A-Wn:** L1 UE 220. Score(158 p.)

Premiere: June 11, 1923, Kassel, Deutsches Tonkünstlerfest des Allgemeinen Deutschen Musikvereins; Robert Laugs, conductor. *See:* B89, B1139, B1205, B1302

First U.S. Performance: December 23, 1943, Minneapolis, MN; Minneapolis Symphony Orchestra; Dimitri Mitropoulos, conductor. *See:* B117, B232, B580, B844, B1225, B1226

Other Performances: K588

Recording: Amadeo 415 825-1. (415 826-1--415 827-1) 2 discs. 33 1/3 rpm. stereo. p1985. Oesterreichische Musik der Gegenwart, v.5. *See:* B154, B927, B1201, B1338
ORF-Symphonieorchester; Lothar Zagrosek, conductor.
Duration: 57 min.
Recorded May 9 - 10, 1985; Grosser Saal des Wiener Konzerthauses.
With his *Symphony, no.1, op.7* and *Symphony, no.3, op.16.*

13. *Toccata und Chaconne über den Choral Ja ich glaub an Jesum Christum.*
(UE) *See:* B163, B638, B752, B1282, B1447
For piano.
Composed: June 20 - 23, 1922
1: *Toccata* (June 20, 1922, Neverstorff) 2: *Chaconne* (June 23, 1922, Neverstorff)
Dedication: Eduard Erdmann.

Manuscripts: **D-brd** Erdmann Estate. **A-Wn:** L1 UE 661. Non-autograph score(66 p.)

Premiere: October 16, 1922, Berlin; Eduard Erdmann, piano. *See:* B1181, B1456, B1457

Publications: B1253

13a. *Eine kleine Suite von Stücken über denselbigen Choral, verschiedenen Charakters = Little suite.* (UE & AMP) *See:* B163
For piano.
Composed: June 30, 1922, Neverstorff.
1: *Allemande.* 2: *Sarabande.* 3: *Gavotte.* 4: *Waltz.* 5: *Fugue.* 6: *Fox trot.*
Dedication: Irene Erdmann.

Manuscripts: **D-brd** Erdmann Estate. **A-Wn:** L1 UE 661. Non-autograph score(66 p.)

Premiere: October 16, 1922, Berlin; Eduard Erdmann, piano. *See:* B1181

Recording: Polydor 95108. 78 rpm. [pre-1931]
Eduard Erdmann, piano.
With Eduard Erdmann *Fox-trot in C-Dur.*

Recording: RCA Victor 15862 ; M646 (set). (Mx. 15862). 78 rpm. [1940] *See:* B488, B984, B1169
Jesús Maria Sanromá, piano.
With Arnold Schoenberg *6 Little Pieces.*

13b. *Lieder.* (unpublished)
For voice & piano. German text by Karl Kraus.
Composed: 1922.
1: *Ich hab von dem fahrenden Zug.* 2: *Fernes Licht.*
Dedication: Irene Erdmann.

Manuscripts: **D-brd** Erdmann Estate.

14. *Die Zwingburg* = *The stronghold*. (UE; dur: 55 min.) *See:* B36, B91, B634, B869, B900, B942, B949, B1008, B1093, B1304, B1442, B1447, K7, K95, K595
Scenic cantata in 1 act; German text by Fritz Demuth, reworked by Franz Werfel. Leiermann (baritone), Ausrufer (tenor), Der Mann (tenor), Die Frau (soprano), Der Ausgezehrte (tenor), Der Bergarbeiter (tenor), Der Trinker (bass), chorus and orchestra: 3.2.4.3 / 4.3.3.1 / timpani / percussion / strings. Composed: July 8 - September 15, 1922, Neverstorff - Breitenstein.

Manuscripts: **A-Wn:** L1 UE 690. Cast list, etc. **A-Wst:** UE deposit Box S-Z. Proof parts. **A-Wst:** MH 10403/c. Sketches(34+5 p.)

Premiere: October 20, 1924, Berlin Staatsoper; Erich Kleiber, conductor; Emil Pirchan, scenery; Dr. Hörth, staging; Friedrich Schorr, Leiermann; Fritz Soot, Mann; Frida Leider, Frau. *See:* B63, B510, B751, B753, B1149, B1207, B1459

Published (Libretto): In *Das musikdramatische Werk, v.1,* hrsg. von Franz Eugen Dostal. Oesterreichische Dramatiker der Gegenwart, v.21. (Wien: Oesterreichische Verlagsanstalt, 1974-77): 11-26.

15. *Lieder*. (UE) *See:* B1041
For voice & piano. German texts by Guido Gezelle (no.1) and Franz Werfel (nos.2 - 5).
Composed: August 6 - September 9, 1922.

1: *Ich wandelt' allein* (August 6, 1922, Breitenstein) **2:** *Allelujah* (August 18, 1922, Breitenstein) "Ist das Licht nicht immer Eines" **3:** *Elevation* (September 7, 1922, Breitenstein) "Welchen Weg bist du gegangen" **4:** *Langsam kommen* (September 9, 1922, Breitenstein) "Langsam kommen schon die Gespenster" **5:** *Das Meer des zweiten Lichts.* "Gross ist und süss der Augenblick"
Dedication (No.3): to M.B.L.

Manuscripts: **A-Wst:** MH 10310. No.1(5 p.) **A-Wst:** MH 10311. No.2(3 p.) **A-Wn:** L1 UE 705. No.3 & 5(4 p.) **A-Wst:** MH 10312. No.4(2 p.)"Copiert von Anna Mahler-Krenek"

Published: No.3 In his *Neun Lieder für Gesang und Klavier.* U.E. 6005. (Wien: Universal Edition, 1927): 13-14.

16. *Symphony, no.3*. (UE; dur: 35 min.) *See:* B78, B417, B1282, K574
For orchestra: 2.2.2.3 / 2.1.0.0 / timpani / strings.
Composed: August 23 - November 16, 1922.

1: *Andante sostenudo* (August 23 - October 9, 1922, Breitenstein - Vienna; Instr. September 20, 1922, Breitenstein) **2:** *Adagio molto* (October 9 - 23, 1922, Berlin; Instr. October 15 - November 2) **3:** *Allegretto commodo* (November 2 - 16, 1922, Berlin; Instr. November 5 - 22)

Manuscripts: **A-Wst:** UE deposit. Score

Premiere: 1924, Berlin; Hermann Scherchen, conductor.

Other Performances: B1213, B1376

Recording: Amadeo 415 825-1. (415 826-1--415 827-1) 2 discs. 33 1/3 rpm. stereo. p1985. Oesterreichische Musik der Gegenwart, v.5. *See:* B927, B1201, B1338 ORF-Symphonieorchester; Lothar Zagrosek, conductor.
Duration: 41 min., 5 sec.
Recorded November 28 - 30, 1985; Grosser Sendesaal des ORF-Funkhauses, Wien.
With his *Symphony, no.1, op.7* and *Symphony, no.2, op.12.*

17. *Der Sprung über den Schatten* = *The leap over the shadow.* (UE; dur: 2 hrs., 30 min.) *See:* B36, B92, B205, B424, B869, B1093, B1164, B1248, B1304, B1447, K595, K838

Comic opera in 3 acts, 10 scenes; text by the composer. Kuno (bass), Prinzessin Leonore (soprano), Gräfin Blandine (mezzosoprano), Odette (soprano), Dr. Berg (baritone), Marcus (tenor), Laurenz Goldhaar (tenor), speaker, chorus, and orchestra: 2.2.4.3 / 3.1.2.0 / timpani / xylophone / banjo / percussion / strings.
Composed: 1923.

Manuscripts: **A-Wn:** L1 UE 671. Piano-vocal score(124 p.) **A-Wn:** L1 UE 674. Libretto(30 p.) **A-Wst:** UE deposit Box K-S. Score(30 p.)"Tempo di foxtrott" **A-Wst:** UE deposit Box K-S. Non-autograph choral parts. **A-Wgm.** Overture, incomplete piano reduction(4 p.)

Premiere: June 9, 1924, Frankfurter Opernhaus, 54. Deutsches Tonkünstlerfest des Allgemeinen Deutschen Musikvereins; Ludwig Rottenberg, conductor; Walther Brüggmann, producer; Ludwig Sievert, scenery; Richard von Schenck, Kuno; Else Gentner-Fischer, Prinzessin; Betty Mergler, Gräfin; Elisabeth Friedrich, Odette; Jean Stern, Dr. Berg; Hermann Schramm, Marcus; Max Roller, Laurenz. *See:* B90, B850, B1140, B1206

Other Performances: B1396

Published **(Libretto):** In *Das musikdramatische Werk, v.1,* hrsg. von Franz Eugen Dostal. Oesterreichische Dramatiker der Gegenwart, v.21. (Wien: Oesterreichische Verlagsanstalt, 1974-77): 27-62.

18. *Concerto, piano, no.1, F-sharp major.* (UE; dur: 30 min.) *See:* B1447
For piano and orchestra: 2.2.2.2 / 2.1.0.0 / strings.
Composed: March 23 - April 21, 1923, Berlin.
Dedication: Eduard Erdmann.

Manuscripts: **A-Wst:** MH 10313. 2-piano score(36 p.) **A-Wn:** L1 UE 665. 2-piano score(49 p.) **US-CA.** Score(101 p.)

Premiere: December 19, 1923, Winterthur, SZ; Eduard Erdmann, piano; Hermann Scherchen, conductor. *See:* B272

Publications: B563, B611, B1400

19. *Lieder.* (UE) *See:* B1041
For voice & piano. German texts by Otfried Krzyzanowski (nos.1 - 2 & 4) and Friedrich Gottlieb Klopstock (no.5).
Composed: April 16 - July 21, 1923.

1: *Erinnerung* (April 16, 1923, Berlin) "Es will kein Baum so wie die Linde blümen!" **2:** *Der Individualist* (April 16, 1923, Berlin) "Ein Weib zu suchen!" **3:** *Erwachen bei der Geliebten* (April 16, 1923, Berlin) "Die Holde schläft" **4:** *Wunsch* (April 16, 1923, Berlin) "Ein einfaches lichtes Kleid" **5:** *Die frühen Gräber* (July 21, 1923, Langballigau; Dedication: Unserem lieben Irenchen [Erdmann]) "Willkommen, o silberner Mond"

Manuscripts: **A-Wn:** L1 UE 714. Nos.1 - 4(1 p.) **A-Wst:** UE deposit Box A-J. No.3(proof, p.18-19) U.E. 6005. **A-Wn:** L1 UE 711. No.5(3 p., non-autograph)

Premiere: March 26, 1926, Berlin; Alice Schäffer-Kutznitzkii, voice.

Published: No.1, 2, 4 & 5 In his *Neun Lieder für Gesang und Klavier.* (Wien: Universal Edition, 1927): 15-20. U.E. 6005.

Recording: No.1, *Erinnerung* ; No.5, *Die frühen Gräber.* EMI Electrola 1C 065-02

677. *Stilwandlungen des Klavierliedes, 1850 - 1950, v.5: Wirkung der Neuen Wiener Schule im Lied.* 33 1/3 rpm. stereo. p1975.
Dietrich Fischer-Dieskau, baritone; Aribert Reimann, piano.
With songs by Joseph Matthias Hauer, Arnold Schonberg, Anton von Webern, Hans-Erich Apostel, Gottfried von Einem, Hanns Eisler, Paul Dessau, Conrad Beck.

Recording: No.2, *Der Individualist.* Preiserrecords SPR 3338. *Humor vokal; heitere Lieder aus Meisterhand.* 33 1/3 rpm. 1983.
Peter Weber, baritone; Erik Werba, piano.
With songs by other composers.

20. *Quartet, strings, no.3.* (UE; dur: 33 min.) *See:* B341, B372, B869, B1282, B1458, B1519
Composed: May 23, 1923, Berlin.

1: *Allegro molto vivace.* **2:** *Adagio.* **3:** *Allegro moderato.* **4:** *Adagio.* **5:** *Walzer comodo.* **6:** *Walzer molto moderato.* **7:** *Tempo I.*
Dedication: Paul Hindemith.

Premiere: August 3, 1923, Salzburg, Internationale Gesellschaft für zeitgenössische Musik; Amar Quartett. *See:* B6, B1387, B1452

First U.S. Performance: March 30, 1940, New York; Galimir Quartet. *See:* B120

Other Performances: B937, B1508

Recording: No.5. *Walze.* Polydor 66201. (B 29057) (Mx: 912 az) 78 rpm. [1923?]
Amar-Hindemith Quartett.
With Igor Stravinsky. *Concertino.*
Also issued on Deutsche Grammophon 66201. (B 29057)

21. *Orpheus und Eurydike.* (UE) *See:* B36, B635, B666, B1093, B1304, B1445, B1447, K41, K595, K662, K850
Opera in 3 acts; German text by Oskar Kokoschka. Orpheus (tenor), Eurydike (soprano), Amor (silent), Psyche (soprano), 3 Furies (mezzosopranos), Drunkard (bass), Soldier (baritone), Sailor (tenor), Clown (baritone), chorus, and orchestra: 3.2.4.3 / 6.4.3.1 / timpani / harp / percussion / strings.
Composed: April 23 - July 31, 1923, Berlin - Langballigau; Instr. July 2 - September 14, 1923, Langballigau - Breitenstein.
Dedication: Oskar Kokoschka.

Manuscripts: **A-Wst:** UE deposit. Score(81 p.) **A-Wn:** PhA 1983. Score (264 p. photocopy) **A-Wst:** UE deposit Box K-S. Non-autograph chorus parts(SATB)

Premiere: November 27, 1926, Kassel, Staatstheater; Ernst Zulauf, conductor; Paul Bekker, producer. *See:* B5, B64, B390, B509, B709, B998, B1208, B1363, B1443, K42.

Published (Piano-vocal score, Act.2, Scene 1, mm.123-160): In *Musik; Ein Unterrichtswerk für die Schule,* hrsg. von Edgar Rabsch und Hans Burkhardt. (Frankfurt: Moritz Diesterweg, 1928-29) v.3, p.173-174.

Published (Libretto): In *Das musikdramatische Werk,* v.1, hrsg. von Franz Eugen Dostal. Oesterreichische Dramatiker der Gegenwart, v.21. (Wien: Oesterreichische Verlagsanstalt, 1974-77): 63-97.

22. *Gemischte a capella-Chöre.* (UE)
For SSAATTBB chorus a cappella. German texts by Matthias Claudius.
Composed: September 20 - October 7, 1923.

1: *Der Mensch* (September 20, 1923, Breitenstein) "Empfangen und genährt vom

Weibe wunderbar" **2:** *Tröstung* (September 21, 1923, Breitenstein) "Der Säemann säet den Samen" **3:** *Die Römer* (October 7, 1923, Breitenstein) "Die Römer, die, vor vielen hundert Jahren"
Dedication: Dem Frankfurter a Capella-Chor 1923 gewidmet.

Manuscripts: **A-Wn:** L1 UE 653. Score(8 p.) **A-Wst:** UE deposit Box A-J. 4 non-autograph parts.

23. *Symphonische Musik, no.2.* (withdrawn)
For chamber orchestra: 1.0.1.1 / 1.0.0.0 / solo strings.
Composed: September 23, 1923, Wien; Instr. October 15, 1923, Breitenstein; Corr. December 2, 1923, Breitenstein.
Alternate title: *Divertimento.*
Dedication: Professor Dr. Georg Schünemann.

Manuscripts: **A-Wst:** MH 10314. Score(45 p.) **A-Wn:** L1 UE 273. Non-autograph parts.

Premiere: February 1, 1924, Berlin, Singakademie; Fritz Stiedry, conductor. *See:* B1032

Other Performances: B715

24. *Quartet, strings, no.4.* (Assmann; dur: 25 min.) *See:* B372, B1519
Composed: December 16, 1923 - January 1, 1924, Vienna - Winterthur, SZ. Fragmentary ending.
1: *Allegro moderato.* **2:** *Adagio.* **3:** *Allegretto grazioso* (December 16, 1923, Vienna) **4:** *Adagio* (December 18 - 23, 1923, Vienna - Zuoz, SZ) **5:** *Allegro vivace* (December 26, 1923, Zuoz, SZ; Dedicated to the memory of the Spanish records.) **6:** *Sostenuto* (December 28, 1923, Zuoz, SZ) **7:** *Allegro deciso* (January 1, 1924, Winterthur, SZ)
Dedication: Werner Reinhart.

Manuscripts: **CH-W:** Dep RS 35/4. **D-brd-**Fassman.

Premiere: August 5, 1924, Salzburg, Internationale Gesellschaft für neue Musik; Amar Quartett.

Other Performances: B479, B937, B1508

Published (Facsimile page from no.5): In *Von neuer Musik, Beiträge zur Erkenntnis der neuzeitlichen Tonkunst* hrsg.v. H. Grues, E. Kruttge, & E. Thalheimer. (Köln: F.J. Marcan-Verlag, 1925): 39-43.

Published (Facsimile page from no.5): In *Musik-Konzepte* 39/40 (October 1984): 107.

25. *Concerto grosso, no.2.* (UE; dur: 30 min.) *See:* K39, K838
For violin, viola, cello and orchestra: 2.2.2.2 / 2.1.0.0 / strings.
Composed: January 1 - February 23, 1924.
1: *Allegro molto moderato e pesante* (January 1 - 23, 1924, Winterthur - Vienna) **2:** *Adagio* (January 3 - February 4, 1924, Milano - Winterthur) **3:** *Allegretto comodo* (February 11 - 12, 1924, Winterthur) **4:** *Andante, quasi adagio* (February 16 - 20, 1924, Winterthur) **5:** *Allegro.*
Dedication: Meinen Freunden in Schweiz.

Manuscripts: **A-Wn:** L1 UE 650. Score(40 p.) **A-Wst:** UE deposit Box A-J. Non-autograph 18 parts.

Premiere: October 14, 1924, Zürich Tonhalle Orchester; Volkmar Andreä, conductor. *See:* B463

First U.S. Performance: February 25, 1926, New York, Carnegie Hall; Damrosch Orchestra; Otto Klemperer, conductor. *See:* B264

Other Performances: B18

26. **Suites, piano.** (UE; dur: 20 min.)
   No.1. Composed: March 29 - April 4, 1924
   1: *Andante* (March 29, 1924, Zürich) **2:** *Andante sostenuto* **3:** *Allegretto* (April 2, 1924, Zürich) **4:** *Andante sostenuto* (August 2, 1923, Bedigliora (Tessin)) **5:** *Allegretto* (April 4, 1924, Winterthur)
   No.2. Composed: April 10 - 23, 1924
   1: *Allegro moderasto* (April 10, 1924, Locarno) **2:** *Andante* (April 17, 1924, Locarno) **3:** *Allegro agitato* (April 19, 1924, Locarno) **4:** *Adagio* (April 20, 1924, Sierre (Valais); alternate version July 23) **5:** *Allegretto* (April 23, 1924, Sierre)
   Dedication: Artur Schnabel.

   Manuscripts: **A-Wn:** L1 UE 652. Suite no.1(12 p.) Includes variant of no.4. **D-brd** Erdmann Estate.

   Premiere: December 12, 1924, Berlin, Blüthnersaal; Eduard Erdmann, piano. *See:* B1033

   First U.S. Performance: January 11, 1938, San Francisco, Fairmont Hotel Red Room; composer, piano. *See:* B231, B366

   Other Performances: B1242

   Published: No.1:4 In *Musik der Zeit*, Vol.5. (Wien: Universal Edition, 1928): 26.

27. **Concertino.** (UE; dur: 20 min.)
   For flute, violin, harpsichord & string orchestra.
   Composed: 1924.
   Dedication: Musikkollegium in Winterthur.

   Manuscripts: **CH-W:** Dep RS 35/7.

   Premiere: February 18, 1925, Winterthur, SZ; Li Stadelmann, harpsichord; Hermann Scherchen, conductor. *See:* B203

   First U.S. Performance: March 24, 1939, Oakland, CA, Oakland Auditorium; Federal Symphony Orchestra; composer, piano; Nathan Abas, conductor. *See:* B450, B835, B1475, B1476

28. **Kleine suite** = *Little suite*. (BA; dur: 8 min.) *See:* B1463
   For clarinet & piano.
   Composed: February 19 - March 3, 1924.
   1: *Praeludium* (February 29, 1924, Gschwand bei Riedtwil, SZ) **2:** *Air* (February 29, 1924, Gschwand bei Riedtwil, SZ) **3:** *Bourré* (March 3, 1924, Zürich) **4:** *Adagio* (March 3, 1924, Zürich) **5:** *Moderner Tanz* (March 3, 1924, Zürich)
   Dedication: Werner Reinhart in Winterthur, March 19, 1924.

   Manuscripts: **CH-W:** Dep RS 35/2. **US** composer Score(6 p.) **D-brd** Kbärenreiter. Blueprint score(6 p.)

   Premiere: January 7, 1967, Bamberg; Karl Dörr, clarinet; composer, piano. *See:* B1145, B1153, B1154

29. **Concerto, violin, no.1.** (UE; dur: 18 min.) *See:* B1447
   For violin and orchestra: 2.0.2.2 / 2.2.0.0 / strings. In one movement.
   Composed: March 9 - 31, 1924, Zürich.
   Dedication: Alma Moodie.

Manuscripts: **A-Wn**: L1 UE 678. Score(33 p.) **A-Wn**: L1 UE 649. Piano-violin score(32 p.) **A-Wst**: UE deposit Box S-Z. Proof score(44 p.) **A-Wst**: UE deposit Box S-Z. Non-autograph parts.

Premiere: January 5, 1925, Dessau, Friedrich-Theater, VII. Abonnement-Konzert; Alma Moodie, violin; Franz von Hösslin, conductor. *See:* B754, B1034, B1218, B1219, B1441

First U.S. Performance: January 16, 1982, Corpus Christi, TX, Bayfront Plaza Auditorium; Corpus Christi Symphony; Goetz Bernau, violin; Eleazar de Carvalho, conductor. *See:* B1349

30. *Lieder.* (unpublished)

For voice & piano. German texts by Gerd Hans Goering (nos.1 - 4 & 9 - 13) and Hans Reinhart (nos.5 - 8).
Composed: April 2 - May 15, 1924.

1: *Epigonen* (April 2, 1924, Zürich) "Dies wär ein Ende" **2:** *Vis á vis du rien* (2 versions [April 2] & May 12, 1924, Zürich) "Tage Wochen, das geht" **3:** *Dämmerung* (April 2, 1924, Zürich) "Wir wollen schweigen" **4:** *Ehrfurcht* (2 versions, April 5 - 6, 1924, Zürich) "Ach, wie es tönet" **5:** *Erkenne deines Wesens* (2 versions, April 9 & May 1, 1924, Zürich) **6:** *Gleich jenem Wind* (3 versions, April 9, May 1 & 12, 1924, Zürich) **7:** *Du schöner Vogel fliegst* (April 9, 1924, Zürich) **8:** *Ich bin mir selbst Gesang* (April 10, 1924, Zürich) **9:** *Schrei* (April 11, 1924, Zürich) "Ein Schrei im Wald" **10:** *Wenn alles hebas hilf in dir zerbricht* (May 15, 1924, Zürich) **11:** *Oft wand der gross* (May 15, 1924, Zürich) **12:** *Epigramm.* "Die lauten Tage sind dahin" **13:** *Die Musen* (April 11, 1924, Zürich) "Niemand beichtet gern in Prosa"

Manuscripts: **A-Wst**: MH 10330. No.1 - 11 & 13(14 p.) **A-Wst**: MH 10331. No.1 - 9 & 12(10 p. non-autograph) **A-Wst**: MH 10332. No.1 - 2(2 p. non-autograph) **A-Wst**: MH 10332. Sketch.

30a. *Lieder.* (unpublished; dur: 12 min.)

For mezzosoprano, clarinet & string quartet. French text by Emile Verhaeren.
Composed: 1924.

1: *La barque* = *The boat.* "Il gêle, et des arbres pâles de givre clair" **2:** *Un soir* = *An evening.* "Avec les doigts de ma torture" **3:** *L'heure mauvaise* = *The evil hour.* "Depuis ces temps troublés d'adieux et de retours"

Manuscripts: **US** composer Score(12 p.) **US** composer Voice part(4 p.)

Premiere: May 28, 1951, Los Angeles City College auditorium; Suzanne Coray, contralto; composer, conductor.

Other Performances: B224

Recording: Orion ORS 79348. 33 1/3 rpm. stereo. [1979] *See:* B1030, B1357, B1462
Neva Pilgrim, soprano; Madison Quartet; William Nichols, clarinet.
Duration: 9 min., 49 sec.
Recorded December 22, 1978, in Ithaca, N.Y.
With his *4 Songs, op.112* and *Zeitlieder*, op.215 and Gladys Nordenstrom *Zeit XXIV.*

31. *Stücke.* (UE; dur: 30 min.)

For orchestra: 3.3.3.3 / 3.3.3.0 / timpani / harp / percussion / strings. In seven movements.
Composed: 1924.

Manuscripts: **CH-W**: Dep RS 35/1.

Premiere: November 4, 1926, Winterthur, SZ; Hermann Scherchen, conductor.

First U.S. Performance: April 22, 1965, Minneapolis, MN; Civic Orchestra of Minneapolis; composer, conductor. *See:* B355, B1232

32. *Vier kleine Männerchöre* = *Four little male choruses.* (UE) *See:* B1192
    Alto solo & TTBB chorus. German texts by Friedrich Hölderlin.
    Composed: November 19, 1924, Zürich.
    1: *Ihr sanftblickenden Berge.* **2:** *Aber es gibt ein finster Geschlecht.* **3:** *Vormals richtete Gott.* **4:** *Der Spaziergang.* "Ihr Wälder schön an der Seite"
    Dedication: Dr. Ludwig Rottenberg.

    Manuscripts: **A-Wn:** L1 UE 663. Score(8 p. non-autograph)

    Premiere: March 25, 1935, Vienna, Ehrbar-Saal, 5. Oesterreichische Studio; Herta Glaz, alto; Wiener Männergesangverein; Professor Grossmann, conductor. *See:* B470, K302

33. *Sonata, violin, no.1.* (Assmann; dur: 30 min.)
    In four untitled movements.
    Composed: October 17, 1924, Zürich - January 21, 1925, Schierke (Harz.)
    Dedication: Alma Moodie.

    Manuscripts: **D-brd-**Fassman.

    Premiere: November 28, 1960, Darmstadt; Klaus Assmann, violin. *See:* B772, B773

    Publications: B298, B1410

34. *Symphony.* (UE; dur: 22 min.) *See:* B417, B1463
    For band: 4.4.4.4 / 4.4.3.1 / percussion.
    Composed: December 4, 1924 - August 30, 1925.
    1: *Allegro* (December 4, 1924, Paris) **2:** *Adagio molto* (December 31, 1924, Zürich) **3:** *Allegro* (January 6, 1925) **4:** *Andante* (August 30, 1925, Cassel)

    Manuscripts: **A-Wst:** UE deposit Box S-Z. Score(30 p.)

    Premiere: February? 1926, Leipzig; Hermann Scherchen, conductor.

    Recording: Thorofon Capella ETHK 341/4. (DTHK 341). *Musik zwischen den Kriegen; Eine Berliner Dokumentation.* 4 discs. 33 1/3 rpm. 1987. *See:* B808
    Radio-Symphonie-Orchester Berlin; Vinko Globokar, conductor.
    Duration: 19 min., 44 sec.
    Recorded: 1970, Berlin, Sender Freies.

35. *Die Jahreszeiten* = *The seasons.* (UE & AMP; dur: 12 min.) *See:* B1192, B1442
    For SATB chorus a cappella. German text by Friedrich Hölderlin; English translation by Virginia Seay and the composer in 1944.
    Composed: September 11 - October 6, 1925, Kassel.
    1: *Der Frühling* = *Spring.* "Der Mensch vergisst die Sorgen aus dem Geiste" = "Now man discards the sorrows from his mind" **2:** *Der Sommer* = *Summer.* "Wenn dann vorbei des Frühlings Blüte schwindet" = "And when the springtime's flowers are slowly fading" **3:** *Der Herbst* = *Autumn.* "Die Sagen, die der Erde sich entfernen" = "The legends of the spirit that departed" **4:** *Der Winter* = *Winter.* "Wenn ungesehn und nun vorüber sind die Bilder" = "The season's features are concealed to man"

    Manuscripts: **US-Wc:** ML96 .K7835 no.11 Case. Score(12 p.) **A-Wst:** UE deposit Box A-J. Non-autograph parts.

Premiere: July 1925, V. Donaueschinger Kammermusikfest; Stuttgarter Madrigalchor; Hugo Holle, conductor. *See:* B755, B799, B1217

Other Performances: B18

Publication: Vremena goda. (Moskva: Izdatel'stvo Muzyka, 1968) 24 p. German and Russian text.

Recording: New Records NRLP 306. *Choral music by the Hamline Choir.* 10 in. 33 1/3 rpm. [1952] *See:* B195, B862, B1172
Hamline University a Cappella Choir; Robert Holliday, conductor.
With his *Lamentatio Jeremiae prophetae* op.93, Lessons 1 & 2 and works by Russell Harris and Carlos Chavez.

Recording: Orion ORS 80377. *Ernst Krenek vocal compositions.* 33 1/3 rpm. stereo. [1980] *See:* B195, B740, B1358
College of the Desert Vocal Ensemble; John L. Norman, conductor.
Duration: 6 min., 52 sec.
Recorded April 13, 1979, University of California, Santa Barbara Krenek Festival.
With his op.61, op.186a, op.210, op.210, op.226, and op.67.

Recording: Excerpts. Austin 6224. [1963] *See:* 195
Texas Tech Choir.

36. *Bluff.* (withdrawn)
Operetta in 3 acts. Text by George Gribble and Carl von Levetzow. Jim, Eleanor, Zena, Bessie, Harry, Toby, Dick, Schreier, Dicher, McGregor, chorus & piano.
Composed: November 7, 1924 - April 5, 1925, Basil - Zürich.
Act I: No.1. *Introduction.* (November 7, 1924, Basil) No.2. *Terzett.* (November 7, 1924, Basil) No.3. *Couplet.* (November 21, 1924, Zürich) No.4. *Duett.* No.5. *Terzett.* No.6. *Duett.* (November 15, 1924, Basil) No.7. *Lied* (Harry) (April 5, 1925, Vienna) No.8. *Septett.* (November 23, 1924, Zürich) No.9. *Schülerrevolution* (Chor u. McGregor) No.10. *Finale I.* (Jim; Eleanor; Zena; Bessie; Harry; Toby; Dick; Schreier; Dicher; Chor)
Act II: No.11. *Introduction zum II. Act; Sextett mit couplets.* (December 15, 1924, Zürich) No.12. *Walzer Duett* (Eleanor, Harry) (January 6, 1925) No.13. *Terzett mit Niggersong.* No.14. *Arie* (Zena) No.15. *Finale II.* No.16. *Duett* (Eleanor, Harry) No.17. *Duett* (Zena, Toby)
Act III: No.18. **Einleitung.** No.19. *Lied* (Bessie) No.20. *Finale III.*
Manuscripts: A-Wst: MH 10377 Sketches(148 p.) A-Wst: MH 10378/c. "Cavatina eroica" sketch(3 p.) A-Wgm. Sketch(7 p.)

37. *Mammon.* (UE; dur: 40 min.)
Ballet; text by Bela Balasz, German translation by Heinrich Kröller. For orchestra: 2.2.2.3 / 3.3.2.1 / harp / xylophone / timpani / percussion / strings.
Composed: April 22 - June 11, 1925, Zürich - Ascona.
1: *Mammon.* 2: *Der Geizige.* 3: *Der Mörder.* 4: *Das Mädchen.* 5: *Der Reiche.* 6: *Die Diebe.* 7: *Aussensprung des Mammon.* 8: *Das Laster.* 9: *Tanz des Goldes.* 10: *Die Kriecher.*
Manuscripts: A-Wst: UE deposit. Score(148 p.) A-Wst Non-autograph piano score(68 p.) A-Wst: UE deposit. Piano score(32 p.)

Premiere: October 1, 1927, Munich, Nationaltheater; Paul Schmitz, conductor; Heinrich Kröller, choreography; Bela Balasz, scenery; Leo Pasetti, costumes. *See:* B67, B728, B819, B922

38. *Der vertauschte Cupido* = *The Exchanged cupid.* (UE; dur: 20 min.) *See:* K13
Ballet after *Les fêtes de l'Hymen et de l'Amour* by Jean Philippe Rameau. For chamber orchestra: 2.2.0.2 / 0.2.0.0 / string quintet.
Composed: 1925.

Premiere: October 25, 1925, Kassel; Grete Margots, choreography; composer, conductor. *See:* B1303

39. *Klavierstücke.* (UE; dur: 10 min.)
October 18 - 22, 1925.
   1: *Allegro ma non troppo* (October 18, 1925, Kassel-Bebra). **2:** *Andante quasi adagio* (October 19, 1925, Karlsruhe). **3:** *Vivace* (October 22, 1925, Kassel). **4-5:** *Moderato affettuoso - Tempo giusto* (October 18, 1925, Karlsruhe).

Manuscripts: **A-Wn:** L1 UE 651. 6 p.

Premiere: November 18, 1925, Kassel; composer, piano.

First U.S. Performance: January 11, 1938, San Francisco, Fairmont Hotel Red Room; composer, piano. *See:* B231, B366

Published (No.1): In *Musik der Zeit*, Vol.5. (Wien: Universal Edition, 1928?): 24-25.

Published (No.5): In *An anthology of piano music*, Vol.5: *The twentieth century*, selected and edited by Denes Agay. (New York: Yorktown Music Press, 1971): 138-139.

Recording: Society of Participating Artists SPA 4. 33 1/3 rpm. mono. [1952] composer, piano.
With his *8 Pieces, op.110* and *Sonata, no.3, op.92, no.4.*

40. *Vom lieben Augustin.* (UE; dur: 10 min.) *See:* K812
Incidental music to a folk play by Dietzenschmidt (pseudonym for Anton Schmidt). For "Schrammel" ensemble (accordion, guitar & clarinet).
Composed: 1925.

Manuscripts: **A-Wst:** UE deposit.

Premiere: November 28, 1925, Kassel; composer, conductor.

41. *Die Rache des verhöhnten Liebhabers.* (unpublished)
Incidental music to a puppet play in two acts by Ernst Toller for voice, violin & piano.
Composed: December 10 - 30, 1925.
   1: *Vorspiel* (December 10, 1925, Cassel) Allegro. **2:** *Canzone veneziana* (December 11, 1925, Cassel) "Rondinella bellegrina" **3:** *Liebende heue* (December 30, 1925, Cassel)

Manuscripts: **A-Wst:** MH 10333. Score(14 p.)

Premiere: 1926, Zürich; performed by puppets.

42. *Das Gotteskind.* (unpublished; dur: 52 min.)
Incidental music to a radio play; written for Radio Kassel.
Composed: 1925.

Premiere: 1925, Kassel; Radio Kassel.

43. *Der Triumph der Empfindsamkeit.* (unpublished; dur: 17 min.) *See:* K38, K812
Incidental music to the Johann Wolfgang von Goethe play. For orchestra: 2.2.2.2 / 0.2.3.0 / mandoline / harp / timpani / percussion / strings.
Composed: 1925.
  I.Teil: *Ouverture* (March 21, 1926, Cassel) **No.1.** *Vivace.* **No.2.** *Alla marcia, Allegretto.* **No.3.** *Andante con moto.* **No.4.** *Moderato.* **No.5.** *Lento* (March 29, 1926)
  II.Teil: No.6. *Largo.* **No.7.** *L'istesso tempo.* **No.7a.** *Andantino.* **No.8.** *Largamente agitato.* **No.9.** *Largamente.* **No.10.** *Allegro capriccioso.* **No.11.** *Marsch, Allegro poco maestoso.* **No.12.** *Finale, Allegro ma non troppo* (April 7, 1926, Cassel)
Commissioned by the Staatstheater, Kassel.
Manuscripts: **A-Wst:** MH 10334. Sketch(4 p.) **US-R.** Score(102 p.) **A-Wst:** UE deposit Box S-Z. Non-autograph score(93 p.)
Premiere: May 9, 1926, Kassel, Staatstheater; composer, conductor. *See:* B1373

43a. *Der Triumph der Empfindsamkeit, Suite.* (UE; dur: 30 min.) *See:* K88
For soprano (in 4th movement) & orchestra: 2.2.2.2 / 0.2.3.0 / mandoline / harp / timpani / strings.
Composed: March 21, 1926 - 1927.
  1: *Overture* (March 21, 1926, Cassel) **2:** *Adagio.* **3:** *Tanzmusik.* **4:** *Einleitung und Finale.*
Manuscripts: **A-Wn:** L1 UE 275. Score(47 p.) **A-Wn:** L1 UE 277. No.4. piano(8 p., non-autograph) **A-Wst:** M 58508. Percussion part.
Premiere: November 28, 1927, Hamburg; Gustav Brecher, conductor. *See:* B1374
First U.S. Performance: February 4, 1932, New York, Carnegie Hall; Jeannette Vreeland, soprano; New York Philharmonic-Symphony; Bruno Walter, conductor. *See:* B268

43a. *Wechsellied zum Tanz.* (UE; dur: 3 min.)
For soprano & piano. German text by Johann Wolfgang von Goethe from *Triumph der Empfindsamkeit.*
1926.
"Lass sie sich drehen und du lass uns wandeln"
Dedication: Maria Ivogün.

43a. *Wechsellied zum Tanz.* (UE; dur: 4 min.)
For soprano & orchestra: 2.2.2.2 / 0.2.3.0 / mandoline / percussion / strings.
1926.

44. *Lustige Märsche* = *Merry marches* = *Märsch für Militärmusik.* (UE; dur: 10 min.) *See:* B1463
Three marches for band: 1.1.4.0 / 2.2.1.1 / timpani / percussion.
Composed: Spring - May 22, 1926.
Commissioned: Donaueschingen Festival 1926.
Manuscripts: **A-Wn:** L1 UE 672. Scores(4, 3, 5 p.) **A-Wst:** UE deposit Box K-S. Non-autograph parts. **A-Wst:** UE deposit Box K-S. Piano(7 p., non-autograph)
Premiere: July 1926, Baden-Baden, Donaueschinger Kammermusikfest; Bataillonskapelle Donaueschingens; Hermann Scherchen, conductor. *See:* B312, B351, B570, B1004, B1005

Recording: Boston Records B 411. 33 1/3 rpm. mono. *Austrian Classical Marches.* [1959] *See:* B170, B195, B196, B252, B1359

Boston Concert Band; Eric Simon, conductor.

Also issued on Boston Records BST 1012 (stereo), Argo 187 (mono), and Argo 5187 (stereo).

With works by E.W. Korngold, Ludwig van Beethoven, Franz Schubert, Alban Berg, and Johann Strauss.

Recording: Louisville Orchestra LS 756. *Music for winds, brass and percussion.* 33 1/3 rpm. stereo. [1975] Louisville Orchestra first edition records [1975, no. 6] *See:* B195, B196, B257, B1127, B1382, B0148

Louisville Orchestra; Jorge Mester, conductor.

Duration: 5 min., 25 sec.

Recorded October 30, 1975, Macauley Theater, Louisville, KY.

With his *Kleine Blasmusik,* op.70a and Peter Maxwell Davies *Saint Michael Sonata.*

Recording: Cornell University Wind Ensemble CUWE 21. 33 1/3 rpm. stereo. [1978?]

Cornell University Wind Ensemble; Marice Stith, conductor.

Recorded March 6, 1977, in Bailey Hall, Cornell University.

With band works by C. L. Mais, J. Goldsmith, J. Gibson, and Henry Cowell.

Recording: Crest CBDNA 77-4. 33 1/3 rpm. quad. [1977].

Eastman Wind Ensemble; Frederick Fennell, conductor.

Recorded at the 19th National Conference of the College Band Directors National Association, The University of Maryland, College Park, Maryland, March 9 - 11, 1977.

With band works by Percy Grainger, Toshira Mayazumi, Keith Foley, Joseph Schwantner, and H. Owen Reed.

Recording: No.1. Gramophone AM 1928 (Austria). 10 in. 78 rpm. [pre-1930]

Orchestra; Dol Dauber, conductor.

45. *Jonny spielt auf.* (UE) *See:* B82, B84, B88, B205, B209, B238, B255, B266, B280, B285, B314, B345, B346, B348, B370, B421, B448, B454, B498, B499, B509, B511, B514, B527, B605, B623, B632, B677, B714, B777, B801, B818, B847, B869, B981, B1039, B1046, B1058, B1059, B1093, B1097, B1130, B1134, B1151, B1197, B1198, B1220, B1249, B1263, B1299, B1300, B1305, B1316, B1326, B1399, B1445, B1447, B1454, B1482, B1492, K66, K67, K68, K69, K72, K73, K74, K79, K100, K105, K206, K493, K516, K523, K595, K662, K904

Opera in 2 acts; text by the composer. Max (tenor), Anita (soprano), Jonny (baritone), Daniello (baritone), Yvonne (soprano), Manager (bass), Hotel director (tenor), Ein Bahnangestellter (tenor), 3 Police (tenor, baritone & bass), chorus, and orchestra: 2.2.3.2 / 2.3.3.1 / piano / xylophone / glockenspiel / timpani / percussion / strings.

Composed: February 9 - June 19, 1926, Cassel; Piano-vocal score May 18 - June 20, 1926.

Dedication: Berta Hermann.

Manuscripts: US-LJ. Sketches(189 p.) A-Wn: L1 UE 641. Score(410 p.) A-Wn: L1 UE 667. Piano-vocal score(210 p.) A-Wn: L1 UE 280. Libretto(45 p.) A-Wst: UE deposit Box A-J. Libretto(60 p.) A-Wn: L1 UE 687. Score([16] p.) "Ergänzung" A-Wn: L1 UE 278. Foxtrot, arranged for piano(3 p.) US-CA. Condensed score(1 p., 9 m.)

Premiere: February 10, 1927, Leipzig; Gustav Brecher, conductor; Walther Brüggmann, producer. *See:* B7, B8, B9, B10, B11, B12, B36, B65, B66, B105,

B265, B541, B628, B839, B1135, B1209, B1278, B1296, B1364, B1444, K47, K48

First U.S. Performance: January 19, 1929, New York, Metropolitan Opera; Arthur Bodanzky, conductor; Michael Bohnen, Jonny; Walther Kirchhoff, Max; Florence Easton, Anita; Editha Fleischer, Yvonne; Friedrich Schorr, Daniello; George Meader, hotelkeeper. *See:* B23, B167, B210, B244, B267, B422, B529, B530, B610, B627, B796, B909, B982, B999, B1220, B1273, B1346, B1403, B1432, B1438, B1439

Composer's English translation: May 12, 1976, Boston, New England Conservatory; Gunther Schuller, conductor. *See:* B1069

First British performance: English translation by Jeremy Sams, October 6, 1984, Leeds, Grand Theater, co-produced by Opera North and the New Opera Company; Anthony Besch, producer; Terry Gilbert, choreography; David Lloyd-Jones, conductor; Jonathan Sprague, Jonny; Penelope MacKay, Anita; Gillian Sullivan, Yvonne; Lyndon Terracini, Daniello; Kenneth Woollam, Max.

Other Performances: B16, B93, B1487, K77

Published (Libretto): In *Prosa, Dramen, Verse.* (Münich: Albert Langen - Georg Müller, 1965): 59-99.

Published (Libretto): In *Das musikdramatische Werk, v.1,* hrsg. von Franz Eugen Dostal. Oesterreichische Dramatiker der Gegenwart, v.21. (Wien: Oesterreichische Verlagsanstalt, 1974-77): 99-137.

Published (English libretto): Translated by Frederick H. Martens. (New York: F. Rullman, 1928) 61 p.

Recording: Amadeo AVRS 5038. 33 1/3 rpm. stereo. [1965] *See:* B77, B111, B363, B443, B466, B660, B991, B1056, B1082, B1114
William Blankenship, Max; Evelyn Lear, Anita; Gerd Feldhoff, Jonny; Thomas Stewart, Daniello; Lucia Popp, Yvonne; Leo Heppe, Manager; Kurt Equiluz, Hotel director; Rudolf Sykora, Train conductor; Anton Wendler, Policeman; Hans Handlos, Policeman; Wiener Volksoper Orchester; Akademie Kammerchor; Heinrich Hollreiser, conductor.
Duration: 23:54 min. & 25:55 min.
Also issued on Philips AL 3498 (mono), Philips SAL 3498 (stereo), Mace MXX 9094 (stereo), and Amadeo AVRS 13 257.

Recording: Hymne des Jonny, Nun ist die Geige mein ; Leb' wohl, mein Schetz, Blues and song. Parlophone E 10698 (England). (Mx: W XXB 7909 ; W XXB 7910). [pre-1936]
Ludwig Hoffmann, bass; Orchestra of the State Opera House, Berlin; Manfred Guritt, conductor.
Also issued on Odeon O-6565 and Decca 25003 (America).
Also issued on Lebendige Vergangenheit LV 51. 33 1/3 rpm. mono. 1979. (With excerpts of other operas).

Recording: Hymne des Jonny, Nun ist die Geige mein ; Leb' wohl, mein Schetz, Blues and song. Electrola EG 690. (Mx: BWR 1264). 10in. 78 rpm. [pre-1936]
Diez Weismann, violin; Johann de Leur, piano.
Also issued on Gramophone 8-47917 and Deutsche Grammophon AM 953 (Austria).

Recording: Hymne des Jonny, Nun ist die Geige mein ; Leb' wohl, mein Schetz, Blues and song. Polydor B 61252-61253. (Mx: 445 & 488) 78 rpm.
Paul Romby Band.
Also issued on Polydor 19808.

Recording: Fantaisie. Parlophone E 11098. (Mx: W XXB 8141 ; W XXB 8142). [pre-

1936] *See:* B0650, B0968
Dajos Bela Künstler Orchester.
Also issued on Odeon 3259, Odeon O-6666, and Decca 25785 (America).

45a. *Rosalinde.* (unpublished)
Song for opera ball at Kassel theatre.
1926.

Manuscripts: US composer 2 p.

Premiere: 1926, Carnival, Kassel.

46. *Ein Sommernachtstraum = A midsummer night's dream.* (UE) *See:* K812
Incidental music to an out-door performance of the William Shakespeare play.
For chamber orchestra: 0.0.2.1 / 2.0.0.0 / percussion / 2 violins.
Composed: 1926.

Premiere: July 1926, Heidelberg; Hermann Scherchen, conductor. *See:* B412

46a. *Herr Reinecke Fuchs.* (unpublished)
Incidental music to a play by Heinrich Anton (pseudonym for Heinrich Simon). For voices (Kantant & Krayant) & ensemble: clarinet, trumpet, violin, piano & percussion.
Composed: 1931.
No.1. *Vorspiel.* **No.2.** *Beginn der 4. Szene.* **No.3.** *Klagegesang für Kantart und Krayant.* **No.4.** *Andante sostenuto.* **No.5.** *O Dank!* **No.6. Trauermarsch.* **No.7.** *5. Szene (Abendstimmung).* **No.8.** *Kinderlied.* **No.9. Aktschluss.* **No.10.** *Einleitung zum 2. Teil.* **No.11.** *Con passione.* **No.12.** *12.Szene, Musik im Spielsaal.* **No.13.** *Cancan für den Schluss der 12. Szene.* **No.14.** *Schlussmusik.*

Manuscripts: **A-Wst:** UE deposit. Score(12 p.) & parts.

Published (Libretto): (Berlin: Oesterheld, 1931) 73 pp.

47. *Vier A-cappella Chöre.* (UE)
For SATB chorus a cappella. German texts by Johann Wolfgang von Goethe.
Composed: July 18 - 31, 1926.
1: *Kläffer* (July 18, 1926, Grasse (Alpes-Maritimes)) "Wie reiten in die Kreuz und Quer" **2:** *Aus den "Inschriften"* (July 29, 1926, Grasse (Alpes-Maritimes)) "Wenn was irgend ist geschehen" **3:** *Guter Rat* (July 30, 1926, Evian-les-bains) "Geschieht wohl, dass man einen Tag" **4:** *Aus den "Zahmen Xenien"* (July 31, 1926, Evian-les-bains) "Wie haben dir Klatsch auf Geklatsche gemacht"
Dedication: Paul Bekker.

Manuscripts: **A-Wn:** L1 UE 682. Score(13 p.)

Premiere: December 7, 1927, Vienna, Mittlerer Konzerthaus-saal; Holles Madrigalvereinigung Stuttgart; Hugo Holle, conductor.

48. *O Lacrymosa.* (UE; 10 min.) *See:* B212, B1041, K82, K414, K908
Songs with piano; 2 versions: high and medium voice. German texts by Rainer Maria Rilke.
Composed: September 8 - 13, 1926.
1: *O Tränenvolle = O tearful you* (September 8 - 10, 1926, Kassel) **2:** *Nichts als ein Athemzug = Nothing but a breath is the emptiness* (September 11, 1926, Kassel) **3:** *Aber die Winter! = But the winters!* (September 13, 1926, Kassel)
Dedication: Rainer Maria Rilke.

Manuscripts: **A-Wn:** L1 UE 657. No.1 - 3(10 p.) **A-Wst:** MH 10335. No.1(4 p.) **A-Wst:** UE deposit Box K-S. No.1 - 3(10 p.) **A-Wn:** PhA 1986. No.1 - 3(9 p.) photocopy.

Premiere: January 29, 1927, Köln, Musikalischen Gesellschaft; Tiny Debüser, soprano; composer, piano. *See:* B756

First U.S. Performance: April 13, 1943, St. Paul, MN, Hamline University, Bridgeman Hall; Alice Gerstl Duschak, soprano; composer, piano. *See:* B116

Publications: B156

Recording: Orion ORS 75204. 33 1/3 rpm. stereo. p1975. *See:* B196, B667, B701, B879, B1331, B1354, B1381
Genevieve Weide, soprano; John Dare, piano.
Duration: 8 min., 25 sec.
Recorded May 17 and June 7, 1975, at California State University, Northridge. With his *Santa Fe timetable,* op.102, *Tape and double,* op.207, and *Toccata, accordion, op.183.*

48a. *O Lacrymosa.* (UE; dur: 10 min.)
For soprano with accompaniment arranged for 2 flutes, 2 clarinets, 2 bassoons & harp.
Composed: 1926.

Manuscripts: **A-Wst:** UE deposit Box K-S. No.1 - 3, score(11 p.) **A-Wn:** PhA 1986. No.1 - 3, score(11 p. photocopy)

Premiere: January 29, 1927, Köln, Musikalische Gesellschaft; Tiny Debüser, soprano; Hermann Abendroth, conductor. *See:* B1389

49. *Der Diktator* = *The dictator.* (UE; dur: 35 min.) *See:* B215, B353, B1093, B1110, B1447, K81, K595
Opera in 1 act, 2 scenes; text by the composer. Dictator (baritone), Charlotte (soprano), Officer (tenor), Maria (soprano), and orchestra: 2.2.2.2 / 1.1.1.0 / timpani / percussion / strings.
Composed: June 23 - August 29, 1926, Cassel - Wien.

Manuscripts: **A-Wn:** L1 UE 673. Libretto(10 p.) **A-Wst:** MH 10406/c. Sketches(51 p.) **A-Wst:** MH 10407/c. Sketch(4 p.) **A-Wn:** L1 UE 656. Piano-vocal score(55 p.) **A-Wn:** L1 UE 668. Score(86 p., stops at m.746)

Premiere: May 6, 1928, Wiesbaden; Joseph Rosenstock, conductor; Paul Bekker, producer. *See:* B13, B79, B83, B274, B451, B573, B934, B1182, B1265, B1365, B1372, B1385, B1446, B1448, B1466, B1525

First U.S. Performance: December 5, 1980, Minneapolis, University of Minnesota, Scott Hall, Opera Theater; Jacqueline Jones, conductor.

Published (Libretto): In *Das musikdramatische Werk, v.1,* hrsg. von Franz Eugen Dostal. Oesterreichische Dramatiker der Gegenwart, v.21. (Wien: Oesterreichische Verlagsanstalt, 1974-77): 139-149.

50. *Das geheime Königreich* = *The secret kingdom.* (UE; dur: 55 min.) *See:* B215, B353, B1093, B1110, B1447, K81, K595
Fairytale opera in 1 act, 2 scenes; text by the composer. King (baritone), Queen (colortura-soprano), Der Narr (baritone), Der Rebell (tenor), 3 women (soprano, mezzosoprano & alto), 2 revolutionaries (tenor & bass), Ein Wächter (tenor), chorus, and orchestra: 2.2.2.2 / 1.1.1.0 / banjo / mandoline / percussion / strings.

Composed: December 7, 1926 - February 17, 1927, Kassel; Instr. February 20, 1927.

Manuscripts: **A-Wst:** MH 10408/c. Sketches(78 p.) **A-Wn:** L1 UE 676. Libretto(16 p.) **A-Wn:** L1 UE 624. Score(188 p.) **A-Wn:** L1 UE 659. Piano-vocal score(97 p.) **A-Wst:** UE deposit Box A-J. Non-autograph parts(SATB hinter der Szene)

Premiere: May 6, 1928, Wiesbaden; Joseph Rosenstock, conductor; Paul Bekker, producer; G.T. Buchholz, staging. *See:* B13, B79, B83, B274, B451, B573, B934, B1182, B1265, B1365, B1372, B1385, B1446, B1448, B1466, B1525

First U.S. Performance: December 5, 1980, Minneapolis, University of Minnesota, Scott Hall, Opera Theater; Jacqueline Jones, conductor.

Published (Libretto): In *Das musikdramatische Werk, v.1,* hrsg. von Franz Eugen Dostal. Oesterreichische Dramatiker der Gegenwart, v.21. (Wien: Oesterreichische Verlagsanstalt, 1974): 151-167.

51. *Kleine Kantate = Little cantata.* (disappeared)
For mixed choir a cappella. Text by Johann Wolfgang von Goethe.
Composed: 1927.

51a. *Intrada.* (unpublished) *See:* B1463
For clarinet, bassoon, trumpet, 2 horns, trombone & timpini.
Composed: April 27, 1927, Kassel.
Written for the 150 jahrige Jubiläum der Staatlichen Künstakademie in Kassel.

Manuscripts: **A-Wst:** MH 10336. Score(8 p.) **A-Wst:** MH 10337. Non-autograph parts.

Premiere: June 1, 1927, Kassel.

52. *Marlborough s'en va-t-en guerre.* (unpublished) *See:* K59, K98, K812
Incidental music to a puppet play after the comedy by Marcel Archard; German translation by the composer. For piano and percussion.
Composed: 1927.

Premiere: May 11, 1927, Kassel, Staatliches Theater Kassel; Paul Hessler, puppets; Grete Klüber, costumes; Paul Schönke, scenery.

53. *Gesänge nach alten Gedichten.* (UE; dur: 15 min.) *See:* B1041
For mezzosoprano & piano. Text by Johann Christian Günther (no.1), Georg Rudolf Weckherlin (nos.2 & 3), and Paul Fleming (no.4).
Composed: May 5 - 16, 1927.

1: *Das unerkannte Gedichte* (May 12, 1927, Kassel) "Man lauert, sitzt und sinnt" **2:** *Ein Rundum* (May 5, 1927, Kassel) "Ein kleine Weil" **3:** *Ein anderes* (May 9, 1927, Kassel) "Ihr wisset, was für schwere Klagen" **4:** *An sich* (May 16, 1927, Kassel) "Sei dennoch unverzagt"

Manuscripts: **A-Wn:** L1 UE 685. Score(9 p.)

Premiere: November 21, 1929, Berlin, Schwechtensaal; Helene Grell, soprano; Friedrich Rolf Albes, piano. *See:* B736

First U.S. Performance: March 1, 1942, Vassar College, Skinner Hall; Olga Forrai, soprano.

Other Performances: B18, B491

53a. *Gesänge nach alten Gedichten.* (UE; dur: 15 min.)
For mezzosoprano with accompaniment arranged for woodwinds.

Composed: 1927.

Premiere: October 1927, Munich, Vereiningung für zeitgenössische Musik; Rosl Baumann, soprano; Bläser des Staatstheater. *See:* B729, B735, B888, B894

54. *Potpourri.* (UE; dur: 12 min.) *See:* B462, K88, K848
For orchestra: 2.2.3.2 / 0.3.2.1 / piano / percussion / strings.
Composed: May 16 - June 24, 1927, Kassel; Revised 1954.
Allegro vivace - Allegro con brio.

Manuscripts: **A-Wn:** L1 UE 648. Score(74 p.) **A-Wst:** UE deposit Box K-S. 3 published scores with revisions. **A-Wst:** UE deposit Box S-Z. Non-autograph parts.

Premiere: November 5, 1927, Köln; Hermann Abendroth, conductor. *See:* B548, B1374

Revised Edition: October 22, 1957, Stuttgart, Süddeutscher Rundfunk, Sendesaal Villa Berg; Südfunk-Unterhaltungsorchester; Otmar Nussio, conductor.

55. *Schwergewicht, oder Die Ehre der Nation* = *Heavyweight, or The pride of the nation.* (UE; dur: 25 min.) *See:* B215, B353, B1093, B1110, B1277, B1447, K81, K595
Operetta in 1 act; German text by the composer. Adam Ochsenschwanz (bass-buffo), Evelyne (soprano), Gaston (tenor), Professor Himmelhuber (baritone), Anna Maria Himmelhuber (mezzosoprasno), Journalist (tenor), Advisor (tenor), and orchestra: 2.2.2.2 / 0.2.2.0 / piano / banjo / percussion / strings.
Composed: March 15 - June 14, 1927, Kassel; Instr. August 20 - September 11, Wiesbaden.

Manuscripts: **A-Wn:** L1 UE 675. Libretto(13 p.) **A-Wgm.** Sketches(28 p.) **A-Wn:** L1 UE 662. Score(95 p.) **A-Wn:** L1 UE 670. Piano-vocal score(45 p.)

Premiere: May 6, 1928, Wiesbaden; Joseph Rosenstock, conductor; Paul Bekker, producer; G.T. Buchholz, staging. *See:* B13, B79, B83, B274, B573, B934, B1182, B1265, B1365, B1372, B1385, B1446, B1448, B1466, B1525

First U.S. Performance: December 5, 1980, Minneapolis, University of Minnesota, Scott Hall, Opera Theater; Vern Sutton, director.

Other Performances: B451

Published (Libretto): In *Das musikdramatische Werk, v.1,* hrsg. von Franz Eugen Dostal. Oesterreichische Dramatiker der Gegenwart, v.21. (Wien: Oesterreichische Verlagsanstalt, 1974): 169-181.

56. *Gesänge.* (UE; dur: 10 min.) *See:* B462, B1041
For baritone & piano. Text by Johann Wolfgang von Goethe.
Composed: November 4 - 8, 1927.
1: *Die Zerstörung Magdeburgs* (November 4, 1927, Kassel) "O Magdeburg, die Stadt" 2: *Der neue Amadis* (November 4, 1927, Kassel) "Als ich noch Knabe war" 3: *Fragment* (November 8, 1927, Kassel-Wiesbaden) "Von mehr als einer Seite verwaist"

Manuscripts: **A-Wn:** L1 UE 658. Score(16 p.)

Premiere: November 5, 1928, Künstlerhaus, Dresden, "Neue Musik - Paul Aron"; Paul Schöffler, baritone; Paul Aron, piano.

Publications: B1006

Recording: Orion ORS 78298. 33 1/3 rpm. stereo. [1978] *See:* B490, B1029, B1355
Michael Ingham, baritone; Carolyn Horn, piano.
Duration: 11 min., 26 sec.
With his *Spätlese*, op.218.

57. **Konzert-Arie** = *Monolog der Stella* = *Stella monologue.* (UE; dur: 10 min.)
See: B462, B1041
For soprano & piano. Text by Johann Wolfgang von Goethe from *Stella* Act 4,
scene 1.
Composed: February 23, 1928, Kassel.
Du blühst schön, schöner als sons
Dedication: Frau Maria Hussa-Greve.

Premiere: June 1928, Berlin; Maria Hussa, soprano.

Other Performances: B224, B1155, B1165

57a. **Monolog der Stella** = *Stella monologue.* (UE; dur: 10 min.)
For soprano with accompaniment arranged for orchestra: 2.2.2.2 / 1.1.0.0 /
strings.

Premiere: August 1928, Hannover; Maria Hussa, soprano.

58. **Kleine Symphonie** = *Little symphony.* (UE; dur: 15 min.) *See:* B215, B417,
B462, K88, K762
For chamber orchestra: 2.0.3.2 / 0.3.2.1 / timpani / guitar / 2 mandolines / 2
banjos / harp / percussion / violins / double bass.
Composed: May 28 - June 30, 1928.

1: *Andante sostenuto* (May 28 - June 8, 1928, Paris; Inst. July 11, 1928, Vienna) **2:**
Andantino (poco lento) (June 28, 1928, Ascona (Ticino)) **3:** *Allegretto, poco grave*
(June 30, 1928, Zürich-Vienna; Instr. June 17, 1928, Vienna)

Manuscripts: **A-Wn:** L1 UE 677. Score(50 p.) **US-CA.** Condensed score(1 p., 6 m.)
A-Wn: L1 UE 686. Non-autograph score(76 p.) **A-Wst:** UE deposit Box S-Z.
Non-autograph parts.

Premiere: November 3, 1928, Berlin, Staatsoperorchester; Otto Klemperer,
conductor. *See:* B595, B1183, B1297, B1526

First U.S. Performance: November 6, 1930, New York, Carnegie Hall; New York
Philharmonic-Symphony; Erich Kleiber, conductor. *See:* B969, B1014, B1131

59. **Sonata, piano, no.2.** (UE & AMP; dur: 20 min.) *See:* B462, B588, B1322,
B1398
Composed: July 21 - 26, 1928.

1: *Allegretto* (July 21, 1928, Vienna). **2:** *Alla marcia, energico* (July 25, 1928, Vienna). **3:**
Allegro giocoso (July 26, 1928, Vienna).

Manuscripts: **A-Wn:** L1 UE 666. 16 p.

Premiere: March 27, 1929, Berlin, Grotrian-Steinweg Saal; Ella Pancera, piano.
See: B558, B1210, B1530

First U.S. Performance: December 12, 1930, Boston. *See:* B487, B489

Other Performances: B116

Publications: B286

Recording: Melodiya CM 03113-4. [1972?] 33 1/3 rpm.
Maria Yudina, piano.

With works by Alban Berg, Andre Jolivet, and Serge Prokofiev.

60. *Leben des Orest.* (UE) *See:* B215, B462, B514, B635, B869, B948, B987, B1046, B1093, B1151, B1299, B1348, B1375, B1527, B1528, K104, K105, K138, K564, K595, K662
Opera in 5 acts; text by the composer. Agamemnon (tenor), Klytaemnestra (alto), Elektra (soprano), Iphigenie (mezzosoprano), Orest (baritone), Aegisth (tenor), Anastasia (alto), King Thoas (baritone), Thamar (soprano), Aristobulos (baritone), Ein Ausrufer (baritone), Ein Hirt (baritone), and orchestra: 2.3.3.2 / 2.3.2.1 / piano / harmonium / banjo / percussion / strings. Composed: August 8, 1928 - May 10, 1929, Štrbské pleso, CSR - Wien; Inst. September 18, 1928 - May 14, 1929, Wien)

Manuscripts: **A-Wst:** MH 10404. Sketch(188 p.) **US-LJ.** Libretto in English translation by Ernst Krenek. **A-Wn:** L1 UE 642. Score(613 p.) **A-Wn:** L1 UE 221. Piano-vocal score(328 p.)

Premiere: January 19, 1930, Neues Theater, Leipzig; Gustav Brecher, conductor; Walther Brüggmann, producer; Oskar Strnad, staging; Ernst Neubert, Agamemnon; Lotte Dörwald, Klytaemnestra; Marga Dannenberg, Elektra; Ilse Koegel, Iphigenie; Karl August Neumann, Orest; Paul Beinert, Aegisth; G. Wentscher-Lehmann, Anastasia; Ernst Oberkamp, King Thoas; Elisabeth Berö, Thamar; Adolf Vogel, Aristobulos. *See:* B14, B214, B237, B313, B542, B743, B744, B745, B746, B783, B986, B1038, B1061, B1108, B1211, B1298, B1306, B1488, K134,

First U.S. Performance (in English): November 20, 1975, Portland, OR, Portland Opera Association; Stefan Minde, conductor; Carey Gordon Wong, designer; Ghita Hager, stage director; Alyce Rogers, Anastasia; Glade Peterson, Agamemnon; Kenneth Riegel, Aegisthos; Sylvia Anderson, Klytaemnestra; Barrie Smith, Iphigenia; Anita Salta, Elektra; Victor Braun, Orestes; William Wildermann, Thoas; Linda Cook, Thamar; David Jimerson, Hawker. *See:* B103, B190, B391, B646, B992, B993

Other Performances: B250, B479, K107, K761

Published (Libretto): In *Orest: Aischylos, Eurpides, Voltaire, Krenek, Sartre, Anouilh,* hrsg. von Joachim Schondorff. (München: A. Lang, 1963)

Published (Libretto): In *Prosa, Dramen, Verse.* (Münich: Albert Langen - Georg Müller, 1965): 101-150.

Published (Libretto): In *Das musikdramatische Werk, v.1,* hrsg. von Franz Eugen Dostal. Oesterreichische Dramatiker der Gegenwart, v.21. (Wien: Oesterreichische Verlagsanstalt, 1974): 183-230.

Published (Facsimilie page): In *Die Musik* 23:8 (May 1931): 609.

61. *Gemischte Chöre.* (UE)
For SATB chorus a cappella. Text by Gottfried Keller.
1: *In der Stadt = In the city* (June 30, 1929, Vienna) "Wo sich drei Gassen kreuzen" "Where three crooked, narrow streets cross" **2:** *Zur Erntezeit = At harvest time* (June 30, 1929, Vienna) "Das ist die üppige Sommezeit" "This is the lush summer time" **3:** *Schifferliedchen = Shipper's song* (June 4, 1929, Vienna) "Schon hat die Nacht" "The night already has opened the silver shrine of the sky"

Manuscripts: **A-Wn:** L1 UE 660. Score(10 p.)

Premiere: November 27, 1932, Vienna, Grosser Konzerthaussaal; Freie Typographia; Erwin Stein, conductor. *See:* B273

Recording: Orion ORS 80377. *Ernst Krenek vocal compositions.* 33 1/3 rpm. stereo.

[1980] *See:* B740, B1358
College of the Desert Vocal Ensemble; John L. Norman, conductor.
Duration: 5 min., 23 sec.
With his op.35, op.186a, op.210, op.210, op.226, and op.67.

Recording: No.2, *Zur Erntezeit*; No.3, *Schifferliedchen*. New Records NRLP 305. *A program of choral excerpts.* 10 in. 33 1/3 rpm. mono. [1951] *See:* B1015
Hamline University a Cappella Choir; Robert Holliday, conductor.
With choral works by Charles Ives, Morales, Benjamin Britten, Heinrich Schütz, and Scarlatti.

62. **Reisebuch aus den österreichischen Alpen** = *Journey through the Austrian Alps.* (UE; dur: 75 min.) *See:* B462, B662, B664, B829, B1040, B1041, B1111, B1150, B1167, B1189, B1326, B1398
   For voice & piano. Text by the composer.
   Composed: July 5 - 26, 1929.
   1: *Motiv = Motive* (July 5, 1929, Vienna) "Ich reise aus, meine Heimat zu entdecken" "To know my land, I now set out to wander" **2:** *Verkehr = Travel* (July 7, 1929, Vienna) "Mit der Bergbahn geht's elektrisch immer höher" "In the Alpland go electric, always higher" **3:** *Kloster in den Alpen = Monastery in the Alps* (July 6, 1929, Vienna) "Riesengross liegt das Kloster da im Tal" "Mighty and vast the abbey stands down there" **4:** *Wetter = Weather* (July 7, 1929, Vienna) "Unverbindlich ist das Wetter in den Alpen" "Unobliging is the weather in the Alpland" **5:** *Traurige Stunde = Sad hour* (July 8, 1929, Vienna) "Nicht jeder Reisetag ist schön und festlich" "Not all my journey days are good and festive" **6:** *Friedhof im Gebirgsdorf = Cemetery in the mountain village* (July 10, 1929, Vienna) "Selbst die Toten in dem kleinen Kirchhof" "E'en the dead lie at an angle" **7:** *Regentag = Day of rain* (July 10, 1929, Vienna) "Es gibt Regentage, die sehr schön sind" "There are rainy days which are delightful" **8:** *Unser Wein = Our wine* (July 13, 1929, Vienna) "Von Süd und Ost belagert stürmisch unsre Alpen" "In South and East the Alps of Austria are under the siege of wine" **9:** *Rückblick = Looking back* (July 13, 1929, Vienna) "Was hab ich bis jetzt nun gefunden?" "What did I so far gain from all this?" **10:** *Auf und ab = Up and down* (July 14, 1929, Vienna) "Auf und ab wie die Narren rennen die Menschen" "Up and down, just like madmen" **11:** *Alpenbewohner = Alpland dwellers* (July 15, 1929, Vienna) "Die Alpen werden von wilden Nomaden bewohnt" "The Alpland shelters mostly wildy behaving nomads" **12:** *Politik = Politics* (July 17, 1929, Vienna) "Ihr Brüder, hört ein ernstes Wort" "O brothers, hear a serious word" **13:** *Gewitter = Thunderstorm* (July 18, 1929, Vienna) "Plötzlich wird es schwarz zwischen den weissen Gipfeln" "Suddenly it is black over the shining summits" **14:** *Heimweh = Nostalgia* (July 19, 1929, Vienna) "Manchmal, in all dem Grossen" "Sometimes, in all the grandeur" **15:** *Heisser Tag am See = Hot day at the lake* (July 22, 1929, Vienna) "Hier ist alles weich und südlich" "Here the spirit of the south reigns" **16:** *Kleine Stadt in den südlichen Alpen = Small town in the Southern Alps* (July 23, 1929, Vienna) "Schmale Gassen, tief und dunkel" "Dark and narrow are ther streets between the houses" **17:** *Ausblick nach Süden = Outlook toward the south* (July 24, 1929, Vienna) "Und über den Bergen liegt Welschland" "And over the mountains lies southland" **18:** *Entscheidung = Decision* (July 25, 1929, Vienna) "Die Sehnsucht wird immer weiter bohren" "The longing will never cease its gnawing" **19:** *Heimkehr = Homecoming* (July 26, 1929, Vienna) "So trägt der schnelle Zug mich wieder heimwärts" "And now the rapid train carries me homeward" **20:** *Epilog = Epilogue* (July 26, 1929, Vienna) "Am Tag nach meiner Heimkehr" "When back in old surroundings"

Manuscripts: **A-Wn:** L1 UE 688. German text(8 p.) **A-Wst:** Nachlass. Text. **A-Wst:**

MH 10338. Sketch(44 p.) **A-Wn:** L1 UE 271. No.7 - 20, score(52 p.) **A-Wn:** L1 UE 271. No.1 - 6, proof(p.1-25) **A-Wst:** UE deposit Box K-S. *Journey through the Austrian Alps* voice part(6 p.)

Premiere: January 17, 1930, Leipzig, Saale des Landeskonservatoriums, Internationale Gesellschaft für neue Musik; Hans Duhan, voice; composer, piano. *See:* B14, B1064, B1108

First U.S. Performance (Incomplete): January 8, 1947, New York, Times Hall; Alice Howland, soprano. *See:* B122, B956

Other Performances: B479

Publications: B287, B812, B1011

Published (Text): In *Prosa, Dramen, Verse.* (Münich: Albert Langen - Georg Müller, 1965): 385-398.

Published: Nos.1, 6, 7, 8, 13, 16, 17, and 19 in English translation by the composer. (Wien: Universal Edition, 1960) 39 p. U.E. 12877.

Recording: Telefunken BLE 14113. [1959] *See:* B216, B940
Rudo Timper, tenor; composer, piano.

Recording: Edition Rhodos ERS 1201-3. (set) 33 1/3 rpm. [1969?] *See:* B245, B697
Rudo Timper, tenor; composer, piano.
Recorded February 28, 1968.
With his *Gesänge des späten Jahres,* op.71 and *The ballad of the railroads,* op.98.

Recording: Oesterreichische Phonothek OPh 10005. 33 1/3 rpm. stereo. [196-]
Osterreichische Musik des 20. Jahrnunderts, v.3.
Franz Lukasovksy, tenor; Roman Ortner, piano.

Recording: Preiserrecords SPR 3269. 33 1/3 rpm. stereo. [197-] *See:* B576, B1083, B1331
Waldemar Kmentt, tenor; Richard Elsinger, piano.

Recording: Preiserrecords SPR 135 007. 33 1/3 rpm. stereo.
Julius Patzak, tenor; Heinrich Schmidt, piano.

Recording: Preiserrecords 120 728. *Krenek Matinee;* Verein der Freunde der Wiener Staatsoper. [1985]
Heinrich Zednik, tenor; Konrad Leitner, piano.
Live performance of October 16, 1983.

Recording: Nos.8, 15, & 17. Philips 6747 061. *Von der Jahrhundertwende bis zur Gegenwart = From the turn of the century to the present time.* 33 1/3 rpm. [1976]
Hermann Prey, tenor; composer, piano.

62b. *Lieder aus Reisebuch aus den oesterreichischen Alpen.* (UE)
For voice & orchestra: 2.2.2.2 / 4.1.1.0 / timpani / harp / percussion / strings.
Nos.1, 7, 8, 10, 5, 15, 17, and 19 orchestrated: 1973.

Manuscripts: **A-Wst:** UE deposit Box K-S. Score(44 p.)

63. *Triophantasie = Trio phantasy.* (withdrawn; dur: 20 min.)
For violin, cello & piano.
Composed: August 15, 1929, Vienna.
In one movement: Andante sostenuto.

Manuscripts: **A-Wst:** MH 10339/c. Score(22 p.)

Premiere: May 15, 1930, Berlin, Beethovensaal; Artur Schnabel, piano; Karl Flesch, violin; and Gregor Piatigorsky, cello. *See:* B559

64. *Fiedellieder*. (UE; dur: 10 min.) *See:* B462, B1040, B1041
For medium voice & piano. Text by Theodor Storm and Theodor Mommsen from *Liederbuch dreier Freund* (Kiel: Schwers'sche Büch Handlung, 1843; Neudruck Leipzig: Bibliophilenabend, 1929)
Composed: February 5 - 6, 1930.

1: *Meine Laute nehm ich wieder* (February 5, 1930, Vienna) **2:** *Musikanten wollen wandern* (February 5, 1930, Vienna) **3:** *Im Walde* (February 5, 1930, Vienna) **4:** *Und so lasst mich weiter wandern* (February 5, 1930, Vienna) **5:** *Nur ein Scherflein in der Runde* (February 5, 1930, Vienna) **6:** *Die Saiten weiss ich zu rühren* (February 6, 1930, Vienna) **7:** *Wiederum lebt wohl* (February 6, 1930, Vienna)

Manuscripts: A-Wn: L1 UE 219. Score(12 p.)

Premiere: April 11, 1930, Dresden, Paul Arons "Neue Musik"; Elisa Stünzner, soprano; Paul Aron, piano. *See:* B1148, B1156, B1157, B1162

Publications: B560, B1460

Recording: New Records NRLP 405. 33 1/3 rpm. mono. [1952] *See:* B99, B142, B195, B326, B556, B863, B1037
Polly Batic, contralto; Robert Leukauf, piano.
With songs by Johann Hauer and Zoltan Kodaly.

65. *Quartet, strings, no.5*. (UE; dur: 45 min.) *See:* B33, B73, B372, B1519
Composed: April 20 - May 3, 1930.

1: *Sonate* (April 20 - 22, 1930, Vienna) **2:** *Thema und Variationen* (April 10 - 17, 1930, Vienna) **3:** *Phantasie* (April 28 - May 3, 1930, Vienna)

Manuscripts: **A-Wst:** MH 10384/c:1. Sketches(24 p.) **A-Wst:** MH 10340. Score(54 p.) **A-Wst:** UE deposit Box K-S. Non-autograph parts. **US** composer Parts(2d mvt.)

Premiere: September 29, 1930, Copenhagen; Kolisch Quartett.

Other Performances: B937, B1508

Recording: Composers Recordings CRI SD 522. 33 1/3 rpm. stereo. p1985. *See:* B408, B534, B1347
Thouvenel String Quartet.
Duration: 40 min.
Recorded July 1983 at Evergreen Studios, Burbank CA.

66. *Kehraus um St. Stephan* = *Cleaning out around St. Stephen*. (unpublished)
Opera, 2 acts; text by Ernst Krenek. Elisabeth Torregiani, Othmar Brandstetter, Alfred Koppreiter, Herr Goldstein, Sebastian Kundrather, Ferdinand Kundrather, Maria Kundrather, Emmerich van Kereszthely, Moritz Fekete, Nora Rittinghaus, Oberwachmann Sachsl, Tobias Lämmergeier, Pepi, chorus, and orchestra: 2.2.4.2 / 2.2.2.1 / timpani / piano / harmonium / guitar / mandoline / percussion / strings.
Composed: June 13 - September 23, 1930, Dölsach; Instr. July 13 - September 28, 1930, Dölsach.

Manuscripts: **A-Wst:** Nachlass. Libretto. **A-Wgm.** Sketches(20 p., incomplete) **A-Wst:** Nachlass. Sketches(14 p.) **A-Wst:** MH 10366. Score(507 p.) **A-Wst:** MH 10367. Scene 15, 2 versions score(pp.407-415, 407-430) **A-Wst:** UE deposit. Piano-vocal score(274 p.)

Published (Libretto): In *Prosa, Dramen, Verse*. (Münich: Albert Langen - Georg Müller, 1965): 151-208.

Published (Libretto): In *Das musikdramatische Werk, v.2*, hrsg. von Franz Eugen

Dostal. Oesterreichische Dramatiker der Gegenwart, v.23. (Wien: Oesterreichische Verlagsanstalt, 1977): 43-97.

Unauthorized First Performance: (Scene) 1982, Hamburg, Hamburger Musikwochen '82; Rolf Nagel, producer. *See:* B759

67. *Durch die Nacht* = *Through the night.* (UE; dur: 18 min.) *See:* B1040, B1041, B1189, K908
For soprano & piano. German text from *Worte in Versen* by Karl Kraus.
Composed: December 6, 1930 - January 19, 1931.
1: *Vor dem Schlaf* (December 31, 1930 - January 1, 1931, Wien) "So spät ist es" "So late, so late, so haunting" **2:** *Vor dem Schlaf* (January 1 - 3, 1931, Wien) "Da weht mich wieder jene Ahnung an" "Now old foreboding breaths on me again" **3:** *Erlebnis* (December 6 - 31, 1930, Wien) "Ich hab von dem fahrenden Zuge geträumt" "I dreamed of the hurring railway train" **4:** *Nächtliche Stunde* (January 7, 1931, Wien) "Nächtliche Stunde, die mir vergeht" "Nocturnal hour that passes from me" **5.** *Fernes Licht mit nahem Schein.* "Distant ray that shineth near" **6.** *Der Tag.* "Wie der Tag sich durch das Fenster traut" "As the day here through the window strays" **7:** *Flieder* (January 19, 1931, Wien) "Nun weiss ich doch, 's ist Frühling wieder" "And now I know that it is Spring again"
Manuscripts: **A-Wst:** MH 10388/c. Sketch(18 p.) **A-Wn:** L1 UE 683. Score(28 p.)
Premiere: April 10, 1931, Dresden, Künstlerhaus; Elisa Stünzner, soprano; composer, piano. *See:* B320
Other Performances: B21, B846, B1383
Recording: Orion ORS 80377. *Ernst Krenek vocal compositions.* 33 1/3 rpm. stereo. [1980] *See:* B740, B1358
Anne Marie Ketchum, soprano; George Calusdian, piano.
Duration: 17 min., 44 sec.
Recorded April 13, 1979, University of California, Santa Barbara Krenek Festival.
With his op.61, op.186a, op.210, op.210, op.226, and op.35.

67a. *Durch die Nacht.* (UE; dur: 18 min.)
For soprano with accompaniment arranged for orchestra: 2.0.2.1 / 0.1.0.0 / piano / strings.
Composed: 1931.
Premiere: June 19, 1932, Vienna, Grosser Musikvereinssaal, Zehntes Musikfest der Internationale Gesellschaft für neue Musik; Wiener Symphoniker; Hedda Kux, soprano; Anton Webern, conductor. *See:* B453, B516, B1017, B1088, B1104

68. *Die Nachtigall* = *The nightingale.* (UE; dur: 8 min.) *See:* B1040, B1041, K908
For soprano & piano. German text from *Worte in Versen* by Karl Kraus.
Composed: February 7 - 10, 1931, Vienna.
1: *Ihr Menschenkinder* = *You human beings.* **2:** *Wir verkünden euch den Wechsel im Jahr* = *We announce to you the change of the year.* **3:** *Zuerst war Eros im goldenen Licht* = *First Eros dwelled in golden light.*
Manuscripts: **A-Wst:** MH 10387/c. Sketch(4 p.) **A-Wn:** L1 UE 655. Score(9 p.)
Premiere: November 26, 1931, Frankfurt.
First U.S. Performance: January 12, 1950, New York, Times Hall; Naomi Ornest, soprano. *See:* B1, B301

Publications: B288, B561, B731, B813

Recording: Carolina Records 712 C-2538. *Contemporary birds.* 33 1/3 rpm. [1971]
Ethel Casey, soprano; Janet Southwick, piano.
With songs by Arnold Schoenberg, Alban Berg, Anton Webern, Frank Martin,
and Roberto Gerhard.

68a. *Die Nachtigall* = *The nightingale.* (UE; dur: 8 min.)
For soprano with accompaniment arranged for orchestra: 2 flutes & strings.
Composed: February 7 - 10, 1931, Vienna.

Manuscripts: **A-Wn:** L1 UE 654. Score(8 p.)

Premiere: October 27, 1931, Bern, Bern Musikgesellschaft, Abonnements-Konzert;
Lucy Siegrist. *See:* B630, B817, B1066

First U.S. Performance: April 25, 1983, New York, Alice Tully Hall; Phyllis Bryn-
Julson, soprano; American Composers Orchestra; Michael Tilson-Thomas,
conductor. *See:* B1106

69. *Theme and 13 variations.* (UE; dur: 20 min.) *See:* B725, K194
For orchestra: 2.2.3.3 / 4.3.2.1 / timpani / harp / percussion / strings.
Composed: Theme March 8, Variations April 21 - May 17, 1931, Vienna.

Manuscripts: **A-Wn:** L1 UE 669. Score(77 p.)

Premiere: October 29, 1931, New York, Carnegie Hall; New York Philharmonic-
Symphony; Erich Kleiber, conductor. *See:* B472

First European Performance: June 10, 1932, Zürich, Allgemeinen Deutschen
Musikvereins. *See:* B1012, B1187

70. *Vier Bagatellen* = *Sonata, piano, 4 hands.* (unpublished; dur: 18 min.)
Composed: July 11 - October 7, 1931.
1: *Overture* (July 11, 1931, Sierre, Valais) **2:** *Minuet* (July 15, 1931, Sierre, Valais) **3:**
Intermezzo (July 21, 1931, Sierre, Valais) **4:** *Rondo* (October 7, 1931, Vienna)

Manuscripts: **A-Wst** Score(24 p.) **A-Wst:** MH 10341. Non-autograph score(37 p.)

Premiere: April 25, 1937, Vienna, Kleinkunstbühne ABC in Cafe Arkaden,
Konzerte moderner Musik; Peter Stadlen, composer, piano.

Other Performances: B224

Recording: Music Library MLR 7014. 33 1/3 rpm. mono. [1952] *See:* B195
Maro Ajemian, piano; composer, piano.
With his *Sonata, piano, no.4, op.114.*

70a. *Kleine Blasmusik* = 4 *Bagatelles.* (UE & AMP; dur: 15 min.) *See:* B1463
Arranged for band: 2.2.3.3 / 2.2.2.1 / timpani / percussion.
Arranged: 1931.

Premiere: June 16, 1932, Frankfurt am Main, Südwestfunk; Hans Rosbaud,
conductor.

Recording: Louisville Orchestra LS 756. *Music for winds, brass and percussion.* 33
1/3 rpm. stereo. [1975] Louisville Orchestra first edition records [1975, no. 6]
See: B148, B196, B257, B1127, B1382
Louisville Orchestra; Jorge Mester, conductor.
Duration: 13 min., 3 sec.
Recorded October 30, 1975, Macauley Theater, Louisville, KY.
With his *Merry marches,* op.44 and Peter Maxwell Davies *Saint Michael Sonata.*

71. *Gesänge des späten Jahres = Songs of the late years.* (UE; dur: 40 min.) *See:* B1041, B1111, B1150, B1189, K208
For voice & piano. German text by the composer.
Composed: September 29 - December 27, 1931.

1: *Wanderlied im Herbst = Walking in Autumn* (September 29 - October 17, 1931, Vienna) "Kalter Regen peitscht die kahle Flur" "Cold rain pelts bare fields" **2:** *Mauern wachsen = Walls grow* (November 11, 1931, Vienna) "Rings um uns wachsen Mauern" "Walls grow around us daily" **3:** *Ballade von den Schiffen = Ballad of the ships* (December 19, 1931, Vienna) "Ich habe alle meine Schiffe ausgesendet" "I launched all my ships" **4:** *Ballade vom Fest = Ballad of the feast* (October 29, 1931, Vienna) "Wir haben von Anbeginn her eine Einladung zum Fest" "We have had from the first an invitation to the feast" **5:** *Heimatgefühl = Sentiment for home* (October 25, 1931, Vienna) "Und ob mein Leben auch eingegraben sei" "And even if my life were entrenched" **6:** *Trinklied = Drinking song* (December 3, 1931, Vienna) "Allein in sonniger Herbstlaube" "Alone in the sunny autumn foliage" **7:** *Liebeslied = Love song* (November 23, 1931, Vienna) "Dass Liebe Raum noch hat" "That love has a space in such a time" **8:** *Und Herbstlaub und Regenschauer = Leaves and rainshowers* (October 14, 1931, Vienna) "Wie traurig du am Gartentore standst" "How sadly you stood at the garden gate" **9:** *Vor dem Tod = Before death* (December 18, 1931, Vienna) "Immer leiser verrinnst du" "Always more softly you slip away" **10:** *Der Augenblick = The instant.* (For piano alone) **11:** *Der Genuss des Unendlichen = The enjoyment of the infinite* (December 27, 1931, Vienna) "Einmal, einmal in vielen hunderttausend Tagen" "Once, once in many hundred thousand days"

Manuscripts: US composer No.1 - 2, 5, 10 - 11 score(pp.3-15, 34-37, 58-67) A-Wst: UE deposit Box A-J. No.1, blueprint score(7 p.) A-Wn: L1 UE 684. No.3 - 4, 6 - 9, score(16-33, 38-57 p.) A-Wst: UE deposit Box A-J. Text(10 p.) & proofs.

Premiere: March 25, 1932, Dresden Tonkünstler-Verein; Elisa Stünzner, soprano; composer, piano. *See:* B71, B321, B428, B686, B1158, B1159

First U.S. Performance: New York, Town Hall, sponsored by the New Friends of Music; Herta Glaz, soprano; composer, piano. *See:* B121

Other Performances: B18, B772, B773, B995

Publications: B782

Published (Text): In *Prosa, Dramen, Verse.* (Münich: Albert Langen - Georg Müller, 1965): 399-406.

Recording: Edition Rhodos ERS 1202-3. (set) 33 1/3 rpm. [1969?] *See:* B245, B697
Rudo Timper, tenor; composer, piano.
Recorded February 28, 1968.
With his *Reisebuch aus den österreichischen Alpen,* op.62 and *The ballad of the railroads,* op.98.

Recording: Orion ORS 78308. 33 1/3 rpm. stereo. [1978] *See:* B208, B1027, B1356
Michael Ingham, baritone; Carolyn Horn, piano.
Duration: 49 min., 36 sec.

72. *Kantate von der Vergänglichkeit des Irdischen = Cantata on the transitoriness of earthly things.* (UE; dur: 20 min.) *See:* B50, B1189
For soprano, mixed chorus & piano. German texts by various seventeenth century authors from *Die Vergessenen; Hundert deutsche Gedichte aus dem XVII. und XVIII. Jahrhunderts* by Heinrich Fischer (Berlin: P. Cassirer, 1926). English translation by the composer.

Composed: April 16, 1932, Vienna.

1: *Tears of the Fatherland*. (Text by Andreas Gryphius). "We now are all destroyed" **2:** *Sta viator!* (Text by Martin Opitz). "Ye foolish mortals" **3:** *On a fountain.* (Text by Johann Klay). "Streaks of shiny silver" **4:** *On a linden tree.* (Text by Johann Klay). "Lovely linden tree" **5:** *New Year 1633.* (Text by Paul Fleming). "Let the bloody battles stop" **6:** *At the end.* (Text by Andreas Gryphius). "In dreads and bitter fear" **7:** *Evening.* (Text by Andreas Gryphius). "The hasty day has gone"

Manuscripts: **A-Wn:** L1 UE 274. Score(24 p.) **US** composer English version.

Premiere: October 9, 1933, Zürich; Mia Peltenburg, soprano; Häusermannscher Privatchor; composer, piano; Hermann Dubs, conductor. *See:* B464, B1188

Publications: B289, B1009, B1098

73. *Karl V.* = *Charles V.* (UE) *See:* B2, B4, B22, B33, B50, B81, B86, B136, B290, B406, B429, B465, B514, B652, B662, B663, B777, B794, B853, B869, B881, B882, B921, B926, B932, B995, B1047, B1058, B1059, B1093, B1105, B1189, B1293, B1299, B1326, B1378, B1500, B1502, B1510, B1513, K221, K229, K231, K240, K247, K251, K285, K286, K295, K329, K345, K354, K434, K480, K493, K523, K577, K586, K595, K830, K893, K894, K926, K927, K933

Opera in 2 parts; text by the composer. Karl V. (baritone), Juana (alto), Eleonore (soprano), Ferdinand (tenor), Isabella (soprano), Juan de Regla (speaker), Francisco Borgia, tenor, Francis I (tenor), Frangipani (tenor), Martin Luther (baritone), Sultan Soliman (baritone), chorus and orchestra: 2.2.3.2 / 4.2.2.1 / harp / percussion / strings.

Composed: June 13, 1932 - May 24, 1933, Velden am Worthersee - Vienna. Revised 1954.

Dedication: Wiener Staatsoper und ihrem Direktor Clemens Krauss.

Manuscripts: **A-Wn:** L1 UE 276. Libretto, proofs. **A-Wst:** MH 10405. Sketch(120 p.) **A-Wn:** L1 UE 729. Piano-vocal score(212 p.) **A-Wst:** UE deposit. Score(251 p.)

Premiere: June 22, 1938, Prague, Neues Deutsches Theater; Karl Rankl, conductor; Franz Schulthes, scenery; Friedrich Schramm, producer; Pavel Ludikar, Karl V; Anton Schmerzenreich, Juan; Martha Cuno, Eleonore; Harriet Henders, Isabella; Lydia Kindermann, Juana; Kurt Baum, Francois; Josef Schwarz, Luther; Hans Grahl, Francisco Borgio. *See:* B474, B475, B733, B734, B920, B1021, B1307, B1308, K488

First German Performance: March 27, 1950, Essen Opera Haus; Gustav König, conductor; Hanns Hartleb, producer; Paul Haferung, scenery; Julius Jüllich, Karl; Ellen Bosenius, Eleonore; Horst Braun, Juan; Fritz Zoellner, Luther; Lutz Walter Miller, Francis I. *See:* B476, B612

Revised version: May 11, 1958, Düsseldorf/Duisburg, Deutsche Oper am Rhein; Reinhard Peters, conductor; Heinz Arnold, scenery; Karl Wolfram, Karl; Ingebord Lasser, Juana; Valerie Bak, Eleonore; Elisabeth Schwarzenberg, Isabella; Hubert Berger, Juan; Paul Späni, Francis I; Thomas Hemsley, Luther. *See:* B52, B53, B75, B157, B296, B790, K711

Original version: October 18, 1984, Vienna, Wiener Staatsoper; Erich Leinsdorf, conductor; Otto Schenk, director; Xenia Hausner, sets; Günther Reich, Karl; Frank Hoffmann, Juan; Karan Armstrong, Eleonore; Margarethe Bence, mother; Thomas Moser, Francis I. *See:* B87, B94, B917, B918, B919, B1109, B1511, K907

Other Performances: B240, B1501, B1504

Publications: B360

Published (Libretto): In *Spectaculum, Texte moderner Opern,* hrsg. von Hans Heinz Stuckenschmidt. (Frankfurt: Suhrkamp, 1962): 199 - 230.

Published (Libretto): In *Prosa, Dramen, Verse.* (Münich: Albert Langen - Georg Müller, 1965): 209-254.

Published (Libretto): In *Das musikdramatische Werk, v.2,* hrsg. von Franz Eugen Dostal. Oesterreichische Dramatiker der Gegenwart, v.23. (Wien: Oesterreichische Verlagsanstalt, 1977): 99-140.

Published (Facsimile page): In *Dank an Ernst Krenek* (Wien: Universal Edition, 1982)

Published (Facsimile page): In *Ernst Krenek, eine Studie,* von Lothar Knessl. Oesterreichische Komponisten des 20. Jahrhunderts, 12. (Wien: Elisabeth Lafite, 1967):between pp.64-65.

Recording: Amadeo AVRS 305. 2 discs. 33 1/3 rpm. stereo. p1981. *See:* B189, B486, B536, B669, B802, B1177
Theo Adam, Karl V; Hanna Schwarz, Juana; Sena Jurinac, Eleonore; Thomas Moser, Ferdinand; Kristine Ciesinski, Isabella; Frank Hoffmann, Juan de Ragla; Helmut Melchert, Francisco Borgia; Peter Schreier, Franz I.; Horst Hiestermann, Fragipani; Siegfried Vogel, Luther; Thomas Moser, Luther desciple; Alfred Sramek, Sultan Soliman; Horst Hiestermann, Astrologer; ORF-Chor, Wien; ORF-Symphonieorchester; Gerd Albrecht, conductor. Also issued on Philips 6769 084. 33 1/3 rpm.

73a. *Fragmente aus dem Bühnenwerk Karl V.* (UE; dur: 20 min.) *See:* K843
For soprano (no.2) & orchestra: 2.2.3.2 / 4.2.2.1 / harp / percussion / strings.
1: *Estremadura [rehearsal nos.1 - 7].* **2:** *Eleonore (Arie der Eleonore) [rehearsal nos.23 - 39].* **3:** *Das letzte Gericht [rehearsal nos.122 - 133].*

Manuscripts: **A-Wn:** L1 UE 272. Proofs.

Premiere: April 19, 1936, Barcelona, Plau de la Musica Catalana, XIV. Festival Internationale Gesellschaft für neue Musik; Leonore Meyer, soprano; Orquestra Pau Casals; Ernest Ansermet, conductor. *See:* B204, B1241, B1266, B1388, K369

Recording: Preiserrecords SPR 10049. 33 1/3 rpm, stereo. [197-?] Dokumentationsreihe des Osterreichischen Komponistenbundes, 24.
Halina Lukomska-Bloch, soprano; ORF-Symphonieorchester; Ernst Bour, conductor.
Duration: 18 min., 25 sec.
With his *Sonata, violin & piano, op.99* and *7 Stucke, string orchestra, op.146*

74. *Jagd im Winter.* (unpublished)
For TTBB chorus, 4 horns & timpani. German text by Franz Grillparzer.
Composed: Fruhjahr, 1933, Vienna
Text: "Der Himmel grau, die Erde weiss"

Manuscripts: **A-Wst:** MH 10342. Score(7 p.)

75. *Das Schweigen* = *Silence.* (unpublished; dur: 8 min.)
For bass & piano. Text by Eberhard Friedrich freiherr von Gemminger.
Composed: July 20, 1933, Vienna
Text: "Einsehafte Gottheit, heil'ges Schweigen"

Manuscripts: **A-Wst:** MH 10343. Score(8 p.)

Premiere: January 24, 1934, Winterthur, SZ, Musikkollegium; Felix Loeffel, bass; composer, piano.

76. *Währed der Trennung.* (unpublished; dur: 4 min.)
For mezzo-soprano, baritone & piano. Text by Paul Fleming.
Composed: July 23, 1933, Vienna.

Manuscripts: A-Wst: MH 10344. Score(8 p.)

Premiere: January 24, 1934, Winterthur, SZ, Musikkollegium; Mia Peltenburg, mezzosoprano; Felix Loeffel, bass; composer, piano.

77. *Cefalo e Procri* = *Cephalus and Procris.* (UE; dur: 35 min.)
Italian opera, prologue & 3 scenes. Text by Rinaldo Küfferle; German translation by the composer. Cephalus (tenor), Procris (soprano), Diana (alto), Aurora (soprano), Kronos (baritone), and orchestra: 1.1.2.1 / 2.1.1.0 / timpani / percussion / piano / strings.
Composed: 1933 - March 8, 1934, Sienna.

Manuscripts: A-Wst: Nachlass. Notes. A-Wst: UE deposit. German libretto(13 p.) A-Wgm. Sketches(42 p.) A-Wst: UE deposit. Piano-vocal score(54 p.) A-Wgm. Piano-vocal score(12 p., unfinished)

Premiere: September 15, 1934, Venice, Goldoni-Theater, III. Internationale Gesellschaft für neue Musik; Hermann Scherchen, conductor; Giovanni Voyer, Cefalo; Sara Scuderi, Procri; Ines Alfani, Aurora; Rhea Toniolo, Diana; Apollo Granforte, Crono. *See:* B352, B410, B1048

77a. *Austrian folksongs.* (unpublished)
Arranged for SATB chorus a cappella; no.3 with soprano solo.
Composed: 1934.
1: *Nachtwächterlied* (Pötsching in Burgenland) "Um achte betrachte" from *25 echte Volkslieder aus dem österr. Burgenland.* (Wien, 1927). **2:** *Es wollt ein Maderl ganz früh aufstehn.* (St.Georgen bei Eisendtadt, Burgenland) "Es wollt ein Maderl ganz früh aufstehen" from *25 echte Volkslieder aus dem österr. Burgenland.* (Wien, 1927). **3:** *Geah i ausse übers Gwänd* (Von der Lavant und Glan) "Aber Diandle" from *"Wulfenia-Blünten" Lieder aus Kärnten.* (Wien, 1932). **4:** *Maria ging in Garten* (Riefensberg im Bregenzerwald) "Maria ging in Garten" from H. Pommer, *Volkslieder und Jodler aus Vorarlberg.* (Wien 1926).

Manuscripts: A-Wst: UE deposit Box A-J. No.1 - 4, non-autograph score(7, 7, 2, 4 p.) A-Wst: MH 10360. No.1, non-autograph score(7 p.) A-Wst: MH 10361. No.2, non-autograph score(6 p.) A-Wst: MH 10362. No.3, non-autograph score(2 p.) A-Wst: MH 10363. No.4, non-autograph score([4] p.)

Premiere: February 25, 1935, Vienna, Ehrbar-Saal, 4. Oesterreichische Studio; Wiener Kaufmännische Gesangsverein; Josefine Weinschenk, soprano; Karl Lahr, piano; Julius Katay, conductor. *See:* B469, K297

77b. *Italian ballads.* (unpublished)
Arranged for voice & piano.
Composed: August 27 - September 1, 1934.
1: *Donna lombarda* (August 29 - 30, 1934, Vienna) **2:** *La monachella e il demonio* (September 1, 1934, Vienna) "Monacella lava nel l'orra" **3:** *Il cavalier di Francia* (August 27, 1934, Vienna) "Chi è chi è che bussa?"

Manuscripts: A-Wst: UE deposit Box A-J. Score(6, 3, 5) **US** composer Non-autograph score(8, 4, 6 p.)

78. *Quartet, strings, no.6.* (UE; dur: 28 min.) *See:* B2, B33, B73, B81, B324, B372, B748, B1050, B1502, B1519, K496, K624, K774
Composed: March 8 - October 13, 1936.

1: *Adagio* (March 8, 1936, Vienna) 2: *Allegro, piuttosto comodo, con grazia* (July 10, 1936, Hochsölden) 3: *Vivace* (August 29, 1936, Serfaus) 4: *Adagio* (September 5, 1936, Tremezzo (Como)) 5: *Fuga a quattro soggetti* (October 13, 1936, Vienna)

Manuscripts: **US-CA.** Sketches(23 p.) **A-Wn:** L1 UE 680. Score(34 p.) **A-Wn:** L1 UE 681. Score(54 p., corrected proofs) **US** composer Parts. **A-Wst:** UE deposit Box K-S. Proof parts.

Premiere: January 16, 1953, Darmstadt, Kranichsteiner Musikgesellschaft; Assmann Quartett. *See:* B200, B278, B599, B764, B765, B1274, B1275

First U.S. Performance: Summer 1959, Tanglewood, CT; Lenox Quartet. *See:* B440, B1023, B1345, K729

Other Performances: B937, B1508

Publications: B349

78a. *Adagio und Fuge.* (UE; dur:15 min.) *See:* K762
Movements 4 and 5 arranged for string orchestra.

Manuscripts: **A-Wst:** UE deposit Box A-J. Score(23 p.)

Premiere: August 28, 1966, Lucerne, SZ, Internationalen Musikfestwochen Luzern 1966; Festival Strings Lucerne; Rudolf Baumgartner, conductor. *See:* B889, B1138

79. *Zwölf Variationen in drei Sätzen* = *Twelve variations in three movements.* (Assmann; dur: 23 min.) *See:* B81, B324, B584, K495, K510, K527, K624, K774
For piano.
Composed: January 27 - April 4, 1937, Lausanne, SZ - Vienna; revised 1940 & 1957.

1: *Allegro, molto moderato, energico - Allegretto, poco misterioso - Allegro corrente - Allegro moderato, energico - Piu allegro.* 2: *Adagio* (endless double canon a 4, by inversion and retrogression) 3: *Allegretto grazioso - Allegro assai - Vivace - Allegretto - Adagio.*

Manuscripts: **CH-W:** Dep RS 35/6. **A-Wst:** MH 10385/c. Sketch(14 p.) **US-Wc:** ML96.K7835 no.25 Case. 1940 revision transparencies(15 p.)

Premiere: December 16, 1937, Los Angeles, home of Mrs.Edgar Baruch, 1222 S.Van Ness Ave., Sponsored by Pro Musica; composer, piano. *See:* B231, B366, B1136, K510

Other Performances: B1242

Publications: B414, B776

80. *Campo Marzio.* (unpublished; dur: 5 min.)
Overture for orchestra: 1.1.1.1 / 2.2.1.0 / timpani / celesta / piano / percussion / strings.
Composed: 1937.

Premiere: Lugano.

80a. *L'incoronazione di Poppea* = *Die Krönung der Poppea.* (UE) *See:* K367, K396, K453, K454, K458, K854
Italian libretto by Giovanni Francesco Busenello; music by Claudio Monteverdi. Orchestration and German translation by Ernst Krenek.

Poppea, Nerone, Ottavia, Ottone, Drusilla, Arnalta, Seneca, captain, Pallade, and soldiers, and orchestra: 1.1.1.1 / 2.1.1.0 / harp / harmonium / piano / strings.
Composed: November 27, 1936, Vienna; Instr. December 12, 1936.

Manuscripts: **A-Wst:** UE deposit Box S-Z. Italian libretto(33 p.) **A-Wgm.** German libretto(6 p., part 2 incomplete) **A-Wgm.** Sketches(56, 30 p.) **A-Wn:** L1 UE 709. Piano-vocal score(144 p.) **A-Wst:** UE deposit. Score(252 p.)

Premiere: September 25, 1937 (in Italian), Vienna, Stadttheater, Internationale Operngesellschaft; Salzburg International Opera Guild; Max Sturzenegger, conductor; composer, between acts music conductor; Eugen Schulz-Breiden, production; Theo Otto, scenery & costumes; Herta Glaz, Poppea; Hans Joachim Heinz, Nerone; Aurora Dolci, Ottavia; Igino Zangheri, Ottone; Grete Menzel, Drusilla; Esther von Ilosvay, Arnalta; Dezsö Ernster, Seneca; Ljubomir Pantscheff, captain; Laszlo Csabai, soldier. *See:* B471, B1133

First U. S. Performance: November 18, 1937, New York; Salzburg International Opera Guild. *See:* B269, B270, B970, B1132, B1350

80b. *L'Incoronazione di Poppea suite.* (UE; dur: 18 min.)
For orchestra: 1.1.1.1 / 2.1.1.0 / harp / piano / strings.
1: *Sinfonia.* **2:** *Molto largo, Act 1.* **3:** *Corrente, Act 2.* **4:** *Sarabande, Act 1.* **5:** *Marcia, Act 2.* **6:** *Intermezzo between Act 1 and 2.*

First U.S. Performance: January 21, 1963, Los Angeles, Fiesta Hall, Plummer Park, Monday Evening Concerts; composer, conductor. *See:* B436, B678

Other Performances: B363

80c. *Ball bei Prinz Eugen, baroque Tanzmusik.* (UE)
Arranged for piano.
Composed: 1935.
1: *Marche sur l'arrivée du Prince Eugène,* by Jacques de St. Luc. **2:** *Gavotta* by Johann Heinrich Schmelzer. **3:** *Minuetto* by Ferdinand Ignaz Hinterleithner. **4:** *Aria* by Johann Heinrich Schmelzer. **5:** *Gigue* by Johann Anton graf Losy von Losintal. **6:** *Balletto* by Johann Heinrich Schmelzer. **7:** *Paesana* by Johann Georg Weichenberger. **8:** *Gigue* by Johann Theodor Herold. **9:** *Fantasia* by Johann Heinrich Schmelzer. **10:** *Carillon d'Anvers* by Jacques de St.Luc. **11:** *Campanella e lamento* by Johann Heinrich Schmelzer. **12:** *Aria* by Johann Joseph Hoffer.

81. *Concerto, piano, no.2.* (UE; dur: 22 min.)
For piano with orchestra: 2.2.2.2 / 4.2.2.1 / timpani / celesta / percussion / strings.
Composed: May 25 - August 2, 1937, Rome - Vent (Tirol).
1: *Andante dolcissimo, celeste* **2:** *Canon in der Urnkehrung. Adagio.* **3:** *Allegretto vivace, molto grazioso e leggiero.*
Commissioned: Concertgebouw Orchestra, Amsterdam.

Manuscripts: **A-Wst:** MH 10386/c. Sketch(23 p.) **A-Wst:** UE deposit Box K-S. Score(59 p.) **A-Wn:** PhA 1988. Non-autograph photocopy score(66 p.)

Premiere: March 17, 1938, Amsterdam; Concertgebouw Orchestra; composer, piano; Bruno Walter, conductor. *See:* B44, B481, B941

First U.S. Performance: November 4, 1938, Boston, Symphony Hall; Boston Symphony Orchestra; composer, piano; Richard Burgin, conductor. *See:* B165, B202, B282, B377, B508, B732, B815, B1243, B1244, B1246, B1468, B1485, B1486

Other Performances: B360, B615, B674, B1238

82. **Lieder nach Worten von Franz Kafka** = *Five songs (Kafka).* (UE & Schott)
    See: B553, B624, B898, K908
    For voice & piano.
    Composed: October 14, 1937 - January 16, 1938.
    1: *Nur ein Wort, nur eine Bitte* (October 14 - 27, 1937, ship "De Grasse" off
    Newfoundland - Worcester-Utica, NY) **2:** *Kämpfte er nicht genug?* (December 2 - 3,
    1937, Chicago) **3:** *Noch spielen die Jagdhunde im Hof* (December 9, 1937, Omaha-
    Cheyenne) **4:** *Du kannst dich zurückhalten von den Leiden der Welt* (January 1,
    1938, Hollywood) **5:** *Ach, was wird uns hier bereitet?* (January 10 - 16, 1938, San
    Francisco)

    Manuscripts: **CH-B**: PSS 8/11. Score(12 p.) **US** composer Sketch(4 p.) **A-Wst**: MH
    14939. Score(9 p.) **US** composer No.3 - 5, score. **A-Wst**: UE deposit Box A-J.
    No.4, score(1 p.)

    Premiere: March 1, 1942, Poughkeepsie, NY, Vassar College, Skinner Recital Hall;
    Olga Forrai, soprano; composer, piano. *See:* B491

    First European Performance: 1957, Mannheim; Carla Henius, soprano; Richard
    Laugs, piano. *See:* B1371

    Other Performances: B253, B1312

    Publications: B1078, B1392

    Published (Facsimile score): In *Ernst Krenek: Fünf Lieder nach Worten von Franz
    Kafka.* (Vienna: Wiener Stadt- und Landesbibliothek, 1985) *See:* B1337

    Recording: Carolina Records 712C-1463. *Casey sings; Town Hall debut.* 33-1/3
    rpm. [1961?]
    Ethel Casey, soprano; Walter Golde, piano.
    Recorded March 5, 1961, New York, Town Hall.
    With songs by Alban Berg, Erich Korngold, Claude Debussy, Joseph Marx,
    Arnold Schoenberg, Anton Webern, Rolfe Liebermann, and Hans Werner
    Henze.

83. **Twelve short piano pieces written in the 12-tone technique.** (Schirmer;
    dur: 11 min.) *See:* B158, B188, B691, B1429, K496
    Composed: December 3 - 17, 1938, Boston - New York.
    1: *Dancing toys.* **2:** *Peaceful mood.* **3:** *Walking on a stormy day.* **4:** *The moon
    rises.* **5:** *Little chessmen.* **6:** *A boat, slowly sailing.* **7:** *Streamliner.* **8:** *Glass
    figures.* **9:** *The sailing boat, reflected in the pond.* **10:** *On the high mountains.*
    11: *Bells in the fog.* **12:** *Indian summer day.*

    Premiere: January 3, 1939, 3:00P.M. National Broadcasting Company, Blue
    Network, from NBC Washington; composer, piano.

    Published (No.4): In *Fifty-one piano pieces from the modern repertoire.* (New York: G.
    Schirmer, 1940): 50.

    Recording: Nos.1 - 3 & 5 - 12. Columbia X 171 (17200-D -- 17201-D) (Mx: CO25698-
    CO25701) 10 in. 78 rpm. [1940] *See:* B488, B704, B1170
    Composer, piano.

    Recording: No.4, *The moon rises.* Paraclete Music Disc 51B. (Mx: 51B) 10 in. 78
    rpm.
    Eunice Eaton, piano.
    With Robert Elmore *Let them praise his name in the dance.*

84. *Suite, cello*. (Schirmer; dur: 10 min.) *See:* B974
Composed: February 18 - 20, 1939, Hollywood, CA.
1: *Andante affettuoso.* **2:** *Adagio.* **3:** *Allegretto.* **4:** *Andante scherzando.* **5:** *Andante, molto liberamente.*

Premiere: November 16, 1939, Poughkeepsie, NY, Vassar College, Skinner Recital Hall; Claus Adam, cello.

Other Performances: B102

Publications: B350

84a. *The night is far spent*. (Schirmer)
For voice & piano. Text from St. Matthew.
Composed: 1939.

85. *Eight column line*. (unpublished; dur: 60 min.) *See:* B555, K494
Ballet by Trude Kaschmann and Alwin Nikolais. For flute, clarinet, bass clarinet, trumpet, piano, 2 violins, viola, and cello.
Composed: March 20 - April 23, 1939, San Francisco, CA - Black Mountain, NC

Manuscripts: US composer Score(104 p.)

Premiere: May 19, 1939, Hartford, CT, Avery Memorial Auditorium, sponsored by the Wadsworth Atheneum and the Committee of Friends and Enemies of Modern Music; Alwin Nikolais, Trude Kaschmann, dancers; composer, conductor. *See:* B792, B955, B1245

85. *School music*. (Belwin)
Composed: 1938 - 1939.
a. *2 Themes by Handel,* oboe & piano. **b.** *Country dance,* 4 clarinets. **c.** *Flute player's serenade,* 4 flutes, by Thornton Winsloe (Allegretto, Moderato, Grazioso). **d.** *Sonatina, bass clarinet & piano,* by Thornton Winsloe (1. Allegretto moderato. 2. Andantino. 3. Allegro). **e.** *Allegro sinfonico,* flute, oboe, clarinet, bassoon & horn. (dur: 6 min.) **f.** *Rhapsody, clarinet & piano,* by Thornton Winsloe. (dur: 6 min.) **g.** *Ballade, horn & piano,* by Dewey Donaldson. (dur: 6 min.) **h.** *Nocturne, flute & piano.* (dur: 6 min.) **i.** *Sarabande, oboe & piano,* by Thornton Winsloe. (dur: 5 min.)

Manuscripts: **A-Wst** No.e, score(13 p.) & 5 parts(2 p.each) **A-Wst** No.f, score(7 p.) & part(2 p.) **A-Wst** No.g, score(6 p.) & part(2 p.) **A-Wst** No.h, score(4 p.) & part(2 p.) **A-Wst** No.i, score(4 p.) & part(2 p.)

Premiere: b. July 27, 1939, Ann Arbor, University of Michigan, Hill Auditorium, sponsored by University Musical Society, Student Recital series; James Lunn, Walter Avis, Ray Schultz, Don Scheid, clarinets.

86. *Symphonic piece* = *Symphonisches Stück*. (Schott/UE; dur: 16 min.) *See:* B417, B1050, B1190, B1515, K503, K520
For string orchestra.
Composed: June 15, 1939, Niagara Falls, NY.
Commissioned: Paul Sacher.
Dedication: Paul Sacher and the Basler Kammerorchester.

Manuscripts: **US** composer Score(14 p.) **A-Wst** Score US-PHf. Non-autograph score **CH-B:** PSS 8/12. Score(19 p.)

Premiere: June 11, 1940, Basel, SZ, Neuer Casino-Saal; Basler Kammerorchester; Paul Sacher, conductor. *See:* B3, B68, K497

First U.S. Performance: August 1, 1939, Ann Arbor, MI, University of Michigan, Hill Auditorium, sponsored by University Musical Society; Summer Session Symphony Orchestra; composer, conductor. *See:* B332

Other Performances: B1025

Published (Facsimile p.1): In *Alte und neue Musik,* von Willi Schuh. (Zürich: Atlantis Verlag, 1952): 86-91.

Published (Facsimile mm.172-190): In *Komponisten des 20. Jahrhunderts in der Paul Sacher Stiftung.* (Basle: Paul Sacher Stiftung, 1986): 220.

87. *Two choruses on Jacobean poems* = 2 *Choruses on Elizabethan poems.* (Rongwen; dur: 6 min.)
For SSAA chorus a cappella. English texts by William Drummond (no.1) and Sir Walter Raleigh (no.2).
Composed: December 16, 1939, Poughkeepsie, NY.
1: *This life, which seems so fair.* 2: *Even such is time.*

Manuscripts: US composer Score(6 p.)

Premiere: December 7, 1940, Poughkeepsie, NY, Vassar College, Skinner Recital Hall; Vassar Glee Club; John Pierce, director.

Recording: Audio Engineering Associates AEA-1094. *The UCSB Dorians in a program of music for women's voices from the 20th century.* 33 1/3 rpm. [197?].
UCSB Dorians; Michael Ingham, conductor.
Recorded at the University of California, Santa Barbara.
With his *Five Prayers* and choral works by Ernst Bacon, Darius Milhaud, Arnold Schoenberg, Milton Babbitt, Igor Stravinsky, and Bernhard Heiden.

88. *Little concerto.* (UE; dur: 10 min.) *See:* B503
For piano and organ (or piano) with orchestra: 1.0.1.0 / 0.0.0.0 / strings.
Composed: December 22, 1939 - January 5, 1940, Charleston, SC - Charlotte, NC.
1: *Andante sostenuto.* 2: *Andantino.* 3: *Allegro energico.* 4: *Andante, liberamente.* 5: *Adagio.* 6: *Allegretto.*

Manuscripts: US composer Score(15 p.) & 2 parts(11 p. each)

Premiere: May 23, 1940, Poughkeepsie, NY, Vassar College, Skinner Recital Hall; Mary Williams, piano; E. Harold Geer, organ; Vassar Orchestra; composer, conductor.

89. *Proprium missae in festo SS. Innocentium martyrum (die 28 Decembris).* (AM; dur: 10 min.)
For SSAA chorus a cappella. Latin text.
Composed: July 4, 1940, Ann Arbor, MI
1: *Introitus* (Psalm 8,3,2) "Ex ore infantium et loctentium" 2: *Graduale* (Psalm 123,7 - 8) "Anima nostra sicut passer erepta est" 3: *Alleluja, laudate* (Psalm 112,1) 4: *Tractus* (Psalm 78.3.10) "Effuderunt sanguinem sanctorum" 5: *Sancti tui domine* (Ecclesiastes 39,19). 6: *Communio* (Matthew 2,18)
Written for the Vassar College Choir.

Manuscripts: US-Wc: ML96 Case. Transparency score(8 p.) US composer Score(8 p.)

Premiere: December 15, 1940, Poughkeepsie, NY, Vassar College Chapel; Vassar College Choir; E. Harold Geer, conductor.

Publications: B302, B950, B1016

90. *Tarquin.* (unpublished) *See:* B944, K508
Chamber opera in 2 parts with 8 scenes. English text by Emmet Lavery;
German text by M.-C. Schulte-Strathaus and P. Funk. Marius (baritone),
Corinna (soprano), Cleon (tenor), Der Erzbischof (bass), Der Kanzler (tenor), 4
speaking rolls & ensemble: 0.0.1.0 / 0.1.0.0 / percussion / 2 pianos / violin.
Composed: January 27 - September 13, 1940, Poughkeepsie, NY - Hollywood,
CA.

Manuscripts: **A-Wst:** UE deposit Box S-Z. German libretto(32 p.) **A-Wst:** MH
14283/c. Piano-vocal score(126 p.) **A-Wst:** MH 14727/c. Sketches(43 + 3 p.)
US composer Score(195 p.)

Premiere: Laboratory demonstration reading (scenes 2 and 7 fully presented):
May 13, 1941, Poughkeepsie, NY, Vassar College, Avery Hall; Emmet Lavery,
Marius; John Pierce, Marius in scene 2; Juliette Harvey, Corinna; Elizabeth
Muir, Corinna in scene 2 & epilogue; Elinor Shutts, Corinna in scene 7;
Richard Brooks, Cleon; Henry Noble MacCracken, Archbishop; Nikander
Strelsky, Chancellor; Charles Gordon Post, Bruno; Francis Matteson,
Reporter; Clair Leonard, Tonio; Francis Matteson, Officer; composer, piano.

First European Performance (in German): July 16, 1950, Cologne, Städtische Bühnen
Köln; Wolfgang von der Nahmer, conductor; Erich Bormann, staging; Walter
Gondolf, scenery; Felix Knäpper, Marius; Charlotte Hoffmann-Pauels,
Corinna; Karl Bernhöft, Cleon; Wilhelm Schirp, Erzbischof; Karl Schiebener,
Kanzler; Fritzleo Liertz, Reporter; Dolf Dolz, Toni; Alexander Schoedler,
Bruno; Anton Germann, Officer; Herbert Anrath, violin; Franz Heil, clarinet;
Hermann Neuhaus, trumpet; Kurt Norden, percussion; Hans Brinkmann,
Herbert Esser, pianos. *See:* B292, B310, B415, B416, B1522

90a. *A contrapuntal excursion through the centuries.* (unpublished)
For student string orchestra.
Composed: June 29, 1941, Madison, WI
1: *Fifteenth century, Chanson.* **2:** *Sixteenth century, Cantus firmus.* **3:**
Eighteenth century, Choral prelude. **4:** *Nineteenth century, Fugue.* **5:**
Twentieth century, Four part canon.

Manuscripts: **A-Wst** Score(7 p.)

91. *La corona.* (BA; dur: 17 min.) *See:* B324, B503, B1301, B1502, K841
Cantata for mezzosoprano, baritone, organ & percussion. English text by
John Donne; later German translation by the composer.
Composed: July 8 - August 23, 1941, Madison, WI - Bear Lake, CO.
1: *Deigne at my hands this crown of prayer and praise.* **2:** *Annunciation.*
"Salvation to all that will is nigh" **3:** *Nativitie.* "Immensitie cloystered in thy
deare wombe" **4:** *Temple.* "With his kinde mother" **5:** *Crucifying.* "By
miracles exceeding power of man" **6:** *Resurrection.* "Moyst with one drop of
thy blood" **7:** *Ascension.* "Salute the last and everlasting day"

Manuscripts: **A-Wst** Score(24 p.) **D-brd** Kbärenreiter: BA 3991. Blueprint score(24
p.)

Premiere: 1958, Copenhagen.

First U.S. Performance: May 24, 1961, Berkeley, University of California, Alfred
Hertz Memorial Hall of Music; Anna Carol Dudley, soprano; Walter Matthes,
bass; Jack Van der Wyk, percussion; Lawrence Moe, organ; composer,
conductor. *See:* B386

91a. *The Holy ghost's ark.* (unpublished; dur: 6 min.)
For mezzosoprano, oboe, clarinet, viola, and cello. Text from a Whitsunday sermon by John Donne, 1626.
Composed: July 5, 1941, Madison, WI.
Text: "When the Holy Ghost hath brought us into the Ark"

Manuscripts: US composer Score(6 p.) US composer 4 parts. US composer 3 transparency parts(2 p. each; viola part lacking) US-CA. Score(4 p.)

Premiere: July 24, 1941, Madison, WI, University of Wisconsin, Music Hall; Clara Bloomfield, soprano; Alfred Barthel, oboe; Robert Woollen, clarinet; Harold Klatz, viola; Arthur Knecht, cello; composer, conductor.

92, no.1. *Sonata, organ.* (Gray; dur: 5 min.) *See:* B247, B503, B807, B1044, B1398, K848, K908
Composed: September 5, 1941, San Clemente, CA.
Allegro ma non troppo, energico - Andante sostenuto - Allegro scherzando.

Manuscripts: US-Wc: ML96 p. US-CA. 8 p.

Premiere: May 3, 1942, Poughkeepsie, NY, Vassar College Chapel; E. Harold Geer, organ.

Published: In *Contemporary masterworks for organ.* (New York: H.W. Gray, 1983) pp.19-28.

Recording: American Society of Composers, Authors and Publishers CB 191. *Pittsburgh International Contemporary Music Festival.* 33 1/3 rpm. microgroove. [1954]
Russell G. Wichmann, organ.
Recorded November 29, 1952, on the Ernest M. Skinner organ, Carnegie Music Hall, Pittsburgh, PA.
With organ works by Paul Hindemith & Walter Piston.

Recording: University of Oklahoma 2. *Organ compositions by Walter Piston, Ernst Krenek, and Roger Sessions.* 33 1/3 rpm. mono. [1953] *See:* B195, B196, B682, B1122, B1174
Mildred Andrews, organ.
Recorded on the Aeolian-Skinner Organ, First Presbyterian Church, Kilgore, TX.
With organ works by Vincent Luebeck, Walter Piston, and Roger Sessions.

Recording: Psallite 66/270 768 PES. 33 1/3 rpm. [1968] Das Orgelporträt, 22. *See:* B135
Werner Jacob, organ.
Recorded on the Willi Peter orgen, St. Nikolai, Hamburg.

Recording: Musica Viva MV 50-1090. *Arnold Schönberg, Ernst Krenek Sämtliche Orgelwerke.* 2 discs. 33 1/3 rpm. stereo. p1980. *See:* B825, B990, B1234
Martin Haselböck, organ.
Recorded January 13, 1980 on the Rieger organ, Frauenkirche, Baden bei Wien.
With his *Orga-nastro,* op.212; *4 Winds suite,* op.223; and *Opus 231* and the complete organ works of Arnold Schoenberg.
Also issued on Colosseum MV 50-1090.

92, no.2a. *Sonatina, flute & viola.* (unpublished)
Composed: January 6, 1942, Poughkeepsie, NY.
1: *Allegretto comodo.* **2:** *Adagio.* **3:** *Vivace.*

Manuscripts: US composer 4 p. **A-Wst:** UE deposit Box K-S. Blueprint score(4 p.)

Premiere: October 22, 1945, Buenos Aires, Teatro del Pueblo; Esteban Eitler, flute; Simon Zlotnik, viola.

92, no.2b. *Sonatina, flute & clarinet*. (BA; dur: 7 min.) *See:* B1463
Arrangement of *Sonatina, flute & viola*.

Manuscripts: **US-Wc:** ML96 Case. Transparency score(4 p.) **D-brd** Kbärenreiter. Blueprint score(4 p.) **A-Wst:** UE deposit Box K-S. Blueprint score(4 p.)

Premiere: October 30, 1944, Buenos Aires, Teatro del Pueblo; Esteban Eitler, flute; Mariano Frogioni, clarinet.

92, no.3. *Sonata, viola*. (Bomart; dur: 10 min.) *See:* K695
Composed: August 12 - 27, 1942.
1: *Allegro moderato, energico* (August 12 - 15, 1942, Bear Lake, CO) **2:** *Adagio* (August 21, 1942, Bear Lake, CO) **3:** *Scherzo, vivace* (August 28, 1942, Bear Lake, CO) **4:** *Chaconne, Allegro con vigore* (August 27, 1942, Bear Lake, CO)

Manuscripts: **US-Wc:** ML96 Case. Transparency(3 p.)

Premiere: April 11, 1947, Chicago, University of Chicago, Leon Mandel Assembly Hall; Germain Prevost, viola.

Other Performances: B253

Published: In *Three compositions for viola solo*. (Boelke-Bomart, 1975) pp.8-11.

92, no.4. *Sonata, piano, no.3*. (AMP) *See:* B29, B72, B159, B409, B447, B588, B1269, B1322, K611, K738,
In four numbered movements.
Composed: December 30, 1942 - May 22, 1943, St. Paul, MN. Revised 1960.

Manuscripts: **A-Wst:** MH 14717/c. Sketch(9 p.) **US-Eu.** Autograph(3 m., dated 1.5.1945, St.Paul, Minn.) **US-Wc:** ML96 Transparency(14 p.)

Premiere: December 1, 1943, Bridgman Hall, Hamline University, ISCM Twin Cities Chapter Concert; composer, piano. *See:* K531

First European Performance: October 2, 1950, Basle, SZ, Theater am Neumarkt, Pro Musica; composer, piano.

Other Performances: B43, B715, K533

Published (Facsimilie of the beginning): In *Musik des 20. Jahrhunderts*, von Alfred Baumgartner. (Salzburg: Kiesel Verlag, 1985): 400-402.

Recording: Society of Participating Artists SPA 4. 33 1/3 rpm. mono. [1952] *See:* B195
composer, piano.
With his *5 Pieces, op.39* and *8 Pieces, op.110*.

Recording: Columbia ML 5336. (Mx. XLP 44530-1A). 33 1/3 rpm. mono. [1958]
See: B195, B385, B425, B485, B647, B1125
Glenn Gould, piano.
With piano works by Alban Berg and Arnold Schoenberg. CBS M3K 42150. *The Glenn Gould legacy, vol.4*. compact disc. p1986.

Recording: First movement. Columbia HML 1009. (Mx: XLP 47959). *Columbia Home Music Library: Encyclopedia of music*, record 9, side B, section 2. 33 1/3 rpm. mono. c1959.
Glenn Gould, piano.
With excerpts of music by many composers.

Recording: First & Fourth movements. Le Chant du Monde LDX 78799. *Concert de Moscou.* [1986] *See:* B307
Glenn Gould, piano.
Recorded at a concert at the Moscow Conservatory, May 12, 1957. Includes a talk about Krenek.
With works by Alban Berg, Anton Webern, and Johann Sebastian Bach.

93. *Lamentatio Jeremiae prophetae.* (BA; dur: 68 min.) *See:* B33, B47, B72, B81, B137, B324, B396, B505, B539, B567, B568, B691, B777, B1050, B1087, B1401, B1408, B1413, B1413, B1502, K520, K611, K692, K730, K738, K740, K774, K839, K841, K872, K908
For SSAATTBB chorus a cappella. Text from the Tenebrae service of the Catholic Church during Holy Week; 3 lessons each for Maundy Thursday, Good Friday, and Holy Saturday.
Composed: November 11, 1941 - May 7, 1942, Poughkeepsie, NY.

1: *In coena Domini* (Ch.I:1 - 14). "Incipit lamentatio Jeremiae Prophetae" 2: *In parasceve* (Ch.II:8 - 15 & III:1 - 9) "De lamentatione Jeremiae Prophetae" 3: *In sabbato sancto* (Ch.III:22 - 30, IV:1 - 6 & V:1 - 11) "De lamentatione Jeremiae Prophetae"

Manuscripts: A-Wst: MH 14735/c. Sketch(22 + 9 p.) A-Wst: MH 14735/c. Text(2 p.) US-Wc: ML96 Case. Transparency score(39 p.) A-Wst: UE deposit Box K-S. Blueprint score(39 p.) D-brd Kbärenreiter. Blueprint score(39 p.) US-CA. Excerpt(2 p.) D-brd Kbärenreiter. Blueprint score(12 p., Flämig version)

Premiere: Excerpts, April 4, 1943, Hamline University, Bridgman Hall; Hamline University Madrigal Singers; Robert Holliday, director. *See:* B115, B140, B566, B886, B1224, B1393

First Complete Performance: October 5, 1958, Kassel, St. Martin Kirche, Kasseler Musiktage; NCRV Vocaal Ensemble Hilversum; Marinus Voorberg, conductor. *See:* B467, B603

Other Performances: B116, B119, B572, B868, B972, B1344

Publications: B1077

Recording: Lessons 1 & 2. New Records NRLP 306. *Choral music by the Hamline Choir.* 10 in. 33 1/3 rpm. [1952] *See:* B862, B1172
Hamline University Singers; Robert Holliday, conductor.
With his *The seasons,* op.35 and works by Roy Harris and Carlos Chavez.

Recording: Lessons 1, 6, & 7. Epic LC 3509. 33 1/3 rpm. mono. [1958] Fromm Music Foundation Twentieth century composers series. *See:* B195, B199, B222, B384, B480, B1124
Choir of the State School of Church Music in Dresden; Martin Flämig, conductor.
With his *Sestina,* op.161.

Recording: Bärenreiter Musicaphon 30 L 1303-4. 2 discs. 33 1/3 rpm. mono. [1961] *See:* B76, B139, B194, B195, B478, B540, B626
NCRV Vocaal Ensemble Hilversum; Marinus Voorberg, conductor.
Recorded January - February 1961 in the Grossen Kirche, Loenen, Holland.
With *Lieder des Abschieds* by Zillig.
Also issued on Bärenreiter LP 059 449.

94. *I wonder as I wander.* (unpublished; dur: 17 min.) *See:* B59, B354, K838
For orchestra: 2.2.2.3 / 4.2.3.1 / timpani / harp / percussion / strings.
Variations on a folktune "collected in North Carolina by John Jacob Niles and
included in his *Songs of the hill folk*" (New York: G. Schirmer, 1934). Niles
actually composed the tune.
Composed: June 6 - July 1, 1942, Poughkeepsie, NY - Madison, WI.

Manuscripts: **A-Wst:** MH 14729/c. Sketch(4 p.) **US** composer Score(40 p.)

Premiere: December 11, 1942, Minneapolis, MN; Minneapolis Symphony
Orchestra; Dimitri Mitropoulos, conductor. *See:* B114, B579, B843, B1223
Broadcast (WABC-CBS): New York, December 20, 1942; New York
Philharmonic-Symphony; Dimitri Mitropoulos, conductor.

First European Performance: November 27, 1951, Darmstadt; Landestheater
Orchester; composer, conductor. *See:* B402, B597, B598, B1339

Other Performances: B1045, B1386

95. *Cantata for wartime = Mitternacht und Tag.* (Schott/UE; dur: 12min.)
For women's chorus and orchestra: 2.2.2.2 / 4.2.2.0 / timpani / percussion /
strings. Text by Herman Melville: A utilitarian view of the *Monitor's* fight, A
Requiem for soldiers lost in ocean transport, Aurora-Borealis, from *Battle
pieces and aspects of the wars*; Dirge and We fish, from *Mardi*. Later German
translation by the composer.
Composed: June 8 - 15, 1943.
Dedication: In gratitude to Hamline University.

Manuscripts: **US-LJ.** Blueprint score(25 p.)

Premiere: March 24, 1944, Minneapolis, MN, Cyrus Northrop Memorial
Auditorium, University of Minnesota; June Peterson, solo; Hamline
University Women's Choir; Minneapolis Symphony Orchestra; Dimitri
Mitropoulos, conductor. *See:* B118, B233, B235, B581, B845, B1227

German translation: October 11, 1954, Hamburg, Nordwestdeutscher Rundfunk;
Frauenchor des NWDR; Sinfonieorchester des NWDR; composer, conductor.
See: B674, B1238

Other Performances: B1025

96. *Quartet, strings, no.7.* (UE; dur: 18 min.) *See:* B73, B324, B372, B1519
Composed: December 20, 1943 - February 7, 1944, St. Paul, MN.

1: *Allegro ma non troppo, grazioso e dolce.* **2:** *Adagio.* **3:** *Allegro ma non
troppo, ben misurato, con passione.* **4:** *Andante sostenuto.* **5:** *Allegretto con
grazia, scherzando e teneramente.*
Dedication: In gratitude to the vivifying spirit of my American students.

Manuscripts: **A-Wst:** MH 14527/c. Sketch(8 p.) **US-Wc:** ML96 Transparency
score(26 p.) & 4 parts(6 p. each) **A-Wst:** UE deposit Box K-S. Blueprint score(27
p.) **A-Wst:** UE deposit Box K-S. Proof miniature score(28 p.) **A-Wst:** UE
deposit Box K-S. Non-autograph parts.

Premiere: November 15, 1944, Indianapolis, World War Memorial Building
Auditorium; Budapest String Quartet.

First European Performance: August 1946, London, 20. Musikfest der
Internationale Gesellschaft für neue Musik; Aeolian Quartet. *See:* B837

Other Performances: B224, B360, B937, B947, B1118, B1508, K712

Publications: B1406, B1480

97. *Five prayers for women's voices over the Pater noster as cantus firmus = Fünf Gebete für Frauenchor a cappella das Pater noster als Cantus firmus.* (UE; dur: 10 min.) *See:* B929, B1408
For SSAA chorus a cappella. English text from John Donne's *A litanie,* no.15, 16, 20, 23, & 27. German translation by the composer.
Composed: June 18 - 28, 1944.

1: *From being anxious = Dass Angst uns* (June 18 - 21, 1944, St.Paul, MN - Ann Arbor, MI) **2:** *From needing danger = Dass durch Gefahr* (June 26, 1944, Bear Lake, CO) **3:** *Through thy submitting all = Wie alles hin du gibst* (June 27, 1944, Bear Lake, CO) **4:** *Heare us, O heare us Lord = Hör uns, o hör uns, Gott* (June 28, 1944, Bear Lake, CO) **5:** *That learning = Dass Wissen* (June 28, 1944, Bear Lake, CO)

Manuscripts: **A-Wst:** MH 14732/c. Text(1 p.) **A-Wst:** UE deposit Box K-S. Text(1 p.) **A-Wst:** MH 14732/c. Sketch(4 p.) **A-Wst:** MH 14797/c. Sketch(1 p.) **US-Wc:** ML96 .K7835 no.28 Case. Transparency score(7 p.) **A-Wst:** UE deposit Box K-S. Blueprint score(7 p.) **A-Wst:** UE deposit Box K-S. Proofs & published score with annotations.

Premiere: June 3, 1945, St. Paul, MN, Hamline University, Hamline Methodist Church; Hamline University Women's Choir; Robert Holliday, director.

Publications: B15, B833, B834, B1407

Recording: University of Illinois CRS 7. [1960?] *See:* B195
University Women's Glee Club; Russell Mathis, conductor.
With choral works by Bruno Maderna, Leslie Bassett, and Thomas Fredrickson.

Recording: Audio Engineering Associates AEA-1094. *The UCSB Dorians in a program of music for women's voices from the 20th century.* 33 1/3 rpm. [197?].
UCSB Dorians; Michael Ingham, conductor.
Recorded at the University of California, Santa Barbara.
With his *Two choruses on Jacobean poems* and choral works by Ernst Bacon, Darius Milhaud, Arnold Schoenberg, Milton Babbitt, Igor Stravinsky, and Bernhard Heiden.

98. *The Ballad of the railroads = Die Ballade von den Eisenbahnen.* (BA; dur: 19 min.) *See:* B1111, K586
For medium voice & piano. English text by the composer; German translation with assistance of the composer.
Text written: March 28 - May 7, 1944, St. Paul, MN; Music composed: May 28 - August 1, 1944, St. Paul, MN - Hollywood, CA

1: *Railroads dinning in my ear = Bahnen, Bahnen, dröhnen mir ins Ohr.* **2:** *Waiting for the train at midday = Warten auf den Zug am Mittag.* **3:** *The engines took me far around = Weit tragen mich Maschinen fort.* **4:** *Cut loose from the ground of grief = Reisst los von dem Kummer euch.* **5:** *Could it be that the trains = Könnt es sein dass die Bahn.* **6:** *All night I hear the trains = Nacht für Nacht hör ich die Züge.* **7:** *As the train runs forth = Wenn der Zug enteilt.* **8:** *Perched on the wall = Hockt an der Wand.* **9:** *Christ the Lord himself is riding = Christus der Herr führt selbst den Zug.* **10:** *I dream and dream = Ich träum und träum.*

Manuscripts: **A-Wst:** MH 14797/c. Text(3 p.) **A-Wst:** MH 14797/c. Sketch(14 p.) **US-Wc:** ML96 .K7835 no.2 Case. Transparency score(20 p.) **D-brd** Kbärenreiter. Blueprint score(20 p.) **D-brd** Kbärenreiter. Proof score(36 p.)

Premiere: April 5, 1950, New York, Carnegie Hall; Eleanor Steber, soprano; Dimitri Mitropoulos, piano. *See:* B316, B329, B571, B957, B1352

First European Performance: 1951, Frankfurt, Kunst-Kabinett; Irmgard Kohlermann, soprano; composer, piano. *See:* B479, K614

Publications: B248, B774

Published (German text): In *Prosa, Dramen, Verse.* (Münich: Albert Langen - Georg Müller, 1965): 407-411.

Recording: Edition Rhodos ERS 1201-3. (set) 33 1/3 rpm. [1969?] *See:* B245, B697
Rudo Timper, tenor; composer, piano.
Recorded March 1, 1968.
With his *Reisebuch aus den österreichischen Alpen,* op.62 and *Gesänge des späten Jahres,* op.71.

99. *Sonata, violin & piano.* (UE; dur: 14 min.) *See:* B555, B616
Composed: September 3, 1944 - February 4, 1945.
1: *Andante con moto* (September 3 - November 25, 1944, Black Mountain, NC - St. Paul, MN) 2: *Adagio* (November 29, 1944 - January 1, 1945, St. Paul, MN - New York) 3: *Allegro assai, vivace* (January 1 - February 4, 1945, New York-Chicago - St. Paul, MN)

Manuscripts: **A-Wst:** MH 14806/c:1. Sketch(13 p.) **US-Wc:** ML96 Case. Transparency score(16 p.) & part(5 p.) **A-Wst:** UE deposit Box S-Z. Blueprint score(16 p.) & part(5 p.) **A-Wst:** UE deposit Box S-Z. Proof score(24 p.) & part.

Premiere: October 21, 1945, Bridgman Hall, Hamline University, ISCM Twin Cities Chapter Concert; Louis Krasner, violin; composer, piano. *See:* K552

First European Performance: December 1950, Hamburg, Nordwestdeutscher Rundfunk Studio concert; Tibor Varga, violin; composer, piano. *See:* B715

Other Performances: K712

Recording: Preiserrecords SPR 10049. 33 1/3 rpm, stereo. [197-?] Dokumentationsreihe des Oesterreichischen Komponistenbundes, 24.
Ernst Kovacic, violin; Adolf Hennig, piano.
Duration: 14 min.
With his *3 Fragmente aus Karl V,* op.73a and *7 Stücke, string orchestra,* op.146.

100. *Hurricane variations.* (unpublished; dur: 15 min.)
For piano. Twenty-two variations and a fugue based on a theme by Virginia Seay.
Theme composed: September 14, 1944, New York; Variations composed: October 1, 1944, New York, NY - St.Paul, MN.

Manuscripts: **A-Wst:** MH 14806/c:2. Sketch(13 p.) **US** composer 10 p.

101. *Tricks and trifles.* (unpublished; dur: 15 min.)
Op.100 arranged for orchestra: 2.2.2.2 / 4.2.2.1 / harp / timpani / percussion / strings.
Orchestrated: June 1945, New York, NY - Bear Lake, CO.

Manuscripts: **US** composer Score(34 p.)

Premiere: March 22, 1946, Minneapolis, MN, Northrop Auditorium; Minneapolis Symphony Orchestra; Dimitri Mitropoulos, conductor. *See:* B500, B582, B1228

102. *Santa Fe time table.* (BA; dur: 15 min.) *See:* K586
For SSAATB chorus a cappella; text from the Atcheson, Topeka and Santa Fe railroad timetable.

Composed: February 25 - April 4, 1945, St.Paul, MN.

Manuscripts: **A-Wst:** MH 14751/c. Sketch(9 p.) **D-brd** Kbärenreiter. Transparency score(21 p.) **A-Wst:** UE deposit Box K-S. Blueprint score(21 p.).

Premiere: (Excerpts) March 12, 1947, Hamline University; Hamline University Singers; Robert Holliday, director. *See:* B583, B1028, B1230

First Complete U.S. Performance: February 20, 1961, Los Angeles, Fiesta Hall, Plummer Park, Monday Evening Concerts; Gregg Smith Singers; Gregg Smith, conductor.

First European Performance: 1961, Darmstadt, Internationale Ferienkurse für neue Musik; Gregg Smith Singers; Gregg Smith, conductor.

Recording: Orion ORS 75204. 33 1/3 rpm. stereo. [1975] *See:* B196, B667, B701, B879, B1331, B1354, B1381
California State University, Northridge, Chamber Singers; John Alexander, conductor.
Duration: 15 min., 20 sec.
Recorded May 17 and June 7, 1975, at California State University, Northridge. With his *O lacrymosa,* op.48, *Tape and double,* op.207, and *Toccata, accordion, op.183.*

103. *Aegrotavit Ezechias* = *The deliverance of Hezekiah.* (Mobart; dur: 8 min.)
Motet for SSA chorus & piano. Latin text from Isaiah 38, 1 - 6; English adaptation by Maurice Wright.
Composed: August 1 - 6, 1945, Gambier, OH.
Text: "In diebus illi" "In the days of Judah"

Manuscripts: **A-Wst:** MH 14781/c. Sketch(4 p.) **US** composer Transparency score(10 p.) **A-Wst:** UE deposit Box K-S. Blueprint score(10 p.)

Premiere: March 12, 1947, Hamline University; Hamline University Singers; Robert Holliday, director. *See:* B583, B1028, B1230

104. *Etude.* (unpublished; dur: 4 min.)
For coloratura soprano & contralto. Text of nonsense syllables.
Composed: September 4, 1945, Gambier, OH.

Manuscripts: **A-Wst:** MH 14771/c. Sketch(3 p.) **US** composer Score(4 p.)

Premiere: 1946, Hamline University; Shirley Hammergreen, soprano; Virginia Cooper, contralto.

105. *Symphonic elegy.* (Elkan-Vogel; dur: 9 min.) *See:* B930, B1369, B1429, B1502, K838
For string orchestra.
Composed: January 1 - 27, 1946, St. Paul, MN.
Allegro.
Dedication: In memorium Anton Webern.

Manuscripts: **A-Wst:** MH 14730/c. Sketch(5 p.) **A-Wst:** MH 14780/c. Sketch(2 p.)

Premiere: September 3, 1946, Saratoga Springs, NY, Saratoga Spa Music Festival; New York Philharmonic-Symphony; F. Charles Adler, conductor.

First European Performance: 1950, Brühler Schlosskonzerte; Jean Meylan, conductor. *See:* B1523

Other Performances: B224, B360, B402, B597, B706, B712, B887, B1118, B1339

Publications: B1370

Published (Facsimile page mm.141-144): In *Musik-Konzepte* 39/40 (October 1984): 112.

Recording: Columbia ML 4524. (Mx. XLP 6989-1E). 33 1/3 rpm. mono. [1952] *See:* B97, B195, B382, B439, B456, B484, B809, B861, B1171, B1215
New York Philharmonic-Symphony; Dimitri Mitropoulos, conductor.
With Arnold Schoenberg *Erwartung.*
Also issued on Philips A 01 495 L. and Philips ABL 3393. 1961.

Recording: Music Library MLR 7029. 33 1/3 rpm. mono. [1952]
San Francisco Chamber Ensemble.
With his *Sonata, piano, no.5, op.121* and *Sonata, viola & piano, op.117.*

105a. *Sargasso.*
Ballet after *Symphonic elegy.*

Premiere: March 24, 1965, New York State Theater; American Ballet Theatre; Glen Tetley, choreography; Kenneth Schermerhorn, conductor. *See:* B590

106. *In paradisum.* (Broude; dur: 3 min.)
Motet for SMzA chorus a cappella.
Composed: April 1, 1946, St. Paul, MN.
Dedication: The Choir of the College of St. Catherine, St. Paul, Minn. in grateful remembrance of the Requiem Mass for the repose of my father's soul.

Manuscripts: **A-Wst:** MH 14779/c. Sketch(4 p.) **US** composer Score(2 p.)

Premiere: May 10, 1946, College of St. Catherine, Jeanne D'Arc Auditorium; College of St. Catherine Liturgical Choir; Ethel Thurston, organ.

107. *Concerto, piano, no.3.* (Schott/UE; dur: 17 min.) *See:* B345, B346, B354
For piano with orchestra: 2.2.3.2 / 4.2.2.1 / harp / timpani / percussion / strings.
Composed: February 3 - 17, 1946, St. Paul, MN.
Allegro, con passione - Andante sostenuto - Poco pui mosso - Adagio - Vivace.

Manuscripts: **A-Wst:** MH 14780/c. Sketch(12 p.) **A-Wst:** UE deposit Box K-S. Blueprint score(35 p.) **US-LJ.** Blueprint score(35 p.)

Premiere: November 22, 1946, Minneapolis, MN, Northrop Auditorium; Minneapolis Symphony Orchestra; Dimitri Mitropoulos, piano & conductor. *See:* B501, B571, B1229

First European Performance: 1960, Vienna; Charlotte Zelka, piano; Wiener Symphoniker; Miltiades Caridis, conductor. *See:* B361

108. *Trio, violin, clarinet & piano.* (AMP; dur: 8 min.) *See:* B555, K638
Composed: June 18 - 28, 1946.
1: *Allegretto moderato, comodo* (June 18 - 21, 1946, Palo Alto, CA) **2:** *Allegro agitato* (June 28, 1946, Palo Alto, CA)

Manuscripts: **A-Wst:** MH 14808/c. Sketch(10 p.) **US-Wc:** ML96 .K7835 no.16 Case. Transparency score(13 p.) & 2 parts(3 p. each) **A-Wst:** UE deposit Box S-Z. Blueprint score(13 p.).

Premiere: November 27, 1946, St. Paul, MN, College of St. Catherine, Jeanne d'Arc auditorium, presented by The Friends of Chamber Music; Krasner Chamber Music Ensemble (Louis Krasner, violin; Walter Thalin, clarinet; composer, piano). *See:* B502, B1294

First European Performance: October 2, 1950, Basle, Theater am Naumarkt, Pro

Musica; Rodolfo Felicani, Oswaldo Mengassini, Karl Engel.

Other Performances: B224, B947

Recording: Crystal Records S 645. 33 1/3 rpm, stereo. [1982] *See:* B256, B633, B1433
Empire Trio. Duraton: 7 min., 36 sec.
With works by Anton Webern, Benjamin Folkman, Francis Poulenc, and Darius Milhaud.

Recording: Laurel Records LR 103. 33 1/3 rpm. stereo. c1974. *See:* B146
Roy D'Antonio, clarinet; Myron Sandler, violin; Delores Stevens, piano.
Recorded in Los Angeles, CA.
Duration: 8 min., 8 sec.
With works by Igor Stravinsky, Charles Ives, and Aaron Khachaturian.

Recording: Supraphon 111 2147. 33 1/3 rpm. stereo. p1977. *See:* B150, B184, B261, B497, B739, B1107
Musici Moravienses.
Duration: 7 min., 5 sec.
Recorded at the National House in Žižkov, Prague, July 12 - 16, 1976.
With works by Paul Hindemith and Darius Milhaud.

109. *O would I were.* (Mercury; dur: 2 min.)
Canon for mixed chorus a cappella.
Composed: 1946.

Published: In *Modern canons.* (New York: Mercury Music, 1947)

110. *Piano pieces.* (Mercury; dur: 10 min.) *See:* B584, B1250
Composed: May 11 - 28, 1946.
1: *Etude* (May 11, 1946, St.Paul, MN) **2:** *Invention* (May 12, 1946, St.Paul, MN) **3:** *Scherzo* (May 13, 1946, St.Paul, MN) **4:** *Toccata* (May 14 - 19, 1946, St.Paul, MN) **5:** *Nocturne.* **6:** *Waltz* (May 22, 1946, St.Paul, MN) **7:** *Air* (May 23, 1946, St.Paul, MN) **8:** *Rondo* (May 28, 1946, St.Paul, MN)

Manuscripts: **A-Wst:** MH 14778/c. Sketch(4 p.) **A-Wst:** MH 14779/c. Sketch(2 p.) **US-Wc:** ML96 .K7835 no.4 Case. Transparency(9 p.)

Premiere: February 9, 1947, Hamline University, Bridgman Hall; Roberta Dresden, piano.

Publications: B821

Recording: Society of Participating Artists SPA 4. 33 1/3 rpm. mono. [1952] composer, piano.
With his *5 Pieces, op.39* and *Sonata, no.3, op.92, no.4.*

111. *What price confidence?* = *Vertrauenssache.* (BA; dur: 45 min.) *See:* B305
Chamber opera in 9 scenes; English text by the composer; later German translation by the composer. Gloria (soprano), Vivian (mezzosoprano), Richard (tenor), Edwin (baritone), and piano.
Text written: July 15, 1945, Bear Lake, CO; Music composed: August 23 - December 24, 1945, Gambier, OH - St.Paul, MN.
Written at the suggestion of Herta Glaz.

Manuscripts: **A-Wst:** MH 14739/c. Sketch(30 p.) **A-Wst:** MH 14797/c. Motive(1 p.) **D-brd** Kbärenreiter. Transparency piano-vocal score(50 p.)

Premiere: (German): May 22, 1962, Saarbrücker Stadttheater; Werner Wilke, conductor; Rüdiger Renn, producer; Franz Weisgerber, staging; Friedel

Towae, costumes; Waltraut Schatzl, Gloria; Hans Riediker, Edwin; Heidi Ferch, Vivian; Phil Sona, Richard. *See:* B26, B108, B800

First U.S. Performance (English): August 2, 1968, Dartmouth Convocation of the Arts, Hopkins Center Theater; Arthur Thompson, Edwin; Diana Hoagland, Gloria; Michael Best, Richard; Joy Blackett, Vivian; Elizabeth Wright, piano. *See:* B371, B1272

Published (German libretto): In *Prosa, Dramen, Verse.* (Münich: Albert Langen - Georg Müller, 1965): 255-270.

Published (German libretto): In *Das musikdramatische Werk, v.2,* hrsg. von Franz Eugen Dostal. Oesterreichische Dramatiker der Gegenwart, v.23. (Wien: Oesterreichische Verlagsanstalt, 1977): 141-155.

112. *Songs on poems by Gerard Manley Hopkins.* (BA; dur: 15 min.)
For tenor & piano.
Composed: December 24, 1946 - January 3, 1947.

1: *Peace = Friede* (December 27, 1946, St.Paul, MN) "When will you ever" "Wann wirst Du jemals" **2:** *Patience = Geduld* (January 3, 1947, St.Paul, MN) "Patience, hard thing!" "Geduld, eine schwere Sache!" **3:** *On a piece of music = Auf ein Stück Musik* (December 26, 1946, St.Paul, MN) "How all's to one thing wrought!" "Wie ist alles in eins gebracht!" **4:** *Moonrise = Mondaufgang* (December 24, 1946, St.Paul, MN) "I awoke in the Midsummer not to call night" "Ich erwachte in der Mitte des Sommers"

Manuscripts: **A-Wst:** MH 14807/c. Sketch(10 p.) **US** composer Transparency score(14 p.) **D-brd** Kbärenreiter. Blueprint score(14 p.)

Premiere: April 25, 1947, Waco, TX, Baylor University, Waco Hall; Leon Wagner, tenor; Russell G. Harris, piano.

Other Performances: B772, B773

Recording: Orion ORS 79348. 33 1/3 rpm. stereo. [1979] *See:* B1030, B1357, B1462
Neva Pilgrim, soprano; Dennis Helmrich, piano.
Duration: 15 min., 32 sec.
Recorded December 22, 1978, in Ithaca, N.Y.
With his *Zeitlieder,* op.215 and 3 *Songs, op.30a* and Gladys Nordenstrom *Zeit XXIV.*

113. *Symphony, no.4.* (unpublished; dur: 30 min.) *See:* B78, B345, B346, B713, K574
For 3.3.3.3 / 4.3.3.1 / piano / timpani / percussion / strings.
Composed: March 1 - July 8, 1947.

1: *Andante, tranquillo* (March 1 - 16, 1947, St. Paul, MN) **2:** *Adagio* (April 22 - May 16, 1947, Austin, TX - St. Paul, MN) **3:** *Allegro pesante* (June 13 - July 8, 1947, Albuquerque, NM; Instr. July 25, 1947, Albuquerque, NM)
Commissioned: Dimitri Mitropoulos.

Manuscripts: **US** composer Score(65 p.)

Premiere: November 27, 1947, New York, Carnegie Hall; New York Philharmonic-Symphony; Dimitri Mitropoulos, conductor. *See:* B271, B495, B636, B1235, B1351
Radio Broadcast: November 30, 1947, New York, Carnegie Hall; New York Philharmonic-Symphony; Dimitri Mitropoulos, conductor.

First European Performance: June 21, 1948, Vienna, Grosser Konzerthaus-Saal; Wiener Symphoniker; Karl Böhm, conductor.

114. *Sonata, piano, no.4.* (Bomart; dur: 19 min., 30 sec.) *See:* B159, B409, B588, B1322, K611
Composed: April 17 - July 5, 1948.

1: *Sostenuto; Allegro ma non troppo; Allegro assai* (April 17 - July 5, 1948, Los Angeles, CA) **2:** *Andante sostenuto, con passione* (May 11 - 18, 1948, Los Angeles, CA) **3:** *Rondo* (May 20 - 28, 1948, Los Angeles, CA) **4:** *Tempo di minuetto, molto lento* (May 31 - June 4, 1948, Los Angeles, CA)

Manuscripts: **A-Wst:** MH 14722/c. Sketch(9 p.) **US-Wc:** ML96 Transparency(17 p.)

Premiere: November 5, 1948, San Francisco, CA, San Francisco Museum of Art, Composers' Forum; Bernhard Abramowitsch, piano. *See:* B169, B951

First European Performance: October 2, 1950, Basle, Theater am Naumarkt; composer, piano.

Publications: B164, B375, B859

Recording: Music Library MLR 7014. 33 1/3 rpm. mono. [1952] *See:* B107, B196, B904, B978
Bernhard Abramowitsch, piano.
With his *4 Bagatelles,* op.70. Earlier alternate issue with his *Fifth sonata* op.121.

Recording: Musical Heritage Society MHS 3874. *Masterpieces of twentieth-century piano music, v.3.* 33 1/3 rpm. stereo. [1978] *See:* B196, B381, B1128
David Burge, piano.
Duration: 18 min., 46 sec.
With Pierre Boulez *Sonata, piano, no.2.*

115. *Sonata, violin, no.2.* (Assmann; dur: 10 min.) *See:* B741
Composed: September - October 1948, Los Angeles, CA.

1: *Allegro deciso.* **2:** *Adagio.* **3:** *Allegretto grazioso, con anima, flessibile.*
Written for Robert Gross.

Manuscripts: US composer 4 p.

Premiere: December 19, 1948, Washington, DC, National Gallery of Art; Robert Gross, violin. *See:* B642

Recording: Orion ORS 73107. *New works for violin.* 33 1/3 rpm, stereo. p1973. *See:* B145, B196
Robert Gross, violin.
Duration: 7 min., 33 sec.
With works by Andrew Imbrie, Leonard Rosenman, Bruno Bartolozzi, & Heinrich J.F. von Biber.

115a. *Remember now.* (Mobart; dur: 5 min.)
Motet for SMzA and piano. English text from Ecclesiastes 12, 1-8.
Composed: September 22, 1947, Los Angeles, CA.
Remember now thy Creator.

Manuscripts: US composer Score(9 p.)

Premiere: 1947, St. Paul, MN.

116. *Short pieces* = *Kurze Stücke.* (BA; dur: 10 min.)
For string quartet or string orchestra.
Composed: October 21 - November 2, 1948, Los Angeles, CA.

1: *Andante.* **2:** *Allegretto moderato.* **3:** *Andante, molto espressivo.* **4:** *Moderato.* **5:** *Molto vivace.*

Manuscripts: **US** composer Transparency score(8 p.) & 4 parts. **D-brd** Kbärenreiter. Blueprint score(8 p.)

Premiere: January 17, 1955, Basel, Konservatoriumssaal; Neues Instrumental-Ensemble Basel; Rudolf Kelterborn, conductor. *See:* B726, B901

117. *Sonata, viola & piano.* (AM; dur:11 min.) *See:* B555
Composed: December 8 - 12, 1948.

1: *Andante* (December 8, 1948, Los Angeles, CA) **2:** *Allegro vivace* (December 12, 1948, Los Angeles, CA) **3:** *Andantino* (December 12, 1948, Los Angeles, CA)
Dedication: Ferenc Molnar and Jane Hohfeld.

Manuscripts: **A-Wst:** MH 14762/c. Sketch(11 p.) **US-Wc:** ML96 .K7835 no.29 Case. Transparency score(12 p.) & part(4 p.) **A-Wst:** UE deposit Box K-S. Blueprint score(12 p.) & part.

Premiere: March 1949, San Francisco; Ferenc Molnar, viola; Jane Hohfeld, piano.

Other Performances: B224, B947, K712

Publications: B46

Recording: Music Library 1/2. (Mx: MLR-1/2). 78 rpm. [1949] *See:* B195
Ferenc Molnar, viola; Jane Hohfeld, piano.
Also issued on Music Library MLR 7029. 33 1/3 rpm. mono. [s1953, lc1952] (With his *Sonata, piano, no.5, op.121* and *Symphonic elegy, op.105*).

Recording: Deutsche Grammophon 36005 A. (Mx: MX2954 72). 78 rpm. *See:* B789, B1340
Michael Mann, viola; Yaltah Menuhin, piano.
Also issued on Polydor 36005. 78 rpm. and Polydor 32034. 45 rpm. Deutsche Grammophon 2954. 33 1/3 rpm. [before 1953] and Deutsche Grammophon LP 19 126. [1960] (With works by Maurice Ravel, Darius Milhaud, Manual de Falla, K. Szymanowski, and Arthur Honegger)

118. *Trio, strings.* (Hansen; dur: 15 min.)
Composed: December 25, 1948 - February 5, 1949, Los Angeles, CA - Palo Alto, CA.
1: *Allegretto vivace.* **2:** *Larghetto.* **3:** *Allegretto vivace.* **4:** *Adagio.* **5:** *Allegretto grazioso.*
Written for the Twentieth Century String Trio: Felix Slatkin, violin, Sven Reher, viola, Kurt Reher, cello.

Manuscripts: **US-Wc:** ML96 .K7835 no.19 Case. Transparency score(13 p.) & 3 parts(5 p. each)

Premiere: April 4, 1949, Los Angeles, Wilshire-Ebell Theater, Evenings on the Roof; Twentieth Century String Trio (Felix Slatkin, violin; Sven Reher, viola; Kurt Reher, cello). *See:* B48, B711

Other Performances: B846, B1383

Publications: B537

Recording: Calig CAL 50 861. *Streichtrios der Neuen Wiener Schule.* compact disc. p1987. *See:*
Wiener Streichtrio.
Duration: 13 min., 13 sec.
Recorded: December 17 - 19, 1986, Studio 3, Bayerischer Rundfunk, München.
With trios by Arnold Schönberg and Anton Webern.

119. *Symphony, no.5.* (Schott/UE; dur: 22 min.) *See:* B78, B345, B346, B874
For orchestra: 2.2.3.2 / 4.2.2.1 / timpani / percussion / strings.
Composed: October 20, 1947 - June 27, 1949, Los Angeles, CA - Albuquerque, NM.

Manuscripts: **A-Wst:** MH 14742/c. Sketch(11 p.)

Premiere: March 16, 1950, Albuquerque, NM; Albuquerque Civic Symphony; Kurt Frederick, conductor. *See:* B571, B1084

First European Performance: September 4, 1950, Venice, 13. Internationale Gesellschaft für neue Musik; and Biennale di Venezia; Kurt Frederick, conductor. *See:* B411, B571, B858

Other Performances: B360, B402, B597, B598, B1339

120. *George Washington variations.* (Southern; dur: 11 min.) *See:* B31, B409, B851
For piano. The tunes of the "Grand March" and the "Martial Cotillion" were found in a manuscript book of the Euterpean Society of Hartford, CT, from about 1800.
Composed: March 21 - 29, 1950, Los Angeles, CA.

1: *Washington's grand march.* **2:** *The same elaborated upon.* **3:** *Battle music.* **4:** *Elegy.* **5:** *The chase* (a canon). **6:** *Sarabande.* **7:** *Grand finale, with the martial cotillion.*
Commissioned: Miriam Molin.
Dedication: Miriam Molin.

Manuscripts: **A-Wst:** MH 14763/c. Sketch(10 p.) **US-Wc:** ML96 .K7835 no.5 Case. Transparency(12 p.)

Premiere: September 24, 1950, Los Angeles, Wilshire Ebell Theatre; Miriam Molin, piano. *See:* B132, B431, B1461

First European Performance: 1951, Paris, American Embassy; Miriam Molin, piano. *See:* B864

Publications: B367

121. *Sonata, piano, no.5.* (unpublished; dur: 20 min.) *See:* B588
Composed: May 8 - July 10, 1950.

1: *Allegretto con grazia* (May 8 - 18, 1950, Los Angeles, CA) **2:** *Andante appassionata* (June 4 - 9, 1950, Los Angeles, CA) **3:** *Vivace; Allegretto con grazia* (July 4 - 10, 1950, New York, NY - Chicago, IL)
Commissioned: Charlotte Zelka.
Dedication: Charlotte Zelka.

Manuscripts: **A-Wst:** MH 14777/c. Sketch(9 p.) **US** composer 20 p.

Premiere: 1950, Cologne?; Charlotte Zelka, piano. *See:* K712

First U.S. Performance: April 1, 1951, Los Angeles County Museum; Charlotte Zelka, piano.

Published (Facsimile mm.1-11): In *Ernst Krenek,* hrsg. von Otto Kolleritsch. Studien zur Wertungsforschung, v.15. (Wien: Universal Edition, 1982): 222.

Recording: Music Library MLR 7029. 33 1/3 rpm. mono. [1952] *See:* B195
Charlotte Zelka, piano.
With his *Sonata, viola & piano, op.117* and *Symphonic elegy, op.105.* First issued on Music Library MLR 7014 with his *Fourth sonata op.114.*

122. *Parvula corona musicalis.* (Bach Quarterly; dur: 10 min.) *See:* K846, K851
For string trio.
Composed: September 3 - 26, 1950.

1: *Argumentum* (September 3, 1950, Venice) **2:** *Symphonia* (September 21, 1950, Innsbruck) **3:** *Invocationes.* **4:** *Contrapuncti varii.* **5:** *Corona.* **6:** *Clausula* (September 26, 1950, Valbella, Rhaetia, SZ)
Commissioned: Italian Radio.
Dedication: Ad honorem Johannis Sebastiani Bach.

Manuscripts: US composer 3 parts. US composer Score(12 p.)

Premiere: January 15, 1951, Rome, Radio Italiana; Vittorio Emanuele, violin; Lodovico Coccon, viola; Giuseppe Selmi, cello.

First U.S. Performance: February 21, 1955, West Hollywood, Los Angeles County Auditorium, Monday Evening Concerts; Dorothy Wade, violin; Louis Kievman, viola; Armand Kaproff, cello. *See:* B37, B916

Publications: K846

Published: In *Bach quarterly* 2:4 (October 1971): 20-31.

Recording: Philips 411 062-1. (411 063-1--411 064-1). *Gidon Kremer Live at Lockenhaus 1982.* 2 discs. 33 1/3 rpm. stereo. p1983. *See:* B1478
Gidon Kremer, violin; Kim Kashkashian, viola; Wolfgang Boettcher, cello.
Duration: 9 min., 34 sec.
Live recording of parts of the Lockenhaus Chamber-Music Festival 1982. With works by Joseph Haydn, Franz Schubert, Arnold Schoenberg, Anton Webern, and others.

123. *Concerto, piano, no.4.* (BA; dur: 22 min.) *See:* B851, B1461
For piano with orchestra: 2.2.2.2 / 4.2.2.0 / percussion / strings.
Composed: July 17 - October 28, 1950.

1: *Allegro, agitato e pesante* (July 17 - August 28, 1950, Needles, CA - Winterthur, SZ) **2:** *Molto adagio* (August 31 - September 19, 1950, Venezia - Vienna) **3:** *Allegro, molto vivace* (October 23 - 28, 1950, Los Angeles, CA)
Dedication: Miriam Molin.

Manuscripts: **D-brd** Kbärenreiter: BA 3498. Transparency score(42 p.) **D-brd** Kbärenreiter: BA 3498a. Transparency 2-piano score(32 p.)

Premiere: October 22, 1951, Cologne, Aula der Universität; Miriam Molin, piano; Städtisches Gürzenich-Orchester; composer, conductor. *See:* B293, B294, B685, B710, B785, B864

First U.S. Performance: April 23, 1965, Minneapolis, MN; Civic Orchestra of Minneapolis; composer, conductor. *See:* B355, B1232

Other Performances: B402, B597, B1339

Recording: Contemporary Records AP 123.
Miriam Molin, piano; composer, conductor.
Announced but not issued.

124. *Double concerto.* (Marks; dur: 17 min.) *See:* B875
For violin and piano with orchestra: 1.1.1.1 / 2.1.0.0 / strings.
Composed: November 19, 1950, Los Angeles, CA.

1: *Andantino.* **2:** *Allegro ma non troppo, deciso.* **3:** *Andantino.* **4:** *Allegretto.* **5:** *Lento.* **6:** *Allegro.*
Dedication: Maro and Anahid Ajemian.

Premiere: October 6, 1951, Donaueschinger Musiktage für Zeitgenössische Tonkunst; Südwestfunkorchester; Anahid Ajemian, violin; Maro Ajemian, piano; Hans Rosbaud, conductor. *See:* B293, B517, B710, B1000, K614

First U.S. Performance: March 9, 1955, Metropolitan Museum of Art, Grace Rainey Rogers Auditorium; Anahid Ajemian, violin; Maro Ajemian, piano; Izler Solomon, conductor. *See:* B737, B814, B1175

Other Performances: B479

Recording: MGM E 3218. 33 1/3 rpm. mono. [1956] *See:* B195
Anahid Ajemian, violin; Maro Ajemian, piano; M-G-M Chamber Orchestra; Izler Solomon, conductor.
With works by Wallinford Riegger and Roger Sessions.

125. *Dark waters = Dunkle Wasser.* (BA; dur: 55 min.) *See:* B304, K593
Opera in 1 act. English text by the composer; later German translation by the composer. Joe (baritone), Claire (alto), Phil (tenor), girl (soprano), 2 gangsters (tenor & bass), Tom (bass), and orchestra: 1.1.1.1 / 2.1.1.0 / piano / percussion / strings.
Composed: January 1 - May 3, 1950, Los Angeles, CA; Instr. February 16, 1951.

Manuscripts: **A-Wst:** MH 14728/c. Sketches(29 p.) **D-brd** Kbärenreiter: BA 4300. Transparency score(105 p.) **D-brd** Kbärenreiter: BA 4300. Transparency piano-vocal score(59 p.) **D-brd** Kbärenreiter: BA 4300. Transparency parts. **A-Wst:** UE deposit Box A-J. Blueprint score(p.1-26)

Premiere: May 2, 1951, Los Angeles, University of Southern California, Bovard Auditorium, Fourth Annual USC Festival of Contemporary Arts; Wolfgang Martin, conductor; Carl Ebert, producer; Kalem Kermoyan, Ava Gjerset, William Olvis, Olive Mae Beach, Donal Combs, Jerome Zidek, and Paul Hinshaw, singers. *See:* B432, B433, B504, B544, B545, B913

First European Performance: August 27, 1954, Darmstadt, Landestheater, Internationale Ferienkurse für neue Musik; composer, conductor. *See:* B518, B671, B672, B673, B1199, B1380

Other Performances: B26, B108, B800

Published (English libretto): (Los Angeles: University of Southern California Press, 1951) 23 p.

Published (German libretto): In *Das musikdramatische Werk, v.2,* hrsg. von Franz Eugen Dostal. Oesterreichische Dramatiker der Gegenwart, v.23. (Wien: Oesterreichische Verlagsanstalt, 1977): 157-171.

126. *Concerto, harp.* (UE; dur: 19 min.)
For harp with chamber orchestra: 1.1.1.1 / 2.1.0.0 / harp / strings.
Composed: February 17, 1951, Los Angeles, CA.
1: *Andante con moto.* **2:** *Allegretto.* **3:** *Adagio.*
Composed for and dedicated to Edna Phillips.

Manuscripts: **A-Wst:** UE deposit Box K-S. Harp-piano score transparency(26 p.) **A-Wst:** UE deposit Box K-S. Harp-piano score blueprint(26 p.) **A-Wst:** UE deposit Box K-S. Proof score(30 p.)

Premiere: December 12, 1952, Philadelphia; Edna Philipps, harp; Philadelphia Orchestra; Eugene Ormandy, conductor. *See:* B831, B1236

First European Performance: November 4, 1954, Vienna, Konzerthaus, Mozart-Saal; Emmy Hürlimann, harp; composer, conductor. *See:* B856, B1118

Other Performances: B360

127. *Concerto, 2 pianos*. (BA; dur: 16 min.)
For 2 pianos with orchestra: 2.2.2.2 / 4.2.2.1 / timpani / percussion / strings.
Composed: May 21, 1951, Los Angeles, CA.
1: *Allegro vivace.* **2:** *Andante.* **3:** *Allegro vivace.* **4:** *Adagio.*
Commissioned by and dedicated to Arthur Whittemore and Jack Lowe.

Manuscripts: **D-brd** Kbärenreiter: BA 4331. Transparency score(40 p.) **D-brd** Kbärenreiter: BA 4331a. Transparency 3-piano score(33 p.)

Premiere: October 24, 1953, New York, Carnegie Hall; New York Philharmonic-Symphony; Jack Lowe and Arthur Whittemore, pianos; Dimitri Mitropoulos, conductor. *See:* B342, B763, B1022, B1173

Other Performances: B224

127a. *Invention*. (Schweizerische Musikzeitung; dur: 1 min.) *See:* B161, B1191
For flute & clarinet.
Composed: 1951.

Premiere: January 7, 1967, Bamberg; members of the Bamberg Bläserquintett. *See:* B1153, B1154

Published: In *Schweizerische Musikzeitung* 93:3 (March 1, 1953): 115.

128. *Sonata, piano, no.6*. (unpublished; dur: 20 min.) *See:* B588
Composed: March 13 - June 26, 1951, Los Angeles, CA - Albuquerque, NM.
1: *Prelude.* **2:** *Andante.* **3:** *Allegretto vivace.* **4:** *Allegro dramatico, appassionato e molto rubato.*

Manuscripts: US composer 16 p.

Premiere: October 1951, Donaueschinger Musiktage für Zeitgenössische Tonkunst; composer, piano. *See:* B293, B710, K614

First U.S. Performance: June 8, 1952, Los Angeles, USC Hancock Auditorium, International Society for Contemporary Music, Los Angeles Chapter; Jacob Gimpel, piano.

Other Performances: B479

129. *Medea*. (BA; dur: 16 min.) *See:* B1090, K807
Monologue for mezzosoprano with orchestra: 2.2.2.2 / 4.2.2.1 / percussion / strings. English text from the free adaptation by Robinson Jeffers of *Medea* by Euripides; German translation by the composer.
Composed: June 9 - 30, 1951, Wickenburg, AZ - Albuquerque, NM; Revised: June 16, 1952, Los Angeles, CA.
Commissioned by and dedicated to Blanche Thebom.

Manuscripts: **US-CA.** Sketch(1 p.) **A-Wst** French libretto & correspondence. **A-Wst** Blueprint score(33 p., original & revised versions) **A-Wst:** MH 14760/c. Blueprint piano-vocal score(20 p., original) **D-brd** Kbärenreiter: BA 3570. Transparency score(35 p.) **D-brd** Kbärenreiter: BA 3570a. Transparency vocal score(21 p.)

Premiere: March 13, 1953, Philadelphia, Academy of Music; Blanche Thebom, mezzosoprano; Philadelphia Orchestra; Eugene Ormandy, conductor. *See:* B239, B832, B1237, B1360

First European Performance: 1954, Darmstadt, Internationale Ferienkurse für neue Musik; Blanche Thebom, mezzosoprano. *See:* B125, B275, B672, B673

130. *Quintet, flute, clarinet, oboe, bassoon & horn.* (unpublished)
Composed: 1952. Rewritten as op.163.
Moderato allegro. (January 1, 1952, Innsbruck)
Exists only on tape at WDR, Cologne.

131. *Sinfonietta a Brasileira* = *The Brazilian.* (UE; dur: 15 min.)
For string orchestra.
Composed: January 10 - February 15, 1952, Teresópolis, Rio de Janeiro, Brazil.
Dedication: Stuttgart Kammerorchester.

Manuscripts: **A-Wst:** MH 14725/c. Sketch(6 p.) **US-Wc:** ML96 Case. Transparency score(14 p.) **A-Wst:** UE deposit Box K-S. Blueprint score(14 p.) **A-Wst:** UE deposit Box K-S. Proof score(30 p.)

Premiere: September 6, 1953, Besançon, France, Festival de Besançon; Stuttgart Kammerorchester; Karl Münchinger, conductor.

First U.S. Performance: March 2, 1983, Los Angeles, Temple Isiah; American Chamber Symphony; Nelson Nirenberg, conductor. *See:* B531, B908

Other Performances: B360

132. *Sacred songs* = *Geistliche Gesänge.* (BA; dur: 12 min.) *See:* B539
For medium voice & piano. English & German Bible texts.
Composed: June 1 - 17, 1952.

1: *The light is sweet* = *Es ist das Licht süss* (Ecclestiatics 11:7-9, 12:1-7) (June 17, 1952, Los Angeles, CA) **2:** *The 104th Psalm* = *Der 104. Psalm* (June 1, 1952, Los Angeles, CA) "Bless the Lord" "Lobe den Herrn"
Dedication: To the memory of Ernst Rubensohn.

Manuscripts: **US-Wc:** ML96 Case. Transparency score(18 p.) **D-brd** Kbärenreiter. Blueprint score(18 p.)

Premiere: January 4, 1953, New York, Town Hall; Herta Glaz, mezzosoprano; composer, piano. *See:* B98, B762, B959, B1418

Other Performances: B772, B773

Recording: Bärenreiter Musicaphon 30 L 1534. 33 1/3 rpm. mono. [1965] *See:* B126, B376
Carla Henius, soprano; Aribert Reimann, piano.
Recorded July 1963, grosser Sendesaal des Kopenhagener Rundfunks.
Durations: 15:50; 13:25.
With Zillig *Lieder des Abschieds.*

133. *Concerto, cello, no.1.* (BA; dur: 22 min.) *See:* B220
For cello with orchestra: 2.2.2.2 / 4.2.2.0 / timpani / harp / percussion / strings.
Composed: December 15, 1952 - March 11, 1953.

1: *Allegro vigoroso* (December 15, 1952, Los Angeles, CA) **2:** *Andante sostenuto* (February 9 - 14, 1953, Los Angeles, CA) **3:** *Allegro vivace* (February 23 - March 11, 1953, Los Angeles, CA)
Commissioned: Margaret Aue.

Manuscripts: **A-Wst:** MH 14811/c. Sketch(12 p.) **A-Wst:** MH 14811/c. Cello part(3 p., incomplete) **D-brd** Kbärenreiter: BA 3826. Transparency score(38 p.) **D-brd** Kbärenreiter: BA 3826. Transparency cello part(8 p.) **D-brd** Kbärenreiter: BA 3826. Transparency piano score(24 p.)

Premiere: March 4, 1954, Los Angeles, Philharmonic Auditorium; Los Angeles

Philharmonic Orchestra; Margaret Aue, cello; Alfred Wallenstein, conductor. *See:* B434, B435, B546, B914, B915

First European Performance: May 1956, Vienna, Ravag; Margaret Aue, cello; composer, conductor. *See:* B1025

Other Performances: B335

134. *Scenes from the West.* (AM, Belwin) *See:* B1250
For school orchestra: 3.1.3.1 / 2saxophones / 2.3.2.0 / piano / percussion / strings.
Composed: 1952 - 1953.
1: *Pageant in Paso Robles.* (dur: 3 min., 45 sec.) **2:** *Hermosa Hills.* (dur: 3 min., 30 sec.) **3:** *Moon over Monterey.* (dur: 4 min.) **4:** *Fresno ferris wheel.* (dur: 4 min.)

135. *Fantasy* = *Phantasiestück.* (unpublished; dur: 10 min.)
For cello & piano.
Composed: 1953.
Commissioned: Hans Blattman.

Manuscripts: US composer Score(16 p.)

Premiere: April 6, 1954, Luzern, Schweizerische Musikforschende Gesellschaft; Hans Battmann, cello; composer, piano. *See:* B867, B897

136. *Miniature.* (New Mexico Quarterly; dur: 2 min.)
For piano. Same as no.20 of op.139.
Composed: 1953.

Manuscripts: US-CA. Sketch(1 p.)

Published: In *New Mexico Quarterly* 23:1 (Spring 1953)

137. *Symphony Pallas Athene.* (Schott/UE; dur: 22 min.) *See:* K640, K751
For orchestra: 2.2.2.2 / 4.2.2.0 / timpani / harp / celesta / piano / percussion / strings. Derived from the opera op.144.
Composed: January 23, 1954, Los Angeles, CA.

Premiere: October 11, 1954, Hamburg, Nordwestdeutscher Rundfunk; NWDR-Sinfonieorchester; composer, conductor. *See:* B613, B614, B615, B1045, B1238, B1386

Other Performances: B360, B856, B1118

Publications: B468, B538, B1489

Published: Facsimile of p.1 In *Melos* 21:7/8 (July/August 1954): 206-208.

138. *Choruses.* (AM, Belwin)
For SATB chorus & organ or piano.
Composed: 1953.
1: *By the sepulchre.* (Matthew 28, 2-3, 5-6) **2:** *On Mount Olivet.* (Matthew 26, 38-39) **3:** *126th Psalm.* **4:** *From the 103rd Psalm. Unison chorus.* (verses 8-11)

Premiere: May 1955, American Guild of Organists, Pasadena and Valley Districts Chapter; Chapman College Madrigal Singers; James M. McKelvy, director.

139. *20 Miniatures.* (Hansen; dur: 19 min.)
For piano.
Composed: January 1953 - March 1954, Los Angeles, CA.
1: *Introduction.* **2:** *Theme.* **3:** *Andante.* **4:** *Andante.* **5:** *Allegretto grazioso.*

6: *Allegro moderato.* **7:** *Andantino.* **8:** *Allegro agitato.* **9:** *Adagio.* **10:** *Moderato.* **11:** *Larghetto.* **12:** *Allegro vivace.* **13:** *Andantino.* **14:** *Allegro moderato.* **15:** *Adagio.* **16:** *Allegretto, capricioso.* **17:** *Allegretto moderato.* **18:** *Vivace.* **19:** *Andante sostenuto.* **20:** *Largo.*

Manuscripts: **US-CA.** Sketches(5 p.) **US-Wc:** ML96 .K7835 no.3 Case. Transparency(20 p.)

Premiere: September 21, 1954, St. Gallen; composer, piano.

First U.S. Performance: April 24, 1955, Los Angeles, Immaculate Heart College, Sigma Alpha Iota, Beta Nu chapter; composer, piano.

Publications: B985

139a. *Six for two.* (unpublished)
2-piano arrangement of nos.3, 16, 7, 9, 8 & 4 from Twenty miniatures.
Arranged: June 13, 1954, Los Angeles, CA.
Dedication: Lowe and Whittemore.

Manuscripts: **US-CA.** Sketches(2 p.) **US** composer Score(9 p.)

Premiere: October 18, 1959, Chicago, Orchestra Hall; Arthur Whittemore and Jack Lowe, piano; Chicago Symphony Orchestra. *See:* B180, B523

140. *Concerto, violin, no.2.* (Schott/UE; dur: 25 min.)
For violin with orchestra: 2.2.2.2 / 4.2.2.0 / timpani / harp / celesta / percussion / strings.
Composed: October 7, 1953 - April 19, 1954, Los Angeles, CA.
In three unnamed movements.
Commissioned: Westdeutscher Rundfunk.
Dedication: Tibor Varga.

Premiere: February 18, 1955, Cologne, Westdeutscher Rundfunk; Tibor Varga, violin; William Steinberg, conductor. *See:* B295, B786

Other Performances: B363

141. *Motette zur Opferung; für das ganze Kirchenjahr.* (Schott; dur: 1 min.)
For SABar chorus a cappella.
Composed: September 27, 1954, Vienna.
Text: "Veni Sanctificator"

Manuscripts: **US-Wc:** ML96 .K7835 no.26 Case. Transparency score(2 p.)

Premiere: March 27, 1955, Basel; Ernst Pfiffner, conductor.

Publications: B639

142. *Eleven transparencies* = *Elf Transparente.* (Schott/UE; dur: 22 min.) *See:* B1398, B1451, K699, K738
For orchestra: 2.2.2.2 / 4.2.2.1 / timpani / harp / percussion / strings.
Composed: May - November 1954, Paris - Los Angeles, CA; Instr. November 14 - 16, SS Liberté, Atlantic Ocean.

1: *Design from darkness.* **2:** *Flashes.* **3:** *Waves.* **4:** *Images and spooks.* **5:** *Rays of warmth.* **6:** *Sparks cascading.* **7:** *Light and shade.* **8:** *Knocks and dashes.* **9:** *Volcano of anguish.* **10:** *Upon hearing the call from far away.* **11:** *The rest is silence.*
Commissioned: Louisville Orchestra.

Manuscripts: **A-Wst:** MH 14809/c. Sketch(22 p.) **A-Wst:** MH 14809/c. Score(p.1-15) **US-PHf.** Non-autograph score

Premiere: February 12, 1955, Louisville, KY; Louisville Orchestra; Robert Whitney, conductor. *See:* B876

First European Performance: December 15, 1955, Düsseldorf; Sinfonieorchester der Stadt Düsseldorf; composer, conductor. *See:* B806, B1137

Other Performances: B224, B1025

Publications: B477

Recording: Louisville Orchestra LOU 56-3. 33 1/3 rpm. mono. [1956] *See:* B195, B877
Louisville Orchestra; Robert Whitney, conductor.
With Robert Caamaño *Magnificat.*

143. *Proprium missae in domenica tertia in quadragesima.* (Schott; dur: 10 min.)
For SABar chorus a capella.
Composed: January 10 - 15, 1955.
1: *Introitus* (January 10, 1955, Los Angeles, CA) "Oculi mei" **2:** *Graduale* (January 11, 1955, Los Angeles, CA) "Exsurge, Domine" **3:** *Tractus* (January 13, 1955, Los Angeles, CA) "Ad te levavi oculos meos" **4:** *Offertorium* (January 13, 1955, Los Angeles, CA) "Justitiae Domini rectae" **5:** *Communio* (January 15, 1955, Los Angeles, CA) "Passer invenit sibi domum"

Manuscripts: US-Wc: ML96 Case. Transparency score(7 p.)

144. *Pallas Athene weint* = *Pallas Athene weeps.* (Schott/UE) *See:* B401, B635, B652, B777, K634, K640, K649, K662, K664, K751, K854, K2, K933
Opera in 3 acts; German text by the composer. Pallas Athene (mezzosoprano), Sokrates (bass-baritone), Alkibiades (tenor), Meletos (tenor), Meton (baritone), Althaea (soprano), Nauarchos (baritone), Senator (tenor or baritone), Agis (bass), Timaea (soprano), Lysander (tenor), Brasidas (baritone), Ktesippos (tenor), and orchestra: 2.2.2.2 / 4.2.2.0 / timpani / harp / piano / percussion / strings.
Composed: July 13, 1952 - June 15, 1953; revised January 2, 1955.

Manuscripts: US-CA. Libretto draft(136 p.) US-CA. Sketches(90 p.) US composer Piano-vocal score(112 p.) A-Wst: MH 14743/c. Blueprint piano-vocal score(21 p., original version) US composer Piano-vocal score(117 p., revised version) US-Wc: ML30.23a.K7 Case. Sketch(1 p., For an interlude between Prologue and 1st act - Bremen, about October 20, 1955 immediately after Premiere) US-Wc: ML96 Case. Transparancy score(3-279 p.; lacking pp. 74-78, 92, 107, 179-183, 224-230, 269)

Premiere: October 17, 1955, Hamburg, Hamburgische Staatsoper; Leopold Ludwig, conductor; Günther Rennert, producer; Alfred Siercke, staging & costumes; Margarete Ast, Pallas Athene; James Pease, Sokrates; Heinz Sauerbaum, Alkibiades; Helmut Melchert, Meletos; Hermann Prey, Meton; Helga Pilarczyk, Althaea; Karl Otto, Nauarchos; Adolf Meyer-Bremen, Senator; Arnold van Mill, Agis. *See:* B309, B617, B618, B674, B675, B676, B911, B1309, B1310, B1420, B1421, B1422

Published (Libretto): In *Prosa, Dramen, Verse.* (Münich: Albert Langen - Georg Müller, 1965): 271-297.

Published (Libretto): In *Das musikdramatische Werk,* v.2, hrsg. von Franz Eugen Dostal. Oesterreichische Dramatiker der Gegenwart, v.23. (Wien: Oesterreichische Verlagsanstalt, 1977): 172-197.

Published (Libretto, Act 1): In *Das Musikleben* 8 (Sepember 1955): 310-312.

145. *Capriccio.* (Schott/UE; dur: 10 min.)
For cello with orchestra: 1.1.1.1 / 1.1.1.0 / timpani / harp / celesta / percussion / strings.
Composed: February 6, 1955, Los Angeles, CA.
Sostenuto.
Commissioned: The City of Darmstadt on the occasion of the X. Internationalen Ferienkurse für Neue Musik, 1955.

Manuscripts: **A-Wst**: UE deposit Box A-J. Blueprint cello-piano score(10 p.) & part(5 p.) **A-Wst**: UE deposit Box A-J. Proof cello-piano score(12 p.) & part(5 p.)

Premiere: May 31, 1955, Kranichsteiner Musikinstitut, Darmstadt, Internationale Ferienkurse für neue Musik; Ludwig Hölscher, cello; Leopold Stokowski, conductor.

First U.S. Performance: May 14, 1957, Bloomington, Illinois Wesleyan University, Presser Hall; Ruth Krieger, cello; Illinois Wesleyan University Orchestra; Mario Mancinelli, conductor. *See:* B935

Recording: Orion ORS 79362. 33 1/3 rpm. stereo. [1979] *See:* B185, B872, B977
Evelyn Elsing, cello; American Camerata for New Music; John Stephens, conductor.
Duration: 11 min., 52 sec.
Recorded Kay Spiritual Center, American University, Washington, DC.
With his *The dissembler,* op.229 and Lawrence Moss *Symphonies, brasses, chamber orchestra.*

146. *Sieben leichte Stücke* = *Seven easy pieces.* (Schott; dur: 8 min.)
For string orchestra.
Composed: 1955.

1: *Ruhig, doch fliessend bewegt.* **2:** *Kräftig, masschartig.* **3:** *Ruhig, zart.* **4:** *Ziemlich schnell.* **5:** *Sehr ruhig, zart.* **6:** *Leicht bewegt, zierlich.* **7:** *Kräftig, entschieden.*

Manuscripts: **US-Wc**: ML96 .K7835 no.6 Case. Transparency score(8 p.)

Premiere: 1955, Mainz.

Recording: Preiserrecords SPR 10049. 33 1/3 rpm, stereo. [197-?] Dokumentationsreihe des Osterreichischen Komponistenbundes, 24.
Orchester des Oesterreichischen Rundfunks Radio Wien; George Singer, conductor.
Duration: 7 min.
With his 3 *Fragmente aus Karl V,* op.73a and *Sonata, violin & piano, op.99.*

147. *Suite, flute & piano.* (Broude; dur: 8 min.) *See:* B555
Composed: 1954.

1: *Andante.* **2:** *Allegretto moderato.* **3:** *Andante con moto.* **4:** *Allegro vivace.*

Premiere: July 5, 1956, Santiago, Universidad Catolica de Chile; Esteban Eitler, flute; Free Focke, piano.

First U.S. Performance: February 9, 1958, Pasadena Art Museum; Paul Horn, flute; Fred Katz, piano.

Publications: B625

Other Performances: B1153, B1154

147a. *Suite, flute & string orchestra*. (Broude; dur: 8 min.)
Composed: 1954.
  1: *Andante*. **2:** *Allegretto moderato*. **3:** *Andante con moto*. **4:** *Allegro vivace*.
Manuscripts: US-Wc: ML96 .K7835 no.22 Case. Transparency score(8 p.)
Publications: B1085

148. *Suite, clarinet & piano*. (Broude; dur: 8 min.) *See:* B555
Composed: 1955.
  1: *Andante sostenuto*. **2:** *Allegro moderato*. **3:** *Andante*. **4:** *Vivace*.
Manuscripts: US-Wc: ML96 .K7835 no.13 Case. Transparency score(9 p.)
Premiere: November 29, 1962, University of Miami, FL, Beaumont Lecture Hall,
  Third Festival of Contemporary International Music; William Klinger,
  clarinet; Jeffrey Stoll, piano. *See:* B1065
Recording: Mark MMF 3355. *20th century masterworks for clarinet, vol.* 2. 33 1/3
  rpm. stereo.
  Paul Drushler, clarinet; Gordon Gibson, piano.
  With clarinet sonatas by Darius Milhaud and Paul Hindemith.
Recording: Educational Music Service (Roncorp) EMS-006. *Allen Sigel, clarinet,*
  live in concert, vol. 2. cassette. c1983.
  Allen Sigel, clarinet; with piano.
  Duration: 8 min., 38 sec.
  With his *Monologue* op.157 and clarinet works by Beethoven/Bellison,
  Kroepsch/Bellison, Luigi Bassi, and Ben-Haim.

148a. *Suite, clarinet & string orchestra*. (Broude; dur: 8 min.)
Composed: 1955.
  1: *Andante sostenuto*. **2:** *Allegro moderato*. **3:** *Andante*. **4:** *Vivace*.
Manuscripts: US-Wc: ML96 .K7835 no.12 Case. Transparency score(10 p.)
Publications: B1085

149. *Psalmenverse zur Kommunion; für das ganze Kirchenjahr*. (Schott; dur:
  10 min.)
  For chorus a capella.
  Composed: 1955.
  1: *Psalm 33:9* "Gustate et videte" SA **2:** *Psalm 33:11* "Divites egerunt et
  esurierunt" SABar **3:** *Psalm 41:2* "Quemadmodum" SATB **4:** *Psalm 80:17*
  "Cibavit illos ex adipe frumenti" SABar **5:** *Johannes 6:56* "Qui manducat
  panem meum" SATB **6:** *Psalm 103:28* "Aperis tu manum tuam" SABar **7:**
  Psalm 112:1 "Laudate pueri Dominum" SATB **8:** *Psalm 116:1* "Laudate
  Dominum omnes gentes" SATB **9:** *Psalm 116:2* "Quoniam confirmata est"
  SATB **10:** *Conclusio* "Sicut erat in principio" SATB
Manuscripts: US composer Score(4 p.)

150. *Sonata, harp*. (BA; dur: 10 min.)
Composed: June 1955, Los Angeles, CA.
Dedication: Nicanor Zabaleta.
  1: *Allegro assai*. **2:** *Adagio*. **3:** *Vivace*.
Manuscripts: US-Wc: ML96 .K7835 no.27 Case. Transparency(7 p.)

Premiere: January 27, 1958, New York, Town Hall; Nicanor Zabaleta, harp. *See:* B496, B960

Publications: B1524

Recording: Klavier KS 507. *20th century harp.* 33 1/3 rpm. stereo. c1972. *See:* B144, B153, B196
Susann McDonald, harp.
Duration: 8 min., 40 sec.
With harp works by Alfredo Casella, Ami Maayani, Alan Hovhaness, Serge Prokofiev, and David Watkins.

151. *Ich singe wieder, wenn es tagt.* (Schott/UE; dur: 3 min.)
For SATB chorus with string orchestra or string quintet. German text by Walther von der Vogelweide.
Composed: November 1955 - January 2, 1956, Stuttgart - Vienna.
Text: "Die Zweifler sage"

Premiere: May 14, 1956, Linz, Kongresssaal der Arbeiterkammer; David-Chor; Kammerorchester der Stadt Linz; composer, conductor.

152. *Spiritus intelligentiae, Sanctus* = *Pfingst-Oratorium.* (UE; dur: 17 min.)
See: B842, B1316, B1408, B1435, K699, K738, K740, K802, K839, K841, K875, K911
Oratorio for Pentecost; for 2 singers, speaker & eletronic sounds.
Composed: October 1955 - March 23, 1956, Hamburg - Köln; Realized at the Westdeutscher Rundfunk, Köln.
Text: "Veni creator spiritu"

Manuscripts: **A-Wst:** MH 14756/c. Sketch(various pages) **A-Wst:** UE deposit Box K-S. Photocopy electronic score(31 p.) **A-Wn:** PhA 1985. Photocopy electronic score(31 p.)

Premiere: May 30, 1956, Cologne, Grosse Sendersaal, Westdeutscher Rundfunk; Käthe Möller-Siepermann, soprano; Martin Häusler, tenor; composer, speaker. *See:* B766, B852, B1311

Other Performances: B43

Published (Facsimile sketch): In *Dank an Ernst Krenek* (Wien: Universal Edition, 1982)

Published (Facsimile pages): In *Ernst Krenek,* hrsg. von Otto Kolleritsch. Studien zur Wertungsforschung, v.15. (Wien: Universal Edition, 1982): 191-192.

Recording: Deutsche Grammophon LP 16 134. 10 in. 33 1/3 rpm. mono. [1959] *See:* B195, B442, B788
Käthe Möller-Siepermann, soprano; Martin Häusler, tenor; composer, speaker; "Elektronische Realisation" by Heinz Schütz, Westdeutscher Rundfunk, Köln.
With G. M. König *Klangfiguren.* Deutsche Grammophon LPE 17 244. 10 in. [1962]

153. *The Belltower* = *Der Glockenturm.* (BA; dur: 58 min.) *See:* B303, K647, K738, K908

Opera in 1 act, 3 scenes; English text by the composer based on the story by Herman Melville; later German translation by the composer. Una (soprano), Bannadonna (baritone), Giovanni (bass), 2 Senators (tenor & baritone), 2 Workmen (tenor & baritone), chorus, and orchestra: 1.2.1.0 / 0.3.2.0 / 2 pianos / percussion / strings.

Composed: December 19, 1955 - April 14, 1956, Linz, Austria - Köln, Germany. Synopsis (1st draft) Bern, completed about 2d half of November 1955 ; Libretto (1st draft) completed about middle December 1955.

Commissioned: Fromm Music Foundation.

Manuscripts: **US-Wc:** ML30.23a .K7 Case. Libretto. **US-Wc:** ML30.23a .K7 Case. Sketch(26 p.) **D-brd** Kbärenreiter: BA 4313. Transparency piano-vocal score(70 p.) **D-brd** Kbärenreiter: BA 4313. Transparency score(102 p.) **US** composer Blueprint score(102 p., with conductor's marks & errata)

Premiere: March 17, 1957, University of Illinois, Urbana, IL, Lincoln Hall Theatre; Ludwig Zirner, producer and director; John Garvey, conductor; Manfred Capell, Bannadonna; Donna Sue Barton, Una; William Olson, Giovanni; Dan MacDonald, Donald Pascher, Senators; John Wilson, statue; Edward Levy, Bruce Govich, workmen. *See:* B441, B600, B953, B1123, B1342, B1464

First European Performance (German translation): December 4, 1958, Duisburg, Deutsche Oper am Rhein; composer, conductor; Günter Roth, staging; Heinz Ludwig, scenery; Hans Frank, Chor; Julius Jüllich, Bannadonna; Helmut Fehn, Giovanni; Elisabeth Schwarzenberg, Una; Walter Beissner, Josef Prehm, workers; Hans Rietjens, Lajos Kendy, Senators. *See:* B54, B217, B297, B791, B1261, B1276, B1390

Published (German libretto): In *Prosa, Dramen, Verse.* (Münich: Albert Langen - Georg Müller, 1965): 299-313.

Published (German libretto): In *Das musikdramatische Werk,* v.2, hrsg. von Franz Eugen Dostal. Oesterreichische Dramatiker der Gegenwart, v.23. (Wien: Oesterreichische Verlagsanstalt, 1977): 199-212.

Recording: University of Illinois CRS 5. 3 discs. 33 1/3 rpm. mono. [1957?] *See:* B193, B195, B221, B263, B383

Donna Sue Burton, Manfred Capell, William Olson, with supporting cast, John Garvey, conductor.

"Works ... commissioned by the School of Music and the Fromm Music Foundation for the 1957 Festival of Contemporary Music."

Duration: about 1 hr.

With works by Burrill Phillips, Irvine Fine, Alan Hovhaness, Wallingford Riegger, and Gunther Schuller.

154. *Tanzstudie.* (unpublished; dur: 3 min.)

For violin, piano, celesta, vibraphone, xylophone & percussion; incorporated into op.162 as no.3.

Composed: January 1956, Wien - Köln.

Commissioned by Norddeutscher Rundfunk, Hamburg.

Manuscripts: **US-Eu.** Sketch(5 p.)

155. *Egregii, carissimi.* (unpublished; dur: 2 min.)

2 voice canon. Latin text by the composer. "I was invited by my old friend, the composer-pianist Edward Erdmann, to celebrate with him his 60th birthday (March 18). As a present, I wrote for him a two-voice canon the Latin

words of which are self-explamatory."
Composed: February 18, 1956, Copenhagen.
Dedication: Eduard Erdmann.

Manuscripts: **D-brd** Erdmann Estate. **US-Wc:** ML30.23a .K7 Case. Sketch(1 p.)

156. *Sonatina, oboe.* (Broude; dur: 6 min.)
Composed: September 21 - 25, 1956, Los Angeles, CA.

Manuscripts: **A-Wst** Sketch(2 p.)

Premiere: May 9, 1960, New York, Circle in the Square, Composers' Showcase.
See: B253

Other Performances: B1153

157. *Monologue.* (Broude; dur: 6 min.)
For clarinet solo.
Composed: August 31 - September 20, 1956.

1: *Moderato* (August 31, 1956, Los Angeles, CA) **2:** *L'istesso tempo.* **3:** *Larghetto*
(September 10, 1956, Los Angeles, CA) **4:** *Allegretto.* **5:** *Allegro appassionato*
(September 20, 1956, Tujunga, CA)

Manuscripts: **A-Wst** Sketch(2 p.)

Premiere: May 9, 1960, New York, Circle in the Square, Composers' Showcase;
Stanley Walden, clarinet. *See:* B253

Recording: Advance Recordings FGR 4. *New music for solo clarinet.* 33 1/3 rpm.
mono. c1964. *See:* B196, B388
Philip Rehfeldt, clarinet.
Duration: 4 min., 27 sec.
With clarinet works by John Cage, Donald Scavarda, Donald Martino, Arline
Diamond & C. Whittenberg.

Recording: Mark Educational Recordings MES 38084. *Unaccompanied solos for
clarinet, v.4.* 33 1/3 rpm. stereo. [198?]
Paul Drushler, clarinet.
Duration: 4 min., 55 sec.
With clarinet works by William O. Smith, Gordon Jacob, Leslie Bassett,
Yvonne Desportes, and F. Gerard Errante.

Recording: MRS 32640. [198?]
Paul Drushler, clarinet.
With clarinet solos by Igor Stravinsky, Osborne, Arnold and Karg-Elert.

Recording: Educational Music Service (Roncorp) EMS-006. *Allen Sigel, clarinet,
live in concert, vol. 2.* cassette. c1983.
Allen Sigel, clarinet.
Duration: 5 min., 43 sec.
With his *Suite for clarinet and piano* op.148 and clarinet works by
Beethoven/Bellison, Kroepsch/Bellison, Luigi Bassi, and Ben-Haim.

158. *Divertimento.* (Broude; dur: 7 min.)
For orchestra: 2.2.3.2 / 2.2.2.0 / percussion / strings.
Composed: October 10 - November 8, 1956, Tujunga, CA.

1: *Allegro vivace.* **2:** *Andante sostenuto.* **3:** *Tempo di menuetto lento.* **4:**
Allegro giocoso.

Premiere: August 23, 1986, Ossiach, Austria; Residentia Orchestra (Hague) Hans
Vonk, conductor.

159. *Guten Morgen, Amerika.* (Schott; dur: 3 min.)
For SATB chorus a cappella. English text by Carl Sandburg; German translation by the composer.
Composed: 1956.
"Nun steht Onkel Sam"

160. *Kette, Kreis und Spiegel, sinfonische Zeichnung = Circle, chain and mirror, symphonic design.* (BA; dur: 16 min.) *See:* B72, B81, B691, B781, B1369, K685, K709, K717, K740, K838, K839
For orchestra: 2.2.2.2 / 2.2.2.1 / harp / timpiani / percussion / strings.
Composed: December 2, 1956 - January 1, 1957, Tujunga, CA; Instr. January 23, 1957.
Commissioned: Paul Sacher.
Dedication: Paul Sacher.

Manuscripts: **A-Wst:** MH 14731/c. Sketch(8 p.) **D-brd** Kbärenreiter. Transparency score(41 p.) **CH-B.** Blueprint score(41 p., presentation)

Premiere: January 23, 1958, Basel, 3. Konzert; Basler Kammerorchester; Paul Sacher, conductor. *See:* B51, B925, B1052, B1053, B1054

First U.S. Performance: March 4, 1965, Boston, New England Conservatory of Music, Brown Hall; Conservatory Symphony Orchestra; composer, conductor. *See:* B1270, B1271

161. *Sestina* (BA; dur: 17 min.) *See:* B2, B33, B81, B405, B662, B1326, B1502, K706, K715, K738, K740, K772, K793, K839
For soprano with ensemble: flute, clarinet, trumpet, 2 percussion, guitar, piano & violin. German text by the composer.
Composed: October 27, 1957, Tujunga, CA.
1: *Vergangen Klang und Klage = Bygone are sound and mourning.* **2:** *In Schritten vorgeordnet durch die Zahl = In stages preordained by number.* **3:** *Das Rad der Welt dreht rätselhafter Zufall = The wheel of the world is turned by riddlesome chance.* **4:** *Noch nicht gekommen ist die Gnadenzeit = Not yet has come the time.* **5:** *In Kreis und Spiegel wandert rings Gestalt = In circle and mirror shape.* **6:** *O grenzenlose Fülle = O fullness without bounds.*
Commissioned by Fromm Music Foundation.
Dedication in friendship to Paul Fromm.

Manuscripts: **A-Wst** Texts **D-brd** Kbärenreiter. Transparency score(60 p.) **US-LJ.** Blueprint score(60 p.)

Premiere: March 9, 1958, New York, New School, "New School Concerts" sponsored by the Fromm Foundation; Bethany Beardslee, soprano; composer, conductor. *See:* B119, B572, B972, B1344

First European Performance: 1958, Berliner Festwochen; Helga Pilarczyk, soprano; Elfriede Hübner, harp; Klaus Billing, piano; members of the Philharmonischen Orchester; composer, conductor. *See:* B123, B1312

Other Performances: B39, B43, B593, B1516

Published (Text): In *Prosa, Dramen, Verse.* (München: Albert Langen - Georg Müller, 1965): 412-413.

Published (Facsimile mm.27-32): In *Ernst Krenek,* hrsg. von Otto Kolleritsch. Studien zur Wertungsforschung, v.15. (Wien: Universal Edition, 1982): 226.

Published (Facsimile pp.18-19): In *Ernst Krenek, eine Studie,* von Lothar Knessl. Oesterreichische Komponisten des 20. Jahrhunderts, 12. (Wien: Elisabeth

Lafite, 1967): 74-75.

Recording: Epic LC 3509. 33 1/3 rpm. mono. [1958] Fromm Music Foundation Twentieth century composers series. *See:* B151, B195, B196, B199, B222, B384, B480, B1026, B1124
Bethany Beardslee, soprano; composer, conductor.
Duration: 19 min., 37 sec.
Recorded March 9, 1958 in New York by CBS Records.
With his *Lamentatio Jeremiae prophetae, op.93. Lessons I, VI, VII.*
Also issued on Orion ORS 78295. stereo. [p1978] (With his *5 pieces, trombone, op.198* and *Flute piece in 9 phases, op.171.*) # MU 8840. #OCLC #RLIN

162. *Marginal sounds* = *Grenzklänge.* (Broude; dur: 14 min.)
For violin, piano, celesta, vibraphone, xylophone & percussion. No.3 is op.154 slightly revised.
Composed: Nov.16, 1957, Tujunga, CA.

1: *Andante.* (October 31, 1957, Tujunga, CA) **2:** *Largo.* **3:** *Comodo.* **4:** *Vivace.*

Manuscripts: US-Eu. Sketchs of nos.1-2 & 4 (5 p.)

Premiere: February 22, 1960, New York, Caspary Auditorium, Manhattan School of Music, presented by Contemporary Music Society and the Rockefeller Institute; Manhattan Percussion Ensemble; Paul Price, conductor. *See:* B218

First European Performance: ca. February 1963, Bonn; Volker Wangenheim, conductor. *See:* B699

Other Performances: B43, B593, B1260

162a. *Jest of Cards* = *Spiel mit Karten.* (unpublished; dur: 20 min.)
Ballet arranged from op.162 for piano, violin, cello & percussion.
Composed: 1962.
Written for the San Francisco Ballet.

Manuscripts: US composer "Introduction to Marginal Sounds" score(10 p.)

Premiere: April 17, 1962, San Francisco, Geary Theatre; San Francisco Ballet; Lew Christensen, choreography; Tony Duquette, scenery; Gerhard Samuel, conductor. *See:* B28, B236, B387, B394

163. *Pentagramm.* (BA; dur: 8 min.) *See:* B1463
For flute, oboe, clarinet, bassoon, and horn. Revision of op.130.
Composed: November 21, 1957; nos.1 - 3 rewritten.

1: *Presto.* **2:** *Andante.* **3:** *Allegretto.* **4:** *Moderato allegro* (January 1, 1952, Innsbruck)

Manuscripts: **A-Wst:** MH 14820/c. Sketch(6 p.) **D-brd** Kbärenreiter: BA 3825. Transparency score(10 p.) & 5 parts.

Premiere: March 31, 1958, Los Angeles, University of California, Schoenberg Hall; Pacific Wind Quintet (Arthur Hoberman, flute; Donald Muggeridge, oboe; Dominick Fera; clarinet; Herman Lebow, horn; Fowler Friedlander, bassoon). *See:* B38

First European Performance: January 7, 1967, Bamberg; Bamberg Bläserquintett. *See:* B1153, B1154

Other Performances: B224, B253, B947

Recording: Lyrichord LL 158. 33 1/3 rpm. mono. [1966] *See:* B196, B368, B389, B684, B939
Soni Ventorum Wind Quintet.

With works by Walter Piston and Joseph Goodman.
Also issued on Lyrichord LLST 7158 (stereo)

164. *Suite, guitar.* (Doblinger; dur: 6 min.) *See:* B460
Composed: Fall 1957, Tujunga, CA.
1: *Allegro moderato.* 2: *Andante sostenuto.* 3: *Allegretto.* 4: *Larghetto.* 5: *Allegro.*
Dedication: Theodore Norman

Manuscripts: US composer 6 p.

Premiere: February 16, 1959, Los Angeles County Auditorium, Monday Evening Concerts; Theodore Norman, guitar. *See:* B39

Recording: Orion ORS 78323. *American guitar.* 33 1/3 rpm. stereo. [1979] *See:* B230, B602, B873
John Kneubuhl, guitar.
Duration: 5 min., 58 sec.
With guitar works by Soulima Stravinsky, John Kneubuhl, Theodore Norman, Albert Harris, and Ernst Bacon.
Also issued on Orion OC 828S cassette.

165. *Missa duodecim tonorum.* (Gregorian Inst.; dur: 20 min.) *See:* B1072, K700, K841
For SSA or TTB chorus & organ.
Composed: December 1957, Tujunga, CA.
1: *Kyrie.* 2: *Gloria.* 3: *Credo.* 4: *Sanctus.* 5: *Benedictus.* 6: *Agnus Dei.*

Manuscripts: US-Wc: ML96 .K7835 no.15 Case. Transparency score(26 p.)

Premiere: 1958?, Vienna, Franciskaner Kirche.

166. *Echoes from Austria.* (Broude; dur: 10 min.) *See:* B409
Austrian folksongs arranged for piano. Nos.1, 2, and 4 are from Carinthia; nos.5 - 7 are from Vorarlberg; and no.3 is original.
Composed: April 26, 1958, Tujunga, CA.
1: *Molto moderato.* 2: *Allegro.* 3: *Allegretto.* 4: *Allegro moderato.* 5: *Moderato.* 6: *Allegretto animato.* 7: *Larghetto.*

Manuscripts: A-Wst: MH 14769/c. Sketch(8 p.) A-Wn: Mus.Hs. 34361. Transparency(10 p.)

Recording: Orion ORS 76246. 33 1/3 rpm. stereo. [1976] *See:* B147, B667, B1331
composer, piano.
Duration: 8 min., 59 sec.
Recorded April 3, 1976, University of California San Diego, La Jolla, CA.
With his *Aulokithara,* op.213a, *Wechselrahmen,* op.189, and *Three sacred pieces,* op.210.
Also issued on Orion OC 676. cassette. [1980?]

167. *Hexahedron* = *Hexaeder.* (unpublished; dur: 12 min.)
Six untitled pieces for ensemble: 1.0.1.0 / 0.1.0.0 / vibraphone / piano / harp / percussion / violin / cello. 2 versions.
Composed: May 21, 1958, Tujunga, CA.

Manuscripts: A-Wst Sketch(65 p. + plan 15 p.) A-Wst Transparency score(3 p.) US composer Score(32 p.) US composer 5 parts.

Premiere: September 7, 1958, Darmstadt, Landestheater, Internationale

Ferienkurse für Neue Musik; Kammerensemble des Kölner Rundfunk-Sinfieorchester; composer, conductor. *See:* B767

First U.S. Performance: May 9, 1960, New York, Circle in the Square, Composers' Showcase; composer, conductor. *See:* B253

168. *Sechs Vermessene = 6 Measurements.* (BA; dur: 12 min.) *See:* B159, B409, B584, K839
Untitled pieces for piano.
Composed: April 1 - July 18, 1958, Borrego Springs, CA.

Manuscripts: **A-Wst:** MH 14816/c. Sketch(26 p.) **A-Wst:** MH 14816/c. Plans(24 p.) **A-Wn:** Mus.Hs. 34362. Transparencies score(12 p.) **D-brd** Kbärenreiter. Blueprint score(12 p.)

Premiere: October 9, 1960, Kasseler Musiktage; Franzpeter Goebels, piano. *See:* B141, B887, B1405

First American Performance: August 9, 1960, Stratford, Ontario, Music Festival.

Other Performances: B253, B386

Publications: B770

Recording: Candide CE 31015. *Avant garde piano.* 33 1/3 rpm. stereo. [1970] *See:* B151, B196, B493, B524, B822, B1026, B1080
David Burge, piano.
Duration: 11 min., 6 sec.
With piano works by Lucian Berio, Pierre Boulez, Luigi Dallapiccola, & Karlheinz Stockhausen.
Also issued on Vox STGBY 637. [1970]

169. *6 Motetten nach Worten von Franz Kafka.* (BA; dur: 18 min.) *See:* B539
For SATB chorus a cappella.
Composed: March 28 - April 1959, Tujunga, CA.

1: *Der Weg* (March 28, 1959) **2:** *Taube auf dem Dach.* "Um was klagst du" **3:** *Die Peitsche.* "Das Tier entwindet Peitsche" **4:** *Der Wagen.* "Läufst du immerfort vorwärts" **5:** *Der Sündenfall.* "Warum klagen wir wegen des Sündenfalles?" **6:** *Müssiggang* (April 1959, Tujunga, CA)
Commissioned: RIAS, Berlin.

Manuscripts: **A-Wst:** MH 14770/c. Sketch(11 p.) **US-Wc:** ML96 .K7835 no.31 Case. Transparency score(33 p.)

Premiere: September 29, 1959, Berlin, Conservatory, Berliner Festwochen; RIAS-Kammerchor; Günther Arndt, conductor. *See:* B124, B427, B868, B1313, B1314

First U.S. Performance: April 4, 1965, San Francisco, Tape Music Center, Composers' Forum; Berkeley Singers; Alden Gilchrist, conductor. *See:* B198, B395

Other Performances: B335

170. *Quaestio temporis = A question of time = Eine frage der Zeit.* (BA; dur: 18 min.) *See:* B2, B72, B1369, K740, K742, K762, K793, K838, K839
For orchestra: 1.1.1.1 / 1.1.1.1 / celesta / guitar / harp / piano / percussion / 1 violin.
Composed: May 25, 1959, Tujunga, CA.
Commissioned: Fromm Music Foundation.

Manuscripts: US composer Transparency score(69 p.)

Premiere: September 30, 1960, Hamburg, Norddeutscher Rundfunk, Studio X,

"Das neue Werk"; Sinfonieorchester des NDR; composer, conductor. *See:* B55, B335, B868, B1256, B1257, B1423, B1424

First U.S. Performance: May 13, 1962, New York, New School for Social Research, Fromm Music Foundation; composer, conductor. *See:* B201, B392, B519, B683, B738, B961

Other Performances: B363, B436, B678

Publications: B492, B528

171. *Flötenstück neunphasig* = *Flute piece in nine phases.* (BA; dur: 12 min.)
See: B262, B555, K793
For flute and piano.
Composed: June 1959, Borrego Springs, CA.
Dedication: Esteban Eitler.

Manuscripts: **US** composer Transparency score(14 p.) **D-brd** Kbärenreiter. Blueprint score(14 p.) & part(12 p.)

Premiere: September 22, 1960, Venice, Venice Festival; Severino Gazzeloni, flute; Piero Scarpino, piano. *See:* B335, B868

First U.S. Performance: January 21, 1963, Los Angeles, Plummer Park, Fiesta Hall, Monday Evening Concerts; Gretel Shanley, flute; Pearl Kaufman, piano. *See:* B436, B678

Publications: B1160

Recording: Orion ORS 78295. 33 1/3 rpm. stereo. [1978] *See:* B149, B151, B196, B880, B976, B1026, B1247
Bernhard Batschelet, flute; composer, piano.
Duration: 12 min., 5 sec.
Recorded December 17, 1977, Palm Springs, CA.
With his *Sestina,* op.161 and *5 pieces, trombone, op.198.*

172. *Hausmusik* = *House music.* (BA; dur: 6 min.) *See:* B555
"Sieben Stücke für die sieben Tage der Woche" (Seven pieces for the seven days of the week)
Composed: August - September 1959, Princeton, NJ.

1: *Moderato.* (For piano, 4 hands) **2:** *Allegretto.* (For soprano recorder & guitar) **3:** *Andantino.* (For 2 recorders & violin) **4:** *Allegro.* (For violin & guitar) **5:** *Animato.* (For soprano recorder & violin) **6:** *Andante con passione.* (For violin & piano) **7:** *Allegretto.* (For piano, soprano recorder, violin & guitar)
Commissioned: RIAS, Berlin for St. Caecilias Day, 1959.

Manuscripts: **D-brd** Kbärenreiter. Blueprint score(12 p., with corrections)

Premiere: November 22, 1959, Berlin, RIAS-Studio VII, Tag der Deutschen Hausmusik; Helmut Roloff, Klaus Billing, Helmut Heller, Siegfried Behrend, Linde Höffer-von Winterfeld, Jeannette Chemin-Petit.

Publications: B771, B840

173. *Basler Massarbeit* = *Basle custom made.* (BA; dur: 6 min.) *See:* K793, K839
For 2 pianos in five numbered movements.
Composed: February 1960, Tujunga, CA.
Commissioned: Werner Batschelet and Dr. Werner Bosshard.

Manuscripts: **US-CA.** Transparency score(12 p.) **D-brd** Kbärenreiter. Blueprint score(12 p.)

Premiere: January 19, 1961, Basel, SZ; Wolfgang Neininger, composer, pianos.

See: B69, B928

First U.S. Performance: Los Angeles, Ojai Festival; Leonard Stein, composer, pianos. *See:* B437

Publications: B248, B774

174. *Children's songs: 3 Madrigals.* (Broude; dur: 3 min.)
For SSA chorus a cappella. Texts by William Shakespeare (no.1), Robert Herrick (no.2), and Alfred Tennyson (no.3).
Composed: Spring 1960, Tujunga & Twenty-nine Palms, CA.
1: *Fairies' song.* "You spotted snakes with double tongue" 2: *The four sweet months.* "First, April, she with mellow showers" 3: *Summer again.* "Summer is coming"

174. *Children's songs: 3 Motets.* (Broude; dur: 3 min.)
For SSA chorus a cappella. Texts from Eccleastics 1:4, 5, 7; Psalm 107:23 - 26, 29; and Psalm 104:24 - 26.
Composed: Easter 1960, Tujunga & Twenty-nine Palms, CA.
1: *The Earth abideth.* 2: *To the sea in ships.* "They that go down to the sea in ships" 3: *Leviathan.* "The earth is full of thy riches"

175. *The flea.* (Marks; dur: 3 min.)
Song for tenor or soprano & piano. English text by John Donne.
Composed: July 4, 1960, Tujunga, CA.

Manuscripts: **A-Wst** ?5 p.

Premiere: 1968, Raleigh, NC, Peace College Auditorium; Ethel Casey, soprano; Janet Southwick, piano.

Published (Facsimile of page 1 of sketch): In *Notations*, by John Cage. (New York: Something Else Press, 1969)

Published: In *New vistas in song.* (New York: E.B. Marks, 1964): 35-40.

176. *Jedermann.* (unpublished)
Incidental music for the play by Hugo von Hofmannsthal. For 2 solo voices, chorus & orchestra: 1.1.2.1 / 2.2.2.0 / guitar / percussion / strings.
Commissioned: Salzburg Festspiel.

Manuscripts: **A-Sfest.** Transparency score(36 p.)

Premiere: July 30, 1962, Salzburg, Salzburger Festspiele; Ernst Hinreiner, musical director; Gottfried Reinhardt, producer.

177. *From three make seven = Aus drei mach sieben.* (BA; dur: 12 min.) *See:* B932, K838, K839, K843
For orchestra: 2.2.2.3 / 4.2.2.1 / harp / piano / percussion / strings.
Composed: 1960 - 1961; Revised 1968.
Commissioned: BMI.

Manuscripts: **A-Wst** Sketch(26 p.) **D-brd** Kbärenreiter. Transparency score(16 p.)

Premiere: March 3, 1965, Berlin, "Musik des 20. Jahrhunderts"; Berliner Philharmonisches-Orchester; Reinhard Peters, conductor. *See:* B128

1968 Version: February 16, 1968, Baden-Baden, Südwestfunk, Hans-Rosbaud-Studio; Sinfonieorchester des Südwestfunk; composer, conductor. *See:* B1376

First U.S. Performance: February 6, 1970, Wyandanch High School Auditorium; Pro Arte Symphony Orchestra; Eleazar de Carvalho, conductor.

84 *Ernst Krenek*

Other Performances: B1213

Recording: Orion ORS 78290. *Krenek conducts Krenek.* 33 1/3 rpm. stereo. [1977]
See: B234
Sinfonieorchester des Südwestfunk; composer, conductor.
Duration: 14 min., 26 sec.
Recorded February 16, 1968.
With his *Horizon circled,* op.196 and *Von vorn herein,* op.219. Deutsche
Grammophon 0629 027-031. 5 discs. 33 1/3 rpm. stereo. p1978.
Accompanies book: *Verehrter Meister, lieber Freund; Begegnungen mit
Komponisten unserer Zeit* by Heinrich Strobel. (Stuttgart: Belser Verlag, 1977-
78) With works by Igor Stravinsky and others.

178. *Jedermann.* (unpublished) *See:* K812
Film score, developed from op.176.
Composed: April 24, 1961.
Commissioned: Duerer Film, Vienna.

Manuscripts: **A-Wst:** MH 14768/c. Sketch(10 p.) **A-Wst:** MH 14821/c. Sketch(19
p.) **A-Wst:** MH 14821/c. "Musiknotizen by Gottfried Reinhardt" 4 p.

Premiere: November 1961, Vienna. *See:* B311

179. *Ausgerechnet und verspielt.* (BA; dur: 80 min.) *See:* B1195, B1286, K772,
K793, K830, K902
Television opera in 1 act. German text by the composer. Markus (baritone),
Ginette (soprano), Fernando (tenor), Lucile (mezzosoprano), Geraldine (alto),
Hamilton (baritone), Bureau chief (baritone), 2 Television cameramen (tenor &
bass), Sestina (mezzosoprano), Marcel (spoken), Casino public (chorus), and
orchestra: 1.1.1.0 / 0.1.1.0 / celesta / harpsichord / harp / harmonium / 2
pianos / guitar / percussion / violin / viola / cello. *Roulette Sestina* for voice
& piano to be played between scenes. *Tornada for Roulette Sestina* for voice, 2
pianos & harmonium.
Text written: December 10, 1960 - June 1961, Friedrichshafen - Palm Springs,
CA; Music composed: June 26 - September 15, 1961, Las Vegas, NV - Lone
Pine, CA; Instr. January 1, 1962, Tujunga, CA.
Commissioned: Osterreichischer Fernsehen.

Manuscripts: **A-Wst:** MH 14755/c. Text(various pages) **A-Wst:** MH 14754/c.
Sketch(109 p.) **D-brd** Kbärenreiter. Transparency score(178 p.) **A-Wst:** UE
deposit Box A-J. Blueprint score(109 p. & rehearsal plan 2 p.) **A-Wst:** UE
deposit Box A-J. "Roulette Sestina" blueprint single staff segments(32 p.) **US**
composer "Tornada for Roulette Sestina" 1 p.

Published (Libretto): In *Prosa, Dramen, Verse.* (Münich: Albert Langen - Georg
Müller, 1965): 315-340.

Premiere: July 25, 1962, Vienna, Oesterreichischer Fernsehen; composer,
conductor; Hermann Lanske, producer; Fritz Wotruba, scenery; Veronika
Kusmin, Mary Richards, Paul Späni, Max Hechenleiter, Paul Schöffler, and
Elisabeth Höngen, singers. *See:* B362, B696, B1471, B1473

Roulette Sestina: October 15, 1964, Mannheim, Aula der Wirtschaftshochschule
im Schloss; Gesellschaft für Neue Musik; composer, conductor.

180. *Alpbach quintet = 5 + 1.* (UE; dur: 20 min.)
Ballet in five untitled movements for flute, oboe, clarinet, horn & bassoon with *Intermezzos* for percussion with solo instrument to be played after each movement.
Composed: February - March 1962, Tujunga, CA.
Commissioned: Austrian College, Alpbach.

Manuscripts: **A-Wst:** MH 14726/c. Sketch(24 p.) **A-Wst:** MH 14563/c. No.4, sketch(2 p.) **A-Wst:** UE deposit Box A-J. Proof parts(6) with corrections. **A-Wn:** PhA 1987. "Intermezzos" photocopy score(5 & 13 p.)

Premiere: August 25, 1962, Alpbach, Austria; Yvonne Georgi, choreography; composer, conductor. *See:* B543

First U.S. Performance: January 21, 1963, Los Angeles, Plummer Park, Fiesta Hall, Monday Evening Concerts; Westwood Wind Quintet. *See:* B436, B678

Other Performances: B102, B1153

180.5 *Organologia.* (unpublished; dur: 15 min.) *See:* B503, B648
For organ. In five untitled movements.
Composed: June 1, 1962, Tujunga, CA.
Commissioned: Stadt Mülheim, Germany.
Dedication: Petri-Kirche zu Mülheim an der Ruhr and Siegfried Reda.

Manuscripts: US composer Transparency(20 p.)

Premiere: November 24, 1968, Mülheim, Petri-Kirche; Gerd Zacher, organ.

181. *Kanon Igor Strawinsky zum 80. Geburtstag = Canon for Stravinsky's 80th birthday.* (BA; dur: 2 min.)
For 2-voice chorus. Latin text by the composer.
Composed: June 1, 1962, Tujunga, CA.

Text: "Igori, carissimo amico"

Manuscripts: **A-Wst:** MH 14738/c. Latin text(1 p.) **A-Wst:** MH 14738/c. Sketch(6 p.) **D-brd** Kbärenreiter. Transparency score(3 p.)

Premiere: March 2, 1962, Los Angeles, Plummer Park, Fiesta Hall, Monday Evening Concerts; Pomona College Glee Club; William F. Russell, conductor. *See:* B40

Publications: B249, K766

Published (Facsimile): In *Musica* 16:4 (April 1962): 4 pages between 176-177.

Published (Text): In *Prosa, Dramen, Verse.* (München: Albert Langen - Georg Müller, 1965): 414.

182. *Nach wie vor der Reihe nach.* (BA; dur: 8 min.)
For orchestra: 2.2.2.2 / 4.2.2.1 / celesta / guitar / harp / vibraphone / xylophone / percussion / strings; includes 2 speakers in the second movement. German text by the composer. In 3 untitled movements
Composed: Text: June 21, 1962, Salzburg; Music: July 1 - August 11, 1962, Wien - Obergurgl (Oetztal).
Commissioned: Süddeutscher Rundfunk, Stuttgart.
Dedication: Süddeutschen Rundfunk and Hermann Scherchen.

Manuscripts: **D-brd** Kbärenreiter. Transparency score(3 p.) Text(5 p.) **D-brd** Kbärenreiter. Transparency score(3 p.) Text(5 p.) Sketch(8 p.) **D-brd** Kbärenreiter. Transparency score(20 p.) BA 4332.

Premiere: October 25, 1962, Stuttgart, Beethovensaal der Stuttgarter Liederhalle, Woche der leichten Musik; Südfunk-Sinfonieorchester; Marianne Simon, Carlo Fuss, speakers; Hermann Scherchen, conductor. *See:* B575, B1176

183. *Toccata.* (Pagani; dur: 6 min.)
  For accordion.
  Composed: Christmas 1962, Tujunga, CA.
  Commissioned: American Accordion Association.

  Manuscripts: **A-Wst:** MH 14767/c. Sketch(11 p.) **US** composer Transparency(9 p.)

  Recording: Orion ORS 75204. 33 1/3 rpm. stereo. [1975] *See:* B196, B667, B701, B879, B1331, B1354, B1381
  Robert Young McMahan, accordion.
  Duration: 5 min., 20 sec.
  Recorded May 17 and June 7, 1975, at California State University, Northridge. With his *Santa Fe timetable*, op.102, *O lacrymosa*, op.48, and *Tape and double*, op.207.

184. *Cello Studien.* (BA; dur: 2 min. each)
  Composed: January 6, 1963, Tujunga, CA.
  a: *Nachdenklich.* For 1 cello. **b:** *Vorkehrungen zur Rückkehr sind getroffen.* For 4 cellos.

  Manuscripts: **A-Wst:** MH 14799/c. Sketch(6 p.) **US** composer Transparency(1 + 4 p.) **D-brd** Kbärenreiter. Blueprint(1 + 3 p.)

  Premiere: April 23, 1968, Riehen, SZ, Hause W. Senn-Dürck.

  Published: In *Violoncello Schule*, hrsg. von Susanne Hirzel. Heft 4. (Kassel: Bärenreiter, 1965), no.47, p.44 & no.87, p.82-85

185. *San Fernando sequence.* (unpublished; dur: 12 min.)
  For electronic tape.
  Composed: 1963.

  Manuscripts: **US-LJ.** Sketch(27 p.)

  Premiere: March 15, 1963, San Fernando State College. *See:* K781

186. *Der goldene Bock* = *The golden ram* = *Chrysomallos.* (BA) *See:* B81, B635, B1090, B1091, K792, K798, K830
  Opera in 4 acts; German text by the composer. Athamas (baritone), Ino (mezzosoprano), Phrixos (tenor), Chairosthenes (tenor), Phineus (baritone), Melachron (baritone), Jason (baritone), Medea (mezzosoprano), Pelias (tenor), Chattahoochie (baritone), Glaukis (mezzosoprano), Abisorontas (mezzosoprano), Nephele (soprano), speakers, chorus and orchestra: 2.2.2.2 / 2.3.3.0 / celesta / harp / piano / electric guitar / timpani / percussion / strings.
  Commissioned: Hamburg State Opera.
  Text written: October - Christmas 1962, Tujunga, CA; English translation: December 8, 1982, Palm Springs, CA; Music composed: January 1 - June 1, 1963.

  Manuscripts: **A-Wst:** MH 14753/c. Libretto drafts **US-LJ.** Libretto in English translation by Ernst & Gladys Nordenstrom Krenek. **A-Wst:** MH 14752/c. Sketch(156 p.) **D-brd** Kbärenreiter. Transparency score(252 p.) **US** composer Piano-vocal score(190 p.) original version.

  Premiere: June 16, 1964, Hamburg State Opera; composer, conductor; Egon Monk, producer; Alfred Siercke, staging; Tom Krause, Jason; Helga Pilarczyk, Medea; Helmut Melchert, Pelias; Toni Blankenheim, Chattahoochie; Elisabeth Steiner, Glaukis; Ria Urban, Abisorontas; Ilse Hollweg, Nephele; Vladimir Ruzdak, Athamas; Cvetka Ahlin, Ino; Jürgen Förster, Phrixos; Anneliese Gerike, Helle; Kurt Marschner, Chairosthenes; Hans-Otto Kloose, Phineus; Hans-Heinrich Hartwig, Melachron. *See:* B56, B57, B58, B100, B223, B438, B520, B521, B565, B587, B606, B620, B621, B708, B803, B1425, B1490, B1496

Published (Libretto): In *Prosa, Dramen, Verse.* (Münich: Albert Langen - Georg Müller, 1965): 341-381.

Published: Facsimile of last page on cover *Generalprogramm, Musikkollegium Winterthur.* (1964/65): 5-16.

Recording: Nicht länger kann ich bleiben (act3). EMI Electrola 1C 195-29 107/109. *Musiktheater Heute; Eine Dokumentation der Hamburgischen Staatsoper.* 3 discs. 33 1/3 rpm. mono. p1972.
Helga Pilarczyk, Medea; Tom Krause, Jason; Chor der Hamburgischer Staatsoper; Philharmonisches Staatsorchester Hamburg; composer, conductor.
With excerpts from his *Sardakai,* op.206 and from operas by Alban Berg, G. Klebe, G. C. Menotti, L. J. Werle, M. Kelemen, M. Kagel.
Label on container: Odeon.

186a. *O Holy Ghost.* (BA; dur: 2 min.)
Motet for SATB chorus a cappella. English text by John Donne from *A litanie,* no.3.
Composed: April 9 - 17, 1964, Los Angeles - Chicago - SS France, New York - Le Havre.
Commissioned: Internationale Heinrich Schütz-Gesellschaft.

Manuscripts: **A-Wst:** MH 14765/c. Sketch(2 p.) **D-brd** Kbärenreiter. Score(3 p.)

Premiere: May 3, 1965, Berlin, 18. Internationale Heinrich-Schütz-Fest; NCRV Vocaal Ensemble Hilversum; Marinus Voorberg, conductor. *See:* B127

Publications: B778

Recording: Orion ORS 80377. *Ernst Krenek vocal compositions.* 33 1/3 rpm. stereo. [1980] *See:* B740, B1358
College of the Desert Vocal Ensemble; John L. Norman, conductor.
Duration: 2 min., 6 sec.
With his op.61, op.35, op.210, op.210, op.226, and op.67.

187. *Fibonacci mobile.* (BA; dur: 16 min.) *See:* B346, B903, B932, K836, K839
For string quartet & piano 4 hands.
Composed: November - December 1964, Tujunga, CA.
Commissioned: Dartmouth College for the Hopkins Center Third Annual Congregation of the Arts by Mario di Bonaventura, Music Director.

Manuscripts: **A-Wst:** MH 14745/c. Sketch(41 p.) **A-Wst:** MH 14764/c. 2-piano score(1 p.). pencil. **D-brd** Kbärenreiter. Transparency(various pages)

Premiere: July 7, 1965, Dartmouth College, Hopkins Center, Spaulding Auditorium, Third Annual Congregation of the Arts; Martin Canin, Anthony di Bonaventura, pianos; Dartmouth String Quartet (Stuart Canin, David Cerone, Ralph Hersh, and Paul Olefsky); composer, coordinator. *See:* B224, B947

188. *König Oedipus.* (unpublished; dur: 20 + 15 min.) *See:* K809, K812
Incidental music to the Sophocles plays: a."Oedipus tyrannus" and b."Oedipus auf Kolonos." German translations by R. Bayer.
Composed: September 12 - December 31, 1964, Vienna.
Commissioned: Salzburger Festspiele.

Manuscripts: **A-Wst:** MH 14772/c. Sketch(21 p.) **A-Sfest.** Transparency scores(24 + 14 p.)

Premiere: July 27, 1965, Salzburg, Salzburg Festspiel; Gustav Rudolf Sellner, producer; Oskar Peter, conductor; Mozarteum-Orchester; Kammerchor der Salzburger Festspiele. *See:* B507, B644

189. *Wechselrahmen = Change of frames.* (BA; dur: 12:30 min.) *See:* B903
For soprano & piano. German text by Emil Barth.
Composed: December 1964 - January 21, 1965, Tujunga, CA.

1: *Schwarze Muse* (January 21, 1965, Tujunga, CA) "Einflüstrerin, Stimme" **2:** *Der Schatten* (January 1 - 7, 1965, Tujunga, CA) "Einziger Augenblick" **3:** *Ihr Schwüre* "Ihr Schwüre gegen das Vergessen" **4:** *Spruchband* (December 25, 1964, Tujunga, CA) "Den Geborenen schreckt das Licht der Welt" **5:** *Wechselrahmen* (December 1964, Tujunga, CA) "Ein Totenhafen" **6:** *Heller als Glassteine* (January 20, 1965, Tujunga, CA) "Heller als Glassteine"
Commissioned: Arbeitsgemeinschaft kultureller Organisationen, Düsseldorf.

Manuscripts: **A-Wst:** MH 14764/c. Sketch(13 p.) **US** composer Transparency score(14 p.) **D-brd** Kbärenreiter. Blueprint score(14 p.)

Premiere: September 9, 1965, Düsseldorf, Kunstverein; Ilse Hollweg, soprano; composer, piano. *See:* B700, B1024

Other Performances: B102

Publications: B129

Recording: Orion ORS 76246. 33 1/3 rpm. stereo. [1976] *See:* B147, B667, B1331
Beverly Ogdon, soprano; composer, piano.
Duration: 11 min., 45 sec.
Recorded April 3, 1976, University of California at San Diego, La Jolla, CA.
With his *Aulokithara,* op.213a, *Three sacred pieces,* op.210, and *Echoes from Austria,* op.166.
Also issued on Orion OC 676. cassette. [1980?]

190. *Quintona.* (unpublished; dur: 9 min.)
For electronic tape.
Composed: 1965.

Manuscripts: **A-Wst:** MH 14737/c. Sketch(14 p.)

Premiere: 1965, San Fernando, CA, San Fernando Valley State College Campus Theater. *See:* K823

Recording: JME ME 1 -- ME 2. *Tercera bienal americana de arte; Primera jornadas americanas de musica experimental.*
Duration: 9 min.

191. *Quintina über die fünf Vokale.* (BA; dur: 12 min.) *See:* B405, B1435, K813, K839, K908
For soprano with ensemble: recorder, vibraphone, xylophone, guitar, viola, percussion & tape. German text by the composer.
Composed: March - April 1965, Cambridge, Mass.

1: *Sprache schenkt Musik das Wort = Language lends the word to music.* **2:** *Es fliesst beredt das Wort = Speech flows eloquently.* **3:** *Werk des Zufalls scheinen sie dem Ohr = A result of chance is what they appear to the ear.* **4:** *Vorbestimmte Klangfigur = Predetermined configuration of sound.* **5:** *Hat, was wir denken, trotz der Stummheit Sinn? = Do our thoughts in spite of muteness have any meaning?* **6:** *Sprache schenkt Musik das Wort = Language lends the word to music.*

Manuscripts: **A-Wst:** MH 14737/c. Sketch(14 p.) **A-Wst:** MH 14741/c. Sketch(12 p.) **D-brd** Kbärenreiter: BA 4187. Transparency score(15 p.) & 6 parts.

Premiere: October 3, 1965, Copenhagen, Danish Radio series "Prisma"; Yolanda Rodio, soprano; composer, conductor. *See:* B604, B810

First U.S. Performance: May 12, 1966, San Francisco Museum, San Francisco Festival of Contemporary Music; Anna Carol Dudley, soprano; composer, conductor. *See:* B113, B213

Other Performances: B102

Published (Facsimile pages): In *Ernst Krenek,* hrsg. von Otto Kolleritsch. Studien zur Wertungsforschung, v.15. (Wien: Universal Edition, 1982): 197-200.

Recording: Orion ORS 80380. 33 1/3 rpm. stereo. [p1980] *See:* B187, B242, B826
Constance Navratil, soprano; Carol Winterbourne, flute; Carrie Holzman, viola; John Kneubuhl, guitar; Fred Lee, Joseph Kucera, Sue Hopkins, percussion; composer, conductor.
Duration: 10 min., 22 sec.
Recorded April 14, 1979, Lobero Theatre, University of California, Santa Barbara.
With his *They knew what they wanted,* op.227.

192. *Der Zauberspiegel = The magic mirror.* (BA; dur: 85 min.) *See:* B932, K830, K902
Television opera in 14 scenes. German text by the composer. A Chinese emperor (bass), Liu Tsao (mezzosoprano), Francesco (tenor), Pierre (bass), Carola (soprano), Rudolf (tenor), Barban (bass), Vera operater 378 (alto), Emperor's servant (tenor), orchestra: 1.1.1.1 / 1.1.1.0 / harp / electric guitar / glockenspiel / vibraphone / xylophone / zither / cymbalum / 3 pianos / harpsichord / celesta / harmonium / percussion.
Text written: March 23 - August 25, 1963, Boulder, CO; Music composed: February 21, 1965 - January 28, 1966, Cambridge, Mass.
Commissioned: Bayerischer Fernsehen, Munich.

Manuscripts: **A-Wst:** MH 14746/c. Libretto drafts. **A-Wst:** MH 14747/c. Sketch(72 p.) **A-Wst:** MH 14747/c. Score(various pages) **D-brd** Kbärenreiter: BA 4169a. Transparency piano-vocal score(88 p.) **D-brd** Kbärenreiter: BA 4169. Transparency score(121 p.)

Premiere: September 6, 1967, Bayerischer Fernsehen, Munich; composer, conductor; Symphonieorchester des Bayerischen Rundfunks; Herbert Kirchhoff, scenery; Joachim Hess, director; Heinz Rehfuss, Chinese ruler; Catherine Gayer, Liu Tsao; Fritz Uhl, Francesco; Willy Ferenz, Pierre; Joan Carroll, Carola; Richard Holm, Rudolf; Horst Günter, Barban; Marylin Tyler, Vera. *See:* B393

First U.S. Showing: April 12, 1979, Santa Barbara, Calif., University of California, Campbell Hall. *See:* B152, B175

193. *Stücke = Pieces.* (BA; dur: 8 min.) *See:* K848
For oboe & piano in four numbered movements.
Composed: March 17 - March 21, 1966, Tujunga, CA.
Dedication: Heinz Holliger.

Manuscripts: US-CA. Sketch(4 p.) US composer Transparency score(8 p.) D-brd Kbärenreiter. Blueprint score(8 p.)

Premiere: May 21, 1967, Zagreb, Fourth Biennale for Contemporary Music; Heinz Holliger, oboe; Jürg Wyttenbach, piano. *See:* B449

First U.S. Performance: February 18, 1969, Los Angeles, County Museum of Art, Bing Theater, Monday Evening Concerts; Barbara Winter, oboe; Charles Fierro, piano. *See:* B42

Other Performances: B43

Publications: B1479

Recording: Philips 6500 202. *The Spectacular Heinz Holliger plays music by Berio, Castiglioni, Holliger, Huber, Krenek [and] Lehmann.* 33 1/3 rpm. stereo. p1970. *See:* B196, B878, B1035, B1430
Heinz Holliger, oboe; Jürg Wyttenbach, piano.
Duration: 5 min., 58 sec.

Recording: Orion ORS 78288. *Four pieces for oboe and piano.* 33 1/3 rpm. stereo. [1977] *See:* B880, B975, B1233
James Ostryniec, oboe; composer, piano.
Recorded March 7, 1977, Georgetown, Washington, DC.
Duration: 5 min., 25 sec.
With works by Charles Wuorinen and Lawrence Moss.

194. *Glauben und Wissen = To believe and to know.* (unpublished; dur: 28 min.) *See:* B1195
Subtitled: *Dialektisches Klang- und Gesangspiel.*
For chorus, 4 speakers & orchestra: 2.2.3.3 / 4.2.2.1 / timpani / harp / piano / harmonium / celesta / guitar / vibraphone / xylophone / glockenspiel / percussion / strings. German text by the composer.
Composed: July 17, 1966, Palm Springs, CA.
1: *Wer in der Höhe.* **2:** *Das macht man uns weis.* **3:** *Nur das Bewiesene wissen wir.* **4:** *Man hofft auf die Tat.* **5:** *Des Glaubens beraubt.*
Commissioned: Norddeutscher Rundfunk.

Manuscripts: US composer Transparency score(53 p.) US composer Choral parts(27 p.)

Premiere: December 21, 1966, Hamburg, Norddeutscher Rundfunk, 101. Abend, 16. Jahr "Das neue Werk"; Chor des NDR; Helmut Franz, director; Sinfonieorchester des NDR; composer, conductor. *See:* B622, B1366, B1426, K826

195. *Proprium für das Dreifaltigkeitsfest = Proprium Missae for Trinity Sunday.* (BA; dur: 25 min.)
For soprano and SATB chorus with ensemble: 2 trumpets, timpani & organ.
Composed: November 9, 1966 - January 26, 1967, Dubrovnik - Schönenberg (Pratteln).
1: *Intrada.* **2:** *Gesang zum Einzug.* "Gepriesen sei der heilige dreifaltige Gott" **3:** *Zwischengesang.* "Gepriesen bist Du, o Herr" **4:** *Gesang zur Gabenbereitung.* "Gott sei gepriesen" **5:** *Gesang zur Kommunion.* "Preiset den Herrn"

Commissioned: St. Johannes Bosco Church, Basel, SZ.

Manuscripts: **A-Wst:** MH 14773/c. Sketch(8 p.) **US-CA.** Electronic sketch(1 p.) **A-Wst:** MH 14773/c. Text & plan(5 p.) **D-brd** Kbärenreiter. Transparency score(19 p.) **A-Wst:** MH 14773/c. No.4, transparency score(p.11-12)

Premiere: July 2, 1967, Basel, SZ; Carmen Prieto, soprano; Chor der Kirche St.Johannes-Don-Bosco; Klaus Deschler, H. Schweizer, trumpets; Leander Schmid, timpani; Joseph Gerwill, organ; François Borer, conductor. *See:* B670

Publications: B1419

196. *Horizon circled* = *Horizont umkreist.* (BA; dur: 20 min.) *See:* B654, B932, B933, K838, K839
   For orchestra: 2.2.3.2 / 4.2.2.1 / timpani / harp / piano / percussion / strings.
   Composed: January 1 - February 20, 1967, Vienna - Baltimore, MD.
   1: *Azimuth.* **2:** *Elevation.* **3:** *Meridian.* **4:** *Innerer Kreis* = *Inner circle.* **5:** *Parabel* = *Parabola.* **6:** *Zenith.*
   Commissioned and dedicated: Meadow Brook Festival, Oakland University, Rochester, MI

   Manuscripts: **A-Wst:** MH 14822/c. Plans(10 p.) **US-CA.** Sketch(13 p.) & electronic sketch(5 p.) **D-brd** Kbärenreiter: BA 6019. Transparency score(40 p.) & parts.

   Premiere: August 12, 1967, Rochester, Mich., Oakland University, Fourth Meadow Brook Festival; Detroit Symphony; Sixten Ehrling, conductor. *See:* B35, B413

   First European Performance: February 16, 1968, Baden-Baden, Südwestfunk, Hans-Rosbaud-Studio; Sinfonieorchester des Südwestfunk; composer, conductor. *See:* B1213, B1376

   Publications: B419

   Published (Facsimile p.1): In *Ernst Krenek,* hrsg. von Otto Kolleritsch. Studien zur Wertungsforschung, v.15. (Wien: Universal Edition, 1982): 229.

   Recording: Orion ORS 78290. *Krenek conducts Krenek.* 33 1/3 rpm. stereo. [1977] *See:* B149, B880, B976, B1247
   Sinfonieorchester des Südwestfunk; composer, conductor.
   Duration: 20 min., 14 sec.
   With his *From three make seven,* op.177 and *Von vorn herein,* op.219.

197. *Piano piece in eleven parts* = *Klavierstück in elf Teilen.* (unpublished; dur: 14 min.)
   Composed: Easter - May 1967, Palm Springs, CA - Baltimore, MD.
   Commissioned: Chicago Musical College.
   Dedication: To the hundreth anniversary of the Chicago Musical College.

   Manuscripts: **US** composer Transparency(14 p.) **D-brd** Kbärenreiter. Blueprint(14 p.)

   Premiere: December 4, 1970, Chicago Musical College of Roosevelt University, Rudolf Ganz Recital Hall; Abraham Stokman, piano. *See:* B608

198. *Pieces* = *Stücke.* (BA; dur: 10 min.) *See:* B980
   For trombone & piano in five numbered movements.
   Composed: June 10 - 12, 1967, Palm Springs, CA.
   Commissioned: Stuart Dempster.

   Manuscripts: **A-Wst:** MH 14779/c. Sketch(4 p.) **US** composer Transparency score(10 p.) **D-brd** Kbärenreiter. Blueprint score(10 p., 2 versions)

Premiere: November 5, 1967, Buffalo, NY, Albright-Knox Art Gallery, Evenings for New Music; Stuart Dempster, trombone; Carlos Alsina, piano. *See:* B291, B1019

Recording: Orion ORS 78295. 33 1/3 rpm. stereo. [p1978]
Stuart Dempster, trombone; composer, piano.
Duration: 9 min., 40 sec.
Recorded June 6, 1968, University of California at San Diego, La Jolla, CA.
With his *Sestina,* op.161 and *Flute piece in 9 phases, op.171.*

199. *Perspektiven = Perspectives.* (BA; dur: 20 min.) *See:* B654, K843
For orchestra: 2.2.3.2 / 4.3.2.1 / timpani / celesta / electric guitar / harp / piano / percussion / strings.
Composed: August 23 - September 1967, Palm Springs, CA; Instr. November 3, 1967.
Commissioned: Ravinia Festival.
Dedication: Ravinia Festival for the Celebration of the Sesquicentennial of the State of Illinois.

Manuscripts: **US** composer Transparency score(43 p.) **D-brd** Kbärenreiter. Photocopy score(43 p.)

Premiere: July 6, 1968, Ravinia Festival, IL; Chicago Symphony Orchestra; Seiji Ozawa, conductor. *See:* B241, B607, B1001

Other Performances: B593

Publications: B207

200. *Exercises of a late hour = Uebungen der späten Stunde.* (BA; dur: 18 min.) *See:* B654, K839
For orchestra: 1.0.2.1 / 1.1.1.0 / timpani / guitar / harp / piano / vibraphone / xylophone / percussion / tape / solo strings (violin, viola, cello & double bass) in 4 untitled movements.
Composed: October 1 - December 24, 1967, Palm Springs, CA; Revised 1969.
Commissioned: John Muir College of the University of California San Diego.

Manuscripts: **A-Wst:** MH 14801/c. Sketch(21 p.) **D-brd** Kbärenreiter: BA 6020. Transparency score(29 p.) & parts.

Premiere: January 19, 1968, University of California, San Diego, Recital Hall, Matthew Campus; composer, conductor.

First European Performance: August 23, 1970, Frankfurt, Hessischer Rundfunk; Radio-Sinfonie-Orchester Frankfurt/Main; composer, conductor. *See:* B251

Other Performances: B1260

201. *Instant remembered = Augenblick erinnert.* (BA; dur: 15 min.) *See:* B654, B1506
For soprano & orchestra: 2.0.2.0 / 2.2.2.0 / timpani / celesta / guitar / harp / piano / vibraphone / xylophone / percussion / tape / violin / viola / cello in 8 untitled movements, the even-numbered movements are readings. *Triple canon = Frame music,* for 2 violins. Spoken text by Plato, Soren Kierkegaard, Johann Wolfgang von Goethe, and Rainer Maria Rilke; sung text by Seneca, Gerard Manley Hopkins, Karl Kraus, and the composer.
Composed: July 18, 1967, Honolulu; Instr. April 11, 1968, Salzburg.
Dedication: To the memory of Anton Webern.
Commissioned: Dartmouth College for the Fourth International Webern Festival, 1968.

Manuscripts: **US-CA.** Sketch(53 p.) **D-brd** Kbärenreiter: BA 6052. Transparency score(26 p.) & parts. **A-Wst** 5 p. US composer *Frame music* Transparency score(11 p. in 6 p.) **US-CA.** *Frame music* Blueprint score(10 p.) with autograph additions.

Premiere: August 1, 1968, Dartmouth College, 4. International Webern Festival; Christina Ascher, soprano; composer, conductor; *See:* B1001

Published (Facsimile pages): In *Ernst Krenek,* hrsg. von Otto Kolleritsch. Studien zur Wertungsforschung, v.15. (Wien: Universal Edition, 1982): 180-185.

202. **Proprium Missae per a le festa de la nativitat de la mare de Deu (8 de setembre)** = *Proprium für Mariae Geburt.* (unpublished; dur: 23 min.)
For chorus, instruments & organ.
Composed: May 31, 1968, Palm Springs, CA.
Commissioned: Abbey of Montserrat.
Dedication: Abadia de Montserrat.

Manuscripts: **US-CA.** Sketches. US composer Transparency score(14 p.) **D-brd** Kbärenreiter: Ms/K30. Blueprint(14 p.)

Premiere: August 22, 1968, Montserrat, Abadia; Capilla y escolania de Montserrat coro de monjes y asamblea; Ireneu Segarra, conductor.

Recording: Vergara 14.013 SL. 33 1/3 rpm. stereo. *Encuentro internacional de compositores en el Monasterio de Montserrat, Septiembre de 1968.* [1968]
Capilla y escolania de Montserrat coro de monjes y asamblea; Ireneu Segarra, conductor.
Recorded in Montserrat, August 22, 1968. Sung in Catalan.
Duration: 22 min., 22 sec.
With *Vespers* by Peter Eben.

203. *Six profiles.* (BA; dur: 12 min.) *See:* B457, B654
For orchestra: 2.2.3.2 / 4.2.2.1 / timpani / celesta / harp / piano / vibraphone / xylophone / percussion / violin in 6 untitled movements.
Composed: 1965 - 1968.
Commissioned: Moorhead-Fargo Symphony Orchestra Association.

Manuscripts: **D-brd** Kbärenreiter. Transparency score(26 p.) & 27 parts.

Premiere: March 14, 1970, Fargo, ND, Center for the Arts Auditorium; Moorhead-Fargo Symphony Orchestra Association; Sigvald Thompson, conductor. *See:* B1002

First European Performance: November 6, 1973, Cologne. *See:* B155

204. *Deutsche Messe (Ordinarium).* (BA; dur: 20 min.)
For SATB chorus, clarinet, trumpet, 2 trombones, tympani & percussion. German text.
Composed: October 14 - 25, 1968, Palm Springs, CA.
1: *Kyrie* "Herr, erbarme dich." 2: *Gloria* "Und auf Erden Friede den Menschen." 3: *Credo* "Wir glauben all an einen Gott." 4: *Sanctus* "Heilig, Heilig, Heilig." 5: *Agnus* "Lamm Gottes du nimmst himweg die Sünden der Welt."
Commissioned: Bildungswoche für katholische Kirchenmusik, Lucerne, SZ

Manuscripts: **A-Wst:** MH 14774/c. Sketch(9 p.) US composer Transparency score(15 p.) **D-brd** Kbärenreiter. Blueprint score(15 p.)

Premiere: October 1969, Luzern, 3. Bildungswoche für katholische Kirchenmusik; Choeur mixte de Bulle; Aargauer Bläserquartett, Guido

Knüsel, organ; P. A. Gaillard, conductor. *See:* B95

Publications: B905

205. *Fivefold enfoldment* = *Fünffache Verschränkung*. (BA; dur: 13 min.) *See:*
B654, K839, K908
For orchestra: 3.2.4.3 / 4.3.2.1 / celesta / electric guitar / harp / 2 pianos /
vibraphone / xylophone / percussion / strings.
Composed: January 18, 1969, Palm Springs, CA.
Commissioned: Serge Koussevitzky Foundation, Library of Congress.
Dedication: To the memory of Serge and Natalie Koussevitzky.

Manuscripts: **A-Wst** Sketch(15 p.) **US-Wc:** ML30.3c .K79 no.1. Transparency
score(24 p.) **D-brd** K**bärenreiter:** BA 6032. Transparency score(24 p.)

Premiere: January 5, 1970, Bonn, Beethovenhalle; Beethovenhalle Orchester;
Volker Wangenheim, conductor. *See:* B284

First U.S. Performance: January 11, 1986, Santa Anna High School; Pacific
Symphony; Keith Clark, conductor. *See:* B532, B965

Recording: ORF 120 423. *Steirischer Herbst, Musikprotokoll 1980.* [1980]
ORF-Symphonieorchester; Leif Segerstam, conductor.
Duration: 11 min., 18 sec.
With his *Auf- und Ablehnung*, op.220 and *They knew what they wanted*, op.227.

206. *Sardakai, oder Das kommt davon* = *Wenn Sardakai auf Reisen geht*. (BA)
See: K903
Opera in 11 scenes. Sardakai (soprano), Urumuru (bass), Dr. Adriano
(baritone), Aminta (mezzosoprano), Carlo (tenor), Heloise (mezzosoprano)
and orchestra: 1.1.2.1 / 1.1.1.0 / timpani / celesta / harp / 2 pianos / electric
guitar / percussion / strings. German text by the composer. Two versions of
the final scenes.
Composed: August 23, 1968 - June 16, 1969, Tanglewood, Mass. - Palm
Springs, CA; Instr. January 23 - June 18, 1969, Palm Springs, CA; Piano-vocal
score: August 19, SS United States, New York-Le Havre; revised: June 8, 1971,
Palm Springs, CA.
Commissioned: Hamburg State Opera.
Dedication: Rolf Liebermann.

Manuscripts: **A-Wst** Libretto(assorted pages) **D-brd** Kbärenreiter. Blueprint
libretto(33 p.) **A-Wst** Sketch(56 p., 1968) **A-Wst:** MH 14723/c. Sketch(22 p.,
1971) **D-brd** Kbärenreiter: BA 6038. Transparency piano-vocal score(91 p.) **D-
brd** Kbärenreiter: BA 6038. Transparency score(127 p.)

Premiere: June 27, 1970, Hamburg State Opera; composer, conductor; Leopold
Lindtberg, producer; Rudolf Heinrich, staging; Jeanette Scovotti, Sardakai;
Raymond Wolansky, Urumuru; Toni Blankenheim, Dr. Adriano; Cvetka
Ahlin, Aminta; Horst Wilhelm, Carlo Murbruner; Elisabeth Steiner, Heloise;
Philharmonisches Staatsorchester. *See:* B226, B380, B779, B784, B793, B871,
B943, B1254, B1258, B1259, B1325, B1427, B1493

Recording: Ich bin Sardakái (Act.1:1-147) and *Mr.Wilson I presume* (Act.2:288-455).
EMI Electrola 1C 195-29 107/109. *Musiktheater Heute; Eine Dokumentation der
Hamburgischen Staatsoper.* 3 discs. 33 1/3 rpm. mono. p1972.
Jeanette Scovotti, Sardakai; Raymond Wolansky, Urumuru; Toni
Blankenheim, Dr. Adriano; Chor der Hamburgischer Staatsoper;
Philharmonisches Staatsorchester Hamburg; composer, conductor.
With excerpts from his *Der goldene Bock*, op.186 and from operas by Alban
Berg, G. Klebe, G. C. Menotti, L. J. Werle, M. Kelemen, M. Kagel.

Label on container: Odeon.

207. *Doppelt beflügeltes Band* = *Tape and double.* (BA; dur: 15 min.) *See:* B654, B903, B1095
    For 2 pianos & tape.
    Composed: November 20, 1969 - January 1, 1970, Palm Springs, CA.
    Commissioned: Oesterreichischer Rundfunk.

Manuscripts: **US-CA.** Sketches(21 p.) **US-Eu.** Sketch(1 p.) **D-brd Kbärenreiter:** BA 6053. Transparency score(19 p.)

Premiere: October 26, 1970, Graz, Steirischer Herbst; Peter Keuschnig, Rudolf Keuschnig, pianos. *See:* B85, B1214

First U.S. Performance: December 7, 1970, Los Angeles, County Museum of Art, Bing Theater, Monday Evening Concerts; Karl Kohn, Margaret Kohn, pianos. *See:* B102, B870

Other Performances: B176

Published (Facsimile p.1): In *Musik-Konzepte* 39/40 (October 1984): 153.

Published (Facsimile p.1): In *Ernst Krenek,* hrsg. von Otto Kolleritsch. Studien zur Wertungsforschung, v.15. (Wien: Universal Edition, 1982): 206.

Recording: Orion ORS 75204. 33 1/3 rpm. stereo. [p1975] *See:* B196, B667, B701, B879, B1095, B1331, B1354, B1381
    Patricia Marcus, William Tracy, pianos.
    Duration: 16 min., 15 sec
    Recorded May 17 and June 7, 1975, California State University, Northridge.
    With his *Santa Fe timetable,* op.102, *O lacrymosa,* op.48, and *Toccata, accordion, op.183.* Bärenreiter Musicaphon 30 SL 5100 in the book *Neue Musik* von Wolfgang Rogge. Musik Aktuell, 1. (Kassel: Bärenreiter, 1979)

208. *Messe Gib uns den Frieden* = *Mass Give us peace.* (BA; dur: 20 min.) *See:* B654
    For SATB chorus & orchestra: 0.0.1.1 / 1.1.0.0 / timpani / organ / percussion / strings. German text.
    Composed: January 29 - November 15, 1970.
    1: *Kyrie* (January 29, 1970, La Jolla, CA) "Herr, erbarme dich" **2:** *Gloria.* "Ehre sei Gott in der Höhe und Friede" **3:** *Credo* (July 12 - November 15, 1970, Vienna) "Ich glaube an den Einen Gott" **4:** *Sanctus* (February - May 30, 1970) "Heilig ist Gott der Herr Zebaoth" **5:** *Verba testamenti* (November 15, 1970, Vienna) "Unser Herr Jesus Christus" **6:** *Agnus* (August 9, 1970, Meran) "Christe Du Lamm Gottes"
    Commissioned: Nordelbische Vereinigung.

Manuscripts: **A-Wst:** MH 14818/c. Text(1 p.) **A-Wst:** MH 14818/c. Sketch(10 p.) **D-brd Kbärenreiter:** BA 6064a. Piano-vocal score(63 p.) **D-brd Kbärenreiter:** BA 6064. Transparency score(48 p.)

Premiere: October 17, 1971, Hamburg, Hauptkirche St. Nikolai, Nordelbische Tage Neue Kirchenmusik; Ernst-Ulrich von Kameke, conductor; Dorothea Förster-Dürlich, soprano; Erika Schmidt, alto; Tadao Yoshie, bass; Kantorei der Hauptkirche St. Petri Hamburg; soloists of Philharmonisches Staatsorchester Hamburg und des Norddeutscher Rundfunk; Hans Bässler, organ. *See:* B758, B816, B1115, B1428, B1494, B1521

First U.S. Performance: April 15, 1979, Santa Barbara, University of California, Lobero Theater; University of California Santa Barbara Singers; Linda Chassman, soprano; Carl Zytowski, tenor; Michael Ingham, conductor. *See:* B152

209. *Duo*. (unpublished; dur: 3 min.)
For flute and double bass with tape.
Composed: November 26, 1970, Palm Springs, CA.
Commissioned: Music Teachers National Association.
Dedication: Nancy and Bertram Turetzky.

Manuscripts: US composer Transparency score(6 p.)

Premiere: January 24, 1971, Palm Desert, College of the Desert, Third Annual Convention, California Association of Professional Music Teachers; Nancy Turetzky, flute; Bertram Turetzky, double bass.

210. *Three sacred pieces*. (Broude; dur: 4 min.) *See:* B1250
For SATB chorus a cappella. English texts: No.1 Ecclesiastics 9:7, 9-10; No.2 Proverbs 30:24-28; and No.3 Proverbs 30:18-19.

1: *Go thy way* ((January 14, 1971, Palm Springs, CA) 2: *There be four things* (January 2, 1971, Palm Springs, CA) 3: *There be three things* (December 29, 1970 - January 1, 1971, Los Angeles, CA - Palm Springs, CA)

Manuscripts: A-Wst: MH 14817/c. Sketch(4 p.)

Premiere: October 18, 1971, Ann Arbor, MI; Marilyn Mason, conductor.

Recording: Orion ORS 76246. 33 1/3 rpm. stereo. [1976] *See:* B147, B667, B740, B1331, B1358
College of the Desert Vocal Ensemble; John L. Norman, conductor.
Duration: 4 min., 7 sec.
Recorded April 11, 1976, College of the Desert, Palm Desert, CA.
With his *Aulokithara*, op.213a, *Wechselrahmen*, op.189, and *Echoes from Austria*, op.166.
Also issued on Orion OC 676. cassette and Orion ORS 80377. 33-1/3 rpm. [1980?] *Ernst Krenek vocal compositions*. [1980] (With his op.35, op.61, op.186a, op.210, op.226, and op.67.)

210. *Three lessons*. (Broude; dur: 6 min.)
For SATB chorus a cappella. English texts by the composer.
1: *Archaeology lesson* (January 25, 1971, Palm Springs) "We bury time capsules underground" 2: *Astronomy lesson* (January 10, 1971, Palm Springs) "Aquarius is the eleventh sign" 3: *Geography lesson* (January 10, 1971, Palm Springs) "Visiting the La Brea tar pits"
No.3 dedicated: Lawrence Morton.

Premiere: October 18, 1971, Ann Arbor, MI; Marilyn Mason, conductor.

Recording: Orion ORS 80377. *Ernst Krenek vocal compositions*. 33 1/3 rpm. stereo. [1980]
College of the Desert Vocal Ensemble; John L. Norman, conductor.
Duration: 4 min., 55 sec.
With his op.35, op.61, op.186a, op.210, op.226, and op.67.

211. *10 Choralvorspiele* = *Choral preludes*. (BA)
For organ.
Composed: February - July 6, 1971, Palm Springs, CA.

Manuscripts: A-Wst: MH 14819/c. Sketch(6 p.) US composer Transparency(8 p.)
D-brd Kbärenreiter. Blueprint(8 p.)

Published: In *Choralvorspiele für den gottesdienstliches Gebrauch, v.4*. (Kassel: Bärentreiter) BA 5484.

212. *Orga-nastro.* (BA; dur: 9 min.) *See:* B503, B836, K908
For organ & tape.
Composed: June 21 - August 4, 1971, Palm Springs, CA.
Commissioned and Dedicated: Marilyn Mason.

Manuscripts: **A-Wst:** MH 14719/c. Sketches(17 p.) **A-Wst:** MH 14719/c. Score(8 p.) **D-brd** Kbärenreiter. Transparency score(16 p.)

Premiere: October 18, 1971, Ann Arbor, University of Michigan, Hill Auditorium, Eleventh Annual Conference on Organ Music; Marilyn Mason, organ. *See:* B1003, B1251

Recording: Musica Viva MV 50-1090. *Arnold Schönberg, Ernst Krenek Sämtliche Orgelwerke.* 2 discs. 33 1/3 rpm. stereo. p1980. *See:* B825, B990, B1234
Martin Haselböck, organ.
Recorded July 12, 1978 on the Rieger organ, Augustinerkirche, Vienna.
With his *4 Winds suite,* op.223; *Sonata,* op.92; and *Opus 231* and the complete organ works of Arnold Schoenberg.
Also issued on Colosseum MV 50-1090.

213. *Kitharaulos.* (BA; dur: 20 min.) *See:* B654, K908
For oboe & harp solo with piano, percussion & strings in five untitled movements.
Composed: September 23 - December 4, 1971, Palm Springs, CA.
Commissioned: Heinz Holliger.
Dedication: Heinz and Ursula Holliger.

Manuscripts: **A-Wst:** MH 14766/c. Sketch(18 p.) **D-brd** Kbärenreiter. Transparency score(30 p.) & oboe-harp part(p.2-26)

Premiere: June 20, 1972, Den Haag, Holland Festival; Ursula Holliger, harp; Heinz Holliger, oboe; Het Radio Kamer Orkest; David Atherton, conductor. *See:* B1402, B1465

First U.S. Performance: October 20, 1974, Philadelphia, Musical Academy; Sarah Dunlap, harp; James Kavanaugh, oboe; Philadelphia Orchestra. *See:* B1434

Recording: Varese Sarabande VR 81200. 33 1/3 rpm. stereo. p1979. *See:* B186
James Ostryniec, oboe; Karen Lindquist, harp; Los Angeles Chamber Orchestra; composer, conductor.
Duration: 19 min., 1 sec.
Recorded April 23, 1979, Ambassador Auditorium, Pasadena, CA
With his *Static and ecstatic,* op.214.
Also issued on Amadeo AVRS 6506.

213a. *Aulokithara.* (BA; dur: 20 min.)
For oboe & harp solo with accompaniment arranged for electronic tape.

Manuscripts: **D-brd** Kbärenreiter. Transparency score(26 p.)

Premiere: October 11, 1972, Mainz, Hilton Hotel, Goldsaal, Ars-Viva-Konzert, Südwestfunk; Ursula Holliger, harp; Heinz Holliger, oboe. *See:* B668, B1377

First U.S. Performance: January 22, 1975, Los Angeles, County Museum of Art, Bing Theater, Monday Evening Concerts. *See:* B593, B1216

Recording: Orion ORS 76246. 33 1/3 rpm. stereo. [1976] *See:* B147, B667, B1331
James Ostryniec, oboe; Karen Lindquist, harp.
Duration: 20 min., 10 sec.
Recorded March 27, 1976, Venice, CA.
With his *Wechselrahmen,* op.189, *Three sacred pieces,* op.210, and *Echoes from Austria,* op.166.
Also issued on Orion OC 676. cassette. [1980?]

214. *Statisch und ekstatisch* = *Static and ecstatic*. (BA; dur: 10 min.) *See:* B654, K908

For orchestra: 1.1.1.0 / 0.1.1.0 / piano / percussion / strings in 10 untitled movements.

Composed: October 29, 1971 - May 18, 1972, Albuquerque, NM - Palm Springs, CA.

Commissioned: Paul Sacher.

Dedication: Paul Sacher in friendship.

Manuscripts: **A-Wst:** MH 14724/c. Sketches(34 p.) **D-brd** Kbärenreiter: BA 6088. Transparency score(46 p.)

Premiere: March 23, 1973, Zürich; Züricher Kammerorchester; composer, conductor. *See:* B890, B1260

First U.S. Performance: January 26, 1975, Palm Springs, Desert Museum; UCSD Chamber Orchestra; composer, conductor. *See:* B172, B593

Recording: Varese Sarabande VR 81200. 33 1/3 rpm. stereo. p1979. *See:* B186 Los Angeles Chamber Orchestra; composer, conductor. Duration: 18 min., 27 sec. Recorded April 23, 1979, Ambassador Auditorium, Pasadena, CA With his *Kitharaulos*, op.213. Also issued on Amadeo AVRS 6506.

215. *Zeitlieder* = *Time songs*. (unpublished; dur: 8 min.)

For mezzosoprano & string quartet. German texts from *Zeit-Gedichte* no.25 & no.16 by Renata Pandula.

Composed: October 6 - 29, 1972.

1: *Kennst du den Augenblick* = *Do you know the moment* (October 6 - 16, 1972, Palm Springs, CA) **2:** *Hab Hände* = *I have hands* (October 29, 1972, Palm Springs, CA)

Manuscripts: **A-Wst:** MH 14776/c. Sketch(6 p.) **US** composer Transparency score(18 p.)

Premiere: May 15, 1974, Augsburg, Tonkünstlerverein, Studio für neue Musik; Eva Maria Wolff-Padros, soprano; Pandula Quartett. *See:* B399, B562

First U.S. Performance: March 10, 1975, La Jolla, University of California at San Diego, Mandeville Recital Hall; Beverly Ogdon, soprano; Feld Quartet.

Published (Facsimile manuscript page): In *Musical Quarterly* 61:3 (July 1975): 467.

Recording: Orion ORS 79348. 33 1/3 rpm. stereo. [1979] *See:* B1030, B1357, B1462 Neva Pilgrim, soprano; Madison Quartet. Duration: 7 min., 38 sec. Recorded December 22, 1978, Ithaca, NY. With his *4 Songs, op.112* and *3 Songs, op.30a* and Gladys Nordenstrom *Zeit XXIV*.

216. *Lieder*. (unpublished; dur: 8 min.)

For soprano & piano. German texts by Lilly von Sauter.

1: *Aber die Nacht* = *But the nights* (November 1, 1972, Palm Springs, CA) "Quer durch die Felder des Schweigens führen zwei silberne Schienen" "Across the silent fields two tracks of silver lead" **2:** *Beschwörung* = *Incantation* (November 13, 1972, Palm Springs, CA) "Wenn Nebel zur Au sinkt" "When mist sinks down to the meadow" **3:** *Der Sternenhimmel* = *The starry sky* (November 16 - 18, 1972, Palm Springs, CA) "Der Tag nimmt nur noch fünfzehn Minuten zu" "The day grows only by fifteen more minutes"

Manuscripts: **US** composer Score(11 p.) **US** composer Score(6 p.)

Premiere: September 22, 1975, Vienna, Oesterreichische Gesellschaft für Musik; Edita Gruberova, soprano; Harald Goertz, piano.

Other Performances: B1330

Recording: Educo 4049. 33 1/3 rpm. stereo. [1985]
Alice Gerstl Duschak, soprano; David Garvey, piano.
With songs by Heinrich Schütz and Franz Schubert.

217. **Flaschenpost vom Paradies, oder Der englische Ausflug** = *Bottled message from paradise.* (unpublished) *See:* K902
Television play; German text by the composer. For tenor, bass, dancers (Himmelsfigur, Junger Mann), 6-8 mimes (Eingeborene von Migo Migo, 3 Ingineure, Kunden, Beamtin, 2 Gangster, 1 Einsiedler, Postbeamte), 1 or more speakers & Musik (electronic tape, percussion & piano)
Composed: August 1972 - February 1973.
Commissioned: Oesterreichischer Rundfunks.

Manuscripts: **A-Wst:** MH 14815/c. Sketch(1 p.) **A-Wst:** MH 14815/c. Cue sheets. US composer Transparency cue sheet(7 p.) & chorus score(3 p.) **A-Wst:** UE deposit Box A-J. Blueprint cue sheet(7 p.) & Musik I.(3 p.)

Premiere: March 8, 1974, Vienna, Oesterreichischer Rundfunk; Hermann Lanske, producer. *See:* B308

218. **Spätlese** = *Late harvest.* (BA; dur: 30 min.) *See:* B33, B903
Songs for baritone & piano. German texts by the composer written January 1 - August 23, 1972.
1: *So spät, so spät = So late, so late* (May 4, 1973, Caslano, TI) **2:** *Spätlese, noch am Stock = Late harvest, still on the vine*
(May 13, 1973, Caslano, TI) **3:** *Ein später Gast tritt ein = A late guest is coming in (March 23, 1973, Caslano, TI)* **4:** *Im Gefälle der Zeit = Running off on its incline the stream of time (June 4, 1973, Caslano, TI)* **5:** *Zu Boden gedrückt von schleichendem Unmut = Beaten down by sneaking depression (July 26 1973, Caslano, TI)* **6:** *Dort, wo in leichter Kurve = Where the road slightly curved (August 23 1973, Caslano, TI)*
Dedication: Dietrich Fischer-Dieskau.

Manuscripts: **A-Wst:** MH 14748/c. Text(19 p.) **A-Wst:** MH 14748/c. Sketch(24 p.) US composer Transparency score(34 p.) **D-brd** Kbärenreiter. Blueprint score(34 p.)

Premiere: July 22, 1974, Munich, Münchner Opernfestspiele; Dietrich Fischer-Dieskau, baritone; composer, piano. *See:* B757

First U.S. Performance: January 22, 1978, La Jolla, University of California at San Diego, Mandeville Recital Hall; Michael Ingham, baritone; Carolyn Horn, piano. *See:* B45

Other Performances: B176, B404, B1152, B1319, B1516

Recording: Orion ORS 78298. 33 1/3 rpm. stereo. [1978] *See:* B490, B1029, B1355
Michael Ingham, baritone; Carolyn Horn, piano.
Duration: 29 min., 27 sec.
With his 3 *Gesänge, op.56.*

219. *Von vorn herein*. (UE; dur: 10 min.) *See:* B446, K908
For chamber orchestra: 1.1.2.0 / 1.0.1.0 / 2 keyboards / strings.
Composed: Begun January 1, 1974.

Manuscripts: **A-Wst:** MH 14736/c. Sketch(15 p.)

Premiere: August 21, 1974, Salzburger Festspiele, Mozarteum; Ensemble 'Die Reihe' Friedrich Cerha, conductor.

First U.S. Performance: June 21, 1976, Los Angeles, Theater Vanguard, ISCM Concert; William Kraft, conductor. *See:* B173, B331, B979

Other Performances: B45

Recording: Orion ORS 78290. *Krenek conducts Krenek.* 33 1/3 rpm. stereo. [1977]
See: B149, B880, B976, B1247
Duration: 9 min., 25 sec.
With his *Horizon circled*, op.196 and *From three make seven*, op.177. ·

220. *Auf- und Ablehnung*. (BA; dur: 18 min.) *See:* B33, K908
For orchestra: 2.2.3.3 / 4.4.3.1 / celesta / harp / piano / percussion / strings.
Composed: June 12 - October 30, 1974, Palm Springs, CA.
Commissioned: Philharmonisches Orchester der Stadt Nürnberg for the Internationale Orgelwoche Nürnberg, 1975.

Manuscripts: **A-Wst:** MH 14757/c. Sketch(17 p.) **D-brd** Kbärenreiter: BA 6707. Transparency score(34 p.)

Premiere: June 13, 1975, Nurenburg, Meistersingerhalle, Internationale Orgelwoche; Philharmonische Orchester der Stadt Nürnberg; Hans Gierster, conductor. *See:* B1146, B1292

Recording: ORF 120 423. *Steirischer Herbst, Musikprotokoll 1980.* [1980]
ORF-Symphonieorchester; Leif Segerstam, conductor.
Duration: 18 min., 20 sec.
With his *Fivefold enfoldment*, op.205 and *They knew what they wanted*, op.227.

221. *Feiertags-Kantate* = *Anniversary cantata*. (UE)
For speaker, mezzosoprano & baritone with SATB chorus and orchestra: 1.1.1.0 / 0.1.1.0 / harp / piano / percussion / strings. German text by the composer.
Composed: December 1, 1974 - March 17, 1975, Palm Springs, CA.
Text:"Man muss, muss man?"
Commissioned: Berliner Festspiel.
Dedication: "Den Berliner Festspielen und mir selbst zum Jubeljahr 1975."

Manuscripts: **A-Wst:** UE deposit Box A-J. Transparency score(60 p.)

Premiere: September 12, 1975, Berlin, Berliner Festspiel; Symphonischen Orchesters Berlin; Kaja Boris, mezzosoprano; Shogo Miyahara, baritone; Stefan Wigger, speaker; Theodore Bloomfield, conductor. *See:* B804, B1320

222. *Two silent watchers*. (unpublished)
Song for voice & piano. English text by Mimi Rudulph.
Composed: June 26, 1975, Palm Springs, CA.
Text: "Two silent watchers side by side

Manuscripts: **US** composer Score(4 p.)

Premiere: 1976, Palm Springs, CA.

223. *Four winds suite* = *Die vier Winde.* (BA; dur: 11 min.) *See:* B503, B836, K908
For organ.
Composed: June - August 11, 1975.

1: *Euros* (June -July 7, 1975, Palm Springs, CA) **2:** *Notos* (August 11, 1975, Palm Springs, CA) **3:** *Zephyros* (July 31, 1975, Palm Springs, CA) **4:** *Boreas* (August 11, 1975, Palm Springs, CA)
Commissioned and dedicated: Marilyn Mason.

Manuscripts: **A-Wst:** MH 14805/c. Sketch(14 p.) **D-brd** Kbärenreiter: Ms/K32. Transparency(14 p.)

Premiere: March 13, 1977, Düsseldorf, Johanniskirche; Marilyn Mason, organ. *See:* B936, B1193

Publications: B855

Recording: Musica Viva MV 50-1090. *Arnold Schonberg, Ernst Krenek Sämtliche Orgelwerke.* 2 discs. 33 1/3 rpm. stereo. p1980. *See:* B825, B990, B1234
Martin Haselböck, organ.
Recorded July 12, 1978 on the Rieger organ, Augustinerkirche, Vienna.
With his *Orga-nastro*, op.212; *Sonata*, op.92; and *Opus 231* and the complete organ works of Arnold Schoenberg.
Also issued on Colosseum MV 50-1090.

224. *Dream sequence.* (UE; dur: 17 min.) *See:* B1067
For symphonic band: 4.3.6.2 / 7 saxophones / 4.10.4.1 / piano / harp / timpani / percussion / double bass.

1: *Nightmare* (December 1, 1975 - January 4, 1976, Portland, OR). **2:** *Pleasant dreams* (December 8, 1975, Portland, OR). **3:** *Puzzle* (November 1975, Portland, OR). **4:** *Dream about flying* (February 13, 1976, Palm Springs, CA).
Commissioned: College Band Directors National Association.

Manuscripts: **US** composer Transparency score(43 p.) **A-Wst:** MH 14804/c. Instrumentation list(1 p.)

Premiere: March 11, 1977, College Park, University of Maryland, 19th National Conference of the College Band Directors National Association; Baylor University Wind Ensemble; composer, conductor. *See:* B74, B535

Recording: Crest CBDNA 77-6. 33 1/3 rpm. quad. 1977.
Baylor Wind Ensemble; Dick Floyd, conductor.
Recorded at the 19th National Conference of the College Band Directors National Association, The University of Maryland, College Park, Maryland, March 9-11, 1977.
With band works by Gustav Holst, M. Tubb, and D. W. Reeves.

225. *Acco-music.* (Ars Nova; dur: 6 min.) *See:* K874, K898
For accordion.
Composed: January 1 - June 3, 1976, Palm Springs, CA.
Slow - Moderato - Animated - Furious.
Commissioned: Accordion Teachers' Guild in memory of Fred Holzhauer.

Manuscripts: **A-Wst:** MH 14804/c. Sketch(11 p.) **US** composer Transparency(8 p.)
Joseph Macerollo, accordion.

Recording: Melbourne Records (Canada) SMLP 4034. *Interaccodinotesta.* 33 1/3 rpm, stereo. p1979. New music series, 14. *See:* B318
Joseph Macerollo, accordion.

Duration: 6 min., 10 sec.
Recorded at Manta Sound, Toronto, Ont.
With accordion works by Barbara Pentland, Arne Nordheim, and R. Murray Schafer.

226. *Settings of poems by William Blake*. (Broude. dur: 3 min.)
For SATB chorus a cappella.
1: *I ask'd a thief* (June 25, 1976, Palm Springs, CA) **2:** *I heard an angel* (June 28, 1976, Palm Springs, CA).
Commissioned: Music Teachers National Association.
Written for the College of the Desert Vocal Ensemble.

Manuscripts: US composer No.1, score(3 p.) US composer No.2, score(5 p.)

Premiere: May 1977, Southwest-Northwest Division of Music Teachers National Association, Honolulu; College of the Desert Vocal Ensemble; John L. Norman, conductor.

Recording: Orion ORS 80377. *Ernst Krenek vocal compositions.* 33 1/3 rpm. stereo. [1980] *See:* B740, B1358
College of the Desert Vocal Ensemble; John L. Norman, conductor.
Duration: 4 min., 5 sec.
With his op.35, op.61, op.186a, op.210, op.226, and op.67.

227. *They knew what they wanted* = *Die wussten was sie wollten*. (Broude; dur: 28 min.) *See:* K908
For narrator with ensemble: oboe, piano, percussion & tape. English text by the composer.
Composed: 1976 - October 30, 1977, Palm Springs, CA.
1: *Ginevra* (after Boccacio *The Decameron*, III.3) **2:** *Tamar* (Genesis 38:1-26) **3:** *Pasiphaë* (Ernst Krenek)
Sponsored by a National Endowment for the Arts Composer/Librettist Fellowship Grant.

Manuscripts: **A-Wst:** MH 14744/c. Text(5 p.) **A-Wst:** MH 14744/c. Sketch(31 p.) US composer Transparency score(38 p.)

Premiere: November 6, 1978, New York, Manhattan School of Music; Group for Contemporary Music; Rheda Becker, speaker; James Ostryniec, oboe; composer, conductor. *See:* B994

Other Performances: B1516

Recording: ORF 120 423. *Steirischer Herbst, Musikprotokoll 1980.* [1980]
Marianne Kopatz, narrator; James Ostryniec, oboe; Adolf Hennig, piano; composer, conductor.
Recorded during the Austrian first performance.
Duration: 27 min., 50 sec.
With his *Auf- und Ablehnung*, op.220 and *Fivefold enfoldment*, op.205.

Recording: Orion ORS 80380. 33 1/3 rpm. stereo. [p1980] *See:* B187, B242, B826
Rheda Becker, narrator; James Ostryniec, oboe; Paul Hoffmann, piano; Mark Goldstein, percussion.
Duration: 27 min., 45 sec.
Recorded September 4, 1979, Georgetown, Washington, DC.
With his *Quintina*, op.191.

228. *Albumblatt.* (unpublished)
For voice & piano. Text by the composer.
Composed: November 6, 1977, Palm Springs, CA.
Dedication: Annegret Batschelet on her 60th birthday.
Text: "Land zwischen Bergen und Wüsten"

Manuscripts: US composer Score(3 p.)

229. *The dissembler* = *Der Versteller.* (BA; dur: 20 min.) *See:* B1168, B1288, K908
Monologue for baritone and ensemble: 1.1.1.1 / 1.1.1.0 / celesta / harp / piano
/ percussion / strings. English text by the composer with quotes from Johann
Wolfgang von Goethe's *Faust* II, Krenek's *Sestina*, Euripides *Hekabe* 488, Psalm
68:15 & 69:14, the *Missale Romanum*, Psalm 101:1.12 & 102:6.11, and
Ecclesiasties 9:4.5.
Text written: January 1 - February 5, 1978; German translation by the
composer: December 25, 1979, Palm Springs, CA. Music composed: February
15 - June 2, 1978, Baton Rouge, LA - Palm Springs, CA.
Text:"I am an actor" "Ich bin ein Akteur"
Commissioned: Chamber Music Society of Baltimore.
Dedication: Michael Ingham.

Manuscripts: **A-Wst:** MH 14720/c. Text(3 p.) **A-Wst:** MH 14720/c. Sketch(30 p.)
D-brd Kbärenreiter. Transparency piano-vocal score(24 p.) **US** composer
Piano-vocal score(24 p.) **D-brd** Kbärenreiter: BA 6759. Transparency score(62
p.) **US** composer Score(62 p.)

Premiere: March 11, 1979, Baltimore, MD, Chamber Music Society; Michael
Ingham, baritone; American Camerata for New Music; John Stephens,
conductor. *See:* B181

First European Performance (German version): September 28, 1980, Berlin, 30.
Berliner Festwochen; Dietrich Fischer-Dieskau, baritone; soloists of the
Berliner Philharmonisches Orchester; Lothar Zagrosek, conductor. *See:* B228,
B1321

Other Performances: B1516

Recording: Orion ORS 79362. 33 1/3 rpm. stereo. [p1979] *See:* B185, B872, B977
Michael Ingham, baritone; American Camerata for New Music; John
Stephans, conductor.
Duration: 20 min., 37 sec.
Recorded at the Kay Spiritual Center, American University, Washington, DC.
With his *Capriccio,* op.145 and Lawrence Moss *Symphonies, brasses, chamber
orchestra.*

230. *Concerto, organ & string orchestra.* (UE) *See:* B503, B903, B1514
In three untitled movements.
Composed: December 13, 1978 - January 1, 1979.
Commissioned: Carinthischer Sommer, 1979.
Dedication: Martin Haselböck.

Manuscripts: **A-Wst:** MH 14813/c. Sketch(14 p.)

Premiere: July 22, 1979, Ossiach, Austria, Stiftskirche; Martin Haselböck, organ.
See: B373, B797, B848

Publications: B854

231. *Opus 231.* (UE) *See:* B503, K908
  For violin & organ.
  Composed: May 13 - June 7, 1979, Palm Springs, CA.
  Commissioned: Wiener Konzerthausgesellschaft.
  Dedication: Ernst Kovacic & Martin Haselböck.

Manuscripts: **A-Wst:** MH 14810/c. Sketch(10 p.) **US** composer Transparency score(16 p.)

Premiere: March 10, 1980, Vienna, Wiener Konzerthausgesellschaft, Mozart-Saal; Ernst Kovacic, violin; Martin Haselböck, organ. *See:* B596, B645

Recording: Musica Viva MV 50-1090. *Arnold Schonberg, Ernst Krenek Sämtliche Orgelwerke.* 2 discs. 33 1/3 rpm. stereo. p1980. *See:* B825, B990, B1234
  Ernst Kovacic, violin; Martin Haselböck, organ.
  Recorded February 2, 1980 on the Rieger organ, Frauenkirche, Baden bei Wien.
  With his *Orga-nastro*, op.212; *4 Winds suite*, op.223; and *Sonata, op.92* and the complete organ works of Arnold Schoenberg.
  Also issued on Colosseum MV 50-1090.

Recording: EMI Electrola Marus ASD 308 531 D. 33 1/3 rpm. 1985.
  Marianne Boettcher, violin; Peter Schwarz, organ.
  Recorded 1984, Kaiser-Friedrich-Gedächtnis-Kirche, Berlin.
  With violin and organ works by Joseph Rheinberger, Max Reger, Heinrich Kaminski, and Wolfgang Steffan.

232. *Im Tal der Zeit = In the valley of time.* (BA; dur: 14 min.) *See:* K908
  For orchestra: 1.1.1.1 / 1.1.1.0 / guitar / piano / percussion / strings.
  Composed: August 23 - October 26, 1979, Palm Springs, CA; Instr. November 18, 1979.
  Commissioned: Steirischer Herbst 1980 zur Eröffnung des Musikprotokolls im Stift Admont.

Manuscripts: **A-Wst:** MH 14812/c. Sketch(14 p.) **D-brd** Kbärenreiter: BA 6778. Transparency score(38 p.) **US** composer Transparency score(39 p.)

Premiere: October 26, 1980, Graz, Steirischer Herbst; Collegium Musicum Instrumentale der Hochschule für Musik und Darstellende Kunst in Graz; Adolf Hennig, conductor. *See:* B727, B891, B1255

First U.S. Performance: January 26, 1981, University of California Los Angeles, Schoenberg Hall, Composers Choice; Los Angeles Philharmonic Orchestra; composer, conductor. *See:* B846, B1383

233. *Quartet, strings, no.8.* (BA; dur: ca.30 min.) *See:* B372, B1519
  In one movement.
  Composed: July 11, 1980 - January 1, 1981, Seefeld (Tirol) - Palm Springs, CA.
  Sponsored by a National Endowment for the Arts Composer/Librettist Fellowship Grant.

Manuscripts: **A-Wst:** MH 14734/c. Sketch(21 p.) **D-brd** Kbärenreiter: BA 7077. Transparency score(31 p.) **US** composer Transparency score(31 p.)

Premiere: June 7, 1981, New York, Carnegie Hall; Thouvenel String Quartet (Eugene Purdue, Teresa Fream, Sally Chisholm, and Jeffrey Levenson) *See:* B240, B526, B937, B1383

Other Performances: B1508

Published (Facsimile pages): In *Musik-Konzepte* 39/40 (October 1984): 103-113.

234. *Arc of life* = *Lebensbogen.* (BA; dur: 17 min.)
For chamber orchestra: 1.1.1.1 / 1.1.1.0 / timpani / piano / percussion / strings.
Composed: June 17 - July 23, 1981, Vienna - Seefeld, Tirol; Instr. August 28, 1981, Palm Springs, CA.

1: *To start with = Um anzuheben.* **2:** *High ground = Hohe Sicht.* **3:** *Somewhat whimsical = Ein wenig launisch* **4:** *Conflict = Widerstreit.* **5:** *With some emotion = Mit etwas Gefühl.* **6:** *Serenity = Heiterkeit.* **7:** *Before sleep = Vor dem Schlaf.* **8:** *Shock and solace = Trauma und Trost.* **9:** *Lighthearted = Mit leichtem Sinn.* **10:** *Stilted = Gestelzt.* **11:** *Strict measure = Strengers Mass.* **12:** *Exit, gracefully = Ab dafür, mit Anmut.*
Commissioned: College of the Desert.

Manuscripts: **A-Wst:** MH 14759/c. Sketch(8 p.) **A-Wst:** MH 14814/c. Score(32 p.) **D-brd** Kbärenreiter. Transparency score(46 p.) **US** composer Transparency score(46 p.)

Premiere: February 24, 1982, Palm Springs, College of the Desert; Los Angeles Chamber Orchestra; Gerard Schwarz, conductor.

First European Performance: November 24, 1983, Aarhus, Musik-Fest. *See:* B760

235. *Concerto, organ.* (BA)
Organ with orchestra: 2.2.2.2 / 4.2.2.1 / timpani / percussion / harp / strings; in four untitled movements.
Composed: January 23 - March 23, 1982, Palm Springs, CA - Vienna; Instr. April 17 - June 17.
Commissioned: Victoria Arts Centre, Melbourne, Australia and Oesterreichischer Rundfunk.

Manuscripts: **US** composer Sketch(16 p.) **US** composer Transparency score(36 p.) **D-brd** Kbärenreiter: BA 7124. Transparency score(36 p.)

Premiere: May 17, 1983, Melbourne Festival, Australia, Melbourne Concert Hall; Martin Haselböck, organ; Melbourne Symphony Orchestra; John Hopkins, conductor. *See:* B110, B430, B594, B924

First European Performance: October 20, 1983, Wiener Konzerthausgesellschaft, Grosser Saal, Festkonzert anlässlich des 70. Jahrestages der Eröffnung des Wiener Konzerthauses; Martin Haselböck, organ; ORF-Symphonieorchester; Lothar Zagrosek, conductor. *See:* B907, B1379

First U.S. Performance: November 1, 1984, New Orleans; Martin Haselböck, organ; New Orleans Symphony. *See:* B407

236. *Concerto, cello, no.2.* (BA; dur: ca.20 min.) *See:* K921
Cello with orchestra: 2.2.0.2 / 4.2.2.0 / percussion / harp / strings.
Composed: July 13 - September 13, 1982, Grindelwald, SZ - Palm Springs, CA; Instr. September 13 - October 3, 1982, Palm Springs, CA.
Commissioned: Oesterreichischer Rundfunk.

Manuscripts: **US** composer Sketch(16 p.) **US** composer Transparency score(29 p.) **D-brd** Kbärenreiter: BA7126. Transparency score(32 p.) & part(8 p.)

Premiere: August 9, 1983, Salzburger Festspiele; David Geringas, cello; ORF-Symphonieorchester; Hans Zender, conductor. *See:* B397, B430

237. *Streichtrio in zwölf Stationen* = *String trio in twelve stations.* (unpublished)
Composed: November 30, 1985, Palm Springs, CA.

Commissioned: Alban Berg Stiftung.
Dedication: Dem Andenken Alban Bergs gewidmet.

Premiere: August 23, 1987, Ossiach, Carinthischer Sommer; Carmina-Streichtrio.
See: B698, B1391

First U.S. Performance: February 16, 1988, Pasadena, Wright Auditorium, Southwest Chamber Music Society; California Trio (Kimiyo Takeya, violin; Jan Karlin, viola; Erika Duke, cello).

238. *Opus sine nomine.*

Oratorio in four movements based upon the Latin text from Genesis 1-3, 32, and 24-29. For soprano, mezzo-soprano, 2 tenors, baritone, narrator, chorus (SATB), and orchestra: 2.2.3.3 / 4.4.4.1 / 3 guitars / percussion / xylophone / vibraphone / piano / celesta / harp / strings.
Composed: Text finished: July 24, 1986, Mödling; Music: January 1, 1980 - November 23, 1986, Palm Springs; Instrumentation: May 12, 1986 - March 12, 1988, Palm Springs.

Manuscripts: **US-LJ.** Libretto typescript(20 p.) **US-LJ.** Transparency piano-vocal score(17, 38 p.) **US-LJ.** Transparency score(139 p.)

238a. *For myself, at eightyfive.*

4 voice canon.
Text: "Die Mechanik ist perfekt"

Published: In *Perspectives of New Music* 24:1 (Fall/Win.1985): 272. *See:* B707

Works Without Opus Number

W1. *Early pieces, 1907.* (unpublished)
For piano.
Composed: 1907.

1: *Christus.* **2:** *Il viaggio a Napoli;* Hochzeitsoper. **3:** *Einleitung zum Wunderbaren Konzert- und Vortrags-stück "Die Seeschlacht bei Lissa."* **4:** *Das Fest des hl. Alexander;* Einleitung zu der gleich. Oper in 10 Akten und Ouverture zu derselben. **5:** *Die Geburt Christi. Ouvertüre.* **6:** *Die Reise über den Ozean.* Grande Fantasie pour le piano. **7:** *Geburtstagsmasch.* **8:** *Die Mühle in Schwarzwald; Ein Idyll.* **9:** *Krönungsmarsch.* **10:** *Die Mühle im Schwarzwald.* **11:** *Wachtparade.*

Manuscripts: **A-Wgm.** P.33-48.

W2. *Early pieces, 1908.* (unpublished)
For piano.
Composed: 1908.

1: *Erzherzog Albrecht-Marsch* (Trauermarsch für Erzhzg. Albrecht). **2:** *Kaiserin Elisabeth Trauermarsch.* **3:** *Leopolds-Marsch "O heiliger Leopold"* **4:** *Spanischer Grenadiermarsch.* **5:** *Pariser Einzugsmarsch, 1814* = *Entry to Paris, 1814.* **6:** *Spanisch-chinesischer Marsch, 801.* **7:** *Kaiser's Geburtsfest.* **8:** *Ol Balaton Haborgaza! (Der Sturm auf dem Plattensee)* Fantasie. **9:** *Aus Oper "Sturm auf dem Meere."*

Manuscripts: **A-Wgm.** 16 p.

W3. *Early pieces, 1908 - 1909.* (unpublished)
Generally for piano.
Composed: 1908 - 1909.

1: *Wachparade;* grosses militärisches Tongemälde. **2:** *Der Untergang von Vineta a 1590.* (2.Jänner 1908 zu Wien). **3:** *Mars und Venus;* grosse Groteske in 5 Akten. **4:** *Seesturm;* Sinphonisches Tongemälde in 5 Akten. **5:** *Am Molo in Triest;* sehr sinnreiche Oper. **6:** *Die Mühle;* Grosse Oper in 5 Acten. **7:** *Tempeldienst in Memphis;* Grosses Oratorium. (26/1/08). For chorus. **8:** *Charfreitags-Sinphonie.* **9:** *Chalif Storch.* **10:** *Der Strassenkampf zu Mailand; Aus dem Jahre 1848.* With trumpet. **11:** *Der 30-jährige Krieg.* **12:** *Lenid de Iaigle.* **13:** *Das Glockenspiel.* **14:** *Missa solemnis in D-moll.* **15:** *I. Russische Rhapsodie;* für Orchester.

Manuscripts: **A-Wgm.** 15 p.

W4. *Waltzes, piano*, op.2. [*sic*] (unpublished)
  Composed: May 1911.
  1: *E-flat major*. **2:** *A-flat major*. **3:** *D-flat major*.

  Manuscripts: **A-Wst:** MH 10411/c. 3 p. **A-Wst:** MH 10412/c. 3 p. "Von meiner Mutter kopiert."

  Published (Facsimile p.1): In *Dank an Ernst Krenek* (Wien: Universal Edition, 1982)

W5. *Oper*. (unpublished)
  Fragment based on an Egyptian subject.
  Composed: 1912/1913.

  Manuscripts: **A-Wst:** MH 10417/c. Incomplete sketch(p.1-16, 51-66 & 2 p.)

W6. *Einsame Rose*, op.3. [*sic*] (unpublished)
  For baritone and piano.
  Composed: July 1913.
  Dedication: Meinem Hochver. Herrn Josef Müller gewidmet.

  Manuscripts: **A-Wst:** MH 10413/c. Score(2 p.)

W7. *Sonata, piano, B-flat minor*, op.5. [*sic*] (unpublished)
  Composed: 1913.
  1: *Allegro*. **2:** *Allegro scherzando*.

  Manuscripts: **A-Wst:** MH 10414/c. 17 p. **A-Wst:** MH 10415/c. 16 p. "Von meiner Mutter kopiert."

W8. *Missa in Festo SS. Trinitatis*. (A-flat major) (unpublished)
  Organ with chorus; no text.
  Composed: 1913.
  1: *Praeludium*. **2:** *Kyrie* **3:** *Gloria*.

  Manuscripts: **A-Wst:** MH 10419/c. Piano score(6 p.)

W9. *Grosse Ostersonate*. (unpublished)
  For chorus and organ.
  Composed: ca.1914.

  Manuscripts: **A-Wst:** MH 10418/c. Movements 2 & 3: piano score(12 p.)

W10. *Die Sterne*. (unpublished)
  For SATB chorus and piano; text by Adolf Fuchs.
  Composed: ca.1914.

  Manuscripts: **A-Wst:** MH 10448/c. Piano-vocal score(7 p.)

W11. *Suite, piano & orchestra*. (unpublished)
  Composed: Winter 1915/16.
  1: *Allegro vivace*. **2:** *Adagio*. **3:** *Tema con variozoni*. **4:** *Finale*.

  Manuscripts: **A-Wst:** MH 10372/c. Piano score(31 p.) black ink.

W12. *Missa symphonica prima, E-flat major*.
  For solos, chorus, orchestra & organ. "Nach der hohen Messe in H-moll von J.S. Bach."
  Composed: ca.1915.

Manuscripts: **A-Wst:** MH 10420/c. Score(54 p., incomplete)

W13. *Suite, piano, F major.* (unpublished)
Composed: ca.1916.
1: *Allegretto.* **2:** *Thema und Variationen.* **3:** *Quasi scherzo.*
Manuscripts: **A-Wst:** MH 10422/c. 16 p.

W14. *Herr Peter Squenz.* (unpublished)
Musik zur Tragödie von Pyramus und Thisbe aus dem Schimpfspiel von Andreas Gryphius (1657). For voice and piano.
Composed: ca.1916.
Manuscripts: **A-Wst:** MH 10424/c. Piano-vocal score(35 p.)

W15. *Mittagsstille.* (unpublished)
Song; text by Georg Ruseler from *Leipziger Illustrierte* number 3815.
Composed: January 1916.
Manuscripts: **A-Wst:** MH 10425/c. #3. Text. **A-Wst:** MH 10428/c. Score(2 p.)

W16. *Abend.* (unpublished)
Song; text by F. Slavik (Teschen).
Composed: January 1916.
Manuscripts: **A-Wst:** MH 10425/c. #7. Text. **A-Wst:** MH 10432/c. Score(2 p.)

W17. *Abendstimmung.* (unpublished)
Song; text by Börries Freiherr von Münchhausen.
Composed: February 1916, Wien.
Manuscripts: **A-Wst:** MH 10425/c. #9. Text. **A-Wst:** MH 10434/c. Score(4 p.)

W18. *Zwischen Erd und Himmel.* (unpublished)
Song; text from *Ghasel* by Robert Hamerling.
Composed: Summer 1916, Teschen.
Manuscripts: **A-Wst:** MH 10425/c. #1. Text. **A-Wst:** MH 10426/c. Score(12 p.)

W19. *Mozart.* (unpublished)
Song; text by Georg Terramare from the *Wiener Sonetten.*
Composed: Summer 1916, Teschen.
Manuscripts: **A-Wst:** MH 10425/c. #2. Text. **A-Wst:** MH 10426/c. Score(12 p.) **A-Wst:** MH 10427/c. Score.

W20. *Stadtpark.* (unpublished)
Song; text by Frieda Schanz from *Gartenlaube* no.20.
Composed: Summer 1916, Teschen.
Manuscripts: **A-Wst:** MH 10425/c. #4. Text. **A-Wst:** MH 10429/c. Score(2 p.)

W21. *Auf einem Berge begraben.* (unpublished)
Song; text by Heinrich Hansjakob.
Composed: Summer 1916, Teschen.
Manuscripts: **A-Wst:** MH 10425/c. #5. Text. **A-Wst:** MH 10430/c. Score(2 p.)

W22. *Variationen über ein lustiges Thema, G major.* (unpublished)
For violin, cello & piano.
Composed: Summer 1916.

Manuscripts: **A-Wst:** MH 10421/c. Score(12 p.) & 2 parts(2 p. each)

W23. *Am Traunsee.* (unpublished)
Song; text by Joseph Victor von Scheffel.
Composed: Summer 1916, Teschen.

Manuscripts: **A-Wst:** MH 10425/c. #6. Text. **A-Wst:** MH 10431/c. Score(4 p.)

W24. *Ein kleines Lied.* (unpublished)
Song; text by Marie Ebner-Eschenbach.
Composed: 1916, Wien.

Manuscripts: **A-Wst:** MH 10425/c. #8. Text. **A-Wst:** MH 10433/c. Score(2 p.)

W25. *Zwischen Erd und Himmel.* (unpublished)
SATB solos, SATB chorus, solo violin & orchestra; text by Robert Hamerling
from *Sinnen und Minnen.*
Composed: Fall 1916, Wien.

Manuscripts: **A-Wst:** MH 10425/c. #10. Text. **A-Wst:** MH 10435/c. Piano-vocal
score(16 p.)

W26. *Der Tod und die Liebe.* (unpublished)
Song; text by Börries Freiherr von Münchhausen.
Composed: Winter 1916, Wien.

Manuscripts: **A-Wst:** MH 10425/c. #12. Text. **A-Wst:** MH 10437/c. Score(3 p.)

W27. *Um Mitternacht.* (unpublished)
For SAT solos, SATB chorus & orchestra; text by Johann Georg Fischer.
Composed: 1916.

Manuscripts: **A-Wst:** MH 10425/c. #13. Text. **A-Wst:** MH 10438/c. Piano-vocal
score(8 p.)

W28. *Der letze Weg.* (unpublished)
Song; text by Börries Freiherr von Münchhausen.
Composed: December 1916, Vienna.

Manuscripts: **A-Wst:** MH 10425/c. #11. Text. **A-Wst:** MH 10436/c. Score(4 p.)

W29. *Ueber einem Grabe.* (unpublished)
Thema mit 5 Variationen und 2 Intermezzi for chorus, soli and orchestra; text
by Konrad Ferdinand Meyer.
Composed: Christmas 1916, Teschen.

Manuscripts: **A-Wst:** MH 10425/c. #14. Text. **A-Wst:** MH 10439/c. Piano-vocal
score(17 p.)

W30. *Sonata, cello & piano, A minor.* (unpublished)
Composed: 1917.
Adagio-Allegro vivace, appassionata. Adagio.

Manuscripts: **A-Wst:** MH 10423/c. Score(18 p., incomplete) & part(6 p.)

W31. *Bühnenmusik zu ?.* (unpublished)
For SATB chorus and orchestra: 2.0.0.0 / 0.2.1.0 / timpani / strings.
Composed: ca.1917.

> **Theil I: 1:** *Allegro.* **2:** *Moderato.* (women/men chorus, 2 flutes, strings) **3:** *Gelächter aus der Trinkstube.* (2 flutes, 2 trumpets, timpani, strings) **4:** *Kanon aus den Trinkstube.* **5-8:** [Untitled]
> **Theil II: 9:** [Untitled] **10:** [Unidentified] **11:** [Unidentified] **12:** [Untitled] **13:** *Dazu hohe Glorie* (Schelle)

Manuscripts: **A-Wst:** MH 10449/c. Score(9 p.)

W32. *Cyrano de Bergerac.* (unpublished)
Incidental music; voice, 4 violins & piano.
Composed: ca.1917.

> **1:** *Prelude.* **2:** *Menuett.* **3:** *Nocturno.* **4:** *Introduction et air.* **5:** *Ballade.*

Manuscripts: **A-Wst:** MH 10450/c. Score(43 p.)

W33. *Doppelfuge, Fünfstimmige, D minor.* (unpublished)
For piano 4-hands.
Composed: February 1917.

Manuscripts: **A-Wst:** MH 10369/c. Score(14 p.)

W34. *Fugen.* (unpublished)
Four-part fugues.
Composed: March 14 - 24, 1917.

> **1:** [lacking] **2:** *Fugen.* (March 18, 1917) **3:** *Fugen. Aeolian.* (March 14, 1917) **4a:** *Fugen. Dorian.* (March 18, 1917) **4b:** *Fugen. Dorian,* transposed up a third. (March 24, 1917)

Manuscripts: **A-Wgm.** Score(30 p.)

W35. *Kanons und Fugen.* (unpublished)
Composed: March 14 - May 12, 1917.

> **1:** *Kanon mit Füllstimme.* 3-voice. **2a:** *Dreistimmige Fuge. Dorian.* (April 4, 1917) **2b:** *Fuge, dreistimmig.* **3:** *Vierstimmige Fuge. Aeolian.* (April 5, 1917) **4:** *Fuge, vierstimmig. Phrygian.* (April 12, 1917) **5:** *Dreistimmiger Kanon.* (April 22, 1917) **6:** *Dreistimmiger endloser Kanon.* (April 22, 1917) **7:** *Vierstimmiger Kanon.* SATB chorus. (April 22, 1917) **8:** *Vierstimmige endloser Kanon.* SAAT chorus. (April 23, 1917) **9:** *Fuge 3.Stimmig.* **10:** *Vierstimmige Fuge.* (May 12, 1917) **11:** *Doppelfuge, 4 stimmig. Dorian.* (April 15, 1917) **12:** *Endloser Kanon in der Oktave* (mit Füllstimme) Dorian, 3 voice.

Manuscripts: **A-Wgm.** Score(30 p.)

W36. *Das 156. Sonett des Petrarca.* (unpublished)
Song; text by K. Förster.
Composed: May - June 1917.
Text: "Ein weisses Reh, dem Goldgeweih verliehen"

Manuscripts: **A-Wst:** MH 10442/c. Score(7 p.)

W37. *Fuge, Dreistimmige, C minor*. (unpublished)
  Composed: May 2 - 6, 1917.

  Manuscripts: **A-Wst:** MH 10453/c. Score(4 p.)

W38. *Fuge, Vierstimmige, F major*. (unpublished)
  Composed: May 26, 1917.

  Manuscripts: **A-Wst:** MH 10454/c. Score(4 p.) **A-Wst:** MH 10455/c. Score(6 p.)

W39. *Fuge, Dreistimmige, C major*. (unpublished)
  Composed: May 30 - June 20, 1917.

  Manuscripts: **A-Wst:** MH 10456/c. Score(4 p.) **A-Wst:** MH 10457/c. Score(4 p.)

W40. *Erlebnis*. (unpublished)
  Song; Text by Hugo von Hofmannsthal.
  Composed: June 25, 1917, Vienna.

  Manuscripts: **A-Wst:** MH 10447/c. Score(14 p.)

W41. *Reiselied*. (unpublished)
  Songs; Text of no.1 by Hugo von Hofmannsthal.
  Composed: July 3, 1917, Vöslau.
  1: *Reiselied*. **2:** [Untitled, no text] **3:** *[Héxanthoucha]*

  Manuscripts: **A-Wst:** MH 10441/c. Score(11 p.)

W42. *[Unidentified.]*
  Song; text by Otto Julius Bierbaum.
  Composed: September 1917, Vöslau.

  Manuscripts: **A-Wgm.** Score(7 p., lacks text)

W43. *Reinigung*. (unpublished)
  Song; Text by Detlev von Liliencron from his collection of poems *Sizilianen*.
  Composed: September 1917, Vöslau.

  Manuscripts: **A-Wgm.** Score(4 p.)

W44. *Waldesstimme*. (unpublished)
  Song; text by Peter Hille.
  Composed: October 14, 1917.

  Manuscripts: **A-Wst:** MH 10443/c. Score(4 p.)

W45. *Lieder*. (unpublished)
  Text of no.2 by Max Jungnickel.
  Composed: October 18 - 29, 1917.
  1: *Götter, keine frostige Ewigkeit*. (October 18, 1917, Vienna) **2:** *Nächtlich*. (October 29, 1917) **3:** *Nachtlied*.

  Manuscripts: **A-Wst:** MH 10444/c. Score(6 p.)

W46. *Die Blüte des Chaos*. (unpublished)
  Song; text by Alfred Mombert.
  Composed: October 21, 1917.

  Manuscripts: **A-Wgm.** Score(3 p.)

W47. *Greek songs.* (unpublished)
Four songs on Greek texts.
Composed: December 22 - 23, 1917.

Manuscripts: **A-Wst:** MH 10446/c. Score(10 p.)

W48. *Der volle Mond steigt aus dem Meer herauf.* (unpublished)
Song.
Composed: ca.1917?

Manuscripts: **A-Wst:** MH 10440/c. Score(4 p.)

W49. *Gott gib dein Gericht dem König.* (unpublished)
Motets for SATB chorus a capella.
Composed: ca.1918

1: *Gott gib dein Gericht dem König.* (Psalm 72) **2:** *Er wird das elende Volk bei Recht erhalten.* **3:** *Wenn den Herr die Gefangen erlösen wird.* (Psalm 126, 1-3). **4:** *Der Herr ist König und herrlich geschmückt* (Psalm 93,1,3-4).

Manuscripts: **A-Wst:** MH 10373/c. Score(39 p.) **A-Wst:** MH 10451/c. No.1, score(4 p., incomplete) **A-Wst** No.1, score(2 p.) **A-Wst:** MH 10452/c. "Schlussfuge" score(18 p.) **A-Wst:** MH 10374/c. Piano score(17 p.) **A-Wst:** MH 10375/c. Organ part(10 p., stops at m.280 of no.4) **A-Wst:** MH 10376/c. Non-autograph parts(S:17 p.; A:18 p.; T:17 p.; B:18 p., all stop at m.280 of no.4)

W50. *Doppelfuge, Fünfstimmige, D-flat major.* (unpublished)
For 2 pianos.
Composed: May 5, 1918.

Manuscripts: **A-Wst:** MH 10370/c. Score(17 p.) **A-Wst:** MH 10371/c. Score(17 p.)

W51. *Pieces, piano.* (unpublished)
Composed: October 8, 1918 - January 1919.

1: *Gavotte, D major.* (October 26, 1918) **2:** *Musette.* **3:** *Marsch, E-flat major.* (October 8 - 9, 1918) **4:** *Scherzo, A major.* (1918) **5:** *Appassionato, D-flat major.* (January 1919) **6:** *Scherzo, G minor.* (1919)

Manuscripts: **A-Wst:** MH 10459/c. No.1-2, 2 p. **A-Wst:** MH 10460/c. No.3, 4 p. **A-Wst:** MH 10461/c. No.4, 7 p. **A-Wst:** MH 10462/c. No.5, 8 p. **A-Wst:** MH 10463/c. No.6, 4 p.

W52. *Leonce und Lena overture.* (unpublished)
For a play by Georg Büchner; piano.
Composed: 1919 or 1920.

Manuscripts: **A-Wst:** MH 10465/c. 9 p.

W53. *Vor dem Schlafe.* (unpublished)
Song; text by Karl Kraus from *Worte in Versen.*
Composed: September 12, 1919, Vienna.

Manuscripts: **A-Wst:** MH 10345. Score(6 p.)

W54. *Albumblatt* = *Stück, violin & piano, F major.* (unpublished)
Composed: 1920.
Nicht schnell, sehr innig.
Dedication: Prof. Franz Xaver Gmeiner, Staatsgymnasium Wien XVIII.

Manuscripts: **A-Wgm.** Score(4 p.) & part(1 p.) **A-Wst:** MH 10416/c. Score(4 p., incomplete)

W55. *Variationen und Fuge über ein Thema von Wilhelm Friedemann Bach, D minor.* (unpublished)
For orchestra; not orchestrated. Theme from the Fourth Polonaise.
Composed: January 1920.

Manuscripts: **A-Wst:** MH 10382/c. Sketch(28 p.) **A-Wst:** MH 10383/c. Sketch(2 p.) **A-Wst:** MH 10466/c. Sketch(10 p.)

W56. *Pieces, piano.* (unpublished)
Composed: February 1 - 4, 1920.
1: *Préambule.* (February 1, 1920) **2:** *Melancholie.* (February 1, 1920) **3:** *Epigramm.* (February 2, 1920) **4:** *Melodie.* (February 2, 1920) **5:** *Arabeske.* (February 3, 1920) **6:** *Linie.* (February 4, 1920)

Manuscripts: **A-Wst:** MH 10468/c. 4 p.

W57. *Lieder.* (unpublished)
Eingereicht für den Zusner-Preis, 1917?. "Das liebliche Vergissmeinnicht."
Composed: April 2 - 10, 1920.
1: [Lacking] **2:** *Den Himmel diesseits trüben die Wolken.* (April 2, 1920) **3:** *Vernichtet ist mein Lebensglück.* (April 2, 1920) **4:** [Untitled] (April 10, 1920)

Manuscripts: **A-Wst:** MH 10445/c 4 p.

W58. *Quartet, strings, D major.* (unpublished)
Composed: May 5, 1920.
1: *Allegro con fuoco.* **2:** *Andantino quassi Intermezzo* **3:** *Finale, Rondo ala Capriccio.*

Manuscripts: **A-Wst:** MH 10467/c. Score(26 p.)

Published (Facsimile pp.1-2): In *Musik-Konzepte* 39/40 (October 1984): 92-93.

W59. *Symphonie, D minor.* (unpublished)
Composed: August 23 - September 23, 1920.
1: *Langsam, schleppend.* **2:** *Allegretto.* (August 23, 1920) **3.** [Lacking] **4:** *Allegro vivace.* (September 23, 1920)

Manuscripts: **A-Wst:** MH 10464. Piano score(52 p.)

W60. *O meine armen Füsse.* (unpublished)
Song; voice and small orchestra.
Composed: ca.1921.

Manuscripts: **A-Wst:** MH 10458/c. Piano score(2 p.)

W61. *6. Sonatine, violin & piano.* (unpublished)
Composed: ca.1921.
1: *Andante molto.* **2:** *Siciliano.* **3:** *Adagio.*
Dedication: Jela Preradovic in Wien.

Manuscripts: **A-Wgm.** Score(6 p.) & part(4 p.)

W62. *6. Sonatina, for violin & viola.* (unpublished)
"In Kanonform".

Composed: September 23, 1921.

1: *Allegretto decisio.* **2:** *Moderato.* **3:** *Tempo Io.* **4:** *Allegro moderato.* **5:** *Tempo Io.* **6:** *Andante molto.*
Dedication: Jela [Preradovic].

Manuscripts: **A-Wst:** MH 10469/c. Score(2 p.)

W63. *Die Büsserin.* (unpublished)
Song; text by Karl Kraus.
Composed: October 18, 1921, Berlin.
Wie viele Lieder bliebe.

Manuscripts: **A-Wst:** MH 10346. [with op.9 songs] Score(2 p.)

W64. *Opfer der Schauspielkunst.* (unpublished)
Song; text by Hellmuth Krüger.
Composed: November 26, 1921, Berlin.

Manuscripts: **A-Wst:** MH 10309. [with op.9 songs] Score(1 p.)

Published: In *Blätter des Deutschen Theaters* (Berlin) 8:1

W65. *Unvollendete Sonate, C-dur, für Piano solo, D.840* by Franz Schubert. (UE)
Last two movements completed by Krenek: December 17, 1921, Berlin.

Manuscripts: **D-brd** Erdmann Estate. **A-Wn.**

Premiere: January 5, 1922, Berlin, Singakademie; Eduard Erdmann, piano. *See:* B694, B827

First U.S. Performance: February 24, 1940, New York, Town Hall; Webster Aitken, piano. *See:* B896

Other Performances: B174, K892

Publications: B300

Recording: Concert Hall Society B-3. (Mx: CHS.127 -- CHS.129, CHS.131). 2 discs. 78 rpm. [194-?]
Ray Lev, piano.
Also issued on Concert Hall Society CHS 1072. 33 1/3 rpm. mono. #WERM

W66. *Musik für kleine Flöte, Bass Tuba und Celesta.* (unpublished)
Composed: ca.1922.

Manuscripts: **A-Wst:** MH 10403/c. Score(2 p.)

W67. *Cadenza for Piano concerto* by Joseph Haydn. (unpublished)
Composed: 1922.

Manuscripts: **D-brd** Erdmann Estate.

W68. *Napoleon.* (unpublished) *See:* K812
Incidental music to a play by Grabbe Christian Dietrich written for the Berliner Staatlichen Schauspielhause.
Composed: 1922.

W69. *Fiesco.* (unpublished) *See:* K812
Incidental music to a play by Schiller Friedrich written for the Berliner Staatlichen Schauspielhause.
Composed: 1922.

W70. *Mädchens Klage.* (unpublished)
    Song; text by Gerd Hans Goering.
    Composed: March 12, 1923, Berlin.
    Text: "Ich hab' eine Katze geliebet"

Manuscripts: **A-Wst:** MH 10347. Non-autograph score(9 p.)

W71. *Kanons.* (unpublished)
    For piano; in two parts.
    Composed: November 23, 1923.

    1: *Kanon in der Oktave.* **2:** *Kanon in der Septime.* **3:** *Kanon in der Sexte.* **4:** *Kanon in der Quinte.* **5:** *Kanon in der Quarte, im doppelten Kontrapunkt.* **6:** *Kanon in der Terz.* **7:** *Krebskanon in der Sekunde, im doppelten Kontrapunkt.*

Manuscripts: **A-Wst:** MH 10470/c. 4 p.

W72. *Symphony, no.10,* by Gustav Mahler; first and third movements edited by Krenek. *See:* B104, B138, B838, B1505

Premiere: October 12, 1924, Vienna, Vienna Staatsoper; Wiener Symphoniker; Franz Schalk, conductor. *See:* B695, B1384

First U.S. Performance: December 6, 1949, Erie, New York; Erie Philharmonic Orchestra; Fritz Mahler, conductor.

Other Performances: B283, B1520

Published (Facsimile of original score): (Wien: Gesellschaft für Graphische Inductrie, 1924) 15 p.

Published (Facsimile page): In *Archiv für Musikwissenschaft* 39:4 (1982): 245-270.

Recording: Epic BC 1024. 33 1/3 rpm. stereo. [1959]
    Cleveland Orchestra; George Szell, conductor.
    With William Walton *Partita.*
    Also issued on Epic LC 3568. 33 1/3 rpm. mono. [1959]

Recording: Society of Participating Artists SPA 31. 33 1/3 rpm.
    Wiener Symphoniker; F. Charles Adler, conductor.
    With Bruckner.

Recording: Gramophone Newsreel . 33 1/3 rpm. mono.
    Zürich Tonhalle; Franz Schmidt [pseud], conductor.

Recording: Westminster WAL 207. 2 discs. 33 1/3 rpm. mono.
    Wiener Staatsoper; Hermann Scherchen, conductor.
    With Mahler's *Symphony, no.5.*
    Also issued on Nixa WLP 6207.

Recording: Columbia M2 31313. 33 1/3 rpm. [1972]
    Cleveland Orchestra; F. Charles Adler, conductor.
    With Mahler's *Symphony, no.6.*

W73. *Das Leben ein Traum.* (unpublished)
    Incidental music to *La vida es sueño* by Franz Grillparzer.
    Composed: 1925.

Premiere: 1925, Kassel.

W74. *Gedicht.* (unpublished)
    For baritone with violin, trumpet, saxophone, percussion & piano; text by Hans Arp.

Composed: January 16, 1926, Kassel.
Text: "O du titulierter Kronen und Wappentattersall"
Manuscripts: **A-Wst:** MH 10471/c. Score(8 p.)

W75. *Die Kaiserin von Neufundland.* (unpublished)
Incidental music to play by Frank Wedekind. For orchestra: 1.1.3.2 / 1.2.1.0 /
timpani / percussion / strings.
Composed: September 16 - 30, 1927, Wiesbaden.
Sketched for the Staatstheater Wiesbaden, commissioned by Paul Bekker.
Manuscripts: **A-Wgm.** Sketch(32 p.) **A-Wst:** MH 10472. Score(3-90 p., incomplete)

W76. *Sonatina, piano,* op.60 [*sic*]. (unpublished)
Composed: December 16, 1928 - January 5, 1929.
1: *Allegro moderato.* (December 16, 1928, St.Moritz) **2:** *Andante sostenuto,*
affetuoso. (January 5, 1929, Vienna)
Manuscripts: **A-Wst:** MH 10349. 9 p.

W77. *Kalender,* op.64 [*sic*]. (unpublished)
For four men's voices a cappella.
Composed: August 30, 1929 - May 13, 1930.
1: *Frülingslied.* *"Der Frühling naht!"* (August 30, 1929, Vienna) **2:** *Winterlied.*
"Das Land hält der Winter gefangen." (September 10, 1929, Aix-en-Provence) **3:** *Ein*
nachdenkliches Tanzlied. (May 13, 1930, Vienna) **4:** *Ein fröhliches Tanzlied. "Ein*
lustiges Liedchen." (May 13, 1930, Vienna)
Manuscripts: **A-Wst:** Nachlass. Plan(2 p.) **A-Wst:** MH 10348/c. Score(8 p.)

W78. *Piece, piano.* (unpublished)
Untitled. Composed: ca.192-.
Manuscripts: **A-Wgm.** Sketches(4 p.)

W79. *Piece, piano.* (unpublished)
Composed: ca.192-.
L'istesso tempo; incomplete.
Manuscripts: **A-Wgm.** 4 p.

W80. *Piece, violin & piano.* (unpublished)
Composed: ca.192-.
Etwas bewegt.
Manuscripts: **A-Wgm.** Score(2 p.)

W81. *Wach auf mein Hort.* (unpublished)
Premiere: June 23, 1930, Berlin; Jugendchor der Staatlichen Akademie für
Kirchen- und Schulmusik; Heinrich Martens, conductor.

W82. *Kantate Von den Leiden des Menschen.* (unpublished)
Cantata; SATB chorus and orchestra: 3.2.3.2 / 2.2.2.1 / timpani / piano / harp
/ strings.
Composed: March 13, 1932. [Start]
Manuscripts: **A-Wst:** Nachlass. Plan(1 p.) **A-Wst:** MH 10389/c. Sketch(16 p.) **A-Wst:** MH 10390/c. Score(17 p., incomplete)

W83. *Vocalise.* (unpublished)
  For voice and piano.
  Composed: March 5, 1934, Vienna.

  Manuscripts: **A-Wst:** MH 10350. Sketch(2 p.) **A-Wst:** MH 10350. Score(4 p.)

W84. *Symeon der Stylit.* (BA) *See:* K347
  Oratorio for soprano, mezzosoprano, tenor, baritone, SATB chorus &
  orchestra: 1.1.1.1 / 1.1.1.0 / pianoi / timpani / strings. German text from
  Byzantinisches Christentum by Hugo Ball alternating with texts from the
  Psalms in Latin.
  Composed: June 3, 1935 - January 21, 1937, Vienna; Instr. September 27, 1935,
  Vienna; Completed April - May 1987, Palm Springs, CA.

  1: *Introduction.* "Ich glaube nicht, dass Symeon ohne Gottes Willen auf
  der Säule gestanden" (June 7, 1935, Wien; Instr. September 27, 1935, Wien [at
  beginning] **2:** *Erste Lesung:* "Wir haben die Hieroglyphensprache verlernt."
  (Text: Hugo Ball, Byzantinisches Christentum, pp.251-2) **3:** *Sonata, Super inventute
  Sancti Symeonis Stylitae.* "Im fünften Jahrhundert nach der Geburt unseres
  Herrn." **4:** "Salvum me fac Domine." **5:** "Im Traume aber erscheint
  Symeon ein Engel." **6:** "Ego autem sum vermis." **7:** "Nach langem Flehen
  ins Kloster." **8:** *Zweite Lesung.* "Geheilt und entlassen." **9:** "Timotheus
  aber, der Archimandrit, wird von Zweifeln erfasst." **10:** "Domini est
  terra et plenitudo eius." (Psalm 23: 1-3, 7 and Psalm 67: 5, 7, 19) **11:** "Symeon
  besteigt den Gipfel des Berges. (February 9, 1936 Wien)

  Manuscripts: **A-Wst:** MH 10364. (UCSD copy) Score(134 p.) **A-Wst:** MH 10365.
  Piano-vocal score(41 p.) **A-Wgm.** Sketch(32 p.)

  Premiere: July 27, 1988, Salzburger Festspiele, Universitätskirche; Eva Csapò,
  soprano; Cornelia Kallisch, mezzosoprano; Werner Hollweg, tenor and
  narrator; Roland Hermann, bass; ORF-Chor Wien; Ensemble Modern
  Frankfurt; Lothar Zagrosek, conductor.

  Published (Facsimile pages): In *Musik-Konzepte* 39/40 (October 1984): 67-75.

W85. *Deep Sea = Lighthouse in the sea.* (unpublished; dur: 6 min.)
  Fantasie for tuba and piano, by Donald M. Hardy [pseud].
  Composed: ca.1939.

  Manuscripts: **A-Wst** Score(10 p.) & part(2 p.)

W86. *Die Vier Lebendigen.* (unpublished)
  Tenor, baritone, and piano.
  Composed: ca.193?.

  Manuscripts: **A-Wgm.** No.2, score(2 p.)

W87. *Prelude.* (Schweizerische Musikzeitung) *See:* K537
  For piano.
  Composed: February 5, 1944, St.Paul, MN.
  Dedication: Werner Reinhart.

  Manuscripts: **CH-W:** Dep RS 35/3.

  Published: In *Schweizerische Musikzeitung* 84:5 (May 1, 1944): 187-189.

W88. *Short piano pieces.* (unpublished)
  Three untitled pieces. Composed: August 1 - 4, 1946, Hollywood, CA.
  Manuscripts: **A-Wst:** MH 14761/c. Sketch(3 p.)

W89. *Spiritus sanctus.* (unpublished)
"First attempt."
Composed: June 25 - September 11, 1948, Albuquerque, NM - Palo Alto, CA.
Text: "And it came to pass that God"
Manuscripts: **A-Wst:** MH 14740/c. Sketch.

W90. *Variation over a Gregorian Chant.* (unpublished)
Composed: ca.1949.
Manuscripts: **A-Wst:** MH 14742/c. Sketch(1 p.)

W91. *Isorhythmic studies.* (unpublished)
Composed: Summer 1955.
Manuscripts: **A-Wst:** MH 14749/c. Sketch(67 p.) **A-Wst:** MH 14750/c. Sketch(35 p.)

W92. *Psalmverse.* (unpublished)
For SATB chorus.
Composed: August 26, 1956, Los Angeles, CA.
Written for Ernst Pfiffner in Basle, SZ.
Manuscripts: **A-Wst** Sketch(2 p.)

W93. *Princeton study.* (unpublished)
Composed: March 1957.
Manuscripts: **A-Wst:** MH 14823/c. Sketch(18 p.)

W94. *Holiday motets* = *Fest Motetten.* (Broude & BA)
For chorus (treble voices) a cappella.
Composed: 1959 - 1966.
1: *Weihnachten* = *Christmas* (1959) "Gloria in excelsis Deo" "Glory to God in the highest" **2:** *Epiphany* = *New year* (Matthew 2:2) (1966) "Vidimus stellam" "We have seen his star in the east" **3:** *Lent* = *Fastenzeit* (Psalm 130:1-2) (1966) "De profundis" "Out of the depths" **4:** *Easter* = *Ostern* (Psalm 118:24) (1960) "Haec dies" "This is the day" **5:** *Thanksgiving* = *Danksagung* (Psalm 136:1 & Psalm 105:14-15) (1966) "Confitemini" "O give thanks unto the Lord"

W95. *Like dew.* (unpublished)
For 3 voices; text by Elisabeth Coatsworth.
Composed: February 23, 1962, Tujunga, CA.
Manuscripts: **US** composer Score(2 p.)

W96. *Piece for H.H. Stuckenschmidt.* (unpublished)
For oboe & piano; written for his 65th birthday.
Composed: April 1966.
Manuscripts: **A-Wst:** MH 14775/c. Sketch(1 p.) **US** composer Score(1 p.)

W97. *Canon.* (unpublished)
Composed: 1969?
Dedication: Dr. Karl Vötterle dem Sechziger sechzig Noten.
Manuscripts: **A-Wst:** MH 14800/c. Sketch(2 p.) **A-Wst:** MH 14799/c. 1 p.

W98. *2 Kanons für Paul Sacher.* (unpublished)
>
> For voices.
> Composed: June 13, 1975 - April 28, 1976.
>
> *Manuscripts:* **A-Wst:** MH 14733/c. Sketches(3 p.) **US** composer Score(1 p.)

W99. *Canon.* (unpublished)
>
> Composed: 1976.
> Text: "From Fromm we have received so many wonderous things / Our best wishes that's all we can return to Fromm"
> Dedication: Paul Fromm on his 70th birthday.
>
> *Manuscripts:* **A-Wst:** MH 14802/c. Sketch(2 p.)

W100. *Amico Sartori.* (unpublished)
>
> Composed: 1976?
> Text: "To friend Sartor..." "Amico Sartori..."
> Written for Friedrich Sartor, editor at Universal Edition.
>
> *Manuscripts:* **A-Wst:** MH 14802/c. Sketch(2 p.) **A-Wst:** MH 14803/c. Sketch(1 p.)

W101. *Deutsche Messgesänge zum 29. Sonntag im Jahreskreis.* (unpublished)
>
> For narrator, chorus (SATB) and organ. Text by Rudolf Henz.
> Composed: March 16 - April 18, 1980, San Francisco, CA.
> Dedication: For Graz 1980.
>
> *Manuscripts:* **A-Wst:** MH 14721/c. Sketch(6 p.)
>
> *Premiere:* October 19, 1980, Graz, Austria, Cathedral, Abteilung Kirchenfunk des ORF; Martin Klietmann, precentor; Emanuel Amtmann, organ; Pro-Arte-Chor Graz; Helmut Guggerbauer, conductor. *See:* B730, B1415

W102. *Gentil aspetto,* by Francesco Landini. (unpublished) (unpublished)
>
> For 3 voices.
> n.d.
>
> *Manuscripts:* **US** composer Score(2 p.)

W103. *De! Dimmi tu* by Francesco Landini. (unpublished) (unpublished)
>
> For 3 voices.
> n.d.
>
> *Manuscripts:* **US** composer Score(3 p.)

W104. *Masses, examples* by Johannes Ockeghem. (unpublished) (unpublished)
>
> n.d.
>
> *Manuscripts:* **US** composer Score(3 p.)

W105. *Amor = Lamento della Ninfa* by Claudio Monteverdi. (unpublished) (unpublished)
>
> For STTB and piano.
> n.d.
> From v.8, p.288. Bass realized by Krenek.
>
> *Manuscripts:* **US** composer Score(6 p.)

Writings

The writings about Krenek are listed alphabetically by author, and subarranged by date. Compositions by Krenek are cited by opus number or, for works without opus number, by "W" number as appropriate. References to citations in the "Bibliography" sections are identified by "B" number for writings about Krenek and by "K" number for writings by him. Abbreviations are explained in the Preface.

-- 1913 -- 24 --

K1. "Der Skorpion." *Unpublished*.

A satirical magazine written during 1913 and 1914 in imitation of Karl Kraus's *Die Fackel*. This is Krenek's first literary effort.

Manuscripts: **A-Wst**.

K2. "Athburg und Sparberg." *Unpublished*.

A fictious political history of two countries modeled on Athens and Sparta written between 1916 to 1919.

Manuscripts: **A-Wst**.

K3. "Das Donaueschinger Programm: Ernst Krenek." *Neue Musik-Zeitung* 42:20 (July 21, 1921): 315.

A brief biographical essay for the program book of the Erste Donaueschinger Kammermusikfest with an analysis, including musical examples, of the *Serenade* op.4.

K4. "Zum Donaueschinger Programm: Ernst Krenek." *Neue Musik-Zeitung* 43:20 (July 20, 1922): 319.

A brief biographical essay for the program book of the Zweite Donaueschinger Kammermusikfest with an analysis of the *Symphonische Musik* op.11. Picture.

K5. "Ernst Krenek." *Der Chorleiter* 4:9/12 (May/June 1923): 11.

Catalog of works and introduction to the *Second symphony* op.12.

K6. "Diskussionsbeitrag." *Pult und Taktstock* 1:4 (July 1924): 67.

Reaction to the article published in the May issue by Florence G. Fidler "Die Besetzung des kleinen Orchesters" discussing three specific points about the use of instruments in chamber music.

K7. "Ernst Krenek." *Blätter der Staatsoper* (Berlin) 5:2 (October 1924): 1.

Brief autobiography for premiere of the opera *Zwingburg* op.14.

-- 1925 --

K8. "Mechanisierung der Musik." *Pult und Taktstock* 2:2/3 (February-March 1925): 35-38.

Reaction (on p.37), with others, to "Mechanisierung der Musik," by Hans Heinz Stuckenschmidt in the January issue. Krenek heard a work by Igor Stravinsky performed by a player piano in Paris and thought it was artistic. The role of the interpreter is not diminished by the phonograph. He thought that his works could be reproduced on the phonograph.

K9. "Zum Problem der Oper." In *Von neuer Musik, Beiträge zur Erkenntnis der neuzeitlichen Tonkunst*, hrsg. von H.Grues, E.Kruttge, und E.Thalheimer. (Köln: F. J.Marcan-Verlag, 1925): 39-43.

Discusses the relationship of text (a specific art form) to music (an abstract art form) in opera. Includes a facsimile of the manuscript of the fifth movement of the *Fourth string quartet* op.24.

   a. ——. *Blätter der Staatsoper* (Berlin) 5:5 (March 1925): 9-13.

   b. ——. *Oesterreichische Musikzeitschrift* 5:9 (September 1950): 178-181.

   Manuscripts: A-Wst typescript ([5] p.)

K10. "Das Donaueschinger Programm: Ernst Krenek." *Neue Musik-Zeitung* 46:20 (July 1925): 466.

Brief biography for the program book of the Donaueschinger Kammermusikfest for the premiere of his chorus *Die Jahreszeiten* op.35.

K11. "Johann Strauss und Wir." *Der Auftakt* (Prague) 5:9 (October 1925): 270.

Comments, with Philipp Jarnach, about the significance of Johann Strauss Jr. He "was the final product and the last breed of a homogeneous audience."

K12. "Musik in der Gegenwart." In *25 Jahre neue Musik, Jahrbuch der Universal-Edition*, hrsg. von Hans Heinsheimer und Paul Stefan. UE Nr.8500 (Wien, 1926): 43-59.

Lecture given at the Kongress für Musikästhetik in Karlsruhe, October 19, 1925. "*Should* we continue to create art, and if so, what kind of art *should* it be? When it comes right down to it, art doesn't have to exist at all, at any rate, it doesn't *have* to exist in any certain way. It either exists or it doesn't. The question about 'what should be' in regard to art is, in my view, the very core of aesthetics ... the artist has no choice in the matter, even if he is clearly aware of living in a time of decadence. Knowledge about what is going on in no way obligates one to act in a certain way. The only thing that is compelling is feeling and belief. Nonetheless, we can discuss what possibilities still exist for at least a limited expression of music. I am of the opinion that the strongest possibilities in this direction lie in the realm of the theater." *See:* B1436

   a. ——. *Blätter der Staatsoper und der Städtischen Oper* (Berlin) 9:10 (December 1928): 8-13.

   Abbreviated.

   b. "Music of today." In *Opera during the Weimar Republic: the Zeitopern of Ernst Krenek, Kurt Weill, and Paul Hindemith*, by Susan C. Cook. (Ph.D.: University of Michigan, 1985), pp.414-425.

c. ——. In *Opera for a new republic: the Zeitopern* of Krenek, Weill, and
Hindemith, by Susan C. Cook. Studies in musicology, no.96. (Ann
Arbor: UMI Research Press, 1988): 193-203.

K13. "Schenck *Der Dorfbabier* und Rameau *Der vertauschte Cupido.*" *[Program: Staatstheater Kassel 1925/26]* no.1 (October 25, 1925)
Notes to the first performance of Krenek's edition of the Rameau ballet op.38.

K14. "Der Darsteller in der Oper." *[Program: Staatstheater Kassel 1925/26]* no.2 (November 7, 1925)
A discussion about the role of acting in operatic performance.

K15. "Beatrice Sutter-Kottlar." *[Program: Staatstheater Kassel 1925/26]* no.3 (November 15, 1925)
An essay about the singer.

K16. "Glucks *Armide.*" *[Program: Staatstheater Kassel 1925/26]* no.3 (November 15, 1925)
Notes to the opera.
a. ——. *Casseler Tageblatt* (May 5, 1926)

K17. "Musik im Schauspiel." *[Program: Staatstheater Kassel 1925/26]* no.4 (November 21, 1925)
A discussion of the role of incidental music to plays.

K18. "Ueber die Operette." *[Program: Staatstheater Kassel 1925/26]* no.5 (December 1925)
A discussion of operetta.

K19. "Das dekorative Element im Theater." *[Program: Staatstheater Kassel 1925/26]* (December 20, 1925)
A discussion of the role of scenery.

K20. "Offenbach-Einakter." *[Program: Staatstheater Kassel 1925/26]* (December 20, 1925)
An examination of the music of Jacques Offenbach.

K21. "[Drei Einführungen zu Kammermusikaufführungen]." *Unpublished.*
Introductory lectures broadcast over Radio Kassel during 1925 and 1926 to three chamber music programs.
Manuscripts: **A-Wst.**

-- 1926 --

K22. "*Boris Godunoff* und die nationale Volksoper." *[Program: Staatstheater Kassel 1925/26]* (1926)
A discussion of the opera by Modest Mussorgsky.

K23. "Cimarosa *Die heimliche Ehe.*" *[Program: Staatstheater Kassel 1925/26]* (1926)
A discussion of the opera *La matrimonio segreto.*

K24. "Das Theater als Bildungsanstalt." *[Program: Staatstheater Kassel 1925/26]* (1926)
Reflections of the role of theater in education.
Manuscripts: **A-Wst** [2] p.

K25. "Die Revue." *[Program: Staatstheater Kassel 1925/26]* (1926)
A discussion of the musical review.

K26. "Pergolesi, Duny, Grétry." *[Program: Staatstheater Kassel 1925/26]* (1926)
A discussion of the three eighteenth century composers.

K27. "Tschaikowsky *Pique Dame*." *[Program: Staatstheater Kassel 1925/26]* (1926)
Notes to the opera.

K28. "Der Ideologe fährt fort." *Unpublished*.
Dated Kassel, 1926.
Manuscripts: **A-Wst** [4] p. ; typescript (3 p.)

K29. "Friedrich der Grosse und die Musik seiner Zeit." *Unpublished*.
Lecture broadcast on Radio Kassel in 1926 concerning the German emperor Frederick the Great and his relationship to the music of his time.
Manuscripts: **A-Wst**.

K30. "Musik im Schauspiel, auf der Bühne und im Rundfunk." *Unpublished*.
Lecture broadcast by Radio Kassel in 1926 concerning the place of incidental music in the theater and on the radio.
Manuscripts: **A-Wst**.

K31. "Ueber Programm und Repertoire in Konzertsaal und Oper." *Unpublished*.
Lecture broadcast on Radio Kassel in 1926 reflecting on programs presented in the concert hall and by the opera.
Manuscripts: **A-Wst**.

K32. "Ein Ideologe über das Theater." *Casseler Tageblatt* (February 16, 1926)
A lecture broadcast on Radio Kassel in 1926 presenting Krenek's opera aesthetic. K. Dietrich responded to Krenek's point of view in his "Ueber Sinn und Zweck des Theaters" (B254), followed by a defense by Krenek under the title "Ueber Ziel und Zweck des Theaters" (K36).
Manuscripts: "Ideologisches und phänomenologisches Theater." **A-Wst** [4] p.

K33. "Das Volkslied." *Rheinische Musik- und Theaterzeitung* 27:7/8 (February 20, 1926): 52.
Reaction, with others, to comments posed in a symposium by F. Max Anton concerning folk music.

K34. "Tanzmusik." *Musikblätter des Anbruch* 8:3/4 (March-April 1926): 170-181.
Responses with F. Wilckens, Alfredo Casella, and others to a question in a symposium regarding the place of dance music in the current culture.

K35. "Beurteilung des Theaters." *[Program: Staatstheater Kassel 1925/26]* no.12 (March 1926)
Comments concerning the role of the theater.
Manuscripts: **A-Wst** [2] p.

K36. "Ueber Ziel und Zweck des Theaters." *Hessischer Kurier* (March 5, 1926): 1.
Lecture broadcast by Radio Kassel in 1926 as a response to K. Dietrich's

reaction to his "Ein Ideologe über das Theater" (K32) published under the title "Ueber Sinn und Zweck des Theaters" (B254). The misconception of what theater is about is based upon the belief that it has a moral function; it is considered a useful institution because it educates the common man. This false premise is derived from the misinterpretation of the Aristotelian statement that tragedy has moral effects upon the listener. The true purpose of theater is the artistic manipulation of its material; not the plot itself, but how all the components of the drama are put together to achieve a theatrical effect.

Manuscripts: "Moderne Formen der Parodie." **A-Wst** [7] p.

A discussion of parody.

K37. "Ferruccio Busoni." *[Program: Staatstheater Kassel 1925/26]* no.15 (May 3, 1926)

Notes about the composer.

K38. *"Der Triumph der Empfindsamkeit."* *Casseler Tageblatt* (May 5, 1926): 2.Blatt, p.[2].

A lecture broadcast over Radio Kassel in May 1926 concerning the forthcoming performance of the Goethe play with his incidental music op.43 in the Kassel Staatstheater on May 9.

  a. "Goethe *Der Triumph der Empfindsamkeit.*" *[Program: Staatstheater Kassel 1925/26]* no.16 (May 9, 1926)

K39. "Mein *Concerto grosso II, op.25.*" *Pult und Taktstock* 3:7/8 (September-October 1926): 140-141.

An analysis of the composition.

K40. "Gegensätzlichkeiten in der Musik." *Allgemeine Musikzeitung* 53:44 (October 29, 1926): 887.

A polemic against Gerhard F. Wehle's article of the same name (B1436) which misquoted Krenek's article "Musik in der Gegenwart" (K12). Krenek notes that his article surveyed music history, especially the period since Beethoven, and pointed out historical trends; Wehle responded (B1437).

K41. *"Orpheus und Eurydike."* *Südwestdeutsche Rundfunk-Zeitung* 2:48 (November 28, 1926): 3.

Lecture about his opera (op.21) given to the Verein der Kunstfreunde in Kassel, November 22, 1926 in anticipation of its premiere.

Manuscripts: **A-Wst**.

K42. "Zur Uraufführung der Oper *Orpheus und Eurydike.*" *[Program: Staatstheater Kassel 1926/27]* (November 27, 1926)

Notes for the premiere of his opera op.21.

K43. "Besprechung G. Torbé, Studie über Krenek." *Unpublished*.
Manuscripts: **A-Wst** 6 p.

K44. "Ueber die Beziehungen von Oper und Schauspiel, I & II." *[Program: Staatstheater Kassel 1926/27]* no.19 (December 1926) ; no.20 (January 1927)

A two-part essay on the relationship between opera and drama. *See:* B315

-- 1927 --

K45. "'Materialbestimmtheit' der Oper." In *Oper, Jahrbuch der Universal Edition; Musikblätter des Anbruch* 9:1/2 (January-February 1927): 48-52.

A discussion of the musical material necessary to give opera life and meaning. The idea of playing, in a verbal sense, is the motor for theatrical creation of today. An opera is theater in the sense that it is played life; as such it must be tailored to the playing actors, the singers. Musical development within the opera has to be easy to understand; emphasis must be on liveliness avoiding moral or political ideologies as well. In these ways, opera is not a problem of our time.

a. ——. In his *Zur Sprache gebracht.* (K707) (München: Albert Langen - Georg Müller, 1958): 25-30.

K46. "Stosseufzer zum *Schwarzen Domino* Auber." *[Program: Staatstheater Kassel 1926/27]* no.21 (January 31, 1927)

Notes to a performance of the opera.

K47. "Krenek *Jonny spielt auf.*" *Neue Leipziger Zeitung* 8:2 (February 6, 1927)

A discussion of the opera op.45 in anticipation of its first performance.

K48. "Zur Uraufführung meiner Oper *Jonny spielt auf.*" *Leipziger neueste Nachrichten* (February 8, 1927)

A discussion of the opera op.45 in anticipation of its first performance.

K49. "Beethoven-Feiern." *[Program: Staatstheater Kassel 1926/27]* no.23 (March 1927)

A brief essay in honor of the centennial of the composer's death.

K50. "Ueber Beethoven." *Der Wiener Tag* no.1514 (March 20, 1927)

A brief note of regard on the centennial of the composer's death.

K51. "Beethoven in der Gegenwart." *Neue Leipziger Zeitung* (March 25, 1927)

A brief note of regard on the centennial of the composer's death.

K52. "Führende Musiker der Zeit über Beethoven." *Neue Preussische (Kreuz-) Zeitung* (Berlin) (March 26, 1927): Sonderbeilage.

A brief note of regard on the centennial of the composer's death.

K53. "Der Opernstoff." *[Program: Staatstheater Kassel 1926/27]* (April 1927) 4 p.

An essay on the subject matter of opera.

a. ——. *[Program: Staatstheater Wiesbaden 1927/28]* no.3.

K54. "Der Operntext." *[Program: Staatstheater Kassel 1926/27]* (Spring 1927)

Discusses the writing of an opera libretto.

a. ——. *[Program: Staatstheater Wiesbaden 1927/28]* no.1.

b. "Von dem Operntext." *Das Theater* 8:20 (October 1927): 476-478.

K55. "Der Zeitgeist." *[Program: Staatstheater Kassel 1926/27]* (April 10, 1927): 2 p. between pp.4-5.

The "current trend" is invented by jealous people to discredit successful new art. In trying to coercively connect a work of art and the time in which it is created, one is bound to misunderstanding, which is proven by the poor judgement contemporaries have historically attributed to important art works of their time.

a. ——. In his *Zur Sprache gebracht.* (K707) (München: Albert Langen - Georg Müller, 1958): 23-24.

K56. "Brief des Dichterkomponisten an den Herausgeber." *Blätter des Hamburger Stadttheater 1926/27* no.15 (May 1927)
Autobiography prepared for a program.

a. "Autobiographische Skizze." *Blätter des Stadt-Theaters Mainz* 1:3 (1927): 3-5.

b. ——. *Sonderheft des Opernhauses Chemnitz* (October 1927)

c. ——. In *Ernst Krenek und seine Oper "Jonny spielt auf"* Sonderheft der *Oper von Heute*, Nachrichtenblätter der Universal Edition 1 (September 1927): 4-6.

d. ——. *Blätter der Staatsoper und der Städtischen Oper* (Berlin) 9:10 (December 1928): 1-3.

e. ——. *Freiburger Theaterblätter* (1928/29): 213.

K57. "Nachträgliches zum Zeitgeist." *[Program: Staatstheater Kassel 1926/27]* no.27 (May 1927)
Reflections on current trends.

K58. "Ueber den Geschmack." *[Program: Staatstheater Kassel 1926/27]* no.28 (May 1927)
Discusses good taste in music.

K59. "*Marlborough zieht in der Krieg.*" *Casseler Tageblatt* (May 6, 1927)
Discusses Marcel Archard's comedy for which Krenek supplied incidental music (op.52) in anticipation of its performance as a puppet play in Kassel.
Manuscripts: **A-Wst** 4 p.

K60. "Musikdramatiker und Sänger." *Der neue Weg* (Berlin) 56:10 (May 16, 1927)
A discussion of the relationship between the opera composer and the singer in performance.

K61. "Die Opernkomposition." *[Program: Staatstheater Kassel 1926/27]* (early Sum.1927) 4 p.
Reflections on the composing of opera.

a. ——. *[Program: Staatstheater Wiesbaden 1927/28]* no.4 or 5.

K62. "Kunst und Sport." *[Program: Staatstheater Kassel 1926/27]* no.29 (June 1927)
On the similarity of art and sports in the public's perceptions.

K63. "Zum Beschluss." *[Program: Staatstheater Kassel 1926/27]* no.30 (June 1927)
Krenek reflects on leaving Kassel for Wiesbaden.

K64. "'Neue Sachlichkeit' in der Musik." *i 10* (Amsterdam) 1:6 (June 1, 1927): 216-218.
The "New objectivity," a term which derives from the plastic arts, does not so much signify the beginning of a new epoch as it means the renewed application of simple, clear, and intelligible music in reaction to abstraction. In this sense, the term can only be applied to German-Middle-European music because abstraction has not been a strong element in "Roman-international" music (neo-Classical music).

K65. "Ueber Sinn und Zweck des Theaters." *Musikblätter des Anbruch* 9:7 (August-September 1927): 281-282.

K66. "Ueber die technische Ausführung meiner Oper *Jonny spielt auf.*" (Vienna: Universal Edition, August 1927) 7 p.

> Pamphlet. Scene by scene examination of the technical requirements of the opera. Date at end: Wien, August 7, 1927.

K67. "Von der Oper." *Ernst Krenek und seine Oper "Jonny spielt auf"* Sonderheft der *Oper von Heute,* Nachrichtenblätter der Universal Edition 1 (September 1927): 7-22.

> From the Universal Edition *Jahrbuch,* 1926 and 1927.

K68. "*Jonny spielt auf* und die Ausführenden." *[Program: Staatstheater Wiesbaden 1927/28]* (October 1927)

> An essay on the opera op.45 and its production.

a. ——. *Sonderheft des Opernhauses Chemnitz* (October 1927)

K69. "Bemerkungen zu meiner Oper *Jonny spielt auf.*" *Das Theater* 8:20 (October 1927): 474-476.

> Discusses the opera op.45 and its themes. Includes photos from several different productions.

K70. "Ernst Krenek über sich und sein Werk." *Blätter der Staatsoper und der Städtischen Oper* (Berlin) 8:4 (October 1927): 2-3.

> Autobiography prepared for the premiere of his opera *Jonny spielt auf* op.45. Picture opposite p.16.

K71. "Mechanisierung der Künste." *i 10* (Amsterdam) 1:10 (October 1927): 376-380.

> Just as painting is influenced by photography, modern music is influenced by mechanical instruments and jazz. Mechanical instruments are not meant to fundamentally change music principals, but to make interesting additions to music.

K72. "*Jonny spielt auf.*" *Blätter der Staatsoper und der Städtischen Oper* (Berlin) 8:4 (October 1927): 4-5.

> Synopsis of the opera op.45.

K73. "*Jonny spielt auf.*" In his *Im Zweifelsfalle.* (K924) (Wien: Europaverlag, 1984): 13-32.

> Lecture given at the Verein der Kunstfreunde in Kassel on October 31, 1927 and at the Kulturbund in Vienna on January 3, 1928 on the staging of the opera op.45, and including Krenek's opinion of its reviews and his intentions. The use of unfortunate terms, such as "jazz opera," "revue," and "operetta," and the characterization of scenes as "comical" or "serious" have led to a broad misunderstanding of the work. He intended to create a lively musical theater reflecting the artistic problems of the time, and as such the character Daniello incorporates the negative state of European art and the false relationship between music and the concert goer. On the other hand, the uncommunicative and solitary Max incorporates a truer and stronger character. Jazz elements are used as an expressive means rather than as a means of musical novelty. The danger in staging the opera is that too much technology on stage overwhelms the opera's concept; the opera is not meant to show the competition between technology and art. *See:* B554

Manuscripts: **A-Wst** typescript(19 p.)

K74. "Wer ich bin." *Neues Wiener Journal* (December 18, 1927)

Comments about himself in anticipation of the first Vienna performance of *Jonny spielt auf* op.45.

K75. "Bühnenwerk, Autor und Interpretation." *Neue Zürcher Zeitung* (December 19, 1927)

A discussion of the relationship between the dramatic creator and the interpreter.

-- 1928 --

K76. "Milhaud und das französische Musiktheater." *[Program: Staatstheater Wiesbaden 1927/28]* (1928)

Notes about the French composer.

K77. "Möglichkeiten der Oper." *Operntheater* [Program: Wiener Staatsoper] (February 4, 1928): 2-5.

Discusses the January 27, 1928 performance of *Jonny spielt auf* op.45 in Vienna.

K78. "Franz Schreker als Lehrer." *Musikblätter des Anbruch* 10:3/4 (March-April 1928): 109-117.

Comments by Krenek, Georg Schünemann, and others in honor of the fiftieth birthday of Franz Schreker.

K79. "Wege des Theaters." *Neue Schweizer Rundschau* 21:3 (March 1928): 235-240.

A discussion of his opera *Jonny spielt auf* op.45 as a direction for contemporary opera to follow.

K80. "Nach Redaktionsschluss eingegangen." *Die Scene* (Berlin) 18:5 (May 1928): 153.

Reaction with others, including Richard Strauss, Felix Weingartner, and Adolf Weissmann, in a symposium entitled "Kapellmeister und Opernregie" on the extent of involvement by the opera conductor in the opera's scenery and staging.

K81. "Meine drei Einakter." *Musikblätter des Anbruch* 10:5 (May 1928): 158-161.

A discussion of the plots of the three one-act operas, *Der Diktator* op.49, *Das geheime Königreich* op.50, and *Schwergewicht* op.55.

a. ——. *[Program: Staatstheater Wiesbaden 1927/28]* (May 6, 1928)

b. ——. *Schweizerische Musikzeitung und Sängerblatt* 68:15 (May 19, 1928): 196-197.

c. ——. *Blätter der Staatsoper und der Städtischen Oper* (Berlin) 9:10 (December 1928): 4-7.

Manuscripts: **A-Wst** typescript copy(5 p.)

K82. "Zur Entstehungsgeschichte der Trilogie *O Lacrymosa*." *Das Inselschiff* 9:3 (Sum.1928): 228-233.

Krenek discusses the origin of the op.48 song cycle. Rainer Maria Rilke sent the poems to Krenek suggesting that he set them; includes the poems and two letters from the poet.

a. ——. *Schweizerische Musikzeitung und Sängerblatt* 69:5 (March 1, 1929): 145-148.

b. ——. In *Rainer Maria Rilke, Stimmen der Freunde, Ein Gedächtnisbuch*, hrsg. von Gert Buchheit. (Freiburg: Urban, 1931): 155-161.

c. "Einkehr bei Rilke." In his *Zur Sprache gebracht.* (K707) (München: Albert Langen - Georg Müller, 1958): 31-34.

K83. "Stimme und Instrument." *Musikblätter des Anbruch* 10:9/10 (November-December 1928): 350-352.

General discussion of the use of voices with and in opposition to instruments.

a. ——. In *Jahrbuch 1929, Gesang* UE Nr.9642 (Wien: Universal Edition, 1929): 36-38.

K84. "Franz Schubert und wir." *Unpublished.*

A lecture given at the Buchhandlung Lechner, Vienna on November 13, 1928.

Manuscripts: **A-Wst** typescript (12 p.)

K85. *"Der weisse Neger." Frankfurter Zeitung Literaturblatt* 61:48 (November 25, 1928): 1.

Review of the book by James Weldon Johnson, translated by Elisabeth von Gans (Frankfurt: Frankfurter Societäts-Druckerei, 1928).

K86. "Franz Schubert und wir." In *Bericht über den internationalen Kongress für Schubertforschung, Wien 25. bis 29. November 1928* (Augsburg: Benno Filser Verlag, 1929): 69-76.

Lecture given at the Schubert-Kongress held in the Nationalbibliothek in Vienna. *See:* B554

-- 1929 --

K87. "Das Schubert-Jahr ist zu Ende." *Anbruch* 11:1 (January 1929): 11-15.

Krenek asks, "What can Franz Schubert's music teach us?" His life coincided with his eminent talent to a homogeneity. His "not wanting to be more than he was," and his roots in folk music did not induce him to search for new materials, but rather to use, in his characteristic way, what he found. As such, Schubert exemplifies the individual living culture, opposed to the sterile masses of humans living today.

a. "Schubert." In his *Zur Sprache gebracht.* (K707) (München: Albert Langen - Georg Müller, 1958): 35-41.

b. ——. In his *Im Zweifelsfalle.* (K924) (Wien: Europaverlag, 1984): 81-87.

K88. "Zu meinen Orchesterwerken, op.43a, 54, 58." *Pult und Taktstock* 6:1/2 (January-February 1929): 11-13.

Discusses his orchestral works, the Suite from *Der Triumph der Empfindsamkeit* op.43a, *Potpourri* op.54, and *Kleine Symphonie* op.58.

K89. "Zu Casellas Aufsatz *Scarlattiana.*" *Anbruch* 11:2 (February 1929): 79-81.

Review, written with G. F.Malipiero, of Alfredo Casella's neo-classic piano and orchestra work based on Scarlatti themes.

K90. "Französisches und deutsches Musikempfinden." *Anbruch* 11:2 (February 1929): 53-57.

A comparison of the differences between French and German attitudes towards music and between the place of music in each culture in an examination of superficiality versus depth in art. French character is more positivistic than the German, always interested in the state of perfection in the arts, while the German stays in the making of it. Altogether German culture has qualitatively and quantitatively more musical talent, but in the present state, not many individually spontaneous creators.

a. ——. *Schweizerische Musikpädagogische Blätter* 18:8/9 (1929): 114-116.

b. ——. In his *Zur Sprache gebracht.* (K707) (München: Albert Langen - Georg Müller, 1958): 42-48.

K91. "Karl Kraus und Offenbach." *Anbruch* 11:3 (March 1929): 135-136.

The Viennese writer Karl Kraus's interest in music was limited to his boundless enthusiasm for the operettas of Jacques Offenbach. *See:* B1332

a. ——. *Die Fackel* 31:806/809 (May 1929): 62-63.

b. ——. *Der Auftakt* (Prague) 10:9/10 (October 1930): 212-213.

K92. "Operette und Revue, eine Diagnose ihres Zustandes." *Anbruch* 11:3 (March 1929): 102-108.

A critical review of the development of the operetta. Burdened with "kitsch" (pseudo-serious borrowings from the genres of opera and drama) operetta has become a dull, bone-headed product. Jacques Offenbach's operettas were always a parody of life; now they are perceived to be an accumulation of platitudes. The musical revue was supposed to revive operetta, but it leads to a new genre, where plot is of little importance, is primitively constructed or even non-existent, and leads to a minimal artistic level. *See:* B554

a. "Operette und Revue." In his *Zur Sprache gebracht.* (K707) (München: Albert Langen - Georg Müller, 1958): 49-56.

K93. "Neue Formen der Oper." *Unpublished.*

A lecture given May 22, 1929.

Manuscripts: **A-Wst**.

K94. "Moderne Komponisten über die Gegenwartsmusik." *Der Wiener Tag* no.2298 (May 26, 1929): 20.

Brief comments by Krenek, Josef Matthias Hauer, Erwin Schulhoff, Egon Wellesz, and Ernst Toch in a symposium about the position of contemporary music in modern society.

K95. "Brief über *Zwingburg* an Schulz-Dornburg." *Der Scheinwerfer* (Essen) 2:18/19 (June 1929)

Discusses the production of the opera op.14.

K96. "Opernerfahrung." *Anbruch* 11:6 (June 1929): 233-237.

Operatic experience can only be obtained through active involvement. A discussion of the opera plot, the dramatic treatment of the plot, and its musical shaping. The singers are the main characters and must not be drowned in orchestral hypertrophy; music is accompaniment. Too much intensity and too much concentration of detail results in fatigue; the general flow of the main line must always be kept in mind. Wagner is a dangerous model; Mozart and Verdi, on the other hand, are unsurpassed in their handling of opera plots. *See:* B554

a. ——. *Blätter des Hessischen Landestheaters* no.18 (1929/30): 141-145.

b. ——. *Die Scene* (Berlin) 20:3 (March 1930): 65-68.

c. ——. *Blätter der Staatsoper und der Städtischen Oper* (Berlin) 10:22 (March 1930): 10-14.

   d. ——. In his *Zur Sprache gebracht*. (K707) (München: Albert Langen - Georg Müller, 1958): 57-63.

   e. ——. *Oper* (Städtische Bühnen, Frankfurt/Main) 2:4 (January 28, 1951) 4 p.

K97. "Freiheit und Technik: Improvisatorischer Stil." *Anbruch* 11:7/8 (July-August 1929): 286-289.

   Explains the meaning of freedom for the artistically active person; the means to exert that freedom lies in one's technique. The danger of technique is its tendency to dominate the act of creation instead of being its tool. The essence of technical ability is the exact realization of the musical idea. The act of improvisation is a specialized technique with maximum flexibility; its use results in the loss of structural complexity.

   a. "Fortschritt und Reaktion." *Die Scene* (Berlin) 21:6 (June 1931): 162-166.

   Extract published in the symposium "Zur Opernproduktion."

   b. "Freiheit und Technik: Improvisatorischer Stil." In *Briefwechsel*, von Theodor W. Adorno und Ernst Krenek. (K862) (Frankfurt am Main: Suhrkamp, 1974): 161-166.

K98. "Bericht über ein Marionettenspiel, op.52." *Die Scene* (Berlin) 19:9 (September 1929): 253-258.

   Description of the production of Marcel Archard's *Marlborough s'en va-t-en guerre* as a puppet play with Krenek's incidental music.

   a. "Bericht über ein Marionettenspiel." In his *Zur Sprache gebracht*. (K707) (München: Albert Langen - Georg Müller, 1958): 64-71.

   b. "A puppet play." In his *Exploring music*. (K817) (New York: October House, 1966): 11-18.

K99. "Ein paar Worte über Johann Strauss." *Die Oper, Blätter des Breslauer Stadttheaters* no.19 (1929/30): 292-294.

   The music of Johann Strauss Jr. is discussed in relationship to Viennese social and political life after 1848. It is due to Strauss's music that the waltz grew from a local, indigenous creation to an entertainment of universal currency. His "operettas are really only an opportunity to use this art of waltz-writing." Strauss differs from Offenbach in that the latter is a dramatist who "has the gift of making contemporary local types so transparent that you can see through the outer shell of absolutely flat, typically obvious reality to the most basic features of human behavior." *See:* B554

   a. ——. *Der Scheinwerfer* (Essen) 3:11 (February 1930): 3-6.

   b. ——. In his *Zur Sprache gebracht*. (K707) (München: Albert Langen - Georg Müller, 1958): 72-75.

   c. "A few words about Johann Strauss." In his *Exploring music*. (K817) (New York: October House, 1966): 19-22.

K100. "Neue Humanität und alte Sachlichkeit." *Neue Schweizer Rundschau* 24:4 (April 1931): 244-258.

   Lecture at the Verein der Studenten der deutschen Technischen Hochschule in Bruenn on December 1929 and in the Lesezirkel Hottingen in Zürich on November 11, 1930. "Our art-epoch differs from" earlier periods because neither the "limited circle" of cognoscenti nor "the living convention exists any longer. [Consequently,] attempts have been made to create an art, particularly an art of the musical theater, which will fit the enlarged society... I conceive of a work of art as the intellectual form of an emotional content...

'Objectivity' is a process but not something to express, and to this extent every art, however Romantic, is 'objective.'" His opera *Jonny spielt auf* is a poor example of the "new objectivity," for although new objects occur in it they do so only as objects surrounding present-day people, without proclaiming any positive attitude concerning them. *See:* B554

a. ——. In his *Zur Sprache gebracht.* (K707) (München: Albert Langen - Georg Müller, 1958): 105-120.

b. "New humanity and old objectivity." In his *Exploring music.* (K817) (New York: October House, 1966): 43-60.

c. "Neue Humanität und alte Sachlichkeit." *Frankfurter Zeitung* 75:855 (November 15, 1930)

   Printed in abbreviated form as notes to the lecture.

K101. "Soll Richard Wagner modern inszeniert werden?" *Der Wiener Tag* no.2478 (December 25, 1929): 21-22.

   Brief note in response to a questionnaire about modern productions of Richard Wagner's operas.

-- 1930 --

K102. "Der schaffende Musiker und die Technik der Gegenwart." In *Kunst und Technik,* hrsg. von Leo Kestenberg. (Berlin: Volksverband der Bücherfreunde, 1930): 141-155.

   Discusses three relationships between technology and the creative artist. Technique provides the reproduction of music, it influences the listener, and produces the artistic performance. Applications of automated or technological music lie in the realm of entertainment, in radio transmission or film presentations. Technique influences the qualitative judgement of the listener, and amateurism vanishes as technology helps everyone to be an average musician. Twelve-tone composition, as pure thinking and the formulation of music, conforms to technological innovation in music composition in general. While technology can hardly influence artistic creation it will be an increasing factor in music. *See:* B554

a. ——. In his *Im Zweifelsfalle.* (K924) (Wien: Europaverlag, 1984): 225-239.

b. "Aus neuerschienenen Büchern." *Zeitschrift für Musik* 98:1 (January 1931): 2 & 4.

   Excerpts from pp.152 and 154.

K103. "Zu Brechts Anmerkungen 'Zur Soziologie der Oper.'" *Unpublished.*
   Written in 1930. Reactions to Bertolt Brecht's observations on the sociology of opera.

Manuscripts: **A-Wst** typescript (3 p.)

K104. "Leben des Orest." *Anbruch* 12:1 (January 1930): 1-4.
   Lecture given on Leipzig Radio in January 1930 and in Mannheim on November 18, 1931. A description of the events surrounding the creation of the opera op.60 and a discussion of its plot.

a. ——. *Blätter der Staatsoper und der Städtischen Oper* (Berlin) 10:22 (March 1930): 1-4.

Manuscripts: **A-Wst** typescript (5 p.)

K105. "Von *Jonny* zu *Orest*." *Leipziger neueste Nachrichten* (January 11, 1930): 16.

Discusses the transition from a "naturalistic contemporary piece in which the whole technical magic of the present day is deployed, to venerable classical material from Greek mythology." The technical props of *Jonny spielt auf* op.45 "were merely the props necessary to present a drama growing out of the every-day life of the present... The duality of the world is presented without being brought to any crisis. [iI *Leben des Orest* op.60,] the ambivalence of the single individual" is presented. *Orest* presents "the bridge between Jonny and Max, instead of the gulf between them, as in *Jonny*."

a. ——. In his *Zur Sprache gebracht.* (K707) (München: Albert Langen - Georg Müller, 1958): 76-78.

b. ——. In his *Im Zweifelsfalle.* (K924) (Wien: Europaverlag, 1984): 33-35.

c. "From *Jonny* to *Orest*." In his *Exploring music.* (K817) (New York: October House, 1966): 23-25.

K106. "Pro domo." *Der Scheinwerfer* (Essen) 3:11 (February 1930): 12-13.

About himself, his music, and his literary works. *See:* B554, B692, B1527

a. ——. *Badische Landeszeitung* (1930?)

K107. "Der 'entlarvte' Orest." *Frankfurter Zeitung* 74:217 (March 22, 1930): 1-2.

Polemic against Bernhard Diebold's criticism of the Berlin performance of Krenek's opera *Leben des Orest* op.60, published as "Singende Tantaliden" (B250) in which he accused Krenek of lacking ideas and of being Wagnerian.

a. ——. In *Experiment Krolloper, 1927-1931*, von Hans Curjel. Studien zur Kunst des neunzehnten Jahrhunderts, Bd.7. (Münich: Prestel-Verlag, 1975): 284-286.

K108. "Banalitäten." *Der Querschnitt* 10:4 (April 1930): 237-238.

Krenek responds to the charge that his recent works are banal and discusses the question of what is banality in a defense of tonality. Picture opposite p.218. *See:* B554

K109. "Darius Milhaud." *Anbruch* 12:4/5 (April-May 1930): 135-140.

Milhaud's operas are reflections of the people and locale of Provence. He uses classical legend as though "it is a possession that must be conserved and must enter directly into present-day life as much as a newly created object. [Other operas] treat material which belongs absolutely to the present day as though it were timeless... Milhaud's technique follows two compositional principles – the tonally cadenced periods of tradition and a sort of heterophony tending towards polytonality."

a. "Darius Milhaud, der Mensch." *Die Musik* 23:8 (May 1931): 630-631.
   Summary of the *Anbruch* article.

b. "Darius Milhaud." In his *Zur Sprache gebracht.* (K707) (München: Albert Langen - Georg Müller, 1958): 84-90.

c. ——. In his *Im Zweifelsfalle.* (K924) (Wien: Europaverlag, 1984): 95-101.

d. ——. In his *Exploring music.* (K817) (New York: October House, 1966): 27-34.

e. "Milhaud." In *The Book of modern composers*, by David Ewen. (New York: Alfred A. Knoff, 1942): 187-193.
   Updated to 1939.

K110. "Zum Missgeschick einer Oper." *Der Scheinwerfer* (Essen) 3:14 (April 1930): 11.

Polemic under the pseudonym Ernst Holzhaus against Stahlburg's (pseudonym for Küpper) "Missgeschick einer Oper" in the March issue, pp.12-13.

K111. "Wagners Beziehungen zu Wien." *Frankfurter Zeitung Literaturblatt* 63:16 (April 20, 1930): 6.

Review of the book *Wagners Kampf und Sieg* by Max Morold, pseudonym for Max Millenkovich (Zurich: Amalthea Verlag, 1930).

K112. "Neue Opern: *Aus einem Totenhaus.*" *Frankfurter Zeitung* 74:296 (April 22, 1930): 1.

Positive review of the opera's first performance in the Brno Nationaltheater of Leoš January ʺ′aček's opera.

K113. "Die Stellung der Musik in der Kultur der Gegenwart." *Die Musikpflege* 1:2 (May 1930)

The main task of music and of the arts in general is to regain humanitarian emphasis in the thoughts of the people; it is the importance of spirit and mind versus pure animalistic pleasure-oriented life. Music today has many faces; its most prominent is its use for an immediate purpose such as entertainment or business, which itself is just a manifestation of an underlying psychological cultural aversion. According to Freud, uneasiness is culture. *See:* B554

a. ——. *National Zeitung* (Basel) (November 8, 1930)

b. ——. In his *Zur Sprache gebracht.* (K707) (München: Albert Langen - Georg Müller, 1958): 79-83.

K114. "Ueber *Gott in Frankreich?* von Friedrich Sieburg." *Der Scheinwerfer* (Essen) 3:17 (May 1930): 18-19.

Review of the book (Frankfurt: Frankfurter Societäts-Druckerei, 1929).

K115. "Bachs Passionen als Dramen." *Frankfurter Zeitung Literaturblatt* 63:18 (May 4, 1930): 13.

Review of the book *Bachs Passionen* by Max Eduard Liehburg (Zürich: Orell Füssli Verlag, 1930). A critical look at Liehburg's ideas on staging Bach's Passions.

K116. "Tonfilm, Opernfilm, Filmoper." *Frankfurter Zeitung* 74:380 (May 23, 1930): 1-2.

Skeptical reaction to the possibilities of opera on film. The problems are economics and aesthetics.

K117. "Fortschritt und Reaktion." *Anbruch* 12:6 (June 1930): 196-200.

A criticism of the labels "progressive" or "reactionary" used to characterize the musical materials used in a composition, and a defense of the use of tonality in contemporary music.

a. ——. In *Briefwechsel*, von Theodor W. Adorno und Ernst Krenek. (K862) (Frankfurt am Main: Suhrkamp, 1974): 181-186.

K118. "Sozialismus und Musik." *Frankfurter Zeitung Literaturblatt* 63:25 (June 22, 1930): 7.

Critical reaction to the naive approach presented in a speech by Walther Howard and published in *Vortrag für den Bund freier Musiklehreskräfte* (Beiln-Hermsdorf: Verlag für Kultur und Kunst, 1930).

K119. "Theater und Musik in Janáčeks *Aus einem Totenhaus*." *Theaterwelt* [Program: Städtischen Bühnen Düsseldorf] 6:13/14 (1930/31): 169-174.
   A discussion of the opera.
   a. ——. [*Program: Deutsche Oper Berlin*] (October 2, 1981): 11-14.

K120. "Komponieren als Beruf." *Die Musikpflege* 1:6 (September 1930)
   Composers in the early 1930's have little market for their music, other than the popular entertainment industry, and need to consider other occupations to support themselves financially. Because of the demands upon a composer to travel extensively, a job with some connection with music is needed, such as teacher, conductor, etc. *See:* B554
   a. ——. In *Festschrift der Deutsche Akademie für Musik und darstellende Kunst in Prag 1920-1930* (Prag, 1931): 32-37.
   b. ——. In his *Zur Sprache gebracht.* (K707) (München: Albert Langen - Georg Müller, 1958): 91-96.
   c. "Composing as a calling." In his *Exploring music.* (K817) (New York: October House, 1966): 35-41.

K121. "Revue der Musikinstrumente, V.Schlaginstrumente." *Frankfurter Zeitung* 75:713 (September 24, 1930): 1-2.
   General description of various percussion instruments. Part 5 in a series on musical instruments by various composers.
   a. "V.Schlaginstrumente." *Revue der Musikinstrumente; Sonderdruck der Frankfurter Zeitung* (1930): 14-16.

K122. "Probleme des Urheberrechts." *Frankfurter Zeitung* 75:806 (October 29, 1930): 1-2.
   Discusses a new copyright regulation and proposes that profits gained from entertainment music should be used to subsidize serious music.

K123. "Geist als Luxus." *Anbruch* 12:9/10 (November-December 1930): 272-273.
   Comments by Krenek decrying the decline of music culture. The fact that music publishers consider it a luxury to edit a string quartet leads him to an analysis of contemporary music sociology and music education. A reaction against the primitive understanding of the music public.

K124. "Arbeitsprobleme des Komponisten." *Frankfurter Zeitung* 75:918 (December 10, 1930): 1-2.
   Discussion about music and the current social situation with Theodor Wiesengrund Adorno broadcast on Frankfurter Sender, November 16th. In discussing musical materials, Krenek sees music solely as the summation of harmony, rhythm, and melody. Adorno goes beyond the naturalistic view, stating that the material is already preformed by history in the artist's mind. They both agree that the means of individual expression cannot be randomly chosen, but is anchored in the social reality of the present.
   a. "Arbeitsprobleme des Komponisten; Gespräch über Musik und soziale Situation." In *Briefwechsel*, von Theodor W. Adorno und Ernst Krenek. (K862) (Frankfurt am Main: Suhkamp, 1974): 187-193.
   b. ——. In *Musikalische Schriften*, von Theodor W.Adorno. Vol.6. Gesammelte Schriften, 19. (Frankfurt: Suhkamp, 1984): 433-439.

K125. "Bedenkliche Sparsamkeit." *Der Autor* (Berlin) 5:12 (December 1930): 4-5.

Reaction to a new policy in which authors receive less for their works from opera houses and theaters.

K126. "Soll ein Künstler publizistisch tätig sein?" *Frankfurter Zeitung* 75:929 (December 13, 1930): 1.

Discusses whether an artist should write for popular magazines, and concludes that there is a pedagogical obligation to do so. *See:* B554

a. ——. *Der Auftakt* (Prague) 14:1/2 (January-February 1934): 14-16.

b. ——. In his *Zur Sprache gebracht.* (K707) (München: Albert Langen - Georg Müller, 1958): 97-99.

K127. "Lernt Musik verstehen!" *Frankfurter Zeitung* 75:942 (December 18, 1930): 3.

Review of the book on applied music aesthetics *Angewandte Musikästhetik* by Hans Mersmann (Berlin: Max Hesse Verlag, 1930). Krenek recommends the book but criticizes the use of subjective terms.

K128. "Thema: Opernetat." *Frankfurter Zeitung* 75:955 (December 23, 1930): 1.

Krenek opposes budget cuts proposed for authors of operas and other theater pieces.

K129. "Musikzeitschriften." *Frankfurter Zeitung Literaturblatt* 63:53 (December 28, 1930): 4.

A review of the music periodicals *Anbruch, Melos, Die Musik, Die Musikpflege,* and *Musik und Gesellschaft.* Krenek concludes that there are too many journals for the market and that their small budgets cannot attract first class writers.

-- 1931 --

K130. "Fahrt ins Waldviertel." *Unpublished.*

Travel article written for the *Frankfurter Zeitung* in 1931.

Manuscripts: **A-Wst** Galley 1 p.

K131. "Wochenschau." *Frankfurter Zeitung* 75:3 (January 2, 1931): 1.

Satirical article criticizing the content of the news reels shown in movie theaters.

K132. "*Perichole,* der elfte Offenbach." *Frankfurter Zeitung* 75:23 (January 9, 1931): 1-2.

Review of the eleventh in a series of readings in Vienna of Jacques Offenbach's operettas by Karl Kraus. Soma Morgenstern reviewed the reading, Krenek reviewed the music.

a. "Zu Offenbach's *Perichole.*" *Die Tribüne* (Cologne) 5:6 (December 1, 1931): 125-128.

K133. "Aus Gründen der Kontrolle." *Frankfurter Zeitung* 75:50 (January 20, 1931): 1-2.

Ironic comments about rigid custom and hotel regulations encountered while traveling.

a. ——. In his *Gedanken unterwegs.* (K720) (München: Albert Langen - Georg Müller, 1959): 24-31.

b. ——. *Neues Wiener Tagblatt* (April 8, 1931)

K134. "Gesinnungsgenossen unter sich." *Anbruch* 13:2/3 (February-March 1931): 66-68.

Reaction to the reviews of his opera *Leben des Orest* op.60 by Fritz Stege "Wandlungen? Zeitstimmen zum Stilproblem" *Allgemeine Musikzeitung* 58:11 (March 13, 1931); Julius Korngold, "Vom Krankenbette der Neumusik." *Neue Freie Presse* (March 18, 1931); and Viktor Zuckerkandl *"Leben des Orest."* *Neue Freie Presse* (January 27, 1930). *See:* B1528

K135. "Von Musik etwas verstehen..." *Frankfurter Zeitung* 75:135 (February 20, 1931): 1.

Discusses why the public has difficulty understanding music, why program guides are poorly written, and how the public can be better guided to understand music. *See:* B554

a. ——. *Neue Leipziger Zeitung* (March 11, 1931): 5.

b. ——. *Die Musik* 25:2 (November 1932): 152-153.

Summary of the article which appeared in the *Neue Leipziger Zeitung*.

c. ——. *Der Auftakt* (Prague) 18:1 (January 1938): 1-4.

d. ——. In his *Zur Sprache gebracht.* (K707) (München: Albert Langen - Georg Müller, 1958): 100-104.

e. ——. *Philharmonische Blätter* (Berlin) no.1 (September 1980)

K136. "Musikzeitschriften; Paul Stefan schreibt uns, Ernst Krenek antwortet." *Frankfurter Zeitung Literaturblatt* 64:9 (March 1, 1931): 7.

Defense by Paul Stefan of the music periodical *Anbruch* in reaction to Krenek's criticism in "Musikzeitschriften," and Krenek's response.

K137. "Zur Frage des Textverstehens in der Oper." *Der Scheinwerfer* (Essen) 4:12 (March 1931): 12-13.

a. ——. *Neues Wiener Journal* (March 17, 1931)

b. ——. *Der Scheinwerfer 1927-1933*, hrsg. von Erhard Schütz und Jochen Vogt. (Essen, 1986): 250-252.

K138. "Nochmals: Gesinnungsgenossen unter sich." *Anbruch* 13:4 (April 1931): 95-97.

Answer to Viktor Zukerkandl's and Julius Korngold's "Zeitgenössisches" (B1528) response to his "Gesinnungsgenossen unter sich" (K134).

K139. "Von der Aufgabe, ein Oesterreicher zu sein." *Die Freyung* (Vienna) 2:2 (April 1931): 1-10.

The title "The task of being an Austrian" implies the admission of an Austrian cultural identity. Historically Austria has been formed by Slavonic and Roman influences rather than by German influences. German culture has historically served, for example through the poet Grillparzer, to strengthen unity in a multinational agglomeration. Instead of just thinking, pan-Germanic Austrians should work against the current degradation of Austrian culture, oppose a general resignation and tendency toward provinciality, and accept the role of keeping up with the heritage of cultural humanism, whose center has been Vienna, not Berlin.

a. ——. In his *Gedanken unterwegs.* (K720) (München: Albert Langen - Georg Müller, 1959): 13-23.

b. ——. In *Das grössere Oesterreich, geistiges und soziales Leben von 1880 bis zur Gegenwart*, hrsg. von Kristian Sotriffer. (Vienna: Edition Tusch, 1982): 15-19.

K140. "Zur heutigen Situation der Neuen Musik." In his *Im Zweifelsfalle.* (K924) (Wien: Europaverlag, 1984): 240-247.

Lecture on Radio Leipzig, April 17, 1931. Discusses how Krenek's generation of composers deals with the contemporary situation of new music. The problem of new music lies in its interpretation rather than in its "newness." The early twenties saw an abstract aesthetic revolt; after 1925 a sociological problem was recognized resulting in the introduction of jazz elements and making music more suitable to the mass taste. Art music, however, should only address the individual without social regards.

Manuscripts: **A-Wst**.

K141. "Künstliche Stimmen." *Die Musik* 23:8 (May 1931): 592-594.

Commentary on an experiment in which the image of a voice recorded onto motion picture soundtrack was magnified so that its component parts could be identified and new voices could be created by drawing directly on the film.

K142. "Generationsterrassen." *Frankfurter Zeitung Literaturblatt* 64:20 (May 17, 1931): 6-7.

Review of the novel *Etzel Andergast* by Jakob Wassermann (Berlin: S.Fischer, 1931).

K143. "Die Erben des Marschkönigs marschieren auf." *Anbruch* 13:5 (June-July 1931): 128-129.

A polemic against the decision by Wiener Radiosender to take off the radio a nationalist march, *Unter dem Doppeladler* by J. F. Wagner.

K144. "Meditation in der Morgendämmerung." *Frankfurter Zeitung* 75:475 (June 29, 1931): 1-2.

Reflections on the noise of a shoemaker's machine heard in the morning in Krenek's house.

a. ——. In his *Gedanken unterwegs.* (K720) (München: Albert Langen - Georg Müller, 1959): 32-35.

K145. "Ein Buch vom '... Leben!'" *Frankfurter Zeitung Literaturblatt* 64:27 (July 5, 1931): 11.

Review of the novel *Ich will leben!* by Peter Flamm, pseudonym for Eric Peter Mosse (Berlin: Verlag Reimar Hobbing, 1931).

K146. "Wiens geistige Situation." *Frankfurter Zeitung* 75:531 (July 19, 1931): 6.

Reflections on Vienna's cultural-intellectual life for the traveler, including a map with points of interest marked.

K147. "Zum Thema 'Musik und Gesellschaft'." *Frankfurter Zeitung* 76:584 (August 8, 1931): 1.

Reaction to Dr. Ernst Emsheimer's "Musik und Gesellschaft" published earlier. Includes Emsheimer's response to Krenek's comments. Krenek disputes Emsheimer's assertion that music practice and education should be ideologically directed to the masses.

K148. "Betrachtungen in den Alpen." *Frankfurter Zeitung* 76:600 (August 14, 1931): 1.

Observations while traveling through the Alps on nature, people, and technology, including an electric piano.

a. "Am Alpensüdrand bemerkt." In his *Gedanken unterwegs.* (K720) (München: Albert Langen - Georg Müller, 1959): 36-40.

K149. "Arbeiterlyrik." *Frankfurter Zeitung Literaturblatt* 64:35 (August 30, 1931): 9.

Review of an anthology of poetry by laborers, *Das proletarishe Schicksal* edited by Hans Muhle (Gotha: Leopold Klotz, 1930).

K150. "Im Wallis." *Frankfurter Zeitung* 76:648 (September 1, 1931): 1-2.

Travel report on a visit to a valley in southern Switzerland.

  a. ——. In his *Gedanken unterwegs.* (K720) (München: Albert Langen - Georg Müller, 1959): 41-47.

K151. "Micky-Mausefalle." *Frankfurter Zeitung* 76:659/660 (September 5, 1931): 3.

Critical remarks regarding cartoons shown before the main feature in motion picture theaters. While they were previously highly amusing, they have become barbaric and distasteful.

K152. "Das Goethe-Jahr steht uns bevor." *Frankfurter Zeitung* 76:688/689 (September 16, 1931): 1.

No author given. Discusses the phenomenon of celebrating a famous person's birth/death centenary in light of the Johann Wolfgang von Goethe centenary.

K153. "Aus Briefen eines österreichischen Freundes." *Frankfurter Zeitung* 76:691/692 (September 17, 1931): 3.

Excepts from three private letters containing travel essays reflecting the contemporary situation in Austria (Salzkammergut) and Germany (Kassel); the editor notes "the sender is unaware of their publication, but since he is well known, they are printed without restraint." The tone of the letters is depressive-aggressive, reflecting upon the old days of Austria and expressing fear at the presence of rising militarism and barbarism.

K154. "Ludwig Thomas *Erinnerungen.*" *Frankfurter Zeitung Literaturblatt* 64:40 (October 4, 1931): 7.

Brief review of a collection of memoirs by the writer (München: Albert Langen, 1931).

K155. "Arzt und Mörder." *Frankfurter Zeitung Literaturblatt* 64:42 (October 18, 1931): 7.

Review of the novel *Georg Letham* by Ernst Weiss (Wien: Paul Zsolnay Verlag, 1931).

K156. "Die Erneuerung Offenbachs durch Karl Kraus." *Theaterwelt* [Program: Städtischen Bühnen Düsseldorf] 7:3 (October 30 1931): 37-39.

The editions and performances by Karl Kraus freshened up the operettas by Jacques Offenbach.

  a. ——. *Die Fackel* 33:864/867 (December 1931): 14-16.

  b. ——. *Bühnen der Stadt Köln,* 1958.

K157. "Ein philiströser Zigeuner." *Frankfurter Zeitung Literaturblatt* 64:44 (November 1, 1931): 7.

Review of the book for young people *Zigeunerfahrt* by Ernst Kromer (Köln: J. P.Bachem, 1931).

K158. "Forderung auch an diese Zeit: Freiheit des menschlichen Geistes." *Anbruch* 14:1 (January 1932): 1-4.

A lecture given in Mannheim on November 17, 1931. Present day art is strongly affected by the political and social life of society, and the artist must remain free. "Spiritual freedom in the widest sense, dignity and worth rooted in religion, is only graciously accorded to separate individuals... Even in the severest crisis the individual responsibility of a man remains fully intact, and every moment he has to choose between better and worse."

a. ——. *Der Scheinwerfer* (Essen) 5:12 (March 1932): 8-11.

b. ——. *Der Scheinwerfer 1927-1933*, hrsg. von Erhard Schütz und Jochen Vogt. (Essen, 1986): 315-319.

c. "Freiheit des menschlichen Geistes." In his *Zur Sprache gebracht.* (K707) (München: Albert Langen - Georg Müller, 1958): 121-126.

d. "The freedom of the human spirit." In his *Exploring music.* (K817) (New York: October House, 1966): 61-67.

Manuscripts: **A-Wst** German typescript (14 p.)

K159. "Arme Musikwissenschaft?" *Frankfurter Zeitung Literaturblatt* 64:48 (November 29, 1931): 5.

Review of the book *Geist und Stoff der Operndichtung* by Max Kraussold (Wien: Ed. Strache Verlag, 1931), disagreeing with its narrow view of opera libretti, and especially its hostile and arrogant attitude toward contemporary music, including that of Igor Stravinsky.

K160. "Gibt es noch eine Universalität." *Frankfurter Zeitung* 76:909 (December 6, 1931): 6.

Response with Ernst Bloch and others to a question in a symposium on the universality of music. Krenek states that "the humanity which we anticipate is a question of spirit."

K161. "Wie der Stadtfrack uns Skiläufer sieht." *Frankfurter Zeitung* 76:909 (December 6, 1931): 7.

Humorous observations on skiers published in the newspaper's travel section.

a. ——. In his *Gedanken unterwegs.* (K720) (München: Albert Langen - Georg Müller, 1959): 48-50.

K162. "*Rundfunk und Musikpflege.*" *Frankfurter Zeitung Literaturblatt* 64:51 (December 20, 1931): 4.

Review of the book by Alfred Szendrei, pseudonym for Alfred Sendrey, about music broadcast on the radio (Leipzig: Kistner und Siegel, 1931).

K163. "Moderne Märchen." *Frankfurter Zeitung Literaturblatt* 64:51 (December 20, 1931): 9.

Review of the book of strange fairy-tales for boys *Die Pforte, Märchen und Sinngebilde* by Hans Boeglin. (Berlin: Verlag Die Runde, 1931).

-- 1932 --

K164. "Rechtfertigung." *23* no.1 (January 1932): 1-2.

Introduction to the new journal edited by Krenek, Alban Berg, Rudolf Ploderer, and Willi Reich. The objective will be to correct misstatements which appeared in the press; therefore, the title of the journal is derived from the number of the paragraph in the Austrian press law which one can call upon for the correction of newspaper articles.

K165. "...... gebeugten Hauptes ...." *23* no.1 (January 1932): 8.

Questions in reaction to a review by Julius Korngold in the *Neuen Freien*

Presse addressed to the conductor Arnold Rosé on his performance of Arthur Honegger's *Pacific 231*.

K166. "Humor des Auslandes." 23 no.1 (January 1932): 9.

> Reaction to an article by "O. K." in the *Neuen Wiener Journal* in honor of Wilhelm Kienzl's 75th birthday in Bern.

K167. "Schön ist die Welt." 23 no.1 (January 1932): 10-11.

> Reaction to an inane and superficial article which appeared in *Musikleben* about the Wiener Lehrer-a capella-Chor.

K168. "Liebe Kinder!" 23 no.1 (January 1932): 13-14.

> Signed "Onkel Jonathan" [not by Ploderer as assigned by W.Reich in the index to the reprint of 23.] Discussion of objectivity and emotion in music in reaction to an article in the *Neuen Freien Presse* by "O. K."

K169. "Zur Geschäftsordnung." 23 no.1 (January 1932): 16.

> Editorial discussion of the volume's contents; with Berg and Ploderer.

K170. "Musikalische Mobilmachung?" *Frankfurter Zeitung* 76:9/11 (January 5, 1932): 3.

> Review of the book *Grundfragen der Schulmusik* edited by Hans Joachim Moser (Leipzig: B. G. Teubner, 1931). Krenek criticizes the author, who advocates a radical reform of high school pedagogy, for longing for an homogeneous people's music culture. Krenek also criticizes the author for preferring a minimal music culture for all to an elitist music for a few.

K171. "Reichtum des Geistes." *Frankfurter Zeitung Literaturblatt* 65:2 (January 10, 1932): 5.

> Review of the collection of four novels published under the title *Nach dem Feuerwerk* by Aldous Huxley in German translation by Herberth E.Herlitschka (Leipzig: Insel-Verlag, 1931).

K172. "Ein merkwürdiger Tierfreund." *Frankfurter Zeitung Literaturblatt* 65:3 (January 17, 1932): 5.

> Review of the book *Freunde aus aller Welt* by Felix Salten (Berlin: P.Zsolnay, 1931).

K173. "Peinliche Memoiren." *Frankfurter Zeitung Literaturblatt* 65:5 (January 31, 1932): 6.

> Review of the book *Tage der Kindheit* by Waldemar Bonsels (Berlin: Ullstein, 1931).

K174. "Grenzen gesinnungsmässiger Passivität." *Frankfurter Zeitung Literaturblatt* 65:6 (February 7, 1932): 5.

> Review of the novel *Die Untat* by Hans Sochaczewer, pseudonym of José Orabuena (Berlin: G.Kiepenheuer, 1931).

K175. "Fröhliche Barbarei." *Frankfurter Zeitung Literaturblatt* 65:7 (February 14, 1932): 8.

> Review of the novel *Mehlreisende Frieda Geier* by Marieluise Fleisser (Berlin: Kiepenheuer, 1931).

K176. "Was es im Tonfilm immer noch gibt." *Frankfurter Zeitung* 76:135/136 (February 20, 1932): 1.

> Review of the film *Wenn ein altes Wiener Lied durch den jungen Frühling zieht.* Ironic, scathing comments on a film whose theme "is a loss of character as well

as of content." Krenek bemoans the artistic level of sound film in general and claims that there hasn't been any trace of artistic responsibility in the medium.

K177. "Erstes Echo." *23* no.2 (February 23, 1932): 1-2.

Editorial restatement of the aims of the journal; with Ploderer and Reich.

K178. "Was der 'Tag' uns zuträgt." *23* no.2 (February 23, 1932): 9-10.

Reaction to the music programming on Viennese Radio which is mostly light operetta.

K179. "Seid verschlungen, Millionen!" *23* no.2 (February 23, 1932): 11-13.

Reaction to Emmerich Kálmán's statements on emotion in music presented in the *Neuen Wiener Tagblatt*.

K180. "Oesterreichischer Prohibitionismus." *23* no.2 (February 23, 1932): 13.

Brief correction to the report on the Internationale Gesellschaft für neue Musik festival which appeared in *Tag* noting that Hans Jelinek, Ernst Krenek, Julius Schloss, and Leopold Spinner also represented Austria.

K181. "Hingegen: Oesterreichischer Annexionismus." *23* no.2 (February 23, 1932): 13-14.

Corrects the erroneous attribution given during a radio concert of Austrian citizenship to Paul Hindemith.

K182. "Aber auch dieses." *23* no.2 (February 23, 1932): 14.

Brief article ridiculing the conductor Karl Alwin and his comments as reported by O. K. in the *Neuen Wiener Journal*.

K183. "Schulisch-Funkisches." *Frankfurter Zeitung* 76:164/165 (March 2, 1932): 1-2.

Ironic reaction to a report broadcast about a German pedagogic experiment. Krenek characterizes an eighth-year High School class as nonsensical, pretentious, and pseudo-pedagogic.

K184. "Von der unzulänglichen Wirklichkeit." *Frankfurter Zeitung Literaturblatt* 65:10 (March 6, 1932): 5.

Review of the book of sketches and novelettes *Männer machen Fehler* by Ulrich Becher (Berlin: E.Rowohlt, 1932).

K185. "Eichendorff und Liliencron von Gottes Gnaden, in einer Person." *23* no.3 (March 23, 1932): 10-12.

Discussion of war poetry and reminiscences of World War I by Eichendorff and Detlev von Liliencron.

K186. "Bundesweinkost." *Frankfurter Zeitung* 76:224/225 (March 24, 1932): 1.

Poetic portrayal of the Viennese food and delicatessen fair which included a giant wine tasting hall surrounded by a large amusement park.

   a. "Vor mir die Sintflut." In his *Gedanken unterwegs.* (K720) (München: Albert Langen - Georg Müller, 1959): 51-54.

K187. "Das fortgesetzte Totenmahl (Haydn-Jubiläum)." *Anbruch* 14:4 (April-May 1932): 76-78.

On the excessive publicity given to Joseph Haydn on his centenary. "This kind of publicity can say nothing valid about a man like Haydn [since] it is the press's job to demonstrate that all our cultural heritage is common property." *See:* B554

a. "Das fortgesetzte Totenmahl." In his *Zur Sprache gebracht.* (K707) (München: Albert Langen - Georg Müller, 1958): 127-129.

b. "The prolonged funeral banquet." In his *Exploring music.* (K817) (New York: October House, 1966): 69-72.

K188. "Die Bombe ins Goethejahr." *Frankfurter Zeitung Literaturblatt* 65:13 (April 3, 1932): 5.

Review of the anti-Nazi/anti-Marxist pamphlet *Kopfschüsse* (Frankfurt: Bücherstube Harau, 1932). The named authors, Viktor Grosshammer, Kuno von Uachitta, and Karlchen Marx, are pseudonyms.

K189. "Verkehrte Welt." *Frankfurter Zeitung Literaturblatt* 65:14 (April 10, 1932): 5.

Review of the Utopian novel *Die Revolution der Reichen* by Martin Maurice translated from the French by Paul Amann (Wien: P.Zsolnay, 1932), which depicts a society with values opposite to reality. The rich want to be poor and consumer goods are in abundance.

K190. "Zwei Seelen wohnen, ach! in seiner Brust." 23 no.4 (May 1, 1932): 5-8.

A critical look at the strange musical criticism of Dr. Joseph Marx in the *Neuen Wiener Journal* exemplified by a review of a concert of Richard Strauss's music. Contradictions are highlighted by rearranging the article to present them in two columns.

K191. "Die Rattenfänger." 23 no.4 (May 1, 1932): 10-13.

Reactions to the proposal in the "Young People's Section" of the *Neuen Wiener Presse* to present Johann Sebastian Bach and Ludwig van Beethoven as gods for young students.

K192. "Ein kurzer Blick ins *Musikleben.*" 23 no.4 (May 1, 1932): 14-15.

A montage of statements from reviews characterizing performances.

K193. "Zur Situation der Oper." *Frankfurter Zeitung* 76:369/370 (May 20, 1932): 1-2.

Shortened from the lecture "Interpretationsstil der neuen Oper," given at the Musikstudio and Radio Frankfurt, February 28, 1932. Discusses what contemporary opera stands for, what the relationships are between text and music, what the opera conveys to the listener, discusses Bertold Brecht's aesthetics and philosophy and his text for Kurt Weill's opera *Mahagonny*, deplores a tendency to place propaganda and pedagogy ahead of musical values, and discusses the lack of humane qualities in contemporary opera.

a. ——. *Der Auftakt* (Prague) 12:5/6 (May/June 1932): 131-137.

b. "Fragen des Opernstils." *Die Bühne* (Vienna) no.365 (December 1, 1933): 30-31.

c. "Problemi di stile nell' opera." *La Rassegna Musicale* 7:3 (May/June 1934): 199-202.

d. "Zur Situation der Oper." In his *Zur Sprache gebracht.* (K707) (München: Albert Langen - Georg Müller, 1958): 130-138.

Manuscripts: **A-Wst** .

K194. "Ernst Krenek: *Thema und 13 Variationen für Orchester, op.69.*" *Zeitschrift für Musik* 99:6 (June 1932): 489-491.

A brief autobiography and analysis written for the Sixty-second Deutsches Tonkünstlerfest des Allgemeinen Deutschen Musikvereins held June 10-14, 1932 in Zürich. Picture opposite p.516.

K195. "Ein dummer Herr." *Frankfurter Zeitung Literaturblatt* 65:24 (June 12, 1932): 5.

A sarcastic review of the novella *Ave Eva* by Hanns Johst (München: Albert Langen, 1932) and its trivial character.

K196. "Legendenhafte Erzählungen." *Frankfurter Zeitung Literaturblatt* 65:26 (June 26, 1932): 7.

Review of the collection of short stories about the occult *Das Opfertier* by Albrecht Schaeffer (Leipzig: Insel Verlag, 1931).

K197. "Der Verwesung lieber als der Freiheit." *23* no.5 (July 1, 1932): 2-9.

Commentary on a dispute in the Viennese press between the critics Julius Korngold and Heinrich Kralik concerning the scenes with Charles V and the auto-da-fe in Giuseppe Verdi's opera *Don Carlos*. The argument concentrates on Verdi and Schiller and involves the entire literary community including Franz Werfel.

K198. "Woher das nur sein mag?" *23* no.5 (July 1, 1932): 18.

A montage of statements from reviews of concerts noting that they only give names and say nothing about the music; consequently they are insignificant.

K199. "Wolkenkitsch." *Frankfurter Zeitung Literaturblatt* 65:27 (July 3, 1932): 5.

Negative review of an adventure book concerning a trip on a Zeppelin *Ziel in den Wolken* by Balder Olden, (Berlin: Universitas Verlag, 1932). Krenek denounces the abundance of "schmaltz."

K200. "Alter Mann, junge Frau." *Frankfurter Zeitung Literaturblatt* 65:30 (July 24, 1932): 5.

Review of the book, a psycho-drama between an old man and a young woman, *Narrenparadies* by Leon Schalit (Berlin: P.Zsolnay Verlag, 1932).

K201. "Ausgeburten der Hundstage." *23* no.6 (October 1932): 10-13.

Response to being branded a Wagnerian romantic.

K202. "Ein preisgekrönter Meister." *23* no.6 (October 1932): 14-16.

Discussion of the organist Louis Dité characterized by the *Neuen Wiener Journal* as a prize-winning Austrian composer.

K203. "Wirklichkeitsgefühl." *Anbruch* 14:8 (October 1932): 156-159.

An analysis of Swiss culture finding its roots more realistic and less abstract than the Austro-German tradition, strongly influenced by the balanced Franco-Italian neighboring cultures, and inspired by the natural scenery. Exponents of Swiss culture can be found in the composer Othmar Schoeck and the writers Gottfried Keller and Jakob Burckhard.

a. "Versuch einer Analyse schweizerischen Geistes." In his *Gedanken unterwegs.* (K720) (München: Albert Langen - Georg Müller, 1959): 55-60.

K204. "Das neue Weltbild der Musik." *Arbeiter Zeitung* (Vienna) (November 15, 1932): 10.

Lecture given in the Sozialdemokratischen Kunststelle in Vienna on November 3, 1932.

Manuscripts: **A-Wst** 16 p.

K205. "Tschechische Erzähler." *Frankfurter Zeitung Literaturblatt* 65:46 (November 13, 1932): 5.

Review of *Dreissig tschechische Erzähler* edited by Anna Auřednícková. (Darmstadt: Darmstädter Verlag, 1932).

K206. "Antwort an Paul Bekker." *Frankfurter Zeitung* 77:880/881 (November 25, 1932): 1-2.

Response to Bekker's "Briefe an Ernst Krenek" (B88). Krenek defends himself against the criticism that his opera *Jonny spielt auf* op.45 was a superficial work, and asserts that his intentions were to illuminate a particular situation in a new light. He also asserts that opera must be more than musical entertainment and that its subject is very important.

K207. "Ueber Sinn und Schicksal der neuen Musikpädagogik." *Die Musikpflege* 3:9 (December 1932): 356-359.

The original purpose of the recent music education reformation was to provide a broad societal base for art music, which had become increasingly isolated. This trend has recently been opposed, the intellectual basis of music has been attacked, and music education is moving in the direction of simplicity, ignoring new music. Music education has developed into the cultivation of amateur music, played by amateurs for amateurs, thereby excluding art music. This new simplicity is hostile towards twelve-tone music and must necessarily result in a lowering of musical taste and sensibility. *See:* B554

a. ——. *Der Auftakt* (Prague) 16:3/4 (1936): 48-51.

b. ——. In his *Zur Sprache gebracht.* (K707) (München: Albert Langen - Georg Müller, 1958): 139-143.

c. ——. In his *Im Zweifelsfalle.* (K924) (Wien: Europaverlag, 1984): 248-252.

K208. "Zu meinem Liederzyklus *Gesänge des späten Jahres.*" *Unpublished.*

Lecture broadcast December 2, 1932 about op.71.

Manuscripts: **A-Wst** typescript (2 p.)

K209. "*Wir von der Oper.*" *Frankfurter Zeitung* 77:931/932 (December 14, 1932): 2.

Review of a collection of photographs of opera personalities edited by Walter Firner (Münichen: F.Bruckmann, 1932). Krenek is critical of the opera star cult and includes ironical citations.

K210. "Das nachgelassene Roman-Fragment Hofmannsthals." *Frankfurter Zeitung* 77:937/938 (December 16, 1932): 1-2.

Review of the novel fragment *Andreas, oder die Vereinigten* by Hugo von Hofmannsthal (Berlin: S.Fischer Verlag, 1932). Krenek lauds the typical Austrian character of the novel, and calls it a continuation of Goethe's classicism which seeks the essential in seemingly trivial occurrences.

K211. "Ein Briefwechsel." *23* no.7 (December 23, 1932): 10-17.

A letter to the editors of *23* from a reader, Dr. Hans W. Heinsheimer an editor of Universal Edition (p.10-12), with a response (p.12-17) by Krenek for the editors. Heinsheimer accuses the journal of indulging in uninteresting local warfare rather than fighting for causes of more than regional importance. Krenek defends and justifies the editorial direction of the journal saying that the small events which it attacks bear the seeds that lead to the global condition.

-- 1933 --

K212. "Altes und neues China." *Frankfurter Zeitung Literaturblatt* 66:7 (February 12, 1933): 5.

Review of the book on China *Yung Fong-ying* by Joseph Maria Frank (Berlin: Sieben Stäbe Verlag, 1932).

K213. "Was sollte Musikkritik leisten?" *23* no.8/9 (February 23, 1933): 1-6.

Criticism "which makes any claim to validity should steer clear of purely atmospheric mood-reports and concentrate on examining the music... What is wanted is analysis rather than value-judgements... Particularly at the present time, when basic changes are occurring in the organization of musical material, musical criticism ought to keep particularly strictly and carefully to these real manifestations of music and try harder than ever to derive its critical standards from the immanent laws within the material itself." *See:* B554

a. ——. *Forum* 4:48 (December 1947): 450-451.

b. ——. *Melos* 25:11 (November 1958): 349-352.

c. ——. *Das Orchester* 6:12 (December 1958): 332-335.

d. ——. In his *Zur Sprache gebracht.* (K707) (München: Albert Langen - Georg Müller, 1958): 144-148.

e. "What should music criticism do?" In his *Exploring music.* (K817) (New York: October House, 1966): 73-77.

f. "Hvad kan man kraeve af musikkritik?" *Dansk Musiktidsskrift* 41:3 (1966): 73-75.

K214. "Die 'braven und vollständig korrekten' Methoden." *23* no.8/9 (February 23, 1933): 8-10.

Corrections to a translation published in an article in *Musikleben*, volume 23, number 7, on a manifesto written by a group of Italian composers opposing the trend of new music. Krenek stresses that the translation is willfully false and polemical, and was derived from *Corriere de la Serra.*

K215. "Teufelsküche der Prominenz." *23* no.8/9 (February 23, 1933): 15-18.

Humorous reaction to an article in the *Neuen Wiener Journal* featuring recipes of prominent musicians.

K216. "Als Nachspeise." *23* no.8/9 (February 23, 1933): 18.

Humorous suggestions for deserts prepared by prominent musicians.

K217. "Roman eines Physikers." *Frankfurter Zeitung Literaturblatt* 66:12 (March 19, 1933): 5.

Review of a book *Der göttliche Ruf* by Ludwig Finckh (Stuttgart: Deutsche Verlags-Anstalt, 1932)

K218. "Musik und Mathematik." *Frankfurter Zeitung* 77:271/272 (April 11, 1933): 1.

Discusses various types of twelve-tone rows and their use, including all-interval rows.

a. ——. *Der Auftakt* (Prague) 13:9/10 (October 1933): 125.

K219. "Der Sachs ist ja da." *23* no.10 (May 15, 1933): 16-17.

Reflections on an article in the *Neuen Wiener Tagblatt* by Carl Lafite about the musician Rudolf Nilius's fiftieth birthday and his claim to fame.

K220. "Italien heute." *Anbruch* 15:6/7 (June-July 1933): 73-76.

Discusses the First International Music Congress held in Florence in the Spring of 1933.

K221. "Mein neues Bühnenwerk." *Neues Wiener Tagblatt* (June 18, 1933): 14.

A discussion of his twelve-tone opera *Karl V.* op.73.

K222. "Zu einigen Thesen des Herrn Dr. Goebbels." *23* no.11/12 (June 30, 1933): 1-6.

A discussion of Nazi Germany's and Dr. Goebbels's artistic philosophies in relation to a request by Wilhelm Furtwängler to allow artists like Bruno Walter and Otto Klemperer to perform in the newly formed Nazi Germany. Krenek states there is no Germanic racially superior music, that atonal music is not anti-Germanic, and that the exponents of the new art act in a primitive pseudo-scientific Darwinism.

K223. "Der Fall Artur Schnabel." *23* no.11/12 (June 30,1933): 7-8.

Laudatory article about the pianist, critical of the mediocrity of Austrian authorities who consistently fail to recognize his eminence in disregard of his world-wide fame and respect.

K224. "Das Wiener Konzertorchester." *23* no.11/12 (June 30, 1933): 11-13.

Admonitions to an orchestra, Das Wiener Konzertorchester formed in 1932 and dedicated to new music. Only superior quality will insure the orchestra's success, and amateurism and self-indulgence must be avoided. The orchestra needs a regular leader with authority.

K225. "Aus dem Schlafcoupé eines Bearbeiters." *23* no.11/12 (June 30,1933): 24-26.

An ironic polemic against Erich Wolfgang Korngold who complained about cuts and arrangements made in his opera *Tote Stadt* in its New York production and yet does the same kind of editing and reinstrumentation to Jacques Offenbach's *A night in Venice.*

K226. "Das lederne Wiener Herz." *23* no.11/12 (June 30, 1933): 27-29.

Attack on an article by Raoul Auernheimer, "Das Herz von Wien," in *Neue Freie Presse* which satirizes the concert halls of Berlin and Vienna in the persons of fictional business men of the leather industry.

K227. "Oesterreichische Phänomene." *23* no.11/12 (June 30, 1933): 29-30.

Satirical reactions to the reports in *Neuen Wiener Journal* of a four-year-old child's hymn to the Zeppelin and the *Neuen Wiener Tagblatt* of a concert by a woman contra bass virtuoso, soprano, and pianist.

K228. "Lesen auf Reisen." *Frankfurter Zeitung* 77:485 (July 2,1933): 8.

A brief survey of travel books.

   a. "Was soll man auf Reisen lesen?" In his *Gedanken unterwegs.* (K720) (München: Albert Langen - Georg Müller, 1959): 61-62.

K229. "Studien zu meinem Bühnenwerk *Karl V.*" *Musik-Konzepte* 39/40 (October 1984): 20-34.

A detailed survey of the historical events surrounding the life of emperor Karl V. with a discussion of their inclusion in his opera. Includes a bibliography of sources.

Manuscripts: **A-Wst** typescript (15 p.) + 2 p.

Written in August 1933.

K230. "Aldous Huxley *Welt - wohin?*" *Die Tatwelt* 9:3 (October 1933): 155-158.
Review of the book.

K231. "Ernst Krenek über seine Oper *Kaiser Karl V.*" *Die Stunde* (Vienna) (October 28 1933)

K232. "Henri Sauguet; Zur geistigen Haltung jüngerer französischer Musik." *Anbruch* 15:9/10 (November-December 1933): 137-140.
Discusses the musical style and influence of Sauget's works since 1922, and especially discusses the opera *Le plumet du colonel* composed in 1924.

K233. "Eine Kleinigkeit vergessen." *23* no.13 (November 1, 1933): 8-10.
Reaction to Bronislau Huberman's letter to Wilhelm Furtwängler in which Huberman declines to perform in Nazi Germany because of the firing of artists based upon their Jewish race or political orientation. The article states that not only interpreters, but especially contemporary composers and important new music, has been strangled in a "cultural catastrophe."

K234. "Der Wiener Verdi." *23* no.13 (November 1, 1933): 17-18.
Humorous article on the relationship between Edmund Eysler, allegedly called the "Verdi of Vienna" by Pietro Mascagni, and his biographer, Kurt Ewald, who attempted to extract uncomfortable information from Eysler.

K235. "Eine begrüssenswerte Erfindung." *23* no.13 (November 1, 1933): 18-19.
Caustic reaction to a brochure by Professor Karl Klein which suggested the use of autohypnosis as a means for instrumentalists to practice music without actually producing sound.

K236. "Ein Dokument abendländischen Empfindens." *Frankfurter Zeitung Literaturblatt* 66:48 (November 26 1933): 7-8.
Review of the book *Mit den Augen des Westens* by Joseph Conrad (Berlin: S.Fischer Verlag, 1933).

K237. "Zivilisierte Magie." *Vossische Zeitung* (November 26, 1933): 31.
Review of the book *Die Geschichten Jaakobs* by Thomas Mann (Berlin: S.Fischer, 1933).

Manuscripts: **A-Wst** typescript ([3] p.)

K238. "Musik im Tonfilm." *Neue Zürcher Zeitung* 154:2267 (December 13, 1933)

a. ——. *Neues Wiener Tagblatt* (December 24, 1933)

K239. "Zerfallendes Imperium." *Vossische Zeitung* (December 24, 1933): 31.
Review of the history book *Paul III, order die geistliche Gegenreformation* by H. W. Edwards (Leipzig: Jakob Hegner, 1933).

K240. "*Karl V.*" *Vossische Zeitung* (December 31, 1933): 25-26.
A synopsis of the opera, including the beginning of the text.

-- 1934 --

K241. "Fortschritt und Reaktion." *Musik-Konzepte* 39/40 (October 1984): 3-13.
Written 1934-1936. A discussion of cultural and political progressive and reactionary tendencies within a sociological framework. The political system influences the cultural shape of a society; for example in a socialist system music, and art in general, is part of the propaganda machine. What has been denounced as "bourgeois decadence" is in reality the core of Western thinking

which was brought about in a liberal, enlightened climate which is the prerequisite for the great masterworks of absolute music.

Manuscripts: **A-Wst** 7 p.

K242. "Venetianische Nacht." *Unpublished.*
Written in 1934.

Manuscripts: **A-Wst** typescript (5 p.)

K243. "Ein Radio-Erlebnis." *Der Querschnitt* 14:1 (January 1934): 33-34.
Impressions of listening to a radio broadcast of Beethoven's *String quartet in C-sharp minor* op.131 while dining in a somber restaurant in a spa.

a. "Lob des Radios." In his *Gedanken unterwegs.* (K720) (München: Albert Langen - Georg Müller, 1959): 63-65.

K244. "Oesterreich." *Anbruch* 16:1/2 (January-February 1934): 1-2.
Sermon-like article on the mission of the Austrian presented as an introduction to an issue on music in Austria. During the Hapsburg years it was up to Austria to maintain the supranational idea of the "empire," based upon humanistic values within a Christian society. Austrian culture is based upon those values; conservatism means to look back to these humanistic values.

a. ——. In his *Zur Sprache gebracht.* (K707) (München: Albert Langen - Georg Müller, 1958): 153-155.

K245. "Schweizerische Musik von aussen gesehen." *Neue Schweizer Rundschau* N.F.1:9 (January 1934): 540-545.
The national characteristics of the Swiss are the basis for a discussion of their (especially Germanic Swiss) music in general and the individual music of Othmar Schoeck in particular.

K246. "Das Nationale und die Kunst." *Neue Zürcher Zeitung* 155:29 (January 7, 1934)
It is the work of art's "autonomous greatness which first gives concrete substance to the concept of a national mentality." The quality of art is universal and not dictated by nationalism.

a. ——. *Wiener Zeitung* 231:33 (February 4, 1934): Sonntagsbeilage 2-3.

b. ——. *Der Auftakt* (Prague) 14:10 (October 1934): 166-169.

c. ——. *Schönere Zukunft* (Vienna) 9:18 (January 28, 1934)
Abbreviated.

d. ——. In his *Zur Sprache gebracht.* (K707) (München: Albert Langen - Georg Müller, 1958): 149-152.
Abbreviated.

e. "Art and nationalism." *Musical Courier* 93:20 (May 19, 1934): 6.

f. "Nationality and art." In his *Exploring music.* (K817) (New York: October House, 1966): 79-82.

K247. "Krenek über die Schwierigkeiten von *Karl V.*" *Wiener Allgemeine Zeitung* (January 20, 1934)

K248. "Freiheit und Verantwortung." *23* no.14 (February 1934): 10-11.
Festschrift in honor of Anton Webern's fiftieth birthday. *See:* B554

a. ——. In his *Zur Sprache gebracht.* (K707) (München: Albert Langen - Georg Müller, 1958): 156-157.

b. ——. *Musik-Konzepte* Sonderband: *Anton Webern II*. (November 1984): 3-4.

K249. "Der Untergang der Habsburgischen Monarchie." *Vossische Zeitung* (February 25, 1934)

Review of the history book *Weder Kaiser noch König* by Bruno Brehm (München: R.Piper Verlag, 1933).

K250. "Konservativ und radikal." *Wiener Zeitung* 231:56 (February 25, 1934): Sonntagsbeilage 1-2. *See:* B358

K251. "Wie ich zu *Karl V.* kam." *Die Furche* no.47 (November 22 1969): 11.

Lecture given March 1934 to a Vienna seminar discussing how he came to compose his opera op.73.

K252. "Zur Situation der Internationalen Gesellschaft für neue Musik." *Anbruch* 16:3 (March 1934): 41-44.

The IGNM reflects the fatigue and indifference found in other international organizations, such as the League of Nations. The idea of having an independently funded group of artists which promotes commercially inviable ideas and works is thwarted by a lack of consensus and a scarcity of funds. More and more, it has become the state which influences ideas rather than the individual artists. Internationale Gesellschaft für neue Musik

K253. "Erfahrungen mit dem 'Zwölftonsystem.'" *Vossische Zeitung* no.53 (March 3, 1934)

Explains the logical and moral foundation of the twelve-tone system. Part 3 of a series which included articles by Josef Rufer (February 3) and Hans Heinz Stuckenschmidt (February 14).

a. ——. In his *Zur Sprache gebracht*. (K707) (München: Albert Langen - Georg Müller, 1958): 158-161.

Abbreviated.

b. ——. In his *Im Zweifelsfalle*. (K924) (Wien: Europaverlag, 1984): 159-162.

K254. "Vesque von Püttlingen." *Anbruch* 16:4 (April 1934): 84.

Review of *Fünfundvierzig Lieder* by Johann Vesque von Püttlingen edited by Helmut Schultz. (Wien: Universal Edition, 1933).

K255. "Eindrücke von einer Spanienreise." *Wiener Zeitung* 231:108 (April 19, 1934): 7-8 ; 231:109 (April 20, 1934): 6-8 ; 231:110 (April 21, 1934): 6-7.

A travel diary of a trip to Spain covering I: Spain in general, Catalonia, The Levante - the Churriguera style and Spanish Gothic. II: African Spain, Granada and the Moors, the language, the imperial era of Charles V.and the Escorial, La Mancha, Toledo, sociological and political impressions. III: Commerce, speech, the bull-fight, Madrid, Goya, the land of the Basques, and departure.

a. "Im Land des Uebermasses." In his *Gedanken unterwegs*. (K720) (München: Albert Langen - Georg Müller, 1959): 66-80.

K256. "Neue Kunst im neuen Staat." *Der Christliche Ständestaat* 1:25 (May 1934): 9-12.

K257. "Ueber die Volksverbundenheit der Kunst." *Wiener Zeitung* 231:139 (May 20, 1934): Pfingstbeilage 1-2.

An article in reaction to the reproach that art has alienated itself from the people. The reasons for this alienation must be sought in the sociological changes which have occurred in the last 200 years. While there used to be an elite group of sponsors for the arts, it has disappeared and has not been replaced. Without financial support for art, the common people have never developed a relationship with new creative art.

a. ———. In his *Zur Sprache gebracht*. (K707) (München: Albert Langen - Georg Müller, 1958): 162-166.

K258. "Probleme der Werdenden." *Wiener Zeitung* 231:145 (May 27, 1934): Sonntagsbeilage 1-2.

A reflection on the problems of youth and the transmission of cultural values between generations.

K259. "Die Bedeutung unserer Genossenschaft." In *Genossenschaft dramatischer Schriftsteller und Komponisten*; Bericht über das Mitgliedsjahr 1933/34. (Vienna: Druckschriftenabteilung, Summer 1934): 10-13.

Inaugural essay upon Krenek's assumption of the post of President of the Austrian Writers Association. He discusses plans for the future and past events.

K260. "Die Musik in der berufsständischen Ordnung." *Anbruch* 16:6 (June 1934): 113-118.

In a discussion of the state of music within the hierarchy of the corporate state, Krenek supports the idea of forming an organization to foster cooperation rather than competition or the formation of unions. Such an organization could be thought of as a chain of organizations uniting through normative contracts everyone who comprises the productive apparatus of music: e.g. authors, publishers, theater directors, stage managers, musicians, and technical personnel.

K261. "Roman der Gottwerdung." *Wiener Zeitung* 231:145 (June 10, 1934): Sonntagsbeilage 1.

Review of a novel *Der junge Joseph* by Thomas Mann (Berlin: S.Fischer, 1934).

K262. "Filmfragen." *Wiener Zeitung* 231:173 (June 24, 1934): Sonntagsbeilage 1.

The low artistic quality of movies is the result of the commercial and economic situation in the film industry. "Problematic" films cannot be commercially successful; consequently they will continue to be the exception. Since film, in trying to represent reality, must be disruptive and cannot present a continuous scene like a theater stage, the director becomes the main responsible artist. Writers and composers can only try to influence the director. One way out of the misery of contemporary film would be to use the income of hits to finance the more problematic and artistic films.

K263. "Ein bürgerlicher König Lear." *Wiener Zeitung* 231:188 (July 9, 1934): 6.

Review of a novel *Der Gerechte* by Hermann Kesten (Amsterdam: Albert de Lange Verlag, 1934).

K264. "Eine Filmrundfrage." *Neue Zürcher Zeitung* 155:1271 (July 15, 1934): 3.

Answers to the question "What do you consider to be the best film?" by Krenek, Rudolf G. Binding, Thomas Mann, and others.

K265. "Im Vorarlberg." *Wiener Zeitung* 231:209 (July 29, 1934): Sonntagsbeilage 3-4.

A travel report about the Vorarlberg in the western part of Austria discussing the different nature of its inhabitants in appearance, mentality, and culture from the rest of Austria.

a. ——. In his *Gedanken unterwegs.* (K720) (München: Albert Langen - Georg Müller, 1959): 81-86.

K266. "Oesterreich und die Schweiz." *Neue Schweizer Rundschau* N.F.2:4 (August 1934): 220-224.

A discussion of Emperor Charles the Fifth and the relationship between Austria and Switzerland.

a. ——. *Wiener Zeitung* 231:279 (October 7, 1934): Sonntagsbeilage 1.

K267. "Musik und Kriminalität." *Wiener Zeitung* 231:223 (August 12, 1934): Sonntagsbeilage 3.

Discusses the power of music, which can stir up emotions and could eventually lead to criminal acts, as exemplified in the case of three arsonists who were members of a band in a rural beer garden.

K268. "Arnold Schönberg." *Wiener Zeitung* 231:251 (September 9, 1934): Sonntagsbeilage 1.

Written to commemorate Arnold Schoenberg's sixtieth birthday. Discusses Schoenberg's musical and historical importance, and explains the development of the twelve-tone technique as a necessary consequent of music history. *See:* B554

a. ——. In his *Zur Sprache gebracht.* (K707) (München: Albert Langen - Georg Müller, 1958): 167-171.

b. ——. In his *Im Zweifelsfalle.* (K924) (Wien: Europaverlag, 1984): 102-106.

c. "Arnold Schoenberg." In *Schoenberg*, edited by Merle Armitage. (New York: G.Schirmer, 1937): 79-88.

English translation by Christel Gang.

K269. "Die verlorene Welt der Väter." *Wiener Zeitung* 231:266 (September 24, 1934): 6.

Review of the book *Tarabas* by Joseph Roth (Amsterdam: Querido-Verlag, 1934).

K270. "'Handwerk' des Komponisten." *Frankfurter Zeitung* 79:510 (October 7, 1934): 1.

A discussion of intuition versus technique in the composition of music, preferring the latter.

a. ——. *Der Tanz* 7:12 (December 1934)

K271. "Harmonie und Atonalität." *Oesterreichische Volkspresse* (October 13, 1934)

Reaction to an article with the same title by Dr. Ernst Hold published September 29, 1934 who responded with "Erwiderung auf den Einwand Ernst Kreneks gegen den Artikel 'Harmonie u. Atonalität'" (B569).

K272. "Zeitgenössische Musik im österreichischen Studio." *Wiener Zeitung* 231:293 (October 21, 1934): 10.

Preview of a series of five concerts of contemporary music initiated by Krenek beginning October 25 in Vienna's Ehrbar-Saal. Each concert is to include a short introductory speech by Krenek and is intended to have a broad appeal to the general public. The first concert will be dedicated to works by the three Austrian masters celebrating their sixtieth birthdays, Arnold Schönberg, Julius Bittner, and Franz Schmidt. The second concert will feature Dr. Lechthaler directing new church music, the third includes significant West European music, the fourth will include new music influenced by folk music, and the last will be dedicated to the youngest Austrian generation.

K273. "Ansprache an einem Abend zeitgenössische Musik." *Der Auftakt* (Prague) 14:11/12 (November-December 1934): 193-197.

Lecture given at the first "Abend des Oesterreichischen Studios" concert on October 25, 1934 in the Ehrbar-Saal, Vienna featuring works by Arnold Schönberg, Julius Bittner, and Franz Schmidt. Krenek sees the concerts unifying different branches of Austrian music without becoming a clique and informing the general public by explaining the music in non-esoteric language pointing out musical relationships.

a. "Ernst Kreneks Einführungsvortrag." 23 no.17/19 (December 15, 1934): 15-16. Excerpt.

Manuscripts: A-Wst typescript (5 p.) ; typescript copy (5 p.)

K274. "Karl Kraus und Arnold Schönberg." 23 no.15/16 (October 25, 1934): 1-4.

Discusses their differences and similarities on their sixtieth birthdays.

a. ——. In his *Zur Sprache gebracht.* (K707) (München: Albert Langen - Georg Müller, 1958): 172-174.

b. ——. In his *Im Zweifelsfalle.* (K924) (Wien: Europaverlag, 1984): 107-109.

c. "Karl Kraus and Arnold Schoenberg." In his *Exploring music.* (K817) (New York: October House, 1966): 83-86.

K275. "Zur Idee eines 'Studios' für zeitgenössische Musik." 23 no.15/16 (October 25, 1934): 9-14.

A series of "Viennese Studio Concerts" for the season 1934-35 to present contemporary music is justified because of the economic depression which discourages the regular music industry from being open to new music and the reactionary direction the Internationale Gesellschaft für neue Musik has taken. The concerts will emphasize communication with the listeners, who will have to discard some of their conventional expectations, through introductory comments before the works.

K276. "Ravag-Sendung und österreichische Sendung." 23 no.15/16 (October 25, 1934): 18-24.

Written under the pseudonym Austriacus; a bitter reaction to a radio festival of new Austrian music which included only the works of a clique of outspoken adversaries of atonal music consonant with the views of Nazi Germany and calling themselves the "Viennese School," a name previously reserved to Schönberg's group. The article stresses a return to the music of the true "Viennese School" and a rejection of the "Pan-Germanic" tonalists. (RAVAG is the Oesterreichische Radio-Vekehrs-AG, now Oesterreichischer Rundfunk)

K277. "Amerikanisches Barock." *Wiener Zeitung* 231:300 (October 28, 1934): 11.

Reflections on two recent American films, *42nd Street* and *Dancing Venus.* Both films are about the theater and were staged with large budgets. Krenek's reaction to the films are overwhelmingly negative; he sees no cultural responsibility in them. The title "American Baroque" alludes to the very expensive production of the films.

a. ——. In his *Gedanken unterwegs.* (K720) (München: Albert Langen - Georg Müller, 1959): 106-109.

K278. "Das Buch vom Antichrist." *Wiener Zeitung* 231:328 (November 25, 1934): Sonntagsbeilage 2.

Review of the book *Der Antichrist* by Joseph Roth (Amsterdam: Albert de Lange, 1934).

K279. "Der Dichter Joseph Roth." *Der Christliche Ständestaat* 1:53 (December 9, 1934): 8-9.

Discusses the work of the novelist and playwright.

K280. "Die Blubo-Internationale." *23* no.17/19 (December 15, 1934): 19-25.

Written under the pseudonym Austriacus. A report and comments on the biannual Internationale Gesellschaft für neue Musik festival in Venice. Krenek protests Richard Strauss's assumption of the role of world music dictator and especially attacks Herbert Gerigk, reviewer of the official Nazi music paper exposing the aspirations of the organizers to exclude new music from future festivals. Blubo is a satirical name for the organization and is derived from the Nazi slogan "Blut und Boden" (Blood and soil).

K281. "Aufbauendes." *23* no.17/19 (December 15, 1934): 31-34.

Compares the new architecture of Adolf Loos and Clemens Holzmeister with new music. Discusses the concepts of "indigenous music," "contra atonalism," "Marxism," "leftism," etc. Krenek concludes that new music has a harder time establishing itself than does architecture.

K282. "Blubo-Sektion Oesterreich." *23* no.17/19 (December 15, 1934): 39-44.

Written under the pseudonym Austriacus. Blubo is the satirical name of a new music organization based upon nationalism as the successor of the Internationale Gesellschaft für neue Musik and is derived from the Nazi slogan "Blut und Boden" (Blood and soil). The article criticizes the foundation and by-laws of the new organization, which differ from the more democratically organized IGNM.

K283. "Die 'Fälle' Furtwängler und Hindemith." *Der Christliche Ständestaat* 1:55 (December 23, 1934): 21-22.

K284. "Der 'geistige Mensch' und die Politik." *Wiener Zeitung* 231:357 (December 25, 1934): Weinachtsbeilage 3-4.

The "spiritual man" is not a mere intellectual, because he is creative in such a way that his products do not possess any economic value. He represents only a very small part of humanity and creates, strictly speaking, only for himself. The relationship between the "spiritual man" and politics is based on the ethical, if not religious approach of the man to the state, represented in the thought of the Christian-Roman imperium.

K285. "*Karl V*; Analyses des Werkes von Autor selbst." *Unpublished.*

A detailed dramatic and musical analysis of the opera op.73 with many examples. Includes a discussion of the twelve-tone rows and the process in which they are derived.

Manuscripts: **US-LJ** typescript copy(10 p., lacks p.2)

-- 1935 --

K286. "Memo on *Karl V* to Dr. Tschulik." *Wiener Zeitung* (1978?)

Krenek describes the circumstances that led to the creation of his opera op.73; it was commissioned without pay for the Vienna State Opera by Clemens Krauss and composed in 1931/32. After initially responding favorably, Krauss changed his mind by Fall 1933, requiring changes which Krenek made, but then cancelled the production. Krenek sees his main adversaries in Josef Rinaldini and the bassoonist Burghauser.

Manuscripts: US-LJ 2 p.

K287. "Zur Psychologie der Micky- und Silly-Welt." *Wiener Zeitung* 232:1 (January 1, 1935): Neujahrsbeilage 4.

A philosophical-psychological analysis of Mickey Mouse cartoons. They idealize technology, have romantic fairy-tale endings, ignore sociological facts such as unemployment, and present the illusion of a prosperous sane world where the weak prevail over the strong.

a. "Micky und Silly." In his *Gedanken unterwegs.* (K720) (München: Albert Langen - Georg Müller, 1959): 110-113.

b. "Svĕt myšaha Mickey." *Masarykuv lid* 11(15) (February 1936) Czech translation.

K288. "Philosophie der Unstimmigkeit." *Wiener Zeitung* 232:14 (January 14, 1935): 6.

Review of the book *Erbschaft dieser Zeit* by philosopher Ernst Bloch (Zürich: Oprecht und Helbling, 1935). The page is misdated January 7.

K289. "Musikleben in Wien." *Schweizerische Musikzeitung und Sängerblatt* 75:2 (January 15, 1935): 41-48.

Discusses the state of new music in Austria and Krenek's efforts to improve it through his "Abende zeitgenössischer Musik," the magazine 23, and the presentation of concerts.

K290. "*Spanien, Ein Land in Gärung* von Fritz Wahl." *Wiener Zeitung* 232:21 (January 21, 1935): 6.

Review of a travel book (Frankfurt: Societäts-Verlag, 1934).

K291. "Einleitung des III Studio-Konzerts, Wien, 21.Jan.1935, Ehrbarsaal." *Unpublished*.

Introduction to the third of Krenek's Oesterreichisches Studio concerts.

Manuscripts: A-Wst typescript (6 p.) ; typescript copy (6 p.)

K292. "Zu Otto Stoessls *Schelmengeschichten.*" *Wiener Zeitung* 232:25 (January 25, 1935): 8-9.

Review of the book (Wien: Saturn-Verlag, 1934).

K293. "*Wir hatten mal ein Kind.*" *Wiener Zeitung* 232:28 (January 28, 1935): 6.

A brief review of the historical novel by Hans Fallada, pseudonym for Rudolf Ditzen (Berlin: Rowohlt, 1934).

K294. "Der Gedanke in der Oper." *Wiener Zeitung* 232:38 (February 7, 1935): 9-10.

A discussion of Alban Berg's opera *Lulu* in honor of his fiftieth birthday, February 9, 1935.

K295. "Künstlerische und wissenschaftliche Geschichtsbetrachtung; Referat in der historisch-soziologischen Arbeitsgemeinschaft (Dr.Georg Fleischer), Wien am 11.Feb.1935." *Wiener Politische Blätter* 3:1 (March 24, 1935): 40-57.

A discussion of ways to approach historical topics derived from his work on the opera *Karl V.* op.73. History cannot be an exact science because it is not reproducible and its interpretations depend upon subjective observations and judgements. The challenge for the artist lies in entering into the aspects of any history where human motivations are ethically analyzed. The dualism of the "individual" and the "total historical event" dominate the artist's interest in history; he does not merely present history but debates it, deliberately interpreting it subjectively.

 a. "Künstlerische und wissenschaftliche Geschichtsbetrachtung." In his *Zur Sprache gebracht.* (K707) (München: Albert Langen - Georg Müller, 1958): 175-196.

 b. ——. *[Program: Staatstheater Braunschweig 1970/71]* no.18.

K296. "Zu Karl Burckhardts *Richelieu.*" *Wiener Zeitung* 232:54 (February 23, 1935): 8.

Review of a biography (München: G. D. W.Callwey, 1935).

K297. "Volkslieder in zeitgenössischer Bearbeitung." *Anbruch* 17:5 (May 1935): 144-147.

Introductory lecture to Krenek's Fourth Abend des Oesterreichische Studio on February 25, 1935 about the folk music arranged by contemporary composers and presented in the concert. Discusses the music of Béla Bartók, Ladislav Vycpálek, Josef Koffler, Jenö Takács, and his own *Austrian folksongs* op.77a.

Manuscripts: A-Wst 4 p. ; typescript (6 p.)

K298. "*Das Atlantisbuch der Musik.*" *Wiener Zeitung* 232:56 (February 25, 1935): 6.

Review of an encyclopedia compiled by Fred Hamel and Martin Hürlimann. (Berlin: Atlantis Verlag, 1934).

 a. "Ein Kompendium der Musik." *Neue Schweizer Rundschau* N.F.3:2 (June 1935): 125-127.

K299. "*Die Uebertragung des musikalischen Urheberrechts an Musikverleger und Musikverwertungsgesellschaften.*" *Wiener Zeitung* 232:56 (February 25, 1935): 6.

Brief review of the book about music copyright by Hans Joachim Hinrichsen (Leipzig: C. F.Peters, 1934).

K300. "Zur Psychologie des musikalischen Schaffens." *Wiener Zeitung* 232:56 (February 25, 1935): 6.

Review of a book on the psychology of musical creativity *Zur Psychologie des musikalischen gestaltens* by Julius Bahle (Leipzig: Akademische Verlagsgesellschaft, 1930).

K301. "Zu Brandis Vortrag über *Karl V.*" *Wiener Zeitung* 232:75 (March 16, 1935): 9.

Review of a lecture by the Göttingen historian Karl Brandis about the Austrian emperor.

K302. "Ansprache zum Abend der zeitgenössischer Musik im Oesterreichischen Studios am 25. März 1935 im Ehrbar-Saal, Wien." In *Briefwechsel*, von Theodor W. Adorno und Ernst Krenek. (K862) (Frankfurt am Main: Suhrkamp, 1974): 199-204.

Introduction to the last of his 1935 Viennese Studio Concerts consisting of songs of Theodor Wiesengrund Adorno, a Sonatina by Erich Apostel, a chamber concerto by Ernst Josef Matheis, a suite by Robert Leukauf, and choral works by Egon Wellesz and Krenek (op.32). He also discusses the problems of publicity and finance he has faced in producing the concerts and explains the termination of the series.

Manuscripts: **A-Wst** typescript (6 p.)

K303. "Chronik der Unzulänglichkeit." *23* no.20/21 (March 25, 1935): 26-29.

Written under the pseudonym Austriacus. Notes on two less-than-exciting French-Austrian exchange concerts, on the awarding of the "Grossen österreichischen Staatspreis" to a painter, on Anton Konrath's statements concerning atonal music, and on an anonymous writer for *Die Glocke* who preaches an anti-modern gospel.

K304. "Volksabstimmung in aner dur." *23* no.20/21 (March 25, 1935): 30-32.

Written under the pseudonym Austriacus. Ironic reaction to a proposed poll organized by the magazine *Illustrierte Kronenzeitung* on what kind of music should be broadcast on the radio.

K305. "Ungarn, Italien, Oesterreich." *Wiener Zeitung* 232:86 (March 27, 1935): 8-9.

Review of two art exhibitions in Vienna, "Ungarischen Volkskunst" (Hungarian folk art) in the Hagenbund and "Futuristischen Malerei" (Futurist art) from Italy in the Neuen Galarie.

K306. "Bruno Walter spricht 'Von den moralischen Kräften der Musik.'" *Wiener Zeitung* 232:108 (April 18, 1935): 10.

A critical review of Walter's speech on the moral force of music. Despite Krenek's regard for the eminent musician, he concludes that Walter is wrong when he asserts that the triad is a naturally given event and that Walter's language, including such phrases as "dark emotions," for example, needs clarification. It is not possible, contrary to Walter's explanations, to prove a connection between musical and ethical value.

K307. "Bemerkungen zum österreichischen Menschen." *Wiener Zeitung* 232:111 (April 21, 1935): Osterbeilage 1-3.

Krenek tries to historically deduce the characteristics of Austrians as distinguished from Germans. He concludes that it is not race that marks the difference but the historic role of Austria to be the leader of the "Reich," which is seen as a supranational entity, a continuation and preservation of Roman-Christian-Occidental humanistic values. The typical Austrian character must be seen as the personification of these values.

K308. "Ernst Krenek über den Maler Rederer." *Profil* (Vienna) 3:5 (May 1935): 224-225.

Krenek briefly discusses the painter's relationship to the Viennese composers, and notes his recent portrait of Alban Berg painted for the composer's fiftieth birthday.

K309. "Der österreichische Dichter." *Wiener Zeitung* 232:120 (May 1, 1935): Beilage 1-2.

A supplement dedicated to Otto Stoessl's sixtieth birthday. Krenek discusses Stoessl's Austrian background and traditions.

K310. "Kunstpolitik im neuen Oesterreich." *Unpublished.*
Lecture given May 14, 1935.
Manuscripts: **A-Wst** 4 p.

K311. "Neue sozialkritische Epik." *Wiener Zeitung* 232:139 (May 20, 1935): 6-7.
Review of the books *Lenz und Jette* by Erik Reger, pseudonym for Hermann Dannenberger (Berlin: Rowohlt, 1935), *Der Dreigroschenroman* by Bertolt Brecht (Amsterdam: A. de Lange, 1934), and *Pardon, wird nicht gegeben* by Alfred Döblin (Amsterdam: Querido-Verlag, 1935)

K312. "Zwischen 'Blubo' und 'Asphalt'." *Der Christliche Ständestaat* 2:22 (June 2, 1935): 520-521.
A discussion of Austrian new music and Nationalsocialism. Blubo is a fictitious satirical new music organization whose name is derived from the Nazi slogan "Blut und Boden" (Blood and soil).

K313. "*Leopold III, Herzog zu Oesterreich.*" *Wiener Zeitung* 232:158 (June 3, 1935): 7.
Review of the book by K. E. Girzberger. (Innsbruck: Universitäts-Verlag Wagner, 1934).

K314. "Alfred Polgar *In der Zwischenzeit.*" *Wiener Zeitung* 232:159 (June 9, 1935): 12.
Review of the book (Amsterdam: A. de Lange, 1935)

K315. "Karl V. als Romanfigur." *Wiener Zeitung* 232:160 (June 11, 1935): 6.
Review of the novel *Karl V.* by Gerhart Ellert, pseudonym for Gertrud Schmirger (Wien: F. G.Speidel, 1935).

K316. "*Orient-Express* Roman von A. den Doolaard." *Wiener Zeitung* 232:160 (June 11, 1935): 7.
Review of the novel; Doolaard is the pseudonym for Cornelius Spoelstra (Amsterdam: Querido-Verlag, 1934).

K317. "Igor Strawinskys Memoiren." *Wiener Zeitung* 232:172 (June 23, 1935): 10-11.
Review of the book *Chroniques de ma vie* by Igor Stravinsky (Paris: Denoël et Steele, 1935).
   a. ——. *Anbruch* 17:8 (August 1935): 222-224.

K318. "Eine Schweinegeschichte." *Wiener Zeitung* 232:173 (June 24, 1935): 7.
Review of the novel *Ein X für ein U* by P. G. Wodehouse in the German translation by Ernst Simon (Zinnen-Verlag).

K319. "Eine soziologische Deutung der zeitgenössischen Musiksituation." *Wiener Zeitung* 232:200 (July 22, 1935): 6.
Review of the book *Die Endkrise der bürgerlichen Musik und die Rolle Arnold Schönbergs* by Hans E. Wind (Wien: Krystall-Verlag, 1935).

K320. "Sommer am Tannberg." *Wiener Zeitung* 232:206 (July 28, 1935): Sonntagsbeilage 3-4.
A poetic, lyric description of the Alpine landscape around Tannberg, at the border between the Austrian states of Vorarlberg and Tirol. Includes a

description of the modern alpine hotel, its guests and their music, which comes by radio.

a. ——. In his *Gedanken unterwegs*. (K720) (München: Albert Langen - Georg Müller, 1959): 87-94.

K321. *"Scharffenberg."* *Wiener Zeitung* 232:206 (July 29, 1935): 6.
Review of the novel by Eckart von Naso. (Berlin: Universitas-Verlag, 1935).

K322. *"Kodansha."* *Wiener Zeitung* 232:206 (July 29, 1935): 7.
Review of the autobiography of the Japanese king Seiji Noma (Berlin: Holle und Co., 1935)

K323. "Entwurf für einen österreichischen Film." *Unpublished*.
Plan for a film. Date at end: Gargellen (Vbg.), July-August 1934.
Manuscripts: A-Wst [4] p.

K324. *"Die Grammatik der Liebe."* *Wiener Zeitung* 232:214 (August 5, 1935): 6.
Review of the book of stories by Ivan Bunin (Berlin: Bruno Cassirer-Verlag, 1935).

K325. *"Tresoreinbruch."* *Wiener Zeitung* 232:228 (August 19, 1935): 6-7.
Review of the novel by Paul Gurk (Berlin: Halle und Co., 1935)

K326. "Alpine Randbemerkungen." *Wiener Zeitung* 232:241 (September 1, 1935): Sonntagsbeilage 1-2.
A philosophical essay comparing nature, represented by the Alps, and music, and the relationship modern man has developed to each. Today people physically use nature, by swimming or skiing for example, rather than merely observing it. Krenek is critical of the intrusion of the radio into nature's environment. He notes that East and West in the Alps is expressed in music, like a theme and its retrograde, while North and South are the inversions.

a. "Der Mensch und die Alpen." In his *Gedanken unterwegs*. (K720) (München: Albert Langen - Georg Müller, 1959): 95-98.

K327. *"Süsse Frucht, bittre Frucht, China."* *Wiener Zeitung* 232:242 (September 2, 1935): 7.
Review of the book by Philadelphian Nora Waln relating her experiences in China at the turn of the century. (Berlin: Wolfgang Krüger-Verlag, 1935).

K328. "Von der Prager Tagung der Intern. Gesellschaft für neue Musik." *Wiener Zeitung* 232:255 (September 15, 1935): 9.
Review of the concerts during the thirteenth music festival and discussion of its organization.

K329. "Neue Wege der Musik im Drama." *Wiener Zeitung* 232:269 (September 29, 1935): Sonntagsbeilage 1.
Discusses Darius Milhaud's *Christophe Colomb* and Krenek's *Karl V.* op.73 as examples of the new interest in historical opera.

a. ——. *Schweizerische Musikzeitung und Sängerblatt* 75:22 (November 15, 1935): 697-701.

b. ——. *Der Auftakt* (Prague) 17:1/2 (January-February 1937): 5-9.

c. "Nuove tendenze della musica nel dramma." *La Rassegna Musicale* 10:4 (April 1937): 125-129.

K330. "Soziologische Kunstbetrachtung." *Unpublished.*
Lecture given at Volkshochschule, October 9, 1935.
Manuscripts: **A-Wst** [2] p.

K331. "Eau de Vichy auf unsere Mühle." 23 no.22/23 (October 10, 1935): 22-29.
Discussion and review of the Thirteenth Music Festival of the Internationale Gesellschaft für neue Musik in Prague.

K332. "Mitteilung über die Studio-Konzerte." 23 no.22/23 (October 10, 1935): 31-32.
Explains that the need for his Viennese Studio Concerts has passed and that they are being discontinued. He urges concertgoers to attend the concerts of the revived Verein für Neue Musik, the Austrian section of the Internationale Gesellschaft für neue Musik.

K333. "Ein Tschaikowskij-Roman." *Wiener Zeitung* 232:291 (October 21, 1935): 6.
Review of the novel *Symphonie pathétique* by Klaus Mann (Amsterdam: Querido-Verlag, 1935).

K334. *"Der Narr aus den Maremmen."* *Wiener Zeitung* 232:298 (October 28, 1935): 6-7.
Review of the novel by Carel and Margo Scharten (Zürich: Rascher & Cie., 1935)

K335. *"Totentanz in Livland."* *Wiener Zeitung* 232:298 (October 28, 1935): 6.
Review of the novel by Siegfried von Vegesack. (Berlin: Universitas, 1935).

K336. "Vortrag zur Einleitung des Konzerts der österreichischen Sektion der IGNM im Hagenbund." *Unpublished.*
Lecture given in Vienna, November 21, 1935.
Manuscripts: **A-Wst.**

K337. "A propos de banalité." *Présence* (Geneva) 3:10 (December 1935): 34-36.
Reaction to Francis Poulenc's "Eloge de la banalité" in this journal. Tonality as such is not bad; however, the twelve-tone system has replaced it.

K338. "England zum ersten Mal gesehen." *Wiener Zeitung* 232:332 (December 1, 1935): Sonntagsbeilage 1-2.
Travel report about London, comparing the city and its atmosphere, way of life, people, and suburbs with Paris and Vienna. The absence of, or aversion to Catholicism has made a significant impact on the English character.
a. ——. In his *Gedanken unterwegs.* (K720) (München: Albert Langen - Georg Müller, 1959): 99-105.
b. ——. *Melos* 27:7/8 (July-August 1960): 212-215.
Picture.

K339. *"Die hundert Tage."* *Wiener Zeitung* 232:340 (December 9, 1935): 7.
Review of the novel by Joseph Roth (Amsterdam: A. de Lange, 1936).

K340. "Blick auf österreichische Lyrik der Gegenwart." *Wiener Zeitung* 232:346 (December 15, 1935): Sonntagsbeilage 1 ; 232:353 (December 22, 1935): Sonntagsbeilage 1.

Lecture "Oesterreichische Lyrik von heute" given in the series Podium im
Hagenbund in Vienna on December 6, 1935. A survey of the current state of
Austrian lyric poetry including the work of Karl Kraus, Georg Trakl, and
Franz Janowitz. Includes a look at the literary periodical *Der Brenner* edited
by Anton Santer and Josef Leitgeb. Examines Berthold Viertel's "Der Ort", a
sonnet by Richard Schaukal, a poem by Herta Staub "Bureau im Gewitter",
and a poem by A. Lernet-Holenia. Krenek sees a characteristic Austrian
element within German language poetry.

Manuscripts: "Vortrag über 'Oesterreichische Lyrik von heute'." **A-Wst**
typescript (11 p.)

K341. "Romantisches Epos der Industrialisierung." *Wiener Zeitung* 232:354
(December 23, 1935): 6.

Review of the novel *Napoleon und der Schmelztiegel* by Erik Reger,
pseudonym for Hermann Dannenberger (Berlin:Rowohlt, 1935).

K342. "Trauer um Alban Berg." *Wiener Zeitung* 232:356 (December 25, 1935):
9.

Memorials to Berg by Krenek, Egon Wellesz, Lilli Claus, and Hans Ewald
Heller accompanying the obituary.

K343. "Betrachtungen bei der Analyse eines Verses." *Wiener Zeitung* 232:356
(December 25, 1935): Weihnachtsbeilage 5.

A phonetic-structural analysis of Richard Schaukal's sonnet "Adalbert
Stifter." Rhythmic conformity relates to poetic meaning, in this case as a
eulogy to the novelist Stifter.

a. ——. In his *Zur Sprache gebracht.* (K707) (München: Albert Langen -
Georg Müller, 1958): 197-199.

K344. "Am Grabe." 23 no.24/25 (February 1, 1936): 17-19.

Eulogies given at Alban Berg's funeral on December 28, 1935; with Hugo
Winter and Willi Reich.

-- 1936 --

K345. "Charles-Quint." *Unpublished.*

Written in 1936 or 1937 concerning his opera *Karl V.* op.73.

Manuscripts: **A-Wst** typescript copy (4 p.)

K346. "Apologie." *Wiener Zeitung* 233:1 (January 1, 1936): Neujahrsbeilage
2-3 ; 233:5 (January 5, 1936): Sonntagsbeilage 2.

Response to Erich Marckhl's "Sinn der Tonalität" in the December 22 and 25,
1935 issues. Marchkl's article argued against atonality, which he branded as
"Bolshevist," "Antichrist," and borne out of rational capriciousness. Krenek
convincingly shows that Marckhl's definition of tonality, which he calls "a
holy untouchable axiom grown from the magic primordial realm of culture,"
is emotionally biased and is no definition at all. In contrast, Krenek quotes
Arnold Schönberg's definition of tonality from his *Harmonielehre.* He defends
Schönberg's atonality and characterizes Marckhl's article as emotionally
biased.

K347. "Journal der musikalischen Arbeit zum Oratorium *Symeon der Stylit,*
3.6.1935 bis 1.1.1936." *Eingebung und Tat im musikalischen Schaffen,* von
Julius Bahle. (Leipzig, 1939)

A diary describing the composition of the oratorio (W84) from the creation
of the all-interval twelve-tone row to the beginning of the orchestration.

a. "Journal der musikalischen Arbeit zu dem Oratorium *Symeon der Stylit* nach Hugo Ball." *Musik-Konzepte* 39/40 (October 1984): 67-77.

Includes facsimiles of pages of the score.

Manuscripts: **A-Wst** 4 p.

K348. "Zur Entwicklung der modernen Oper." *Unpublished.*

Lecture given at the Wiener Stadt-Stimmen on January 10, 1936. The range of modern opera extends from Alban Berg's social commentary in *Wozzeck* to Darius Milhaud's religious commentary in *Christophe Colomb.*

Manuscripts: **A-Wst.**

K349. "Ein Rilke-Sonderheft." *Wiener Zeitung* 233:22 (January 23, 1936): 10.

Review of an issue of the periodical *Philobiblon* dedicated to the sixtieth birthday of the poet Rainer Maria Rilke.

K350. "Tiefe und Distanz." *Wiener Zeitung* 233:25 (January 26, 1936): Sontagsbeilage 3.

Discusses the opposing approaches of subjective commentary and academic objectivism in the reviewing of intellectual creations, such as theater, films, etc. The role of prejudice and resentment, as well as the term "relativism," are explored. Deep radical analysis always poses religious questions, which are beyond everyday propaganda.

a. ——. In his *Gedanken unterwegs.* (K720) (München: Albert Langen - Georg Müller, 1959): 114-116.

K351. "Cromwell, ein Mann seiner Zeit." *Wiener Zeitung* 233:26 (January 27, 1936): 6.

Review of the book *Oliver Cromwell, ein Mann seiner Zeit* by Hilaire Belloc in the German translation by B. Deermann (Einsiedeln (SZ): Benziger, 1935).

K352. "*Der sozialen Kundgebungen der Päpste, 1832-1931.*" *Wiener Zeitung* 233:33 (February 3, 1936): 7.

Review of the book by Theodor Willi Stadler exploring the social edicts of the Papacy (Einsiedeln: Benziger, 1935).

K353. "Rückkehr zum Thomismus." *Wiener Zeitung* 233:33 (February 3, 1936): 7.

Review of a religious lecture by the Dominican P. M. Gillet entitled *Le retour au Thomisme.*

K354. "Vorbemerkung zur Vorlesung von *Karl V.* in Graz, 3. Februar 1936." *Musik-Konzepte* 39/40 (October 1984): 35-37.

A lecture tracing the beginnings of the opera op.73 and discussing its political problems.

K355. "*Die schweigsame Frau* in Graz." *Wiener Zeitung* 233:34 (February 4, 1936): 8.

Review of the first performance of the opera by Richard Strauss based upon a libretto by Stephan Zweig.

K356. "Kritik als Schoepferisches Vermoegen." *Musica viva* 1:1 (April 1936): 9-17.

Discussion of the idea of "criticism as a creative power" presented by Willy Tappolet with responses by Egon Wellesz, Krenek and others. Krenek asserts that criticism can be creative because it transmits the inner meaning of a work and can throw light upon artistic intentions. The basis of sound judgement can only be achieved by the comparison of the creative ideal with the results. (Letter dated: 8.2.36, Wien)

K357. *"Der Major."* *Wiener Zeitung* 233:40 (February 10, 1936): 6.
Review of the novel by Ruth Schaumann (Berlin: G.Grote, 1935).

K358. "Alban Berg zum Gedächtnis." *Wiener Zeitung* 233:45 (February 15, 1936): 10.
A memorial for the deceased composer discussing his importance to music. An announcement of a memorial concert to be performed that evening is also included.

K359. "Von der Würde der abendländischen Musik." *Wiener Zeitung* 233:53 (February 23, 1936): Sonntagsbeilage 1-2 & 233:60 (March 1, 1936): Sonntagsbeilage 1-2.
Newspaper text expanded for a lecture broadcast May 4, 1936 on Radio Zürich. Music in Western culture is autonomous, that is it exists for itself and is not *used* for anything because it has long-ago escaped the magical taboo of having been given to man by a deity when Christianity became the religion of the West. "Christianity is not a tribal faith, but a universal message of salvation." Krenek traces the development of Western music through its Christian beginnings to the twelve-tone system.
a. ——. *Neue Zürcher Zeitung* (January 21, 1937)
b. ——. In his *Zur Sprache gebracht.* (K707) (München: Albert Langen - Georg Müller, 1958): 200-208.
c. "On the status of Western music." In his *Exploring music.* (K817) (New York: October House, 1966): 87-95.
d. "Von der Würde der abendländischen Musik." In his *Im Zweifelsfalle* (K924) (Wien: Europaverlag, 1984): 253-261.
e. ——. *Unknown*, pp.9-15.
Manuscripts: **A-Wst** typescript (2 p.)

K360. *"John Law; Roman der Banknote."* *Wiener Zeitung* 233:54 (February 24, 1936): 7.
Review of the book by Stephan Pollatschek (Wien: Saturn-Verlag, 1936).

K361. "Béla Bartók 5. *Streichquartett.*" *Pester Lloyd* (February 25, 1936)
Review of its first performance in Vienna.

K362. "Zum internationalen Kongress für Musikerziehung in Prag." *Wiener Zeitung* 233:62 (March 3, 1936): 10-11.
Discusses the main theme "Education for musical listening and musical understanding" presented at the International Congress for Music Education.

K363. *"Adolf Loos privat."* *Wiener Zeitung* 233:68 (March 9, 1936): 6.
Review of the book by Claire Loos (Wien: Johannes Presse, 1936).

K364. "Richard Götz *Licht und Landschaft.*" *Neues Wiener Tagblatt* (March 15, 1936)
Review of the book (Wien: Johannes Presse, 1936).

K365. "Eine Monographie über Karl V." *Wiener Zeitung* 233:75 (March 16, 1936): 6.
Review of the book *Karl V.* by Walter Fritsch (Leipzig: Julius Kittle Nachfolge, 1936).

K366. "Was erwartet der Komponist von der Musikerziehung?" *23* no.26/27 (June 8, 1936): 19-26.

A lecture on the problems of music education given at the First Internationale Kongress für Musikerziehung, April 8, 1936 in Prag. "It may be said that the new endeavors of music education are conducive to replacing our public audience with something much better, with a community of actively musical people who, being educated to singing and playing together, will generate a new, more profound and more vital musical culture. I cannot conceal that, from the vantage point of a creative musician, this ideal does not at all appear desirable. No matter how sincere the efforts of communal singers, lute and recorder players may be, they will always conquer only the exterior fringe, the lowest level of the realm of music. If their achievement as measured against the total of music, is nearly nothing, there is the danger that those who measure it against the effort they have expended in reaching it may take it for a maximum. And even if their teachers may not think so, they may come to feel that music beyond their reach is an intellectual plaything not worthy of their attention." *See:* B19

a. ——. In *Briefwechsel,* von Theodor W. Adorno und Ernst Krenek. (K862) (Frankfurt am Main: Suhrkamp, 1974): 208-214.

b. "Skladatel a problémy všeobecné hudební výchovy." *Rytmus* (Prag) 1:9 (April 1936): 106-107.

Summary in Czech prepared by M. F.

K367. "Zur textlichen Bearbeitung von Monteverdis *Poppea.*" *Wiener Zeitung* 233:102 (April 12, 1936): Osterbeilage 5-7.

Discusses the text by Giovanni Francesco Busenello and its dramatic implications in his edition of the opera op.80a to be produced in Vienna in 1937; includes selections from the libretto.

a. "Meine Textbearbeitung von Monteverdis *Poppea.*" *Anbruch* 18:4/5 (June-July 1936): 106-108.

Abbreviated essay, including an excerpt from the libretto.

K368. "Erster Internationaler Kongress für Musikerziehung in Prag." *Wiener Zeitung* 233:104 (April 15, 1936): 7-8 ; 233:105 (April 16, 1936): 7-8.

Discusses the principal themes of the conference on music education and reviews its concerts.

K369. "Krenek *Karl V.*" *Mirador* (Barcelona) 8:374 (April 16, 1936)

In Catalan. Program note for the premiere of *Fragmente aus dem Bühnenwerk "Karl V."* op.73a.

a. ——. [*Program: IGNM-Konzert Barcelona]* (April 19, 1936)

K370. "Kongress für Musikerziehung in Prag." *Neues Wiener Tagblatt* (April 20, 1936)

Discusses the Erster Internationale Kongress für Musikerziehung.

K371. "Notizen aus Barcelona." *Wiener Zeitung* 233:128 (May 9, 1936): 8-9 ; 233:131 (May 12, 1936): 7-8.

Travel report about Barcelona on the occasion of the Internationale Gesellschaft für neue Musik festival discussing the festival, Catalonia, the local language, its unique architecture, the dance-play "La Platum," and fireworks.

a. "Stadt zwischen Traum und Wirklichkeit." In his *Gedanken unterwegs.* (K720) (München: Albert Langen - Georg Müller, 1959): 117-120.

K372. "Notizen aus Südfrankreich." *Wiener Zeitung* 233:136 (May 17, 1936): Sonntagsbeilage 1-2.

A travel report about spring in Southern France, Avignon, and including impressions of the rain in Narbonne.

a. "Regen über Narbonne." In *Querschnitt; 10 Jahre Langen-Müller 1952-1962.* (München: Albert Langen/Georg Müller, 1962): 372-376.

b. ——. In his *Gedanken unterwegs.* (K720) (München: Albert Langen - Georg Müller, 1959): 121-125.

K373. "*Chroniques de ma vie* (II. Teil)." *Wiener Zeitung* 233:151 (June 2, 1936): 6.

Brief review of the second volume of Igor Stravinsky's autobiography (Paris: Denoël et Steele, 1936).

K374. "Beiträge zu Fragen der Musikästhetik." *Wiener Zeitung* 233:163 (June 14, 1936): Sonntagsbeilage 1-2.

Extensive review of the book by Ernst Georg Wolff *Grundlagen einen autonomen Musikästhetik.* Sammlung musikwissenschaftlicher Abhandlungen, Bd.15. (Strassburg: Heitz & Co., 1934). A generally appreciative response to Wolff's proposal to create a separate, autonomous field of music aesthetics within philosophy. There exists a primordial phenomenon to musical medium, poised between sound reality and psyche, whose basic cell is the musical interval. All musical rules can be constructed out of this general realm. Krenek disagrees with Wolff when the author validates only one construction scheme, the major scale, and states that this is a contradiction to his philosophy. *See:* B1484

K375. "*Diabolus in musica.*" *Wiener Zeitung* 233:164 (June 15, 1936): 6.

Review of a book of essays on music by Désiré Emile Inghelbrecht. (Paris: E.Chiron, 1933).

K376. "*Ein schweigsamer Held.*" *Wiener Zeitung* 233:164 (June 15, 1936): 6.

Review of the novel by James Hilton in a German translation by Elizabeth Arten. (Einsiedeln SZ: Benziger, 1936).

K377. "R.Schneider-Schelde *In jenen Jahren.*" *Wiener Zeitung* 233:164 (June 15, 1936): 6.

Brief review of a novel by Rudolf Schneider-Schelde (Leipzig: Zeitbild Verlag, 1935).

K378. "Aischylos in Breitensee." *Wiener Zeitung* 233:165 (June 16, 1936): 7.

Review of a production of the play *Perser*.

K379. "Blätter aus einem alpinen Tagebuch." *Wiener Zeitung* 233:197 (July 19, 1936): Sonntagsbeilage 1-2 & 233:211 (August 2, 1936): Sonntagsbeilage 1-2.

The first two of four travel reports about a trip in the Austrian Alps, including impressions and reflections on the effects of Alpine nature on the city traveller.

a. "Geborgen in den Bergen." In his *Gedanken unterwegs.* (K720) (München: Albert Langen - Georg Müller, 1959): 126-135.

K380. "Der Autor und die Premiere." *Neues Wiener Tagblatt* (June 21, 1936)

K381. "Karl Kraus." *Der Christliche Ständestaat* 3:25 (June 21, 1936)

K382. "Neue Beiträge zur Musikästhetik." *Wiener Zeitung* 233:170 (June 21, 1936): Sonntagsbeilage 1-2.

Continues the extensive review of the book by Ernst Georg Wolff *Grundlagen einen autonomen Musikästhetik. Sammlung musikwissenschaftlicher Abhandlungen,* Bd.15. (Strassburg: Heitz & Co., 1934). *See:* B1484

K383. *"Der musikalische Schaffensprozess."* *Wiener Zeitung* 233:171 (June 22, 1936): 8.

Review of the book by Julius Bahle concerning the psychological study of the creative experience and stimulus (Leipzig: S.Hirzel, 1936).

K384. "Die Musikalischen Systeme der Nachkriegszeit, I: Das Zwölftonsystem, b: Thesen." *Musica viva* 1:2 (July 1936): 4-7.

General discussion of his use of the twelve-tone system and the attitudes one must have to use it. He discusses the relationship between the twelve-tone system and tonality, its structural peculiarities, harmony, and form. He concludes that the twelve-tone system only establishes a relationship between its elements and therefore approaches the spirit of mathematics and modern physics. "Thus it expresses a more elevated liberty of mind but at the same time represents a more rigorous obligation... The balance between liberty and obligation remains to be found." German text with English, French, and Italian translations. *See:* B1414

K385. *"Der Stadtpark."* *Wiener Zeitung* 233:184 (July 6, 1936): 6.

Review of the novel by Hermann Grab (Wien: Zeitbild Verlag, 1935).

K386. *"Tobias und die Goldvögel."* *Wiener Zeitung* 233:184 (July 6, 1936): 6.

Review of the novel by Otto Helmut Lienert (Einsiedeln, SZ: Verlag Benziger, 1936).

K387. *"Der arme Verschwender."* *Wiener Zeitung* 233:191 (July 13, 1936): 6.

Review of the novel by Ernst Weiss (Amsterdam: Querido Verlag, 1936).

K388. "Rechenschaft über ein Leben." *Wiener Zeitung* 233:205 (July 27, 1936): 7.

Review of the book *Viele reden, einer ruft; Das Zeugnis eines rastlosen Lebens* by Fritz Rudolf Könekamp (Einsiedeln, SZ: Benziger, 1936).

K389. "Fünfundzwanzig Jahre *Brenner.*" *Wiener Zeitung* 233:207 (July 29, 1936): 7.

Celebrates the twenty-fifth anniversary of the periodical from Innsbruck which emphasizes Christian life and the German language.

K390. *"Dschung Kue; oder, Der Bezwinger der Teufel."* *Wiener Zeitung* 233:212 (August 3, 1936): 7.

Review of a Chinese folk tale in the German translation by Claude du Bois-Reymond (Berlin: S.Fischer Verlag, 1936).

K391. *"Ein Mensch fällt aus Deutschland."* *Wiener Zeitung* 233:219 (August 10, 1936): 6.

Review of the novel by Konrad Merz (Amsterdam: Querido-Verlag, 1936).

K392. "Blätter aus einem alpinen Tagebuch, III." *Wiener Zeitung* 233:231 (August 23, 1936)

The third report of a trip in the Austrian Alps; this installment focuses on the Bregenzer Wald in the Western part of Austria.

a. "Vom Bregenzer Wald." In his *Gedanken unterwegs*. (K720) (München: Albert Langen - Georg Müller, 1959): 136-141.

K393. "Blätter aus einem alpinen Tagebuch, IV." *Wiener Zeitung* 233:252 (September 13, 1936): Sonntagsbeilage 1-2.

The last of four travel reports concerning a trip in the Austrian Alps. This installment focuses on a valley high in the Alps describing the landscape and its society, comparing urbane society with rural society, and condemning clichéd opinions about the people and the existence of the radio in the mountain resorts.

a. "Die sublime Zone." In his *Gedanken unterwegs*. (K720) (München: Albert Langen - Georg Müller, 1959): 142-147.

K394. *"Die Kunst, anständig zu sein."* *Wiener Zeitung* 233:253 (September 14, 1936): 7.

Review of the book by Arkas [pseud.] (Einsiedeln, SZ: Benziger, 1936).

K395. "Notizen aus dem Burgenland." *Wiener Zeitung* 233:273 (October 4, 1936): Sonntagsbeilage 1.

Travel report about Burgenland, the Eastern-most part of Austria bordering on Hungary, comparing the landscape with Africa and other southern landscapes.

a. "Nähe des Südens." In his *Gedanken unterwegs*. (K720) (München: Albert Langen - Georg Müller, 1959): 148-153.

K396. "Zur musikalischen Bearbeitung von Monteverdis *Poppea*." *Schweizerische Musikzeitung und Sängerblatt* 76:20 (October 15, 1936): 545-555.

His edition (op.80a) was intended for practical purposes. "The problem, therefore, is not to reconstitute, as in the case of *Orfeo*, but to interpret Monteverdi's music as expressive music with a wide range of psychological differentiation." A detailed description with many musical examples of Krenek's orchestration.

a. "Ernst Krenek on Monteverdi's *Poppea*." *Musical Times* 77:1126 (December 1936): 1082.

English summary.

K397. "Was nennt man neue Musik, und warum?" In his *Ueber neue Musik*. (K418) (Wien: Ringbuchhandlung, 1937): 5-17.

The first lecture given in the Vienna series "Neue Musik" on October 23, 1936 in the Klubsaal des Oesterreichischen Ingenieur- und Architekten-Vereins. Repeated in Zurich and Basel in January 1937. Krenek surveys contemporary music, looking at the "new objectivity," surrealism, expressionism, neo-classicism, and folk music influences. Krenek concludes that new music is that music composed using the twelve-tone technique of the Viennese School of Arnold Schönberg. *See:* B20, B160, B168, B219, B369, B574, B679, B795, B811, B830, B1051, B1089, B1200, B1221, B1222

K398. *"Das Problem der Theodizee im philosophischen Denken des Abendlandes, Bd.1: Von Platon bis Thomas von Aquino."* *Wiener Zeitung* 233:309 (November 6, 1936): 7.

Review of the book by Friedrich Billicsich (Innsbruck: Tyrolia Verlag, 1936).

K399. "*Dr. Renaults Versuchung.*" *Wiener Zeitung* 233:309 (November 6, 1936): 6.

Review of the novel by Johannes V. Jensen in the German translation by Julia Koppel (Vienna: Bermann-Fischer Verlag, 1936).

K400. "Ueber Musik reden." *Der Wiener Tag: Der Sonntag* Nr.138 (November 8, 1936): [2].

A discussion of how one talks about music, both in the specifics of notes and form, and in the generalities of emotion.

K401. "Erinnerung an Karl Kraus." 23 no.28/30 (November 10, 1936): 1-16.

Tells of Krenek's feelings of great personal loss caused by Kraus's death. Although a non-musician, Kraus profoundly influenced Krenek through the organization of his thought. A radical-conservative, Kraus's thought is close to new music, although he himself did not perceive the relationship. *See:* B554

a. ——. In his *Zur Sprache gebracht.* (K707) (München: Albert Langen - Georg Müller, 1958): 229-240.

K402. "Hoch vom Olymp." 23 no.28/30 (November 10, 1936): 44-47.

Written under the pseudonym Austriacus. Reflecting on the ideas of world peace and the community of nations, the article ironically compares the attention given to the Olympic athletes and to athletes in general with the lack of attention accorded composers. The situation is especially ironic in a country like Austria which has produced so many "Olympic" composers.

K403. "Grundideen einer neuen Musikästhetik." In his *Ueber neue Musik.* (K418) (Wien: Ringbuchhandlung, 1937): 17-35.

The second lecture given in the Vienna series "Neue Musik" on November 11, 1936 in the Klubsaal des Oesterreichischen Ingenieur- und Architekten-Vereins. Repeated in Zurich and Basel in January 1937. A musical aesthetic must be general enough to encompass tonality and atonality. The musical thought or Gestalt or entity-concept is the basis of music; from the thoughts' complete transformation of the raw material at the level of articulation and relation emerges tonality or atonality. These musical thoughts, when combined, become the form of a composition, and the form provides its outline. The aesthetic is derived from concepts by Leonhard Deutsch, Ernst Georg Wolff, Christian von Ehrenfels, Julius Bahle, and Arnold Schönberg.

a. ——. In his *Zur Sprache gebracht.* (K707) (München: Albert Langen - Georg Müller, 1958): 257-276.

b. ——. In his *Im Zweifelsfalle.* (K924) (Wien: Europaverlag, 1984): 163-182.

c. "Basic principles of a new theory of musical aesthetics." In his *Exploring music.* (K817) (New York: October House, 1966): 129-149.

K404. "Atonalität." In his *Ueber neue Musik.* (K418) (Wien: Ringbuchhandlung, 1937): 37-51.

The third lecture given in the Vienna series "Neue Musik" on November 13, 1936 in the Klubsaal des Oesterreichischen Ingenieur- und Architekten-Vereins. Repeated in Zurich and Basel in January 1937. An examination of the development of atonal music; tonal music has defined form through the use of dissonant intervals in dominant harmonies. Krenek defines atonality and postulates an atonal harmonic system. He also discusses the development from atonality to the twelve-tone technique.

K405. "Zwölftontechnik." In his *Ueber neue Musik*. (K418) (Wien: Ringbuchhandlung, 1937): 51-70.

The fourth lecture given in the Vienna series "Neue Musik" on November 20, 1936 in the Klubsaal des Oesterreichischen Ingenieur- und Architekten-Vereins. Repeated in Zurich and Basel in January 1937. A definition of the twelve-tone technique and a detailed examination of its use.

    a. "Atonalita a dvanáctitónová technika." *Tempo* (Prague) 17:1 (October 8, 1937): 2-3.

    Extract from *Ueber neue Musik* concerning the twelve-tone technique. Translated by J. L. Přel.

K406. "Ein neuer Roman von Joseph Roth." *Wiener Zeitung* 233:327 (November 27, 1936): 11.

Review of the book *Berichte eines Mörders; erzählt in einer Nacht* (Amsterdam: A. de Lange Verlag, 1936).

K407. "Ueber die gesellschaftliche Bedeutung von Wahrheit und Lüge." *National Zeitung* (Basel) (November 29, 1936)

Citing as an example the Oxford University rule punishing lying, Krenek comes to the conclusion that motives for lying are related to the sociological power structure. One is expected to lie and still respect truth as a high ethical value; only powerlessness requires truth.

    a. ——. In his *Gedanken unterwegs*. (K720) (München: Albert Langen - Georg Müller, 1959): 154-157.

K408. "Ansprache bei der Trauerfeier für Karl Kraus." In *Trauerfeier für Karl Kraus, Wien, 30.11.1936*. (Vienna: Saturn-Verlag, 1937) 13 p.

Eulogy given during a memorial service held in the Vienna Konzerthaus for the Viennese moralist, critic, satirist, and journalist.

    a. ——. In his *Zur Sprache gebracht*. (K707) (München: Albert Langen - Georg Müller, 1958): 224-228.

Manuscripts: US-LJ typescript (4 p.)

K409. "Musik und Mathematik." In his *Ueber neue Musik*. (K418) (Wien: Ringbuchhandlung, 1937): 71-89.

The fifth lecture given in the Vienna series "Neue Musik" in December 1936 in the Klubsaal des Oesterreichischen Ingenieur- und Architekten-Vereins. Repeated in Zurich and Basel in January 1937. Krenek continues his discussion of the twelve-tone technique with a look at its mathematical basis. He explains the construction of all-interval rows and other row formations, and discusses the role of the row in musical form.

K410. "Léon Bloy: *Briefe an seine Braut*." *Wiener Zeitung* 233:337 (December 7, 1936): 7.

Review of the book in a German translation by Karl Pfleger (Salzburg: Anton Pustet, 1935).

K411. "*Isabella, Begründerin der Weltmacht Spanien*." *Wiener Zeitung* 233:348 (December 18, 1936): 10.

Review of the book by A. St. Wittlin (Erlenbach-Zurich: Eugen Rentsch-Verlag, 1936).

K412. "Musik und Humanität." In his *Ueber neue Musik.* (K418) (Wien: Ringbuchhandlung, 1937): 90-108.

The sixth lecture given in the Vienna series "Neue Musik" on December 18, 1936 in the Klubsaal des Oesterreichischen Ingenieur- und Architekten-Vereins. Repeated in Zurich and Basel in January 1937. Krenek examines the role of "new music" composed in the twelve-tone technique and discusses its relationship to the current musical environment. He examines its role in religious and secular music, and discusses the political forces which are arrayed against "new music." He also discusses the need for relavant music education, and the aesthetics of "new music" and its social role. *See:* B554

a. ——. *Anbruch* 19:6 (May.1937): 128+

K413. "Elegie auf Spanien." *Wiener Zeitung* 233:355 (December 25, 1936): Weihnachtsbeilage 5-6.

Reflections on war, terrorism, and the destruction of culture occurring in the Spanish Civil War.

a. "Spanische Elegie." In his *Gedanken unterwegs.* (K720) (München: Albert Langen - Georg Müller, 1959): 158-164.

K414. "Zu Rilkes zehntem Todestag." *Wiener Zeitung* 233:357 (December 29, 1936): 6.

An appreciation of the poet Rainer Maria Rilke mentioning Krenek's setting of his *O Lacrymosa* op.48.

-- 1937 --

K415. "Analyse der *Altenberg-Lieder* Bergs." In *Alban Berg,* von Willi Reich. (Wien: Herbert Reichner, 1937): 43-46.

Analysis of *Fünf Orchester-Lieder nach Ansichtskartentexten von Peter Altenberg* op.4 by Alban Berg.

K416. "Ist Oper heute noch möglich?" In [Unknown] (Wien: [Unknown], 1937): 273-288.

A consideration of operas from all periods with an investigation of the problems peculiar to modern operas. The characteristic of opera is that it is basically a nonsensical art product, and that fact has always raised questions about its viability. Opera reform has generally concentrated upon the conflict of music versus language, and reforms have only been gradually adopted.

a. ——. In his *Zur Sprache gebracht.* (K707) (München: Albert Langen - Georg Müller, 1958): 209-223.

b. ——. In his *Im Zweifelsfalle.* (K924) (Wien: Europaverlag, 1984): 36-50.

c. ——. *[Program: Hamburgische Staatsoper]* no.6 (1961/2): 41-48.

d. "Is opera still possible today?" In his *Exploring music.* (K817) (New York: October House, 1966): 97-112.

K417. "Vorwort," In his *Ueber neue Musik.* (K418) (Wien: Ringbuchhandlung, 1937): 3-4.

Krenek mentions that his book is based upon a series of lectures which he gave in Vienna. He notes that his friend Theodor W. Adorno helped him clarify his thought, and he thanks Willi Reich for his assistance in producing the book.

K418. *Ueber neue Musik; sechs Vorlesungen zur Einführung in die theoretischen Grundlagen.* Universal Edition no.10,876. (Wien: Ringbuchhandlung, 1937) 108 p.

Collection of six lectures: *Was nennt man neue Musik, und warum?* (K397), *Grundideen einer neuen Musikästhetik* (K403), *Atonalität* (K404), *Zwölftontechnik* (K405), *Musik und Mathematik* (K409), *Musik und Humanität* (K416). *See:* B554

a. ——. (Reprint. Darmstadt: Wissenschaftliche Buchgesellschaft, 1977)

K419. "Ueber neue Musik." *Anbruch* 19:1 (January 1937): 23-24.

A summary of the important points of the lectures given in Vienna in 1936 and published under this title.

K420. "Die Sitzung." *Wiener Zeitung* 234:1 (January 1, 1937): Neujahrsbeilage 3.

A humorous article on the various forms of meetings, their names (conference, enquête, congress, talk, audience, etc.), their purposes, and their results.

K421. "*Die Antwort des Herrn.*" *Wiener Zeitung* 234:18 (January 18, 1937): 6.

Review of the novel by Alphonse de Châteaubriant in the German translation by James Schwarzenbach (Einsiedeln, SZ: Benziger, 1936).

K422. "*Das Blut des Armen.*" *Wiener Zeitung* 234:18 (January 18, 1937): 6.

Review of the book by Léon Bloy in the German translation by Clemens ten Holder (Stuttgart: Anton Pustet, 1936).

K423. "Ein Korsika-Roman." *Wiener Zeitung* 234:25 (January 25, 1937): 6.

Review of the book *Heimweh nach der Hölle* by Erik Reger, pseudonym for Hermann Dannenberger (Berlin: Rowohlt, 1936).

K424. "*So einfach ist es nicht.*" *Wiener Zeitung* 234:25 (January 25, 1937): 6.

Review of the book by Otto Michael (Einsiedeln, SZ: Benziger, 1936).

K425. "Roman der Prüfung." *Wiener Zeitung* 234:46 (February 15, 1937): 7.

Review of the book *Joseph in Aegypten* by Thomas Mann (Wien: Bermann Fischer, 1936).

K426. "Notizen aus der Schweiz." *Wiener Zeitung* 234:53 (February 21, 1937): Sonntagsbeilage 2-3.

Comparing Switzerland with Austria, Krenek describes several cities and especially Basel, mentioning its Institute for Music Research and the conductor Paul Sacher.

a. "Auf der Suche nach der Heimat." In his *Gedanken unterwegs.* (K720) (München: Albert Langen - Georg Müller, 1959): 165-169.

K427. "Reise durch westliche Länder." *Anbruch* 19:3 (March 1937): 56-59.

Observations regarding the musical situation in small countries such as Belgium and Holland. Small countries have to look beyond their borders because their own cultural production is not sufficient. Radio stations in these countries do a lot to propagate their new music.

a. ——. In his *Gedanken unterwegs.* (K720) (München: Albert Langen - Georg Müller, 1959): 170-172.

K428. "Linksrheinisch." *Wiener Zeitung* 234:73 (March 14, 1937): Sonntagsbeilage 1-2.

Travel report on the countries on the left bank of the Rhine: Switzerland, Alsance, and the Netherlands. Discusses the languages and dialects, cities and their peculiarities, climate, museums, and people, as well as their histories and cultural identities.

a. ——. In his *Gedanken unterwegs.* (K720) (München: Albert Langen - Georg Müller, 1959): 173-177.

K429. "Othmar Schoecks neue Oper." *Wiener Zeitung* 234:77 (March 18, 1937): 10.

Review of the first performance of Schoeck's opera *Massimilla* in Zurich. It is one of the most original and charming of the characteristically light Swiss music dramas. Its clear parlando is presented with an agility and intensity which is in no way inferior to Strauss; the distinction is in the fluffy transparent orchestration, an observance of the forceful tempos, and the clarity of every word.

K430. "*The green pastures.*" *Wiener Zeitung* 234:85 (March 26, 1937): 9.
A review of the American film.

K431. "Tonal-Atonal." *Neues Wiener Journal* no.15576 (March 31, 1937)
Extracts from a lecture.

K432. "Oesterreichische, tschechische, belgische Musik in Prag." *Wiener Zeitung* 234:106 (April 17, 1937): 11.

Review of a series of concerts by two musical societies. Přítomnost under the leadership of Alois Hába presented concerts of Arnold Schönberg's Suite for chamber orchestra op.29 and Haba's *Sechstelton Musik.* Umělecká beseda presented an evening of Belgian music, including the Second string quartet of Jean Absil.

K433. "Die Prager Avantgarde-Bühnen." *Wiener Zeitung* 234:110 (April 21, 1937): 9.

A discussion of two avant garde theaters in Prague, the Befreite Theater and D-37, and a review of the productions which Krenek attended.

K434. "The new music and today's theatre." *Modern Music* 14:4 (May/June 1937): 200-203.

"If opera is to follow a new path ... it must take its bearings from ... the really new music," that is, it must use the twelve-tone technique. "By their very nature the principles of the new music lead away from the closed form, and realize instead the idea of 'fragments.'" Krenek's opera *Karl V.* op.73 makes use of these principles to interrupt the opera with the historical accomplishments of the emperor in order to probe their political and religious implications. "A second formal characteristic arising from this ideology of the music drama, is the tendency to divide the dramatic action between diverse simultaneous scenes and the device of an all-enclosing treatment." Consequently, the new opera will make extended use of historical subjects to search out "the true political significance of events and [develop] the conflicts that are essential to dramatic construction."

a. ——. In *The Essence of opera,* edited by Ulrich Weisstein. (New York: The Free Press of Glencoe, 1964): 348-353.

K435. "Rapport sur le point de vue du compositeur contemporain au sujet de l'attitude du public vis à vis des oeuvres modernes." *Unpublished.*

A lecture given May 11, 1937 in Brussels. [Publication information unknown; exists in **A-Wsb** B 141609]

Manuscripts: **A-Wst**.

K436. "Tintoretto-Ausstellung in Venedig." *Wiener Zeitung* 234:130 (May 12, 1937): 9.

Discusses the exhibition Mostra del Tintoretto in the Venetian gallery Ca' Pesaro.

K437. "S. Kracauer *Jacques Offenbach und das Paris seiner Zeit.*" *National Zeitung* (Basel) (May 16, 1937)

Review of the book (Amsterdam: A. de Lange, 1937).

K438. "Musikerbiographie ohne Musik." *Wiener Zeitung* 234:135 (May 18, 1937): 6.

Review of a book on the social conditions in Paris *Jacques Offenbach und das Paris seiner Zeit* by Siegfried Kracauer (Amsterdam: A. de Lange, 1937).

K439. "*Von Pythagoras bis Hilbert.*" *Wiener Zeitung* 234:135 (May 18, 1937): 6-7.

Review of a book surveying the history of mathematics and its masters by Egmont Colerus (Wien: Paul Zsolnay Verlag, 1937).

K440. "Musikkongress in Florenz." *Wiener Zeitung* 234:136 (May 19, 1937): 9 & 234:137 (May 20, 1937): 9.

Discusses the Second Internationale Musik-Kongress held in the Maggio Musicale in Florence. The topic of the first day was the relation between contemporary music and publications, and the Austrian participants were Egon Wellesz, Willi Reich, and Krenek. The second day was devoted to the question of music and film. See "Eine italienische Reise und ihre Folgen" (B315) by Hans Eisler for a reaction to Krenek's comments.

b. ——. *Anbruch* 19:6 (June 1937): 159-161.

K441. "Giotto-Ausstellung in Florenz." *Wiener Zeitung* 234:138 (May 21, 1937): 10.

Krenek visited the Mostra Giottesca near the Maggio Musicale in Florence while he attended the Second Internationale Musik-Kongress. He discusses the exhibition.

K442. "Musikkongress in Florenz." *Neues Wiener Tagblatt* (May 23, 1937)

K443. "Paul Hindemith spricht über 'die Komposition'." *Wiener Zeitung* 234:144 (May 27, 1937): 9-10.

Krenek reports on and discusses a series of three lectures given by Paul Hindemith during the Internationale Musik-Kongress in which he presented the harmonic theory published in his book *Unterweisung im Tonsatz*.

K444. "Alban Bergs *Lulu.*" *Wiener Zeitung* 234:154 (June 6, 1937): Sonntagsbeilage 1-2.

Lecture given in the Grossen Saal of the Tonhalle in Zurich on May 31st at the premiere of the opera. Examines the dramatic and musical background of *Lulu*.

a. ——. *Opernhaus Zürich Jahrbuch 1937/38*, p.16.

b. ——. In his *Zur Sprache gebracht.* (K707) (München: Albert Langen - Georg Müller, 1958): 241-250.

c. ——. *Opernhaus Zürich Jahrbuch 1979/80*, p.58.

d. ——. In his *Im Zweifelsfalle; Aufsätze über Musik.* (K924) (Wien: Europaverlag, 1984): 115-124.

e. ——. In *Querschnitt; 10 Jahre Langen-Müller 1952-1962.* (München: Albert Langen/Georg Müller, 1962): 161-170.

f. "Alban Berg's *Lulu.*" In his *Exploring music.* (K817) (New York: October House, 1966): 113-122.

K445. "*Vereinigung durch den Feind hindurch.*" *Wiener Zeitung* 234:148 (May 31, 1937): 7.

   Review of the novel by Rudolf Borchardt (Wien: Bermann-Fischer Verlag, 1937).

K446. "Die neue Mozart-Biographie." *Wiener Zeitung* 234:169 (June 7, 1937): 7.

   Review of the biography *Mozart* by Annette Kolb (Wien: Bermann-Fischer Verlag, 1937).

K447. "Christliche Philosophie." *Wiener Zeitung* 234:169 (June 21, 1937): 7.

   Review of the book *Von der christlichen Philosophie* by Jacques Maritain in a German translation by Balduin Schwarz. (Salzburg: Anton Pustet, 1935).

K448. "*Der Gemmenschneider.*" *Wiener Zeitung* 234:183 (July 5, 1937): 6.

   Review of the book of poems by Ernst Waldinger (Wien: Saturn Verlag, 1937)

K449. "*Prag heute.*" *Wiener Zeitung* 234:211 (August 2, 1937): 7.

   Review of the book by Frank Warschauer (Prag: Orbis, 1937).

K450. "Soll die Jugend mit der neuen Musik bekannt gemacht werden?" *Wiener Zeitung* 234:217 (August 8, 1937): Sonntagsbeilage 1-2.

   Lecture given for the Gesellschaft für Musikerziehung during Musikpadagogischen Tagung in Paris on June 28, 1937.

K451. "*Annerl.*" *Wiener Zeitung* 234:225 (August 16, 1937): 6.

   Review of the novel by Max Brod (Amsterdam: Verlag A. de Lange, 1937).

K452. "*Erbauungsbuch für den deutschen Spiesser.*" *Wiener Zeitung* 234:246 (September 6, 1937): 6.

   Review of the book by Herbert Schneider (Wien: Richard Lenni, 1937).

K453. "Meine Bearbeitung von Monteverdis *Poppea.*" *Der Wiener Tag* (September 12, 1937): 9.

K454. "Zur dramaturgischen Bearbeitung von Monteverdis *Poppea.*" *23* no.31/33 (September 15, 1937): 22-30.

   Discussion of his dramatic edition and the production of Monteverdi's *Poppea* in Vienna in 1937.

K455. "Von der Pariser Tagung der IGNM." *23* no.31/33 (September 15, 1937): 40-42.

   Report on the re-organization of the Internationale Gesellschaft für neue Musik at a meeting in Paris and the changes in its by-laws affecting the selection of juries, election of its president, place for its next meeting, etc.

K456. "Fallobst." *23* no.31/33 (September 15, 1937): 46-48.

   Written under the pseudonym Austriacus. A collection of three short articles concerning actual events. The first article ridicules Dr. Wilhelm Furtwängler's comments about jazz in an interview; the second attacks Josef Wenzl-Traunfels, a mediocre composer who managed to get a composition job at the Vienna Staatsakademie; and the third is in the form of a pamphlet about tonality to be sold as a pharmaceutical agent.

K457. "Notizen zur Gesamtausgabe von Franz Kafkas Schriften." *Wiener Zeitung* 234:273 (October 3, 1937): Sonntagsbeilage 1-2.

Discusses the theme of bureaucracy and the Austrian characteristics represented in several Kafka stories.

a. ———. In his *Zur Sprache gebracht.* (K707) (München: Albert Langen - Georg Müller, 1958): 251-256.

b. "Notes on Kafka's collected works." In his *Exploring music.* (K817) (New York: October House, 1966): 123-128.

K458. "Zum Text von Monteverdis *Poppea.*" *Der Wiener Tag* (October 3, 1937)

K459. "Auf dem Wasser zu singen." *Wiener Zeitung* 234:297 (October 27, 1937): 9.

Impressions of the ocean voyage which brought the Salzburg Opera Company to America. Includes a description of the ship, complaints about hardships, and reports on nautical technology and immigration procedures.

a. ———. In his *Gedanken unterwegs.* (K720) (München: Albert Langen - Georg Müller, 1959): 178-181.

b. ———. *Hannoversche Presse* (April 29, 1960)

K460. "Zehn Tage Broadway." *Wiener Zeitung* 234:305 (November 5, 1937): 7-8.

A report on his stay in New York with the Salzburg Opera Company. Includes a short description of Times Square, reflections on American customs and eating habits in restaurants, and a comparison of American and European mentalities.

K461. "*Die Macht des Scharlatans.*" *Wiener Zeitung* 234:309 (November 9, 1937): 7.

Review of the book by Grete de Francesco on the history of medicine. (Basel: Bruno Schwabe)

K462. "Acht Tage Kanada." *Wiener Zeitung* 234:331 (December 2, 1937): 7-8.

Describes his visit to Canada and to the cities Montreal and Toronto. Krenek finds Canada is influenced more by Europe than by the United States.

K463. "Zur amerikanischen Mentalität, I." *Wiener Zeitung* 234:348 (December 19, 1937): 9.

An attempt to analyze why the American and European mentality are different. Business is seen as a sociological substitution for the more sublime relationships of European society; the business mind is considered to be the primary problem solver. Artistic programs are consequently closely bound up with commercial enterprises.

a. ———. In his *Gedanken unterwegs.* (K720) (München: Albert Langen - Georg Müller, 1959): 182-186.

K464. "Zur amerikanischen Mentalität, II." *Wiener Zeitung* 234:354 (December 25, 1937): 11-12.

Further discussion of the American business mentality; there is no requirement for credentials to hold a job, economic success is the important factor. The artist is viewed as one who does a job expecting profit and success.

a. ——. In his *Gedanken unterwegs*. (K720) (München: Albert Langen - Georg Müller, 1959): 186-190.

-- 1938 --

K465. "Fliegertod und Mädchenschule." In his *Gedanken unterwegs*. (K720) (München: Albert Langen - Georg Müller, 1959): 195-198.

Written in 1938. Review of the American films *Too hot to handle* and *Girls school*. Krenek states that the underlying theme in both films, whether intentional or unintentional, is human dread, though he has not seen this mentioned in any American review; one examines the business of reporting death and killing while the other emphasizes the act of bribery.

K466. "Ein politischer Prozess in New York." *Unpublished*.

Written in 1938 probably for the *Wiener Zeitung*. Discusses the election campaign of Thomas Dewey against Tammany Hall.

Manuscripts: US-LJ 4 p.

K467. "Nothing sacred." *Unpublished*.

A review written in German in 1938 of the films *Nothing sacred* and *Manhattan melodrama*; both films are mirrors of American psychology. The irony of *Nothing sacred* lies in the fact that success can be achieved even by rigorously attacking the very means that underlie commercial success, that is, a business attitude and shallow ethics.

Manuscripts: US-LJ 5 p.

K468. "The three overcoats of Anton K." *New Mexico Quarterly* 25:1 (Spr.1955): 9-43.

A story originally written in German in 1938. Depicts the plight of "K", an alien resident, and his conflict with bureaucracy.

a. "Die drei Mäntel des Anton K." In his *Prosa, Dramen, Verse*. (Münich: Albert Langen - Georg Müller, 1965): 11-57.

Manuscripts: US-LJ 35 p. ; various pages.

K469. "Bemerkungen zur Rundfunkmusik." *Zeitschrift für Sozialforschung* 7:1/2 (1938): 148-165.

Reflections on the problems of radio broadcasting. Because radio is a business, or a general service of propagandistic means, its function is directed toward banality and everyday use according to its sociological-political environment. The almost exclusive broadcasting of tonal music as well as the almost exclusive abuse of such music as mere entertainment accelerates the general banalization of tonal music. Instead of providing new forms of progressive artistic quality, which it could, the radio only pours out huge quantities of what has already been there.

a. ——. In *Kritische Kommunikationsforschung; Aufsätze aus der Zeitschrift für Sozialforschung*, hrsg. von Dieter Prokop. Reihe Hanser 141. (Munich: Carl Hanser Verlag, 1973): 47-65.

b. ——. In his *Im Zweifelsfalle*. (K924) (Wien: Europaverlag, 1984): 262-280.

K470. "Amerikanische Städtebilder, I." *Wiener Zeitung* 235:1 (January 1, 1938): Neujahresbeilage 1-2.

Impressions of the American cities New York and Chicago, their skylines and traffic systems.

K471. "Was ist gut in Amerika?" *Wiener Zeitung* 235:5 (January 6, 1938): 7-8.

After criticizing much of what he experienced in America from Hollywood, Krenek discusses some of the high points of his trip: the railway system with its beautiful stations and the high quality of service and comfort on the transcontinental trains, the exemplary hygiene and comfort supplied by electricity in hotels, and the luxury of the average home with two or three bathrooms. In general, food is pretty bad, except for fruits and ice cream.

K472. "Die 'Idee' (Zur amerikanischen Mentalität, III)." *Wiener Zeitung* 235:14 (January 15, 1938): 7-8.

People with "ideas" are trouble-makers because they expect more and disturb the general way of life; as a result, they cannot be successful and are despised.

a. "Zur amerikanischen Mentalität, III." In his *Gedanken unterwegs.* (K720) (München: Albert Langen - Georg Müller, 1959): 190-194.

K473. "Amerikanische Städtebilder, II." *Wiener Zeitung* 235:15 (January 16, 1938): Sonntagsbeilage 1.

Impressions of the American cities Saint Paul with its lakes and harsh climate; Salt Lake City and its altitude, the great Salt Lake, the Mormon Temple, and polygamy; and Los Angeles with its great dimensions which require owning a car, the beautiful mountains, the mild climate, and the people who are restless due in part to the film industry.

K474. "Bemerkungen zum amerikanischen Filmwesen." *Wiener Zeitung* 235:29 (January 30, 1938): Sonntagsbeilage 1-2.

A critical look at American movie theaters with a comparison of the trivial feature films and news-reels with German counterparts. An ironic look at American tastes as reflected in popular movie themes.

a. "Amerikanisches Filmwesen." *Der kleine Bund* (Bern) 19:24 (June 12, 1938): 1-2.

Expanded to include critical remarks about the American business mentality in the film industry; concludes that commercial considerations determine "culture."

K475. "Musik in Amerika." *Unpublished.*

Written in February 1938 for the *Wiener Zeitung.* Impressions of the state of music in America.

Manuscripts: **A-Wst** 7 p.

K476. "Nach fünf Monaten Amerika." *Unpublished.*

Written in February 1938 for the *Wiener Zeitung.* Reflections on his stay in America.

Manuscripts: **A-Wst** ink (6 p.)

K477. "*Frauen nach Jakatra.*" *Wiener Zeitung* 235:37 (February 7, 1938): 6.

Review of the novel by A. den Hertog, translated from the Dutch by Heinz V. Rövari. (Einsiedeln (SZ): Verlag Benziger)

K478. "Amerikanische Landschaft." *Wiener Zeitung* 235:38 (February 8, 1938): 8.

Description of Zion Canyon while traveling by train and bus from Salt Lake City to Los Angeles. Krenek discusses Cedar City, the Mormon style of house building, and his impressions of the scenery, especially of the layers of color, while visiting the canyon.

a. ——. In his *Gedanken unterwegs*. (K720) (München: Albert Langen - Georg Müller, 1959): 199-202.

K479. "Amerikanische Städtebilder, III." *Wiener Zeitung* 235:47 (February 17, 1938): 9-10.

Impressions of the American cities: San Francisco with its cable car system, China town and the Japanese quarter, and the Golden Gate Bridge, Seattle with its beautiful bay, and Denver. Krenek emphasizes his impressions on viewing the San Francisco Bay Area from the top of Mount Tamalpais; the European enjoys landscape for itself, while the American enjoys landscape only in so far as he can do something with it.

K480. "L'atonalité." *Les Cahiers de la musique* 2:3/4 (March-April 1938): 51-63.

Lecture in French given in Brussels on March 31, 1938. A discussion of atonality and twelve-tone music with musical examples drawn from his opera *Karl V*. op.73.

Manuscripts: "Musique nouvelle." **US-LJ** 8 p.

K481. "Ostwärts." In his *Gedanken unterwegs*. (K720) (München: Albert Langen - Georg Müller, 1959): 212-215.

Written in March 1938 for the *Wiener Zeitung*, but not published. Impressions on the voyage across the ocean leaving New York and returning to Europe; includes a meditation on Schubert. Article has a melancholic character.

Manuscripts: **A-Wst** 4 p.

K482. "American mixed grill, I & II." *Wiener Zeitung* 235:62 (March 4, 1938): 8 ; 235:63 (March 5, 1938): 10.

In German. Discusses American societal peculiarities: the drugstore is a relic from pioneer days that developed into a multipurpose store combining coffee shop, pharmacy, and general store. American manners and everyday language are examined, especially the effects of phrases such as "I am sorry" which provides a complete lack of social responsibility and having the good effect of being patient to the non-fluent foreigner. Also examines the manner in which one introduces oneself, contests and gambling, and death and the funeral.

a. ——. In his *Gedanken unterwegs*. (K720) (München: Albert Langen - Georg Müller, 1959): 203-211.

K483. "Is there reaction in contemporary music?" *Musical America* 38 (April 25, 1938): 5.

Reaction to atonal music is tending toward a "normalization" of musical language reflected in the twelve-tone style and the use of folk materials. Picture.

K484. "Contemporary problems, functions of the I.S.C.M. Festival." *London Daily Telegraph and Morning Post* (May 28, 1938)

"When the International Society for Contemporary Music was founded some seventeen years ago, the gentle breeze of peaceful minds and high ideals waved through the world. The international entente of creative musicians seemed to complete in the artistic sphere the task undertaken by the League of Nations, and the Austrian group of composers, who were the most active in promoting the idea of the society, believed that Salzburg, its birth-place and scene of the first festival, would become the Geneva of music... The I.S.C.M.'s most serious difficulty lies in the fact that the internal activity of many sections is handicapped by the lack of financial means and obstructed by aesthetic and political reaction."

K485. "Wie steht es um die neue Musik?" *Basler Nachrichten* (July 24, 1938): 119-120.

Reviews the problems of the London Festival of the International Society for Contemporary Music without mentioning names or specific works. Hearing many new compositions in a short time requires considerable concentration, but the real reason most of the music failed to convey an impression of a whole must be sought in the problem of personality. Though it should be expected that not all pieces in such an event can be masterworks, there were two groups of compositions which best succeeded: those which used a variation of a well-tried scheme in a witty way and those which revealed new intentions using tried techniques. The presence of personality also needs a balance of theory and system; the inspired musical idea is not alone sufficient for a successful piece. Evidence of deeper values justifies the continuation of new music festivals.

K486. "Plea for modern opera: A way out of the stagnation of present times." *London Daily Telegraph and Morning Post* (August 27, 1938)

Printed in "The world of music" column edited by Richard Capell. Proposes two solutions to the lack of new operas, one is a chamber opera to be performed by touring companies where the long preparation time would be off-set by many performances, the other is an opera requiring extraordinary forces to be performed at a festival. England presents the opportunities for these kinds of operas.

K487. "The Viennese school." *Unpublished.*

Lecture given at Boston University on October 25, 1938. "If one would identify the so-called Viennese School of modern music with atonality and twelve-tone technique it would be right only in a narrow, more technical sense... The main idea realized by Arnold Schoenberg, the head of this school, was to make music more music-conscious again, after the spectacular features of the high romanticism which connected music more and more with extramusical conceptions."

Manuscripts: **US-LJ** typescript copy (5 p.)

K488. "The transplanted composer." *Modern Music* 16:1 (November-December 1938): 23-27.

Music is universal, and the immigrant composer can contribute to American musical life. The situation of new music depends upon the mental attitude of those in control of the mechanism of distribution which in turn is dependant upon public taste. Education of laymen and musicians is important, and the immigrant, if at all articulate, can play a useful role. Picture of scenes from the Prague production of *Karl V.* op.73.

K489. "Musik für die Ewigkeit." *Basler Nachrichten* (November 2, 1938)

Reflections on the contents of a time capsule buried at the New York Exposition of 1938 which contained music from contemporary culture: *Finlandia, Stars and Stripes Forever,* and *Flat Foot Floozie.* "When one thinks of the cultural mish-mash in New York, one almost feels that the barbarians who set fire to the library of Alexandria did more to preserve classical culture than the manager of the Olympic Games would have done had he buried a little fire-proof, earthquake-proof, poison-proof box containing all the pop songs of Alcibiades' day."

a. ——. In his *Zur Sprache gebracht*. (K707) (München: Albert Langen - Georg Müller, 1958): 277-278.

b. "Music for eternity." In his *Exploring music*. (K817) Geoffrey Skelton. (New York: October House, 1966): 151-153.

K490. "Lecture." *Unpublished*.

Lecture given at Wesleyan University, Middletown, CT, November 9, 1938. "There are especially three statements which I wish to make the main issue of the present discussion. The first would be that the Sonata-form is the standard form of tonality and as such bound to the conditions of tonality... [Second] the efforts of resolving the problem of the form in the realm of atonality by re-establishing the Sonata-form or other traditional forms failed necessarily to reach their aim. Thirdly, I will try to demonstrate that only the twelve-tone technique was able to furnish new means for developing a new and adequate idea of form."

Manuscripts: US-LJ 4 p.

K491. "The place of contemporary music in general education." *American Musicological Society Papers* 3 (1938): 25-29.

Lecture at the American Musicological Society meeting, Washington, DC, December 1938 concerned with the widening gap between the composer and audience and the burden that rests on music educators for attempting to close that gap. "When teachers are asked about how real modern music could be introduced in their plans, even those who are willing to do it point out that modern music raises two main difficulties: the difficulty of understanding and that of performing. The first one is particularly puzzling because under normal circumstances, everybody should more readily perceive the features of his own time than those of the past which require obviously a great deal of historical perspective and self-adaptation on the part of the observer... Of course, listening, explanation, analysis, would not be sufficient to awaken the permanent interest of young people in modern music. The general trend in modern education is to handle everything practically... But there is still another means for making young people acquainted with modern music: that is the piano."

-- 1939 --

K492. "'Information please' on modern music." *Unpublished*.

Written in 1939 concerning the lack of information about atonal and twelve-tone music in American encyclopedias and dictionaries. A book review of *The Macmillan Encyclopedia of Music and Musicians* edited by Albert E. Wier (New York, 1938) and *International Cyclopedia of Music and Musicians* edited by Oscar Thompson (New York: Dodd, Mead & Co., 1939).

Manuscripts: US-LJ typescript copy (5 p.)

K493. "Opera." *Unpublished*.

Lecture given at Stanford University, March 8, 1939. An historical survey of the development of opera in Germany and Italy by repertory companies as opposed to touring companies. Opera is still indebted and influenced by the work of Richard Wagner and his concept of operatic style as illusion and the artificial world of *Gesamtkunstwerk*. Krenek's approach to a new opera led to a revival of its primitive characteristics as a stage play with song and dance, of which *Jonny spielt auf* op.45 is an example, with the intent of destroying illusion by bringing realistic objects (such as the telephone, a railway station, etc.) on stage. Wagner's principal achievement was raising opera to a level of philosophical presentation which resulted in a new interest in historical subjects, such as Darius Milhaud's *Christoph Colomb* and Krenek's *Karl V.* op.73. Another modern style was introduced by Kurt Weill influenced by the techniques of motion pictures. Krenek concludes the idea of a touring opera ensemble instead of the repertory theater would fit well in the United States.

Manuscripts: **US-LJ** 6 p.

K494. "American experiences." *Tempo* 1:3 (May 1939): 1-2.

From a lecture given in 1937-38. Based upon his visit to America with the Salzburg Opera Guild, he finds there is an interest in touring opera and thinks chamber opera could fill that need. It is as difficult to write what one likes in America as it is in Europe, but there are a few progressive institutions fostering the cause of new music. There is a need for school music which a composer can fill if he is willing to forgo his "radicalism." Mentions he is writing *Eight column line* op.85 and teaching at the University of Michigan and about to start at Vassar.

K495. *Music here and now,* translated by Barthold Fles. (New York: W. W.Norton, 1939) 306 p.

An expansion, translation, and re-writing of *Ueber neue Musik*. Dated at end: Boston, October 1938 - Ann Arbor, June 1939. Contents: 1. *Who is musical?* "The musical person is someone who is directly affected by music ...[and] able to understand musical construction." On the inadequacies of program notes and suggestions for educating the public. 2. *Modern music is unpopular.* Music is affected by social conditions and economics. Royalties tend to favor the established repertoire against new music. European radio is supported by taxes and plays new music, American radio is supported by the market place and consequently plays little new music. 3. *Not all contemporary music is new music.* Distinguishes between "Contemporary," "Modern," and "New" music; decries popular music and its banality; discusses Ferruccio Busoni, Igor Stravinsky, Paul Hindemith, Béla Bartók, Charles Ives, Arnold Schoenberg, and their characteristic styles; and supports atonality because of its richness. 4. *The concept of music in the Western world.* Contrasts Western music, which is a reflection if Western culture, to music of other cultures. Form is important as opposed to iteration, rhyme and symmetrical formations, polyphony and balances, and harmony. 5. *Rise and decline of tonality.* Music before Bach is unpopular because it is not based upon tonality and requires a different way of listening. Discusses the beginnings of tonality in opera and Monteverdi, the tonal cadence, harmonic modulation and tempered pitch, chromaticism, Johann Sebastian Bach, the sonata form, Beethoven, Schubert, the return of chromaticism in Wagner, to culminate in Schoenberg's Three piano pieces, op.11. 6. *Atonality.* It is identified by a lack of the cadential and dominant functions, and the absence of a definite key-consciousness. Defines atonality with its free rhythm; examines polytonality, athematicism of Alois Hába, and the super-nationality of twelve-tone music. 7. *Music under construction.* Free, prose-like diction and dissonance means a tightening of nuances and a refinement of the sound language. Balance and iteration are re-defined. Defines the basic features of the twelve-tone technique and its search for new forms. Describes his *Variations* op.79 as an example of twelve-tone music. Reacts to various objections to the use of twelve-tone music. 8. *Music and mathematics.* Because something can be described with mathematical figures does not make it mathematical. Discusses the relationship of the overtones to a scale and Paul Hindemith's theory of combination tones, and notes that music controls the raw materials of tones. Discusses the relativity of scientific systems and axioms, and the relationship of theory to practice. 9. *New Media.*

Discusses the differences between composer and performer, the development of orchestration, the role of the conductor, strict adherence to the score, the training of performers, and the role of radio, recordings, and films. 10. *From minuet to swing.* The difference between popular and serious music was not always so distinct; art music absorbed folk music elements and entertainment music absorbed art music elements. The break widened with the difference between Offenbach and Wagner, the Viennese operetta, jazz, and improvisation. 11. *What must we do?* Raise the listener to a higher state of consciousness, organize new music groups like the International Society for Contemporary Music, change opera to small forms, improve the teaching of music to the public, encourage piano playing, and emphasize musical work as art. *See:* B70, B588, B681, B723, B724, B761, B893, B1051, B1343, B1353, B1394, K503

a. ——. (Reprint. New York: Russell & Russell, 1967) 306 p.

K496. *Studies in counterpoint based on the twelve tone technique.* (New York: G.Schirmer, 1940) 37 p.

A textbook. "The author wishes to set forth the elementary principles of the twelve-tone technique as he has applied it in a number of his own works." Krenek mentions the *Sixth string quartet* op.78 and *Twelve short piano pieces* op.83. Dated: Washington, DC, January 1939 - Estes Park, CO, August 1939. *See:* B177, B398, B400, B883, B1051, B1060, K565, K602

a. *Studi di contrappunto basati sul sistema dodecafonico,* traduzione italiana di Rodolfo Rueck. (Milano: Edizioni Curci, 1948) 43 p.

b. *Studi di contrappunto basati sul sistema dodecafonico,* traduzione italiana di Rodolfo Rueck. Rev. ed. (Milano: Edizioni Curci, 1954) 43 p.

c. *Zwölfton-Kontrapunkt Studien,* Deutsche Uebertragung von Heinz Klaus Metzger. Edition Schott, 4203. (Mainz: B.Schott's Söhne, 1952) 51 p.

d. *Studies in counterpoint based on the twelve tone technique.* (Tokyo: [Unknown], 1955)

Japanese translation.

e. ——. Libros de música, 4. (Madrid: Ediciones Rialp, 1965)

Spanish translation; published with the Spanish translation of *Selbstdarstellung* (K569-b).

f. *Studije dvanaesttonskog kontrapunkta.* Prevod: Vasilije Mokranjac. (Beograd: Univerzitet umetnosti u Beogradu, 1978)

Yugoslavian translation prepared as a dissertation.

K497. "Students in America." *New York Times* 88:29821 (September 17, 1939): 10:5.

"When I set out for my first teaching activity in this country, at the Summer school of the University of Michigan, I was warned... 'Don't expect too much of the students!'" In fact, American students are very good. In seven rehearsals his just completed *Symphonic piece* op.86 for string orchestra was convincingly presented in a try-out concert. "The absolutely unexpected fact [is] that a students' orchestra was able to perform most satisfactorily and without any strain a full-fledged modern score... The students did not feel at all harassed by the awesome feature of atonality and twelve-tone technique."

-- 1940 --

K498. "Ant story." *Unpublished.*

Written about 1940? A short story in English told from the point of view of

ants. Depicts the relationship of ants with people, who try to annihilate them.
Manuscripts: US-LJ 6 p.

K499. "Nationalism in Music." *Unpublished*.

Written 1940-1944. "By restoring music to its function as an expression of universal human experience, by breaking down the tendency toward dull and narrow provincialism, composers may contribute more than they think to establishing a peaceful community of nations."

Manuscripts: US-LJ typescript copy (10 p.)

K500. "Harmonie, Kontrapunkt, Komposition." *Unpublished*.

Course lecture notes, examples, and tests dated 1940.

Manuscripts: US-LJ various pages.

K501. "Teaching the atonal idiom." *Music Teachers National Association Proceedings* 34 (1940): 306-312.

A lecture given at a meeting of the Music Teachers National Association, in Cleveland on January 19, 1940, describing his teaching of atonality to Vassar College students; includes brief compositions by two students: Jill Markell and Katherine Schaefer.

a. "Unterweisung in der atonalen Tonsprache." *Schweizerische Musikzeitung* 85:7 (July 1945): 321-322.

Extract.

K502. "Teaching composition." *Modern Music* 17:3 (March-April 1940): 148-153.

The aim of education is to enable a student to express himself in music. Two methods are available: one follows historical progression and requires the student to master the style of each period; the other begins with contemporary music materials. Present music teaching uses both methods.

K503. "Ernst Krenek." In *Letters of composers; an anthology*, compiled and edited by Gertrude Norman and Miriam Lubell Shrifte. (New York: Grosset & Dunlap, 1946): 397-400.

A letter to George Perle, dated Poughkeepsie, NY, March 13, 1940, reacting to his article "The Twelve-Tone Modal System" later published in the *Music Review* (November 1941). "Your contention is obviously that the present stage of composition needs regulations to the effect that only certain sound-relationships may be utilized... The predicament is exactly this: working along the lines of the 'classical' technique, we find ourselves every now and then embarrassed by the necessity of locating remaining tones of the series... The only imaginative way out of the dilemma seems to be a freer treatment of the series as I indicated in my book [*Music here and now* (K495)], and practiced in my *Symphonic piece*" op.86.

a. ——. In *Letters of composers; an anthology*, compiled and edited by Gertrude Norman and Miriam Lubell Shrifte. (New York: Knopf, 1946): 397-400.

b. ——. In *Letters of composers; an anthology*, compiled and edited by Gertrude Norman and Miriam Lubell Shrifte. (Reprint: Westport, CT: Greenwood Press, 1979): 397-400.

K504. "Choir concert features music of many eras." *Vassar Miscellany News* (March 20, 1940)

Review of the Easter concert.

K505. "Schnabel played Schubert's sonatas with unique skill." *Vassar Miscellany News* (April 20, 1940)

Review of a concert.

K506. "The Music Department." *Vassar Alumnae Magazine* 25:6, pt.1 (June 1940): 25-26.

Description of the department and its activities during a recent "Open house."

K507. "Cadential formations in atonal music." *AMS Bulletin* no.6 (August 1942): 5.

A lecture given at the meeting of the Greater New York Chapter of the American Musicological Society in New York on November 13, 1940. An examination of "the 'motival' and the 'extra-motival' functions of the series used in the twelve-tone technique, the former being manifest in purely melodic phenomena, the latter in more homophonic texture. Is it possible that these functions could be classified by means of a system of 'functional twelve-tone modes'? Investigation of the medieval modal system and of the Psalm-Tones shows that the essence of the modes was revealed particularly in the cadences. Similar analysis of various cadences in atonal music indicates tentatively the existence of three main cadence types... It appears doubtful that functional twelve-tone modes can be derived from the cadential formations in atonal music."

Manuscripts: "A study of cadential formations in atonal music." **US-LJ** typescript (9 p.) ; typescript copy (9 p.)

K508. "New opera style." *Music Clubs Magazine* 20:4 (April 1941): 7-8.

A lecture given at the National Federation of Music Clubs luncheon meeting held during the Music Teachers National Association meeting in Cleveland in December 1940. The new style calls for a small orchestra of no more than six instruments with spoken dialogue. Krenek is about to finish an opera, *Tarquin* op.90, meeting these criteria.

Manuscripts: **US-LJ** typescript (5 p.)

K509. "The survival of tradition." *Modern Music* 18:3 (March-April 1941): 143-146.

American music is a continuation of European musical tradition. The influences on a composer by external events are only superficial. "What [the composer] needs is shelter, food, and time to write music. Nothing short of the physical lack of these admittedly primitive prerequisites can seriously disturb him."

K510. "Krenek to play original variations at faculty concert." *Vassar Miscellany News* (March 8, 1941)

Discusses *12 Variationen in drei Sätzen* op.79. Krenek notes that the first performance was given at a concert sponsored by the Pro Musica Chapter in Los Angeles on January 1938.

K511. "Dance recital has whimsy, grandeur." *Vassar Miscellany News* (April 12, 1941)

Review of a performance by the Dance Group.

K512. "Gustav Mahler" In *Gustav Mahler,* by Bruno Walter; translated by James Galston. (New York: Greystone, 1941): 155-220.

Biographical essay, dated at end: Poughkeepsie, NY, May - June 1941.

Sections are entitled "Bohemian, Jew, German, Austrian;" "Mahler and Bruckner;" "Odyssey through the operatic province;" "Prague and Leipzig;" "Professional dilemma: creator and interpreter;" "Operas: why did Mahler not write any?" "Budapest: Mahler is for the first time his own master;" "Hamburg: *The youth's magic horn;*" "Foretokens of surrealism;" "Mahler and Strauss;" "Mahler in Vienna: The Austrian paradox;" "Life in Vienna: Mahler's conversion to Catholicism;" "On the threshold of 'new' music;" "Mahler leaves Vienna;" "Mahler and America;" and "Exit." Krenek notes that "the fundamental feature of Mahler's music is the army march, running the whole gamut from the triumphal cortege to the muffled sounds of the funeral service... His propensity for striking symbols made him choose again and again the martial rhythm of bugle and drum."

a.   ——. In *Gustav Mahler*, by Bruno Walter; translated by James Galston. (Reprint: New York: Da Capo, 1970): 155-220.

b.   ——. In *Gustav Mahler*, by Bruno Walter; translated by James Galston. (Reprint: New York: Vienna House, 1973): 155-220.

K513. "The role of inspiration in music." *Bulletin of Hamline University* 33:1 (January 1943): 2-6.

Lecture given at Yale University's Pierson College on December 10, 1941; the Hamline University Faculty Club on November 10, 1942; University of New Mexico, Albuquerque on August 31, 1943; and Vassar College. Music is composed by a combination of imagination and intellect through a process of working out musical ideas. "The creative process is essentially one of selection and elimination, no matter to what extent its different phases are conscious and possibly protracted labor, or quick, seemingly inspired decisions. The criteria applied in the selective processes are inner logic and originality." *See:* B554

a.   "Ueber die Inspiration." *Melos* 22:3 (March 1955): 68-71.

German translation by Helmut von Bracken.

b.   ——. In his *Zur Sprache gebracht*. (K707) (München: Albert Langen - Georg Müller, 1958): 279-285.

Manuscripts: **US-LJ** 7 p.

K514. "The composer speaks." In *The Book of modern composers*, edited by David Ewen. (New York: Alfred A. Knopf, 1942): 354-355.

A short survey of his stylistic development. "Looking back over the evolution of my musical style, I am not astonished that even benevolent observers became confused and vacillating in their faith. Whenever they thought I had comfortably settled down in some stylistic district, I was not at the expected place the next time, and the business of classifying had to start all over again... I have been striving for an ever-freer and more incisive articulation of musical thought. Liberation of this thought from harmonic conventions and rhythmic patterns, and preparation of a new, genuinely polyphonic way of thinking which makes full and conscious use of the tremendous experience of tonality, appear to me as guiding factors in my present endeavors."

a.   ——. In *The Book of modern composers*, by David Ewen. 2d ed. (New York: Alfred A. Knoff, 1950): 354-355.

K515. "Busoni then and now." *Modern Music* 19:2 (January-February 1942): 88-91.

Reminiscences about Ferruccio Busoni, whom Krenek met in Berlin in the early 1920's, with a discussion of his creed: neo-classicism. Krenek concludes that "it is fitting that he should be little known at present, lest he be quoted as the originator of a way of thinking which, against his will, has become the vehicle of reaction."

K516. "Where to begin? Operatic production or produce." *Opera News* 6:14 (January 19, 1942): 8-10, 30.

Should the opera composer wait until production facilities exist for new opera or should the composer write new opera? Krenek thinks the composer should wait, but "it is both the privilege and the risk of the creative artist to confront the naturally inert production apparatus with so powerful a vision that practical requirements will eventually be adapted to meet it." Krenek outlines the essentials of an operatic style which can be performed in America: 1. An opera dealing "with subjects commanding the vital interest of large and greatly diversified groups of listeners." 2. A sufficiently complex musical idiom to satisfy the intellectual standards of adult audiences. 3. Rigorously limited technical apparatus as far as scenery, number of singers, and instruments. Picture of a scene from *Jonny spielt auf* op.45.

K517. "Music and text, reflections of a modern composer on Lied and libretto." *Jahrbuch des Wiener Goethe-Vereins* 84/85 (1980-81): 97-104.

Lecture given during the Second American Congress for Aesthetics held at the Catholic University of America, Washington, DC, April 24, 1942; rewritten for Composers' Symposium, University of New Mexico, March 1984. Reflections on the dependence of stage action and musical time; stage action is a stylized replica of the biological continuity of life while music sets up its own time system.

a. "Persönliches." In his *Opera librettos*, Vol.3 (unpublished).

Manuscripts: "Music meets life in opera." **US-LJ** typescript (5 p.)

K518. "Die Amerika Reise." *Unpublished.*

A diary begun with his trip to America with the Salzburg Opera Company. Written between October 3, 1937 and September 17, 1939 and between December 18, 1939 and November 1940 in German, and from April 28, 1941 to August 29, 1942 in English.

Manuscripts: **US-LJ** 12 & 61 p.

K519. "On the enjoyment of music." *Unpublished.*

Lecture given in Bridgman Hall, Hamline University, Saint Paul, MN on October 5, 1942. "It is obvious that the difference between hearing and listening is expressed in the amount of attention devoted to the phenomenon. Now what is it precisely to what we should pay attention in order to enjoy music? It is no more and no less than the musical process itself. Actually it should be easier to enjoy music than any other art, because music does not refer to anything but itself."

Manuscripts: **US-LJ** typescript copy (6 p.)

K520. "New developments of the twelve-tone technique." *Music Review* 4:2 (May 1943): 81-97.

Dated at end: Saint Paul, MN, October-November 1942. Discusses the motivic function of the row, secondary series derivation by means of rotation, and twelve-tone modality using works of Anton Webern, Arnold Schoenberg, George Perle, and Roy Harris as well as his *Symphonic piece for string orchestra* op.86 and *Lamentatio Jeremiae prophetae* op.93.

Manuscripts: **US-LJ** typescript copy (15 p.)

K521. "A composer teaching." *Unpublished*.

Lecture given at the Minnesota Music Teacher's Association, Nicollet Hotel, Minneapolis, MN, November 2, 1942. The composer in the liberal arts college must teach theory to "illiterate" students; a survey of the available sources and proposals for new ones. "Whenever a composer is teaching at a liberal arts college, there is some apprehension likely to develop lest he may overemphasize the significance of creative endeavors and give the music department that famous conservatory slant which seems to many college people particularly distasteful."

Manuscripts: US-LJ typescript copy(7 p.) ; typescript copy (7 p.)

K522. "Music and football: Krenek advises knowing the rules." *Minneapolis Sunday Tribune* (November 15, 1942)

In listening to music, entertainment is a passive attitude, while enjoyment is an active one. New music requires several listenings to be comprehended.

-- 1943 --

K523. "Opera between the wars." *Modern Music* 20:2 (January-February 1943): 102-111.

Opera between the First World War and the Second World War was a reaction to Wagner's operas resulting in many different styles pointing toward a greater division between action and reflection; surveys opera styles from 1920 to 1940, including mention of the place of his opera *Jonny spielt auf* op.45. Notes that his opera *Karl V*. op.73 emphasized the division between action and reflection, and that "the business of music is now to underline the un-reality of the action and strengthen its articulation, instead of magically transfiguring it."

K524. "Music as a profession, vocation, and avocation." *Unpublished*.

Lecture given in Saint Paul, MN at the Lowry Hotel during a meeting of the American Interprofessional Institute, Saint Paul Chapter on April 29, 1943. Krenek discusses the place of the composer in society.

Manuscripts: US-LJ 16 p.

K525. "Traditional and new techniques in teaching theory." *Unpublished*.

Lecture given in Saint Paul, May 1943.

Manuscripts: US-LJ 7 p.

K526. "Europa nach dem Krieg." *Aufbau* (New York) 9:19 (May 7, 1943): 4.

Response with others to a question concerning the prospects of the rebirth of European culture following the Second World War.

K527. "The music of Ernst Krenek." *New Mexico Quarterly Review* 13:4 (Winter 1943): 415-419.

A lecture given at the University of New Mexico, Albuquerque, August 29, 1943, augmented with notes taken by John D. Robb. Krenek reacts to being labeled an "expressionist"; notes that the new music is expressive. Robb's notes continue with the contrast between the terms atonality and tonality, pointing out that new music has only continued the break-down of tonality already begun by Wagner. The twelve-tone system allows much creative activity. Includes a brief description of the *Variations for piano* op.79 written in 1937.

K528. "Universalism and nationalism in music." *New Mexico Quarterly* 14:1 (Spring 1944): 47-58.

Lecture given at the University of New Mexico, Albuquerque, August 30, 1943. Explores nationalism in the music of the Americas, and concludes that "the sooner Americans rid themselves of national self-consciousness, which is an embarrassing hang-over from nineteenth-century attitudes, the sooner they will be able to live up to the high purpose of Americanism, that is, to show the world the degree of happiness possible of attainment once the nationalistic poison is eliminated from the organism."

a. ——. In his *Gedanken unterwegs.* (K720) (München: Albert Langen - Georg Müller, 1959): 216-228.

b. ——. In his *Im Zweifelsfalle.* (K924) (Wien: Europaverlag, 1984): 281-291.

German translation by Friedrich Saathen.

Manuscripts: US-LJ typescript copy (17 p.)

K529. "The ivory tower and the common man." *Music* no.1 (November 1944): 32-34.

A lecture given at Hamline University, Saint Paul on September 27, 1943. The place of the artist "is in the watch-tower of civilization" in this age of the "common-man." Those "studying the grammar and syntax of that language of art are called upon to spread its knowledge and thus contribute to bringing to an end the proverbial loneliness of the Ivory Tower." *See:* B554

a. "Der elfenbeinerne Turm und der Mann von der Strasse." In his *Zur Sprache gebracht.* (K707) (München: Albert Langen - Georg Müller, 1958): 286-294.

b. "The ivory tower." In his *Exploring music.* (K817) Geoffrey Skelton. (New York: October House, 1966): 155-165.

Manuscripts: US-LJ typescript copy (7 p.) ; typescript copy (6 p.)

K530. "Announcement of the I.S.C.M. concert at Hamline University, December 1, 1943." *Unpublished.*

A lecture broadcast over station WLB, University of Minnesota in preparation for the concert.

Manuscripts: US-LJ typescript copy(6 p.)

K531. "Introductory remarks at the first concert of the Twin Cities Chapter of the International Society for Contemporary Music, Bridgman Hall, Hamline University, Saint Paul, MN, December 1, 1943." *Unpublished.*

A pre-concert lecture including a brief discussion of the *Third piano sonata* op.92, no.4 which he premiered.

Manuscripts: US-LJ typescript copy(4 p.)

-- 1944 --

K532. "Little remarks on a great work." *Unpublished.*

Review, written about 1944, of the book *Joseph, the provider* by Thomas Mann translated into English by H. T. Lowe-Porter (New York: Alfred A. Knopf, 1944). Mentions his review of about ten years earlier.

Manuscripts: US-LJ typescript copy(3 p.).

K533. "Introductory remarks at the Concert at the School of Design, Chicago, Illinois, February 19, 1944." *Unpublished.*

Briefly discusses each work on the program, including his *Third piano sonata* op.92, no.4.

Manuscripts: US-LJ typewritten (2 p.)

K534. "Homage to Schoenberg: The idiom and the technique." *Modern Music* 21:3 (March-April 1944): 131-134.

"The impact of Arnold Schoenberg's creative genius upon the evolution of contemporary music was felt mainly in two instances. The first was the publication of the *Three piano pieces* op.11, in 1910. The second, the invention of the Twelve-tone technic, [sic] was made known to the world at large approximately in 1923... [The technique] can generate new constructive principles and inspire the musical mind to even broader generalizations of basic ideas, and so it is of the very essence of life."

K535. "Introductory remarks at the Concert of compositions by students of Mr. Krenek's classes in composition." *Unpublished.*

A lecture for the March 9, 1944 concert at Hamline University introducing Elisabeth Clark, Robert Erickson, Russell G. Harris, Virginia Seay, and undergraduate composers Marie Guthrie, Gladys Nordenstrom, Martha Johnson, and Roque Cordero.

Manuscripts: US-LJ typescript(6 p.)

K536. "ISCM newsletter, March 20, 1944." *Unpublished.*

Krenek reports on the activities of the Twin Cities Chapter during the previous year.

Manuscripts: US-LJ typescript copy(3 p.)

K537. "Nachtrag zum Werner Reinhart-Heft." *Schweizerische Musikzeitung* 84:5 (May 1, 1944): 187-189.

A two-page facsimile of *Prelude* (W87) for piano dedicated to his long-time friend and patron (dated Saint Paul, MN, February 5, 1944), and including a brief discussion of the twelve-tone structure of the work.

K538. "Contemporary music." *Unpublished.*

A lecture given at the Los Angeles campus of the University of California on August 1, 1944. Krenek examines Igor Stravinsky's Harvard University lectures given during 1939/40 and the composer's concept of musical time. Krenek distinguishes between ontological and psychological time; Stravinsky obviously adheres to the first type, which is intellectually easier to grasp than the second because it consists of repetitions of rhythmical and other patterns. Ontological time also corresponds to the non-emotional type of music which Krenek opposes. He sees his own music fitting into the second group characterized by emotional expression through carefully organized constructions.

Manuscripts: US-LJ 16 p.

K539. "Music and social crisis." *Journal of Aesthetics and Art Criticism* 3:9/10 (1944): 53-58.

Discussion of the effect of war on music; concludes "that by and large music develops independently from the vicissitudes of war."

a. "Soziale Krise und Musik." *Die Furche* no.14 (April 12, 1947): 5-6.

b. "Musik und soziale Krise." *Prisma* (Stockholm) 1:10 (1947): 41-43.

   German translation by E. Schlubach.

Manuscripts: "How does war affect music?" US-LJ English typescript (6 p.)

K540. "The composer and the interpreter." *Black Mountain College Bulletin* 3:2 (December 1944). 10 p.

Lecture given at the Black Mountain College Summer Music Institute on September 4, 1944. Krenek explores the relationship between the interpreter and the composer in presenting new music and offers suggestions for performers as they interpret compositions. The means by which a composer communicates his intentions to the performer "has become literature; that is, the written score has meaning, aesthetic value and the full dignity of an art object, no matter whether, or how often, it is made audible, and it retains all those qualities even when it is only sitting on the book-shelves of the library... Although a musical score is infinitely more exact than a literary text in regard to the elementary facts of pitch level, rhythm, dynamics and the like, there is still a wide margin left for interpretation... If there is any trouble with interpretation, it is mainly due to the fact that interpreters are trying too hard to suppress their own imagination."

a. ——. In his *Exploring music.* (K817) (New York: October House, 1966): 167-183.

b. "Komponist und Interpret." In his *Zur Sprache gebracht.* (K707) (München: Albert Langen - Georg Müller, 1958): 295-308.

K541. "Arnold Schoenberg at seventy" *Black Mountain College Bulletin* 3:1 (November 1944). 8 p.

A lecture given at the Black Mountain College Summer Music Institute on September 6, 1944. Krenek compares Arnold Schoenberg to Claudio Monteverdi in their revolutionary effects upon the music of their times and in their synthesizing roles. He also discusses Schoenberg's role in fostering excellence in performance and interpretation of new music.

K542. "Announcement of the ISCM concert at Hamline University, Oct.22, 1944." *Unpublished.*

A lecture broadcast over station WLB, University of Minnesota, October 17, 1944.

Manuscripts: **US-LJ** typescript copy(4 p.)

K543. "Introductory remarks at the third concert of the Twin Cities Chapter of the International Society for Contemporary Music, Bridgman Hall, Hamline University, Saint Paul, MN, October 22, 1944." *Unpublished.*

A pre-concert lecture.

Manuscripts: **US-LJ** typescript copy(3 p.)

K544. "The appeal to conscience." *Modern Music* 22:1 (November-December 1944): 6-9.

Part of a symposium "On artists and collaboration" consisting of responses by emigrant composers to the question "Who are collaborators and what should be done with them?" Krenek discusses the questions that need to be raised in deciding the fate of European artists who collaborated with the oppressors while in Nazi-dominated countries.

a. "Appell an das Gewissen." In his *Gedanken unterwegs.* (K720) (München: Albert Langen - Georg Müller, 1959): 229-232.

German translation by Friedrich Saathen.

-- 1945 --

K545. "That noise called music." In his *Exploring music.* (K817) (New York: October House, 1966): 185-193.

Written about 1945 in German; English translation by Geoffrey Skelton. Music on the radio is presented as background noise. "We are dissipating our musical heritage for the sake of one ingenious machine and are heading for a musical famine." *See:* B554

a. ——. In *Writings of German composers,* edited by Jost Hermand and James Steakley. (New York: Continuum, 1984): 269-276.

b. "Das unaufhörliche Raunen." In his *Zur Sprache gebracht.* (K707) (München: Albert Langen - Georg Müller,

K546. "Mahler the composer." *Listen* 8:2 (February 1945): 3-4.

Examines the symphonies of Gustav Mahler in an attempt to dispel some of the existing prejudices about them.

K547. "Introductory remarks at the concert of contemporary composers at Hamline University, Bridgman Hall, February 28, 1945." *Unpublished.*

Manuscripts: US-LJ typescript copy(2 p.)

K548. "Music composition, life work or sideline?" *Listen* 8:6 (June 1945): 3-6.

Response (with other composers) to the questions "Does part of your income result from royalties, is it sufficient to keep you at an existence level, and by what other means do you make your living?" Krenek's royalties do not supply him enough for a single person; he makes his living through giving lectures and writing articles.

K549. "How not to appreciate music." *Unpublished.*

Lecture given at Kenyon College, August 15, 1945 on the process of teaching music appreciation.

Manuscripts: US-LJ typewritten copy(19 p.)

K550. "Preface." *Hamline studies in musicology* 1 (September 1945): i-vii.

"Of all the individuals engaged in the widely diversified branches of music it is probably contemporary composers that will be found among those most vitally interested in, and best equipped with understanding of musicological thought." A survey of theoretical and historical studies by composers including autobiographical reminiscences. *See:* B379, B547, B591, B747, B1450

K551. "Conversation past midnight." In his *Exploring music.* (K817) (New York: October House, 1966): 231-244.

A reaction written in 1945 in the form of a dialogue to *Time* magazine's reportage of Béla Bartók's death; Krenek reflects on the importance of composers, their music, and musical immortality.

a. "Gespräch nach Mitternacht." In his *Zur Sprache gebracht.* (K707) (München: Albert Langen - Georg Müller, 1958): 379-391.

German translation by Friedrich Saathen.

b. "Das Aergernis der Unsterblichkeit." *Neue Schau* (Kassel) 19:10 (October 1958): 346.

Excerpt from the end of the essay published in *Zur Sprache gebracht.* Picture.

c. "Unsterblichkeit?" In *Gespräche mit Komponisten,* hrsg. von Willi Reich. (Zürich: Manesse Verlag, 1965): 251-272.

Reprinted from *Zur Sprache gebracht.*

d. "Gespräch nach Mitternacht." In his *Im Zweifelsfalle.* (K924) (Wien: Europaverlag, 1984): 144-155.

e. "Ejszakai párbeszéd." In *A huszadik század zenéje,* edited by Imre Fábián. (Budapest: Gondolat, 1966): 93-102.
Hungarian translation. Picture.
Manuscripts: US-LJ 11 p. ; typescript copy (15 p.)

K552. "Introductory remarks at the fifth concert of the Twin Cities Chapter of the International Society for Contemporary Music, Bridgman Hall, Hamline University, St. Paul, Minn., October 21, 1945." *Unpublished.*
Includes a brief discussion of the *Sonata for violin and piano* op.99.
Manuscripts: US-LJ typescript copy(2 p.)

K553. "Letter to John H. Harvey." *Saint Paul Pioneer Press* (December 9, 1945)
An angry response to the assertion of Dr. Frank Black that nothing worthwhile has been written by composers in Europe since World War I.

-- 1946 --

K554. [Definitions of musical terms], In *Encyclopedia of the arts,* by D.D. Runes and H. G.Schrickel (New York: Philosophical Library, 1946)
Brief definitions appear under the following headings: Accent (p.6.), Articulation (p.70), Cadence (p.129), Canon (p.138), Chord (p.206), Climax (p.232), Consonance, dissonance (p.253), Counterpoint (p.263), Design (2) (p.280), Drive (p.291-292), Enharmony (p.329), Fugue (p.375), Harmony (2) (p.420), Homophony (p.441), Horizontal (p.443), Idiom (p.450-452), Imitation (p.454), Inversion (p.478), Melody (p.602), Meter (p.615), Mode (p.622), Monody (p.629), Monophony (p.629), Motif (p.630), Part (p.724), Phrase (p.756), Polyphony (p.775), Polytonality (p.775), Resolution (p.850), Rhythm (Music) (p.855), Structure (p.973), Style (3) (p.975), Symmetry (2) (p.985), Tension (1) (p.1000-1001), Texture (p.1004), Theme (2) (p.1014), Twelve-tone technique (p.1028), Variation (p.1043), and Vertical (p.1046). Definitions for Form, Key, and Scale were incorporated into larger articles.
Manuscripts: US-LJ typescript copy (11 p.)

K555. "Review." *Unpublished.*
Review of Jacques Maritain's book *Art and scholasticism* (1946).
Manuscripts: US-LJ typescript(1 p.).

K556. "Introductory remarks at the sixth concert of the Twin Cities Chapter of the I.S.C.M., April 1, 1946, Bridgman Hall, Hamline University, St. Paul, Minn." *Unpublished.*
Discusses the music of Mark Brunswick and Roque Cordero, and Arnold Schoenberg's *Book of the hanging gardens.*
Manuscripts: US-LJ typescript copy(3 p.)

K557. "Preface." *Unpublished.*
Preface to the Hebrew edition of *Music here and now;* dated: September 1946, St.Paul, MN. Also published by Alfred A. Knopf, 1946.
Manuscripts: US-LJ typescript(1 p.)

K558. "Anpassung an Amerika." *Oesterreichische Musikzeitschrift* 1:12 (December 1946): 390-392.
Immediately following the annexation of Austria by Germany in March 1938, Krenek applied for immigration to America, having already spent five months traveling around the country. He discusses his adaptation to

American life, and describes American musical life during the Second World War contrasting it to pre-war Europe.

Manuscripts: US-LJ typescript (3 p.)

K559. "Preface." *Hamline studies in musicology* 2 (1947): i.

Krenek briefly discusses the contents of the second collection of papers on musicological topics prepared by his graduate students at Hameline University and himself. "We have again tried to discuss the phenomena which attracted our interest in [the ideas outlined in the first volume] to the problems of composition." *See:* B317, B592, B747

K560. "A discussion of the treatment of dissonances in Okeghem's masses as compared with the contrapuntal theory of Johannes Tinctoris."
Hamline studies in musicology 2 (1947): 1-26.

"Observation of numerous examples of conspicous treatment of dissonance in Johannes Okeghem's Masses prompted an investigation of the question whether and to what extent the composer's technique was in keeping with the pertinent teachings of the contemporary theorists... The treatment of dissonance in Okeghem's work appears as a remnant of that older style which Tinctoris passionately wishes to see discarded... It seems that theorists are likely to be progressive when the trend of evolution is in the direction of simplification and 'classical' orientation. In such periods composers whom later ages call bold and forward looking appear to be absolute. When the general trend is toward complexity and 'romantic' orientation, theorists usually become conservative... Thus the concepts of progress and reaction are inextricably intertwined in the history of art."

K561. "Review." *Unpublished.*

Review of the book *The Works of the mind* edited for the University of Chicago Committee on Social Thought by Robert B. Heywood (Chicago: University of Chicago Press, 1947). "It is somewhat embarrassing to notice that of the four artists only one, the composer Arnold Schoenberg [in his essay 'The Musician'], seems to have understood the assignment."

Manuscripts: US-LJ typescript copy(2 p.).

K562. "ISCM activities." *Unpublished.*

A report discussing the activities of the Twin Cities Chapter from 1943 to 1947.

Manuscripts: US-LJ typescript copy(2 p.)

K563. "Introductory remarks at the eighth concert of the Twin Cities Chapter of the International Society for Contemporary Music, Bridgman Hall, Hamline University, St. Paul, Minn., March 12, 1947."
Unpublished.

A pre-concert lecture.

Manuscripts: US-LJ typescript copy(2 p.)

K564. "*Das Leben des Orest.*" *Die Komödie* (Vienna) 2:3 (December 1947): 109.

A discussion of the opera op.60.

-- 1948 --

K565. "Amerika." *Stimmen* 1:6 (1948): 179-181.

It is difficult to write twelve-tone music in America because an entire generation of American composers studied under Nadia Boulanger and are adherents of neoclassicism. Consequently, they have a suspicious, intolerant attitude toward twelve-tone composition. Arnold Schönberg is respected as a teacher and Alban Berg's *Violin concerto* is accepted because of its romantic sound, but otherwise the idiom is under attack. He mentions his *Studies in counterpoint based on the twelve tone technique* (K496) and his students Russell G. Harris, Robert Erickson, George Perle, Will Ogdon, Martha Johnson, and Roque Cordero. He also notes that of the older generation of American composers, only Wallingford Riegger uses the twelve-tone technique.

Manuscripts: US-LJ typescript (2 p.)

K566. "Review." *Unpublished.*

Review of the book *Theory of harmony* by Arnold Schoenberg translated by Robert D. W. Adams (New York: Philosophical Library, 1948).

Manuscripts: US-LJ typescript copy(3 p.).

K567. "Review." *Unpublished.*

Review of the book *The art of judging music* by Virgil Thomson (New York: Knopf, 1948).

Manuscripts: US-LJ typescript(3 p.).

K568. "Introduction to music." *Unpublished.*

The first third of a projected history of music.

Manuscripts: US-LJ typescript(64 p. & musical examples)

K569. *Selbstdarstellung.* (Zürich: Atlantis Musikbücherei, 1948) 66 p.

An extensive autobiography. *See:* B322, B358, B554, B857, B1050, B1051, B1112, B1113, K577, K578, K621

a. "Self analysis." *New Mexico Quarterly* 23:1 (Spring 1953): 5-57.

Expansion and translation. Dated at end: Aptos - Palo Alto, CA, June 1946; revised and brought up to date in Los Angeles, July 1952.

b. *Autobiografia y estudios.* Libros de musica, 4. (Madrid: Ediciones Rialp, 1965)

Spanish translation; published with the Spanish translation of *Studies in counterpoint* (K496-e).

Manuscripts: US-LJ German typescript (42 p. & corrections) ; English typescript (44 p.)

K570. *Musik im goldenen Westen; das Tonschaffen der U.S.A.* Orpheus Bücher, 4. (Wien: Brüder Hollinek, 1949) 73 p.

A history and survey of American new music and its institutions from 1900 to the present, mentioning specific composers whom he thinks are significant to the musical scene. Dated at end: Los Angeles, February 1948. *See:* B1051

Manuscripts: US-LJ 51 p. ; typescript(27 p.)

K571. "*The making of yesterday;* the diaries of Raoul de Roussy de Sales." *Tomorrow* 8 (March 1948): 58.

A book review of the diaries published by Reynal and Hitchcock.

Manuscripts: US-LJ typescript copy (2 p.)

K572. "Problems in California." *Musical Digest* 29 (April 1948): 14-15, 36.

Surveys the musical institutions of Northern and Southern California and concludes that there is a great potential but that it is hampered by provincial traits. Picture.

K573. "Something old, something new." *WABF Program Magazine* (New York) 1:4 (April 1948): 16-17.

The public today is very interested in the latest art, but can only tolerate old music. "The average music lover has only very little opportunity to transcend the narrow circle mapped out for him by the combined forces of concert management, radio, gramophone industry, and music appreciation literature."

Manuscripts: US-LJ typescript (3 p.)

K574. "Bemerkung zum Problem der Symphonie in der Gegenwart." *Festschrift des Konzerthauses* (Vienna, 1948)

Krenek looks at his four symphonies in relation to the monumental symphonies of the twentieth century starting with Mahler's *Eighth symphony.*

a. "Symphonie in der Gegenwart." *Der Standpunkt* (Meran) (September 10, 1949)

Manuscripts: US-LJ typescript (2 p.)
Dated at end: April 4, 1948.

K575. "Ist Los Angeles eine Stadt?" In his *Gedanken unterwegs.* (K720) (München: Albert Langen - Georg Müller, 1959): 233-243.

An analysis of the urban character of the city written in 1948, shortly after he moved to Southern California. The focus of urban life is the supermarket which assumes the role of a mini-city center, and consequently Los Angeles is an extended suburban area. The film industry holds the whole aggregation together and creates a pseudo-intellectual elite of writers and artists. The climate is the only motivation which justifies the presence of the area which is otherwise very provincial.

-- 1949 --

K576. "Technique de douze sons et classicisme." *Polyphonie* Paris 4 (1949): 64-67.

French translation by René Leibowitz of "Twelve-tone technique and classicism." "If historical parallels are allowed, it would seem that Schoenberg's position today has much in common with that of Johann Sebastian Bach at the end of the 1740s. At that time Bach was not regarded as a prophet opening up new avenues of the development of music, but rather as a composer who tenaciously clung to the aesthetic and technical ideals of the past and spent his uncontested mastery in perfecting a style that had become obsolete. There are more than a few observers and commentators in our day who think very much the same about Schoenberg."

Manuscripts: US-LJ English typescript (2 p.)

K577. "Vom *Jonny* zur Zwölftonmusik." *Melos* 16:2 (February 1949): 33-38.

Excerpt from *Selbsdarstellung* (K569). Discusses the development of his compositional technique and the change to twelve-tone music in *Karl V.* op.73.

K578. "Der musikalische Fortschritt." *Melos* 16:3 (March 1949): 71-75.

Last chapter from *Selbsdarstellung* (K569). Krenek describes himself as an "anti-mainstream" composer, always moving contrary to expectations. Picture.

a. ——. *Darmstädter Tagblatt* Feuilleton (August 18, 1950): 4.

K579. "Teaching as a composer's craft." *Composers News Record* no.9 (Spring 1949): 1-2.

A symposium in response to questions about the composer's role in an educational institution with responses by Krenek, Henry Cowell, Walter Piston, and Edwin Gerschefski. Krenek thinks the composer should be fully integrated into the institution, and should develop attitudes and skills in the students.

K580. "Arnold Schönberg 75år." *Prisma* (Stockholm) 2:4 (July-August 1949)

K581. "Rundfragen über Film." *Biografbladet* (Stockholm) (Winter 1949/50): 242-243.

Responses with others printed in Swedish with an English summary to a question about film music. Krenek thinks that film is considered a commercial mass-product, not art, and consequently has no audience.

-- 1950 --

K582. "Ockeghem." *Unpublished.*

A brief survey of the life and works of the composer written around 1950 as a perspectus for a book.

Manuscripts: US-LJ 3 p.

K583. "Fernseh-Oper." *Neue Zürcher Zeitung* (1950): 1, 3.

A discussion of the problems of producing opera for television.

K584. "The Neighbors; or, The Test." In *Freundesgabe für Friedrich T. Gubler zum sechzigsten Geburtstag am 1. Juli 1960.* (Winterthur, SZ: Buchdruckerei, 1960): 103-120.

Libretto in English for a chamber opera set in the Middle West sometime before the Civil War. Dated at end: Chicago, Ill., 1950.

Manuscripts: US-LJ English synopsis typescript (3 p.) ; German synopsis (1955) typescript (3 p.)

K585. "The future of opera: two questions." *Musical America* 70 (February 1950): 113.

The discussion of opera in the future needs to answer two questions: what are the practical conditions of operatic production and what kind of musical plays will composers write? "Opera can have a future when enough opera houses exist, willing and able to produce new works." Picture.

a. "The future of opera." *Musical Digest* no.17 (1950/51): 37-40.

K586. "Die Reise nach Westen." *Der Mittag* (Düsseldorf) no.72 (March 25/26, 1950)

Essay on the similarities between the empire of Charles V and the United States, and between Vienna and Hollywood. After discussing his opera on the subject of emperor Charles V, Krenek explains his motivations in writing the song cycle *The ballad of the railroads* op.98. Inspired by the motet by Josquin des Prez "Liber generationis Jesus Christi," *The Santa Fe time table* op.102 is set for six part a capella choir with its text taken from the railroad's timetable.

a. ——. In his *Gedanken unterwegs.* (K720) (München: Albert Langen - Georg Müller, 1959): 244-247.

b. "Westwärts." *Frankfurter Neue Presse* (August 21, 1960)

K587. "The transplanted composer." *Los Angeles Times* 69 (May 21, 1950): IV:6.

A symposium on the emigré composer. Krenek does not think that the style of the music written by emigré composers in America differs from the music they wrote in Europe. Circumstances have, however, controlled opportunities which affect the the forces for which he writes.

K588. "On meaning in music." *Measure* 1:3 (Sum.1950): 311-322.

Rejects the idea of music possessing meaning outside itself while supporting the idea of music as the self expression of the composer. Includes his reactions to a performance of his *Second symphony* op.12 twenty years after its composition. "The significance of contemporary music depends on the ability of the composers to write music that the expert can in technical terms demonstrate to be new, on the ability of the listener to experience its newness through sympathetic observation of the expressive content, and possibly, through not necessarily, on the listener's inclination to visualize great and important ideas as being related to the expressive features of the particular musical process." *See:* B1112, B1113

a. "Ueber die Bedeutung von Musik." *Schweizerische Musikzeitung* 93:3 (March 1, 1953): 108-113.

b. ——. In *Musiker über Musik*, Ausgewählt und kommentiert von Josef Rufer. (Darmstadt: Stichnote Verlag, 1956), pp.223-226.

c. "Ueber die Bedeutung der Musik." In his *Zur Sprache gebracht.* (K707) (München: Albert Langen - Georg Müller, 1958): 317-330.

K589. "Kurzer Rechenschaftsbericht." *Schweizerische Musikzeitung* 90:6 (June 1, 1950): 299-301.

Discusses the use of the twelve-tone technique in his works from 1939 to 1950.

K590. "Introductory remarks." *Unpublished.*

Lecture given at a concert by the Los Angeles chapter of the International Society for Contemporary Music on July 30, 1950 honoring Roger Sessions.

Manuscripts: US-LJ 7 p.

K591. "Ein paar Worte zu meinen letzten Werken." *Darmstädter Echo* (August 23, 1950)

K592. "Ueber eigene Werke." *Unpublished.*

A lecture broadcast over Norddeutscher Rundfunk, Hamburg on December 7, 1950 surveying his compositional styles up to his adoption of twelve-tone music. He discusses atonality and his early atonal style, characterized by *Symphonische Musik* op.11, which was reminiscent of middle Schoenberg. The unifying elements of his early symphony works were rhythmic uniformity and polyphonic technique. His turn to neoclassicism by the mid-1920s was hesitatingly followed by his "Schubert" period, which by the early 1930s was replaced by his desire for a more intellectually demanding way of composition and hence his turn toward twelve-tone composition.

Manuscripts: US-LJ 9 p.

-- 1951 --

K593. "Soll die Oper einen Sinn haben?" *Das Neue Forum* (Darmstadt) 1:2 (1951): 31-32.

A discussion of the relationship of the composer to his libretto. Krenek doubts whether opera is supposed to convey rational or philosophical sense; many successful operas contain nonsensical texts. Nevertheless, Krenek tries to make sense in his new opera *Dark waters* op.125 by working on a text based upon rational thought.

K594. "Wenn man den Stand der Musik..." *Unpublished.*

A lecture for Salzburg given in 1951 about music in America and the sociological and musical differences between the established East Coast musical society and the mobile immigrant society characteristic of the West Coast. Krenek discusses the emerging generation of American composers.

Manuscripts: US-LJ typescript(4 p.) ; 5 p.

K595. "Freiheit und Rechtfertigung." *Oper* (Städtische Bühnen, Frankfurt/Main) 2:4 (January 28, 1951): [1-2]

Surveys the themes of his operas from his earliest opera *Zwingburg* op.14 to the first twelve-tone opera *Karl V.* op.73, pointing out a continuing concern with freedom.

K596. "Europäische Komponisten über Verdi." *Melos* 18:2 (February 1951): 35-41.

Responses from composers about their personal reactions to Giuseppe Verdi and his relationship to our time. Krenek's reactions to Verdi were formed at a time when he was very much in the shadow of Wagner, but Verdi's treatment of the orchestra is still valid.(pp.36-37). With Luigi Dallapiccola, Wolfgang Fortner, etc.

K597. "Sprengstoff für 'ewige Werte.'" *Die Welt* (Essen) (February 16, 1951)

Observations on the sociological development of music during the last 500 years. The radio and recording industries have revolutionized the sociology of music listeners, yet the repertoire has remained unchanged. Facing the ever-increasing commercial attitude of music publishers, contemporary composers are seeking refuge in music festivals, symposia, and music broadcasts as it becomes more and more difficult for them to enter the repertoire. This situation leads to the isolation of the contemporary composer.

a. ——. *Die Welt* (Hamburg) (February 17, 1951)

K598. "New attitudes toward new music." *WABF Program Magazine* (New York) 4:3 (March 1951): 5-6.

A discussion of the waning influences of European music and the rapid emergence of American composers. The community of listeners has not yet fully appreciated the presence of such composers.

K599. "Fünfzig Jahre Komponierhandwerk." *Melos* 18:4 (April 1951): 97-99.

Briefly surveys the development of music from 1900 to 1950, and compares it to the changes which occurred during the period 1550 to 1600. *See:* B1112

a. ——. In his *Zur Sprache gebracht.* (K707) (München: Albert Langen - Georg Müller, 1958): 331-334.

K600. *In memoriam Adolph Koldofsky.* (Los Angeles: privately printed, April 10, 1951)

Eulogy at the funeral in Rosedale Chapel.

K601. "Was ist 'esoterische' Musik?" *Der Mittag* (Düsseldorf) (April 18, 1951)

Twelve-tone music is thought to be esoteric and require training to enjoy; film music can be as complex, and is enjoyed by millions of people without training.

K602. "Die Zwölftonmusik als Lehre." *Melos* 18:5 (May 1951): 141-143.

A discussion of the literature of twelve-tone music and a comparison of Krenek's *Studies in counterpoint* (K496) with Herbert Eimert's *Lehrbuch der Zwölftontechnik.*

K603. "Introductory remarks at the concert of the Los Angeles Chapter, I.S.C.M., May 6, 1951, Hancock Auditorium, University of Southern California." *Unpublished.*

Manuscripts: **US-LJ** typescript copy(1 p.)

K604. "An exceptional musician: Kurt Frederick." *New Mexico Quarterly* 21:1 (Spring 1951): 26-35.

A tribute to the conductor of the Albuquerque Civic Symphony Orchestra including reminiscences of Frederick's youth in Vienna and praise for his championing of new music.

K605. "On writing my memoirs." *Berkeley* no.10 (June 1951): 2.

Discusses writing his memoirs (K609) which he began in 1942 and which now covers up to 1932. He starting writing his memoirs because he began to forget a great deal about his life before emigrating to America, and the reality of his life in this country was so strong that it obliterated memory of his previous life in Europe. While the immediate motivation is his pleasure in writing them, he has the conviction that his musical work will someday be considered far more significant than it is now. He will donate his memoirs to the Library of Congress, to remain unopened until fifteen years after his death. *See:* B554

a. ——. In his *Exploring music.* (K817) (New York: October House, 1966): 7-10.

b. "Ueber meine Memoiren." In his *Zur Sprache gebracht.* (K707) (München: Albert Langen - Georg Müller, 1958): 17-21.

K606. "Botschaft an den II.Internationalen Zwölftonkongress." *Unpublished.*

Written for Darmstadt, 1951; dated Albuquerque, NM, June 23, 1951. Surveys his twelve-tone music since coming to America.

Manuscripts: **US-LJ** 1 p. ; typescript copy (1 p.)

K607. "Die Zwölfton Musik." *Unpublished.*

Lecture broadcast over RIAS, Berlin September 22, 1951.

Manuscripts: **US-LJ** 20 p.

K608. "Vortrag für Berlin RIAS." *Unpublished.*

Reminiscences broadcast November 1951.

Manuscripts: **US-LJ** 10 p.

-- 1952 --

K609. "Memoirs." *Unpublished.*

Memoirs of his life before emmigrating to America written between 1942 and 1952. They are to remain sealed until fifteen years after his death. See his "On writing my memoirs" (K605).

Manuscripts: **US-Wc.**

K610. "New methods in teaching counterpoint." *Hinrichsen's Musical Yearbook* 7 (1952): 116-128.

Counterpoint is taught more now because of the melodic tendencies of modern music, but counterpoint based upon Giovanni Palestrina's style is too dull. His study of Johannes Ockeghem with the fifteenth century mensuration scheme makes for more interesting exercises and is more relevant to twentieth century music.

Manuscripts: **US-LJ** typescript copy (3 p.)

K611. "Anhang I: Ernst Krenek." In *Die Komposition mit Zwölf Tönen,* von Josef Rufer. Stimmen des XX.Jahrhunderts, 2. (Berlin: Max Hesses Verlag, 1952), pp.170-172.

Discusses his use of row rotation in the *Lamentatio Jeremiae prophetae* op.93 and the *Third piano sonata* op.92, no.4, and his use of three-note groups in the *Fourth piano sonata* op.114. Omitted from the second edition.

a. "Contemporary composers on their experiences of composing with twelve tones: Ernst Krenek." In *Composition with twelve notes related only to one another,* by Josef Rufer; translated by Humphrey Searle. (London: Rockliff, 1954): 188-191.

K612. "A roving composer in Western Germany." *Musical America* 72 (February 1952): 12, 164.

Reactions to his trip to Europe and the importance that German radio and tape recording have upon the contemporary musical scene. Discusses the significance of the chamber symphony by Pierre Boulez performed at the Donaueschingen festival.

K613. "Porque devemos conhecar melhor a musica antiga." *Intercambio* (Rio de Janeiro) 10:3/4 (March-April 1952): 29-31.

Lecture originally given under the title "Why study music history" at the College of St. Catherine, Saint Paul, MN. A study of music within the context of its own time brings out its unique and special qualities; there is music beyond the nineteenth century.

Manuscripts: **US-LJ** English typescript (3 p.)

K614. "Letter to the Editor." *Music News* 44:5 (May 1952): 19.

Reports in detail on his trip to Europe and South America; he mentions the premieres of the *Double concerto* op.124 and the *Sixth piano sonata* op.128, the first German performance of the *Ballad of the railroads* op.98, and other performances.

K615. "The problem of creative thinking in music." In *The Nature of creative thinking, a lecture at the meeting of the Industrial Research Institute, Skytop Mt., PA, May 5-7, 1952.* pp.51-57.

Manuscripts: **US-LJ** 1 p.

K616. *Johannes Ockeghem.* Great religious composers, edited by John J.Becker. (London: Sheed & Ward, 1953) 86 p.

A biography intended for the general reader, including a study of the music within the context of its time. "His music reveals a man who was by no means a conformist, who dared to venture into territories off the beaten track according to his own lights, a man whose interior being was shaken by sudden, unpredictable impulses, and who had an unusual sensitivity for fine, delicate shadings of sentiment which he did not hesitate to express in rather unconventional ways." Date at end: Los Angeles, May 25, 1952. *See:* B27, B130, B162, B279, B473, B643, B860, B884, B910, B1036, B1283

Manuscripts: **US-LJ** 56 p. ; typescript (65 p. & changes 2 p.) ; corrections (15 p.)

K617. "The roving composer pays a short visit to Brazil." *Musical America* 72 (June 1952): 13, 17.

A travel note on his trip to Teresópolis where he taught in a six week summer institute sponsored by Pro Arte Brasil.

K618. "Musik im Kreuzfeuer der Meinungen." In *Sieben Jahre Internationale Ferienkurse für neue Musik, 12.-24. Juli 1952.* (Darmstadt): [1].

K619. "Erfahrungen in Amerika." *Unpublished.*

A lecture recorded by radio station KFAC in Los Angeles in October 1952 for broadcast by Radio Salzburg. Discusses the circumstances which caused him to seek refuge in the United States in 1938 and his first teaching positions in universities which provided him an opportunity to become acquainted with medieval and Renaissance music through their libraries. He also discusses his decision to move to California. He does not believe that his immigration to the United States affected any change in his compositional philosophy.

Manuscripts: US-LJ 5 p. ; typescript (3 p.)

K620. "Landslide misleading." *Los Angeles Daily News* (December 1, 1952)

A letter to the editor. Krenek thinks the term "landslide" used in the report of the defeat of Adlai Stevenson by Dwight Eisenhower was incorrect.

-- 1953 --

K621. "Ueber die Einzigkeit eines Werkes." In *Allgewalt Musik*, hrsg. von H. Barth. 2.erweiterte Aufl. (München: Wilhelm Langewiesche-Brandt, 1953): 136-137.

Brief extract from *Selbstdarstellung* (K569). No analysis, psychological research, or aesthetic investigation will ever be able to explain the vitality that marks the uniqueness of a great composition. Beset with that unknown factor called "inspiration," the composer can only search his own conscience about what he has written and leave it with the assurance that there is nothing he might want to change.

K622. "Authentisch, doch liberal." *Oesterreichische Musikzeitschrift* 8:1 (January 1953): 11-16.

Review of the book *Die Komposition mit zwölf Tönen* by Josef Rufer (Berlin: Max Hesses Verlag, 1952).

Manuscripts: US-LJ typescript copy (4 p.)

K623. "Well, maybe next season..." *Musical America* 73 (February 1953): 7, 183.

Satirical discussion on the relationship between performer and composer; specifically examines the question of why performers don't play what the composer writes.

Manuscripts: US-LJ typescript (4 p.)

K624. "Zu meinen Kammermusikwerken 1936-1950." *Schweizerische Musikzeitung* 93:3 (March 1, 1953): 102-104.

Discusses the suitability of the sonata form to twelve-tone music, the use of two tone-rows in the same piece, and the division of the row into sub-groupings. He also discusses the rotation procedures used in the *Seventh string quartet* op.96. He considers the *Sixth string quartet* op.78 and the *Piano variations* op.79 the high points of that period.

K625. "Letter." *Los Angeles Times* 72 (March 5, 1953)

"When the hucksters begin to take music so seriously that they think an analogy ... might promote sale of the product under their care, we are really getting somewhere."

K626. "Lulu." *Blätter der Städtischen Bühnen Essen, 1952/1953* 13:13 (March 7, 1953): 167.

A discussion of the characterization of Lulu; she is drawn as a tragic figure by a harsh moralist, and Alban Berg's music adds sadness and sympathy to the work.

K627. "Letter." *Los Angeles Times* 72 (March 8, 1953)
Whisky-Beethoven.

K628. *Modal counterpoint in the style of the sixteenth century.* (Lynbrook, NY: Boosey & Hawkes, 1959) 21 p.

A textbook. "Observance of the rules in this manual will produce a style close enough to the compositional procedures of Palestrina as to make it possible for the student to achieve, even in his elementary exercises, some of the flavor of living great music... Special emphasis is placed on the development of the student's sense for freely articulated melody." Dated: Los Angeles, June 1953. *See:* B206, B820, B963

Manuscripts: US-LJ 10 p. ; typescript copy (9 p.) ; typescript copy (7 p.)

K629. "Music mail box." *Los Angeles Times* 72 (September 27, 1953)

A letter to Albert Goldberg stating that his August 2 column about opera in concert "expresses to perfection my own ideas on the subject."

K630. "Letter." *Time* (Canadian edition) 62:13 (September 28, 1953)

A reaction to A.Lynd's article "Quackery in the public schools" *Time* (September 7, 1953) and its comments concerning the need to know mathematics.

K631. "Is the twelve-tone technique on the decline?" *Musical Quarterly* 39:4 (October 1953): 513-527.

Comments that the twelve-tone technique is on the decline because there is no "authentic" method are erroneous because it is a technique and not a system. "The brief survey of recent happenings in the realm of dodecaphony tends to show that through the increasing number of composers who have tried their hands at the twelve-tone technique and who were not associated with the 'founding fathers' a wide variety of technical procedures and stylistic results was revealed as lying within the possibilities of this technique." Surveys the literature about twelve-tone music and discusses the use of hexachords, row permutation and rotation, and totally organized serial music. *See:* B161

a. "Decadenza della dodecafonia?" *Diapason* 7 (May 1956): 12-20.

Manuscripts: US-LJ 17 p. ; typescript copy (16 p.)

K632. *Tonal counterpoint in the style of the eighteenth century.* (Lynbrook, New York: Boosey & Hawkes, 1958) 44 p.

A textbook. "This outline discusses actual compositional procedure as far as the writing of brief two-part and three-part inventions requires it, including the application of double counterpoint and canonic devices." Dated: Los Angeles, November 1953. *See:* B30, B277, B820, B962, B1013

Manuscripts: US-LJ 24 p. ; typescript(20 p.) ; Examples 6 p. ; Examples 10 p. ; galleys.

K633. "Letter to John N. Burk." *[Program: Boston Symphony Orchestra]* no.8 (December 11, 1953)

Discusses his edition of Gustav Mahler's *Tenth symphony*.

-- 1954 --

K634. "So schreibt man eine Oper." *Die Welt* no.23 (January 28, 1954): 6.

Discusses writing opera in general, and the writing of his opera *Pallas Athene weint* op.144.

K635. "Project of a museum of modern music." *Unpublished*.

A proposal dated Los Angeles March 1954, and directed to BMI, for the creation of an institution for music to be housed in New York similar to the Museum of Modern Art.

Manuscripts: US-LJ typescript copy(3 p.)

K636. "*Anleitung zur Zwoelftonkomposition*. By Hanns Jelinek." *Musical Quarterly* 40:2 (April 1954): 250-256.

Book review of an introduction to twelve-tone music. "As far as premises, principles, and presentation are concerned, Jelinek's book is eminently suited for the purpose announced in its title. The author is circumspect and conservative in the choice of his assumptions." Jelinek's books are the first two of a three-part manual of composition in twelve-tone music.

Manuscripts: US-LJ 6 p.

K637. "Composer Krenek joins the fray." *Los Angeles Daily News* (April 15, 1954): 22.

Letter to Mildred Norton's column "Stage and screen." "As long as Mr. Wallenstein performs new music as well as he knows how, it seems to me to be a matter of subordinate interest whether or not he likes to do so."

K638. "Ein Brief zur Zwölftontechnik." *Schweizerische Musikzeitung* 94:5 (May 1, 1954): 173-174.

A reply to questions on the audibility of twelve-tone music posed in Willy Burkhard's "... Auseinandersetzung mit der Zwölftontechnik" (March 1, 1954). Mentions the *Trio for violin, clarinet & piano* op.108 in which one movement uses the twelve-tone technique and the other does not.

K639. "Mr. Krenek answers Mr. Toch." *Musical Courier* 149:9 (May 1, 1954): 5.

A reaction to an interview with Ernst Toch by the *Los Angeles Times*. "I am more concerned about Toch's desperate and defeatist attitude toward contemporary music. His attack against the twelve-tone technique reveals the sad spectacle of a man whom we respected as a sensitive and erudite artist aligning himself with those sinister characters who denounce as an 'ism' everything that transcends their feeble intellectual capacities."

K640. "*Pallas Athene weint*." *Melos* 21:7/8 (July-August 1954): 206-208.

Discusses the relationship of *Symphonie Pallas Athene* op.137 to the opera *Pallas Athene weint* op.144 from which it is derived. Includes a facsimile of the first page of the Symphony.

K641. "'Krise' und 'Experiment.'" *Darmstädter Echo* (August 21, 1954)

Discusses contemporary opera versus "traditional" opera; a crisis in opera has always existed, and experiments have always been necessary. In that sense, the repertory consists of successful experiments, and therefore, the new successful experiments gradually change the repertory.

a. ——. *Hessische Nachrichten* (October 14, 1954)

K642. "Second things first." *Time* 64:17 (October 25, 1954): 2.

Letter objecting to *Time*'s characterization of Charles Ives (September 27, 1954) as "an insurance broker who pioneered polytonal music in the U.S. in his spare time." Krenek responded "Ives was able to become a great composer because he was intelligent enough to become an insurance man at a time when [his music] was still less productive of ... commercial success than it is now."

K643. "Ein neues Blatt ist aufgeschlagen." *Melos* 21:11 (November 1954): 305-307.

Young composers have adopted serial music as a continuation of twelve-tone music.

K644. "Sinn und Unsinn der modernen Musik." *Forum* 2:16 (April 1955): 152.

Notes to a speech given on November 8, 1954, in the Vienna Oesterreichische Kulturvereinigung. There are three levels of listening: a. the sensual level, simple sensual enjoyment, b. the emotional level, perceived evaluation of moods expressed in timbres, texture, and rhythm, and c. the structural level, formal relationships of musical elements. Amateurs and non-musicians generally relate to levels a and b, musicians relate to level c. Since tonality was established around 1600, sense meant reasonable music, a music which followed certain rules and could be anticipated, and which was enriched by the genius who added something unexpected to the old scheme. In modern music, and especially twelve-tone music, the genius's contribution is at the extreme, and in electronic music everything must start from scratch, that is the making of the musical elements. The layman hears this music as nonsense because he can't relate it to his prelearned rules; in music where nothing is unexpected, the difference between "sense" and "nonsense" can be hard to perceive.

-- 1955 --

K645. "Ueber Mozart." *Unpublished.*

A book review written about 1955?

Manuscripts: US-LJ 2 p.

K646. "Den Jüngeren über die Schulter geschaut." *Die Reihe* 1 (1955): 31-33.

Twelve-tone composers of the middle generation "found that the justification and purpose of the technique lay in the ... development and variation of clearly defined musical ideas, without being limited by functional harmony... One comes to the conclusion that the extraordinary directness of appeal of so many twelve-note compositions is due to the conflict ... of apparently contradictory principles: desire for spontaneous utterance and restriction imposed by technical procedure... It does not seem that the younger composers ... want to limit serial pre-composition but rather to extend its scope... The extension of the serial pre-formation of intervals into the domains of rhythm, dynamic and to a certain extent, sound aspects in music, has brought the younger composers to a complete liberation from the offerings of nature ... at the cost of an acceptance of total pre-determination... To the superficial observer it appears that the phenomena demonstrated so far in electronic music: levels of color, texture, density, consistency and mass of sound material, are of a considerably lower intellectual level of musical consciousness than the aspirations which were associated with the demanding music of the past."

a. "Alle spalle dei giovani." *Incontri musicali* 1:1 (December 1956): 51-54.

b. "A glance over the shoulders of the young." *Die Reihe* (English) 1 (1958): 14-16.

Manuscripts: US-LJ German 5 p.

K647. *"Bell tower." Unpublished.*
Notes on the opera op.153.

Manuscripts: US-LJ 1 p.

K648. "[Lecture]." *Unpublished.*
A lecture written for broadcast over RIAS, Berlin. Discusses his interest in serial music and defends the young composers who use it.

Manuscripts: US-LJ 3 p.

K649. *"Pallas Athene weint." Oesterreichische Musikzeitschrift* 10:1 (January 1955): 8-9.
Includes part of the libretto of the opera op.144.

K650. "Die Zauberlehrlinge." *Schweizerische Musikzeitung* 95:1 (January 1,1955): 5-6.
The students at the Darmstadt Summer School in 1954 were intellectually better prepared than were the students Krenek encountered in 1950.

K651. "Gino Contilli: *Suite per orchestra d'archi...* Wallingford Riegger: *Music for orchestra,* op.50. Nikos Skalkottas: *Little suite for strings.* Karlheinz Stockhausen: *Kontra-Punkte, Nr.1." Notes* 2d series, 12:2 (March 1955): 327-328.
Review of the music. "The four compositions under this heading are, with one possible exception, based on the twelve-tone technique. Apart from this, they have little in common, which may again demonstrate how much leeway this technique allows to the individual composer for unfolding his ideas freely in the style of his choosing."

Manuscripts: US-LJ 4 p.

K652. "Charles Ives, 1874-1954." *Schweizerische Musikzeitung* 95:4 (April 1, 1955): 141-144.
A biography of the composer and an appreciation of his work on the occasion of his eightieth birthday. In German.

a. ——. In his *Im Zweifelsfalle.* (K924) (Wien: Europaverlag, 1984): 129-135.

K653. "Column conductor takes a back seat and lets the volunteers run the show." *Los Angeles Times* 74 (April 10, 1955)
Letter to Albert Goldberg's column "The sounding board." Krenek reacts to the positive review accorded Henry Pleasants's *The agony of modern music* which misquotes him.

K654. "Kranichsteiner Musikinstitut." *Unpublished.*
Notes for two lectures given in May 1955.

Manuscripts: US-LJ 5 p.

K655. *"Neue Musik in der Entscheidung.* Von Karl H. Wörner." *Notes* 2d series, 12:3 (June 1955): 443-444.
Review of the book (Mainz: B.Schott's Söhne, 1954).

Manuscripts: US-LJ 3 p.

K656. "Der Stein, den die Bauleute verworfen haben, der ist zum Eckstein worden." *Die Reihe* 2 (1955): 19.

> Dated at end: Los Angeles, June 1955. Reminiscences on Anton Webern's conviction of his own greatness and his anonymity.

a. ——. *Kommentare zur Neuen Musik* 1 (Cologne, 1961): 33-34.

b. "The same stone which the builders refused is become the headstone of the corner." *Die Reihe* (English) 2 (1958): 12.

Manuscripts: **US-LJ** English typescript copy (12 p.)

K657. "Tradition in Europa und Amerika." *Das Musikleben* 8:7/8 (July-August 1955): 284-285.

> Response to "Tradition ist Schlamperei" by Schriftleiter von Glosse (in volume 8, number 3, March 1955, pp.84-85) which discusses Krenek's article "Die Zauberlehrlinge" (K650).

K658. "New development in electronic music." *Musical America* 75 (September 1955): 8.

> Discusses the elements of electronic music as produced by Karlheinz Stockhausen at the Nordwestdeutscher Rundfunk studio in Cologne as a new and important step in the development of music. "Inspired by Anton Webern in whose work [a younger generation of dodecaphonists] saw the promise of a farther searching concept of serial composition, they tried at first to include the rhythmic aspect of the musical process into the area of premeditation... What we seem to be able to observe in the electronic endeavors at Cologne is another logical step in the same direction. Here the area of premeditation is further extended so that it now includes even the structure of the sound itself."

Manuscripts: "A new vista." **US-LJ** 5 p.

K659. "Musik und Entropie." *Unpublished*.

> A lecture given in the Fall of 1955.

Manuscripts: **D-bdr DSim** typescript (1 p.)

K660. "Musikleben in Kalifornien." *Neue Zeitschrift für Musik* 116:10 (October 1955): 32-33.

> Contrasts music in Northern California and its center, San Francisco, with music in Los Angeles. Mentions specific performing organizations, composers, conductors, etc.

Manuscripts: **US-LJ** 6 p.

K661. "Betrachtungen zur gegenwärtigen Situation der neuen Musik." *Unpublished*.

> Lecture given October 11, 1955 in Darmstadt on his view of the current situation of new music.

Manuscripts: **D-bdr DSim** typescript copy (3 p.)

K662. "Warum *Pallas Athene weint*?" [*Program: Hamburgische Staatsoper 1955*] no.1 (October 15, 1955): 35-41.

> An examination of the themes of Krenek's operas based on classic Greek drama exhibits the connection between the events of antiquity and the problems of today. Oskar Kokoschka's text for *Orpheus und Eurydike* op.21 presented myth in a completely modern interpretation. The physical and

dramatic tension in *Jonny spielt auf* op.45. Krenek discusses the plot and the historical basis of *Pallas Athene weint* op.144, written for the opening of the new Hamburg opera house, in detail.

a. ——. In his *Zur Sprache gebracht*. (K707) (München: Albert Langen - Georg Müller, 1958): 335-341.

b. ——. In his *Im Zweifelsfalle*. (K924) (Wien: Europaverlag, 1984): 51-57.

c. "Why *Pallas Athene weeps*." In his *Exploring music*. (K817) (New York: October House, 1966): 195-201.

c. ——. *Unpublished*.

Manuscripts: US-AUS typescript (9 p.)

K663. "In eigener Sache." *Unpublished*.

A lecture broadcast on Radio Bremen on October 19, 1955. Krenek explains and justifies the many changes in his musical style and discusses why he is not considered a member of the avant garde.

Manuscripts: US-LJ 10 p. ; typescript (4 p.)

K664. "Letter to Leopold Ludwig." In *Leopold Ludwig*, von Berndt W. Wessling. (Bremen: Carl Schünemann Verlag, 1968): 93.

Facsimile of a letter dated October 19, 1955 thanking the conductor of the premiere of his opera *Pallas Athene weint* op.144 for "bringing the ship safely into port."

Manuscripts: US-LJ ink 1 p.

K665. "Klang, der nichts Menschliches hat." *Die Welt* (October 22, 1955)

A discussion of electronic music and its relation to atonal and serial music.

K666. "Zur Eröffnung der Wiener Staatsoper." *Wiener Staatsoper* (November 1955): 75.

K667. "Letzte Nachricht vom Sterbebett der ernsten Musik." *Melos* 22:11 (November 1955): 322-324.

Review of the book *The Agony of Modern Music* by Henry Pleasants.

a. "Lieber Herr Doktor Strobel." *Melos* 23:3 (March 1956): 77-78.

A letter of correction.

Manuscripts: US-LJ English 14 p. ; English typescript(7 p.). English.

K668. "Some outstanding American composers." In *Composers on music, an anthology of composer's writings from Palestrina to Copland*, edited by Sam Morgenstern. (New York: Pantheon Books, 1956): 540-545.

Translation of "Die Anfänge der Generation vor 1900" from his book *Musik im goldenen Westen*. Discusses the music of Aaron Copland, Roger Sessions, George Antheil, Virgil Thomson, and Charles Ives.

K669. "Stravinsky and surrealism." In *Composers on music, an anthology of composer's writings from Palestrina to Copland*, edited by Sam Morgenstern. (New York: Pantheon Books, 1956): 537-539.

An excerpt from his book *Music here and now*, Chapter 3 (pp.71-73). Discusses *Histoire du soldat* as an example of surrealism and Igor Stravinsky's change of style to neoclassicism. "The clinging to traditional means is just as systematic as in the case of neoclassicism, although the share of progressiveness is larger here than in the latter, since destruction, not restoration, is the object. The old material is not treated as if it were still intact and as useful as before, but is regarded as a conglomeration of wreckage, to be built up into a system contradicting the original arrangement. Surrealism causes a shock very similar to that produced by the introduction of really new features... The movement has deteriorated until it has become a craft, and by this deterioration has surrendered the essential individuality required for a really new style of art. Stravinsky shakes hands with neoclassicism by way of Jean Cocteau and Surrealism."

K670. "Schoenberg and atonality." In *Composers on music, an anthology of composer's writings from Palestrina to Copland,* edited by Sam Morgenstern. (New York: Pantheon Books, 1956): 539-540.

An excerpt from his book *Music here and now,* Chapter 3 (pp.80-83). New music is characterized by atonality; Arnold Schoenberg originated a system of atonality in Vienna which is the logical step following tonality.

    a. "Komponisten über Musik." *Forum* 4:46 (October 1957): 364-366.

German translation of several excerpts from the book including "Schönberg und die Atonalität." (p.366)

K671. *De rebus prius factis.* (Frankfurt: Hansen Musikverlag, 1956)

Krenek investigates the connection between medieval contrapuntal techniques and modern serial methods. The composer is interested in the electronic medium for two reasons: firstly, it enables him to extend his control over a region of musical elements which remains inaccessible while he still uses conventional instruments. With the help of the electronic apparatus he can even bring timbres into his constructional design... Furthermore, he can realize highly complex time-relationships with a degree of precision that an ensemble of human performers can never be guaranteed to provide, even after strenuous and protracted rehearsal. *See:* B787, B1409

K672. "Mozart." *Blätter der Städtischen Bühnen Düsseldorf 1955/56* no.9 (March 5, 1956)

The facsimile of a letter printed in a program booklet dedicated to Wolfgang Amadeus Mozart briefly discussing Mozart's immortality.

K673. "Doch 'Tag der Arbeit.'" *Kölnische Rundschau* (March 24, 1956)

Letter to the newspaper correcting their translation of "Thanksgiving Day."

K674. "Text an der Kassa; zur Problematik des Opernlibrettos." *Forum* 3:28 (April 1956): 152-154.

Singers, orchestras, and composers have all reduced the clarity of the libretto, and modern opera has become more intellectually complex. "Nevertheless it is still true that the best operas are those in which one can satisfactorily follow the text with one's logical and critical faculties *and* the emotional line with one's purely sensual powers of enjoyment."

    a. "Zur Problematik des Librettos." In his *Zur Sprache gebracht.* (K707) (München: Albert Langen - Georg Müller, 1958): 342-349.

    b. ——. In his *Im Zweifelsfalle.* (K924) (Wien: Europaverlag, 1984): 58-65.

    c. ——. In *Vom Wesen der Oper; Opernkomponisten in Autobiographien,* hrsg. von Heinz Krause-Graumnitz. (Berlin: Henschelverlag, 1969): 436-441.

    d. "The libretto problem." In his *Exploring music.* (K817) (New York: October House, 1966): 203-210.

K675. "Cherub mit selbstgestutzten Flügeln; Das Bildnis Mozarts aus seinen Briefen." *Forum* 3:31/32 (July-August 1956): 275-279.

A picture of Mozart through his letters; review of the book *Wolfgang Amadeus Mozart, Briefe,* edited by Willi Reich (Zurich: Manesnse Verlag, 1948).

a. "Das Bildnis Mozarts aus seinen Briefen." In his *Zur Sprache gebracht*. (K707) (München: Albert Langen - Georg Müller, 1958): 350-360.

K676. "[Beethoven's *Eroica* sketches]." *Unpublished*.
Lecture given July 1956 at the Darmstadt Ferienkursen.
Manuscripts: **D-bdr BNba** stenographic notes. **US-LJ** Musical examples 13 p.

K677. "Dignified levels." *Time* 68 (July 16, 1956)
A letter to the editor referring to an article about the artist Josef Albers and commenting "it is regrettable that your Music section hardly ever rises to such a sober and dignified level."

K678. "Was ist und wie entsteht elektronische Musik?" *Forum* 3:33 (September 1956): 330-333.
An introduction to the production of electronic music. It "is made up of sounds that are not made by a man directly causing a substance to vibrate, but by electric impulses in vacuum tubes... Electronic music differs from *musique concrète* in that it is fundamentally made up of electronically produced sounds. *Musique concrète* ... is essentially a montage of existing acoustic phenomena." After a thorough examination of the method of composing with electronic sounds, Krenek concludes that "the aleatoric element is no longer the function of an individual 're-creating' the music, but the direct expression of its creator's imagination." *See:* B554

a. ——. In his *Zur Sprache gebracht*. (K707) (München: Albert Langen - Georg Müller, 1958): 361-370.

b. ——. In his *Im Zweifelsfalle*. (K924) (Wien: Europaverlag, 1984): 198-207.

c. "What electronic music is and how it is made." In his *Exploring music*. (K817) (New York: October House, 1966): 211-220.

d. ——. In *Twentieth-Century Views of Music History*, edited by William Hays. (New York: Charles Scribner's Sons, 1972): 373-382.
Translated by Margaret Shenfield and Geoffrey Skelton.

K679. "Vom Altern und Veralten der Musik." *Forum* 3:36 (December 1956): 446-448.
The constant striving of "New Music" for the new and novel tends to obscure the fact that it grows old, but it does not have to become senile. Theodor Wiesengrund Adorno's concept of "language-similarity" of music is discussed and his belief in its negation by "New Music" is refuted. *See:* B554

a. ——. In his *Zur Sprache gebracht*. (K707) (München: Albert Langen - Georg Müller, 1958): 371-378.

b. "On the ageing and obsolescence of music." In his *Exploring music*. (K817) (New York: October House, 1966): 221-229.

-- 1957 --

K680. "Warum komponieren Sie Opern?" *Blätter der Städtischen Bühnen Düsseldorf 1957*
A personal statement explaining his motivation to compose operas. Opera is a difficult subject to discuss because successful opera may contain a nonsensical message; however, Krenek has always felt the need to communicate his dramaturgical and musical talent in a logically consistent and intellectually clear manner. This contrast may be the reason why opera continues to fascinate him.

a. "Das vertrackte Medium." *Musik der Zeit* Neue Folge:3 (1960): 29.

Manuscripts: "Musik der Zeit." **US-LJ** 2 p.

K681. "On Artur Schnabel's compositions." In *Artur Schnabel, a biography,* by César Saerchinger. (New York: Dodd, Mead & Co., 1957): 317-319.

An appreciation of Artur Schnabel the composer, to whom "composing music was just as important and permanent a vehicle of self-expression as piano playing. In the last two decades of his life the creation of music subjectively even took precedence over its interpretation... He could afford to write music not only unpopular but also impractical according to current standards of performance."

a. ——. In *Artur Schnabel, a biography,* by Cesar Saerchinger. (London: Cassell & Co., 1957): 317-319.

b. ——. In *Artur Schnabel, a biography,* by Cesar Saerchinger. (Reprint Westport, CT, 1973): 317-319.

Manuscripts: **US-LJ** 20 p. & correspondence

K682. "Wie beurteilen Sie die Zukunft des Musiktheaters? Glauben Sie an einen Fortbestand der Oper?" *Oper* [Program: Opernhaus Mannheim] (January 1957)

A brief letter of appreciation for the Festschrift to the opening of the new Mannheimer Nationaltheater.

K683. "Mahler's *Ninth Symphony.*" *Unpublished.*

A lecture broadcast by the CBC, Vancouver, January 20, 1957. Krenek briefly discusses the emotional situation surrounding Gustav Mahler's composition of this symphony followed by a general appreciation of Mahler's later works. His adherence to the classical model, yet colossally expanding the form, creates a dialectical tension. He foreshadows future principles of composition by pushing the classical form beyond its limits; in a way his colossal symphonic monsters lead directly to Webern's minimalism. Krenek thoroughly analyzes the individual movements of the symphony and points out that the adherence to the classic Rondo form in all movements provides a new meaning for features such as theme and development establishing stability versus fluidity.

Manuscripts: **US-LJ** 11 p.

K684. "Der gesunde Menschenverstand." *Melos* 24:2 (February 1957): 33-34.

Extracted from *De Rebus prius factis.* New music is a continuation of old music.

K685. "*Kette, Kreis und Spiegel.*" In *Alte und Neue Musik* Vol.2: *Das Basler Kammerorchester 1926-1976.* (Zürich: Atlantis Verlag, 1977): 247-248.

Briefly discusses the meaning of the title of the work and its rhythmic elements. Extract from a letter to Paul Sacher, February 1, 1957, printed in program no.76, 16.January 1958.

K686. "Mein schweres Dasein als 'ernster Komponist'." *Frankfurter Allgemeine Zeitung* (February 19, 1957)

Excerpt from *De rebus prius factis.*

K687. "Riccardo Malipiero: *La donna è mobile.*" *Notes* 2d series, 14:2 (March 1957): 196.

Review of the music.

Manuscripts: **US-LJ** 2 p.

K688. "Konrad Roetscher: *Suite in fünf Sätzen für grösseres Orchester*, op.26." *Notes* 2d series, 14:2 (March 1957): 196-197.

Review of the music.

K689. "Lydteorier, betragtninger over elektron-musik." *Dansk Musiktidsskrift* 32:2 (May 1957): 31-33.

Danish translation of Chapter 9 from *De rebus prius factis*. Picture.

K690. "Time and time again." *Schweizerische Musikzeitung* 97:6 (June 1957): 261-262.

The complex determination of serial music loses any appearance of regularity and sounds like utterly spontaneous improvisation, like the life-process. In English.

K691. "Der elektronische Klang." *Neue Zürcher Zeitung Sonntagausgabe* no.1607 (June 2, 1957): 5-6.

A brief introduction to the electronic music being produced in the Nordwestdeutscher Rundfunk studio in Cologne.

K692. "*Lamentatio Jeremiae prophetae*." *Alte und Neue Musik* Vol.2: *Das Basler Kammerorchester 1926-1976*. (Zürich: Atlantis Verlag, 1977): 246-247.

Very brief discussion of the text, form, and rhythm of the work from the program notes: Extrakonzert, 20. June 1957.

K693. "Kitsch und Kunst." *Forum* 4:43/44 (July-August 1957): 290-297.

Response, with others, to a request for a brief definition and comparison between "Kitsch" and Art. For Krenek (page 293) the essence of "Kitsch" lies in the presentation of traditionally sophisticated art work in a banal context, or when traditionally primitive means are used to claim "depth" or a deeper meaning. "Kitsch," for example, is the use of a Mahler symphony as background music for a cartoon movie. Twelve-tone music is hard to imagine as "Kitsch" because it lacks traditional associations.

K694. "*Alban Berg; The man and his music*. By H.F. Redlich." *Musical Quarterly* 43:3 (July 1957): 403-406.

Book review pointing out errors and augmenting information from his personal acquaintance with Berg. Concludes that "a carefully drawn up catalogue of works and an 'exhaustive' discography make this lively and concise book a valuable tool of reference."

Manuscripts: US-LJ 2 p.

K695. "Krenek's music." *Unpublished*.

A lecture broadcast over KPFA, Berkeley, CA, August 1957. An analysis of the *Viola sonata* op.92, no.3.

Manuscripts: US-LJ 3 p.

K696. "Webern *Symphony*." *Unpublished*.

Lecture broadcast over CBC Vancouver on September 29, 1957. A discussion and analysis of the music.

Manuscripts: US-LJ 17 p.

K697. "Der ganze Webern in drei Stunden." *Melos* 24:10 (October 1957): 304-305.

A review of the Columbia recording of Anton Webern's complete works.

Manuscripts: US-LJ 3 p.

K698. Number unused.

K699. "Krenek profile." *Unpublished.*

A lecture broadcast by the CBC, Vancouver, on December 22, 1957. Krenek reviews the latest developments in music and provides a view into the future of composition with examples from his own music. He discusses the compositional basis for *Eleven transparencies* op.142 where brevity of form is related to serial thinking. He discusses serialism and the younger generation of composers, and the replacement of the traditional role of the phrase/sentence and other speech-like features with ideas of pure construction and design. He also discusses tape and electronic music using *Spiritus inteligentiae, Sanctus* op.152 as an example.

Manuscripts: US-LJ 15 p.

-- 1958 --

K700. "Atonalität und Zwölftontechnik." *Unpublished.*

Written about 1958? Discusses twelve-tone technique during his years at Hamline University and analysizes his *Missa duodecim tonorum* op.165 written for the Gregorian Institute.

Manuscripts: US-LJ pp.2-4

K701. "Bericht über Versuche in total determinierter Musik." *Darmstädter Beiträge zur neuen Musik* 1 (1958): 17-21.

Discusses serial music and describes the development of rhythmic sets from a twelve-tone row.

a. ----. In his *Im Zweifelsfalle.* (K924) (Wien: Europaverlag, 1984): 183-189.

K702. "Gestiftete Musik." *Musik und Szene; Theaterzeitschrift der Deutschen Oper am Rhein* 3:6 (1958/59): 61-65.

The role of foundation support for music in America is contrasted with the financial support for music available in Europe. Picture.

K703. "Komponist im Exil." *Kontrapunkte* 2 (1958): 141-146.

Describes his experiences teaching music to American veterans studying under the G.I. Bill in California. Extracted from *De rebus prius factis.*

K704. "Was mich heute beschäftigt." *Almanach auf das Jahr 1958* (Hollywood: Cultural Exchange Center, 1958): 12-15.

Since 1954 he has written electronic music; a discussion of what it is and how he uses it. Picture.

K705. "Zwölftonmusik für Chor." In *112. Niederrheinisches Musikfest in Duisburg Jahrbuch 1958.* (Darmstadt: Mykenae, 1958)

A discussion about intonation problems in serial and atonal choral compositions. The assertion of the impossibility of singing equal tempered intervals was already refuted by late romantic compositions with their frequent enharmonic changes which made equal temperament a necessity.

Manuscripts: US-LJ 1 p.

K706. "Neue Anwendungsmöglichkeiten in der seriellen Technik." *Unpublished.*

Lecture broadcast over Norddeutscher Rundfunk, Hamburg in 1958. Beginning with a ridiculing description of John Cage's *Piano concert*, Krenek launches into an explanation of the principles and philosophy of chance music as a "willful withdrawing from the idea of 'rule.' It cannot be seen why chance music claims to be related to serial music, where all aspects are determined."

He discusses the characteristics of serial music and the planned "element of surprise" in an examination of *Sestina* op.161.

Manuscripts: **US-LJ** typescript copy(7 p.)

K707. *Zur Sprache gebracht,* hrsg. von Friedrich Saathen. (München: Albert Langen - Georg Müller, 1958) 398 p.

A collection of essays: *Ueber meine Memoiren* (K605-b); *Der Zeitgeist* (K55-a); *'Materialbestimmtheit' der Oper* (K45-a); *Einkehr bei Rilke* (K82-c); *Schubert* (K87-a); *Französisches und deutsches Musikempfinden* (K90-b); *Operette und Revue* (K92-a); *Opernerfahrung* (K96-d); *Bericht über ein Marionettenspiel* (K98-a); *Ein paar Worte über Johann Strauss* (K99-b); *Von "Jonny" zu "Orest"* (K105-a); *Die Stellung der Musik in der Kultur der Gegenwart* (K113-b); *Darius Milhaud* (K109-b); *Komponieren als Beruf* (K120-b); *Soll ein Künstler publizistisch tätig sein?* (K126-b); *Von Musik etwas verstehen...* (K135-d); *Neue Humanität und alte Sachlichkeit* (K100-a); *Freiheit des menschlichen Geistes* (K158-c); *Das fortgesetzte Totenmahl* (K187-a); *Zur Situation der Oper* (K193-d); *Ueber Sinn und Schicksal der neuen Musikpädagogik* (K207-b); *Was sollte Musikkritik leisten?* (K213-d); *Das Nationale und die Kunst* (K246-d); *Oesterreich* (K244-a); *Freiheit und Verantwortung* (K248-a); *Erfahrungen mit dem 'Zwölftonsystem'* (K253-a); *Ueber die Volksverbundenheit der Kunst* (K257-a); *Arnold Schönberg* (K268-a); *Karl Kraus und Arnold Schönberg* (K274-a); *Künstlerische und wissenschaftliche Geschichtsbetrachtung* (K295-a); *Betrachtungen bei der Analyse eines Verses* (K343-a); *Von der Würde der abendländischen Musik* (K359-b); *Ist Oper heute noch möglich?* (K416-b); *Ansprache bei der Trauerfeier für Karl Kraus* (K408-a); *Erinnerung an Karl Kraus* (K401-a); *Alban Bergs "Lulu"* (K444-b); *Notizen zur Gesamtausgabe von Franz Kafkas Schriften* (K457-a); *Grundideen einer neuen Musikästhetik* (K403-a); *Musik für die Ewigkeit* (K489-a); *Ueber die Inspiration* (K513-b); *Der elfenbeinerne Turm und der Mann von der Strasse* (K529-a); *Komponist und Interpret* (K540-b); *Das unaufhörliche Raunen* (K545-b); *Ueber die Bedeutung der Musik* (K588-c); *Fünfzig Jahre Komponierhandwerk* (K599-a); *Warum "Pallas Athene weint"?* (K662-a); *Zur Problematik des Librettos* (K674-a); *Das Bildnis Mozarts aus seinen Briefen* (K675-a); *Was ist und wie entsteht elektronische Musik?* (K678-a); *Vom Altern und Veralten der Musik* (K679-a); *Gespräch nach Mitternacht* (K551-a). *See:* B506, B619, B640, B866, B1043, B1055, B1397, B1470

a.   ——. (Reprint Berlin: Deutsche Buch Gemeinschaft, 1965)

K708. "Ein 'moderner' Meister des XV. Jahrhunderts." *Neue Zeitschrift für Musik* 119:1 (January 1958): 3-8.

Discusses his interest in Johannes Ockeghem, which began during his years at Vassar College, and the importance of Ockeghem's music for his own music. He concludes that the music of the Renaissance can provide a direction to the composer of today.

a.   ——. In his *Im Zweifelsfalle.* (K924) (Wien: Europaverlag, 1984): 75-80.

Manuscripts: "Meine Beziehung zu Johannes Ockeghem." **US-LJ** typescript (8 p.)

K709. "Neuere musikalische Denkweisen." *Basler Nachrichten* (January 19, 1958)

Discusses the background and analyzes *Kette, Kreis und Spiegel* op.160 in preparation for its premiere by the Basel Kammerorchester.

K710. "Ein 'verwirrter' Zeitgnosse meldet sich zu Wort." *Melos* 25:2 (February 1958): 70.

A reaction to Andreas Briner's "Verwirrung um Zeit" in volume 24 (November 1957) on the static qualities of serial music.

K711. "Ueber mein Werk." *Musik und Szene; Theaterzeitschrift der Deutschen Oper am Rhein* 2:13 (1957/58): 145-146.

Briefly discusses *Karl V.* op.73 and its 1954 revision. Dated at end: March 1958. Picture, facsimilie score.

K712. "[Communication from Ernst Krenek]." In *Amendment to communications act of 1934*, United States Senate hearings, Committee on Interstate and Foreign Commerce, Eighty-fifth Congress, Second Session. (Washington: Government Printing Office, 1958. [Y4.In8/3:C73/34/958]): 997-1001.

Refutes the comments made during the hearings implying "that the present organization of BMI promotes the creation and dissemination of predominantly inferior music" and supports the BMI management. Includes the program from an April 1, 1951 concert held at the Los Angeles County Museum which included the first Los Angeles performances of the *Fifth piano sonata* op.121 and the *Seventh string quartet* op.96, and performances of the *Sonata for viola and piano* op.117 and the *Sonata for violin and piano* op.99. Also includes a chronology of Krenek's life.

K713. "Was ist 'Reihenmusik'?" *Neue Zeitschrift für Musik* 119:5 (May 1958): 278-281 & 119:8 (August 1958): 428-430.

Comments on serial music in reaction to Josef Rufer's article "Was ist Zwölftonmusik?" in volume 118, number 1 (January 1957). Includes a discussion of pitch and octave serialization using as examples the music of Anton Webern and Karlheinz Stockhausen.

Manuscripts: **US-LJ** 9 p.

K714. "Syllepsis." *Los Angeles Evening Mirror News* 10:218 (June 21, 1958): 1:7.

A letter to the editor; Krenek disagrees with the definition given for the winning word in the June 12th report of the Washington spelling contest.

K715. "Sestina." *Melos* 25:7/8 (July-August 1958): 235-238.

A technical analysis of the serial composition op.161; includes the text.

K716. "Roman Vlad *Storia della dodecafonia*." *Notes* 2d series, 15:4 (September 1958): 568-569.

Review of the book. "To a composer it is always exhilarating to read another composer on the art of composition... It is like sitting down with an old friend for a long discussion of a subject that had been on our minds for the better part of our lives." Krenek's principal criticism of the book is with its "lack of proportion." Too much space is taken up with Schoenberg, Berg, and Webern and not enough with younger composers. Also too much emphasis is placed upon Italian music.

Manuscripts: **US-LJ** 3 p.

K717. "Vortrag für Radio Bremen, Oct.31, 1958." *Unpublished.*

Discusses *Kette, Kreis und Spiegel* op.160.

Manuscripts: **US-LJ** 5 p.

-- 1959 --

K718. "Unterwegs im grossen Südwesten." In his *Gedanken unterwegs.* (K720) (München: Albert Langen - Georg Müller, 1959): 248-295.

Travel essays written in 1959 giving his impressions of nature, landscape, people, and culture in Utah, New Mexico, Arizona, Nevada, and California. Mentions the missions of Santa Barbara, San Xavier del Bac, and Isleta and the atomic test area of Los Alamos; discusses the American school system, advertising, and commercialism; describes the peculiarities of the American language and the Mormon culture; describes the Grand Canyon, gold-rush ghost towns, Nevada and gambling, San Francisco, the Sierra Nevada, Death Valley, and the Imperial Valley.

K719. "Vom Verfall des Einfalls." In *Prisma der gegenwärtigen Musik,* hrsg. von Joachim E. Behrendt und Jürgen Uhde. Soziale Wirklichkeit, Bd.6 (Hamburg: Furche-Verlag, 1959): 137-144.

Observations on the decline of the musical idea. Musical inspiration, which is difficult to define in any case, is dependant upon the imagination of its inventor. The composer of serial music does not depend upon inspiration but rather upon the predetermination of all the musical events, which provokes the rise of "accidental" music as exemplified by Karlheinz Stockhausen and John Cage. In both instances of serialist and aleatoric music the musical idea is present within the "system." The musical idea under the previous system could not be planned ahead, but occurred unpredictably within a musical emotion; now this has been replaced by a system in which randomness can be controlled.

a. ——. In his *Im Zweifelsfalle.* (K924) (Wien: Europaverlag, 1984): 190-197.

K720. *Gedanken unterwegs; Dokumente einer Reise,* hrsg. von Friedrich Saathen. (München: Albert Langen - Georg Müller, 1959) 296 p.

A collection of travel essays: *Von der Aufgabe, ein Oesterreicher zu sein* (K139-a), *Aus Gründen der Kontrolle* (K133-a), *Meditation in der Morgendämmerung* (K144-a), *Am Alpensüdrand bemerkt* (K148-a), *Im Wallis* (K150-a), *Wie der Stadtfrack uns Skiläufer sieht* (K161-a), *Vor mir die Sintflut* (K186-a), *Versuch einer Analyse schweizerischen Geistes* (K203-a), *Was soll man auf Reisen lesen?* (K228-a), *Lob des Radios* (K243-a), *Im Land des Uebermasses* (K255-a), *Im Vorarlberg* (K265-a), *Sommer am Tannberg* (K320-a), *Der Mensch und die Alpen* (K326-a), *England zum ersten Mal gesehen* (K338-a), *Amerikanisches Barock* (K277-a), *Micky und Silly* (K287-a), *Tiefe und Distanz* (K350-a), *Stadt zwischen Traum und Wirklichkeit* (K371-a), *Regen über Narbonne* (K372-b), *Geborgen in den Bergen* (K379-a), *Vom Bregenzer Wald* (K392-a), *Die sublime Zone* (K393-a), *Nähe des Südens* (K395-a), *Ueber die gesellschaftliche Bedeutung von Wahrheit und Lüge* (K407-a), *Spanische Elegie* (K413-a), *Auf der Suche nach der Heimat* (K426-a), *Reise durch westliche Länder* (K427-a), *Linksrheinisch* (K428-a), *Auf dem Wasser zu singen* (K459-a), *Zur amerikanischen Mentalität* (K463-a, K464-a & K472-a), *Fliegertod und Mädchenschule* (K465), *Amerikanische Landschaft* (K478-a), *American mixed grill* (K482-a), *Ostwärts* (K481), *Universalism and nationalism in music* (K528-a), *Appell an das Gewissen* (K544-a), *Ist Los Angeles eine Stadt?"* (K575), *Die Reise nach Westen* (K586-a), *Unterwegs im grossen Südwesten* (K718). *See:* B768, B1472, K734

K721. "Ernst Krenek." *Carré rouge* (Lausanne, SZ) no.11 (May/June 1959) A note of appreciation with others for Ernest Ansermet.

K722. "Egon Wellesz: *5 Sinfonie, op.75.*" *Notes* 2d series, 16:3 (June 1959): 473. Review of the music.

Manuscripts: **US-LJ** included in 5 p.

K723. "Rolf Liebermann: *Sinfonie 1949*. Rudolf Wagner-Regeny: *Drei Orchestersätze*, 1952." *Notes* 2d series, 16:3 (June 1959): 473.
Review of the music.
Manuscripts: US-LJ included in 5 p.

K724. "Luigi Nono: *Incontri*. Luigi Nono: *Varianti*." *Notes* 2d series, 16:3 (June 1959): 473-474.
Review of the music.
Manuscripts: US-LJ included in 5 p.

K725. "Riccardo Malipiero: *Concerto per violoncello e orchestra*." *Notes* 2d series, 16:3 (June 1959): 474.
Review of the music.
Manuscripts: US-LJ included in 5 p.

K726. "Giselher Klebe: *Rhapsodie für Orchester*, op.17. Giselher Klebe: *Römische Elegien*. Giselher Klebe: *Moments musicaux*, op.19." *Notes* 2d series, 16:3 (June 1959): 474-475.
Review of the music.
Manuscripts: US-LJ included in 5 p.

K727. "Das Licht unterm Scheffel." *Forum* 6:67/68 (July-August 1959): 292-293.
A discussion of the difficulties in achieving recognition by young Austrian serial composers.

K728. "Ernst Krenek." In *Für Heinz Tiessen, 1887-1971*. Schriftenreihe der Akademie der Künste, Bd.13. (Berlin: Akademie der Künste, 1979): 294-295.
The transcript of a letter to Tiessen dated September 17, 1959 thanking him for his history of the Internationale Gesellschaft der neue Musik.

K729. "Amerikanischer Musiksommer." *Forum* 6:70 (October 1959): 377-378.
A description of his attendance at two Fromm Foundation sponsored seminars at Tanglewood and Princeton, mentioning the first American performance of his *Sixth string quartet* op.78 at Tanglewood, the music faculty at Princeton, especially Roger Sessions, Milton Babbitt, and Edward Cone, and the RCA Music Synthesizer.

K730. "Amerikas Einfluss auf eingewanderte Komponisten." *Musica* 13:12 (December 1959): 757-761.
"America has sharpened the sense of reality of the European composers that came to its shores. Yet at the same time it seems to have made them neglect ... the 'sense of possibility.'" The emigré composer fleeing the Nazis had to fight against a defensive attitude of the native American composers, yet most undertook teaching posts which placed them in an environment with a defensive attitude toward the new. The American public had a mentality of pragmatism which tends toward conformity. As a result of these influences, the emigré composer was inhibited. Only when Krenek returned to Europe in the early 1950s was he revitalized and the path, including rotation which he had begun with *Lamentatio Jeremiae prophetae* op.93, could again be followed. *See:* B554

a. ——. In his *Im Zweifelsfalle*. (K924) (Wien: Europaverlag, 1984): 136-143.

b. "America's influence on its émigré composers." *Perspectives of New Music* 8:2 (Spring/Summer 1970): 112-117.

Translation by Don Harren with slight revisions.

c. ——. In *Writings of German composers*, edited by Jost Hermand and James Steakley. (New York: Continuum, 1984): 276-283.

Translated by Don Harran.

K731. "Die grosse Musikmaschine." *Forum* 6:72 (December 1959): 466-467.

A report on Krenek's visit to the RCA Music Synthesizer at the Columbia-Princeton Electronic Music Center including a "layman's" explanation of how the studio works (using additive synthesis) and what the computer does (punched cards give the computer instructions on how to control the synthesizer.) This system is different from the European music studios where electronic music was recorded, processed, mixed, and re-recorded by hand rather than through computer instructions. His over-all aesthetic judgement of the Synthesizer's sound is skeptical.

a. ——. In his *Im Zweifelsfalle.* (K924) (Wien: Europaverlag, 1984): 208-212.

-- 1960 --

K732. "Ueber Schuberts *Winterreise*." *Unpublished*.

A lecture broadcast over Radio Hannover about 1960.

Manuscripts: US-LJ 1 p.

K733. "Franz Schreker." *Unpublished*.

Reminiscences about his teacher broadcast on Sender Freies Berlin about 1960.

Manuscripts: US-LJ 4 p.

K734. "Gedanken zwischen Hollywood und Wien." In *Literaturkalender Spectrum des Geistes 1960*. (Ebenhausen bei München: Hartfrid Voss Verlag, 1960): 94-95.

An illustrated calendar with a brief excerpt from *Gedanken Unterwegs* (K720).

K735. "Serial music." *Unpublished*.

Lecture given at a meeting of the Los Angeles chapter of the American Musicological Society in 1960. "The more parameters are regulated by serial premeditation, the less predictable is the result in all its details. Thus the element of improvisation is built into the process of strict prearrangement, and the unexpected occurs by necessity."

Manuscripts: US-LJ 1 p.

K736. "Ueber eigene Werke." *Unpublished*.

Lecture discussing his concept of and use of time in his own works. He continues with further discussions of the concepts of serialism, randomness, and row principles supported with musical examples.

Manuscripts: US-LJ 6 p.

K737. "Anton von Webern, a Profile." In *Anton von Webern perspectives*, compiled by Hans Moldenhauer; edited by Delmar Irvine. (Seattle: University of Washington Press, 1966): 3-14.

Lecture entitled "Profile on Webern" for the Fromm Foundation and given February 1960; adapted for the Seattle Webern Festival May 25, 1962. Surveys

Webern's life and works noting that "there is no other composer of similar significance in the whole history of music whose entire life's work (as left by himself to posterity) takes not more than about three hours of performance time, as does that of the Austrian Anton von Webern."

a. "Webern in perspective, a profile of the music." *Saturday Review* 49:22 (May 28, 1966): 47-49.

b. "Anton von Webern, a Profile." In *Anton von Webern perspectives,* compiled by Hans Moldenhauer; edited by Delmar Irvine. (Reprint New York: Da Capo Press, 1978): 3-14.

Manuscripts: US-LJ 5 p.

K738. "Profile on myself." *Unpublished.*

A radio broadcast prepared for the Fromm Foundation, February 1960, presenting an outline of Krenek's compositional personality and briefly introducing the works before they are played: the *Third piano sonata* op.92, no.4 demonstrates his early twelve-tone technique; he explains the time and circumstances of the composition of *Lamentatio Jeremiae prophetae* op.93; the *Eleven transparencies* op.142 are miniature forms dependent upon classical models; *Spiritus intelligentiae, Sanctus* op.152 for two voices and electronic sounds is a religious work focused about the manifestation of the Holy Ghost; the *Sestina* op.161 is his realization of the serial concept; and he concludes with an explanation of the story of his opera *The Bell tower* op.153.

Manuscripts: US-LJ 10 p.

K739. "Ein Fall von Hinterhofkunst." *Forum* 7:75 (March 1960): 112-113.

A discussion of the Watts towers as a reflection of life in Los Angeles.

K740. "Extents and limits of serial technique." *Musical Quarterly* 46:2 (April 1960): 210-232.

Krenek reviews the principles of serial rotation, indeterminacy and other serial techniques used in his compositions *Lamentatio Jeremiae prophetae* op.93, *Spiritus intelligentiae Sanctus* op.152, *Kette, Kreis und Spiegel* op.160, *Sestina* op.161, and *Quaestio temporis* op.170. *See:* B997

a. ——. In *Problems of Modern Music; The Princeton Seminar in Advanced Musical Studies,* edited by Paul Henry Lang. (New York: W.W. Norton, 1960): 72-94.

K741. "Mit dem Wohlstand schwindet die Heiterkeit." *Magnum* (Köln) no.29 (April 1960): 58.

Reflection on the changes which have taken place in Germany and with the German people since World War II. Generally the changes are considered improvements as the people before 1932 who gave the impression of "Angst," distrust, arrogance, and aggressiveness are now polite and friendly. The rapid Americanization of the country is a cause for some concern.

K742. "*Quaestio temporis.*" *Musica* 14:7 (July 1960): 415-419.

Analysis of the work op.170 including a discussion of serial transformation and its rhythmic and duration serialization.

K743. "Zeit und Ewigkeit." *Forum* 7:79/80 (July-August 1960): 281-283.

Philosophical observations on musical time in honor of the centennial of Gustav Mahler's birthday. Krenek notes that Mahler's music was directed toward infinity, characterized by elements representing steadiness and perpetual reoccurrence, as well as the march as a journey to infinity. Although it seeks timelessness it moves in ontological time. On the other hand, serial or twelve-tone music lives, moves, and changes in its own time. The idea of retrograde, for example, is time flowing backwards; in this sense twelve-tone music has no time direction and is not ontological.

a. ——. In his *Im Zweifelsfalle*. (K924) (Wien: Europaverlag, 1984): 88-94.

K744. "Serialism." In *The Modern Composer and His World*, edited by John Beckwith and Udo Kasemets. (Toronto: University of Toronto, 1961): 65-71.

Lecture given at the Shakespearean Festival in Stratford, Ontario, Canada, August 9, 1960 on the lack of a sense of tempo in serial music.

Manuscripts: "Serial music today." US-LJ 9 p. ; typescript(6 p.)

K745. "Notizen zum eigenen Geburtstag." *Forum* 7:81 (September 1960): 340.

Reflections and reminiscences prompted by his receiving the Silver Medal of Honor from the Austrian government on his sixtieth birthday.

K746. "Der wandelbare Komponist." In *Das musikalische Selbstportrait von Komponisten, Dirigenten, Instrumentalisten, Sängerinnen and Sängern unserer Zeit*, Josepf Müller-Marein & Hannes Reinhardt. (Hamburg: Nannen Verlag, 1963): 175-192.

Autobiographical lecture written for the Norddeutscher Rundfunk in Hamburg, and broadcast September 30, 1960 as "Das musikalische Selbstportrait." Picture.

a. "Den alsidige komponist." In *Musikalske selvportraetter*, Josef Müller-Marein & Hannes Reinhardt; Danish translation by Torben Meyer. (Kobenhavn: July Gjellerups Forlag, 1966): 157-174.

K747. "'Stochastische' Musik." *Musikalische Jugend* 9:5 (October-November 1960): 1-2.

Serial music is a result of the composer's desire to strictly control a performance.

K748. "Komponiste und Hörer." *Musikalische Zeitfragen* 12 (1964)

Lecture given at the Kasseler Musiktagen, October 7, 1960 examining why composers compose and the role of the listener. Krenek asks: do composers compose for themselves, for listeners, or for performers? Those who cannot find listeners nevertheless feel the urge to compose and are wrongfully thought to be arrogant. The middle ages had a different philosophy; art was not made for the people, but for God. Our own art-making is dominated by an historical consciousness which compels us to permanent change; only new contributions are thought to characterize an epoch. This attitude explains the development of serial music; however, it is not so radically new and shares certain similarities with medieval music and thought such as retrograde musical time, rhythmic independence from a meter, and the recent approach of music to ways of thinking similar to the natural sciences. The role of the listener is to try to listen without prejudice and to judge the music as it is. *See:* B246, B775

a. "Komponist und Hörer." In his *Im Zweifelsfalle*. (K924) (Wien: Europaverlag, 1984): 298-318.

Manuscripts: US-LJ typescript copy (20 p.)

K749. "Letter to A. Goldberg." *Los Angeles Times* 79 (October 16, 1960)

K750. "Musik und Sprache." *Forum* 7:84. (December 1960): 461-463.

Lecture given for the Feierstunde der Wiener Konzerthausgesellschaft and the Oesterreichischen College on October 24, 1960 for Krenek's sixtieth birthday on the differences in the communicative capabilities of music and speech and the similarity of pre-serial music to the patterns of speech.

a. "Musik und Sprache (I)." In his *Im Zweifelsfalle.* (K924) (Wien: Europaverlag, 1984): 328-333.

K751. *"Sinfonie Pallas Athene."* In *Alte und Neue Musik* Vol.2: *Das Basler Kammerorchester 1926-1976.* (Zürich: Atlantis Verlag, 1977): 248-251.

Briefly discusses the relationship of the symphony to the opera. Extracted from program Nr.92, 29.October 1960.

K752. "Proportionen und pythagoräische Hämmer." *Musica* 14:11 (November 1960): 708-712.

Draws a relationship between Johannes Tinctoris's proportional notation and rhythm in modern music.

-- 1961 --

K753. "Ist Oper heute noch möglich?" *[Program: Hamburgische Staatsoper]* no.6 (1961/2): 41-48.

K754. "Grussworte der Komponisten." *Musik und Szene; Theaterzeitschrift der Deutschen Oper am Rhein* 6:3 (1961/62): 27.

A facsimile of a brief handwritten note from Krenek congratulating the Deutschen Oper am Rhein during their festival week "Musiktheater des XX. Jahrhunderts." Picture.

K755. "Zwölftontechnik." *Unpublished.*

A lecture broadcast over Südwestfunk, Baden-Baden about 1961.

Manuscripts: **US-LJ** 10 p.

K756. "Die Moderne Musik und ihr Publikum." *Die Kultur* 9 (February 1961)

K757. "Franz Schubert Liedkompositionen." *Unpublished.*

A lecture broadcast over Südwestfunk, Baden-Baden, March 3-4, 1961 presenting a portrait of the composer and discussing the relative indifference with which he was generally received, his futile attempts to write a successful opera, and the erroneous assessment of later musicologists of his compositional importance. Krenek uses a number of songs in which the piano includes the singer's part as examples to explain Schubert's compositional genius. Each example contains hints on the architecture of rhythm, melody, harmony, and motive. Krenek mentions the problematic relationship between composition and text in Schubert's songs, and notes that his totally lyrical devotion to the text may explain his failure as an opera composer.

Manuscripts: **US-LJ** 20 p.

K758. "Jahre des Kulturpessimismus." *Magnum* (Köln) no.35 (April 1961): 42.

A brief response to a question about life in the 1920s consisting of his personal view of what happened and how it is seen today.

Manuscripts: "Die zwanziger Jahre." **US-LJ** 6 p.

K759. "Stravinsky." *Unpublished.*

A lecture broadcast over RIAS, Berlin on June 19, 1962, for Igor Stravinsky's eightieth birthday. Krenek reminiscenes about their first meetings in Berlin and Geneva around 1923. He mentions Stravinsky's influence on his neo-romantic period, but notes that his turn to twelve-tone music caused a rift between the two composers. Only twenty-five years later, when Stravinsky turned to serialism, did they resume friendly relations.

Manuscripts: US-LJ 2 p.

K760. "Kann man serielle Musik hören?" *Melos* 28:7/8 (July-August 1961): 223-229.

The transcript of a round-table discussion between Krenek, Claus-Henning Bachmann, Franz Willnauer, and Fritz Winckel in Alpbach Austria on whether the listener can hear the serialized elements in serial music.

K761. "Beherrschtes Lächeln; Ernst Kreneks Nachwort zur Darmstädter Orest-Krise." *Darmstädter Tagblatt* (November 24, 1961)

Reactions to the dispute on the occasion of the Darmstadt production of his opera *Leben des Orest* op.60 in September. After viewing the rehearsals, Krenek refused to attend the opening night performance which led to a conflict between the state theater and the Kranichsteiner Musikinstitut. His comments reflect an attitude of standing above the tumult, giving advice on how to respect new music in general, and on how the opera should have been received. He points out the contradictory remarks of Wolfgang Steinecke made in articles printed before and after the performance.

-- 1962 --

K762. "In eigener Sache." *Unpublished.*

Lecture broadcast on Bayrische Rundfunk in 1962 discussing his own music: *Kleine Symphonie* op.58, *Adagio und Fuge* op.78a, and *Quaestio temporis* op.170.

Manuscripts: US-LJ 7 p.

K763. "Das Gesetz der Serie." *Unpublished.*

Lecture given to the Oesterreichischen Kulturvereinigung, January 4, 1962 concerning the twelve-tone row and serialism.

Manuscripts: US-LJ 3 p.

K764. "Bemerkungen zur Wiener Schule." *Oesterreichische Musikzeitschrift* 17:4 (April 1962): 184-185.

Additions and comments to the article "Die Wiener Schule und die Gegenwart" (B182) by Friedrich Cerha on the relationship of the serial composers to Schoenberg and his circle, and a reaction to Cerha's comment about Krenek's isolation in America and his relationship to the new generation of Austrian composers. *See:* B182

K765. "Verlegen, verlegt, verlogen." *Forum* 9:100 (April 1962): 171-173.

A humorous article about the difficulties of the publisher selling contemporary music and the distrust of the composer regarding the publisher. Composers overestimate the means and power of the publisher, and feel cheated when they do not receive evidence (money) of rapid publication. Most publishers are unaware that there is little to be made by the composer through the sale of printed music; the bulk of a composer's income comes from commissions, which are supported by philanthropists and institutions, and rarely from publishing companies. The title is a play on words: publisher and mislay, lost, and a lie.

K766. "Kanon, Igor Strawinsky zum 80. Geburtstag." *Musica* 16:4 (April 1962): 4 pages between 176-177.

Facsimile of the manuscript of his eighty note canon op.181 in honor of the composer.

a. ——. *Basler Nachrichten* no.467 (November 4, 1962)

K767. "Das musikalische Klima Oesterreichs." *Musica* 16:3 (May/June 1962): 103-106.

Surveys musical life in Vienna before the Second World War and discusses its generally conservative character. Picture.

Manuscripts: **US-LJ** typescript (13 p.)

K768. "New dimensions of music." In *Anton von Webern perspectives,* compiled by Hans Moldenhauer; edited by Delmar Irvine. (Seattle: University of Washington Press, 1966): 102-107

A lecture given at the Seattle Webern Festival on May 25, 1962. Discusses the changes in music since the death of Anton Webern, and the development of serial and chance music. "Just as the twelve-tone technique was constantly reviewed, revised, reshaped, remodeled, and applied in countless varying situations without ever being abandoned, so will the serial concepts govern musical thinking for a long time to come, even if their application should still be less obvious than it has been so far. Undoubtedly Anton von Webern will continue to be recognized as the fountainhead of this kind of musical thinking."

a. ——. In *Anton von Webern perspectives,* compiled by Hans Moldenhauer; edited by Delmar Irvine. (Reprint New York: Da Capo Press, 1978): 102-107.

Manuscripts: **US-LJ** Editor's summary typescript (2 p.)

K769. "Igor Strawinsky 80 Jahre." *Die Welt* no.138 (June 16, 1962)

Reminiscences and good wishes by a number of composers, including Krenek.

K770. "Der Wille zur Ordnung." *Forum* 9:103/4 (July-August 1962): 330-331.

Written in honor of Stravinsky's eightieth birthday. A discussion of Stravinsky's acceptance and subsequent use of serialism.

a. ——. In his *Im Zweifelsfalle.* (K924) (Wien: Europaverlag, 1984): 110-114.

K771. "Tradition in perspective." *Perspectives on Ideas and the Arts* 11:10 (October 1962): 32-38.

Serial music and "neoclassicism" are seen as continuations of the recent musical tradition. Krenek points out that conformity and non-conformity are dictated by the age in which one lives and briefly examines some of the turning points in music history in order to determine our present relationship with tradition. He concludes that tradition "is made evident in the existence of 'schools' -- not so much in the sense of established institutions, but of groups of individuals who in the sequence of a few generations exhibit a kind of teacher-student relationship... In an age that attaches high value to originality, the formation of such groups is not as common a phenomenon as we assume it to have been in ages past." Picture. *See:* B378

a. ——. *Perspectives of New Music* 1:1 (Fall 1962): 27-38.

K772. "Ausgerechnet, aber sehr verspielt." *Forum* 9:107 (November 1962): 467-470.

Describes the basis of his first serial work *Sestina* op.161 and its relationship to his television opera *Ausgerechnet und verspielt* op.179, which uses the poetic sestina form for the roulette scenes.

a. ——. In his *Im Zweifelsfalle*. (K924) (Wien: Europaverlag, 1984): 66-72.

-- 1963 --

K773. "Schönberg *Violinkonzert*." *Unpublished*.
Lecture broadcast by Westdeutscher Rundfunk, Cologne about 1963.
Manuscripts: US-LJ 3 p.

K774. "*Lamentatio Jeremiae prophetae*." In *The Composer's point of view; essays on twentieth-century choral music by those who wrote it*, by Robert Stephan Hines. (Norman: University of Oklahoma Press, 1963): 22-34.
Discussion of the inception and construction of op.93. "When I decided on the style and character of my work, I went much further than just giving up the idea of making it fit for liturgical use. I had in mind to write a work that would express as purely as possible certain ideas and ideals of composition that I had developed in those years, and to do so without compromise and concessions to so-called practical demands. This attitude was a result partly of my becoming increasingly involved in the formidable constructional possibilities of the twelve-tone technique, partly again of the despondent mood of a period that seemed to make the future of cultural activities such as performances of new music look rather hopeless... In my opinion my *Sixth String Quartet* [op.78] (1936) and my *Twelve Variations* for piano [op.79] (1937) mark the high points of my preoccupation with the problems of the 12-tone technique. The *Lamentatio*, taken up after the circumstances attending my emigration from Europe had, for a while, diverted me from the main line of my creative efforts, stands at a crossroads, as it were, in that in its intransigency it continues and perhaps exceeds the uncompromising attitude of the earlier works mentioned above."

K775. "Brief an Theodor W. Adorno, II: Ernst Krenek." In *Zeugnisse; Theodor W. Adorno zum sechzigsten Geburtstag*, hrsg. von Max Horkheimer. (Frankfurt: Europäische Verlagsanstalt, 1963): 361-364.
Letter to Adorno on his sixtieth birthday reflecting on their relationship which goes back to a meeting during the rehearsals for his opera *Der Sprung über den Schatten* in Frankfurt in 1924. They have remained friends ever since, although they became estranged during the fifties when Adorno was accepted in Darmstadt as the leader of the avant garde while Krenek became increasingly isolated. Krenek also reflects on their philosophical discussions.

a. "Briefe 62." In *Briefwechsel*, von Theodor W. Adorno und Ernst Krenek. (K862) (Frankfurt am Main: Suhrkamp, 1974): 151-155.

K776. "Electronic music." In *Book of Knowledge* (New York: Grolier, 1963)
A survey and description of electronic music.
Manuscripts: US-LJ 2 p. ; typescript (2 p.)

K777. "Elements of music." In *Book of Knowledge* (New York: Grolier, 1963)
A discussion and definition of pitch, dynamics, rhythm, tempo, melody, polyphony, consonance, and dissonance.
Manuscripts: US-LJ 11 p. ; typescript (5 p.)

K778. "Modern music." In *Book of Knowledge* (New York: Grolier, 1963)
An extensive historical survey of modern music since Gustav Mahler. Includes a discussion of the neo-classic (most prevalent in America), twelve-tone, serial, and chance styles. "Modern music of the neo-classical and

folkloristic types has found its place in the programs of tradition-bound institutions... The more advanced forms of modern music (dodecaphonic, serial, etc.) naturally have a more limited appeal and are cultivated by special interest groups."

Manuscripts: US-LJ 14 p. & additions. ; typescript (11 p.)

K779. "Musical forms." In *Book of Knowledge* (New York: Grolier, 1963)
An historical survey of musical forms.

Manuscripts: US-LJ 5 p. ; typescript (5 p.)

K780. "Tomas Luis de Victoria." In *Book of Knowledge* (New York: Grolier, 1963)
A biography and survey of his works.

K781. "Electronic music." *Unpublished.*
Program notes for the San Fernando Valley State College performance on March 15, 1963 of the *San Fernando sequence* op.185.

Manuscripts: US-LJ 5 p.

K782. "13. Januar: Ludwig Stecker 80 Jahre alt." *Melos* 30:1 (January 1963): 1-15.
Brief notes of appreciation from many people for the retiring editor of the publishing firm Schott, including a poem by Krenek (p.10). "Man muss sich strecken nach der Decke, | der gute Strecker misst sie zu. | Wenn sie uns manchmal kurz erscheint, | so hoffen wir, 's its gut gemeint. | Lang war sein Walten über Schott, | und noch setzt er sich nicht zu Ruh'. | Dass es noch länger sich erstrecke, | das wünschen wir; das walte Gott."

K783. "Ernst Krenek's random thoughts on today's music and composers." *Newsletter of American Symphony Orchestra League* 14:4-5 (July-August 1963): 25-26.
A lecture given at the ninth annual Composer's Luncheon in June 1963 in San Francisco. The problem of the composer of new music is that the music is complex and consequently only appeals to a small group of listeners. Regardless of this condition, the composer is generally respected today.

Manuscripts: US-LJ 7 p. ; typescript (6 p.)

K784. "Weltfernes Festival." *Forum* 10:114 (June 1963): 302-303.
Discusses the Seattle Webern Festival and its lectures and concerts.

K785. "Gesang der Greise." *Forum* 10:115/6 (July-August 1963)
Reaction to Heinz-Klaus Metzger's article "Das Altern der jüngsten Musik" (volume 10, number 112/113) in which he describes new music as "senile chant." The argument of degenerative senility in new music was brought up by Theodor Wiesengrund Adorno in 1954 and opposed at that time by Metzger; both men, from different points of view, accept and acknowledge only subversive music. Metzger's critique on aging focuses on Luigi Nono, the revolutionary who became a bureaucrat, Pierre Boulez, who retired in a "Debussy-cloud," and Karlheinz Stockhausen, who turned to infantility. Krenek believes that the possibilities of serial music have not yet been exploited and considers the article biased propaganda for some young composers.

K786. "Atonality retroactive." *Perspectives of New Music* 2:1 (Fall/Winter 1963): 133-136.
Review of the book *Tonality and atonality in sixteenth century music* by

Edward E. Lowinsky (Berkeley: University of California Press, 1961). "Lowinsky has a very special gift for projecting the results of his assiduous research in the limited field of musicology onto the wider horizon of history and philosophy."

K787. "Composizione." In *Enciclopedia della musica* Vol.1 (Milan: Ricordi, 1963): 512-513.

Surveys the many meanings of the term "composition" and the many techniques available to the composer. In addition, Krenek also discusses the teaching of composition.

Manuscripts: US-LJ English 4 p. ; Italian typescript (5 p.)

K788. "Orlando di Lasso." In *Enciclopedia della musica* Vol.2 (Milan: Ricordi, 1964): 571-572.

Describes the Renaissance composer's musical style and concludes that he is a "romantic" because of the expressivity of the music.

Manuscripts: US-LJ English 4 p. ; Italian typescript copy (4 p.)

K789. "Johannes Ockeghem." In *Enciclopedia della musica* Vol.3 (Milan: Ricordi, 1964): 297-298.

Examines the composer's music and his place in fifteenth century music.

Manuscripts: US-LJ English 3 p. ; Italian typescript copy (3 p.)

K790. "Ritmo e metro." In *Enciclopedia della musica* Vol.4 (Milan: Ricordi, 1964): 25-26.

Examines the relationship between the terms rhythm and meter and notes that the two terms should be considered distinct: meter is concerned with musical stress and accentuation while rhythm is concerned with duration and speed.

Manuscripts: US-LJ English 3 p. ; Italian typescript copy (3 p.)

K791. "Giovanni Pierluigi da Palestrina." In *Enciclopedia della musica* Vol.4 (Milan: Ricordi, 1964): 362-363.

A description of the composer's musical style in the context of the music of the twentieth century.

Manuscripts: US-LJ English 6 p. ; Italian typescript copy (7 p.)

K792. "Alt und neu im graphischen Bild der Musik." *Generalprogramm, Musikkollegium Winterthur.* (1964/65): 5-16.

A survey of changes in rhythmic notation from the earliest music to electronic and graphic music. Includes a facsimile of the final page from his opera *Der goldene Bock* op.186 in manuscript score on cover.

K793. "Ueber eigene Werke." *Unpublished.*

A lecture broadcast over Westdeutscher Rundfunk, Cologne, in 1964 discussing the concept of serialism using examples from *Sestina* op.161 and *Quaestio temporis* op.170. He also discusses how the row and other parameters, including text, are serialized. His last strictly serial work was *Flötenstück neunphasig* op.171. In his later works, the *Basler Massarbeit* op.173 and the comic opera *Ausgerechnet und Verspielt* op.179, he felt the necessity to somewhat loosen up the concept of total determination.

Manuscripts: US-LJ 10 p.

K794. "Remarks on the influence of the new technical media (electronics, cinema) on the conception of works for the music stage (Opera)." In

Zeitgeössisches Musiktheater, Hamburg, 1964. Internationaler Kongress,
hrsg. von Ernst Thomas. (Hamburg: Deutscher Musikrat, 1966): 108.

"1) Electronic music has influenced above all the image of sound.
Composers having had experience in working with electronic sound
equipment have frequently felt the urge to create similar sound effects while
dealing with traditional instruments... 2) Electronic sounds are being
introduced into the musical sector of the stage work a) as background ... [and]
b) as musical elements of the foreground... 3) The influence of the cinema on
the musical theater (opera) may be seen in a tendency toward further breaking
up the still lingering Aristotelian concept of the stage work... It affects the
sense and meaning of the drama as such."

K795. "Hol' der Henker eure beiden Häuser!" *Forum* 11:121 (January 1964):
43-46 ; 11:122 (February 1964): 106-109.

Reflections on why theoretical writings about contemporary music are so
difficult to read using as examples the discussions of the serialism of pitch
and rhythm by Karlheinz Stockhausen, Pierre Boulez, and Milton Babbitt.
See: B1453

a. "Zur Geheimsprache der modernen Musikliteratur." *Musica* 18:6
(November-December 1964): 287-296.

b. "Om roversproget i den moderne musiklitteratur" *Dansk Musiktidsskrift*
40:2 (March 1965): 29-36.

Danish translation.

K796. "Neue Perspektiven in der amerikanischen Musik." *Unpublished.*

A lecture broadcast over Westdeutscher Rundfunk, Cologne, on April 27,
1964 on the development of American music. The true American composer
only emerged in the generation born around 1900, and their father figure has
been Igor Stravinsky who, along with Nadia Boulanger, exerted his influence
to establish neo-classicism. Jazz has had almost no influence on this
generation of composers as it was regarded an African decadence, and they
have approached twelve-tone composition with utmost distrust. Since World
War II the picture has drastically changed with a turning to serialism and a
study of Webern along with a strong interest in jazz. Krenek's students
George Perle and Robert Erickson have both successfully integrated serialism
into their personal styles, but the first real serialist composer is Milton
Babbitt, whom Krenek finds too mathematically oriented.

Manuscripts: US-LJ 11 p.

K797. "Es rieselt, es knistert, es kracht." *Forum* 11:125 (May 1964): 272-273.

Discusses the revolutionary developments of Claude Debussy, Alexander
Scriabin, Charles Ives, Igor Stravinsky, and Arnold Schoenberg which
resulted in strong public reactions to their music. *See:* B554

a. ———. In his *Im Zweifelsfalle.* (K924) (Wien: Europaverlag, 1984): 292-
297.

K798. "Notizen zum *Goldenen Bock.*" *[Program: Hamburgische Staatsoper
1963/64]* no.16 (June 15-30, 1964): 124-126.

Notes written for the Hamburg State Opera premiere of *Der goldene Bock*
op.186. Includes excerpts from the correspondence commissioning the opera
and developing its ideas.

Manuscripts: US-LJ 5 p.

K799. "A composer's influences." *Perspectives of New Music* 3:1 (Fall/Winter 1964): 36-41.

A survey of the various influences on Krenek and their effects on his music. During Krenek's student days in Vienna in 1918 he encountered the *Lineare Kontrapunkt* by Ernst Kurth which "turned my entire musical orientation inside out. I was fascinated by the notion that music was not just a vague symbolization of *Gefuehl* instinctively conjured up into pleasant sounding matter, but a precisely planned reflection of an autonomous system of streams of energy materialized in carefully controlled tonal patterns." When he turned from his atonal style around 1924 to "the neoclassical posturing of the Baroque concerto, and shortly afterwards to the neoromantic attitudes displayed in *Jonny spielt auf* op.45 and the song cycle of the *Reisebuch aus den österreichischen Alpen* op.62, the first move was touched off by the exhilarating experience of Igor Stravinsky's *Pulcinella* and by my contacts with the seemingly carefree, unspeculative, straightforward music of my French contemporaries." This change was also influenced by his friend Eduard Erdmann's introduction to the music of Franz Schubert. His introduction to twelve-tone music can be seen as the "adoption of the musical technique that the tyrants hated most of all [and] may be interpreted as an expression of protest."

a. ——. In *Perspectives on American composers,* edited by Benjamin Boretz and Edward T. Cone. (New York: W. W. Norton, 1971): 125-130.

-- 1965 --

K800. "Vortrag für Baden-Baden." *Unpublished.*

A lecture written about 1965 for Südwestfunk, Baden-Baden concerning American radio, and disscussing the Hooper Ratings used to determine American listeners' preferences. Krenek discusses the general characteristics of the American and German radio systems and represents the general differences between the two audiences.

Manuscripts: US-LJ 6 p.

K801. "Die kulinarische Oper." *Hier* (Dortmund) no.6/7 (1965/66): 57.

The title means "opera for the gourmet," a sarcastic remark, perhaps going back to Bertold Brecht, intended to discredit traditional opera as a musical delicatessen for the upper class. A short philosophical essay about the sensual enjoyment of opera versus the higher claim of art. Opera reform has been concerned with carrying the ethical message on the vehicle of sensual music to insure its acceptance; but opera has no message to transmit, it only reflects a state of senselessness which, in fact, the world is.

Manuscripts: US-LJ 3 p.

K802. "Köln-WDR." *Unpublished.*

A lecture written for broadcast on Westdeutscher Rundfunk, Cologne in 1965. Discusses music and language and their relationship to electronic music. Focuses on his electronic work *Spiritus intelligentiae, Sanctus* op.152 composed in the Cologne Radio studio in 1955 and 1956.

Manuscripts: US-LJ 20 p.

K803. "Krenek's early music." *Unpublished.*

A lecture in German broadcast over Südwestfunk, Baden-Baden, in 1965 discussing his early years, the *First piano sonata* op.2, and his early *Lieder.*

Manuscripts: US-LJ 5 p.

K804. *Prosa, Dramen, Verse.* (München: Albert Langen - Georg Müller, 1965) 413 p.

A collection of Krenek's writings including the story *Die drei Mäntel des Anton K.;* the opera librettos *Jonny spielt auf* op.45, *Leben des Orest* op.60, *Kehraus um St. Stephan* op.66, *Karl V.* op.73, *Vertrauenssache* op.111, *Pallas Athene weint* op.144, *Der Glockenturm* op.153, *Ausgerechnet und verspielt* op.179, and *Der goldene Bock* op.186; and the song texts *Reisebuch aus den österreichischen Alpen* op.62, *Gesänge des späten Jahres* op.71, *Die Ballade von den Eisenbahnen* op.98, *Sestina* op.161, and *Kanon* op.181. *See:* B1068, B1196, B1497

K805. "Vorbemerkung." In his *Prosa, Dramen, Verse.* (Münich: Albert Langen - Georg Müller, 1965): 7-10.

Brief introduction to each of the writings selected for the volume and covering the period from 1925 to 1963.

Manuscripts: US-LJ 3 p.

K806. "'Zeitgemässe' Betrachtungen." *Oesterreichische Musikzeitschrift* 20:1 (January 1965): 6-8.

A discussion of the concept of musical time and its serial ordering by contemporary composers.

K807. "Medea." In *Alte und Neue Musik* Vol.2: *Das Basler Kammerorchester 1926-1976.* (Zürich: Atlantis Verlag, 1977): 251-252.

Krenek briefly discusses the creation of the monologue op.129 and its construction. Extracted from program number 118, January 16, 1965.

K808. "Rätselhaftes Spanien." *Forum* 12:138/9 (June-July 1965): 322-324.

Travel notes on a trip to Spain.

K809. "Meine Begegnungen mit der griechisichen Antike." *Salzburger Festspiele 1965* (Salzburg, 1965): 29.

Program notes written for the premiere on July 27, 1965 of his incidental music to the two *Oedipus* Sophocles plays op.188.

K810. "The composer as an interpreter of his own works." *Music Austria* (Vienna) 6 (July-September 1965): 1-2.

Krenek asserts that an authentic performance of a musical composition results when the composer conducts his own works.

a. "Der Komponist als Interpret seiner Werke" In *Beiträge der Oesterreichischen Gesellschaft für Musik.* (1968): 61-62.

K811. "Anton Weberns magisches Quadrat." *Forum* 12:140/141 (August-September 1965): 395-396.

A lecture given at the Webern-Gedenkfeier in Mittersill, Austria, on August 4, 1965 at the unveiling of a plaque on the house in which Webern died. Krenek explains the magic square "SATOR;" its interpretation refers to a citation of the old testament by the prophet Ezekiel and is directly connected to Webern's tragic premature death. *See:* B902

a. ——. In his *Im Zweifelsfalle.* (K924) (Wien: Europaverlag, 1984): 125-128.

Manuscripts: US-LJ 7 p. ; typescript (13 p.)

K812. "Musik im Schauspiel." *Oesterreichische Musikzeitschrift* 20:8 (August 1965): 415-418.

Discusses the writing of music for plays following the performance of his incidental music op.188 for Sophocles's *Oedipus* plays given during the Salzburg Festival. His first incidental music was written in 1922 for the director of the Berliner Staatlichen Schauspielhauses, Leopold Jessner, for productions of Grabbe's *Napoleon* (W68) and Schiller's *Fiesco* (W69). Later, in Kassel, he wrote incidental music for Goethe's *Der Triumph der Empfindsamkeit*, the comedy *Vom lieben Augustin*, Shakespeare's *Ein Sommernachtstraum*, and Archard's comedy *Marlborough s'en va-t-en guerre*. In 1961 he wrote incidental music to Gottfried Reinhardt's film *Jedermann*. Some of the problems with incidental music are that it is short lived and it is difficult to synchronize with the play. Tape and electronic music are attractive media to use for incidental music.

Manuscripts: US-LJ 4 p.

K813. "Musik und Sprache." *Die Zeit* 20:38 (September 17, 1965): Feuilleton:17-18.

Lecture given to the Arbeitsgemeinschaft Kultuteller Organisationen, Dusseldorf, September 9, 1965 on the relationship of music and speech, and serial operations which can be used on text. Includes the text of *Quintina* op.191 for six instrumentalists and electronic sounds. Picture.

a. "Musik und Sprache (II)." In his *Im Zweifelsfalle*. (K924) (Wien: Europaverlag, 1984): 334-342.

Manuscripts: US-LJ 16 p.

K814. "En gammel rovers bekendelser." *Dansk Musiktidsskrift* 40:8 (December 1965): 254-256.

Krenek responds to Svend Westergaard's reaction (B1453) to Krenek's "Om roversproget i den moderne musiklitteratur" (K795) on the complexity of writings about serial music.

Manuscripts: US-LJ German 4 p.

K815. "Arnold Schoenbergs *Orchestervariationen*, op.31." *Unpublished*.

Lecture broadcast over Norddeutscher Rundfunk, Hamburg, December 17, 1965.

Manuscripts: US-LJ 6 p. ; typescript copy (17 p.)

K816. "Möbel hinauswerfen." *Kontraste* 6:4 (1966): 1.

Responses to questions posed to several personalities concerning juke boxes, modern music which could be played by amateurs, "light-music," and rock music. Krenek expresses his negative reactions to these questions and thinks that amateurs should become enlightened by listening to modern music instead of playing "watered-down" modern music. He also thinks that some operetta music is good, especially that by Jacques Offenbach.

K817. *Exploring music*, essays translated by Margaret Shenfield and Geoffrey Skelton. (New York: October House, 1966) 245 p.

A collection of essays selected in part from *Zur Sprache gebract*; many are translated into English: *On writing my memoirs* (K605-a), *A puppet play* (K98-b), *A few words about Johann Strauss* (K99-c), *From "Jonny" to "Orest"* (K105-c), *Darius Milhaud* (K109-d), *Composing as a calling* (K120-c), *New humanity and old objectivity* (K100-b), *The freedom of the human spirit* (K158-d), *The prolonged funeral banquet* (K187-b), *What should music criticism do?* (K213-e) *Nationality and art* (K246-f), *Karl Kraus and Arnold Schoenberg* (K274-c), *On the status of Western music* (K359-c), *Is opera still possible today?* (K416-e) *Alban Berg's "Lulu"* (K444-f), *Notes on Kafka's collected works* (K457-b), *Basic principles of a new theory of musical aesthetics* (K403-c), *Music for eternity* (K489-b), *The ivory tower* (K529-

b), *The composer and the interpreter* (K540-a), *That noise called music* (K545), *Why Pallas Athene weeps* (K662-c), *The libretto problem* (K674-d), *What electronic music is and how it is made* (K678-c), *On the ageing and obsolescence of music* (K679-b), *Conversation past midnight* (K551). *See:* B41, B101, B133, B211, B403, B444, B522, B718, B719, B841, B892, B945, B946, B1361

b. *Exploring music,* essays translated by Margaret Shenfield and Geoffrey Skelton. (London: Calder & Boyars, 1966) 245 p.

c. *Exploring music,* essays translated by Margaret Shenfield and Geoffrey Skelton. (Reprint New York: October House, 1969) 245 p.

K818. "Erinnerungen an einen Freund." In *Begegnungen mit Eduard Erdmann,* hrsg. von Christof Bitter und Manfred Schlösser. (Darmstadt: Erato Presse, 1968): 70-83.

Lecture broadcast over Westdeutscher Rundfunk, Cologne, February 28, 1966. Krenek reminiscences about his life-long friendship with the pianist and composer which began in Berlin when Krenek was a student in the Staatliche Hochschule für Musik in 1920. Pictures.

Manuscripts: US-LJ 15 p. (p.1 missing) ; typescript copy (13 p.)

K819. "Talking about music: Some current terms." *Perspectives of New Music* 4:2 (Spring/Summer 1966): 81-84.

Examines the use of the terminology used in *Perspectives of new music* assuming a readership of "educated" musicians with a common "jargon." Krenek opposes the mathematical terminology used in the writings about music employed by Milton Babbitt and the graduates of Princeton University because it makes the discussion of musical problems "not understandable, the problems remain unsolved, and consequently it is rarely possible to surmise whether a different approach might have been more useful." Mathematical terminology makes music appear too complex.

K820. "*Matthäus gibt Ärgernis.*" *Neues Forum* 13:150/151 (June-July 1966): 411-412.

Review of the film directed by Paolo Pasolini with a comparison to other religious films.

Manuscripts: US-LJ 10 p.

K821. "Ueber die Natur des Ausgezeichneten." In *Bach-Preis 1966 der freien und Hansestadt Hamburg* (Hamburg: Th.Dingwort & Sohn, 1967): 10-23.

The acceptance speech given upon the conferment of the Bach-Preis in Hamburg on September 30, 1966. Krenek examines the career and the aesthetics of the Hamburg drama critic Gotthold Lessing which leads him to a comparison of the relationship of composers to "rules" of composition in the Eighteenth century and today.

a. "Lessing, Bach, Gegenwart." *Musica* 21:1 (January-February 1967): 1-5. Excerpt.

Manuscripts: US-LJ 20 p. ; typescript (7 p.)

K822. "Ueber eigene elektronische Musik." *Unpublished.*

A lecture broadcast over Westdeutscher Rundfunk, Cologne, in October 1966 concerning his electronic music.

Manuscripts: D-bdr KNwdr .

K823. "*Quintona* Einführung." *Unpublished.*

Lecture broadcast over Westdeutscher Rundfunk, Cologne, October 18,

1966 to introduce a performance of op.190.

Manuscripts: US-LJ 6 p.

K824. "Komponist und Schallplatte." *Fono Forum* 11:11 (November 1, 1966): 558-561.

A lecture given to the Akademie der Künste in Berlin on October 1, 1966. Krenek discusses the many kinds of recordings and their functions, examining the spectrum from the recording of Karl Kraus's voice played at his funeral to reflections on the possible uses of recordings by composers. Krenek also touches on the problems of defining and achieving high fidelity, the place of recordings in current musical life, and the industry's responsibility towards new music. Picture.

a. ——. In his *Im Zweifelsfalle.* (K924) (Wien: Europaverlag, 1984): 319-327.

b. "Skladatel a desk." *Hudebni rozhledy* 19:23/24 (1966): 744-746.
   Czech translation.

Manuscripts: US-LJ 23 p.

K825. "Ockeghem." *Unpublished.*

Lecture broadcast over Bayerischer Rundfunk, München, November 2, 1966. Discusses the place of the composer in his own time and compares it with the condition of the composer today.

Manuscripts: US-LJ 12 p.

K826. "Im Zweifelsfalle." *Forum* 14:159 (March 1967): 273-276.

A lecture given during the 101st concert in the series "Das neue Werk" by the Norddeutscher Rundfunk in Hamburg, December 21, 1966 which presented the premiere of *Glauben und Wissen* op.194. Krenek presents an analysis of the chorus and orchestra work and prints his text.

a. ——. In his *Im Zweifelsfalle.* (K924) (Wien: Europaverlag, 1984): 343-347.

Manuscripts: US-LJ 2 p.

K827. "Lecture." *Unpublished.*

Given at Goucher College, Towson, MD, on May 15, 1967. Traces the development of music through the twentieth century to serial and chance music.

Manuscripts: US-LJ 10 p.

K828. "Commentary." In *Anton von Webern sketches (1926-1945).* (New York: Carl Fischer, 1968): 1-7.

Dated at end: August-November 1967, Palm Springs, California. An examination and discussion of the sketches in the volume concluding: "the basic simplicity of Webern's compositional procedure is certainly the cause of that crystalline clarity that has made his music so widely accepted after the shock induced by its formidable concentration had subsided. It is fortunate that his elaborate and painstaking sketches allow us to observe the genesis of his admirable work." *See:* B80, B680, B1318, B1431

-- 1968 --

K829. "Ernst Krenek." In *Begegnungen mit Eduard Erdmann,* hrsg. von Christof Bitter und Manfred Schlösser. (Darmstadt: Erato Presse, 1968): 260-283.

The correspondence between Krenek and Erdmann from 1924 to 1932.

K830. "Musiktheater - Fernsehen - Film." *IMZ Bulletin* no.3/4 (1968): 21-28.

In German with English (translated by William Arnold) and French translations. An explanation of the film-like character of his operas. *Karl V.* op.73 shows scenic thinking reminiscent of film making through the use of flash backs. These characteristics are even stronger in *Der goldene Bock* op.186 with its continuous succession of short scenes. The one-act opera *Dark waters* was primarily conceived for television, but it has only been produced on the stage. The video and audio of the television opera *Ausgerechnet und verspielt* op.179 was simultaneously recorded, and *Der Zauberspiegel* op.192, which requires special video effects, was recorded on colored sound track film. "The great appeal ... which the camera has as a medium for the opera composer lies therein in that he has the possibility to quickly change locales, perspectives, distances and high light accents etc., thus giving completely new dimensions to the field of musical drama... The possibilities of this medium are unlimited and exciting. They go far beyond what one can imagine a 'film opera' to be like. The so-called 'total opera' attains its greatest possibilities whenever the recording can be done by means of the audio-visual sound camera."

K831. "Ueber Schuberts *Unvollendete Sinfonie.*" *Unpublished.*

A lecture broadcast over Südwestfunk, Baden-Baden, in 1968 examining why Schubert's *Unfinished symphony* is still extremely popular. The answer may lie in the gentle melancholic atmosphere it conveys, yet today we tend to believe that such emotional content is exclusively produced by the listener, not by the music itself which is merely sound, and is learned by the listener through experience. In fact, Krenek asserts, it is the composition's technical details which are responsible for the aesthetic value of the piece. The lecture is supported by musical examples elucidating the differences in composition techniques between Beethoven and Schubert and how these techniques affect the music.

Manuscripts: US-LJ 21 p.

K832. "Moderne Musik." In *Musik und Verlag, Karl Vötterle zum 65. Geburtstag am 12. April 1968,* hrsg. von Richard Baum und Wolfgang Rehm. (Kassel: Bärenreiter, 1968): 92-100.

Krenek briefly discusses the place of contemporary music in Bärenreiter's catalog of publications, and includes a list of contemporary music published between 1928 and 1968.

Manuscripts: US-LJ 4 p.

K833. "Moderne Kirchenmusik." *Unpublished.*

Written for Montserrat, July 1968. "For the last few decades the contemporary composer who was interested in writing ecclesiastical music was looking with envy at the architect who was allowed to build churches of the most unconventional type while 'modern' music was not permitted to cross the doorstep of the cathedral."

Manuscripts: US-LJ 1 p.

K834. "R4 - What for?" *Perspectives of New Music* 7:1 (Fall/Winter 1968): 152-155.

A reaction to Michael Kassler's "Toward a theory that is the twelve-note-class system" volume 5, number 2. Krenek questions whether the theory presented by Kassler is necessary and sufficient and objects to the unnecessarily theoretical structures and jargon in the analysis of twelve-tone pieces by Webern and Schoenberg. He concludes "we would face the considerable fatigue of penetrating the thicket of Kassler's discourse with resigned equanimity if we could be convinced that the effort was inevitable in order to reveal some hitherto unknown phenomena of musical construction in the most recent compositional ventures. However, his work taxes our patience to the degree of exasperation because he expects the reader to learn a formidable corpus of totally unfamiliar terms and symbols only to realize in the end that the possible results of the theory's application were known long before, and the theory is not even adequate to accomplish the task it was assigned." Kassler responds on pages 155-156.

Manuscripts: US-LJ 4 p.

K835. "Gustav Mahlers *IV. Symphonie.*" *Unpublished.*

A lecture broadcast over Südwestfunk, November 1968, consisting of a detailed analysis of the symphony.

Manuscripts: US-LJ 16 p.

-- 1969 --

K836. "Mobilisierte Musik." *Beiträge der Oesterreichischen Gesellschaft für Musik* 1 (1968/69): 52-55.

Although serial and aleatoric music superficially appear to produce the same results, serial music presents a logical development in the history of music. Includes a discussion of the serial aspects of *Fibonacci mobile* op.187.

-- 1970 --

K837. "Bemerkungen eines stehengebliebenen Nachläufers."
Philharmonische Blätter (Berlin) no.3 (1970/1): 16-19.

A general description of the state of new music and an attempt to justify his own place in new music. He presents a pessimistic outlook about recent compositional developments which he considers to be primitive compared with the high intellectual demands of serialism.

K838. "Ernst Krenek." In *The Orchestral composer's point of view, essays on twentieth century music by those who wrote it,* by Robert Stephan Hines. (Norman: University of Oklahoma Press, 1970): 105-127.

Briefly discusses his orchestral music including the first three *Symphonies* op.7, op.12 and op.16, the two *Concertos grosso* op.10 and op.25, *I wonder as I wander* op.94, *Symphonic elegy* op.105, *Circle, chain, and mirror* op.160, *Quaestio temporis* op.170, *From three make seven* op.177, and *Horizon circled* op.196. "In my early orchestral works I tried above all to get away from the late Romantic, neo-Germanic pseudo-contrapuntal hubbub of the Straussian type as well as from the mistiness of Impressionistic mixtures. I took my cue from Mahler and used orchestral color to set off melodic lines against each other in dry and harsh textures... In the later works, especially since *Quaestio temporis*, I have tried to re-create with traditional instruments some of the sounds so characteristic of electronic music... Timbre takes on a new significance. Since in serial and post-serial music polyphonic continuity appears only exceptionally, color becomes frequently the essential vehicle of design."

Manuscripts: US-LJ 11 p.

K839. "Circling my horizon." In his *Horizons circled; reflections on my music.* (K864) (Berkeley: University of California Press, 1974): 16-87.

Four lectures entitled "A composer viewing this century's music" given at the University of California at San Diego, January 19 to February 2, 1970. "The first is concerned with the position in history of the contemporary composer and with the varying degrees of his historical consciousness and the ways in which his work is influenced by these factors. In the second I discuss the composer's involvement in the problems of the society of which he is a member. This subject matter I have mainly illustrated by referring to my operas, ... since a good number of these works have very outspoken political implications. In the third section I talk about the sociological and economic background of the composer's work as it has unfolded in our century. [In the fourth] I focus on the particular situation of composition at the present time, discussing the concept of serialism, and investigating how it developed and what became of it." Includes a detailed discussion of the serial aspects of *Spiritus intelligentia, sanctus* op.152, *Lamentatio Jeremiae prophetae* op.93, *Kette, Kreis und Spiegel* op.160, *Sestina* op.161, *Quaestio temporis* op.170, *Basler Massarbeit* op.173, *Sechs Vermessene* op.168, *Fivefold enfoldment* op.205, *Fibonacci mobile* op.187, *From three make seven* op.177, *Horizon circled* op.196, *Exercises of a late hour* op.200, and *Quintina* op.191.

Manuscripts: "UCSD lecture outline." **US-LJ** Outline 5 p. ; Lecture I 17 p. ; Lecture II 17 p. ; Lecture II typescript (18 p.) ; Lecture III 16 p. ; Lecture IV 16 p. ; Lecture IV typescript (19 p.) ; "Circling my horizon" typescript (175 p.)

K840. "Anton Weberns Skizzenbücher." *Musica* 24:2 (March-April 1970): 121-123.

A discussion of the six composition notebooks which cover the last twenty years of Webern's life and the facsimile publication to which he supplied an introduction.

Manuscripts: **US-LJ** 3 p.

K841. "Vom Geiste der geistlichen Musik." *Sagittarius* 3 (1970): 17-28.

A lecture given during the 22. Internationalen Heinrich Schütz-Fest in Breda, Holland, on June 13, 1970. Krenek discusses the relationship of twelve-tone music to sacred music and his own sacred compositions *La Corona* op.91, *Lamentatio Jeremiae Prophetae* op.93, *Spiritus intelligentiae, Sanctus* op.152, and *Missa Duodecim Tonorum* op.165.

K842. "Selbstporträt." *Melos* 37:9 (September 1970): 340-346.

A lecture broadcast by Südwestfunk, Baden-Baden. Krenek discusses his life and musical works.

K843. "Ernst Krenek on his own work." *The Listener* 85:2199 (May 20, 1971): 657.

Dated September 30, 1970. Discussion of his orchestral works *Fragments from Karl V* op.73a, *From three make seven* op.177, and *Perspectives* op.199 broadcast May 22 over BBC Radio 3.

Manuscripts: **US-LJ** 5 p.

K844. "Serialism." In *Dictionary of contemporary music,* edited by John Vinton. (New York: E.P. Dutton & Co., 1971): 670-674.

A survey of serialism, including a discussion of its precedents, compositional methods, and perspectives. Krenek mentions specific compositions by Milton Babbitt, Pierre Boulez, himself, and others.

Manuscripts: **US-LJ** 6 p.

K845. "Stravinsky, a composer's memorial." *Perspectives of New Music* 9:2 (Spring/Summer 1971): 7-9.

A eulogy to Igor Stravinsky discussing his importance as the last of the twentieth century's founding fathers of contemporary music and mentioning Krenek's relationship with the composer.

Manuscripts: US-LJ 2 p.

K846. *"Parvula corona musicalis."* Bach 2:4 (October 1971): 18-31.

Two pages of commentary about the trio op.122 with reference to its B-A-C-H theme and a facsimile of the manuscript score.

K847. "Notwendige Entscheidungen." *Musica* 25:6 (November-December 1971): 557-561.

Based on Krenek's lectures given during the Kasseler Musiktage 1970. Reminiscences about the most important developments of his artistic life and works.

-- 1972 --

K848. "Broadcast: The selection of works ..." *Unpublished.*

Probably written in 1972 to introduce a concert of his chamber music consisting of *Potpourri* op.54, the *Organ sonata* op.92, no.1, and *Four pieces for oboe and piano* op.193.

Manuscripts: US-LJ 1 p.

K849. "What we learn from modern music" *American Music Teacher* 21:6 (June-July 1972): 16-18, 32.

A lecture given at the Music Teachers National Association meeting in Portland, Oregon on March 22, 1972 discussing the shortcomings of various approaches to teaching music to laymen, performers, and composers. Music education has approached new music from two points of view: ignore it or "prepare its charges technically and philosophically, emotionally and intellectually for their encounter with progressive contemporary music, on the assumption that people so prepared will have no problems when they are faced with music of the past... Listening to truly new music and studying it carefully, we observe that it is not only in its appearance, but also in its essence, fundamentally different from traditional music. Therefore, if we approach it with the plan of learning from it something that may be profitably applied elsewhere, we shall never be disappointed. If such is our disposition, we should better stay away from it and leave it to those who come to it with open ears and open minds, intent upon experiencing the excitement which it holds in store for those who learn how to hear and to perform genuine new music."

a. "Was lernen wir von moderner Musik?" *Oesterreichische Musikzeitschrift* 27:10 (October 1972): 517-524.

German translation by Rudolf Klein.

Manuscripts: US-LJ 14 p.

K850. *"Orpheus and Eurydice."* *Unpublished.*

A lecture broadcast over the BBC, London on June 4, 1972, including a synopsis of the opera op.21. He reminisces about the origins of the opera and its composition, and discusses the important themes of the work.

Manuscripts: US-LJ 7 & 3 p.

K851. "Postscript to the *Parvula corona*." Bach 3:3 (July 1972): 21-26.

A detailed analysis of op.122.

Manuscripts: US-LJ 12 p.

K852. "Kritik und Würdigung: Ernst Krenek." In *50 Jahre Musik im Hörfunk; Beiträge und Berichte,* hrsg. auf Anlass des 9. Internationalen IMZ-Kongresses von Kurt Blaukopf, Siegfried Goslich, und Wilfried Scheib. (Wien: Jugend und Volk, 1973): 130.

Brief reminiscence of the early years of the Hessischer Rundfunk in Frankfurt and its importance in presenting contemporary music.

Manuscripts: US-LJ 1 p. ; 7 p.

K853. "The massive bombing of North Vietnam." *Los Angeles Times* 93 (January 5, 1973)

A letter to the editor with other letters under this heading praising an editorial.

K854. "Einführung in die *Poppea*-Bearbeitung und in *Pallas Athene weint.*" *[Program: ORF-Konzert in Wien]* (April 13, 1973)

The plot of his re-setting of Claudio Monteverdi's *L'incoronazione di Poppea* op.80a, which was not meant to be a reconstruction, is related to his opera *Pallas Athena weint* op.144, which is about the decline of democracy in ancient Athens. He discusses the opera plots in relation to the historical events of ancient Greece around 400 B.C.

Manuscripts: US-LJ 3 p.

K855. "Gespräch mit meinem zweiten Ich." *Melos* 40:4 (July-August 1973): 204-207.

An interview with himself about composing and the present state of the arts. Generally, the article reflects the resentment of the composer at not being appropriately judged by the music world, his disappointment at not having been accepted by the younger generation of composers, and his pessimism about the state of music composition in general. He also discusses the motivations which led him to switch from his twelve-tone style of the 1940s to serialism in the 1950s, his dislike of improvisation, and his experimentation with electronic music.

Manuscripts: US-LJ 5 p. ; typescript (7 p.).

K856. "Schubert *Streichquintett C-dur.*" *Unpublished.*

A lecture broadcast over Südwestfunk, Baden-Baden, August 1973 examining in detail the string quintet which was not published or performed during Franz Schubert's lifetime. The detailed analysis emphasizes the rhythmic motives, harmonic progressions, and the changes of mood of each of the musical sections. He mentions Schubert's incredible capacity of writing so much music in so little time.

Manuscripts: US-LJ photocopy(14 p.).

K857. "From a composer, reminiscing about Artur Schnabel." *Piano Quarterly* 22:84 (Winter 1973/4): 44.

Krenek got to know Schnabel in 1921 at the Hochschule für Musik in Berlin; he saw in Schnabel an avant garde composer with a kind of "Jekyll and Hyde" personality who loved to compose but never performed new music on his programs.

Manuscripts: US-LJ 2 p.

K858. "Schubert *Streichquartett G-dur, op.161.*" *Unpublished.*

A lecture broadcast over Südwestfunk, Baden-Baden, November 1973 examining in detail Franz Schubert's last string quartet. Characteristically for

Schubert's music is his boldness which lies in subtle finesse which the average listener can overlook without being deprived of a musical experience; Beethoven, on the other hand, scares some of his listeners through his grand dramatic gestures.

Manuscripts: US-LJ photocopy(15 p.).

K859. "Schönberg lebt." *Unpublished.*

A lecture broadcast over Südwestfunk, Baden-Baden, December 1973 in defense of criticisms against Arnold Schoenberg contending that he couldn't escape his own traditionalism and join the budding serialist movement. Krenek praises Schönberg as an aesthetic who attempted to make each composition, such as his *Piano pieces* op.11 and *Survivor from Warsaw,* significant.

Manuscripts: US-LJ 5 p. ; photocopy (3 p.)

K860. "Epilog." In *Arnold Schönberg Gedenkausstellung 1974,* hrsg. von Ernst Hilmar. (Vienna: Universal Edition, 1974): 135-136.

An evaluation and appreciation of the composer on the centenary of his birth. He was important for the emancipation of dissonance which led to twelve-tone music.

Manuscripts: US-LJ 2 p.

K861. *Das musikdramatische Werk,* hrsg. von Franz Eugen Dostal. Vol.1-3. Oesterreichische Dramatiker der Gegenwart, Vol.21, Vol.23-24. (Wien: Oesterreichische Verlagsanstalt, 1974-77)

A collection of the opera librettos; the third volume was never published. Contents **Vol.1:** *Zwingburg* op.14, *Der Sprung über den Schatten* op.17, *Orpheus und Eurydike* op.21, *Jonny spielt auf* op.45, *Der Diktator* op.49, *Das geheime Königreich* op.50, *Schwergewicht oder die Ehre der Nation* op.55, and *Leben des Orest* op.60. **Vol.2:** "Die Realität spielt mit," by Wolfgang Rogge. *Kehraus um St. Stephan* op.66, *Karl V.* op.73, *Vertrauenssache* op.111, *Dunkle wasser* op.125, *Pallas Athene weint* op.144, and *Der Glockenturm* op.153. **Vol.3 (Unpublished):** *Ausgerechnet und verspielt* op.179, *Der goldene Bock* op.186, *Der Zauberspiegel* op.192, *Sardakai* op.206, and *Flaschenpost vom Paradies* op.217

K862. *Briefwechsel,* von Theodor W. Adorno und Ernst Krenek; hrsg. von Wolfgang Rogge. (Frankfurt: Suhrkamp, 1974) 273 p.

A collection of correspondence between the two men including essays by Krenek and Adorno. Krenek's essays are: *Vorwort* (K863), *Briefe 62* (K775-a), *Freiheit und Technik: Improvisatorischer Stil* (K97-b), *Fortschritt und Reaktion* (K117-a), *Arbeitsprobleme des Komponisten* (K124-a), *Ansprache zum Abend des zeitgenössischen Musik im Oesterreichischen Studios am 25. März 1935 im Ehrbar-Saal, Wien* (K302), and *Was erwartet der Komponist von der Musikerziehung?* (K366-a). Adorno's essays include his discussion of twelve-tone music *Zur Zwölftontechnik,* the essay he wrote in conjunction with K117 *Reaktion und Fortschritt,* and his writings about Krenek: *Zur Deutung Kreneks* (B17-a), *Ernst Krenek* (B18-a), *Musikpädagogische Musik* (B19-a), *Krenek, Ernst, "Ueber neue Musik"* (B20-a), and *Zur Physiognomik Kreneks* (B22-b). *See:* B143, B687, B1252, B1279, B1280

K863. "Vorwort." In *Briefwechsel,* von Theodor W. Adorno und Ernst Krenek. (K862) (Frankfurt am Main: Suhrkamp, 1974): 7-10.

Krenek reflects, in this introduction to the volume of letters and articles by the two men, on their relationship, on Adorno's philosophical writings, and on his own writings.

K864. *Horizons circled; reflections on my music.* With contributions by Will Ogdon and John Stewart. (Berkeley: University of California Press, 1974)

Contains the four lectures given by Krenek while Regent's lecturer at the San Diego campus of the University of California January 19 to February 2, 1970 entitled "Circling my horizon" (K839); *Preface* (B1284) and *The composer views his time* by John L. Stewart (B1285); and *A master composer and a foremost musician of our time* (B931-a), *Minutes of a conversation between Will Ogdon and Ernst Krenek* (B932-a), and "*Horizon circled*" *observed* by Will Ogdon (B933). *See:* B183, B259, B445, B459, B667, B720, B721, B722, B865, B954, B1081

K865. "Horizont umkreist." *Oesterreichische Musikzeitschrift* 31:3 (January 1976): 2-11.

Excerpt from the first part of the book *Horizons circled* (K864), translated by Rudolf Klein.

K866. "Schönberg wird hundert." *Melos* 41:1 (January 1974): 2-5.

Compares the status of Schoenberg's music on the centenary of his birth to that of Mahler's and Wagner's at their centenaries. Between Wagner's death in 1883 and his centenary, Schoenberg had transformed musical language beyond recognition, while during the period following Schoenberg's death and centenary, it has remained relatively unchanged. "At the time of his crossing the magic centennial line Schoenberg's fame is tied to one deed which he performed in the early years of this century -- the radical change of the musical language used by the composers of the Western world."

a. "Schoenberg the centenarian" *Journal of the Arnold Schoenberg Institute* 1:2 (February 1977): 87-91.

Translated by Paul A. Pisk.

Manuscripts: US-LJ 11 p.

K867. "Looking back on 75 years as a mainstream misfit." *Los Angeles Times* 94 (February 2, 1975): Calender:50-53.

Lecture given at the Krenek Festival held at the College of the Desert, Palm Desert, California on January 23, 1975. Reflections on his life and the fact that he has not been a mainstream composer.

Manuscripts: US-LJ typescript copy (8 p.).

K868. "Teaching composition in America: reminiscences." *American Music Teacher* 24:4 (February-March 1975): 6-11.

Surveys his teaching assignments in America including the Malkin Conservatory in Boston, the University of Michigan Summer Sessions, Vassar College, Hamline University, Los Angeles City College, and Brandeis University.

Manuscripts: US-LJ 10 p.

K869. "Offener Brief." *Musica* 29:2 (March-April 1975): 151-152.

Letter addressed to "Herr [Wolfram] Schwinger" in reaction to "Der andere Mund" (B404) by g.r., a review of the Berlin performance of *Spätlese* op.218 by Dietrich Fischer-Dieskau and the composer, and the reviewer's comments about the performance by the "old piano-player." Krenek's use of finger nails and elbows were part of the extended techniques required of the pianist and not a result of his age. *See:* B404

K870. "Russell's *Mahler*." *Los Angeles Times* 94 (March 16, 1975): Calender:23-24.

A letter about the film. Krenek objects that it miss-uses his name, miscasts Emperor Franz Joseph, and distorts Mahler's conversion to Catholicism.

K871. "Zum 75. Geburtstag." *Unpublished*.

Lecture broadcast over Bayerischer Rundfunk, München, August 23, 1975 surveying his compositional output.

Manuscripts: US-LJ 2 p.

K872. "Ueber Ockeghem und meine *Lamentatio*." *[Program: Donaueschinger Musiktage]* (October 17-19, 1975): 15-17.

Drawing a parallel between Johannes Ockeghem (who had a reputation of one who composes only to solve intellectual problems rather than for sensual beauty) and himself, Krenek praises the polyphonic and rhythmic complexities of Ockeghem's *Missa prolationem*. He notes that the freely accented composition is only revealed with the omission of modern bar-lines, and that he followed the same procedure in his *Lamentatio Jeremiae prophetae* op.93. He explains the derivation of modal scales out of the twelve-tone domain, as well as the relationship of Gregorian chant to his work.

Manuscripts: US-LJ 3 p.

K873. "[Reminiscences]." In *Othmar Schoeck im Selbstzeugnissen und Zeitgenossenberichten*, von Werner Vogel. (Zürich: Atlantis, 1976): 160, 166, 184, 237-238, 267.

Reminiscences about the composer and their relationship.

Manuscripts: US-LJ typescript (2 p.) ; 3 p.

K874. "Krenek on Krenek's new piece." *Accordion Art* 2:1 (1976): 9.

A discussion of *Acco-music* op.225.

K875. "In 1954." *Talea* Mexico (March 1976)

The electronic composition *Spiritus intelligentiae, Sanctus* op.152, which was commissioned by Herbert Eimert at the Westdeutscher Rundfunk, Cologne, in 1954, is examined; Krenek used old rhythmic formulas from Josquin des Prez as the basis of the work. He also discusses the changing attitude toward electronic music and the establishment of an electronic music studio in his home in Palm Springs.

Manuscripts: US-LJ 4 p.

In English.

K876. "Humanitarians wanted." *Los Angeles Times* 95 (June 27, 1976): Calendar:2.

A letter to the editor in reaction to Martin Bernheimer's June 18 article on *Norma*. "If a humanitarian foundation would collect all available scores of this most imbecile of all operas and have them buried in a very remote salt mine, ... intelligent and brilliant singers such as Beverly Sills might become tempted to ... more exciting and important projects."

Manuscripts: US-LJ 1 p.

K877. "Neue Strömungen in der zeitgenössischen Musik." *Der Zeitgeist* Nr.445 (3 June 1977): 17.

Written for the Basler Kammerorchester, August 1976 surveying his compositions.

Manuscripts: US-LJ 4 p.

K878. "Ansprache." *Unpublished.*

A lecture given at CISAC, Paris, in September 1976 concerned with protecting the rights of composers.

Manuscripts: US-LJ 3 p.

K879. "Wo ist die Avantgarde bloss hingeraten?" *Die Welt* (29 December 1976)

Krenek answers the question "What happened to the avant garde?" with a critical look at the negative influences of John Cage's philosophy on new music and the emergence of minimal music with its hypnotic effect. The characteristic hostility of the avant garde toward the established arts, and the shock effect, which used to be the most formidable weapon of the avant garde, has become blunt because the avant garde have become the mainstream.

a. "Das Gesellschaftsspiel der Avantgarde." *Zeitbühne* 6:2 (February 1977): 54-57.

b. "Wo ist die Avantgarde bloss hingeraten?" *Musik und Kirche* 47:2 (March-April 1977): 76-77.

c. ——. *Ex libris* (Zürich) 33:3 (March 1978)

Manuscripts: US-LJ typescript copy (5 p.)

K880. "Neue Strömungen in der zeitgenössischen Musik." In *Alte und Neue Musik* Vol.2: *Das Basler Kammerorchester 1926-1976.* (Zürich: Atlantis Verlag, 1977): 156-160.

Discusses the different directions of contemporary music, including the turning away from serialism toward indeterminacy, the turn toward oriental philosophy, the abandonment of polyphony in favor of sound blocks, and the influence of electronics in a search for new timbres and sounds. Krenek sees the turn to nostalgic forms and ways of music making and more extended use of aleatoric music as directions for the future.

a. ——. *Aufbau* (New York) (June 3, 1977).

K881. "Vorwort zum Neudruck." In his *Ueber neue Musik; sechs Vorlesungen zur Einführung in die theoretischen Grundlagen.* (Darmstadt: Wissenschaftliche Buchgesellschaft, 1977): 1-2.

Preface to the reprint edition, dated Palm Springs, CA, February 1977. Krenek notes that the 'new' music he talked about in his lectures is no longer new. His lectures were concerned with the music of the Second Viennese School and the twelve-tone technique of Arnold Schoenberg which persisted to the end of World War II. Since 1945, serial music has taken the place of twelve-tone music.

Manuscripts: US-LJ 1 p.

K882. "Strauss' *Salome.*" *Los Angeles Times* 96 (March 6, 1977): Calendar:2.

A letter to the editor in reaction to Martin Bernheimer's review on February 2 of the television production of the opera. "I have always found [television] particulary attractive because it allows me to focus the viewer's attention on details which even in a normal-sized opera house are inevitably lost."

Manuscripts: US-LJ typescript copy (1 p.)

K883. "Composers-Librettists." *Los Angeles Times* 96 (July 23, 1977): Calendar:2.

A letter to the editor in reaction to an article by Robert Musel on June 30 which included the statement that Michael Tippett "is unique among operatic composers ... in that he writes his own librettos." Krenek lists seven other composers who also wrote their own librettos, including himself.

K884. "Zur Vollendung von Alban Bergs *Lulu*-Fragment." *Musica* 31:5 (September-October 1977): 401-403.

Discusses the performance of *Lulu* without a third act and Krenek's belief that it could be completed from the existing sketches.

Manuscripts: US-LJ typescript copy (5 p.)

K885. "Beethoven *Streichquartette*." *Unpublished*.

A lecture broadcast over Westdeutscher Rundfunk, Cologne, October 4, 1977.

Manuscripts: US-LJ 2 p. ; typescript (2 p.)

K886. "Small screen *Figaro*." *Los Angeles Times* 96 (October 16, 1977): Calendar:2.

"Sharing Martin Bernheimer's enthusiasm about *Le nozze di Figaro* on KCET Channel 28 [published in the *Los Angeles Times's*] "View" October 5, I'd like to go as far as to say that this is *the* way to stage an opera... It is possible only for the little screen, where the director can focus the viewer's attention onto any detail that even in a medium-sized opera house would be lost."

K887. "Letter." *Unpublished*.

Discusses the etymology of the word sláva in reaction to its use in *Time* (October 24, 1977).

Manuscripts: US-LJ.

K888. "Letter." *Unpublished*.

Krenek protests the stopping of the advertising of X-rated movies in the *Los Angeles Times* (October 25, 1977).

Manuscripts: US-LJ typescript copy(1 p.)

-- 1978 --

K889. "Bärenreiter Jubiläum." *Unpublished*.

Laudatory comments on the occasion of the fiftieth anniversary of the publishing house.

Manuscripts: US-LJ 1 p.

K890. "Address." *Unpublished*.

Lecture given at the inauguration of the Ernst Krenek Archive at the University of California, San Diego, January 22, 1978 discussing his relationship with the University.

Manuscripts: US-LJ 1 p.

K891. "Letter." *Los Angeles Times* 97 (August 13, 1978)

A reaction to Martin Bernheimer's essay in memory of Bruno Walter.

K892. "Letter." *Los Angeles Times* 97 (September 12, 1978)

Comments in reaction to Daniel Carriaga's review of R. Haag's Schubert recital and Krenek's completion of the *C major piano sonata* (W65).

Manuscripts: US-LJ typescript copy (1 p.)

K893. "Erinnerungen an die Entstehung meiner Oper *Karl V*. vor 45 Jahren." *[Program: Staatstheater Darmstadt]* no.19 (October 27, 1978): [1-2]

A description of the circumstances and ideas which led to the creation of his opera op.73, and a discussion of his motivations to take up the twelve-tone technique. He also discusses the relationships he developed in adapting an historical libretto to the twelve-tone idiom.

Manuscripts: **US-LJ** 1 p. ; typescript copy (2 p.)

K894. *"Karl V.* ein Jux?" *Süddeutsche Zeitung* (November 9, 1978)

A lecture broadcast over Bayerischer Rundfunk, München, on the Musikprogramm, October 31, 1978.

-- 1979 --

K895. "Interview with myself." In *The Krenek Festival, April 8 to 15, 1979* (B705) (Santa Barbara): 5-6.

Dated January 12, 1979. Discusses his working method both as a young man during the 1920s and later with his serial music. *See:* B705

Manuscripts: **US-LJ** 2 p.

K896. "Letter to Jack Smith." *Los Angeles Times* 98 (May 1, 1979)

About Lupanar.

Manuscripts: **US-LJ** typescript copy (1 p.)

K897. "Music and text, reflections of a modern composer on lied and libretto." *Jahrbuch des Wiener Goethe-Vereins* 84/85 (1980-81): 97-104.

Lecture given at Stanford University, May 19, 1979. "It seems that music in the process of assembling a text to produce an opera somehow brings it down from the higher levels of literature." A discussion of the aesthetic implications of setting text to music.

Manuscripts: **US-LJ** 3 p.

K898. "Accordion." *Unpublished.*

Written in July 1979 concerning his associations with the instrument and the composition of *Acco-music* op.225.

Manuscripts: **US-LJ** 1 p.

K899. "Der Komponist Ernst Krenek erinnert sich". *Der Landbote* (Winterthur, SZ) no.255 (November 3, 1979): 28-29.

Krenek reminisces on the occasion of the 350th anniversary of the Musik-Kollegium in Winterthur on his stay in Switzerland made possible through a grant by Werner Reinhart. He discusses his beginnings as a composer in Berlin at which time his friendly relations with Werner Reinhart and the Musik-Kollegium began. He talks about his friendship with Georg Wolff and the Reinhart brothers, meeting Rainer Maria Rilke, Oskar Kokoschka, and Friedrich T. Gubler (who later became chief editor of the feuilleton section of the *Frankfurter Zeitung*), and the works he composed in Switzerland.

Manuscripts: **US-LJ** 3 p. ; typescript (6 p.)

K900. "Letter (Nov.24, 1979)." *Unpublished.*

For *Time* magazine. On the etymology of "Zigeuner."

Manuscripts: **US-LJ** typescript copy(1 p.)

-- 1980 --

K901. *Elektro-Ton und Spharenklang.* (Linz: Linzer Veranstaltungsgesellschaft, 1980) 14 p.

Lecture given at the opening of the International Bruckner Festival, Linz in 1980. After reflecting upon the history of entertainment and serious music,

Krenek reminds the reader that the planned action of "ars electronica" (to have the whole city participating in a "musical cloud") is not a new idea. It was propagated, in a way, by Paul Hindemith's *Gebrauchsmusik* and is present in everyday radio background-music. He draws a line from the middle ages to the problems of new music, and questions whether electronic music can solve those problems. *See:* B554

a. "Elektro-Ton und Sphärenklang." In his *Im Zweifelsfalle.* (K924) (Wien: Europaverlag, 1984): 213-221.

Manuscripts: US-LJ 7 p.

K902. "Persönliches zur Oper." *Jahrbuch des Wiener Goethe-Vereins* 84/85 (1980-81): 275-281.

Krenek discusses his personal experiences dealing with the difficulties of composing opera. The choice of the text is crucial because it is the vehicle which allows the music to redraw the intensity curve of the emotion. Intelligibility of the text is only partly the responsibility of the composer and his orchestration; it is especially the responsibility of the conductor and performers. Television is seen as a very favorable medium for opera because video technique adds new dimensions, but there is the added problem of synchronization between audio and video. He briefly discusses his television operas *Zauberspiegel* op.192, *Ausgerechnet und verspielt* op.179, and *Flaschenpost vom Paradies* op.217.

K903. "Remarks on *Sardakai.*" *Unpublished.*

A lecture given at the University of California, Santa Barbara, in 1980 about composing the opera op.206.

Manuscripts: US-LJ 1 p.

K904. "*Jonny* erinnert sich." *Oesterreichische Musikzeitschrift* 35:4/5 (April-May 1980): 187-189.

Reflections on the first performance in Vienna of *Jonny spielt auf* on the occasion of its revival at the Theater an der Wien under the auspices of the Wiener Festwochen and the Steirischen Herbst on June 3. The opera was very successful in Europe; however, the intentions of the composer were lost in the Austrian production. After 1930 the opera disappeared from the repertory. Picture: scene.

a. ——. *[Program: Opernhaus Graz, Wiener Festwochen]* (June 3, 1980): [2-3] & (October 26, 1980): [2-3]
Abbreviated.

Manuscripts: US-LJ typescript copy (2 p.)

K905. "Marginal remarks to *Lulu.*" *Alban Berg Studien* 2 (1981): 8-11.

Lecture given at the Internationalen Alban-Berg-Symposion, Vienna on June 2, 1980. "In *Lulu* we are transported by the magic charm of its nostalgic beauty, full of admiration for a work so passionately conceived and lovingly completed by its maker, notwithstanding the flaws it has inevitably inherited from the unwieldy model to which it was inextricably wedded from its inception." Krenek goes on to discuss Friedrich Cerha's completion of the opera and its performance in Santa Fe, New Mexico, and concludes that Berg would have made some changes in the opera had he finished it.

a. "Randbemerkungen zu *Lulu.*" *Das Orchester* 29:12 (December 1981): 1013-1016.

Manuscripts: US-LJ 3 p. ; typescript copy (7 p.)

K906. "Die Musik ist der Urgrund des Gedankens." *Salzburger Nachrichten* (August 23, 1980): 5.

K907. "Nach fünfzig Jahren." *Diners Club Magazin* (Vienna) (September 1980): 6.

Krenek discusses the first production of his opera *Karl V.* op.73 in Vienna fifty years after its cancelled premiere.

K908. "Programmnotizen zum Musikprotokoll Graz 1980." *[Program: Musikprotokoll 1980: Ernst Krenek 23.-26. Oktober]*, pp.430-433.

Brief program notes on the works performed during the Steirischer Herbst, 1980: *Statisch und Ekstatisch* op.214; *The Dissembler* op.229; *Kitharaulos* op.213; *Durch die Nacht* op.67; *Die Nachtigall* op.68; *O Lacrymosa* op.48; *Fünf Lieder* op.82; *Fünfache Verschränkung* op.205; *Auf- und Ablehnung* op.220; *Symphony no.2*, op.12; *Sonata, organ* op.92; *Die vier Winde* op.223; *Opus 231*; *Orga-Nastro* op.212; *The bell tower* op.153; *Im Tal der Zeit* op.232; *Quintina* op.191; *Die wussten was sie wollten* op.227; *Von vorn herein* op.219; and *Lamentatio Jeremiae prophetae* op.93.

   a. ——. *Oesterreichische Musikzeitschrift* 35:9 (September 1980): 430-433.

K909. "Von Krenek über Krenek zu Protokoll gegeben." In *Ernst Krenek*, hrsg. von Otto Kolleritsch. Studien zur Wertungsforschung, Bd.15. (Wien: Universal Edition, 1982): 9-14.

Lecture given at the Musiksymposion, Graz, October 24, 1980. Autobiographical details covering his ancestry, name, studies with Franz Schreker, and taking-up the twelve-tone technique. Even though he is an American citizen he is not considered an American composer, and he wonders how a composer should be classified, in relation to his place of birth or to his working locale, as he examines several multi-national composers.

Manuscripts: US-LJ 1 p.

K910. "Ist Komponieren lehrbar/lernbar? Antworten von Komponisten." *Musica* 35:4 (July-August 1981): 349-353.

Answers by eleven composers to the question, "Can composition be taught/learnt?" Krenek says that technique can be.

-- 1982 --

K911. "Mi experiencia en la composicion electronica." *Pauta* (Mexico) 1:1 (January-March 1982): 16-22.

Detailed discussion of the composition of *Spiritus intelligentiae, Sanctus* op.152 at the electronic music studio of the Westdeutsche Rundfunk.

K912. "Reminiscences." *Unpublished.*

About Vienna in the 1920's.

Manuscripts: US-LJ typescript copy 2 p.

-- 1983 --

K913. "Changes, as they come and go." *Unpublished.*

Written for *Confronting Stravinsky* edited by Jann Pasler but not published. "Variety of styles within one person's output is either praised as proving the richness and versatility of his imagination, or held against him as a sign of fickleness and lack of orientation." A reflection on Stravinsky's style changes.

Manuscripts: US-LJ typescript copy (1 p.)

K914. "Keintate." *Unpublished*.

English translation of Friedrich Cerha's *Keintate*, with explanatory footnotes.

Manuscripts: US-LJ typescript copy(8 p.)

K915. "Makulatur." *Spinario-Gesellschaft, Salzburg*.

Letter to Rupert Huber.

K916. "Komponisten und Interpreten von heute äussern sich zu Webern." In *Anton Webern, 1883-1983; Eine Festschrift zum hundertsten Geburtstag* hrsg. von Ernst Hilmar. (Vienna: Universal Edition, 1983): 29-56.

Brief expressions of admiration by many composers; Krenek's contribution (p.44) refers to his 1955 article "The same stone which the builders refused is become the headstone of the corner" (K656) and notes that Webern's influence has become stronger over the years.

K917. "Two views of the 'Ring.'" *Los Angeles Times* 102 (February 6, 1983): Calendar:99.

A letter to the editor in reaction to Martin Bernheimer's article on January 16 about the PBS broadcast of Richard Wagner's *Der Ring des Nibelungen*. "I realized for the first time in my life that *Das Rheingold* is a suspenseful and exciting theater piece. TV is an ideal medium for it."

K918. "Vorwort." In his *Im Zweifelsfalle*. (K924) (Wien: Europaverlag, 1984): 7-10.

An introduction to the collection of essays written between 1927 and 1980. *See:* B554

K919. "Literarischer Lebenslauf." *Jahrbuch des Wiener Goethe-Vereins* 86/88 (1982-84): 9-19.

Dated Mödling, June 24, 1983; includes a facsimile of the manuscript of the article, pp.15-19. A reflection on his literary efforts beginning with an unpublished quasi-satirical magazine which he wrote as a teenager and on his literary influences.

Manuscripts: US-LJ typescript copy (5 p.)

K920. "Zu Anton Weberns 100. Geburtstag." *Musik-Konzepte* Sonderband: *Anton Webern II* (November 1984): 26-50.

Lecture broadcast over Westdeutsche Rundfunk, August 1983. Discusses his relationship with Webern, examines Webern's musical legacy, and discusses in detail the characteristic, of his compositions, including many examples. Includes a facsimile of the manuscript of the first page of *Symphonic elegy* op.105.

Manuscripts: US-LJ.

K921. "Ernst Krenek *Konzert für Violoncello und Orchester, op.236* Salzburger Festspiele, Kleines Festspielhaus, 9.8.1983." *Oesterreichische Musikzeitschrift* 38:7/8 (1983): 406.

A brief program note from its first performance.

K922. "Between two worlds." *Unpublished*.

An autobiographical lecture given at the Austrian Music Festival in New York, November 1983.

Manuscripts: US-LJ typescript(4 p.)

K923. "Einsiedler-Kongress." *Oesterreichische Musikzeitschrift* 38:11 (November 1983): 605.

Humorous introduction to an issue devoted to Anton Webern's one-hundredth birthday.

-- 1984 --

K924. *Im Zweifelsfalle; Aufsätze über Musik.* (Wien: Europaverlag, 1984) 352 p.

Collection of essays in four parts, 1. On the possibilities of opera, 2. About composers, 3. The rules of music, and 4. General considerations: *Vorwort* (K918). I. Möglichkeiten der Oper: *Jonny spielt auf* (K73), *Von "Jonny" zu "Orest"* (K105-b), *Ist Oper heute noch möglich?* (K416-c), *Warum Pallas Athene weint?* (K662-b), *Zur Problematik des Librettos* (K674-b), *Ausgerechnet, aber sehr verspielt* (K772-a). II. Ueber Komponisten: *Ein "moderner" Meister des XV. Jahrhunderts* (K708-a), *Schubert* (K87-b), *Zeit und Ewigkeit* (K743-a), *Darius Milhaud* (K109-c), *Arnold Schönberg* (K268-b), *Karl Kraus und Arnold Schönberg* (K274-b), *Der Wille zur Ordnung* (K770-a), *Alban Bergs "Lulu"* (K444-d), *Anton Weberns magisches Quadrat* (K811-a), *Charles Ives, 1874-1954* (K652-a), *Amerikas Einfluss auf eingewanderte Komponisten* (K730-a), *Gespräch nach Mitternacht* (K551-d). III. Regeln der Kunst: *Erfahrungen mit dem "Zwölftonsystem"* (K253-b), *Grundideen einer neuen Musikästhetik* (K403-b), *Bericht über Versuche in total determinierter Musik* (K701-a), *Vom Verfall des Einfalls* (K719-a), *Was ist und wie entsteht elektronische Musik?"* (K678-b), *Die grosse Musikmaschine* (K731-a), *Elektro-Ton und Sphärenklang* (K901-a). IV. Allgemein betrachtet: *Der schaffende Musiker und die Technik der Gegenwart* (K102-a), *Zur heutigen Situation der Neuen Musik* (K140), *Ueber Sinn und Schicksal der neuen Musikpädagogik* (K207-c), *Von der Würde der abendländischen Musik* (K359-d), *Bemerkungen zur Rundfunkmusik* (K469-b), *Universalism and nationalism in music* (K528-b), *Es rieselt, es knistert, es kracht* (K797-a), *Komponist und Hörer* (K748-a), *Komponist und Schallplatte* (K824-a), *Musik und Sprache* (K750-a & K813-a), *Im Zweifelsfalle* (K826-a). *See:* B601, B690

K925. "Letter." *Unpublished.*

To Martin Bernheimer concerning his "New Romanticism" article in the *Los Angeles Times* (February 6, 1984).

Manuscripts: **US-LJ** typescript copy 1 p.

K926. "Aus der Mappe eines Opernschreibers." *Oesterreichische Musikzeitschrift* 39:10 (October 1984): 506-509.

Discusses his interest in writing operas, from his student days in Berlin to the present. Includes a brief discussion of each of his operas and the events surrounding the premiere of *Karl V.*

K927. "Das Gefühl, wie in einem Dornenbusch zu arbeiten." *[Program: Staats-Oper Wien]* (October 18, 1984): 62-66.

A discussion about writing *Karl V.* op.73

-- 1985 --

K928. "Vortrag über Anton Webern für den WDR." *Unpublished.*

A lecture broadcast over Westdeutscher Rundfunk, Cologne, in August 1985.

Manuscripts: US-LJ typescript 12 [i.e. 17] p.

-- 1986 --

K929. "Anton Webern." In *Komponisten des 20. Jahrhunderts in der Paul Sacher Stiftung.* (Basel: Paul Sacher Stiftung, 1986): 127-129.

Webern came from a family whose characteristic was nationalism, but he remained an independent spirit. His conduct was reserved and modest, and he showed a love for order bordering on pedantry. The sketchbooks show his meticulous work and the titles of the works show his extra-musical associations. The *Symphony,* op.21 and the unfinished cantata demonstrate his economy of musical means.

K930. "Offener Brief an Claus Helmut Drese." *Die Presse* (Vienna) (April 18, 1986)

K931. "Schubert-Portrait." *Unpublished.*

Dated: Palm Springs, January 1986 - Mödling, June 20, 1986. A three-part lecture broadcast by Westdeutscher Rundfunk, Cologne of Krenek's impressions of Franz Schubert's songs.

Manuscripts: US-LJ 18 p. ; typescript(27 p.)

K932. "Foreword." In *Gustav Mahler's American years, 1907-1911,* by Zoltan Roman. (Stuyvesant, NY: Pendragon Press, 1988)

Krenek compares the America he found to that encountered by Mahler thirty years earlier.

-- 1988 --

K933. "Ansprache fuer die Gedenkstunde in der Wiener Staatsoper am 13. Maerz 1988." *Unpublished.*

Written to be read at the comemoration of the fiftieth annerversary of the Anschluss. Krenek reflects on the events depicted in his operas *Pallas Athene weint* op.144 and *Karl V.* op.73 in relationship to the Nazi take-over of Austria.

Manuscripts: US-LJ typescript photocopy(1 p.)

Bibliography

The writings about Krenek are listed alphabetically by author, and subarranged by date. Compositions by Krenek are cited by opus number or, for works without opus number, by "W" number as appropriate. References to citations in the "Bibliography" sections are identified by "B" number for writings about Krenek and by "K" number for writings by him. Abbreviations are explained in the Preface.

B1. A.B. "Naomi Ornest, soprano." *Musical America* 70:2 (January 15, 1950): 70.
   Review of a recital which included the first New York performance of the song *Die Nachtigall* op.68.

B2. ——. "Return of a serialist." *Music and Musicians* 19:4 (December 1970): 22.
   Report of an interview before a BBC concert in honor of Krenek's seventieth birthday. Briefly discusses his important works: *Karl V.* op.73, the *Sixth string quartet* op.78, *Questio temporis* op.170, and *Sestina* op.161.

B3. A.H. "Fünftes Konzert des Basler Kammerorchesters." *Basler Volksblatt* (June 13, 1940)
   Review of the premiere of *Symphonisches Stück* op.86.

B4. A.W. "Kreneks *Karl V.*" *Neues Wiener Tagblat* (March 1, 1936):
   Discussion of the opera op.73.

B5. A.W.B. *"Orpheus und Eurydike."* *Hamburger Acht Uhr Abendblatt* (November 30, 1926)
   Review of the premiere of the opera.

B6. Aber, Adolf. "Internationales Kammermusikfest in Salzburg." *Berliner Tageblatt* (August 14, 1923)
   Review of the premiere of the *Third string quartet* op.20.

B7. ——. "Ernst Krenek: *Jonny spielt auf.*" *Leipziger neueste Nachrichten* (February 11, 1927)
   Review of the premiere of the opera.

B8. Aber, Adolf. *"Jonny spielt auf."* *Schweizerische Musikzeitung und Sängerblatt* 67:7 (February 19, 1927): 83.
Review of the premiere of the opera op.45.

B9. ——. "Ernst Krenek: *Jonny spielt auf."* *Musikblätter des Anbruch* 9:3 (March 1927): 127-132.
Review of the premiere of the opera op.45.

B10. ——. "Ernst Krenek: *Jonny spielt auf."* *Signale für die musikalische Welt* 85:9 (March 2, 1927): 286-288.
Review of the premiere of the opera op.45.

B11. ——. *"Jonny spielt auf* by Ernst Krenek in Leipsic, Germany." *Musical Courier* 94 (March 10, 1927): 5.
Review of the premiere of op.45.

B12. ——. "Le dernier opera de Krenek." *La Revue Musicale* 8:8 (June 1927): 305.
Review of the premiere of the opera *Jonny spielt auf* op.45.

B13. ——. "Die neuen Krenek-Opern." *Die Musikwelt* 8:6 (1930): 314-315.
Review of the premiere of the three one-act operas *Der Diktator* op.49, *Das geheime Königreich* op.50, and *Schwergewicht, oder Die Ehre der Nation* op.55.

B14. ——. "Uraufführungen, zwei neue Krenek-Werke." *Die Musik* 22:6 (March 1930): 443-444.
Review of the Leipzig premieres of the opera *Das Leben des Orest* op.60 and the song cycle *Reisebuch aus den österreichischen Alpen* op.62. Picture facing p.440.

B15. Abraham, Gerald. "Ernst Krenek. *Five Prayers."* *Music Review* 16 (August 1955): 262.
Review of the publication.

B16. Adorno, Theodor Wiesengrund. "Frankfurt a.M." *Die Musik* 20:3 (December 1927): 221-222.
Review of a performance of the opera *Jonny spielt auf* op.45.

B17. ——. "Zur Deutung Kreneks." *Anbruch* 14:2/3 (February-March 1932): 42-45.
A discussion from a radio broadcast of the significance of Krenek's works and his change in musical styles. Picture by Oskar Kokoschka.

    a. ——. In *Briefwechsel,* von Theodor W. Adorno und Ernst Krenek. (K862) (Frankfurt: Suhrkamp, 1974): 194-198.

    b. ——. In his *Musikalische Schriften.* Vol.5, hrsg. von Rolf Tiedemann und Klaus Schultz. Gesammelten Schriften, Bd.18. (Frankfurt: Suhrkamp Verlag, 1984): 571-575.

B18. ——. "Ernst Krenek." *The Listener* (October 23, 1935): 735-736.
Announces an upcoming BBC concert of vocal music (to include *Die Jahreszeiten* op.35; *Gesänge nach alten Gedichten* op.53; *Gesänge des späten Jahres* op.71; and excerpts from *Lieder* op.9) and the *Second concerto grosso* op.25. Krenek "may have made a brief incursion into jazz opera but he has done a great many other things, and the comparative popularity of *Jonny* should not be allowed to brand him permanently as a follower of the American romantics who have succeeded in commercializing primitive emotions."

a. ——. In *Briefwechsel*, von Theodor W. Adorno und Ernst Krenek. (K862) (Frankfurt: Suhkamp, 1974): 205-207.

b. ——. In his *Musikalische Schriften*. Vol.5, hrsg. von Rolf Tiedemann und Klaus Schultz. Gesammelten Schriften, Bd.18. (Frankfurt: Suhkamp Verlag, 1984): 531-534.
German translation.

c. ——. *Musik-Konzepte* 39/40 (B895) (October 1984): 11-13.
German translation.

B19. ——. "Musikpädagogische Musik." 23 no.28/30 (November 10, 1936)
Cast in the form of a letter from Hektor Rottweiler in reaction to Krenek's article "Was erwartet der Komponist von der Musikerziehung?" (K366).

a. ——. In *Briefwechsel*, von Theodor W. Adorno und Ernst Krenek. (K862) (Frankfurt: Suhrkamp, 1974): 215-223.

b. ——. In his *Musikalische Schriften*. Vol.5, hrsg. von Rolf Tiedemann und Klaus Schultz. Gesammelten Schriften, Bd.18. (Frankfurt: Suhrkamp Verlag, 1984): 805-812.

B20. ——. "Kreneks *Ueber neue Musik*." *Zeitschrift für Sozialforschung* (1938): 294-296.
Review of the book (K397).

a. "Krenek, Ernst, *Ueber neue Musik*." In *Briefwechsel*, von Theodor W. Adorno und Ernst Krenek. (K862) (Frankfurt: Suhrkamp, 1974): 224-226.

b. ——. In his *Gesammelten Schriften*. Vol.20 (Frankfurt: Suhrkamp, 1984)

c. "Zu Kreneks Buch *Ueber neue Musik*." *Musik-Konzepte* 39/40 (B895) (October 1984): 125-128.

B21. ——. "Zum Rundfunkkonzert vom 22. Februar 1940." In his *Musikalische Schriften*. Vol.5, hrsg. von Rolf Tiedemann und Klaus Schultz. Gesammelten Schriften, Bd.18. (Frankfurt: Suhkamp Verlag, 1984): 576-580.
Introduction to a radio concert which included *Durch die Nacht* op.67.

B22. ——. "Zur Physiognomik Kreneks." *Musik und Szene; Theaterzeitschrift der Deutschen Oper am Rhein* 2:13 (1957/58): 146-151.
Discusses Krenek as a twelve-tone composer and his opera *Karl V.* op.73.

a. ——. In his *Moments musicaux*. (1964): 125-131.

b. ——. In *Briefwechsel*, von Theodor W. Adorno und Ernst Krenek. (K862) (Frankfurt: Suhrkamp, 1974): 227-231.

c. ——. In his *Musikalische Schriften*. Vol.4, hrsg. von Rolf Tiedemann. Gesammelten Schriften, Bd.17. (Frankfurt: Suhrkamp Verlag, 1982): 109-113.

B23. **"Al Jolson greets 'Jonny'."** *New York Times* 78:25929 (January 20, 1929): 8:28.
Jolson meets the black-faced star of *Jonny spielt auf*. Includes information about the production costs of the opera.

B24. **Altmann, Wilhelm.** "[Review]." *Allgemeiner Zeitung* (Königsberg) (March 29, 1922)
Review of the premiere of the *First symphony* op.7.

B25. Altmann, Wilhelm. "Ernst Krenek." In *Von neuer Musik, Beiträge zur Erkenntnis der neuzeitlichen Tonkunst,* hrsg. von H. Grues, E. Kruttge, and E. Thalheimer. (Köln: F.J. Marcan, 1925): 296-298.
A bibliography of works to op.27 with title, genera, and poet indices.

B26. Ammel, Winfried. "Zwei Kurzopern von Ernst Krenek." *Opernwelt* 3:7/8 (1962): 72
Review of the premiere of the chamber opera *Vertrauenssache* op.111 and performance of *Dunkle Wasser* op.125.

B27. Anderson, Dale. "*Johannes Ockeghem* by Ernst Krenek." *Etude* 71:10 (October 1953): 8.
Review of the book (K616). "Krenek has rendered a valuable service in bringing Ockeghem a little nearer to 1953."

B28. Anderson, Jack. "San Francisco Ballet's new ballet." *Dance Magazine* 36:6 (June 1962): 43, 58.
Review of the premiere of the ballet *Jest of cards* op.162a and an interview with Krenek. Pictures.

B29. Anderson, Janet M. "An analysis of the sonata form and rotation technique in Ernst Krenek's *Piano sonata no.3* op.92, no.4, first movement." (Master's thesis: Moorhead State University, 1984) 83 pp.
Discussion of Krenek's use of rotation as an aspect of twelve-tone technique.

B30. Andrews, H. K. "*Tonal counterpoint in the style of the eighteenth century.*" *Music and Letters* 40:4 (October 1959): 378-379.
Review of the book (K632).

B31. Anson, George. "More contemporary piano music of the Americas." *Inter-American Music Bulletin* no.28 (March 1962): 1-21.
Includes a brief description of the *George Washington variations* op.120.

B32. Antheil, George. *Bad boy of music.* (Garden City, NY: Doubleday, Doran & Co., 1945)
An autobiography; mentions meeting Krenek who later became very friendly and helped him prepare the opera *Ivan the terrible.* Also mentions trying to influence Sam Goldwyn to hire Krenek to write music for the movies.

B33. Antoniou, Theodore. "Das Interview." *Musica* 34:2 (March-April 1980): 145-147.
An interview with Krenek discussing his life and works. He considers his masterpieces to be the *Second symphony* op.12, the *Fifth string quartet* op.65, the opera *Karl V.* op.73, the *Sixth string quartet,* op.78, the chorus *Lamentatio Jeremiae prophetae* op.93, *Sestina* for voice and chamber ensemble op.161, the song cycle *Spätlese* op.218, and the orchestra work *Auf- und Ablehung* op.220.

B34. Antonova, O. "25-ia general'naia assembleia MMS." *Sovetskaia muzyka* 37:12 (1973): 135-142.
Interviews with the "revolutionary" musicians, Paul Dessau, Ernst Krenek, Michael Tippett, and Rolf Lieberman.

B35. Appleton, Jon. "Current chronicle: Rochester, Michigan." *Musical Quarterly* 54:1 (January 1968): 92-96.
Extensive review of the premiere of *Horizon circled* op.196. "For although the work uses principles of rotation, ... it also illustrates Krenek's approach

to the coloristic effects so prevalent in the more avant-garde works of the past decade."

B36. Argus. "Ernst Krenek und sein Opernschaffen." *Leipziger Bühnenblätter* no.8 (1926/27): 60-62.

Program of the premiere of the opera *Jonny spielt auf* op.45. Surveys Krenek's operas.

B37. Arlen, Walter. "Large premiere quota lends glow to concert." *Los Angeles Times* 74 (February 22, 1955): III:9.

Review of the first American performance of *Parvula corona musicalis ad honorem J.S.Bach* op.122.

B38. ——. "Wind quintet, pianist in UCLA performance." *Los Angeles Times* 77 (April 1, 1958): IV:10.

Review of the premiere of *Pentagramm* op.163.

B39. ——. "Monday Eve Concert debuts Krenek work." *Los Angeles Times* 78 (February 18, 1959)

Review of the premiere of the *Guitar suite* op.164. The concert also included a performance of *Sestina* op.161 conducted by the composer and sung by Marni Nixon.

B40. ——. "Chorus and woodwind quartet give concert." *Los Angeles Times* 81 (March 4, 1962): 4:13.

Review of the premiere of the *Canon for Stravinsky* op.181.

B41. ——. "Two composers speak." *Los Angeles Times* 85 (August 7, 1966): Calendar:25 & 37.

Review of the book *Exploring music* (K817).

B42. ——. "Pianist Fierro in Monday Eve Concert." *Los Angeles Times* 88 (February 19, 1969): 4:14.

Review of the first American performance of *Four pieces* op.193.

B43. ——. "Krenek tribute by college." *Los Angeles Times* 93 (November 12, 1974): 4:12.

Review of the first concert in the Krenek Festival held at the California State University, Northridge Campus Theater. The concert included *Marginal sounds* op.162; *Spiritus intelligentiae Sanctus* op.152; *Four Pieces for oboe* op.193; the *Third piano sonata* op.92, no.4; and *Sestina* op.161.

B44. Arntzenius, L. M. G. "Afscheid van Walter." *De Telegraaf* (Amsterdam) (March 18, 1938)

Review of the premiere of the *Second piano concerto* op.81.

B45. Arthur, Bill. "Krenek assists at UCSD concert." *Los Angeles Times* 97 (January 24?, 1978)

Review of the January 22, 1978 concert which celebrated the opening of the Ernst Krenek Archive with the bestowal of his papers to the University of California, San Diego. The concert included the American premiere of *Spätlese* op.218 and a performance of *Von vorn herein* op.219 played by the SONOR Ensemble conducted by Bernard Rands.

B46. Avshalomov, Jacob. "René Bernier: *Sonatine pour violon et alto...* Ernst Krenek: *Sonata for viola and piano*." *Notes* 2d ser. 12:1 (December 1954): 142-143.

Review of the publication of op.117.

B47. B.M. "Ernst Krenek kommt wieder nach Kassel." *Hessische Nachrichten* (October 2, 1958)

An interview with the composer in anticipation of the performance of *Lamentatio Jeremiae prophetae* op.93.

B48. B.R. "Concert at Roof features string trio, piano music." *Los Angeles Times* 68 (April 5, 1949): I:15.

Review of the premiere of the *String trio* op.118.

B49. "Der Bach Preis der Freien und Hansestadt Hamburg 1966 ist Ernst Krenek zugesprochen worden ..." *Das Orchester* 14:4 (April 1966): 167.

Announcement of the award of the Hamburg Bach Prize to Krenek. Picture.

B50. Bach, David Joseph. "New music by Berg, Webern, Krenek." *Modern Music* 12:1 (November-December 1934): 31-38.

Discusses the *Kantate von der Vergänglickeit des Irdischen* op.72 and *Karl V.* op.73, which "apart from its lyric and musical value, ... is very Austrian and Catholic minded, in keeping with the ideas of the ruling class."

B51. Bachmann, Claus-Henning. "Das wandernde Crescendo." *Frankfurter Rundschau* (March 29, 1958)

Announces the forthcoming premiere of *Kette, Kreis und Spiegel* op.160 in Switzerland.

B52. ——. "Festwoche 'Musiktheater des XX. Jahrhunderts'." *Oesterreichische Musikzeitschrift* 13:6 (June 1958): 280-282.

Review of the first performance of a new version of *Karl V.* op.73 in Düsseldorf.

B53. ——. "Düsseldorf." *Schweizerische Musikzeitung* 98:7/8 (July 15, 1958): 318-319.

Review of the first performance in the revised version of the opera *Karl V.* op.73.

B54. ——. "Düsseldorf." *Schweizerische Musikzeitung* 99:1 (January 1, 1959): 37-38.

Review of the first European performance of the chamber opera *Der Glockenturm* op.153.

B55. ——. "*Quaestio temporis*." *Musica* 14:11 (November 1960): 723-724.

Review of the premiere of the chamber orchestra work op.170.

B56. ——. "*Der goldene Bock* in Hamburg uraufgeführt." *Die Bühne* (Vienna) no.7 (1964): 20-21.

Review of the premiere of the opera op.186.

B57. ——. "Das Gespräch: Krenek, Monk und *Der goldene Bock*." *Opernwelt* 5:6 (June 1964): 30-31.

An interview with the composer of the opera op.186 and the premiere's producer, Egon Monk.

B58. ——. "Held Jason." *Opernwelt* 5:8 (August 1964): 24-26.
Review of the premiere of the opera *Der goldene Bock* op.186. Pictures.

B59. **Bager, Robert.** "Ernst Krenek." In *The Concert Companion,* by Robert
Bager and Louis Biancolli. (London: McGraw-Hill, 1947): 377-378.
Quotes the program notes for the orchestral variations *I Wonder as I wander*
op.94 as the basis of a brief discussion about the composer.

B60. **Bahle, Julius.** *Der musikalische Schaffensprozess.* (Leipzig: S. Hirzel,
1936)
An examination of the creative process of composers based upon their own
comments, including many quotations from Krenek. About thirty composers
were sent several poems to consider setting to music; they were asked to
report on their reactions to the poems and to the process by which they
evaluated them. Krenek responded that he is influenced more by imperative
phrases than by wishful statements in the poems and that rhythmical
suggestions in the text are welcome incentives. He believes that outside
events which affect the emotional balance should not find their way into the
compositional process, and he explains his desire for musical order which led
him to adopt the twelve-tone technique.
a. ——. 2d.ed. Schöpferisches Menschentum, Bd.1. (Konstanz: Paul
Christiani, 1947) 203 pp.

B61. **Bailey, Olive Jean.** "The influence of Ernst Krenek on the musical
culture of the Twin Cities." (Ph.D. diss.: University of Minnesota, 1980)
573 pp.
Examines the effect of Krenek's presence from 1942 through 1947 at
Hamline University and the St. Paul community through oral history
interviews with thirty-five people. The study concludes that the "golden age
of music" during Krenek's tenure provided a momentum toward acceptance
and promotion of new music.
a. ——. *Dissertation Abstracts* 41:5 (November 1980): 1824-A.

B62. **Ballstaedt, Andreas.** "*Ernst Krenek.* Hrsg. von Otto Kolleritsch."
Musikforschung 38:3 (July-September 1985): 240-241.
Review of the book (B328).

B63. **Band, Lothar.** "Ernst Kreneks *Zwingburg.*" *Neue Musik-Zeitung* 46:5
(December 1925): 117.
Review of the premiere of the opera op.14.

B64. **Baresel, Alfred.** "Kreneks *Orpheus.*" *Der Auftakt* (Prague) 6:11/12
(1926): 233-234.
Review of the premiere of the opera op.21.

B65. ——. "*Jonny spielt auf.*" *Der Auftakt* (Prague) 7:2 (1927): 43-44.
Review of the premiere of the opera op.45 in Leipzig.

B66. ——. "*Jonny spielt auf.*" *Neue Musik-Zeitung* 48:13 (April 1927): 293-294.
Review of the premiere of the opera op.45.

B67. **Bartels, W. von.** "*Mammon,* Ballet von Ernst Krenek." *Rheinische Musik-
und Theaterzeitung* 28:35/36 (October 8, 1927): 408-409.
Review of the premiere of the ballet op.37.

B68. "Des Basler Kammerorchester holt sein V., Konzert nach." *Basler Nachrichten* (June 12, 1940)

Review of a performance of *Symphonisches Stück* op.86.

B69. Batschelet, Werner. "Zum Kompositionsabend von Ernst Krenek." *National Zeitung* (Basel) no.21 (January 13, 1961)

Surveys Krenek's works and discusses the forthcoming premiere of *Basler Massarbeit* op.173 which Dr.Batschelet participated in commissioning.

B70. Bauer, Marion. "Krenek on *Music here and now.*" *Modern Music* 17 (January-February 1940): 121-123.

Review of the book (K495).

B71. Baum, Günther. "Neue Musik in Dresden, I: Jacobi und Krenek." *Der Auftakt* (Prague) 12:4 (1932): 104-105.

Review of the premiere of the song cycle *Gesänge des späten Jahres* op.71.

B72. Baumgartner, Alfred. "Ernst Krenek." In his *Musik des 20. Jahrhunderts.* (Salzburg: Kiesel Verlag, 1985): 400-402.

Brief biography, summary of his works, and brief discussion of the *Second symphony* op.12, *Kette, Kreis und Spiegel* op.160, *Questio temporis* op.170, and *Lamentatio Jeremiae prophetae* op.93. Picture; facsimile of the beginning of the manuscript of the *Third piano sonata* op.92, no.4.

B73. Baumhof, Wendelin. "Untersuchungen zum Streichquartett bei Ernst Krenek." (Thesis: Staatlichen Hochschule für Musik, Köln, 1971) 84 pp.

Thorough examination of *String quartets* no.1, op.6; no.5, op.65; no.6, op.78; and no.7, op.96. Points out the development from the Bartok-inspired First quartet to the twelve-tone Seventh quartet.

B74. "Baylor Wind Ensemble at CBDNA National Conference." *The School Musician* 48:8 (April 1977): 42.

Brief announcement of the premiere of *Dream sequence* op.224.

B75. Beard, Harry R. "Modern works presented by the Deutsche Oper am Rhein." *Musical Times* 99:1384 (June 1958): 330.

Review of a performance of the revised version of *Karl V.* op.73 during the 1958 May Week of Modern Opera in Düsselforf.

B76. Beaujean, Alfred. "Ernst Krenek: *Lamentatio Jeremiae Prophetae.*" *Hi Fi Stereophonie* 3:3 (March 1964): 128-129.

Record review of the chorus op.93 on Bärenreiter Musicaphon 30 L 1303-4.

B77. ——. "Ernst Krenek: *Jonny spielt auf.*" *Hi Fi Stereophonie* 3:12 (December 1964): 615.

Record review of the opera op.45 on Amadeo AVRS 5038.

B78. ——. "Die Symphonie nach Mahler." *Hi Fi Stereophonie* 15:6 (June 1976): 611-616.

Brief survey of the development of the symphony in the 20th century, including Krenek's symphonies. Picture.

B79. Beck, Joachim. "Schreker und Krenek." *Die Weltbühne* 25:1 (1929): 22-25.

Review of the premiere of Krenek's three one-act operas, *Der Diktator* op.49,

Das geheime Königreich op.50, and *Schwergewicht* op.55. They are compared to Krenek's teacher's opera *Singende Teufel*.

a. "Schrecker und Krenek." *Deutsche Tonkünstlerzeitung* 27:493.

B80. Beck, R. T. "Sketches." *Music and Letters* 50:4 (October 1969): 548-549.

Review of *Anton von Webern Sketches (1926-1945)* with Krenek's "excellent commentary" (K828).

B81. ——. "Krenek, Wellesz, Hauer." In *Music in the Modern Age*, edited by F. W. Sternfeld. (London: Weidenfeld & Nicolson, 1973): 180-191.

Discusses the serial aspects of Krenek's works and especially traces his use of row "rotation" from his opera *Karl V.* op.73 through the *Lamentatio Jeremiae prophetae* op.93, the *Twelve variations for piano* op.79, the *Sixth string quartet* op.78, *Kette, Kreis und Spiegel* op.160, *Sestina* op.161 and *Der goldenen Bock* op.186.

B82. Becker, Harry Cassin. "Krenek's *Jonny* journeys west." *Musical America* 47:19 (February 25, 1928): 5, 25.

Discussion of the opera in anticipation of the first American performance at the Metropolitan Opera. Picture.

B83. ——. "Krenek goes to Paris." *Musical America* 47:21 (March 10, 1928): 3, 17.

An interview; includes a discussion of the forthcoming premiere of the three one-act operas *Der Diktator* op.49, *Das geheime Königreich* op.50, and *Schwergewicht* op.55.

B84. ——. "Opera to tame Negro-White love." *New York Evening Graphic* (January 18, 1929)

Discusses the plot of the opera *Jonny spielt auf* in an American context in anticipation of the forthcoming first American performance.

B85. Becker, Wolfgang. "Da Graz." *Nuova revista musicale italiana* 5:1 (January-February 1971): 125-126.

A brief review of the premiere of *Doppelt beflügeltes Band* op.207. Italian translation by Luigi Andrea Gigante.

B86. Beer, Otto Fritz. "Ernst Krenek." *Der Auftakt* (Prague) 15:1/2 (1935): 7-10.

Survey of the vocal works leading up to the opera *Karl V.* op.73.

B87. ——. "Kreneks *Karl V.* nach fünfzig Jahren an der Wiener Staatsoper." *Musica* 39:1 (1985): 48-49.

Discussion of the Vienna premiere of op.73 fifty years after the cancellation of its premiere.

B88. Bekker, Paul. "An Ernst Krenek." In his *Briefe an zeitgenössischer Musiker.* (Berlin: Max Hesses Verlag, 1932): 91-102.

Discusses Krenek's work during his time as Bekker's assistant in Kassel and ponders where Krenek will go stylistically after the opera *Jonny spielt auf*. Cast in the form of a letter. See Krenek's "Antwort" (K206).

B89. ——. "*Zweite Symphonie* von Krenek." *Musikblätter des Anbruch* 5:6/7 (June-July 1923): 198-199.

A review of the premiere of op.12.

B90. Bekker, Paul. "Ernst Krenek." *Musikblätter des Anbruch* 6:6 (June-July 1924): 241-245.
Review of the premiere of the opera *Der Sprung über den Schatten* op.17.

B91. ——. "Ernst Krenek: *Zwingburg.*" *Musikblätter des Anbruch* 6:10 (November-December 1924): 414-417.
Discussion of the opera op.14.

B92. Belaiev, Viktor. "Kshenek i problema opery." *Novaia muzyka* (Leningrad) 1:2 (1927): 8-13.
Discusses Krenek, the problem of modern opera, and the opera *Der Sprung über den Schatten* op.17.

B93. ——. "Leningrad takes to *Jonny.*" *Christian Science Monitor* (February 16, 1929)
Review of the Russian production of the opera op.45.

B94. "Belated production." *New York Times* 133:46141 (August 19, 1984): 2:18.
Announcement of the first Viennese performance of the opera *Karl V.* op.73 starting on October 18.

B95. Benary, Peter. "Neue Werke für dir katholische gottesdienstliche Praxis." *Schweizerische Musikzeitung* 109:6 (November-December 1969): 359-360.
Review of a performance of the *Deutsches Ordinarium* op.204 during a festival of Catholic church music in Lucerne.

B96. Berg, Alban. "Vorstellung Ernst Kreneks." In *Alban Berg*, von Willi Reich. (Wien: Herbert Reichner, 1937): 195-196.
Brief lecture given January 3, 1928 in the Vienna Kleinen Musikvereinssaal.

B97. Berger, Arthur. "Spotlight on the moderns." *Saturday Review* 35:26 (June 28, 1952): 46-47.
Record review of the *Symphonic elegy* op.105 on Columbia ML 4524.

B98. ——. "New Friends." *New York Herald Tribune* (January 5, 1953)
Review of the premiere of *Two sacred songs* op.132.

B99. ——. "Spotlight on the moderns." *Saturday Review* 36:26 (June 27, 1953): 59.
Record review of *Fiedellieder* op.64 on New Records NRLP 405.

B100. Berges, Ruth. "The view from Germany." *Opera News* 29:5 (December 12, 1964): 31.
Brief review of the premiere of the opera *The Golden ram* op.186.

B101. Bergquist, Peter. "*Exploring music.* By Ernst Krenek." *Music Educators Journal* 53:8 (April 1967): 114-115.
Review of the book (K817).

B102. Bernheimer, Martin. "Birthday salute to Krenek." *Los Angeles Times* 90 (December 9, 1970): 4:1 & 22.
Review of the American premiere of *Tape and double* op.207. The concert, a celebration of Krenek's seventieth birthday by the Monday Evening Concerts, also included *Wechselrahmen* op.189, *Quintina* op.191, the *Cello suite* op.84, and the *Alpbach quintet* op.180. Picture.

B103. Bernheimer, Martin. "Two operatic revelations in Multnomah county." *Los Angeles Times* 94 (December 7, 1975): Calendar:76-77.

Review of the first American performance in English by the Portland Opera of the *Life of Orestes* op.60.

a. ——. "Portland: Triumph for Krenek." *Opera* 27:2 (February 1976): 126-128.

B104. ——. "Bruno Walter: Some missing themes and variations." *Los Angeles Times* 97 (August 6, 1978): Calendar:60-61.

An extensive review of a small collection of letters by Walter published by Educational Media Associates of America including a letter to Alma Mahler. "You gave permission years ago to Krenek for completion of the *Tenth [symphony* (W72)] ... The uncompleted work of a musical genius must not be touched, even by the most gifted and devoted musician."

B105. Bie, Oscar. "*Jonny spielt auf.*" *Berliner Börsen-Courier* (February 12, 1927)

Review of the premiere of the opera op.45.

B106. Bischof, Rainer. "Von der Würde der abendländischen Musik ..." In *Ernst Krenek: Fünf Lieder nach Worten von Franz Kafka.* (Vienna: Wiener Stadt- und Landesbibliothek, 1985): 7-12.

A brief survey of Krenek's philosophical development from his youth in *fin de siècle* Vienna to the present.

B107. Biskind, Joseph. "Music." *The Argonaut* (San Francisco) (September 18, 1953)

Record review of the *Fourth piano sonata* op.114 on Music Library MLR 7014.

B108. Bitz, Albert-Peter. "Der Mut hat sich gelohnt." *Saarbrücker Zeitung* no.121 (May 25, 1962)

Review of the premiere of *Vertrauenssache* op.111 with a performance of *Dunkle Wasser* op.125.

B109. "Bla-Bla zum Pizzicato?" *Die Welt* (October 23, 1969)

An interview.

B110. Blanks, Fred R. "Australia." *Musical Times* 124:1688 (October 1983): 634.

Review of premiere of the *Organ concerto* op.235 during the Thirteenth Melbourne International Festival.

B111. Blaukopf, Kurt. "Spielt Jonny heute wieder auf?" *Phono* 11:1 (September-October 1964): 5-6.

Record review of the opera op.45 on Amadeo AVRS 5038.

B112. Bloomfield, Arthur. "New workshop." *Musical America* 80:9 (August 1960): 39.

Characterizes Krenek's lecture "The crises in inspiration" given during the American Composers' Workshop at the San Francisco Conservatory of Music June 20-24 as "soft sell for serialism."

B113. ——. "Musical joking plus." *San Francisco Examiner* (May 13, 1966): 32.

Review of the first American performance of *Quintina* op.191.

B114. Boardman, Frances. "Technical skill delights audience." *Saint Paul Pioneer Press* (December 12, 1942): 8.

Review of the premiere of *I wonder as I wander* op.94.

B115. ——. "Distinguished concert given at Hamline." *Saint Paul Pioneer Press* (April 6, 1943): 11.

Review of the performance of excerpts from *Lamentatio Jeremiae prophetae* op.93 performed April 4th.

B116. ——. "Variety of music - Recital presents Minnesota talent." *Saint Paul Pioneer Press* (April 14, 1943)

Review of a Bridgmen Hall concert which included *Lamentatio Jeremiae prophetae* op.93 sung by the Hamline Madrigal Singers conducted by Robert Holliday (heard within the past few months); the *Second piano sonata* op.59 played by Winifred Bolle; and the first U.S. performance of *O Lacrymosa* op.48.

B117. ——. "Symphony performance 'Superb'." *Saint Paul Pioneer Press* (December 24, 1943): 5.

Review of the American premiere of the *Second symphony* op.12.

B118. ——. "Symphony gives striking performance." *Saint Paul Pioneer Press* (March 25, 1944)

Review of the premiere of the *Cantata for wartime* op.95.

B119. Boeringer, James L. "New School." *Musical Courier* 157:6 (May 1958): 27.

Review of a concert which included a performance of *Lamentatio Jeremiae prophetae* op.93 and the premiere of *Sestina* op.161.

B120. Bohm, Jerome D. "Modern music marks third in concert series." *New York Herald Tribune* (March 30, 1940)

Review of a performance of the *Third string quartet* op.20 performed by Galimir Quartet.

B121. ——. "Sessions work and Krenek songs given in concert of New Friends." *New York Herald Tribune* (June 27, 1941)

Review of a performance of the first American performance of *Gesänge des späten Jahres* op.71 and four songs.

B122. ——. "Howland recital." *New York Tribune* (January 9, 1947): 19.

Review of the first New York performance of five songs from *Travelogue from the Austrian Alps* op.62.

B123. Bollert, Werner. "Kammerkonzerte." *Musica* 12:12 (December 1958): 736-737.

Review of the first European performance of *Sestina* op.161.

B124. ——. "Festwochen." *Musica* 13:12 (December 1959): 760-778.

Review of the premiere of *Sechs Motetten nach Worten von Franz Kafka* op.169.

B125. ——. "Musikspiegel." *Musica* 16:5 (1962): 260-261.

Includes a brief review of the first European performance of the monologue *Medea* op.129.

B126. ——. "Winfried Zillig: *Lieder des Abschieds*; Ernst Krenek: *Zwei geistliche Gesänge*." *Phonoprisma* 8:5 (1965): 145-146.

Record review of op.132 on Bärenreiter Musicaphon 30 L 1534.

B127. ——. "18. Internationales Heinrich Schütz-Fest." *Musica* 19:4 (July-August 1965): 198-201.
Includes a brief review of the premiere of *O holy ghost* op.186a.

B128. ——. "Konzertspiegel." *Musica* 19:4 (July-August 1965): 209-210.
Includes a review of the Berlin Philharmonic premiere of *Aus drei mach sieben* op.177.

B129. ——. "Neue Lieder von Krenek." *Musica* 22:2 (March-April 1968): 116.
Review of the publication of *Wechselrahmen* op.189.

B130. Bonaccorsi, Alfredo. "Ernst Krenek, *Johannes Ockeghem*." *La rassegna musicale* 24 (1954): 176-177.
Review of the book (K616).

B131. ——. "Walter Grandi. *Il sistema tonale ed il contrappunto dodecafonico di Ernst Krenek.*" *La rassegna musicale* 27:3 (Sept.1957): 256.
Review of the book (B452).

B132. Bongard, David. "Music review: Miriam Molin." *Los Angeles Daily News* (September 25, 1950)
Review of the premiere of *George Washington variations* op.120.

B133. "Book reviews." *Strad* 77:919 (November 1966): 283.
Review of the book *Exploring music* (K817).

B134. Boone, Charles. "Krenek, Ernst." In *Dictionary of Contemporary Music,* edited by John Vinton. (New York: E. P. Dutton & Co., 1971): 408-409.
A biographical essay surveying his life and works, especially discussing his twelve-tone works.

B135. Borek, Christoph. "Das Orgelportrait." *Hi Fi Stereophonie* 8:5 (May 1969): 326-363.
Record review of the organ music series which includes Krenek's *Sonata* op.92 on Psallite 66/270 768 PES.

B136. Borio, Gianmario. "Fortschritt und Geschichtsbewusstsein in den musik-theoretischen Schriften von Krenek und Adorno." *Musik-Konzepte* 39/40 (B895) (October 1984): 129-148.
Examines Theodor Wiesengrund Adorno's and Krenek's writings about music using Krenek's opera *Karl V.* op.73 as an example.

B137. Borris, Siegfried. "Geist und Gestalt der Kirchenmusik in den 50er Jahren." In *Meilenstein eines Komponistenlebens.* (Kassel: Bärenreiter, 1977): 38-44.
Discusses the composition of Günter Bialas's *Im Anfang* in relation to Krenek's *Lamentatio Jeremiae prophetae* and other works.

B138. Bouwman, F. "Kan en mag Mahlers *Unvollendete* worden voltooid?" *Mens en melodie* 41 (October 1986): 408-428.
Discussion of Mahler's *Tenth symphony* (W72) and Krenek's edition.

B139. Branscombe, Peter. "Krenek: *Lamentatio Jeremiae prophetae.*" *Hi-Fi News & Record Reviews* 26:1 (January 1981): 96.
Record review of op.93 on Bärenreiter Musicaphon 30 L 1303-4.

B140. Brennecke, Wilfried. "Musiktage." *Musica* 12:11 (November 1958): 673-675.

Review of the premiere of the complete *Lamentatio Jeremiae prophetae* op.93.

B141. ———. "Betont modern." *Musica* 14:12 (December 1960): 789-791.

The Kasseler Musiktage included two lectures by Krenek, "Komponist und Hörer" and "Neue Aspekte der seriellen Musik", an evening of his songs composed between 1921 and 1952 sung by Rudo Timper accompanied by the composer, and the premiere of *Sechs Vermessene* op.168. Picture.

B142. Briggs, John. "Records: Singers." *New York Times* 102:34847 (June 21, 1953): 2:9.

Record review of *Fiedellieder* op.64 on New Records NRLP 405.

B143. Brinkmann, Reinhold. "Theodor W. Adorno und Ernst Krenek: *Briefwechsel.*" *Die Musikforschung* 30:3 (July-September 1977): 353-354.

Review of the book (K862).

B144. Bronston, Levering. "20th century harp." *The New Records* 40:11 (January 1973): 12-13.

Record review of the *Harp sonata* op.150 on Klavier KS 507.

B145. ———. "Violin." *The New Records* 41:3 (May 1973): 15.

Record review of the *Second violin sonata* op.115 on Orion ORS 73107.

B146. ———. "Stravinsky: *L'histoire du soldat.* Ives: *Largo.* Krenek: *Trio.* Khachaturian: *Trio.*" *The New Records* 43:4 (June 1975): 8-9.

Record review of op.108 on Laurel Records LR 103.

B147. ———. "Chamber music." *The New Records* 44:8 (October 1976): 6.

Record review of *Aulokithara* op.213a, *Wechselrahmen* op.189, *Three sacred pieces for chorus* op.210, and *Echoes from Austria* op.166 on Orion ORS 76246.

B148. ———. "Krenek: *Kleine Blasmusik, op.70a.* Krenek: *Merry marches, op.44.* Davies: *Saint Michael sonata.*" *The New Records* 45:8 (October 1977): 2.

Record review of Louisville Orchestra LS 756.

B149. ———. "Krenek: *Horizon circled, op.196.* Krenek: *From three make seven, op.171.* Krenek: *Von vorn herein, op.219.*" *The New Records* 46:2 (April 1978): 3.

Record review of the orchestral works on Orion ORS 78290.

B150. ———. "Chamber music." *The New Records* 46:8 (October 1978): 5.

Record review of the *Trio for clarinet, violin and piano* op.108 on Supraphon 111 2147.

B151. ———. "Krenek: *Sestina for voice and instrumental ensemble.* Krenek: *Pieces for trombone.* Krenek: *Flute piece in (9) phases.*" *The New Records* 47:2 (April 1979): 7-8.

Record review of op.161, op.168, and op.171 on Orion ORS 78295.

B152. Brown, Kenneth. "Ernst Krenek: A dozen concerts do him honor." *High Fidelity/Musical America* 29:11 (November 1979): MA34, MA39.

Review of the eight-day festival held on the campus of the University of California, Santa Barbara which included a dozen concerts, lectures by eminent scholars, an exhibit of Krenek's paintings, and an exhibition of memorabilia and manuscripts. The television opera *Der Zauberspiegel* op.192

received its first American screening, and the mass *Gib uns den Frieden* op.208 received its American premiere.

B153. Brown, Royal S. "Twentieth-Century Harp." *High Fidelity* 23:11 (November 1973): 134.

Record review of the *Harp sonata* op.150 on Klavier KS 507.

B154. ———. "Krenek: *Symphonies No.1, op.7; No.2, op.12.*" *Fanfare* 9:5 (May/June 1986): 165-166.

Record review of Amadeo 415 825-1. The review omits mention of the *Third symphony* op.16 which is included on the record.

B155. Bruck, Werner. "Ein Rausch mit Pomp und Pathos." *Kölner Stadt-Anzeiger* (November 7, 1973): 31.

Review of the first European performance of *Six Profiles* op.203.

B156. Brust, Felix. "Ernst Krenek. *O Lacrymosa*, op.48." *Allgemeine Musikzeitung* 54:15 (April 8, 1927): 406.

Review of the publication of the songs.

B157. Brust, Fritz. "Politische Oper im Zwölftönesystem." *Frankfurter Allgemeine Zeitung* (March 28, 1950)

Review of the first German production of *Karl V.* op.73.

B158. Buccheri, John Stephen. "An approach to twelve-tone music; Articulation of serial pitch units in piano works of Schoenberg, Webern, Krenek, Dallapiccola, and Rochberg." (Ph.D. diss.: Eastman School of Music, 1975) 339 pp.

An attempt to develop an approach to twelve-tone music focused on serial pitch units in context, the extent to which such units are articulated by non-pitch aspects, and the potentials of the pitch set. Includes an analysis of *Twelve short piano pieces* op.83 (pp.155-190).

a. ———. *Dissertation Abstracts* 37:2 (August 1975): 679-A.

B159. Burge, David. "Contemporary piano: Ernst Krenek." *Contemporary Keyboard* 6:2 (February 1980): 80.

Burge reminiscences about his meetings with Krenek and discusses the piano music, especially *Six Vermessene* op.168, and the *Third sonata* op.92, no.4 and *Fourth sonata* op.114.

B160. Burkhard, Willy. "Grenzen des musikalischen Hörens." *Schweizerische Musikzeitung und Sängerblatt* 77:22 (November 15, 1937): 589-593.

Burkhard, a middle of the road tonal (not twelve-tone) composer, expresses his reservations with Krenek's book *Ueber neue Musik* (K397).

B161. ———. "Versuch einer kritischen Auseinandersetzung mit der Zwölftontechnik." *Schweizerische Musikzeitung* 94:3 (March 1, 1954): 85-93.

Questions the audibility of twelve-tone music in reaction to Krenek's article "Is the twelve-tone technique on the decline?" (K631) using Krenek's *Invention* op.127a as the example.

B162. Burkley, Francis J. "Medieval Musician." *The Commonweal* 58:15 (July 17, 1953): 375-376.

Review of the book *Johannes Ockeghem* (K616).

B163. Busoni, Ferruccio. "Letter to Emil Hertzka, 21.4.1923." In his *Selected Letters*, translated, edited, and with an introduction by Antony Beaumont. (London: Faber and Faber, 1987): 362.

Busoni thanks the editor of Universal Edition, for sending him the publication of *Toccata und Chaconne* op.13 and *Eine kleine Suite* op.13a, and discusses the pieces. "It is a pleasing demonstration of energy, built on diversified foundations. The composer's character is not yet fully established."

B164. C.S. "Twelve-tone scores published by Bomart." *Musical America* 70:9 (August 1950): 28.

Review of the publication of the *Fourth piano sonata* op.114. "It will perhaps be a labor of love for pianists to perform this sonata, but it deserves to be known and understood, for it is one of the best works Krenek has written in the past few years."

B165. C.W.D. "Symphony Hall." *Boston Globe* (November 5, 1938)

Review of the American premiere of the *Second piano concerto* op.81.

B166. Cahn, Geoffrey Stephen. "Weimar culture and society as seen through American eyes: Weimar music -- the view from America." (Ph.D. diss.: St. John's University, 1982) 493 pp.

Reception by Americans was generally poor when they first encountered the musical compositions of the Weimar Republic during the nineteen-twenties and early nineteen-thirties. Tastes in America were influenced by the nation's own cultural directions which ran counter to those of Weimar Germany and German music disturbed more American critics and audiences than any other phase of Weimar culture. The composers discussed in this study, including Krenek, mirrored the political, social, and cultural climate of the Weimar Republic. Much of their music was either cerebral and dissonant or overly romantic and antiquated and thus ill-suited for American adaptation. Though some works were better received than others, and a few American composers, critics, and select audiences were enthusiastic, Weimar music was not well received until after World War II, when Weimar culture generally had a greater influence on our own arts. This study concludes that tastes do vary between national cultures and different epochs, and just as social phenomena can be linked with a specific time and place, so may our cultural preferences be conditioned by the forces of history.

a. ——. *Dissertation Abstracts* 43:5 (1982): 1641-A.

B167. Calloway, Inez. "*Johnny strikes up the band.*" *The Literary Digest* 100:6 (February 9, 1929): 20-21.

Surveys the reviews of the American premiere. Picture.

B168. Calvocoressi, M.-D. "*Ueber neue Musik.* By E. Krenek." *Musical Times* 78:1137 (November 1937): 956-957.

Review of the book (K397).

B169. Campbell, Francean. "New music program well performed." *San Francisco Examiner* (November 6, 1948)

Review of the premiere of the *Fourth piano sonata* op.114.

B170. Canby, Edward Tatnall. "Korngold: *Much ado about nothing* suite. Austrian classical marches (Beethoven, Schubert, Krenek, Berg, Strauss)." *Audio* 43:12 (December 1959): 70.

Record review of Boston Records BST 1012 which includes op.44.

B171. Candra, Zdeněk. "Krenek." *Hudebni rozhledy* 21:10 (1968): 296.
Biographical essay. Picture.

B172. Cariaga, Daniel. "Krenek festival at Palm Springs." *Los Angeles Times* 94 (January 27, 1975): 4:1 & 12.
Review of the festival and the first American performance of *Static and ecstatic* op.214.

B173. ——. "Finale for series of contemporary works." *Los Angeles Times* 95 (June 22, 1976): 4:10.
Review of the American premiere of *Von vorn herein* op.219. William Kraft conducted because Krenek, who was scheduled to conduct the work, was ill.

B174. ——. "Haag begins 'A Schubert Festival'." *Los Angeles Times* 97 (September 12, 1978): IV:11.
Review of a performance by Robert Haag of Krenek's edition of Schubert's *Piano sonata in C major* (W65).

B175. ——. "Channel city for Krenek." *Los Angeles Times* 98:140 (April 22, 1979): Calender:78-80.
Review of the Krenek Festival at the University of California, Santa Barbara and the first showing in America of his television opera *Der Zauberspiegel* op.192.

B176. ——. "Krenek esoterica heard in Pasadena." *Los Angeles Times* 103:154 (May 5, 1984): 5:8.
Review of a concert in the Pasadena Conservatory of Music of *Spaetlese* op.218 sung by Michael Ingham with Carolyn Horn, piano; the first American performance of *Serenade* op.4; and *Doppelt Beflügeltes Band* op.207 played by Margaret Kohn and Karl Kohn.

B177. Carner, Mosco. *"Studies in counterpoint based on the twelve-tone technique."* *Music and Letters* 22:1 (January 1941): 84-87.
Review of the book (K496). It "ought to be used not only by the student-composer for whom it was primarily written, but by all those who are alive to the various problems of modern music in general. It is true that Krenek shows us only the bare bones of atonal music, but after all anatomy is the foundation of the whole body."

B178. ——. *"Ernst Krenek. By Lothar Knessl."* *Music and Letters* 50:1 (January 1969): 196-198.
Review of the book (K662).

B179. ——. "Krenek." *Musical Times* 124:1685 (July 1983): 427-428.
Review of *Ernst Krenek Katalog zur Ausstellung der Wiener Stadt- und Landesbibliothek, May/June 1982* (B550) by Ernst Hilmar and *Ernst Krenek Studien zur Wertungsforschung* edited by Otto Kolleritsch (B328).

B180. Cassidy, Claudia. "Notes on Whittemore and Lowe, the second *Carmen*, other things." *Chicago Tribune* (October 19, 1959)
Review of the premiere of *Three short twelve-tone pieces* op.139a.

B181. Cera, Stephan. "Performance." *The Sun* (Baltimore) (March 12, 1979)
Review of the premiere of *The Dissembler* op.229.

B182. Cerha, Friedrich. "Die Wiener Schule und die Gegenwart" *Oesterreichische Musikzeitschrift* 16:1 (January 1961): 43-54
　　Discusses the relationship of serial composers to Arnold Schoenberg and his circle, and comments that Krenek's influence on the younger generation of Austrian composers is limited because he lives in America. Krenek responds in "Bemerkungen zur Wiener Schule" (K764).

B183. Chadwick, Nicholas. "*Horizons circled; Reflections on my music.*" *Music and Letters* 57:2 (April 1976): 190-192.
　　Review of the book (K864).

B184. Charles, John W. "Hindemith: *Quartet for Clarinet, Violin, Cello, and Piano.* Krenek: *Trio for Violin, Clarinet, and Piano.* Milhaud: *Suite for Violin, Clarinet, and Piano.*" *Fanfare* 2:2 (November-December 1978): 71-72.
　　Record review of op.108 on Supraphon 111 2147.

B185. Chase, William W. "American Camerata for New Music." *The New Records* 48:3 (May 1980): 15.
　　Record review of Orion ORS 79362 which includes the *Capriccio for cello* op.145 and *The Dissembler* op.229.

B186. ——. "Krenek: *Static and ecstatic,* op.214 ..." *The New Records* 48:6 (August 1980): 8.
　　Record review of Varese Sarabande VR 81200 which also includes *Kitharaulos* op.213.

B187. ——. "Krenek: *They knew what they wanted* and Krenek: *Quintina.*" *The New Records* 48:10 (December 1980): 11.
　　Record review of op.227 and op.191 on Orion ORS 80380.

B188. Chissell, Joan. "Ernst Krenek and the twelve-tone system." *Monthly Musical Record* 72:836 (May 1942): 84-87.
　　A discussion of twelve-tone technique as used in *Twelve Short piano pieces* op.83.

B189. Christen, Norbert. "Nicht angemessen realisiert." *Musica* 36:5 (September-October 1982): 468-469.
　　Record review of *Karl V.* op.73 on Amadeo AVRS 305.

B190. Clark, Martin. "Portland Op.: *Life of Orestes.*" *High Fidelity/Musical America* 26:3 (March 1976): MA28.
　　Review of the American premiere of the opera.

B191. Cleman, Tom. "Ernst Krenek. *Serenade für Klarinette, Violine, Viola, Violoncello* op.4. *Streichquartett, Nr.2,* op.8." *Notes* 39:3 (March 1983): 702-703.
　　Review of the publications.

B192. "CMC appoints Krenek, Fletcher to composition faculty." *Music News* 41:6 (June 1949): 15.
　　Announcement of Krenek's appointment at the Chicago Musical College.

B193. Cohn, Arthur. "Six from Illinois." *American Record Guide* 25:4 (December 1958): 271-273.

Record review of the chamber opera *The bell tower* op.153 on University of Illinois CRS 5.

B194. ——. "Krenek: *Lamentario Jeremiae prophetae, op.93.*" *American Record Guide* 26:7 (March 1962): 558-560.

Record review of Bärenreiter Musicaphon 30 L 1303-4.

B195. ——. "Ernst Krenek." In his *Twentieth Century Music in Western Europe.* (Philadelphia: J.P. Lippincott, 1965): 175-181, 443-447.

Briefly discusses *Eleven transparencies* op.142, *Music for string orchestra* op.105, *Drie lustige Märsche* op.44, *Double concerto* op.124, *Organ sonata* op.92, *Third piano sonata* op.92, no.4, *Fourth piano sonata* op.114, *Fifth piano sonata* op.121, *Four Bagatelles* op.70, *Sonata for viola and piano* op.117, *Fiedellieder* op.64, *Sestina* op.161, *Die Jahreszeiten* op.35, *Five prayers over the Pater noster as cantus firmus* op.97, *Lamentatio Jeremiae prophetae* op.93, *Spiritus intelligentiae Sanctus* op.152, and *The bell tower* op.153 on pages 175-181. Briefly reviews the recordings of Krenek's music on pages 443-447: Austin 6224, Bärenreiter Musicaphon 30 L 1303-4, Boston Records B 411, Columbia ML 5336, Deutsche Grammophon LP 16 134, Epic LC 3509, Louisville Orchestra LOU 56-3, MGM E 3218, Music Library MLR 7014, Music Library MLR 7029, New Records NRLP 405, University of Illinois CRS 5, University of Illinois CRS 7, and University of Oklahoma 2.

B196. ——. "Ernst Krenek." In his *Recorded Classical Music.* (New York: Schirmer Books, 1981): 1013-1016.

Record reviews of Advance Recordings FGR 4, Klavier KS 507, Louisville Orchestra LS 756, Lyrichord LL 158, Musical Heritage Society MHS 3874, Orion ORS 73107, Orion ORS 75204, Orion ORS 78295, Philips 6500 202, and University of Oklahoma 2.

B197. Colucci, Matthew Joseph. "A Comparative study of contemporary musical theories in selected writings of Piston, Krenek, and Hindemith." (Ph.D. diss.: University of Pennsylvania, 1957) 195 pp.

Twentieth century composers have found it necessary to express themselves in words partly because of the need to explain or defend their convictions to their listeners and partly due to the demand of their new patroness, the university. The importance of the theoretical writings of the three composers lies in the approach to musical theory and its relationship to composition. Krenek views music as always having progressed through the use of new, arbitrary ideas by the composer; he has accepted the twelve-tone technique and its speculative methods of theory as a new basis of music. Colucci concludes that the three composers will achieve eminence as composers and not through any theoretical codifications that attempt to justify them.

a. ——. *Dissertation Abstracts* 17:11 (1957): 2628-2629.

B198. Commanday, Robert. "Singers' triumph -- Kafka to music." *San Francisco Chronicle* (April 6, 1965)

Review of the first American performance of *Six Motets on words by Franz Kafka* op.169.

B199. "Comment in Brief on Recent LP Disks." *New York Times* 108:36912 (February 15, 1959): 2:15.

Record review of *Sestina* op.161 and excerpts from *Lamentatio Jeremiae prophetae* op.93 on Epic LC 3509.

B200. **"Commissions, awards, new hearings of works."** *Musical Courier* 147:1 (January 1, 1953): 6.

Announcement of the forthcoming premiere of the *Sixth string quartet* op.78.

B201. **"Composers and performers in concert of new music at New School next Sunday."** *New York Times* 111:38088 (May 6, 1962): 2:9

Announcement of upcoming first American performance of *Quaestio temporis* op.170. Picture.

B202. **"Concertgebouw te Amsterdam: Het tweede piano-concert van Ernst Krenek."** *Nieuwe Rotterdamsche Courant* (March 18, 1938)

Review of the premiere of the *Second piano concerto* op.81.

B203. **"*Concertino*."** *Musikblätter des Anbruch* 7:6/7 (June-July 1925): 343.

Announcement of the premiere of the *Concertino for flute, violin and harpsichord with string orchestra* op.27.

B204. **"Conversa amb Ernst Krenek."** *Mirador* (Barcelona) 8:377 (May 7, 1936)

An interview following the premiere of *Fragmente aus dem Bühnenwerk "Karl V."* op.73a.

B205. **Cook, Susan C.** "Opera during the Weimar Republic: the *Zeitopern* of Ernst Krenek, Kurt Weill, and Paul Hindemith." (Ph.D. diss.: University of Michigan, 1985) 520 pp.

With the resumption of musical life in Germany following World War I, three young composers came to the fore as the dominant members of the new generation: Ernst Krenek, Kurt Weill, and Paul Hindemith. Krenek was the first of the three to produce what came to be called a *Zeitoper* (topical opera) with his *Jonny spielt auf* op.45, which attained an unprecedented success following its premiere in 1927. The *Zeitoper* emerges as a genre which arose directly out of concerns on the part of these composers to prove their commitment to opera and to bring modern opera into line with the spirit which characterized the new republican age. Thus *Zeitopern* are of modern life in their choice of subject matter and characters, scene settings, staging, and musical idioms. Examines the operas *Der Sprung über den Schatten* op.17 and *Jonny spielt auf* op.45, and jazz in light of the changing opera aesthetic of the time.

a. ——. *Dissertation Abstracts* 46:7 (1986): 1771-A.

b. *Opera for a new republic: the Zeitopern* of Krenek, Weill, and Hindemith. Studies in musicology, no.96. (Ann Arbor: UMI Research Press, 1988)

B206. **Cooke, Francis Judd.** "*Modal counterpoint in the style of the sixteenth century.*" *Journal of music theory* 4:1 (April 1960): 112-115.

Review of the text book (K628).

B207. **Cope, David.** "Ernst Krenek. *Perspektiven*, op.199." *Notes* 36:4 (June 1980): 986-987.

Review of the publication.

B208. **Corleonis, Adrian.** "Krenek: *Gesaenge des Spaeten Jahres*, op.71." *Fanfare* 3:2 (November-December 1979): 92.

Record review of Orion ORS 78308.

B209. *"Cosi fan tutte* in *Jonny*-Auffassung." *Zeitschrift für Musik* 94:12 (December 1927): 707.

Discusses the Mozartian elements in Krenek's opera op.45.

B210. Cowell, Henry. "Why the ultra-modernists frown on Krenek's opera." *Singing and Playing* 4:2 (February 1929): 15, 39.

"Scathing review of *Jonny spielt auf* after its American premiere." Cf. Bruce Saylor *The writings of Henry Cowell.* (1977)

B211. Cox, Ainslee. *"Exploring music,* by Ernst Krenek." *Music Journal* 24:8 (October 1966): 75.

Review of the book (K817).

B212. Cremonese, Adriano. "Rilke - *O Lacrymosa* - Krenek." *Musik-Konzepte* 39/40 (B895) (October 1984): 114-124.

Analysis of the three songs of op.48 and the text which Rilke asked Krenek to set.

B213. Cunningham, Carl. "Contemporary music: Festival ends on a lyric note." *San Francisco Chronicle* (May 14, 1966): 34.

Review of the first American performance of *Quintina* op.191.

B214. Curjel, Hans. "Zu Giorgio di Chiricos Berliner Bühnenbildern." *Du* (Zürich) 24 (November 1964): 12-16.

Brief reminiscence of employing the artist Giorgio di Chirico to design the sets for the premiere of *Leben des Orest* op.60. Pictures.

B215. ——. *Experiment Krolloper, 1927-1931.* Studien zur Kunst des neunzehnten Jahrhunderts, Bd.7. (Münich: Prestel-Verlag, 1975) 504 pp.

A history of the Berlin Krolloper which included premieres of the three one-act *Der Diktator* op.49, *Das geheime Königreich* op.50, and *Schwergewicht* op.55, the opera *Leben des Orest* op.60, and *Kleine Sinfonie* op.58. Includes reprints of reviews of the premieres.

B216. D.H. "Ernst Krenek: *Reisetagbuch aus den österreichischen Alpen.*" *Melos* 29:6 (June 1962): 205.

Record review of the song cycle op.62 on Telefunken BLE 14113.

B217. D.H.G. "Kreneks Oper: *Der Glockenturm.*" *Ruhr-Nachrichten und Westfalierpost* (December 5, 1958)

Review of the first German performance of *Der Glockenturm* op.153.

B218. D.J.B. "Manhattan School group performs in new hall." *Musical America* 80:4 (March 1960): 29.

Review of the premiere of *Marginal sounds* op.162.

B219. Dahlhaus, Carl. "Ernst Krenek und das Problem des musikalischen Sprachwechsels." In *Ernst Krenek,* hrsg. von Otto Kolleritsch. (B328) Studien zur Wertungsforschung, Bd.15. (Wien: Universal Edition, 1982): 36-46.

An examination of the aesthetic background of twelve-tone music as discussed in a series of letters and articles between Theodor Wiesengrund Adorno and Krenek and in Krenek's *Ueber neue Musik* (K397).

B220. Dale, S. S. "Contemporary cello concerti, LXXI: Krenek and Hajdu." *Strad* 89:1064 (December 1978): 713-719.

Discussion and analysis of the *Cello concerto* op.133.

B221. Daniel, Oliver. "Champaign, '57." *Saturday Review* 41:37 (Sept.13, 1958): 69.

Brief record review of the chamber opera *The bell tower* op.153 on University of Illinois CRS 5.

B222. ——. "Joy in problems." *Saturday Review* 42:9 (February 28, 1959): 68-69.

Record review of *Sestina* op.161 and *Lamentatio Jeremiae prophetae* op.93 on Epic LC 3509. Picture.

B223. ——. "The International Music Council's Tenth General Assembly." *National Music Council Bulletin* 25:1 (1964): 10.

Includes a review of the premiere of the opera *Der goldene Bock* op.186.

B224. ——. "Dartmouth's congregation." *Saturday Review* 48:31 (July 31, 1965): 35, 44-45.

Review of a series of concerts which included *Bagatelles* op.70 and *Verhaeren* songs op.30a on the opening concert; *Monologue for Stella* op.57 and *Eleven Transparencies* op.142 conducted by the composer; a chamber music all-Krenek program featuring the premiere of *Fibonacci mobile* op.187 with *Pentagram* op.163, *Sonata for viola and piano* op.117, *Trio for clarinet, violin & piano* op.108, and the *Seventh string quartet* op.96; and *Symphonic elegy* op.105 and *Concerto for two pianos* op.127 on the concluding concert.

B225. ——. "Krenek, Ernst." In *The New Grove Dictionary of Music and Musicians,* edited by Stanley Sadie. Vol.10. (London: Macmillan, 1980): 253-256.

Biographical essay with list of works. Picture.

B226. Dannenberg, Peter. "Hamburg." *Opera* 21:10 (October 1970): 959-600.

Review of the premiere of the opera *Das kommt davon* op.206.

B227. ——. "Gegen die Dummheit in der Musikkritik; eine historische Betrachtung der oesterreichischen Musikzeitschrift 23." *Neue Musikzeitung* 22 (April-May 1973): 15.

Discussion of the music perdiodical founded by Krenek, Alban Berg, Willi Reich, and Rudolf Ploderer, and its attack against the stupidities of music critics's statements.

B228. Danuser, Hermann. "Berliner Herbst." *Schweizerische Musikzeitung* 120:6 (November-December 1980): 366-368.

Review of the Berlin Festival which included the first performance in German of *The Dissembler* op.229.

B229. ——. "Krenek, Ernst. *A composer in exile.*" *Literature, Music, Fine Arts* 16:1 (1983): 67-69.

Review of the book by Cludia Maurer Zenck (B1502).

B230. Darrell, R. D. "The Tape Deck." *High Fidelity* 30:8 (August 1980): 87.
Record review of Orion OC 328S which includes the *Guitar suite* op.164.

B231. Davidson, Marie Hicks. "Krenek gives recital." *San Francisco Call* (January 12, 1938)
Review of a lecture presented by Pro Musica entitled "Common ideology of classical and modern music" and a piano recital in the Fairmont Hotel Red Room on January 11 consisting of *Two suites* op.26, *Five pieces* op.39, and *Variations* op.81 [sic op.79] "completed last year and never before played by him to any audience".

B232. Davies, Grace. "Music." *Minneapolis Daily Times* (December 24, 1943)
Review of the first American performance of the *Second symphony* op.12.

B233. ——. "Symphony Concert." *Minneapolis Daily News* (March 25, 1944)
Review of the premiere of *Cantata for war time* op.95.

B234. Davis, Peter G. "The Diaghilev of contemporary music: Heinrich Strobel's lively legacy." *High Fidelity* 32:10 (October 1982): 70.
Record review of Deutsche Grammophon 0629 027-031 which includes *Aus drei mach sieben* op.177.

B235. "Debussy, Krenek works feature women's choir." *Minneapolis Star Journal* (March 14, 1944)
A discussion of the forthcoming premiere of the *Cantata for wartime* op.95.

B236. "Deck of dancing cards." *Life* 52:23 (June 8, 1962): 91-92.
Review of *Jest of cards* op.162. "The biggest ballet hit on the West Coast in years, it has enjoyed smash appearances in San Francisco and a sell-out two weeks at the Seattle World's Fair." Includes three color picture.

B237. De Courcy, Geraldine. "Krenek unites jazz and classic myth in new opera." *Musical America* 50:4 (February 25, 1930): 5,18.
Review of the premiere of *Leben des Orest* op.60. "On the whole, the work has been characterized generally as an unsatisfactory accumulation of ideas without any definite object or connection." Pictures: p.5.

 a. "What they read twenty years ago." *Musical America* 70:4 (March 1950): 17.
Brief excerpts from the review of the premiere.

B238. Decsey, Ernst. "Jazz in Vienna." *Neues Wiener Tagblatt* (January 7, 1928)
General discussion of the opera *Jonny spielt auf* op.45 in anticipation of its first performance in Vienna.

 a. ——. In *Two Hundred Years of Opera*, pp.441-445.

B239. de Schauensee, Max. "Blanche Thebom Sings New Krenek Work." *The Philadelphia Evening Bulletin* (March 14, 1953)
Review of the premiere of *Medea* op.129. Picture.

B240. "The desert and Ernst Krenek." *MadAmimA* 2:2 (Fall 1981): 7.
Announces the Fourth Annual Joanna Hodges Piano Conference and Competition will occur in Palm Desert, February 20 through March 1, 1982; contestants must each play a work of Krenek. Also mentions that the opera

Karl V. op.73 was broadcast over NPR in June, the Thouvenel String Quartet gave the premiere of the *Eighth string quartet* op.233, and that Vassar College has scheduled a concert of Krenek's music on which the Composers String Quartet also will play the *Eighth string quartet*.

B241. Dettmer, Roger. "Premiere days for Ravinia fans." *Chicago's American* (July 8, 1968)

Review of the premiere of *Perspectives* op.199 on July 6th.

B242. ——. "Krenek: *They Knew What They Wanted*, Op.227; *Quintina*, Op.191." *Fanfare* 4:3 (January-February 1981): 133-134.

Record review of Orion ORS 80380.

B243. Deutsch, Otto Erich. "Der Wiener Schubert-Kongress." *Zeitschrift für Musikwissenschaft* 11 (1928/29): 238-240.

The Congress opened with Krenek's talk "Schubert und wir."

B244. "Deutschland nun auch in Amerika durch *Jonny spielt auf* blossgestellt!" *Zeitschrift für Musik* 96:3 (March 1929): 160-162.

The New York reception of the opera was not a success, just like the Paris reception.

B245. Dibelius, Christoph. "E. Krenek: *Reisebücher*." *Hi Fi Stereophonie* 8:3 (March 1969): 200.

Record review of the song cycle op.62 on Edition Rhodos ERS 1201-3.

B246. Dibelius, Ulrich. "Krenek hat sich verspätet." *Melos* 32:2 (February 1965): 51.

Review of the book *Komponist und Hörer* (K748).

B247. Dickinson, Peter. "Krenek's *Organ sonata*." *Musical Times* 104:1439 (January 1963): 54-55.

Analysis with performance notes of op.92.

B248. ——. "Krenek." *Musical Times* 104:1441 (March 1963): 199.

Review of the publications of *The ballad of the railroad* and *Basler Massarbeit*.

B249. ——. "Birthday canon." *Musical Times* 104:1445 (July 1963): 501.

Review of the publication of op.181.

B250. Diebold, Bernhard. "Singende Tantaliden." *Frankfurter Zeitung* (March 12, 1930)

Review of the Berlin performance of the opera *Leben des Orest* op.60. Krenek responds in "Der 'entlarvte' Orest" (K107).

   a. ——. In *Experiment Krolloper, 1927-1931*, von Hans Curjel. Studien zur Kunst des neunzehnten Jahrhunderts, Bd.7. (Münich: Prestel-Verlag, 1975): 282-284.

B251. Dierks, Donald. "UCSD composer presents inventive, interesting work." *San Diego Union* (January 20, 1968)

Review of the premiere of *Exercises of a late hour* op.200.

B252. Diether, Jack. "Korngold's *Much ado*." *American Record Guide* 26:1 (September 1959): 43-45.

Record review of *Three Merry marches* op.44 on Boston Records BST 1012.

B253. Diether, Jack. "Music of Ernst Krenek." *Musical America* 80:7 (June 1960): 37.

Review of a "Composers' Showcase" concert in the Circle in the Square on May 9th, during which *Hexahedron* op.167 was given its first American performance in a thorough revision conducted by the composer. The concert also included *Pentagram* op.163, *Sonata for violin, Sechs Vermessene* op.168, *Songs on texts by Franz Kafka* op.82, and *Sonata for viola* op.92, no.3. Both *Monologue* op.157 and *Sonatina for oboe* op.156 received their premiere performances.

B254. Dietrich, K. "Ueber Sinn und Zweck des Theaters (Nach Krenek, Hebbel und Schiller)." *Hessischer Kurier* (February 18, 1926)

A reaction to Krenek's "Ein Ideologe über das Theater" (K32). Krenek responded to Dietrich in his "Ueber Ziel und Zweck des Theaters" (K36).

B255. Diettrich, Eva. "Auf den Spuren zu Jonnys Erfolg." In *Ernst Krenek*, hrsg. von Otto Kolleritsch. (B328) Studien zur Wertungsforschung, Bd.15. (Wien: Universal Edition, 1982): 119-124.

An examination of the reception of *Jonny spielt auf* op.45 and its success.

B256. Ditsky, John. "Krenek: *Trio for Violin, Clarinet, and Piano* ..." *Fanfare* 6:2 (November-December 1982): 302-303.

Record review of op.108 on Crystal Records S 645.

B257. ———. "Krenek: *Kleine Blasmusik*, Op.70a; *Drei Lustige Märsche*, Op.44." *Fanfare* 1:4 (March-April 1978): 44-45.

Record review of Louisville Orchestra LS 756.

B258. Dobner, W. "Carinthischer Sommer; Eine Ernst Krenek-Woche als Höhepunkt." *Musica* 39:5 (1985): 469+

Review of the week-long Festival devoted to Krenek.

B259. Dömling, Wolfgang. "Ernst Krenek: *Horizons circled.*" *Melos/NZ* 1:5 (September-October 1975): 415.

Review of the book (K864).

B260. Doflein, Erich. "51. Deutsches Tonkünstlerfest vom 13.-18. Juni in Nürnberg." *Signale für die musikalische Welt* 79:27 (July 6, 1921): 699-703.

Review of the premiere of the *First string quartet* op.6.

B261. Dommett, Kenneth. "Hindemith: *Quartet for clarinet, violin, cello and piano.* Krenek: *Trio for violin, clarinet and piano.* Milhaud: *Suite for violin, clarinet and piano.*" *Hi-Fi News & Record Reviews* 23:7 (July 1978): 96.

Record review of op.108 on Supraphon 111 2147.

B262. Dow, William Bradford. "Structural implications of dynamics in *Flute pieces in nine phases.*" (Master's thesis: University of California San Diego, 1977) 67 pp.

A thorough analysis of the serialization of the dynamics of op.171.

B263. Downes, Edward. "Records: American." *New York Times* 107:36639 (May 18, 1958): 2:15.

Record review of *The bell tower* op.153 on University of Illinois CRS 5.

B264. Downes, Olin. "Music" *New York Times* 75:24871 (February 27, 1926): 12.

Review of the first American performance of the *Second concerto grosso* op.25.

B265. Downes, Olin. "European concert series given by Mrs. E.S. Coolidge
-- Krenek jazz opera." *New York Times* 77:25453 (October 2, 1927): 8:8.
Review of the premiere of the opera *Jonny spielt auf* op.45.

B266. ——. "The generation of Krenek." *New York Times* 78:25922 (January
13, 1929): 8:9.
Discussion of the opera *Jonny spielt auf* op.45 in anticipation of the first
American performance. Picture of Krenek by Shoemaker.

B267. ——. "*Jonny spielt auf* opera of the age." *New York Times* 78:25929
(January 20, 1929): 8:28.
Review of the first American performance of the opera op.45.

B268. ——. "Bruno Walter conducts Philharmonic-Symphony in new
German compositions by Krenek and Schmidt." *New York Times*
81:27040 (February 5, 1932): 24.
Review of the first American performance of the suite from *Der Triumph der
Empfindsamkeit* op.43a.

B269. ——. "A modern version of 'Poppea'." *New York Times* 87:29142
(November 7, 1937): 11:7.
Information about Monteverdi's opera in anticipation of its first American
performance in Krenek's version.

B270. ——. "17th century opus by Salzburg Guild." *New York Times* 87:29145
(November 10, 1937): 28.
Review of the first American performance of Krenek's version of
Monteverdi's *Poppea*.

B271. ——. "Elman is soloist at Philharmonic." *New York Times* 97:32815
(November 28, 1947): 37.
Review of the premiere of the *Fourth symphony* op.113.

B272. Draber, H. W. "Uraufführung des *Klavierkonzertes* von Ernst Krenek."
Musikblätter des Anbruch 6:1 (January 1924): 35.
Review of the premiere of op.18.

B273. "3 *Chöre nach Texten von Gottfried Keller*." *Anbruch* 14:12 (December
1932): 223.
Review of the premiere of the *Choruses for mixed voices* op.61.

B274. "3 Einakter." *Allgemeine Musikzeitung* 55 (April 27, 1928): 516.
Brief announcement of the forthcoming premiere of the three one-act operas
Der Diktator op.49, *Das geheime Königreich* op.50, and *Schwergewicht, oder Die
Ehre der Nation* op.55.

B275. Drew, David. "The Darmstadt Summer School of New Music, 1954."
Score 10 (December 1954): 77-81.
Includes a review of the first European performance of *Medea* op.129.

B276. ——. "Musical theater in the Weimar Republic." *Proceeding of the Royal
Musical Association* 88 (1961/62): 89-108.
Surveys musical theater in Germany from 1920-1929 by examining the
teachers and playwrights pointing out the impact of contemporary theater on
the composers Krenek, Paul Hindemith, and Kurt Weill and their theater
music. Krenek's opera *Jonny spielt auf* was the classic of the *Zeitoper* genera.

B277. Druckman, Jacob. *"Tonal counterpoint in the style of the eighteenth century.* By Ernst Krenek." *Juilliard Review* 6:3 (Fall 1959): 22.
Review of the text book (K632).

B278. dt. "Kreneks 6. *Streichquartett." Darmstädter Tagblatt* (January 20, 1953)
Review of the premiere of op.78.

B279. Duckles, Vincent. *"Johannes Ockeghem." Notes* 2d ser. 10:4 (Sept.1953): 622-623.
Review of the book (K616).

B280. "Due opere dell'ora presente." *Musica d'oggi* 9:5 (May 1927): 142-143.
Summarizes various reviews of the premiere of the opera *Jonny spielt auf* op.45.

B281. Dümling, Albrecht. "Ernst Krenek zum 80. Geburtstag; ein Komponist zwischen den Stilen." *Deutsches Allgemeines Sonntagsblatt* (Hamburg) (August 23, 1980)
Discusses Krenek as writer of his own texts and his various styles in celebration of his eightieth birthday. Picture.
a. ——. *Das Orchester* 28:11 (November 1980): 910-911.

B282. Durgin, Cyrus. "Boston Orchestra premieres Krenek and Hill concertos." *Musical Courier* 118:11 (December 1, 1938): 18.
Review of the first American performance of the *Second piano concerto* op.81.

B283. ——. "Burgin, Munch, Posselt appear with symphony." *Boston Globe* (December 12, 1953)
Review of a concert which included Krenek's edition of Mahler's *Tenth symphony* (W72) conducted by Richard Burgin.

B284. Duvenbeck, Gunter. "Nach dem Gesetz der Serie." *Bonner Rundschau* (January 7, 1970)
Review of the premiere of *Fünffache Verschränkung* op.205.

B285. Dv. *"Jonny spielt auf." Schweizerische Musikzeitung und Sängerblatt* 67:26 (November 12, 1927): 395-396.
Discusses the opera op.45 in anticipation of its Zurich production.

B286. ——. "Besprechungen." *Schweizerische Musikzeitung und Sängerblatt* 69:12 (June 15, 1929): 479-480.
Includes a brief review of the publication of the *Second piano sonata* op.59.

B287. ——. "Besprechungen: Ernst Krenek. *Reisebuch aus den österreichischen Alpen." Schweizerische Musikzeitung und Sängerblatt* 70:4 (February 15, 1930): 157.
Review of the publication of the song cycle op.62.

B288. ——. "Besprechungen: Ernst Krenek. *Die Nachtigall." Schweizerische Musikzeitung und Sängerblatt* 71:14/15 (August 1, 1931): 585.
Review of the publication of the song op.68.

B289. ——. "Ernst Krenek. *Kantate von der Vergänglichkeit des Irdischen." Schweizerische Musikzeitung* 72:21 (November 21, 1932): 660-661.
Review of the publication of op.72.

B290. Dv. "Besprechungen." *Schweizerische Musikzeitung und Sängerblatt* 74:3 (February 1, 1934): 104-105.

A brief description of the opera *Karl V.* op.73 which Krenek had just finished.

B291. Dwyer, John. "The Gallery: Foss, UB artists offer innovations on far-out series." *Buffalo Evening News* (November 6, 1967): IV:54.

Review of the premiere of *Five pieces for trombone* op.198.

B292. E. "Ernst Kreneks *Tarquin.*" *Melos* 17:9 (September 1950): 262.

Review of the German premiere of the opera. Picture, p.261.

B293. ——. "Erstaufführung von Kreneks 4. Klavierkonzert." *Melos* 18:11 (November 1951): 330.

Review of the premiere of the *Fourth piano concerto* op.123. Also mentions that the month of October saw the premieres of *Double concerto* op.124 in Donaueschingen and the *Sixth piano sonata* op.128.

B294. ——. "Ein neues Klavierkonzert von Krenek." *Das Musikleben* 4:12 (December 1951): 357.

Review of the premiere of the *Fourth piano concerto* op.123.

B295. ——. "Kreneks neues Violinkonzert." *Melos* 22:4 (April 1955): 114.

Review of the premiere of the *Second violin concerto* op.140.

B296. ——. "Musikdrama um *Karl V.*" *Melos* 25:9 (Sept.1958): 294-295.

Review of the premiere of the new edition of the opera op.73 in Düsseldorf. Picture.

B297. ——. "Ernst Kreneks Oper *Der Glockenturm.*" *Melos* 26:1 (January 1959): 15-16.

Review of the first performance of the German translation of op.153.

B298. E.A.S. "Ernst Krenek: *Sonate für Violine solo, op.33.*" *Melos* 33:1 (January 1966): 34.

Review of the publication.

B299. E.F. "Europa ist seine Heimat." *Die Welt* (October 17?, 1951)

Interview in which Krenek describes his current activities.

B300. E.H. "Ergänzung von Schuberts unvollendeter Sonate C dur von Ernst Krenek." *Musikblätter des Anbruch* 5:9 (November 1923): 276-277.

Review of the publication of Schubert's *Piano sonata D.840* (W65) completed by Krenek.

B301. E.L. "Ornest, soprano, heard in recital." *New York Times* 99:33592 (January 15, 1950): 18.

Review of the first New York performance of *Die Nachtigall* op.68.

B302. E.Q. "Krenek, Ernst, *Proprium Missae: Dom.III i Quadr..*" *Musik und Alter* (May/June 1957): 191.

Review of the publication of the score of op.89.

B303. Eaton, Quaintance. "*The bell tower.*" In her *Opera Production; A Handbook.* (Minneapolis: University of Minnesota Press, 1961): 168-169.

Performance information and synopsis of the opera op.153.

B304. ——. *"Dark waters."* In her *Opera Production II; A Handbook.* (Minneapolis: University of Minnesota Press, 1974): 264-265. Performance information and synopsis of the opera op.125.

B305. ——. *"What price confidence."* In her *Opera Production II; A Handbook.* (Minneapolis: University of Minnesota Press, 1974): 332-333. Performance information and synopsis of the opera op.111.

B306. Eberle, Gottfried. "Klangkomplex, Trope, Reihe; Materialien zu einer vergleichenden Theorie der Zwölftonkomposition." *Musica* 34:2 (March-April 1980): 139-144.

The description in the article on twelve-tone technique in the encyclopedia *Musik in Geschichte und Gegenwart* is too narrow in the light of actual practices by Arnold Schoenberg, Alban Berg, and Krenek which actually reflect the theories proposed by Nicolas Obuchow and Joseph Matthias Hauer.

B307. ——. "Concert de Moscou." *Neue Zeitschrift für Musik* 147:10 (October 1986): 62.

Record review of Glenn Gould's May 12, 1957 performance of two movements from the *Third piano sonata* op.92, no.4 on Le Chant du Monde LDX 78799.

B308. Effenberger, E. "Krenek lässt den Engel aus der Flasche." *Salzburger Nachrichten* (March 9, 1974)

Review of the premiere of *Flaschenpost vom Paradies* op.217 on Austrian Television. It was awarded the 1974 Salzburger Fernsehopernpreis.

B309. Ehinger, Hans. *"Pallas Athene weint."* *Schweizerische Musikzeitung* 95:12 (December 1, 1955): 504-505.

Review of the premiere of the opera op.144.

B310. Eimert, Herbert. "Kreneks 'Tarquin'-Uraufführung." *Kölnische Rundschau* (July 18, 1950)

Review of the first European performance of *Tarquin* op.90.

B311. Einge, Hans. *"Jedermann* für jerdermann." *Die Presse* (Vienna) (November 25, 1961)

Review of the film and Krenek's incidental music (op.178).

B312. Einstein, Alfred. "Donaueschingen 1926." *Zeitschrift für Musik* 93:9 (September 1926): 495-497.

Review of the festival which included the premiere *Drei lustige Märsche* op.44.

B313. ——. "Krenek's new opera." *New York Times* 79:26321 (February 16, 1930): 9:8.

Review of the premiere of *Leben des Orest* op.60.

B314. ——. "L'opera tedesca d'oggi." *La rassegna musicale* 5 (1932): 26-37.

Includes a discussion of Krenek's opera *Jonny spielt auf* op.45.

B315. Eisler, Hans. "Eine italienische Reise und ihre Folgen." In his *Musik und Politik, 1: Schriften 1924-1948,* hrsg. von Günter Mayer. (München: Rogner & Bernhard, 1973): 194-197.

A reaction to Krenek's article "Musikkongress in Florenz" (K44) discussing the Maggio musicale florentino festival April 30-May 4, 1933. Eisler objects to many of Krenek's political characterizations.

B316. "Eleanor Steber and Dimitri Mitropoulos." *Musical Courier* 141:9 (May 1, 1950): 20.

Review of the premiere of the song cycle *Ballad of the railroads* op.98.

B317. Ellinwood, Leonard. "*Hamline studies in musicology*, vol.II." *Notes* 2d ser. 4:4 (September 1947): 465-466.

Review of the second volume edited by Krenek (K559).

B318. Ellis, Stephen W. "Interaccodinotesta." *Fanfare* 4:2 (November-December 1980): 218-219.

Record review of the Canadian recording Melbourne Records SMLP 4034 which includes *Acco-music* op.225.

B319. Engel, Carl. "Views and reviews." *Musical Quarterly* 9:2 (April 1923): 287-302.

Includes a negative review of the publication of the *First piano sonata* op.2 and mentions the good review of his *First string quartet* op.6 by Torbe (B1368).

B320. Engländer, Richard. "Ernst Krenek op.67 *Durch die Nacht*." *Anbruch* 13:4 (May 1931): 99.

Review of the premiere of the songs.

B321. ——. "Ernst Krenek: *Gesänge des späten Jahres*, op.71." *Anbruch* 14:4/5 (April-May 1932): 85.

Review of the premiere of the song cycle op.71 in Dresden.

B322. ——. "Ernst Krenek: *Selbstdarstellung*." *Svensk tidskrift för Musikforskning* 32 (1950): 222-223.

Review in Swedish of Krenek's autobiography (K569).

B323. Engle, Susan Stancil.
"A Harmonic analysis and comparison of selected twelve-tone compositions of Krenek and Cordero". (Master's thesis: Indiana University, 1969) 145 pp.

A comparison of twelve-tone works by Krenek and his student Roque Cordero.

B324. Erickson, Robert. "Krenek's later music." *Music Review* 9 (1948): 29-44.

Surveys the music from 1930 to 1947, with emphasis on the *Sixth string quartet* op.78, the *Twelve variations in three movements for piano* op.79, *La corona* op.91, *Lamentatio Jeremiae prophetae* op.93, and the *Seventh string quartet* op.96.

B325. ——. "Kreneks amerikanische Texte." *Schweizerische Musikzeitung* 93:3 (March 1, 1953): 104-108.

Discusses Krenek's American vocal works. German translation by Willi Reich.

B326. Ericson, Raymond A. "Hauer, Johann Matthias: *Hölderlin Lieder*, Op.32. Krenek, Ernst: *Fiedellieder*, Op.64. Kodaly, Zoltan: *Sappho's Love Song at Night* and *The Forest*, Op.9." *Musical America* 73:14 (November 15, 1953): 18.

Record review of New Records NRLP 405.

B327. "Ernst Krenek." *Musica* 34:2 (March-April 1980): 116-117.

Chronological table of his life. Picture.

B328. *Ernst Krenek,* hrsg. von Otto Kolleritsch. Studien zur *Ernst Krenek,* hrsg. von Otto Kolleritsch. Studien zur Wertungsforschung, Bd.15. (Wien: Universal Edition, 1982)

A collection of essays about the composer: *Der verletzliche Komponist* by Claudia Maurer Zenck (B1507), *Ueber Ernst Kreneks musikästhetische Vorstellungen* by Otto Kolleritsch (B679), *Ernst Krenek und das Problem des musikalischen Sprachwechsels* by Carl Dahlhaus (B219), *Geschichtsphilosophische Motive im Musikdenken Kreneks* by Reimar Klein (B651), *Krenek as an essayist* by John L. Stewart (B1289), *Wie schlafende Uhren blicken uns des Lebens Bilder an* by Wendelin Schmidt-Dengler (B1150), *Die Rezeption der Antike in Kreneks Operntexten* by Roswitha Vera Karpf (B635), *Einzelheiten zur Musik des jungen Krenek* by Rudolf Stephan (B1282), *Auf den Spuren zu Jonnys Erfolg* by Eva Diettrich (B255), *Subjekt - Objekt/Erläuterungen zur Dramaturgie epischen in "Karl V"* von Ernst Krenek by Ivanka Stoieanova (B1293), *Kreneks drei Einakter von 1928* by Wolfgang Ruf (B1110), *Ernst Kreneks Liederzyklus "Reisebuch aus den österreichischen Alpen"* by Karin Marsoner (B829), *Krenek und Ockeghem* by Wolf Frobenius (B396), *Bruch und Summe* by Claudia Maurer Zenck (B1506), *wärs ein neuer Anfang* by Rainer Wehinger (B1435), *Bemerkungen zu einigen späteren Werken Ernst Kreneks* by Gösta Neuwirth (B903), and *Krenek als Problem der Avantgarde* by Martin Zenck (B1518), *See:* B62, B179, B689, B828, B1186

B329. "Ernst Krenek: *Ballad of the railroads.*" *Music News* 42:7 (July 1950): 22.

Excerpts from reviews of the premiere of the song cycle op.98 by Virgil Thomson (B1352) and Ross Parmenter (B957).

B330. "Ernst Krenek commissioned to write opera." *Musical Leader* 82:2 (February 1950): 16.

Dimitri Mitropoulos gave $2,000 to the Chicago Musical College to commission a tv opera from Krenek, who will be on leave second semester.

B331. "Ernst Krenek conducts his own work." *Los Angeles Times* 95 (June 20, 1976): Calender:75.

Announcement of the premiere of *Von vorn herein* op.219. Picture.

B332. "Ernst Krenek conducts own musical score." *Ann Arbor* (August 2, 1939)

Review of the first performance of *Symphonic piece for string orchestra* op.86 at the University of Michigan.

B333. "Ernst Krenek, Daten und Fakten." *Oesterreichische Musikzeitschrift* 35:9 (September 1980): 428-429.

A chronology of Krenek's life and works.

B334. "Ernst Krenek erhielt den Bach-Preis." *Musica* 20:6 (November-December 1966): 289-290.

Discusses Krenek's receipt of the Hamburg Bach Preis.

B335. "Ernst Krenek honored in his 60th year." *The World of Music* 2:3 (June 1960): 56.

Krenek honors include election to membership in the U.S. National Institute of Arts and Letters and honorary membership in the Austrian State Academy of Music in Vienna. The premiere of *Ninephase piece for flute* op.171 will be performed by Severino Gazzelloni and Piero Scarpino at the Venice Festival in September. He will conduct *A question of time* op.170 at the

Norddeutscher Rundfunk in Hamburg later in September. The *Cello concerto* op.133 was performed by Ludwig Hoelscher and the Dresden Philharmonic in March. The Süddeutscher Rundfunk performed *Six Motets on texts by Franz Kafka* op.169 in the series "Music of Our Time."

B336. "Ernst Krenek: II. Sinfonie, op.12." *Allgemeine Musikzeitung* 50:22/23 (June 8, 1923): 381-383.

Detailed analysis in the series "Analysen der zur Aufführung kommenden Orchesterwerke." Picture.

B337. "Ernst Krenek ist nach Wien übersiedelt." *Wiener Allgemeine Zeitung* (October 25, 1928)

An interview.

B338. "Ernst Krenek of Vassar faculty is famed as composer, pianist, conductor." *Hudson Valley Courier* (November 23, 1941): 13.

General information about Krenek as he began teaching at Vassar College. Picture.

B339. "Ernst Krenek quits as Dean at Hamline." *Minneapolis Sunday Tribune* (January 4, 1948)

Announces Krenek's resignation and his move to Los Angeles.

B340. "Ernst Krenek wurde 60 Jahre alt." *Kirchenchor* 20:5 (September-October 1960): 77.

Surveys Krenek's sacred music in an appreciation of his sixtieth birthday.

B341. Evans, Edwin. "Krenek, Ernst." In *Cobbett's Cyclopedic Survey of Chamber Music*, edited by Walter Willson Cobbett. 2d ed. Vol.2. (London: Oxford University Press, 1963): 76-79.

A brief biography up to the composition of the opera *Jonny spielt auf* in 1927, and a detailed analysis of the *First string quartet* op.6 and *Third string quartet* op.20.

B342. Evett, Rober. "New music in New York." *New Republic* 129:15 (November 9, 1953): 20.

Review of the premiere of the *Two-piano concerto* op.127.

B343. Ewen, David. "Krenek, Ernst." In his *American Composers; a Biographical Dictionary.* (New York: G. P. Putnam's Sons, 1982): 389-393.

A biography and discussion of his works to 1978.

B344. ——. "Ernst Krenek." In his *The Book of Modern Composers*. (New York: Alfred A. Knoff, 1942): 351-353, 535-537.

A brief biographical essay, portrait, and list of works.

B345. ——. "Ernst Krenek." In his *The Complete Book of 20th Century Music*. New & rev.ed. (Englewood Cliffs, NJ: Prentice Hall, 1959): 210-213.

A brief biographical essay with an examination of *Jonny spielt auf* op.45, the *Third piano concerto* op.107, the *Fourth symphony* op.113, and the *Fifth symphony* op.119.

   a. ——. In his *The Complete Book of 20th Century Music*. New & rev.ed. (Englewood Cliffs, NJ: Prentice Hall, reissued 1963): 210-213.

B346. Ewen, David. "Ernst Krenek." In his *The World of Twentieth-Century Music.* (Englewood Cliffs: Prentice Hall, 1968): 430-433.

A brief biography and examination of *Jonny spielt auf* op.45, *Third piano concerto* op.107, *Fourth symphony* op.113, *Fifth symphony* op.119, and *Fibonacci mobile,* op.187.

B347. ———. "Ernst Krenek." In his *Composers Since 1900.* (New York: H.W. Wilson Co., 1969): 322-325.

Biographical essay surveying his life to the mid-1960s.

B348. ———. *"Jonny spielt auf."* In his *The New Encyclopedia of the Opera.* (New York: Hill and Wang, 1971): 333-334.

A synopsis of the opera op.45.

B349. F.B. "Chamber music." *Musical Times* 78:1136 (October 1937): 887-888.

Review of the publication of the *String quartet* op.78.

B350. ———. "New music." *Musical Times* 83:1193 (July 1942): 208-209.

Review of the publication of the *Cello suite* op.84.

B351. Felber, Erwin. "Le festival de Donau-Eschingen." *La revue musicale* 7:11 (October 1926): 255-256.

Includes a brief review of *Les trois marches pour musique militaire* op.44 noting allusions in the music to Igor Stravinsky, Gustav Mahler, and jazz.

B352. ———. "Musikdramatische Uraufführungen in Venedig." *Neue Freie Presse* (Vienna) Nr.25151 (September 19, 1934)

Review of the premiere of the opera *Cefalo e Procri* op.77.

B353. Feldens, Fr. "Zu den Einaktern von Krenek, Hindemith, Milhaud und Weill." *Der Scheinwerfer* (Essen) 2:18/19 (June 1929): 3-6.

Compares the three one-act operas of Krenek (*Der Diktator* op.49, *Das geheime Königreich* op.50, and *Schwergewicht* op.55) with those of Paul Hindemith, Darius Milhaud, and Kurt Weill.

B354. Ferguson, Donald W. "Krenek." In his *Masterworks of the Orchestral Repertoire.* (Minneapolis: University of Minnesota Press, 1954): 305-310.

Discusses the *Second symphony* op.12, the orchestral variations *I Wonder as I wander* op.94, and the *Third piano concerto* op.107. Primarily extracted from the notes prepared for the program books of the Minneapolis Symphony Orchestra.

B355. "Festival will honor composer Ernst Krenek." *Minneapolis Sunday Tribune* (April 11, 1965)

Discusses the forthcoming four-day festival sponsored by the Civic Orchestra of Minneapolis and the first American performances of *Stücke* op.31 and the *Fourth piano concerto* op.123.

B356. "Die Festspielstadt 1980; Die Musik ist der Urgrund des Gedankens." *Salzburger Nachrichten* (August 23, 1980): 5.

Interview on Krenek's eightieth birthday.

B357. Fiechtner, Helmut A. "Ernst Krenek, Persönlichkeit und Werk." *Oesterreichische Musikzeitschrift* 2:11/12 (November-December 1947): 291-294.

A survey of his life with specific mention of his recent works up to opus 110.

B358. Fiechtner, Helmut A. "Authentisches von und über Ernst Krenek." *Oesterreichische Musikzeitschrift* 7:11/12 (November-December 1952): 342-346.

Includes excerpts from Krenek's *Selbstdarstellung* (K569) and "Konservativ und Radikal" (K250), and a catalog of his compositions up through 1952.

B359. ——. "Ernst Krenek." *Musica* 7:1 (January 1953): 7-10.

Biographical essay, with a catalog of works written after his arrival in America, op.83-132.

B360. ——. "Krenek dirigiert und spricht." *Melos* 22:1 (January 1955): 27-28.

Krenek returned to Vienna, and there were many performances of his music: a concert by the Wiener Symphoniker in the Vienna Sendesaal der Ravag included the *Second piano concerto* op.81, with Arno Erfurth, piano, and *Sinfonietta a Brasileira* op.131; the concert in the Vienna Konzerthaus Mozartsaal consisted on the *Symphonic elegy* op.105, the *Harp concerto* op.126, with Emmy Hürlimann, harp, and *Symphony Pallas Athene* op.137, *Fifth symphony* op.119, and *Seventh string quartet* op.96. Universal Edition issued a new edition of the opera *Karl V.* op.73, and Krenek gave a lecture "Sinn und Unsinn in der modernen Musik" in the Oesterreichischen Kulturvereinigung.

B361. ——. "Oesterreich: Kleines Musikfest." *Musica* 14:5 (May 1960): 301-302.

Review of the first Euopean performance of the *Third piano concerto* op.107.

B362. ——. "Ausgerechnet -- und gewonnen." *Musica* 17:1 (1963): 25-26.

Review of the premiere of the television opera *Ausgerechnet und verspielt* op.179.

B363. ——. "Eine Krenek-Woche." *Musica* 18:6 (1964): 317-318.

During a week's celebration in Vienna, Krenek gave a lecture "Die dunklen Wasser der schönen blauen Donau" concerning new music in Vienna and his music since 1957, a commentary to the recording of *Jonny spielt auf* op.45 on Amadeo AVRS 5038 entitled "Jonny aus einiger Distanz," and conducted a concert which included his *Poppea* suite op.80b, the *Second violin concerto* op.140, and *Quaestio temporis* op.170.

B364. ——. "Ernst Krenek." *Oesterreichische Musikzeitschrift* 19:1 (January 1964): 29-30.

Surveys Krenek's importance to music on the occassion of his receipt of the Vienna State Prize for Music.

B365. Finch, A. E. "Ernst Krenek." (Thesis, 1969?) 46 pp.

Detailed survey of his works period by period; concludes that while he has written in many styles, there was only one principal change to twelve-tone technique.

B366. Fisher, Marjory M. "Composer Ernst Krenek is introduced by Pro Musica." *San Francisco News* (January 12, 1938)

Review of lecture entitled "Common ideology of classical and modern music" and a piano recital in the Fairmont Hotel Red Room on January 11 consisting of *Two suites* op.26, *Five pieces* op.39, and *Variations* op.81 [sic op.79] "completed last year and never before played by him to any audience."

B367. Flanagan, William. "Ernst Krenek: *George Washington variations*." *Notes* 2d ser. 13:4 (Sept.1956): 706.

Review of the publication of op.120.

B368. ——. "Goodman: *Quintet for Wind Instruments.* Piston: *Three Pieces for Flute, Clarinet, and Bassoon.* Krenek: *Pentagram for Winds.*" *Hi Fi/Stereo Review* 17:6 (December 1966): 88.

Record review of op.163 on Lyrichord LLST 7158 and Lyrichord LL 158.

B369. Fleischer, H. "Ernst Krenek, *Von neuer Musik.*" *La Rassegna Musicale* 10:9/10 (1937): 353-354.

Review of the book *Ueber neue Musik* (K397).

B370. Fleischmann, Hugo R. "The first jazz opera and operetta." *The Chesterian* 9:69 (March 1928): 152-155.

Discussion of the jazz elements of the opera *Jonny spielt auf* op.45.

B371. Fleming, Shirley. "Hanover, N.H.: Webern, Krenek & a new violin." *High Fidelity/Musical America* 18:10 (October 1968): MA23, MA31.

Review of the American premiere of the opera *What price confidence* op.111 with Krenek narrating. Picture.

B372. ——. "The Thouvenel String Quartet." *High Fidelity/Musical America* 31:3 (March 1981): MA6-7.

Interview with the ensemble centered on their relationship with Krenek and their performances of his eight string quartets.

B373. Flich, Ludwig. "Neue Musik in Ossiach." *Oesterreichische Musikzeitschrift* 34:9 (September 1979): 440.

Review of the premiere of the *Concerto for organ and string orchestra* op.230.

B374. Flotzinger, Rudolf. "Apropos Ernst Krenek." *Oesterreichische Musikzeitschrift* 35:9 (September 1980): 425-427.

Briefly surveys his life and artistic development. The inconsistencies in his music, for which his critics reproach him, are rooted in the contradictions of his time and therefore actually represent an expression of a higher consistency.

B375. "For piano solo." *Musical Courier* 141:8 (April 15, 1950): 31.

Review of the publication of the *Fourth piano sonata* op.114.

B376. Forchert, Arno. "Zillig, *Lieder des Abschieds*; Krenek, *Zwei geistliche Gesänge.*" *Fono Forum* 10:1 (January 15, 1965): 26.

Record review of op.132 on Bärenreiter Musicaphon 30 L 1534.

B377. "Fort-holder." *Time* 32:20 (November 14, 1938): 50-51.

Review of the first American performance of the *Second piano concerto* op.81. Picture.

B378. Forte, Alan. "*Perspectives of new music,* vol.1, no.1." *Journal of the American Musicological Society* 17:1 (September 1964): 110-113.

Review of the first issue of the journal which includes Krenek's "Tradition in perspective" (K771). Forte notes that "the article presents a curious oscillation between a view of history from the standpoint of the composer *qua* historian and from the standpoint of the historian *qua* composer... In the end, however, the former view prevails."

B379. Fox, Charles Warren. "Guide to new books on music." *Saturday Review* 29:4 (January 26, 1946): 14-15.

An annotated selection of the year's books on music, including *Hamline Studies in musicology* volume one edited by Krenek (K550).

B380. Francis, William M. "Krenek's 12-tone pop-art 'Result'." *Christian Science Monitor* 62:198 (July 20, 1970): 4.

Review of the premiere of *That's the result, or, When Sardakai goes traveling* op.206. Picture: scene.

B381. Frank, Peter. "Masterpieces of Twentieth Century Music, Vol.3." *Fanfare* 3:4 (March–April 1980): 184-188.

Record review of Musical Heritage Society MHS 3874 which includes the *Fourth piano sonata* op.114.

B382. Frankenstein, Alfred. "Schoenberg: *Erwartung,* Op.17. Krenek: *Symphonic Elegy."* *High Fidelity* 2:2 (September–October 1952): 57.

Record review of op.105 on Columbia ML 4524.

B383. ——. "University of Illinois Festival of Contemporary Music, 1957." *High Fidelity* 8:9 (Sept.1958): 78.

Record review of the opera *The bell tower* op.153 on University of Illinois CRS 5.

B384. ——. "Krenek, Ernst. *Sestina for Voice and Instrumental Ensemble; Lamentatio Jeremiae Prophetae."* *High Fidelity* 9:1 (January 1959): 55.

Record review of op.161 and op.93 on Epic LC 3509.

a. ——. *High Fidelity Annual* 5 (1959): 98.

B385. ——. "Schoenberg, Arnold: *Piano Pieces,* Op.11. Berg: *Sonata for Piano,* Op.1. Krenek: *Sonata for Piano, No.3,* Op.93." *High Fidelity* 9:9 (April 1959): 66, 68.

Record review of Columbia ML 5336.

a. ——. *High Fidelity Annual* 5 (1959): 160-161.

B386. ——. "Gripping Cantata By Ernst Krenek." *San Francisco Chronicle* (May 26, 1961)

A review of the first American performance of *La Corona* op.91. The composer also played *Sechs Vermessene* op.168 which had been performed at the Stratford Music Festival in Ontario "last summer."

B387. ——. "New S.F. ballet a war of cards." *San Francisco Chronicle* (April 19, 1962)

Review of the premiere of *Jest of cards* op.162a.

B388. ——. "Phillip Rehfeldt: *New Music for Solo Clarinet."* *High Fidelity* 16:2 (February 1966): 100-101.

Record review of *Monologue* op.157 on Advance Recordings FGR 4.

B389. ——. "Goodman: *Quintet for Wind Instruments.* Piston: *Three Pieces for Flute, Clarinet, and Bassoon.* Krenek: *Pentagram for Winds."* *High Fidelity* 16:10 (October 1966): 140.

Record review of op.163 on Lyrichord LLST 7158 and Lyrichord LL 158.

a. "Goodman, Joseph. *Quintet for Wind Instruments.* Piston: *Three Pieces for Flute, Clarinet, and Bassoon.* Krenek: *Pentagram for Winds."* *High Fidelity Annual* 12 (1967): 177.

B390. **Frankfurter, Johannes.** "*Orpheus und Eurydike* im szenischen Urwald." *Neue Zeit* (October 23, 1973): 13.

Review of a performance of the opera op.21 in Graz.

B391. **Freeman, John W.** "Dagli stati uniti." *Nuova rivista musicale italiana* 9:4 (October-December 1975): 645-647.

Includes a brief announcement of the Portland production of *Leben des Orest* op.60.

B392. **French, Richard F.** "Current chronicle: New York." *Musical Quarterly* 48:3 (July 1962): 387-392.

Review of a Concert of New Music commissioned by the Fromm Foundation which opened with the first American performance of *Quaestio temporis* op.170. "Krenek predetermines certain elements of the composition ... [and] says, in effect: all music accepts certain limitations and produces certain surprises... The first surprise is that certain aspects of the works should make themselves so accessible... The second surprise is that the choice and combination of instrumental timbres - ... not serially predetermined - should in turn produce no surprises."

B393. **Fricke, Florian.** "Eine missglückte Uraufführung." *Süddeutsche Zeitung* (September 8, 1967)

Review of the premiere broadcast of the television opera *Der Zauberspiegel* op.192.

B394. **Fried, Alexander.** "'Card' ballet a grand slam." *San Francisco Examiner* (April 18, 1962)

Review of the premiere of *Jest of cards* op.162a.

B395. ———. "Concert of fine new music." *San Francisco Examiner* (April 5, 1965)

Review of the first American performance of *Six Motets on words by Franz Kafka* op.169.

B396. **Frobenius, Wolf.** "Krenek und Ockeghem." In *Ernst Krenek*, hrsg. von Otto Kolleritsch. (B328) Studien zur Wertungsforschung, Bd.15. (Wien: Universal Edition, 1982): 153-173.

An discussion of the influences of Johannes Ockeghem's compositional techniques on Krenek's style with a detailed examination of *Lamentatio Jeremiae prophetae* op.93, including Krenek's use of the rotation on the twelve-tone row.

B397. **Fuhrmann, Peter.** "Neue Musik beim alten Festspiel." *Neue Musikzeitung* 32:5 (October-November 1983): 6.

Review of the premiere of the *Cello concerto* op.236.

B398. **Fussan, Werner.** "Ernst Krenek, *Zwölfton-Kontrapunkt-Studien.*" *Musikleben* 6:1 (January 1953): 31.

Review of the German translation of *Studies in counterpoint* (K496).

B399. **G.** "Krenek-Uraufführung." *Süddeutsche Zeitung* (May 18, 1974)

Review of the premiere of *Momenta vitae* op.215.

a. ———. *Das Orchester* 22:7/8 (July-August 1974): 467-468.

B400. **G.A.** "*Studies in counterpoint.* By Ernst Krenek." *Musical Times* 81:1171 (September 1940): 373.

Review of the book (K496).

B401. ghjk. "Ernst Krenek: *Pallas Athene weint.*" *Der Opernfreund* 2:9 (May 1, 1957): 9-10.

Discussion of the opera op.144, its themes, and structure in the series "Die Oper unseres Jahrhunderts, 3." Picture on cover.

B402. G.I. "Konzert mit Werken von Ernst Krenek." *Darmstädter Tagblatt* (November 28, 1951)

Review of a performance of *Symphonische Elegie* op.105, *Fourth piano concerto* op.123 played by Miriam Molin, *Fifth symphony* op.119, and *I wonder as I wonder* op.94 all conducted by the composer.

B403. G.M.W. "*Exploring music,* by Ernst Krenek." *Recorded Sound* no.26 (April 1967): 196.

Review of the book of essays (K817).

B404. g.r. "Der andere Mund." *Musica* 28:6 (1974): 557-558.

Review of a performance of *Spätlese* op.218 in Berlin by Dietrich Fischer-Dieskau and the composer reprinted from the *Frankfurter Allgemeine Zeitung.* Comments on the "old piano-player's" poor technique. See Krenek's "Offener Brief" (K869).

B405. Gábor, György. "Ernst Krenek szeriális versei." *Muzsika* 11:5 (May 1968): 22-24.

Discussion of the serial works for voice and instruments *Sestina* op.161 and *Quintina* op.191. Picture.

B406. Gagel, Walter. "Karl V. - Kaiser zwischen den Zeiten." *Musik und Szene; Theaterzeitschrift der Deutschen Oper am Rhein* 2:13 (1957/58): 151-155.

The place of the Emperor in history and Krenek's opera op.73.

B407. Gagnard, Frank. "Symphony pumps the organ with variety." *Lagniappe* (November 2, 1984): 11.

Review of the first American performance of the *Organ concerto* by Martin Haselbock with the New Orleans Symphony.

B408. Gann, Kyle. "Krenek: *String Quartet No.5.*" *Fanfare* 9:2 (November-December 1985): 188.

Record review of op.65 on Composers Recordings CRI SD 522.

B409. Ganz, Rudolph. "Ernst Krenek." In his *Rudolf Ganz Evaluates Modern Piano Music; A Guide for Amateur and Student.* (Evanston: The Instrumentalist Co., 1968): 23.

Brief comments about the *Third piano sinata* op.92, no.4, *Fourth piano sonata* op.114, *George Washington variations* op.120, *Echoes from Austria* op.166, and *Sechs Vermessene* op.168.

B410. Gavazzeni, Gianandrea. "Lettera da Venezia: Il III Festival di Musica." *La rassegna musicale* 7 (1934): 371-377.

Includes a brief review of the opera *Cefalo e Procri* op.77.

B411. Genêt. "Letter from Venice." *New Yorker* 26:31 (September 23, 1950): 59-66.

Review of a performance of the *Fifth symphony* op.119 at the Festival of Contemporary Music.

B412. Georg, Manfred. "Heidelberger Festspiele." *Neue Freie Presse* (Vienna) (August 10, 1926)

Review of the premiere of the incidental music to *Ein Sommernachtstraum* op.46.

B413. George, Collins. "Meadow Brook Festival: A distinctive sound." *Detroit Free Press* (August 14, 1967)

Review of the premiere of *Horizon circled* op.196.

a. "Premieres." *BMI, the Many Worlds of Music* (November 1967): 17. Excerpts. Picture.

B414. ger. "Ernst Krenek: *Zwölf Variationen in drei Sätzen, op.79.*" *Melos* 32:7/8 (July-August 1965): 278.

Review of the publication.

B415. Gerbracht, Wolfram. "Des Teufels General singt Arien." *Die Welt* no.164 (July 17, 1950)

Review of the first German performance of the chamber opera *Tarquin* op.90.

B416. Gerbracht, Wolfram. "Ernst Krenek: *Tarquin.*" *Musica* 4:10 (October 1950): 393-394.

Review of the German premiere of the opera in Cologne. Picture.

B417. Gervink, Manuel. *Die Symphonie in Deutschland und Oesterreich in der Zeit zwischen den beiden Weltkriegen.* Kölner Beiträge zur Musikforschung, Bd.140. (Regensburg: Gustav Bosse Verlag, 1984) 313 pp.

An extensive survey of German and Austrian symphonic music with analysis of specific works. Discusses Krenek's *First symphony* op.7, *Symphonische Musik* op.11, *Second symphony* op.12, *Third symphony* op.16, *Symphony for band* op.34, *Kleine Symphonie* op.58, and *Symphonisches Stück* op.86. (pp.113-128 & 246-258).

B418. "Gespräch mit Krenek." *Leipziger Abendpost* (January 14, 1930)

An interview.

B419. Gieseler, Walter. "Neue Partituren von 1967 bis 1978." *Musica* 34:2 (March-April 1980): 181-183.

Includes a review of the publication of the orchestral score of *Horizont umkreist* op.196.

B420. ——. "Was an der Zeit ist ..." *Musica* 34:2 (March-April 1980): 127-131.

While still remaining independent, Krenek's thinking about music has been influenced by the ideas of Arnold Schoenberg, Karl Kraus, and Theodor Wiesengrund Adorno.

B421. Gilman, Lawrence. "*Jonny* über alles." *New York Herald Tribune* (January 13, 1929)

Discusses the opera in anticipation of the first American performance.

B422. ——. "Music." *New York Herald Tribune* (January 20, 1929)

Review of the first American performance of the opera *Jonny spielt auf* op.45.

B423. Ginzburg, Simon. "Ernst Krenek biograficheskaia notiz." *Novaia muzyka* (Leningrad) 1:2 (1927): 5-7.

Brief survey in Russian of the published compositions, including *Jonny spielt auf*. Picture.

B424. Glebov, Igor. "Pryzhok cherez ten'." *Novaia muzyka* (Leningrad) 1:2 (1927): 14-22.

Detailed discussion in Russian of the opera *Der Sprung über den Schatten* op.17.

B425. "Glenn Gould's other 'E'." *Saturday Review* 42:9 (February 28, 1959): 50.

Record review of the *Third piano sonata* op.92, no.4 on Columbia ML 5336.

B426. "Glosse: Künstlerische Reifeprüfung." *Neue Zeitschrift für Musik* 144:6 (June 1983): 27-28.

Facsimilie of a letter from Krenek to Lorin Maazel expressing outrage at being asked to submit an opera for a contest sponsored by the Vienna Staatsoper. The letter is used as the basis of a satirical dialogue between a young composer and an opera director discussing the problems of securing performances of contemporary music.

B427. Goebel, Walter F. "Neue Musik bei den Berliner Festwochen." *Oesterreichische Musikzeitschrift* 14:11 (November 1959): 481-483.

Review of the eight premieres presented during the festival, including *Motetten nach Texten von Franz Kafka* op.169.

B428. Göhler, G. "Dresden." *Zeitschrift für Musik* 99:5 (May 1932): 433-434.

Review of the premiere of the song cycle *Gesäng des späten Jahres* op.71.

B429. Goertz, Harald. "Es wuerde mich nicht interessieren, ein klassisches Drama als Oper aufzumöbeln." *Oper 1980; Jahrbuch der Zeitschrift Opernwelt* 21 (1980): 99-100.

Interview with Krenek on his eightieth birthday covering the opera *Karl V.* op.73, film and television opera, and the writing of his own librettos.

B430. ——. "Salzburger Festspiele: Bodengewinne Neuer Musik." *Musica* 37:5 (September-October 1983): 432-433.

Review of the premieres of the *Second cello concerto* op.236 and *Organ concerto* op.235.

B431. Goldberg, Albert. "Young pianist opens debut season at Ebell." *Los Angeles Times* 69 (September 25, 1950): 3:7.

Review of the premiere of *George Washington variations* op.120.

B432. ——. "SC School of Music gives one-act operas." *Los Angeles Times* 70 (May 4, 1951): III:8.

Review of the premiere of the opera *Dark waters* op.125.

B433. ——. "Southern California festival presents new Krenek opera." *Musical America* 71:8 (June 1951): 16.

Review of the premiere of *Dark waters* op.125.

B434. ——. "Margaret Aue plays new Krenek concerto." *Los Angeles Times* 73 (March 5, 1954): II:9.

Review of the premiere of the *Cello concerto* op.133.

B435. Goldberg, Albert. "Los Angeles Philharmonic season ends." *Musical America* 74:6 (April 1954): 22.

Review of the premiere of the *Cello concerto* op.133.

B436. ——. "Krenek works heard in Monday concert." *Los Angeles Times* 82 (January 23, 1963): 4:6.

Review of the American premiere of *Flute piece in nine phases* op.171 and *Alpbach quintet* op.180, and performances of *Quaestio temporis* op.170 and *L'incoronazione di Poppea suite* op.80b in a Monday Evening Concert.

B437. ——. "Ojai Festival returns to tradition format." *Los Angeles Times* 82 (May 28, 1963): 4:8.

Reviews the festival and a performance of *Basler Massarbeit* op.173 by Leonard Stein and the composer on May 25th.

B438. *"Der goldene Bock."* *Die Welt* (June 17, 1964)

Review of the premiere of the opera op.186 concentrating on the problem concerning plot and music. The opera has a convincing plot but the music is placative, it does not substantiate the story.

B439. Goldman, Richard Franco. "Schoenberg: *Erwartung.* Krenek: *Symphonic Elegy for String Orchestra (In Memoriam Anton von Webern.*" *Musical Quarterly* 38:4 (October 1952): 671-673.

Record review of op.105 on Columbia ML 4524. "The *Elegy* has real nobility and breadth; it has clarity, pace, and sensitive dark sonorities."

B440. ——. "Current chronicle: New York." *Musical Quarterly* 46:1 (January 1960): 71-76.

Review of the American premiere of the *Sixth string quartet* op.78.

B441. Goldthwaite, Scott. "Current chronicle: Urbana, Illinois." *Musical Quarterly* 43:3 (July 1957): 390-398.

Survey of the Eighth Festival of Contemporary Arts at Urbana and brief review of the premiere of *The bell tower* op.153.

B442. Goodwin, Noël. "The new music of Germany." *Records and Recording* 2:9 (June 1959): 12-15.

Includes a record review of *Spiritus intelligentiae, Sanctus* op.152 on Deutsche Grammophon LP 16 134.

B443. ——. "Curiosity corner." *Music and Musicians* 13:12 (August 1965): 29.

Record review of the opera *Jonny spielt auf* op.45 on Philips AL 3498 and Philips SAL 3498.

B444. ——. "Three moderns." *Music and Musicians* 15:7 (March 1967): 58-59.

Review of the book of essays *Exploring music* (K817).

B445. Gould, Glenn. "A Festschrift for 'Ernst who'???" *Piano Quarterly* 24:92 (Winter 1975-76): 16-18.

Review of the book *Horizons circled* (K864).

a. ——. In *The Glenn Gould Reader.* (Toronto: Lester & Orpen, 1984): 189-194.

b. ——. In *The Glenn Gould Reader.* (New York: Alfred A. Knopf, 1984): 189-194.

B446. Gould, Glenn. "Hommage á Ernst Krenek." *Musik-Konzepte* 39/40 (B895) (October 1984): 14-19.

Reminiscence of Krenek's visit to the Toronto Conservatory while Gould was a student, and an assessment of his works, noting that he had not lost any of his rhythmic vitality as demonstrated by his recent work *Von vorn herein* op.219. Translation of a Westdeutscher Rundfunk in Cologne broadcast by Johannes Goehl and Patricia Goehl-Kew.

B447. ——. "Piano music of Berg, Schoenberg, and Krenek." In *The Glenn Gould Reader*. (Toronto: Lester & Orpen, 1984): 195-200.

Reprint of the liner notes for Columbia ML 5336 which includes the *Third piano sonata* op.92, no.4.

   a. ——. In *The Glenn Gould Reader*. (New York: Alfred A. Knopf, 1984): 195-200.

B448. Gräner, Georg. "Bruckner und der Geist des *Jonny*." *Allgemeine Musikzeitung* 54:47 (November 25, 1927): 1215-1217.

Contrasts the superficial spirit of *Jonny spielt auf* op.45 with Bruckner's truly spiritual nature.

B449. Graf, Milan. "Biennale für Neue Musik." *Musica* 21:5 (September-October 1967): 228-229.

Review of the premiere of *Vier Stücke für Oboe und Klavier* op.193.

B450. Gran, Arnold. "Bat Symphony scores again in Oakland concert." *Post Enquirer* (Oakland, CA) (March 25, 1939)

Review of the first U.S. performance of the *Concertino* op.27.

B451. Grandchamp, Kathleen. "Minneapolis." *Opera News* 45:14 (March 7, 1981): 27.

Review of the first American performances of the one-act operas *Das geheime Königreich* op.50 and *Der Diktator* op.49 and the local revival of *Schwergewicht* op.55 given on alternate nights in German and English at the University of Minnesota Opera Theater with the composer in attendance.

B452. Grandi, Walter. *Il sistema tonale ed il contrappunto dodecafonico di Ernst Krenek*. (Rome: Edizioni musicali Ortipe, 1954) 124 pp. *See:* B131

B453. Green, L. Dunton. "The International Music Festival in Vienna." *The Chesterian* 13:104 (July-August 1932): 230-233.

Includes a review of a performance of the song cycle *Durch die Nacht* op.67a.

B454. Green, Marcia S. "Ravel and Krenek: Cosmic music makers." *College Music Symposium* 24:2 (1984): 96-104.

Discusses the similarities between *Jonny spielt auf* op.45 and Ravel's *L'Enfant et les sortilèges* comparing their structure, symbols of technology, use of the descending fourth, the depiction of America and the use of jazz, the effect of neo-classicism, autobiographical elements, and their relationship to modernism. Green concludes that "the structural similarities and thematic resemblances between [the two works] are significant, not so much in terms of one artist's influence upon the other, but rather, because both Krenek and Ravel were alive and creating during the same historical period."

B455. Greene, David Mason. "Krenek, Ernst." In *Greene's Biographical Encyclopedia of Composers*. (Garden City, NY: Doubleday, 1985): 1148-1149.

Biographical essay surveying his life to the 1980s with a list of works appearing on recordings.

B456. Greenfield, Edward. "Gramophone records." *Musical Times* 102:1423 (September 1961): 571.

Includes a record review of *Symphonic elegy* op.105 on Philips ABL 3393.

B457. Grewe, Dietolf. "Mit dem Komponieren ist es wie mit Tennis." *Kölner Stadt-Anzeiger* (November 7, 1973): 31.

Interview covering Krenek's life and focused on his *Six Profiles* op.203.

B458. Griffiths, Paul. "Ernst Krenek." *Music and Musicians* 23:12 (August 1975): 24-26.

Survey of Krenek's life on his 75th birthday. Picture.

B459. ———. "Krenek mirrored." *Musical Times* 116:1591 (September 1975): 795.

Review of the book *Horizons circled* (K864).

B460. Grün, Andreas. "Ernst Krenek, *Suite für Gitarre allein, op.164*; eine analytische Betrachtung." *Gitarre und Laute* 7:3 (May/June 1984): 34-43.

Extensive analysis with notes on interpretation. Picture.

B461. Gubler, Friedrich T. "Ein Brief an Ernst Krenek." *Schweizerische Musikzeitung* 93:3 (March 1, 1953): 101-102.

Introduces the "Ernst Krenek-Heft" by discussing Krenek's activities since leaving Europe.

B462. Günther, Siegfried. "Der Kurs in Kreneks jüngstem Schaffen." *Die Musik* 23:8 (May 1931): 587-591.

A discussion of Krenek's tonal works including *Potpourri* op.54, *Drei Gesängen* op.56, *Konzertarie* op.57, *Kleine Sinfonie* op.58, *Zweite Klaviersonate* op.59, *Leben des Orest* op.60, *Reisebuch aus den österreichischen Alpen* op.62 and *Fiedellieder* op.64. Picture opposite p.593; facsimile of a page from the full score of *Leben des Orest* opposite p.609.

B463. Gysi, Fritz. "Zürich." *Allgemeine Musikzeitung* 52:10 (March 6, 1925): 214.

Includes a review of the premiere of the *Second concerto grosso* op.25.

B464. ———. "Musikbriefe: Zürich." *Allgemeine Musikzeitung* 61:9 (March 2, 1934): 108.

Includes a review of the premiere of *Kantate von der Vergänglichkeit des Irdischen* op.72.

B465. h. "Vorlesung Ernst Krenek in Graz." *Wiener Zeitung* 233:38 (February 8, 1936): 9.

Review of a lecture by Krenek concerning his unperformed opera *Karl V.* op.73.

B466. ———. "Die 'Jazzoper der goldenen zwanziger Jahre' auf Schallplatte." *Phonoprisma* 7:5 (1964): 157.

Discusses the forthcoming recording of *Jonny spielt auf* op.45 by Amadeo AVRS 5038. Picture of Alfred Jerger as Jonny in 1928.

B467. H--s. "Kreneks *Lamentatio Jeremiae prophetae*." *Kasseler Post* (October 7, 1958)

Review of the first complete performance of *Lamentatio Jeremiae prophetae* op.93.

B468. H.D.H. "Ernst Krenek: *Symphonie Pallas Athene*." *Melos* 29:9 (September 1962): 303.

Review of the publication of op.137.

B469. H.E.H. "Konzerte." *Wiener Zeitung* 232:62 (March 3, 1935): 15.

Review of Krenek's fourth Austrian Studio Concert which included the premiere of his Austrian folksongs op.77a.

B470. ——. "Das fünfte Studiokonzert." *Wiener Zeitung* 232:87 (March 28, 1935): 11.

Review of Krenek's Fifth Austrian Studio Concert in honor of Alban Berg's fiftieth birthday which included the premiere of *Vier kleine Männerchöre* op.32.

B471. ——. "Kreneks *Poppea*-Erneuerung." *Wiener Zeitung* 234:266 (September 26, 1937): 11.

Review of the premiere of Krenek's edition of the Monteverdi opera op.80a.

B472. H.H. "Music: Novelties by Philharmonic." *New York Times* 81:26942 (October 30, 1931): 8:27.

Review of the premiere of *Variations* op.69.

B473. ——. "From the dark ages before Bach." *Musical Opinion* 77:916 (January 1954): 221.

Review of the book *Johannes Ockeghem* (K616).

B474. H.H.S. "Die Krenek-Premiere." *Prager Tagblatt* No.146 (June 26, 1938)

Review of the premiere of *Karl V*. op.73.

B475. ——. "Krenek's *Karl V*. at Prague." *Daily Telegraph* (London) (July 2, 1938)

Review of the premiere of the opera op.73.

B476. H.J.K. "*Karl V*." *Westdeutsche Nachrichten* (Essen) (March 30, 1950)

Review of the first German production of op.73 in Essen.

B477. H.J.S. "Ernst Krenek: *Elf Transparente*." *Melos* 27:2 (February 1960): 63.

Review of the publication.

B478. H.L. "Ernst Krenek: *Lamentatio Jeremiae prophetae*." *Melos* 29:6 (June 1962): 205.

Record review of the choral work op.93 on Bärenreiter Musicaphon 30 L 1303-4.

B479. H.P. "Ernst Krenek in Frankfurt." *Melos* 19:1 (January 1952): 19-20.

Review of the performance of the opera *Leben des Orest* op.60 during the composer's recent visit; in addition, Krenek conducted his *Double concerto* op.124, and *Symphonische Musik* op.11 on the radio. There was also a performance at the Frankfurter Amerikahaus of the song cycle *Reisebuch aus den österreichischen Alpen* op.62, by Willy Berling, baritone, and Walter Faith, piano. The visit concluded with a "Composition Evening" which included the *First string quartet* op.6 and the *Fourth string quartet* op.24 performed by the Assmann Quartett, the first European performance of the song cycle *The ballad of the railroads* op.98, and a performance of the *Sixth piano sonata* op.128.

B480. ——. "Krenek: *Sestina for voice and instrumental ensemble*." *The New Records* 26:12 (February 1959): 13.

Record review of *Sestina* op.161 and excerpts from *Lamentatio Jeremiae prophetae*

prophetae op.93 on Epic LC 3509.

B481. H.R. "Walter's Afscheid." *Algemeen Handelsblad* (Amsterdam) (March 18, 1938)

Review of the premiere of the *Second piano concerto* op.81.

B482. Haefeli, Anton. *Die Internationale Gesellschaft für Neue Musik (IGNM); Ihre Geschichte von 1922 bis zur Gegenwart.* (Zürich: Atlantis Musikbuch-Verlag, 1982) 767 pp.

A history of the society including discussion of the performances of Krenek's works during the festivals of 1923, 1924, 1925, 1932, 1933, 1936, 1938, and 1946. Also documents Krenek's involvement with the society as a jurist in 1934 and 1941, his leadership of the Austrian Section, and his writings about the society and its congresses.

B483. Häusler, Josef. "Ernst Krenek." In his *Musik im 20. Jahrhundert, von Schönberg zu Penderecki.* (Bremen: Carl Schünemann Verlag, 1969): 252-259.

Biographical essay and list of works.

B484. Haggin, B.H. "Records." *The Nation* 175:4 (July 26, 1952): 78.

Brief record review of *Symphonic elegy* op.105 on Columbia ML 4524.

B485. ——. "From Gesualdo to Schoenberg." *New Republic* 140:23 (June 8, 1959): 22.

Record review of the *Third piano sonata* op.92, no.4 on Columbia ML 5336.

B486. Halasz, Gabor. "Ein Meisterwerk der Wiener Schule." *Opernwelt* 23:12 (December 1982): 72.

Record review of the opera *Karl V.* op.73 on Amadeo AVRS 305.

B487. Hale, Philip, "Symphony concert." *The Boston Herald* 168:166 (December 13, 1930): 14.

Review of the first American performance of the *Second piano sonata* op.59.

B488. Hall, David. *The Record Book; A Music Lover's Guide to the World of the Phonograph.* (New York: Smith & Durrell, 1940): 305, 322-323.

Includes record reviews of *Eine kleine Suite* op.13a on RCA Victor 15862 and the *Short piano pieces* op.83 on Columbia X 171.

B489. Hall, R. Albert. "Maria Yudina Plays." *Fanfare* 1:3 (January 1978): 71-72.

Record review of Melodiya CM 03113-4 which includes the *Second piano sonata* op.59.

B490. ——. "Krenek: *Spätlese,* Op.218; *Drei Gesänge,* Op.56," *Fanfare* 2:3 (January-February 1979): 62.

Record review of Orion ORS 78298.

B491. Hallinan, Nancy. "Faculty interpret Krenek and Brahms." *Vassar Miscellany News* 26 (March 4, 1942)

Review of the premiere of *Fünf Lieder nach Worten von Franz Kafka* op.82 and a performance of *Vier Gesänge nach alten Gedichten* op.53.

B492. Hambraeus, Bengt. "Krenek: *Quaestio temporis.*" *Musikrevy* 16:3 (1961): 90.

Review of the publication of the score of the orchestral work op.170.

B493. Hamilton, David. "Berio, Luciano. *Sequenza IV*... Krenek: *Sechs Vermessene*..." *High Fidelity Annual* 16 (1971): 65-67.
Record review of op.168 on Candide CE 31015.

B494. "Hamline signs Ernst Krenek." *Minneapolis Star Journal* (May 24, 1942)
Announces that Krenek will begin teaching at Hamline University in the Fall semester.

B495. Harmon, Carter. "Composer's position in this country." *New York Times* 97:32817 (November 30, 1947): 2:7.
"Public opinion must learn to be impressed by the composer's integrity" says Krenek in an interview before the premiere of the *Fourth symphony* op.113.

B496. Harrison, Jay S. "Nicanor Zabaleta, harpist, gives recital at Town Hall." *New York Herald Tribune* (January 28, 1958)
Review of the premiere of the *Harp sonata* op.150.

B497. Harrison, Max. "Hindemith: *Quartet for clarinet, violin, cello and piano.* Krenek: *Trio for violin, clarinet and piano.* Milhaud: *Suite for violin, clarinet and piano.*" *Gramophone* 56:662 (July 1978): 214.
Record review of op.108 on Supraphon 111 2147.

B498. Harry, Walter. "Zeitliches und Ueberzeitliches in *Jonny spielt auf.*" *Musikblätter des Anbruch* 10:1 (January 1928): 14-17.
General discussion of the opera op.45 and its themes. Krenek used Jung's theories of personality archetypes for his characters; for example, Max is a composer not only fleeing from life but from himself.

B499. Hartmann, Rudolf. "Operndramaturgische Glossen über Kreneks *Jonny spielt auf.*" *Neue Musik-Zeitung* 48:17 (June 1927): 382-384.
Discusses the opera and its libretto.

B500. Harvey, John H. "Symphony in lively performance." *Saint Paul Pioneer Press* (March 23, 1946)
Review of the premiere of *Tricks and trifles* op.101.

B501. ——. "New Krenek concerto proves excellent work." *Saint Paul Pioneer Press* (November 23, 1946)
Review of the premiere of the *Third piano concerto* op.107.

B502. ——. "Shure and ensemble acclaimed." *Saint Paul Pioneer Press* (November 29, 1946)
Review of the premiere of the *Trio* op.108.

B503. Haselböck, Martin. "Die Orgelwerke Ernst Kreneks; eine Ueberschau zum 80. Geburtstag des Komponisten am 23. August 1980." *Musik und Kirche* 50:3 (1980): 114-122.
Analyses and recommendations for performance of those works which include organ: *Little Concerto* op.88; *La Corona* op.91; *Sonata* op.92, no.1; *Organologia,* op.180-1/2; *Orga-nastro* op.212, *Four winds suite* op.223, *Concerto* op.230; and *Opus 231.*

B504. Hausdorff, Martin. "Opera premiere in Los Angeles." *Overture* (June 1951)
Review of the premiere of the chamber opera *Dark waters* op.125.

B505. Hausswald, Günter. "Musica sacra in Zwölftontechnik." *Musik und Kirche* 28:1 (January-February 1958): 9-13.

Discussion of the sacred choral work *Lamentatio Jeremiae prophetae* op.93.

B506. ——. "Essays über Musik." *Musica* 12:10 (October 1958): 638.

Review of the book of essays *Zur Sprache gebracht* (K707).

B507. ——. "Grosses Welttheater." *Musica* 19:5 (September-October 1965): 249-251.

Includes a brief review of the plays *König Oedipus* and *Oedipus auf Kolonos* performed during the Salzburg Festival with incidental music by Krenek op.188.

B508. Heinsheimer, Hans W. "The little old lady in Boston." *Musical Courier* 135:8 (April 15, 1947): 5.

An account of the first American performance of the *Second piano concerto* on November 4, 1938 and a reflection on the audience's reaction to the music. An old lady said "'Conditions in Europe must be dreadful'... She has said all that was to be said about the music she had just heard: the fear in the music, the confusion, the shock, the tension, the despair, the emptiness, the decaying philosophy of the dead end."

a. "Passenger on the Arc." In his *Menagerie in F Sharp*. (Garden City, NY: Doubleday & Co., 1947): 1-7.

B509. ——. "Giselda is a bad girl." In his *Menagerie in F Sharp*. (Garden City, NY: Doubleday & Co., 1947): 119-137.

Impressions of the premiere of the opera *Orpheus und Euridike* op.21 and the financial success of *Jonny spielt auf* op.45.

B510. ——. "A medal from the empress." In his *Menagerie in F Sharp*. (Garden City, NY: Doubleday & Co., 1947): 49-60.

Reminiscence of his first meeting with Krenek at the premiere of his opera *Zwingburg* and impressions of its premiere.

B511. ——. "The sweet cup of success." In his *Menagerie in F Sharp*. (Garden City, NY: Doubleday & Co., 1947): 138-162.

Discusses the success of the opera *Jonny spielt auf* op.45. "Its melodies and rhythms were plugged on the radio, fiddled in cafés, and whistled on the streets. The Tobacco Monopoly operated by the Austria Government brought out a new cigarette ... and called it Jonny. And to top it all, a boisterous Prussian lawyer ... bought the picture rights ... for Warner Brothers in Hollywood."

B512. ——. "What is happening to music in Europe." *Etude* 69:1 (January 1951): 14-15, 57.

Surveys musical life in Europe. Picture of Krenek.

B513. ——. *Best regards to Aida; the defeats and victories of a music man on two continents*. (New York: Alfred A. Knopf, 1968)

Reminiscences about his work at the publishers Universal Edition in Vienna, Boosey and Hawkes in New York, and G. Schirmer and of his life-long friendship with Krenek whom he met at the premiere of *Zwingburg* op.14.

B514. ——. "Ernst Krenek, Away from the mainstream." *Opera News* 40:5 (November 1975): 34-36.

A survey of Krenek's operas based upon an interview; the operas *Jonny spielt auf* op.45, *Karl V.* op.73, and *Life of Orestes* op.60 are especially mentioned.

B515. Heller, Friedrich C. "Claudia Maurer Zenck: *Ernst Krenek - ein Komponist im Exil.*" *Oesterreichische Musikzeitschrift* 35:12 (December 1980): 680-681.

Review of the book about Krenek (B1502).

B516. Heller, H. E. "Kammerorchesterkonzert." *Wiener Zeitung* 229:142 (June 21, 1932): 6.

Review of the premiere of *Durch die Nacht* op.67a with accompaniment arranged for orchestra.

B517. Helm, Everett. "Current chronicle: Germany." *Musical Quarterly* 38:1 (January 1952): 136-145.

Review of the 1951 Donaueschingen festival and the premiere of the *Concerto for violin and piano* op.124, which opened the festival on October 6. "This twelve-tone work is serious in nature and extremely well written, but is academic and frequently downright boring." (p.143)

B518. ——. "Germany." *Musical Times* 95:1340 (October 1954): 557.

Review of the German premiere of the opera *Dunkle Wasser* op.125.

B519. ——. "Fromm Music Foundation." *Musical America* 82:7 (July 1962): 25-26.

Review of a concert sponsored by the Foundation at the New School which included the first American performance of *Quaestio temporis* op.170.

B520. ——. "New Krenek opera needs editing." *Minneapolis Sunday Tribune* (July 5, 1964): 9.

Review of the premiere of the opera *Der goldene Bock* op.186.

B521. ——. "Krenek opera places Jason in America." *New York Times* 113:38886 (July 12, 1964): 2:9.

Review of the premiere of the opera *Der goldene Bock* op.186.

B522. ——. "*Exploring music* by Ernst Krenek." *Music Review* 30:3 (1969): 243-244.

Review of the book of essays (K817).

B523. Henahan, Donald. "2-piano concert is politely pleasant." *Chicago Daily News* (October 19, 1959)

Review of the premiere of *Three short 12-tone pieces* op.139a.

B524. ——. "When Masselos plays Satie: simplicity, not monotony." *New York Times* 119:40909 (January 25, 1970): 2:30.

Record review of *Sechs Vermessene* op.168 on Candide CE 31015.

B525. ——. "On being an 'accessible' composer." *New York Times* 130:44972 (June 7, 1981): D:21.

Comparison of Krenek with Gian Carlo Menotti and their popularities. Picture.

B526. ——. "Music: The Thouvenel String Quartet." *New York Times* 130:44972 (June 8, 1981): C:12.

Review of a Carnegie Recital Hall concert which included a performance of the *First string quartet* op.6 and the premiere of the *Eighth string quartet* op.233.

B527. Henderson, Ray. "Jazz mixes with opera in Germany." *Boston Evening Transcript* 98:234 (October 8, 1927): 3:8.

General discussion of Krenek's opera *Jonny spielt auf* and its jazz elements. Pictures.

B528. ——. "A question of time." *Musical Times* 102 (June 1961): 355.

Review of the publication of *Questio temporis* op.170.

B529. Henderson, W. J. "Music and musicians." *New York Sun* (January 12, 1929)

Discussion of the opera *Jonny spielt auf* in anticipation of American premiere.

B530. ——. "Music and musicians." *New York Sun* (January 26, 1929)

Reflections on the opera *Jonny spielt auf* following its performance in New York.

B531. Henken, John. "Krenek work in American premiere." *Los Angeles Times* 102:90 (March 3, 1983): 6:5.

Review of the first American performance of the *Brazilian sinfonietta* op.131.

B532. ——. "Clark's Pacific Symphony gives Mahler his due." *Los Angeles Times* 105:41 (January 13, 1986)6:3.

Review of the first American performance of *Fivefold enfoldment* op.205.

B533. Henry, Helen. "Atonal approach: Krenek composer in vanguard of advanced music." *The Sun* (Baltimore) (April 16, 1967): C:1.

Interview conducted while Krenek was visiting professor at Peabody Conservatory.

B534. Herbert, Clayton. "Krenek: *String quartet no.5*, op.65." *The New Records* 53:10 (December 1985): 9.

Record review of Composers Recordings CRI SD 522.

B535. "Here & there." *High Fidelity/Musical America* 27:8 (August 1977): MA31.

Review of the premiere of *Dream sequence* op.224.

B536. Herman, Roland. "Von der Art des Zugangs angetan." *Fono Forum* 27:9 (September 1982): 6.

Letter in reaction to Lück's review (B802) of the Amadeo AVRS 305 recording of *Karl V.* op.73.

B537. Herrmann, Horst Dietrich. "Ernst Krenek: *Streichtrio für Violine, Viola und Violoncello*." *Melos* 28:10 (October 1961): 336.

Review of publication of op.118.

B538. ——. "Ernst Krenek: *Symphonie Pallas Athene*." *Neue Zeitschrift für Musik* 124:10 (1963): 410.

Review of the publication of the score op.137.

B539. Herrmann, Joachim. "Vokalwerke von Ernst Krenek." *Musica* 15:12 (December 1961): 702-703.

Briefly traces the choral music from *Lamentatio Jeremiae prophetae* op.93 through the *Zwei geistliche Gesänge* op.132 to the *Kafka motets* op.169.

B540. Hermann, Joachim. "Ernst Krenek: *Lamentatio Jeremiae prophetae.*"
Phonoprisma 5:1 (1962): 14.
Record review of op.93 on Bärenreiter Musicaphon 30 L 1303-4.

B541. Heuss, Alfred. "Ernst Kreneks Jazz-Oper, *Jonny spielt auf.*" *Zeitschrift
für Musik* 94:3 (March 1927): 168-169.
Review of the premiere of the opera op.45.

B542. ——. "Wo stehen wir heute?" *Zeitschrift für Musik* 97:3 (March 1930):
163-167.
Review of the premiere of the opera *Leben des Orest* op.60.

B543. hhr. "*Fünf plus eins* unter Yvonne Georgi." *Kurier* (August 29, 1962): 7.
Review of the premiere of the ballet op.180.

B544. Hickman, C. Sharpless. "In the key of C sharp." *Music of the West* 6
(June 1951): 7.
Review of the premiere of the chamber opera *Dark waters* op.125.

B545. ——. "Krenek opera world premiered on Coast." *Musical Courier* 144:1
(July 1951): 5.
Review of the premiere of *Dark waters* op.125.

B546. ——. "Los Angeles." *Musical Courier* 149:7 (April 1, 1954): 30-31.
Review of the premiere of the *Cello concerto* op.133.

B547. Hill, Richard S. "*Hamline studies in musicology.*" *Notes* 2d ser. 3:1
(December 1945): 42-43.
Review of the first volume edited by Krenek (K550).

B548. Hiller, Paul. "Aus dem Westdeutschen Musikleben: Köln."
Allgemeine Musikzeitung 54:47 (November 25, 1927): 1226-1227.
Includes a review of the premiere of *Potpourri* op.54 for orchestra.

B549. Hilmar, Ernst. "Krenek-Bestände in Wien." *Oesterreichische
Musikzeitschrift* 35:9 (September 1980): 458-460.
Surveys the music manuscripts and letters donated by Krenek in 1950 to the
Wiener Stadt- und Landesbibliothek and the materials owned by Universal
Edition which were deposited in the Austrian National Library and the
Stadtbibliothek.

B550. ——. *Dank an Ernst Krenek, Katalog zur Ausstellung der Wiener Stadt-
und Landesbibliothek im Historischen Museum der Stadt Wien, Mai/Juni
1982.* (Wien: Universal Edition, 1982)
The catalog of an exhibition of materials related to Krenek, including music
and literary manuscripts, photographs, and correspondence. *See:* B179,
B1186

B551. ——. "Eine Ernst Krenek Ausstellung im Historischen Museum der
Stadt Wien." *Oesterreichische Musikzeitschrift* 37:5 (May 1982): 256-257.
Announcement and description of an exhibition of materials related to
Krenek.

B552. ——. "Ernst Krenek in eigner Sache." *Oesterreichische Musikzeitschrift*
40:7/8 (July-August 1985): 377-387.
Excerpts of letters from Krenek to his publisher Universal Edition, 1921-
1937. Picture.

B553. ——. "Ach, was wird uns hier bereitet?" In *Ernst Krenek: Fünf Lieder nach Worten von Franz Kafka.* (Vienna: Wiener Stadt- und Landesbibliothek, 1985): 40-41.

A brief discussion of the circumstances surrounding the composition of op.82; it was the first work Krenek composed during his first trip to America. Also includes a brief discussion of the facsimile, the reproductions of Krenek's paintings, and the reproductions of Krenek portraits.

B554. ——. "Es rieselt, es knistert, es kracht." In *Ernst Krenek: Fünf Lieder nach Worten von Franz Kafka.* (Vienna: Wiener Stadt- und Landesbibliothek, 1985): 23-38.

Brief quotes in German from Krenek's writings on himself, art, imagination and music, New Music, "U-Musik," the theater, composition, composers, composer's jubilees, music critics and publishers, literature, and the audience from unpublished manuscripts in the Krenek-Archiv of the Wiener Stadt- und Landesbibliothek, and from *Jonny spielt auf* (K73), *Operette und Revue* (K92), *Opernerfahrung* (K96), *Franz Schubert und wir* (K86), *Ein paar Worte über Johann Strauss* (K99), *Der schaffende Musiker und die Technik der Gegenwart* (K102), *Soll ein Künstler publizistisch tätig sein?* (K126), *Die Stellung der Musik in der Kultur der Gegenwart* (K113), *Pro domo* (K106), *Banalitäten* (K108), *Komponieren als Beruf* (K120), *Von Musik etwas verstehen...* (K135), *Neue Humanität und alte Sachlichkeit* (K99), *Das fortgesetzte Totenmahl* (K187), *Ueber Sinn und Schicksal der neuen Musikpädagogik* (K207), *Was sollte Musikkritik leisten?* (K213), *Freiheit und Verantwortung* (K248), *Arnold Schönberg* (K268), *Erinnerung an Karl Kraus* (K401), *Ueber neue Musik* (K418), *Musik und Humanität* (K412), *Der elfenbeinerne Turm und der Mann von der Strasse* (K529), *Ueber die Inspiration* (K513), *Das unaufhörliche Raunen* (K545), *Selbstellung* (K569), *Ueber meine Memoiren* (K605), *Vom Altern und Veralten der Musik* (K679), *Was ist und wie entsteht elektronische Musik?* (K678), *Amerikas Einfluss auf eingewanderte Komponisten* (K730), *Es rieselt, es knistert, es kracht* (K797), *Elektro-Ton und Sphärenklang* (K901), and *Vorwort: Im Zweifelsfalle* (K918).

B555. Hinson, Maurice. "Ernst Krenek." In *The Piano in Chamber Ensemble; An Annotated Guide.* (Bloomington: Indiana University Press, 1978): 54, 111, 195, 244, 379, 440.

Brief performance notes on the *Violin and piano sonata* op.99, *Viola and piano sonata* op.117, *Suite for flute and piano* op.147, *Flute piece* op.171, *Sonatina for bass clarinet and piano* op.85, *Suite for clarinet and piano* op.148, *Trio* op.108, and *Hausmusik* op.172.

B556. Hinton Jr., James. "Hauer: *Hölderlin Lieder*, Op.32. Krenek: *Fiedellieder.* Kodaly: *Drei Lieder*, Op.9." *High Fidelity* 3:5 (November-December 1953): 74.

Record review of the song cycle op.64 on New Records NRLP 405.

B557. Hirschberg, Walther. "Dritter Vortragsabend der Hochschule." *Signale für die musikalische Welt* 79:25 (June 22, 1921): 660.

Review of the premiere of the *Sonata for violin and piano* op.3 and a performance of *Serenade* op.4 during a concert of Franz Schreker's students at the Berlin Staatliche Akademische Hochschule für Musik, Konzertsaal on June 21, 1921; Oskar Schubert, clarinet; Gustav Havemann, violin; Hans Mahlke, viola; Hermann Hopf, cello.

B558. Hirschberg, Walther. "Ella Pancera." *Signale für die musikalische Welt* 87:14 (April 3, 1929): 482.

Review of the premiere of the *Second piano sonata* op.59.

B559. ——. "Artur Schnabel, Karl Flesch, Gregor Piatigorsky." *Signale für die musikalische Welt* 88:21 (May 21, 1930): 644.

Review of the premiere of the *Trio phantasy* op.63.

B560. ——. "Neue Lieder." *Signale für die musikalische Welt* 88:48 (November 26, 1930): 1400-1402.

Includes a brief review of the publication of the *Fiedellieder* op.64 songs.

B561. ——. "Neue musikalien etc." *Signale für die musikalische Welt* 90:8 (February 24, 1932): 175-176.

Includes a review of the publication of *Die Nachtigal* op.68.

B562. Höe. "Hochgezüchtete Klangartistik." *Augsburger Allgemeine* no.113 (May 16, 1974): 23.

Review of the premiere of the songs *Momenta vitae* op.215.

B563. Hoerée, Arthur. "Ernst Krenek: *Concert pour piano et orchestre* (Fa diéze majeur)." *La revue musicale* 6:1 (November 1924): 75.

Review of the publication of the *First piano concerto* op.18.

B564. Hoffmann, S. "Der Komponist Ernst Krenek wird 85 Jahre alt." *Orchester* 33 (November 1985): 1078.

An appreciation of the composer on his eightyfifth birthday.

B565. Hofmann, Holger. "Ausklang der Hamburger Spielzeit." *Madame* (Munich) (October 1964)

Review of the premiere of the opera *Der goldene Bock* op.186.

B566. Hofmann, Klaus. "Kreneks *Lamentatio Jeremiae prophetae* von den Grenzen der Musik." *Gottesdienst und Kirchenmusik* 10:1 (January 1959): 12-13.

Review of the premiere of the complete op.93.

B567. Hogan, Clare. "An examination of Stravinsky's contribution to serialism in the light of the theories, music and personality of Ernst Krenek." (Master's thesis: University of Keele, 1982) 121 pp.

A study of Igor Stravinsky's adoption of the twelve-tone technique of transposition-rotation developed by Krenek in 1941 in his *Lamentatio Jeremiae prophetae* op.93. Stravinsky used the technique in his *Threni* and other works. The thesis also studies the personal relationship between the two composers and clarifies Stravinsky's comments about that relationship.

B568. ——. "*Threni*: Stravinsky's 'debt' to Krenek." *Tempo* no.141 (June 1982): 22-29.

A detailed examination of the similarities of the two composers settings of the *Lamentations of Jeremiah*. The author concludes that "despite their various similarities, Stravinsky's and Krenek's aims were fundamentally quite different ... For Krenek the rotation technique was the solution to a self-imposed problem, namely, to integrate certain principles of the twelve-tone technique with those of ancient modality. Once this had been solved, as far as he was concerned, the technique could not be used in a similar way again without being repetitive." However, Krenek used rotation in his *Third piano sonata* op.92, no.4 and his *Seventh string quartet* op.96 written shortly after *Lamentatio Jeremiae prophetae* op.93, as well as several works written in the late 1950s.

B569. Hold, Ernst. "Erwiderung auf den Einwand Ernst Kreneks gegen den Artikel 'Harmonie u. Atonalität." *Oesterreichische Volkspresse* (October 20, 1934)

A polemic against Krenek's reactions in his "Harmonie und Atonalität" (K271) against Hold's article of the same name in the September 29 issue.

B570. Holde, Artur. "Das Donaueschinger Musikfest." *Allgemeine Musikzeitung* 53:32/33 (August 6, 1926): 627-628.

Review of the premiere of *Lustige Märsche* op.44.

B571. ———. "Neue Werke von Ernst Krenek." *Melos* 17:12 (December 1950): 349-351.

Discusses three recent premieres. The Albuquerque performance of the *Fifth symphony* op.119 at the University of New Mexico by the Civic Orchestra was a "school performance"; the Vienna performance conducted by Kurt Frederick should be considered its premiere. Also discusses the premiere of the *Third piano concerto* op.107 at Minneapolis, MN, played and conducted by Dimitri Mitropoulos, who had recently performed it with the New York Philharmonic; and the recent premiere of *The ballad of the railroads* op.98.

B572. ———. "Kammermusik in der New School." *Aufbau* (New York) (March 14, 1958)

Review of a concert sponsored by the Fromm Music Foundation on March 9 of *Lamentatio Jeremia prophetae* op.93 by Hugh Ross and his Schola Cantorum and the premiere of *Sestina* op.161.

B573. Holl, Karl. "Kreneks Opern-Einakter." *Der Auftakt* (Prague) 8:5/6 (1928): 129-132.

Review of the premieres of the one-act operas *Der Diktator* op.49, *Das geheime Königreich* op.50, and *Schwergewicht, oder Die Ehre der Nation* op.55.

B574. Holländer, Hans. "Ernst Kreneks Buch *Ueber neue Musik.*" *Wiener Zeitung* 234:110 (May 5, 1937): 10.

Review of the book (K397).

B575. Honolka, Kurt. "Woche leichter Musik." *Musica* 17:1 (January 1963): 28-29.

Review of the premiere of *Nach wie vor der Reihe nach* op.182.

B576. ———. "Der romantische Krenek." *Opernwelt* 18:6 (1977): 52.

Record review of the song cycle *Reisebuch aus den österreichischen Alpen* op.62 on Preiserrecords SPR 3269.

B577. "Hotelgespräch mit Krenek." *Tempo* (Berlin) no.53 (March 5, 1930)

An interview.

B578. Houk, Norman C. "Krenek, Czech modernist, sees firm link with past." *Minneapolis Morning Tribune* (September 13, 1942)

An interview with Krenek. "I have never felt there was a complete break, a gap, between the old masters and present music."

B579. Houk, Norman C. "Music review." *Minneapolis Morning Tribune* (December 12, 1942): 10.

Review of the premiere of *I wonder as I wander* op.94.

B580. ——. "Krenek Symphony stirs controversy." *Minneapolis Morning Tribune* (December 24, 1943): 11.

Review of the first American performance of the *Second symphony* op.12.

B581. ——. "Choir and Symphony draws applause." *Minneapolis Morning Tribune* (March 25, 1944): 5.

Review of the premiere of the *Cantata for wartime* op.95.

B582. ——. "Orchestra members shine as soloists." *Minneapolis Morning Tribune* (March 23, 1946)

Review of the premiere of *Tricks and trifles* op.101.

B583. ——. "*Time table* wins audience approval." *Minneapolis Morning Tribune* (March 13, 1947)

Review of the premieres of the *Santa Fe time table* op.102 and *Aegrotavit Ezechias* op.103.

B584. Houser, James D. "The evolution of Ernst Krenek's twelve-tone technique." (Master's thesis: Eastman School of Music, 1977) 131 pp.

Traces Krenek's changing compositional style, defines three periods, and examines closely a representative piano work from each period. The First period, extending from 1930 to 1937, is represented by *Zwölf Variationen in drei Sätzen* op.79; the second period extending from the late 1930s through the 1940s, is represented by *Eight piano pieces* op.110, and the third period extending from the 1950s to the present, is represented by *Sechs Vermessene* op.168.

B585. Hucke, Helmut. "Zwei Meister der Kirchenmusik." *Musik und Alter* 13 (1960/61): 105-106.

Krenek's sixtieth birthday is recognized, along with Johann Nepomuk David.

B586. "Hudba a obraz světa." *Tempo* (Prague) 16:14 (May 24, 1937): 182-184.

Interview between Pavel Nettl, Krenek, and Alois Hába.

B587. Hürlimann, Martin. "Vom Musiktheater im Festspielsommer 1964." *Du* (Zürich) 24 (September 1964): 68-74.

Review of the premiere of *Der goldene Bock* op.186.

B588. Huetteman, Albert George. "Ernst Krenek's theories on the sonata and their relations to his six piano sonatas." (Ph.D. diss.: University of Iowa, 1968) 402 pp.

Reviews Krenek's theories presented in *Ueber neue Musik* (K397) and *Music here and now* (K495) related to his piano sonatas and presents an analysis of their formal structure. The study concludes that his sonatas strongly resemble late nineteenth-century text-book schemes of the form, his main and second themes begin lyrically and proceed to build climaxes, he re-works the exposition material in the development sections, his recapitulations are usually normal, each sonata includes at least one movement in sonata form, and while preferring three movements he avoids any particular tempo scheme.

a. ——. *Dissertation Abstracts* 30:2 (August 1969): 751-A -- 752-A.

B589. **Hughes, Allen.** "The Krenek method." *New York Times* 109:37360 (May 8, 1960): 2:9.

Discusses the forthcoming all-Krenek concert at Circle in the Square.

B590. ——. "Ballet: New dance work." *New York Times* 114:39142 (March 25, 1965): 43.

Review of the premiere of the ballet *Sargasso* based on *Symphonic elegy* op.105.

B591. **Hughes, Charles W.** "Krenek, Ernst (ed.) *Hamline studies in musicology.*" *Journal of Aesthetics and Art Criticism* 4:4 (June 1946): 254.

Review of volume one of the book (K550).

B592. ——. "Krenek, Ernst (ed.). *Hamline studies in musicology. Vol.II.*" *Journal of Aesthetics and Art Criticism* 6:1 (September 1947): 72-73.

Review of volume two of the book (K559).

B593. **Hughes, Jean.** "Current chronicle: Ernst Krenek festival concerts." *Musical Quarterly* 61:3 (July 1975): 464-470.

There were 36 works presented during several Southern California festivals honoring Krenek's 75th birthday. A festival in November at California State University, Northridge, presented *Marginal sounds* op.162, *Sestina* op.161, and *Perspectives* op.199. *Aulokithara* op.213a, was presented in January at a Monday Evening Concert. At the official festival concert in Palm Springs, Krenek conducted the U.C.S.D. Chamber Orchestra in the American premiere of *Static and ecstatic* op.214. Facsimile: *Static and ecstatic* manuscript page.

B594. **Hunt, Ian.** "Ideas in search of composition." *The Australian* (May 19, 1983).

Review of the premiere of the *Organ concerto* op.235.

B595. **Huth, A.** "Neue Orchestermusik in Berlin." *Neues Wiener Tagblatt* (November 8, 1928)

Review of the premiere of *Kleine Symphonie* op.58.

B596. **I.R.** "Neue Werke - junge Künstler." *Oesterreichische Musikzeitschrift* 35:4/5 (April-May 1980): 233.

Review of the premiere of *Opus 231.*

B597. **Ilgner, Gerhard.** "Krenek in Darmstadt." *Zeitschrift für Musik* 113:1 (January 1952): 56-57.

Review of a performance by the Darmstädter Landestheater-Orchester conducted by the composer of the *Symphonic elegy* op.105, the *Fourth piano concerto* op.123, and the first German performances of the *Fifth symphony* op.119 and the orchestral variations *I wonder as I wander* op.94.

B598. ——. "Zwei Erstaufführungen von Ernst Krenek." *Melos* 19:1 (January 1952): 20.

The composer conducted the Darmstädter Landestheater-Orchester in his *Fifth symphony* op.119 and the first European performance *I wonder as I wander* op.94.

B599. ——. "Kreneks 6. *Streichquartett*, Darmstadt." *Melos* 20:3 (March 1953): 87.

Review of the premiere in Darmstadt.

B600. "Illinois." *Opera* 8:6 (June 1957): 361.

A brief announcement of the first performance of the chamber opera *The bell tower* op.153.

B601. "*Im Zweifelsfalle.*" *Musik und Bildung* 17 (February 1985): 139.

Review of the book of essays (K924).

B602. J. "American guitar." *The New Records* 48:7 (September 1980): 11.

Record review of the *Guitar suite* op.164 on Orion ORS 78323 disc and Orion OC 828S cassette.

B603. J.Q. "Gipfel neuer Kirchenmusik." *Hessische Nachrichten* (October 6, 1958)

Review of the first complete performance of *Lamentatio Jeremiae prophetae* op.93 during the Kasseler Musiktage.

B604. J.R. "Dänisches Ensemble spielt 34mal Boulez an 28 Tagen." *Melos* 33:11 (November 1966): 382.

Review of the premiere of *Quintina* op.191 by Jolanda Rodio and conducted by the composer in the Danish Radio series "Prisma."

B605. Jacob, Walter. "Ueber den Realismus in Kreneks *Jonny spielt auf.*" *Die Musik* 20:3 (December 1927): 182-185.

Discussion of the opera op.45.

B606. Jacobs, Arthur. "Music and words in Hamburg." *Opera* 15:8 (August 1964): 515-517.

Review of the congress "Contemporary Music Theater" held in Hamburg, June 16-23 and featuring the premiere of the opera *Der goldene Bock* op.186. Picture.

B607. Jacobson, Bernard. "2 imaginative works premiere at Ravina[*sic*]." *Chicago Daily News* (July 8, 1968)

Review of the premiere of *Perspectives* op.199.

B608. ———. "Two big pianists, two big recitals." *Chicago Daily News* (December 7, 1970): 31.

Review of the premiere of *Piano piece in eleven parts* op.197.

B609. Jarustovskii, Boris. *Očerki po dramaturgii opery XX veka, II.* (Moskva: Muzyka, 1978) 261 pp.

Discusses, in Russian, the development of European opera during the period between the two world wars. Connects the fate of musical theater in various countries with social, political, and cultural change. Includes analyses of Krenek's operas.

B610. "Jazz orchestra jars New York." *Music News* 21:6 (February 8, 1929): 26.

Review of the first American performance of *Jonny spielt auf* op.45. Reprinted from the *Chicago Tribune*.

B611. Jemnitz, Alexander. "Ernst Krenek: *Konzert für Klavier und Orchester (Fis-dur)* op.18." *Die Musik* 17:11 (August 1925): 853-854.

Review of the publication.

B612. Joachim, Heinz. "Herz als Schauplatz der Geschichte." *Die Welt* (March 28, 1950)

Review of the first German production of *Karl V.* op.73 in Essen.

B613. ——. "[Review]." *Die Welt* (October 12, 1954)
Review of the premiere of *Symphony Pallas Athene* op.137.

B614. ——. "Hamburg weltoffen." *Melos* 21:11 (November 1954): 321-322.
Report on a visit to Hamburg by Krenek and several concerts, including the premiere of *Symphonie Pallas Athene* op.137.

B615. ——. "Ur- und Erstaufführungen von Ernst Krenek." *Melos* 21:11 (November 1954): 321-322.
Review of a concert by the Sinfonieorchester des NWDR conducted by the composer which included his *Second piano concerto* op.81, with pianist Arno Erfurth, and the premiere of *Symphony Pallas Athene* op.137. Krenek also conducted Robert Erickson's *Fantasy for cello & orchestra* with cellist Siegfried Palm.

B616. ——. "Ernst Krenek." *Schweizerische Musikzeitung* 95:1 (January 1, 1955): 1-5.
Discusses his place in modern music and analyzes the *Sonata for violin and piano* op.99.

B617. ——. "Hamburgische Staatsoper auf neuen Wegen." *Melos* 22:11 (November 1955): 328-329.
Review of the premiere of the opera *Pallas Athene weint* op.144. Picture.

B618. ——. "Current chronicle: Germany." *Musical Quarterly* 42:1 (January 1956): 92-98.
Review of the first performance of *Pallas Athene weint* op.144. "Stirred by the opera's largeness of conception and by the ethical seriousness of its attitude and artistic *Gestalt*, in part even grateful for the entirely justified intellectual demands, the international audience turned the Hamburg premiere into a big, unqualified success for the work and its composer, who was present."

B619. ——. "Anmerkungen zur Musik unserer Tage." *Die Welt* (July 1958)
Review of the book of essays *Zur Sprache gebracht* (K707).

B620. ——. "Antike ohne Illusionen." *Neue Zeitschrift für Musik* 125:7-8 (1964): 310-311.
Review of the premiere of the opera *Der goldene Bock* op.186. Picture.

B621. ——. "Germany: Season of moderns." *Musical America* 84:7 (Sept.1964): 26.
"Concurrently with the International Congress for Contemporary Music Theater, the Hamburg State Opera put on performances of ... its modern repertoire... The high point of the series was the premiere of ... *The Golden ram*" op.186.

B622. ——. "Meditation über den Zweifel." *Die Welt* no.301 (December 27, 1966): 11.
Review of the premiere of *Glauben und Wissen* op.194.

B623. Johnson, H. Earle. "Krenek, Ernst." In his *Operas on American Subjects.* (New York: Coleman-Ross, 1964): 67.
Briefly surveys the early performances of *Jonny spielt auf* op.45.

B624. Johnson, June Durkin. *Analysis of selected works for the soprano voice written in serial technique by living composers.* (D.M.A. thesis: University of Illinois, 1967) 189 pp.

Investigates and evaluates six works, including Krenek's *Fünf Lieder nach Worten von Franz Kafka* op.82.

B625. Jones, Charles. "Ernst Bacon: *Burnt cabin branch...* Ernst Krenek: *Suite for flute and piano...*" *Notes* 2d ser. 13:3 (June 1956): 524.

Review of the publication of op.147.

B626. Jones, Ralph E. "Krenek: *Lamentations of the prophet, Jeremiah.*" *The New Records* 29:12 (February 1962): 6-7.

Record review of op.93 on Bärenreiter Musicaphon 30 L 1303-4.

B627. "*Jonny spielt auf* by Ernst Krenek in New York Jan.19, 1928." *Musical Courier* 98 (January 24, 1929): 7.

Review of the first American performance of op.45.

B628. "*Jonny spielt auf.*" *Allgemeine Musikzeitung* 54:4 (January 28, 1927): 89.

Brief announcement of the forthcoming premiere of the opera op.45 in Leipzig.

B629. K. "Ernst Krenek 80." *Musikhandel* 31:6 (September 1980): 281.

Brief biography and a list of festivals honoring his eightieth birthday.

B630. K.J. "Bern." *Schweizerische Musikzeitung und Sängerblatt* 71:22 (November 15, 1931): 798-799.

Review of the premiere of *Die Nachtigall* op.68a for soprano and orchestra.

B631. K.K. "Einzelgänger der neuen Musik." *Musikhandel* 21:5 (August 1970): 199.

General survey and appreciation of Krenek's life.

B632. Kaltat, L. "Fokstrot spasaet Europe opera *Dzhoui naigryvaet.*" *Proletarskii muzykant* no.2 (1929): 20-27.

Fox trot saves Europe, a discussion of Krenek and his opera *Jonny spielt auf* op.45.

B633. Kanny, Mark N. "Krenek: *Trio for violin, clarinet and piano;* Webern: *Four pieces for violin and piano* op.7..." *American Record Guide* 47:2 (January 1984): 71-72.

Record review of op.108 on Crystal Records S 645 which includes op.108.

B634. Kapp, Julius. "*Zwingburg.*" *Blätter der Staatsoper* (Berlin) 5:2 (October 1924): 2-5.

Synopsis of the opera op.14.

B635. Karpf, Roswitha Vera. "Die Rezeption der Antike in Kreneks Operntexten." In *Ernst Krenek*, hrsg. von Otto Kolleritsch. (B328) Studien zur Wertungsforschung, Bd.15. (Wien: Universal Edition, 1982): 79-94.

An examination of Krenek's use of themes from ancient Greece in the plots of his operas including *Orpheus und Eurydike* op.21, *Leben des Orest* op.60, *Pallas Athene weint* op.144, and *Der goldene Bock* op.186.

B636. Kastendieck, Miles. "Krenek's 4th an intellectual gesture." *New York Journal-American* (November 28, 1947): 14.

Review of the premiere of the *Fourth symphony* op.113.

B637. ——. "Ernst Krenek." *Mens en melodie* 22:7 (December 1967)

"Time and time again commentators have found Ernst Krenek's music fascinating, but he remains an enigma among composers... Krenek may be unique as an intellectual *and* a composer, to say nothing of being a splendid lecturer, a highly acclaimed teacher, a fine pianist and a skillful, meticulous conductor." Surveys the musical works written in America. Picture.

a. ——. *BMI, the Many Worlds of Music* (December 1967): 17.

B638. Katz, Erich. "Ernst Kreneks *Toccata und Chaconne* für Klavier, op.13." *Melos* 4:1 (August 1, 1924): 39-58.

Detailed analysis of the composition.

B639. Kaufmann, Ferdinand. "Ernst Kreneks *Motette zur Opferung.*" *Musica sacra* 83 (1963): 282-285.

Review of the publication of op.141.

B640. Kaufmann, Harald. "Musik als Sprache und Stammeln." *Forum* 6:72 (December 1959): 461-463.

Review of the book of essays *Zur Sprache gebracht* (K707).

B641. ——. "Den österrikiska musiken under de sista trettio aaren." *Musikrevy* 16:8 (1961): 262-265.

Surveys Austrian music between the wars and Krenek's position in it.

B642. Keith, Richard. "Symphony, choir give Yule concert." *Washington Post* (December 20, 1948): 10.

Review of the premiere of the *Second violin sonata* op.115.

B643. Keller, Hans. "Education marches on." *Music Review* 15 (February 1954): 71-73.

Review of the book *Johannes Ockeghem* (K616).

B644. Kellermayr, Rudolf E. "Sellners *Oedipus* erfror in der Felsenreitschule." *Kleine Zeitung* 62:171 (July 29, 1965): 10.

Review of the premiere of Aeschylus's *Oedipus* cycle with incidental music by Krenek op.188.

B645. Khittl, Klaus. "Keine Mondscheinsonate." *Die Presse* (Vienna) (March 12, 1980)

Review of the premiere of *Opus 231.*

B646. Kinkaid, Frank. "Portland." *Opera News* 40:11 (January 17, 1976): 30.

Review of the English translation of *Life of Orestes* op.60 performed at the Portland Opera. Picture.

B647. Kipnis, Igor. "Berg: *Sonata for piano, op.1*; Schönberg: *Three piano pieces, op.11*; Krenek: *Sonata no.3 for piano, op.92, no.4.*" *American Record Guide* 25:8 (April 1959): 518.

Record review of Columbia ML 5336.

B648. Kirchberg, Klaus. "Neue Musik für Orgel." *Musica* 23:1 (January-February 1969): 32.

Review of the premiere of *Organologia* op.180.5 in Mülheim Petrikirche by Gerd Zacher.

B649. Kirchmeyer, Helmut. "Lothar Knessl: *Ernst Krenek.*" *Die Musikforschung* 29:1 (January-March 1976): 122.

Review of the book about Krenek (B662).

B650. Klein, Herman. "Operatic and foreign songs." *Gramophone* 6:61 (June 1928): 19-20.

Record review of excerpts from *Jonny spielt auf* op.45 on Parlophone E 10698.

B651. Klein, Reimar. "Geschichtsphilosophische Motive im Musikdenken Kreneks." In *Ernst Krenek*, hrsg. von Otto Kolleritsch. (B328) Studien zur Wertungsforschung, Bd.15. (Wien: Universal Edition, 1982): 47-55.

An examination of Krenek's attitudes and discussions of the role of music history in new music as demonstrated in his writings.

B652. Klein, Rudolf. "Neue Musik in Oesterreich." *Musica* 16:3 (1962): 107-115.

Survey of Austrian music in which Krenek's relationship to Schoenberg is discussed with the assertion that the operas *Karl V.* op.73 and *Pallas Athene weint* op.144 are his important works. Picture, p.105.

B653. ——. "Contemporary music in Austria." *Musical Quarterly* 51:1 (1965): 180-190.

Survey of Austrian music after the First World War. Of those composers who stood on both sides of 1945, "the most important of all is without doubt Ernst Krenek... He was the only one of those composers who formed the first inner circle of the Viennese School who was later in close and continuous contact with the developments of today and tomorrow. This explains, most probably, why Krenek tried to come to grips with all forms of musical expression, including the serial and aleatory experiments."

a. ——. In *Contemporary Music in Europe: A Comprehensive Survey* edited by Paul Henry Lang and Nathan Broder. (New York: G. Schirmer, 1965): 180-190.

B654. ——. "Informationen zu Kreneks jüngsten Werken." *Oesterreichische Musikzeitschrift* 28:4 (April 1973): 161-166.

Describes the compositional processes, structural principles, and serial techniques in Krenek's works from 1967 to 1971: *Horizon circled* op.196, *Perspektiven* op.199, *Exercises of a later hour* op.200, *Instant remembered* op.201, *Six profiles* op.203, *Fivefold enfoldment* op.205, *Doppelt beflügeltes Band* op.207, *Messe Gib uns den Frieden* op.208, *Kitharaulos* op.213, and *Statisch und ekstatisch* op.214.

B655. ——. "Krenek, Ernst." In *Sohlmans Musiklexikon*. Vol.4. (Stockholm: Sohlmans Förlag, 1977): 185-186.

Biographical essay with list of works. Picture.

B656. "Kleines Komponisten-Lexikon." *Oesterreichische Musikzeitschrift* 16:6/7 (June-July 1961): 322-326.

Brief biographies of Krenek, Arnold Schönberg, Alban Berg, Anton Webern, Egon Wellesz, Hans Erich Apostel, Hanns Jelinek, and Karl Schiske.

B657. "Kleines Lexikon." *Oesterreichische Musikzeitschrift* 15:5 (May 1960): 266-268.

Brief biographies of composers represented in the Wiener Festwochen including Krenek.

B658. Klemm, Eberhardt. "Gespräch mit Ernst Krenek. *Jahrbuch Peters* 3 (1981): 203-218.

An interview with the composer.

B659. ——. "Die gute alte Musik -- ich habe sie noch gekannt." *Musik und Gesellschaft* 36 (September 1986): 461+

Sketches of German and Austrian emigramt composers, including Krenek.

B660. Knessl, Lothar. "Ernst Krenek." *Oesterreichische Musikzeitschrift* 19:11 (November 1964): 539-541.

Discusses Krenek's recent visit to Vienna during which he gave several lectures, conducted concerts of his recent music, and saw the issuance of recording Amadeo AVRS 5038 of his opera *Jonny spielt auf* op.45.

B661. ——. "Wien: *Das dunkle Wasser,* Krenek zwischen *Jonny* und Zeitfragen." *Neue Zeitschrift für Musik* 125:12 (December 1964): 553-554.

Report of Krenek's lecture "Dunklen Wasser an der schönen blauen Donau" [Dark waters on the beautiful blue Danube] surveying Krenek's works from *Jonny spielt auf* op.45 to serialism pointing out that freedom is a major theme of his operas. Emphasizes the serial works.

B662. ——. *Ernst Krenek, eine Studie.* Oesterreichische Komponisten des 20. Jahrhunderts, 12. (Wien: Elisabeth Lafite, 1967)

Biographical essay with a detailed examination of the *Second symphony* op.12, *Reisebuch aus den österreichischen Alpen* op.62, *Karl V.* op.73, and *Sestina* op.161 as examples of each of his major creative periods. Includes facsimiles and photos. *See:* B178, B649, B938, B1092

B663. ——. "Dir reflektierte Historie." *Forum* 14:160/161 (April-May 1967): 399-404.

Analysis of the themes in the opera *Karl V.* op.73.

B664. ——. "Kreneks Reise in die Tonalität." *Oesterreichische Musikzeitschrift* 22:6 (June 1967): 335-338.

Reisebuch aus den österrrechischen Alpen op.62, Krenek's 1929 song cycle which was influenced by Schubert's *Winterreise,* is examined in detail.

B665. ——. "Den Horizont umkreist; Ernst Krenek zum Fünfundsiebzigsten." *Musica* 29:4 (July-August 1975): 344-346.

Essay celebrating Krenek's seventy-fifth birthday and surveying the importance of the works composed during the previous ten years. Picture.

B666. Knoch, Hans. *Orpheus und Eurydike, der antike Sagenstoff in den Opern von Darius Milhaud und Ernst Krenek.* Kölner Beiträge zur Musikforschung, 91. (Regensburg: Gustav Bosse, 1977) 277 pp.

This Ph.D. dissertation surveys the Orpheus myth and discusses Krenek's setting of Oskar Kokoschka's play in his opera *Orpheus und Eurydike* op.21.

B667. Knussen, Oliver. "Ernst Krenek: *The Santa Fe Timetable,* Op.102..." *Tempo* No.122 (September 1977): 38-42.

Reviews the recordings Orion ORS 75204 and Orion ORS 76246 and the book *Horizons circled* (K864). Includes a discography of recordings available in Britain.

B668. Koch, Gerhard R. "Blasen, Schlagen, Taumeln." *Frankfurter Allgemeine Zeitung* no.246 (October 23, 1972): 19.

Review of the premiere of *Aulokithara* op.213a.

B669. ——. "Kaiser-Verklärung." *Frankfurter Allgemeine Zeitung* (January 27, 1982)

Record review of the opera *Karl V.* op.73 on Amadeo AVRS 305.

B670. Kö. "Musikalische Gottesdienst-Gestaltung auf neuen Wegen." *Basler Nachrichten* no.277 (July 4, 1967): 3.

Review of the premiere of *Proprium für das Dreifaltigkeitsfest* op.195.

B671. Koegler, Horst. "Germany." *Musical Courier* 150:4 (October 1954): 25.

Review of the German premiere of *Dark waters* op.125.

B672. ——. "Germany." *Opera* 5:11 (November 1954): 678-679.

Includes a review of the German premiere of *Dark waters* op.125 and mentions the performance of the monologue *Medea* op.129 at Darmstadt.

B673. ——. "*Dark Waters* in Darmstadt." *Opera News* 19:3 19 (November 15, 1954): 21.

Review of the German premieres of the opera op.125 and the monologue *Medea* op.129 during the International Holiday Courses of New Music.

B674. ——. "Germany." *Musical Courier* 150:6 (November 15, 1954): 33.

Brief review of the premiere of *Pallas athene symphony* op.137 by the NWDR Symphonie-Orchester conducted by the composer. The concert also included a performance of the *Second piano concerto* op.81 and the first European performance of the *Hermann Melville cantata* op.95.

B675. ——. "Hamburg." *Musical Courier* 152:6 (November 15, 1955): 27-28.

Review of the opening of the Hamburg Opera house and the premiere of *Pallas Athene weint* op.144. Picture.

B676. ——. "Modern Hamburg." *Opera News* 20:6 (December 12, 1955): 12-13.

Review of the premiere of the opera *Pallas Athene weint* op.144, the most important event in the celebration of the opening of the new Hamburgische Staatsoper.

B677. Köhler, Heinrich. "Jazz." *Blätter des Stadt-Theaters Mainz* 1:3 (1927): 13-14.

Explores the themes of jazz and Jonny in Krenek's opera *Jonny spielt auf.*

B678. Kohn, Karl. "Current chronicle: Los Angeles." *Musical Quarterly* 49:3 (July 1963): 360-369.

Surveys the 1962/63 season of Monday Evening Concerts noting that three works by Krenek had their first America performances: *Flute piece in nine phases* op.171, a suite from his adaptation of Monteverdi's *L'Incoronazione* op.80b, and *Alpbach Balletmusik* op.180. In addition, *Quaestio temporis* op.170 was performed.

B679. Kolleritsch, Otto. "Ueber Ernst Kreneks musikästhetische Vorstellungen." In *Ernst Krenek*, hrsg. von Otto Kolleritsch. (B328) Studien zur Wertungsforschung, Bd.15. (Wien: Universal Edition, 1982): 29-35.

An examination of the aesthetic principles presented in *Ueber neue Musik* (K397).

B680. Kolneder, Walter. "Anton Webern: *Sketches.*" *Die Musikforschung* 23:4 (October-December 1970): 497-498.

Review of the book of sketches and Krenek's introductory essay (K828).

B681. Kolodin, Irving. "Krenek spielt auf." *Saturday Review* 21:13 (January 20, 1940): 18.

Review of the book *Music here and now* (K495).

B682. ——. "From campus, studio and library." *Saturday Review* 37:11 (March 13, 1954): 30-31.

Brief record review of the Organ sonata op.92 on University of Oklahoma 2.

B683. ——. "Music to my ears." *Saturday Review* 45:21 (May 26, 1962): 39.

Review of the first American performance of *Quaestio temporis* op.170.

B684. ——. "Recordings reports II: Miscellaneous LPs." *Saturday Review* 49:39 (September 24, 1966): 76.

Brief record review of *Pentagram* op.163 on Lyrichord LLST 7158.

B685. "Der Komponist Ernst Krenek." *Münsterländische Zeitung* (Cloppenburg) (October 30, 1951)

Review of the premiere of the *Piano concerto* op.123.

B686. "Komponisten." *Anbruch* 14:2/3 (February-March 1932): 62.

Brief announcement of the premiere of *Gesänge des späten Jahres* op.71 on March 25 in Dresden sung by Elisa Stünzner. On April 4 it will be sung in Berlin and broadcast over the radio.

B687. Konold, Wulf. "Druckreifer Gedankenaustausch." *Musica* 29:4 (July-August 1975): 347.

Review of the book by Krenek and Theodor Wiesengrund Adorno, *Briefwechsel* (K862).

B688. ——. "Ernst Krenek." *Musica* 36:3 (May/June 1982): 270-271.

Review of the biography *Ernst Krenek, ein Komponist im Exil* (B1502) by Claudia Maurer Zenck.

B689. ——. "Ueber Ernst Krenek." *Musica* 37:1 (January-February 1983): 66-67.

Review of the book of essays by Otto Kolleritsch (B328).

B690. ——. "Als Literat und Mittelpunkt." *Musica* 39:2 (March-April 1985): 198-199.

Reviews of Krenek's book of essays *Im Zweifelsfalle* (K924) and a book of essays about Krenek *Musik-Konzepte 39/40* (B895).

B691. Kopp, Sister Bernadette. "Ernst Krenek." In her "The Twelve-tone technique of Adolph Weiss." (Ph.D. diss.: Northwestern University, 1981): 125-127.

Briefly discusses the twelve-tone technique used in *Twelve short piano pieces* op.83 and *Suite for cello* op.84. Also briefly discusses Krenek's use of rotation in his *Lamentatio Jeremiae prophetae* op.93 and *Kette, Krise, und Spiegel* op.160.

B692. Korngold, Julius. "Vom Krankenbette der Neumusik." *Neue Freie Presse* (Vienna) (March 18, 1931)

Reactions to Krenek's article "Pro domo" (K106).

B693. "Konzert-Rundschau." *Berliner Zeit am Mittag* (February 21, 1921)
Review of the premiere of the *Serenade* op.4.

B694. "Konzertrückschau." *Deutsche Zeitung* Berlin (January 18, 1922)
Review of the premiere of Schubert's *Piano sonata* D.840 (W65) completed by Krenek and preformed by Eduard Erdmann in the Singakademie.

B695. Kouta, Robert. "Mahlers Zehnte Symphonie." *Der Auftakt* (Prague) 4:10 (1924): 288-289.
Review of the premiere of Krenek's edition of the symphony (W72) at the Vienna Staatsoper on October 12.

B696. Kraus, Egon. "Musik im Fernsehen, internationale Tagung in Salzburg." *Musik im Unterricht* 53:10 (October 1962): 294-297.
Discusses the festival which included the awarding of the Salzburger Opernpreis 1962 to television operas, including *Ausgerechnet und verspielt* op.179. Picture.

B697. Kraus, Gottfried. "Krenek, *Reisebücher*." *Fono Forum* 14:3 (March 1969): 152-153.
Record review of op.62 on Edition Rhodos ERS 1201-3.

B698. ——. "Die Kraft der eigenen Ordnung." *Die Presse* (Vienna) (August 25, 1987)
Review of the premiere of the *String trio* op.237 on a concert in celebration of Krenek's eightyseventh birthday during the Carinthian Summer festival.

B699. Krellmann, Hanspeter. "Bonn: *Grenzklänge* von Ernst Krenek." *Melos* 30:3 (March 1963): 95.
Review of the first European performance of *Marginal sounds* op.162.

B700. ——. "Dialog mit Ernst Krenek." *Musica* 19:6 (November-December 1965): 310-311.
Interview focusing on Krenek's operas and changing styles. Includes a review of the premiere of *Wechselrahmen* op.189. Picture.

B701. ——. "Ein Krenek-Document." *Musica* 30:4 (July-August 1976): 354-355.
Record review of Orion ORS 75204.

B702. "Krenek." *Musical America* 83:10 (October 1963): 39.
Announcement of the three day festival honoring Krenek's sixty-third birthday held by the North Carolina Music Society in the State Legislative Building in Raleigh.

B703. "Krenek Archiv in USA eroeffnet." *Oesterreichische Musikzeitschrift* 33:6 (June 1978): 304-305.
Announcement of the opening of the Ernst Krenek Archive at the University of California, San Diego with a deposit of correspondence covering the years 1938 through 1973 and manuscripts and copies of his writings over the same period.

B704. "Krenek *Eleven short piano pieces,* **from op.83."** *The Steinway Review of Permanent Music* (August 1940)
Record review of Columbia X 171.

B705. *The Krenek Festival.* (Santa Barbara, CA, 1979) 167 pp.

Program book of the festival held at the University of California, Santa Barbara from April 8 to 15. Includes "Interview with myself" (K895), program notes and texts of the 47 compositions performed during the festival, and many photographs.

B706. "Krenek festival at University of Wisconsin." *Musical Courier* 149:6 (March 15, 1954): 44.

Announcement of the festival beginning March 14; it will open with Krenek's lecture "A composer accounts for himself" and close with *Symphonic elegy* op.105 conducted by the composer. University of Wisconsin

B707. "A Krenek Festschrift." *Perspectives of New Music* 24:1 (Fall-Winter 1985): 270-423.

The scores of twenty compositions presented to Krenek by his students and admirers at a concert on December 7 during a three-day festival held at the University of California, San Diego. The scores included *For myself, at eighty-five* op.238a by Krenek, and works by Theodore Antoniou, Tom Benjamin, William Bland, Garrett Bowles, David Burge, Sergio Cervetti, Marc-Antonio Consoli, Roque Cordero, Aurelio de la Vega, Grant Fletcher, Glen Glasow, Beverly Grigsby, Dennis Kam, Christopher Kuzell, Peter Odegard, Will Ogdon, Nikola Ovanin, George Perle, Jerome Rosen, and Richard Swift. Picture.

B708. "Krenek new opera transports Jason to America." *The Times* (London) no.56068 (July 20, 1964): 5.

Review of the premiere of the opera *Der goldene Bock* op.186. Picture.

B709. "Krenek opera brings dissonance-orgy." *Musical America* 45:12 (January 8, 1927)

Review of the premiere of *Orpheus und Eurydike* op.21. Picture.

B710. "Krenek performs own works." *Music News* 43:9 (November 1951): 6.

Brief announcement of the premiere of the *Fourth piano concerto* op.123, the *Double concerto* op.124, and the *Sixth piano sonata* op.128. Also mentions that Krenek will visit the Teresopolis (Brazil) Art Institute to teach in January.

B711. "Krenek trio premiered." *Musical Courier* 139:8 (April 15, 1949): 15.

Review of the premiere of the *String trio* op.118.

B712. "Krenek work to get Hamline premiere." *Minneapolis Sunday Tribune* (May 8, 1949)

Discusses the forthcoming May 19th performance of the *Symphonic elegy* op.105 by the Hamline Symphony Orchestra conducted by Thomas Nee.

B713. "Krenek writing symphony here." *New Mexico Music* (July-August 1947)

Interview with Krenek discussing the composition of the *Fourth symphony* op.113 and including a survey of recent performances of his works.

B714. "Krenek, der Freudenbringer." *Zeitschrift für Musik* 94:11 (November 1927): 641.

Discusses the opera *Jonny spielt auf* op.45 which was programmed in about sixty opera houses during the Winter of 1927/8.

B715. "Krenek-Ehrung." *Hamburger Abendblatt* (December ?, 1950)
Review of a Nordwestdeutscher Rundfunk (NWDR) studio concert "Neues Werk" of *Sinfonischen Musik für 9 Soloinstrumente* op.23, the *Third piano sonata* op.92, no.4, and the first European performance of *Sonata for violin and piano* op.99.

B716. "Krenek, Ernst." *Current Biography* (1942): 472-474.
Biographical essay and portrait.

B717. "Krenek, Ernst." *Contemporary Authors* 57-60 (1976): 330.
Brief biographical essay listing his career, books, and operas.

B718. "Krenek, Ernst. *Exploring Music.*" *The Booklist and Subscription Books Bulletin* 63:3 (October 1, 1966): 148.
Review of the book of essays (K817).

B719. "Krenek, Ernst. *Exploring Music.*" *Choice* 3:9 (November 1966): 781.
Review of the book of essays (K817).

B720. "Krenek, Ernst. *Horizons Circled.*" *The Booklist* 71:17 (May 1, 1975): 889.
Review of the book (K864).

B721. "Krenek, Ernst. *Horizons Circled.*" *Choice* 12:4 (June 1975): 546.
Review of the book (K864).

B722. "Krenek, Ernst. *Horizons circled.*" *Kirkus* 42:11 (June 1, 1974): 614.
Review of the book (K864).

B723. "Krenek, Ernst. *Music Here and Now.*" *The Booklist* 36:9 (February 1, 1940): 210-211.
Review of the book (K495).

B724. "Krenek, Ernst. *Music Here and Now.*" *Choice* 5:4 (June 1968): 495.
Review of the Russel & Russel reprint of the book (K495).

B725. "Krenek, Ernst. *Thema und 13 Variationen für Orchester,* op.69." *Allgemeine Musikzeitung* 59:22/23 (June 10, 1932): 317.
Analysis of the composition and a list of works. Picture.

B726. "Eine Krenek-Uraufführung des neuen Instrumentalensembles." *Basler Nachrichten* (January 18, 1955)
Review of the premiere of *Five short pieces for strings* op.116.

B727. Kriechbaum, Reinhard. "Aus facettenreichem Schaffen." *Wiener Zeitung* (October 28, 1980)
Review of the premiere of *Im Tal der Zeit* op.232.

B728. Krienitz, Willy. "*Mammon.*" *Allgemeine Musikzeitung* 54:41 (October 14, 1927): 1042.
Review of the premiere of the ballet op.37.

B729. ——. "Musikbriefe: München." *Allgemeine Musikzeitung* 54:47 (November 25, 1927): 1221-1222.
Includes a review of the premiere of the songs *Gesänge nach alten Gedichten* op.53a.

B730. Kröll, Karl. "Krenek-Uraufführung im Dom Messgesänge für die neue Liturgie." *Süd-Ost Tagespost* (Graz, Austria) (October 21, 1980)

Review of the premiere of *Deutschen Messgesänge zum 29. Sonntag im Jahreskreis* (W101) at the beginning of a week-long festival devoted to Krenek at the Graz Steirischer Herbst.

B731. Kuznitzky, Hans. "Ernst Krenek. *Die Nachtigall aus 'Worte in Versen' von Karl Kraus*, op.68." *Allgemeine Musikzeitung* 59:2 (January 15, 1932): 26.

Review of the publication of the songs.

B732. L.A.S. "Krenek Symphony soloist." *Christian Science Monitor* 30:290 (November 5, 1938): 11.

Review of the first American performance of the *Second piano concerto* op.81.

B733. L.S. "Kreneks *Karl V.*" *Bohemia* (Prague) (June 23, 1938)

Review in German of the premiere of the opera op.73.

B734. la. "Pražská premiéra Křenkova *Karla V.*" *Ceske Slovo* (June 24, 1938)

Review of the premiere of the opera op.73.

B735. Lade, Ludwig. "Ein neue Konzertwerk." *Frankfurter Zeitung* (October 1927)

Review of the premiere of the *Vier Gesänge nach alten Gedichten* for mezzosoprano and woodwinds op.53a.

B736. ———. "Neue Musik: München." *Musikblätter des Anbruch* 9:10 (December 1927): 446-447.

Review of the premiere of *Vier Gesänge für Mezzosopran mit Blässern* op.53a.

B737. Lang, Paul Henry. "Ajemian sisters." *New York Herald Tribune* (March 10, 1955)

Review of the first American performance of the *Double concerto* op.124.

B738. ———. "Music: Fromm Foundation." *New York Herald Tribune* (May 14, 1962)

Review of the first American performance of *Quaestio temporis* op.170.

B739. Lange, Art. "Hindemith: *Quartet for Clarinet, Violin, Cello, and Piano*; Krenek: *Trio for Violin, Clarinet, and Piano*; Milhaud: *Suite for Violin, Clarinet, and Piano.*" *American Record Guide* 42:2 (December 1978): 53.

Record review of op.108 on Supraphon 111 2147.

B740. ———. "Krenek: *Die Jahreszeiten*, Op.35; *Drei Gemischte Choere*, Op.61; *Durch die Nacht*, Op.67; *O Holy Ghost*, Op.186a; *Three Sacred Pieces*, Op.210; *Three Lessons*, Op.210; *Two Settings of Poems by William Blake*, Op.226." *American Record Guide* 44:2 (December 1980): 35-36.

Record review of Orion ORS 80377.

B741. Langham, Nancy Clarke. "A study of two sonatas for the 1940s: *Sonata no.2 for solo violin* op.115 (1948) by Ernst Krenek and *Sonata for solo violin* op.10 (1940) by Vincent Persichetti." (Ph.D. diss.: Louisiana State University, 1985) 142 pp.

Concluded that both sonatas are chromatic and formally tight, Baroque appearances in thematic construction and overall style are apparent, and both are conservative in their use of special effects.

B742. Langrock, Klaus. "Krenek, Ernst." In *Das Grosse Lexikon der Musik*, hrsg. von Marc Honegger und Günther Akkord. Bd.5. (Freiburg: Herder, 1981): 8-10.
A biographical essay with list of works. Picture.

B743. Latzko, Ernst. "Ernst Kreneks *Leben des Orest.*" *Leipziger Bühnenblätter* no.9 (1929/30): 84-88.
Program book of the premiere of the opera.

B744. ——. "Ernst Krenek: *Leben des Orest.*" *Rheinische Musik- und Theaterzeitung* 31:2 (January 25, 1930): 22-23.
Review of the premiere of the opera op.60.

B745. *"Leben des Orest.*" *Allgemeine Musikzeitung* 57:1 (January 3, 1930): 19.
Brief announcement of the forthcoming premiere of the opera op.60.

B746. *"Leben des Orest.*" *Leipziger neueste Nachrichten* (January 26, 1930): Welt im Bild, p.8.
Four pictures of the premiere of the opera op.60.

B747. Leibowitz, René. "La musicologie est-elle possible?" *Critique* no.33 (Winter 1945/46): 125-138.
Extensive review of both volumes of the *Hamline studies in musicology* (K550 & K559).

B748. ——. "Les nouvelles générations de compositeurs 'dodécaphonistes'." In his *Introduction à la musique des douze sons*. (Paris: L'Arche, 1949): 250-270.
An analysis of the *Sixth string quartet* op.78 in a discussion of twelve-tone technique by several composers.

B749. Leichtentritt, Hugo. "Die Wochen vor Ostern im Berliner Musikleben." *Hannover Courier* (April 10, 1922)
Review of the premiere of the *First symphony* op.7.

B750. ——. "Glazounoff the center of interest in Berlin." *Musical Courier* 84:16 (April 20, 1922): 40.
Includes a review of the premiere of the *First symphony* op.7. Caricature sketch by Maria Wetzel.

B751. ——. "Kreneks *Zwingburg.*" *Der Auftakt* (Prague) 4:10 (1924): 285-287.
Review of the premiere of the opera op.14.

B752. ——. "German music of the last decade." *Musical Quarterly* 10:2 (April 1924): 193-218.
Survey intending to show "that music in Germany is still alive, that in spite of the most unfortunate and deplorable conditions of life, an enthusiasm surpassing in intensity the efforts of the older generation" exists. Discusses Krenek as "a typical child of his generation ... [whose] real talent is not to be questioned." Mentions his "much admired" *Symphonic music* op.11, that his two symphonies op.7 and op.12 "proved a sensation at their first performances," that several string quartets have been performed, and that *Toccata and Chaconne* op.13 showed "Krenek's powerful architectural ability." (pp.215-216)

B753. ——. "Krenek's *Die Zwingburg*, crude and chaotic, has Berlin premiere." *Musical Courier* 89:20 (November 13, 1924): 16-17.

Review of the premiere of the opera op.14. Picture.

B754. ——. "Krenek's new violin concerto shows retreat from radicalism." *Musical Courier* 90:8 (February 19, 1925): 6.

Review of the premiere of op.29. Includes caricature of Alma Moodie playing the concerto.

B755. **Lemacher, Heinrich.** "Das V. Donaueschinger Kammermusikfest." *Allgemeine Musikzeitung* 52:32/33 (August 7, 1925): 688-689.

Review of the premiere of the chorus *Die Jahreszeiten* op.35.

B756. ——. "Aus dem Westdeutschen Musikleben: Köln." *Allgemeine Musikzeitung* 54:7 (February 18, 1927): 157-158.

Review of the premiere of the songs *O lacrymosa* op.48.

B757. **Lesch, Helmut.** "Dir Knaben machen kühnen Krach." *Abend Zeitung* (Munich) (July 24, 1974)

Review of the premiere of the song cycle *Spätlese* op.218.

B758. **Lesle, Lutz.** "Eine neue Kirchenmusik." *Die Welt* (October 19, 1971): 23.

Review of the premiere of *Messe Gib uns den Frieden* op.208.

B759. ——. "Zwischen den Künsten; 1. Intermediale in Hamburg." *Musica* 37:1 (January-February 1983): 49-50.

Review of a performance of a scene from the uncompleted opera *Kehraus um St. Stephan* op.66.

B760. ——. "Zwischen den Stühlen." *Die Zeit* no.48 (November 25, 1983): 56.

Review of the performance of *Arc of life* op.234 for orchestra during the Aarhus Musik-Fest.

B761. **Levant, Oscar.** "I like music books." *Publishers' Weekly* 137 (February 24, 1940): 883-885.

An interview in which he discusses the recent books he likes; *"Music here and now* [K495] excited me the most of any recent book."

B762. **Levinger, Henry W.** "New Friends of Music." *Musical Courier* 147:2 (January 15, 1953): 22-23.

Review of the premiere of *Two sacred songs* op.132.

B763. ——. "Carnegie Hall." *Musical Courier* 148:6 (November 15, 1953): 10.

Review of the premiere of the *Concerto for two pianos* op.127.

B764. **Lewinski, Wolf-Eberhard von.** "Auf suche nach neuer Kammermusik." *Düsseldorfer Nachrichten* (January 28, 1953)

Review of the premiere of the *Sixth string quartet* op.78.

B765. ——. "Uraufführung in Darmstadt: Ernst Kreneks 6. *Streichquartett*." *Das Musikleben* 6:3 (March 1953): 102.

Review of the premiere of op.78.

B766. ——. "Kölner Lautsprecher-Konzert in Kranichstein." *Darmstädter Tagblatt* (July 21, 1956)

Review of an electronic music concert which included the premiere of *Spiritus intelligentiae, Sanctus* op.152.

B767. Lewinski, Wolf-Eberhard von. "Musik der Zeit - Musik der Zukunf."
Darmstädter Tagblatt (September 9, 1958)
Review of the premiere of *Hexaeder* op.167.

B768. ——. "Reiseschriftsteller Krenek." *Musica* 14:1 (January 1960): 53-54.
Review of the book of travel essays *Gedanken unterwegs* (K720).

B769. ——. "Ernst Krenek 60. Jahre." *Musica* 14:8 (August 1960): 527-528.
Brief biographical essay in honor of his sixtieth birthday.

B770. ——. "Vom Musikalienmarkt." *Musica* 14:9 (September 1960): 610.
Review of the publication of *Sechs Vermessene* op.168 for piano.

B771. ——. "Kreneks *Hausmusik*." *Musica* 15:10 (October 1960): 579.
Brief review of the publication of op.172.

B772. ——. "Der Liederkomponist Ernst Krenek." *Darmstädter Tagblatt*
(November 30, 1960)
Review of the premiere of the *First violin sonata* op.33; the songs, sung by
Rudo Timper and accompanied by the composer, were *Ballade vom Fest* op.71,
no.4, *Zwei geistliche Gesäng* op.132, the *Hopkins Lieder* op.112, and five songs
from 1921-23.

B773. ——. "Krenek unterwegs: Darmstadt." *Musica* 15:1 (January 1961): 30-
31.
Review of two Darmstadt concerts including a vocal concert of the *Hopkins
songs* op.112 along with songs from 1921 and 1931 sung by Rudo Timper and
accompanied by the composer, and the premiere of the *First violin sonata op.33*.

B774. ——. "Neue Werke von Krenek." *Musica* 16:6 (1962): 331-332.
Review of the Baerenreiter publications of *Ballad of the railroads* op.98 and
Basler Massarbeit op.173.

B775. ——. "Krenek: *Komponist und Hörer*." *Musica* 18:6 (1964): 332.
Review of the book (K748).

B776. ——. "Ernst Krenek: *Zwölf Variationen*." *Musica* 19:2 (March-April
1965): 89.
Review of the publication of op.79.

B777. ——. "Zum 65. Geburtstag Ernst Kreneks." *Musica* 19:4 (July-August
1965): 219-220.
Surveys Krenek's life on his sixty-fifth birthday noting his early success
with *Jonny spielt auf* op.45. Other important works are *Lamentatio Jeremiae
prophetae* op.93, *Karl V.* op.73, and *Pallas Athene weint* op.144.

B778. ——. "Neue Chormusik." *Musica* 20:2 (March-April 1966): 88-89.
Includes a brief review of the publication of *O Holy Ghost* op.186a.

B779. ——. "Hamburg: Eine neue Oper von Krenek." *Schweizerische
Musikzeitung* 110:4 (July-August 1970): 261.
Review of the premiere of the opera *Das kommt davon* op.206.

B780. Lichtenhahn, Ernst ; Seebass, Tilman. *Musikhandschriften aus der
Sammlung Paul Sacher*. (Basel: Hoffmann-La Roche, 1976) 200 pp.
A Festschrift for Paul Sacher's seventieth birthday discussing his activities
as patron, conductor, and collector. Includes a catalog of his collection of
musical autographs containing several by Krenek.

B781. Lichtenhahn, Ernst. "Zum Wesen und zur Geschichte von Paul Sachers Kompositionsaufträgen." *Alte und neue Musik,* Vol.2: *Das Basler Kammerorchester 1926-1976.* (Zürich: Atlantis Verlag, 1977): 127-155.

The Festschrift for the Basle Symphony Orchestra and its conductor Paul Sacher includes a discussion and documentation of the commissions, including *Kette, Kreis und Spiegel* op.160 with a facsimile of a letter, pp.147-148.

B782. Liebling, Leonard. "New publications." *Musical Courier* 107:1 (July 1, 1933): 20.

Review of the publication of *Gesänge des Späten Jahres* op.71.

B783. *"The Life of Orestes* by Ernst Krenek." *Musical Courier* 100 (March 8, 1930): 7.

Review of the premiere of the opera op.60.

B784. Limmert, Erich. "Hamburg: Eine Opernbagatelle, Kreneks *Wenn Sardakai auf Reisen geht.*" *Neue Zeitschrift für Musik* 131:7/8 (1970): 326-327.

Review of the premiere of the opera op.206. Picture of a scene.

B785. Lindlar, Heinrich. "Krenek-Uraufführung." *Zeitschrift für Musik* 112:12 (December 1951): 673-674.

Review of the premiere of the *Fourth piano concerto* op.123.

B786. ——. "Kreneks 2. *Violinkonzert.*" *Das Orchester* 3:5 (May 1955): 147.

Review of the premiere of op.140.

B787. ——. "Betrachtungen eines Komponisten." *Musica* 11:4 (April 1957): 235.

Review of the book *De rebus prius factis* (K671).

B788. ——. "Elektrogene Musik: Neue Klangprobleme." *Phonoprisma* 1:1 (1958): 9

Record review of *Spiritus intelligentiae, Sanctus* op.152 on Deutsche Grammophon LP 16 134.

B789. ——. "Die Moderne hat das Wort." *Phonoprisma* 1:6 (1958): 89-90.

Record review of *Viola and piano sonata* op.117 on Deutsche Grammophon Gesellschaft LPEM 19 126.

B790. ——. "Moderne Oper über Kaiser Karl III. *[sic]*" *Die Welt* (May 15, 1958)

Review of the first performance of the new version of *Karl V.* op.73.

B791. ——. "Kreneks *Glockenturm.*" *Musica* 13:2 (February 1959): 117-118.

Review of the first European performance of the chamber opera *Der Glockenturm* op.153.

B792. Lindstrom, Carl E. "Krenek ballet at Avery proves vital experience." *The Hartford Times* (May 20, 1939)

Review of the premiere of the ballet *Eight column line* op.85.

B793. Linke, Norbert. "Zum Glück Zitate von Gluck, Kreneks Oper *Das Kommt Davon* in Hamburg uraufgefuehrt." *Neue Musikzeitung* 19:4 (August-September 1970): 2.

Review of the premiere of the opera *Sardakai, oder Das kommt davon* op.206.

B794. List, Kurt. "Political art, notes on Krenek's *Karl V.* [op.73]." *Modern Music* 15 (May/June 1938): 233-235.

Asserts that Krenek "has not only turned to political art but to the art of politics. For anyone who ventures to use the twelve-tone technic as a material in his musical works today has yielded to political art."

B795. Lockspeiser, Edward. "*Ueber neue Musik.*" *Music and Letters* 18:4 (October 1937): 421.

Review of the book (K397).

B796. Loeb, Madeleine. "Jazzing grand opera." *Musical Digest* (October 1928): 18, 48.

Review of the first American performance of *Jonny spielt auf* op.45.

B797. Lorenz, Paul. "In Hochform: Der Corinthische Sommer in Ossiach." *Opernwelt* 20:10 (October 1979): 31-32.

Mentions the Colloquium held to celebrate Krenek's seventy-ninth birthday and the premiere of the *Concerto for organ and string orchestra* op.230.

B798. Lossen-Freytag, Joseph. "Zweites Donaueschinger Kammermusikfest zur Förderung zeitgenössischer Tonkunst." *Signale für die musikalische Welt* 80:35 (August 30, 1922): 949-951.

Includes a review of the premiere of *Symphonische Musik* op.11.

B799. ——. "Donaueschinger Kammermusik-Aufführungen 1925." *Zeitschrift für Musik* 92:9 (September 1925): 524-525.

Review of the festival including a brief review of the premiere of *Die Jahreszeiten* op.35.

B800. Ludewig, Wolfgang. "Zwei Kurzopern von Ernst Krenek in Saarbrücken." *Melos* 29:9 (Sept.1962): 289.

Review of the premiere of the opera *What price confidence?* op.111 and a performance of *Dunkle Wasser* op.125 in the Landestheater.

B801. ——. "Ueber Strömungen und Entwicklungen in der Musik der zwanziger Jahre." *Musica* 31:5 (September-October 1977): 412-415.

Discusses Krenek's opera *Jonny spielt auf* op.45 and the music of other composers written during the twenties in relation to the dissolution of functional tonality brought about by Claude Debussy and Arnold Schönberg and the economic and political events following World War I.

B802. Lück, Hartmut. "*Karl V.* von Ernst Krenek." *Fono Forum* 27:6 (June 1982): 68-71.

Record review of the opera op.73 issued on Amadeo AVRS 305 and Philips 6769 084. Pictures. *See:* B536.

B803. Lüdicke, Heino. "Hamburg." *Musik und Gesellschaft* 14:10 (October 1964): 622-623.

Review of the premiere of the opera *Goldene Bock* op.186.

B804. ——. "Kurt-Weill-Zyklus und anderes von den Festwochen." *Musik und Gesellschaft* 26:1 (January 1976): 58-59.

Includes a brief review of the premiere of *Feiertagskantate* op.221.

B805. Lüttwitz, Heinrich von. "Krenek in Köln." *Musica* 4:11 (November 1950): 434.

A report on various performances of his music during his visit to Cologne.

B806. ——. "Ernst Krenek und Erich Walter." *Musica* 10:2 (February 1956): 133.

Review of the first European performance of *Elf Transparente* op.142.

B807. **Lukas, Viktor.** "Ernst Krenek." In *Reclams Orgelmusikführer.* 2. Aufl. (Stuttgart: Philipp Reclam June , 1967): 212-213.

A brief analysis of the *Organ sonata* op.92.

B808. **Lumpe, Vera.** "Zum Berlin-Jubiläum." *Musica* 41:4 (July-August 1987): 380-381.

Review of record set Thorophon Capella ETHK 341/4 which includes the *Symphony for winds and percussion* op.34.

B809. **Luten, C.J.** "Schoenberg: *Erwartung.* Krenek: *Symphonic elegy for string orchestra.*" *American Record Guide* 18:10 (June 1952): 299-300.

Record review of op.105 on Columbia ML 4524.

B810. **Lykkebo, Finn.** "Ernst Krenek i MpF." *Dansk Musiktidsskrift* 40:8 (December 1965): 288.

Review of the premiere of *Quintina* op.191.

B811. **M.C.** "Ernst Krenek: *Ueber neue Musik.*" *Monthly Musical Record* (September 1937): 159.

Review of the book (K397).

B812. **M.C.T.** "Ernst Krenek, *Reisebuch aus den österreichischen Alpen.*" *La rassegna musicale* 3:5 (September 1930): 429-431.

Review of the publication of the song cycle op.62.

B813. ——. "Ernst Krenek, *Die Nachtigall,* op.68, per canto e pianoforte." *La rassegna musicale* 4 (1931): 237.

Review of the publication of the song.

B814. **M.D.L.** "Ajemians offer concertos for two." *Musical America* 75:6 (April 1955): 15.

Review of the first New York performance of Double concerto op.124.

B815. **M.S.** "Introduction to a new work from the Schoenberg school." *Boston Evening Transcript* 109:258 (November 3, 1938): 20.

Discusses the forthcoming American premiere of the Second piano concerto op.81. Lists other performances: April 8, BBC Orchestra, Sir Adrian Boult, London; May 16, Stockholm radio; in January it will be performed by the Chicago Symphony Orchestra, Frederick Stock, conductor. Picture.

B816. **Maack, Rudolf.** "Report from Germany: Hamburg." *American Choral Review* 14:4 (1972): 24-26.

Review of the convention devoted to the performance of contemporary church music sponsored by the Lutheran Churches recently merged under the name "Nordelbien." The premiere of the Mass *Give us peace* op.208 was the most impressive of the three commissions.

B817. **Mai, Julius.** "Bern." *Die Musik* 24:5 (February 1932): 371-372.

Review of the premiere of *Die Nachtigall* op.68a by Lucie Sigrist, soprano.

B818. **Majut, Rudolf.** "Kreneks Jonny-Dichtung im geistesgeschichtlichen Zusammenhang des Weltschmerzes und der Rousseauismus." *Germanisch-Romanische Monatsschrift* 16 (1928): 437-458.

A detailed examination of the symbols used in *Jonny spielt auf.*

B819. "*Mammon* by Ernst Krenek in Munich, Oct.1927." *Musical Courier* 95 (November 10, 1927): 6.

Review of the premiere of the ballet op.37.

B820. Mann, Alfred. "*Der neue Gradus.* Von Ernst Tittel. *Modal counterpoint in the style of the sixteenth century.* By Ernst Krenek. *Tonal counterpoint in the style of the eighteenth century.* By Ernst Krenek." *Notes* 2d ser. 17:4 (September 1960): 577-578.

Review of Krenek's text books (K628 & K632). "In spite of its deficiencies, his practical attitude succeeds because it is paired with historical insight. The composer speaks as true theorist, and thus he speaks with unquestionable authority."

B821. Mann, Robert. "Ernst Krenek: *Eight piano pieces.*" *Notes* 2d ser. 4:2 (March 1947): 193-194.

Review of the publication of op.110. "Aside from their aesthetic charm and vivacity these affecting pieces clearly illustrate the effectiveness of twelve tone technique."

B822. Mann, William S. "Avant-Garde Piano Music." *Gramophone* 48:572 (January 1971): 1207.

Record review of *Sechs Vermessene* op.168 on Vox STGBY 637.

B823. Manzoni, Giacomo. "Krenek, Ernst." In *Enciclopedia della musica.* Vol.2. (Milan: G. Ricordi, 1964): 546-547.

A biographical essay with list of works. Picture.

B824. Marckhl, Erich. *Rede für Ernst Krenek.* (Graz: Akad. Druck- und Verlagsanstalt, 1969) 11 pp.

Lecture given at the Akademie für Musik und Darstellende Kunst in Graz on October 13, 1969. Discusses the polarities evident in Krenek's music and the ways in which they reflect the crisis of modern music in a pluralistic society. Provides a biographical sketch and offers an estimate of him as a man and artist.

B825. Mardirosian, Haig. "Complete Organ Works of Arnold Schoenberg and Ernst Krenek." *Fanfare* 6:5 (May-June 1983): 214-215.

Record review of Musica Viva MV 50-1090.

B826. Mark, Michael. "Krenek: *They Knew What They Wanted,* Op.227; *Quintina for Soprano, Instruments and Electronic Tape,* Op.191." *American Record Guide* 44:7 (May 1981): 21.

Record review of Orion ORS 80380.

B827. Marschalk, Max. "Eine Tanzsuite." *Vossische Zeitung* (January 7, 1922)

Review of the premiere of the Schubert *Piano sonata* D.840 (W65) completed by Krenek.

B828. Marschall, Gottfried R. "*Ernst Krenek,* éd. par Otto Kolleritsch." *Revue de musicologie* 69:2 (1983): 249-251.

Review of the book of essays about Krenek (B328).

B829. Marsoner, Karin. "Ernst Kreneks Liederzyklus *Reisebuch aus den österreichischen Alpen.*" In *Ernst Krenek,* hrsg. von Otto Kolleritsch. (B328) Studien zur Wertungsforschung, Bd.15. (Wien: Universal Edition, 1982): 144-152.

A discussion of the influences of Franz Schubert's music on Krenek's song cycle op.62.

B830. Martin, Frank. "A propos du langage musical contemporain." *Schweizerische Musikzeitung und Sängerblatt* 77:18/19 (October 1, 1937): 501-505.

Reaction to Krenek's book *Ueber neue Musik* (K397) and its espousal of twelve-tone music.

B831. Martin, Linton. "4 Symphony soloists join in orchestra's program." *Philadelphia Inquirer* (November 13, 1952)

Discussion of the *Harp concerto* op.126 in anticipation of its premiere.

B832. ——. "Blanche Thebom presents striking Academy concert." *Philadelphia Inquirer* (March 14, 1953)

Review of the premiere of the monologue *Medea* op.129.

B833. Mason, Colin. "*Divertimento per 111 strumenti.* By Roman Vlad... *Five prayers.* By Ernst Krenek..." *Music and Letters* 36:3 (July 1955): 306-308.

Review of the publication of op.97.

B834. ——. "New music." *Musical Times* 97:1355 (January 1956): 24-26.

Includes a review of the publication of *Five prayers* op.97.

B835. Mason, Jack. "*Concertino* by Krenek played here." *Oakland Tribune* (March 26, 1939)

Review of the first American performance of op.27.

B836. Mason, Marilyn. "Fifty years commissioning organ music." *American Organist* 20:4 (April 1984): 101-102.

Discusses her inter-relations with the composers and the works she commissioned and premiered. She commissioned *Orga-nastro* op.212 and the *Four wind suite* op.223.

B837. Mathis, Alfred. "Das 20. Musikfest der I.G.N.M. in London." *Oesterreichische Musikzeitschrift* 1:8 (August 1946): 281-282.

Includes a review of the first European performance of the *Seventh string quartet* op.96.

B838. ——. "Mahler's *Unfinished symphony.*" *The Listener* 40:1033 (November 11, 1948): 740.

Discusses Krenek's edition (W72) of the "Adagio" and "Purgatorio," and discusses the status of the manuscript sketch.

B839. ——. "Elisabeth Schumann and the Vienna Opera." *Opera* 24:11 (November 1973): 968-979.

A biography of one of the singers in the first Vienna performance of Krenek's opera *Jonny spielt auf* op.45; includes a discussion of the events surrounding the production of the opera and the opposition to it by Julius Korngold, music critic for the *Neue Freie Presse* (a publication of the wealthy Jewish bourgeoisie), and the *Deutsch-oesterreichische Tageszeitung*, the Nazi paper.

B840. Maw, Nicholas. "Krenek. *Hausmusik.*" *Musical Times* 103:1431 (May 1962): 335.

Review of the publication of op.172.

B841. Mayer, George Louis. "Krenek, Ernst: *Exploring music*." *Library Journal* 91:12 (June 15, 1966): 3213.

Review of the book of essays (K817).

B842. Mayer-Rosa, Eugen. *Musik und Technik; Vom Futurismus bis zur Elektronik.* Beiträge zur Schulmusik, 27. (Wolfenbüttel: Möseler, 1974) 104 pp.

Discusses the relationship between music and technology, and includes an analysis of Krenek's *Pfingstoratorium* op.152 (pp.43-44).

B843. McNally, William J. "More or less personal." *Minneapolis Morning Tribune* (December 11, 1942): 4.

Discusses Krenek's life and position in contemporary music in preparation for the premiere of *I wonder as I wander* op.94.

B844. ———. "More or less personal." *Minneapolis Morning Tribune* (December 23, 1943): 4.

Discusses the forthcoming American premiere of the *Second symphony* op.12.

B845. ———. "More or less personal." *Minneapolis Morning Tribune* (March 24, 1944): 4.

Discusses the forthcoming premiere of the *Cantata for wartime* op.95.

B846. McQuilkin, Terry. "Ernst Krenek in composer series." *Los Angeles Times* 100:56 (January 28, 1981): 6:3.

Review of a Los Angeles Philharmonic Composer's Choice concert on January 26 at UCLA's Schoenberg Hall with performances of the *String trio* op.118 and *Durch die Nacht* op.67, and the first American performance of *In the valley of time* op.232.

B847. McSpadden, J. Walker. "Ernst Krenek." In his *Operas and Musical Comedies.* Enlarged edition. (New York: Thomas Y. Crowell, 1954): 84-86.

A synopsis of his opera *Jonny spielt auf* op.45.

B848. Meckna, Michael. "Ernst Krenek zwischen Kalifornien und Kärnten." *Oesterreichische Musikzeitschrift* 34:7/8 (July-August 1979): 360-361.

Report on the festival held at the University of California, Santa Barbara in April 1979 and the premiere of the *Concerto for organ and string orchestra* op.230 in Carinthia.

B849. ———. "Santa Barbara." *Musical Times* 120:1637 (July 1979): 597.

Review of the festival held at the University of California, Santa Barbara, April 8-15 during which fifty of his works were performed in twelve concerts. Krenek's "presence and participation was decisive for the festival's success, with his energetic conducting, his graceful pianoism, and his commentary demonstrating a keen intellect tempered with a lively wit."

B850. Meisterbernd, Max. "Ernst Krenek: *Der Sprung über den Schatten*." *Frankfurter Nachrichten* (June 10, 1924)

Review of the premiere of the opera op.17.

B851. "Mephisto's musings: Dodecaphonist." *Musical America* 70:8 (July 1950): 11.

Report of an encounter and interview with Krenek on his way to Europe.

He is writing his *Fourth piano concerto* op.123 and has just finished the *George Washington variations* op.120 which will be premiered in Los Angeles by Miriam Molin in September. Krenek gave his impressions of the forthcoming Second International Congress for Twelve-Tone Music in Locarno, Switzerland.

B852. Metzger, Heinz-Klaus. "Vokal, Instrumental, Elektronisch, Neue Musik im Kölner Funkhaus." *Melos* 23:7/8 (July-August 1956): 220-223.

Review of the series "Musik der Zeit" in the Grossen Sendesaal des Westdeutscher Rundfunk (WDR) in Cologne, which included the premiere of *Spiritus intelligentiae, Sanctus* op.152.

B853. ——. "Plus ultra." *Musik-Konzepte* 39/40 (B895) (October 1984): 53-66.

Discusses the social conditions prevalent during the early 1930s and their effect on Krenek's opera *Karl V.* op.73.

B854. Meurs, Norbert. "Neuere Orgelmusik." *Musica* 35:4 (July-August 1981): 390-392.

Includes a review of the publication of the score of the *Organ concerto* op.230.

B855. Meyers, Klaus. "Liturgisches und Konzertantes, Neues für die Orgel." *Musica* 33:5 (September-October 1979): 479-481.

Includes a brief review of the publication of *Die vier Winde* op.223.

B856. mg. "Krenek dirigiert Krenek." *Weltpresse* (Vienna) (November 5, 1954)

Review of a performance in the Mozart-Saal of the Konzert conducted by the composer of *Symphonie Pallas Athene* op.137 and the first European performance of his *Harp concerto* op.126.

B857. Mila, Massimo. "Ernst Krenek, *Selbstdarstellung*." *La rassegna musicale* 19 (January 1949): 77-79.

Review of Krenek's autobiography (K569).

B858. ——. "Lettra da Venezia." *La rassegna musicale* 20:4 (October 1950): 325-329.

Includes a review of the first European performance of Krenek's *Fifth symphony* op.119 during the Biennal di Venezia.

B859. ——. "Ernst Krenek. *Piano sonata, n.4*." *La rassegna musicale* 22:4 (October 1952): 349.

Review of the publication of op.114.

B860. Miller, Catharine Keyes. "Music." *Library Journal* 78:13 (July 1953): 1238.

Review of the book *Johannes Ockeghem* (K616).

B861. Miller, Philip L. "Mixed programs -- with reservations." *Library Journal* 77:14 (August 1952): 1298.

Record review of *Symphonic elegy* op.105 on Columbia ML 4524.

B862. ——. "Mostly choral and partially American." *Library Journal* 78:11 (June 1, 1953): 984.

Record review of *Die Jahreszeitung* op.35 and *Lamentatio Jeremiae prophetae* op.93 on New Records NRLP 306.

B863. ———. "Hauer: *Hoelderlin Lieder, op.32*; Krenek: *Fiedellieder, op.64*; Kodaly: *Sappho's love song; At night; The forest, op.9*." *American Record Guide* 20:1 (September 1953): 27-28.

Record review of New Records NRLP 405.

B864. "Miriam Molin gives premieres." *Musical Courier* 145:2 (January 15, 1952): 21.

Review of the premiere of the *Fourth piano concerto* op.123 in Cologne in two performances, followed by performances in Brussels, Darmstadt, Berlin and Vienna; all performances except the one at Darmstadt were recorded for future broadcast. She also performed and recorded for broadcast the *George Washington variations* op.120 at the American Embassy in Paris.

B865. Mitchell, Donald. "The emancipation of the dissonance." *Hinrichsen's Musical Yearbook* 7 (1952): 141-152.

A bibliography of the writings by composers, theorists and critics with brief biographies of the composers, including Krenek.

B866. Mittag, Erwin. "Ernst Krenek und die Zur Sprache gebrachte Musik." *Wort und Wahrheit* (December 1958)

Review of the book of essays *Zur Sprache gebracht* (K707).

B867. "Moderne Kompositionen für Cello." *Luzerner neueste Nachrichten* (April 8, 1954)

Review of the premiere of *Phantasiestück* op.135.

B868. Moldenhauer, Hans. "Noted composer's birthday marked by first performance of new work." *Music of the West* 16:4 (December 1960): 14.

Pieces performed during Krenek's sixtieth year included premieres of *Flute piece in nine phases* op.171, *A question of time* op.170, and *Six Motets on texts by Franz Kafka* op.169. *Lamentatio Jeremiae prophetae* op.93, was also performed.

B869. Molkow, Wolfgang. "*Der Sprung über den Schatten*; zum Opernschaffen Ernst Kreneks in den 20er und 30er Jahren." *Musica* 34:2 (March-April 1980): 132-135.

Discusses Krenek's operas written during the twenties and thirties, and demonstrates that he was much more radical than his contemporaries in his search for a contemporary form.

B870. Monson, Karen. "Ernst Krenek music offered." *Los Angeles Herald-Examiner* (December 9, 1970): C-12.

Review of the first American performance of *Tape and double* op.207.

B871. Moor, Paul. "Ernst Krenek's new opera." *High Fidelity/Musical America* 20:11 (November 1970): MA19.

Review of the premiere of *That's what happens, or When Sardakai goes traveling* op.206.

B872. Moore, David W. "Krenek: *Capriccio for Cello and Orchestra; The Dissembler*. Moss: *Symphonies for Brass Quintet and Chamber Orchestra*." *American Record Guide* 43:9 (July-August 1980): 27-28.

Record review of Orion ORS 79362.

B873. Moore, J.S. "Guitar." *The New Records* 47:8 (October 1979): 14-15.

Record review of the *Guitar suite* op.164 on Orion ORS 78323.

B874. Mooser, R. Aloys. "Ernst Krenek: *5e Symphonie.*" In his *Panorama de la musique contemporaine, 1947-1953.* (Geneve: Rene Kister, 1953), 166-168.
Brief discussion and analysis of the symphony.

B875. ——. "Ernst Krenek: *Doppelkonzert.*" In his *Panorama de la musique contemporaine, 1947-1953.* (Geneve: Rene Kister, 1953), 249-251.
Brief discussion and analysis of the concerto.

B876. Mootz, William. "[Unknown]." *Louisville Courier-Journal* (February 14, 1955)
Review of the premiere of *Eleven Transparencies* op.142.

B877. "More Briefly Noted." *High Fidelity* 6:8 (August 1956): 50-51.
Record review of *Eleven transparencies* op.142 on Louisville Orchestra LOU 56-3.

B878. Morgan, Robert P. "Heinz Holliger -- Spectacular indeed!" *High Fidelity* 24:5 (May 1974): 98.
Record review of *Four pieces for oboe and piano* op.193 on Philips 6500 202.

B879. ——. "Krenek: Various Works." *High Fidelity* 26:6 (June 1976): 80-81.
Record review of Orion ORS 75204.

a. ——. "Krenek, Ernst. *O Lacrymosa; The Santa Fe timetable; Tape and double; Toccata.*" *High Fidelity Annual* 22 (1977): 190-192.

B880. ——. "Krenek, Ernst. *From three make seven,* Op.171; *Horizon circled,* Op.196; *Von vorn herein,* Op.219 & *Four Pieces for oboe and piano,* Op.193. Wuorinen: *Composition for oboe and piano.* Moss: *Unseen leaves.*" *High Fidelity* 29:1 (January 1979): 80-81.
Record review of Orion ORS 78290 and Orion ORS 78288.

a. ——. *High Fidelity Annual* 25 (1980): 168-169.

B881. Morgenstern, Soma. "Motivenbericht zu einen Opernbuch." *Frankfurter Zeitung* 78:4 (January 4, 1934): 1.
Discussion of the text and plot of *Karl V.* op.73 in anticipation of its premiere in Vienna at the end of February (which was cancelled).

B882. ——. "Oper in Wien." *Frankfurter Zeitung* 78:52 (January 30, 1934): 2.
Brief discussion of the cancellation of the premiere of *Karl V.* op.73.

B883. Morris, R.O. *"Studies in counterpoint."* *Music Review* 2:3 (August 1941): 248.
Review of the text book (K496).

B884. Morton, Lawrence. "Krenek's friends." *Frontier* (October 1953): 27.
Review of the book *Johannes Ockeghem* (K616).

B885. Motto, David. "Emigre composers in the United States: Teaching in American universities." (Batchelor's thesis: University of California, Berkeley, 1986) 103 pp.
Surveys Krenek's teaching career in a chapter entitled "Teaching twelve-tone: Ernst Krenek." Concludes that "Krenek believed that [his students] must be actively involved in the creation of music themselves. At the same time, however, Krenek felt that not everyone had the gift to be thoroughly creative in his compositions."

B886. Müllmann, Bernd. "Kreneks *Lamentatio* für Chor a cappella." *Melos* 26:1 (January 1959): 19.

Review of the first complete performance of *Lamentatio Jeremiae prophetae* op.93.

B887. ———. "Kassel Musiktage 1960, Nun auch serielle Musik." *Neue Zeitschrift für Musik* 121:12 (1960): 434.

Review of the festival which included a performance of the *Symphonischer Elegie* op.105 and the premiere of *Sechs Vermessene* op.168.

B888. "Münchener Konzerte." *Münchener Post* (October 10, 1927)

Review of the premiere of *Vier Gesänge nach alten Gedichten* op.53a in the version for voice and winds.

B889. Müry, Albert. "Neue Musik." *Musica* 21:1 (January-February 1967): 28-29.

Review of the concerts held during the Internationalen Musikfestwochen Luzern 1966 which included the premiere of *Adagio und Fuge* op.78a.

B890. Muggler, Fritz. "Zuerich: Uraufführungen von Krenek und Nordenstrom." *Schweizerische Musikzeitung* 113:3 (May/June 1973): 160-161.

Review of the premiere of *Statisch und ekstatisch* op.214.

B891. ———. "Krenek-Musikprotokoll; Konzerte und Symposion Steirischer Herbst 80." *Musica* 35:1 (January-February 1981): 38-39.

Review of the "Ernst Krenek Symposium" in Graz, Austria October 23-26, during which twenty-two works were performed, including the premiere of *Im Tal der Zeit* op.232.

B892. "Music and 'music'." *Times Literary Supplement* 67:3436 (January 4, 1968): 1.

Review of the book of essays *Exploring music* (K817).

B893. "Musik und Humanität." *Anbruch* 19:4/5 (May 1937): 128-130.

Review of the book *Ueber neue Musik* (K495).

B894. "Musik und Musiker." *Münchener Zeitung* (October 12, 1927)

Review of the premiere of *Vier Gesänge nach alten Gedichten* op.53a in the version for voice and winds.

B895. *Musik-Konzepte* 39/40 (Oct.1984)

A special issue devoted to Ernst Krenek and containing the essays: *Ernst Krenek* by Theodor Wiesengrund Adorno (B18-c), *Hommage à Ernst Krenek* by Glenn Gould (B446), *Schöne und "scheene" Musik* by Claudia Maurer Zenck (B1510), *Auswahlbibliographie* by Rainer Riehn (B1075), *Plus ultra* by Heinz-Klaus Metzger (B853), *ROTAS-SATOR* by Gösta Neuwirth (B902-a), *Die Ungleichzeitigkeit des Neuen* by Martin Zenck (B1519), *Rilke - "O Lacrymosa" - Krenek* by Adriano Cremonese (B212), *Zu Kreneks Buch "Ueber neue Musik"* by Theodor Wiesengrund Adorno (B20-c), *Fortschritt und Geschichtsbewusstsein in den musik-theoretischen Schriften von Krenek und Adorno* by Gianmario Borio (B136), *Bemerkungen zu einigen späteren Werken Ernst Kreneks* by Gösta Neuwirth (B903-a), and *Chronologisches Werkverzeichnis* by Rainer Riehn and Claudia Maurer Zenck (B1076). *See:* B690

B896. N.S. "Aitkin gives recital." *New York Times* 89:29982 (February 25, 1940): 1:38.

Review of the first New York performance of Schubert's *Piano sonata* D.840 (W65) completed by Krenek.

B897. ——. "Cello-Abend." *Vaterland* (Lucern) (April 12, 1954)

Review of the premiere of *Phantasiestück* op.135.

B898. Neeb, Hans. "Kreneks *Kafka Lieder*; ein Beitrag zur Zwölftontechnik ausserhalb der Wiener Schule." (Thesis?, 197-?) 58 pp.

Explores Krenek's use of the twelve-tone row in the songs op.82 and his setting of the text.

B899. Nestler, Gerhard. "Ernst Kreneks Opern." *Melos* 36:5 (May 1971): 197.

Review of the book *Ernst Krenek*, by Wolfgang Rogge.

B900. "Neue Kunst im Spiegel der Zeit." *Blätter der Staatsoper* (Berlin) 5:4 (December 1924): 15-19.

Impressions of Feruccio Busonis's *Arlecchino*, Egon Wellesz's *Die Nächtlichen*, and Krenek's opera *Zwingburg* op.14.

B901. "Neues Instrumental-Ensemble." *National Zeitung* (Basel) (January 19, 1955)

A Review of the premiere of *Five short pieces for strings* op.116.

B902. Neuwirth, Gösta. "*Rotas-sator*; für Ernst Krenek zum 23. August 1980." *Oesterreichische Musikzeitschrift* 35:9 (September 1980): 461-472.

Investigation of the palindrome used in Webern's *Concerto, op.24* and discussed by Krenek in his 1965 speech (K811). It comes from an ancient stone in Pompeii, but perhaps also has some Christian significance.

    a. "ROTAS-SATOR." *Musik-Konzepte* 39/40 (B895) (October 1984): 78-91.

B903. ——. "Bemerkungen zu einigen späteren Werken Ernst Kreneks." In *Ernst Krenek*, hrsg. von Otto Kolleritsch. (B328) Studien zur Wertungsforschung, Bd.15. (Wien: Universal Edition, 1982): 202-215.

Surveys Krenek's late works with special emphasis on *Fibonacci mobile* op.187, *Doppelt beflügeltes Band* op.207, *Wechselrahmen* op.189, and *Spätlese* op.218 and the *Organ concerto* op.230.

    a. ——. *Musik-Konzepte* 39/40 (B895) (October 1984): 149-160.

B904. "New classical records." *Time* 62:10 (September 7, 1953): 100-104.

Includes a brief record review of the *Fourth piano sonata* op.114 on Music Library MLR 7014.

B905. Newlin, Dika. "Ernst Krenek: *Deutsche Messe für Chor, Gemeinde und Instrumente*." *Notes* 27:1 (Sept.1970): 162-163.

Review of the publication of op.204.

B906. ——. "Krenek, Ernst." In *McGraw-Hill Encyclopedia of World Biography*, edited by D.I. Eggenberger. (New York: McGraw-Hill, 1973): 251-252.

A biographical essay.

B907. Nezbeda, Ottokar. "70 Jahre Wiener Konzerthaus." *Oesterreichische Musikzeitschrift* 38:12 (December 1983): 712-713.

Includes a review of the first European performance of the *Organ concerto* op.235.

B908. **"Nirenberg and the American Chamber Symphony."** *Israel Today* (March 11, 1983): 35.
   Review of the first American performance of *Brazilian Sinfonietta* op.131.

B909. **Noble, Hollister.** "At last, *Jonny* arrives." *Musical America* 49:3 (January 19, 1929): 5, 32.
   A survey of the reviews of the first American performance of op.45. Picture.

B910. **Noble, Jeremy.** *"Johannes Ockeghem."* *Music and Letters* 35:3 (July 1954): 252.
   Review of the book (K616). "Krenek's own experience as a composer helps him to put himself in the composer's position and to understand his problems; there are one or two sections, in fact, which might be refreshing to a jaded musicological palate."

B911. **Nölter, Wolfgang.** "The new Hamburg Opera." *Opera* 6:12 (December 1955): 752-760.
   Review of the three premieres which opened the new Hamburg State Opera house. "The greatest event of the festival week was the performance of Ernst Krenek's new opera *Pallas Athene weint* op.144." Pictures.

B912. **Norton, Mildred.** "Drama, Music Editor." *Los Angeles Daily News* (June 22, 1949): 10.
   Discusses Krenek's exit from Los Angeles to a position at the Chicago Musical College.

B913. ——. "Opera reviews." *Los Angeles Daily News* (May 3, 1951)
   Review of the premiere of the opera *Dark waters* op.125.

B914. ——. "Still hope for Modern music." *Los Angeles Daily News* (March 4, 1954)
   Interview with the composer in anticipation of the forthcoming premiere of the *Cello concerto* op.133. Picture.

B915. ——. "Krenek's new work heard." *Los Angeles Daily News* (March 5, 1954)
   Review of the premiere of *Cello concerto* op.133.

B916. ——. "West Coast report." *Saturday Review* 38:18 (April 30, 1955): 61.
   Review of the first American performance of *Parvula corona musicalis* op.122.

B917. Norton-Welsh, Christopher. "Austria: Krenek's *Karl V.*" *Opera* 36:1 (January 1985): 50-51.
   Review of the first performance of the opera op.73 in Vienna after fifty years.

B918. ——. "Vienna." *Opera News* 49:9 (January 19, 1985): 42.
   Review of the first performance in Vienna of the opera *Karl V.* op.73.
   a. ——. *Opera News* 49:10 (February 2, 1985): 35.

B919. ——. "Vienna." *Opera News* 49:10 (February 2, 1985): 35.
   Review of the first performance in Vienna of the opera *Karl V.* op.73.

B920. O.B. "Ernst Krenek *Karl V.*" *Prager Presse* (June 24, 1938)
   Review of the premiere of the opera op.73.

B921. o.st. "Ernst Kreneks *Karl V.*" *Wiener Zeitung* 233:59 (February 29, 1936): 7.

Review of a lecture in the series Podium im Hagenbund.

B922. O.v.P. "Kreneks *Mammon.*" *Musikblätter des Anbruch* 9:10 (December 1927): 439.

Review of the premiere of the ballet op.37.

B923. Obermaier, Walter. "Nur ein Wort, nur ein Gedanke ..." In *Ernst Krenek: Fünf Lieder nach Worten von Franz Kafka*. (Vienna: Wiener Stadt- und Landesbibliothek, 1985): 14-19.

A discussion of Krenek's interest in setting texts to music, his acquaintence with writers, and the influence of Franz Kafka on him.

B924. O'Connell, Clive. "Festival off to a promising start." *The Age* (Melbourne) (May 19, 1983)

Review of the premiere of the Organ concerto op.235.

B925. oe. "Zwei Uraufführungen im dritten Konzert des Basler Kammerorchesters." *National Zeitung* (Basel) (January 27, 1958)

Review of the premiere of *Kette, Kreis und Spiegel* op.160.

B926. Oehlmann, Werner. "Ernst Krenek." In his *Oper in vier Jahrhundert*. (Stuttgart: Belser, 1984): 818-821.

Discussion of *Karl V.* op.73 with musical examples and synopsis.

B927. Oehlschlägel, Reinhard. "Geglückter Start." *MusikTexte* 12 (December 1985): 62-63.

Record review of the series Oesterreichischer Musik der Gegenwart which includes the first three symphonies on Amadeo 415 825-1.

B928. Oesch, Hans. "*Basler Massarbeit.*" *National Zeitung* (Basel) (January 20, 1961)

Review of the premiere of *Basler Massarbeit* op.173.

B929. Ogdon, Will. "The twelve-tone series as cantus firmus: A discussion of Ernst Krenek's *Five Prayers*." *Bulletin of the American Musicological Society* nos.11-13 (September 1948): 86-87.

Abstract of a paper read at a meeting of the Texas chapter, November 8, 1947, in Waco. The twelve-tone series is used as a cantus firmus and generates the harmonic scheme of the composition. "The *Five Prayers* op.97 is only one example of how the later uses of the twelve-tone technique differs from the earlier 'classical' concept."

B930. ——. "Series and structure: An investigation into the purpose of the twelve-tone row in selected works of Schoenberg, Webern, Krenek, and Leibowitz." (Ph.D. diss.: Indiana University, 1955) 341 pp.

Examines how series and series method conform to, coordinate with, or determine other factors of composition in the works of Krenek, Arnold Schoenberg, and René Leibowitz. The *Symphonic Elegy* op.105 is examined in detail, and Ogdon concludes that Krenek breaks with Schoenberg by reducing and even disregarding the form function of the row in favor of its potential as a source of motival characterization and variation.

a. ——. *Dissertation Abstracts* 16:2 (1956): 351.

B931. ——. "An appreciation of master composer Ernst Krenek." *American Music Teacher* 21:4 (February-March 1972): 26-27.

"Krenek has always been regarded as a man of his time. Only once did Krenek attempt to escape from his responsibility when, in the later 1920's, he tried to revivify the language of tonality through rapprochement with the lyricism of Franz Schubert. Even then Krenek could not really escape for Schubert inevitably led him, about 1930, to the technical regions inhabited by Arnold Schönberg, not over the usual path of later converts, a way of mechanistic and dissonant neo-classicism but, rather, through the lyrical, expressive Austrian tradition as it matured from Schubert through Mahler and on through Schönberg, Berg and Webern."

   a. "A master composer and a foremost musician of our time." In *Horizons Circled; Reflections on My Music,* by Ernst Krenek. (K864) (Berkeley: University of California Press, 1974): 1-16.

B932. ——. "Conversation with Ernst Krenek." *Perspectives of New Music* 10:2 (Spring-Summer 1972): 102-110.

Wide-ranging interview covering Krenek's life and works. "I feel that the film has become more and more the only medium for dealing seriously with the problems of our time... In my early operas I was mainly concerned with the idea of social freedom from oppression and personal freedom from inhibitions ... in *Charles V* [op.73] the concept of justification is the hinge on which the play revolves... The strong emphasis on Christian universality made this opera utterly intolerable to the Nazis... Through my preoccupation with serial music I became more and more intrigued with the philosophical problems of time and space... In *Charles V* [I] applied some dramaturgical devices that suggest techniques more germane to moving pictures than to the stage, such as for instance splitting the place of the action, rapid changes of locale, flashbacks, and the like." Another opera which uses cinematic devices is *Golden ram* op.186. The interview discusses the opera *Karl V* op.73; *The magic mirror* op.192; *Horizon circled* op.196; *From three make seven* op.177; *Fibonacci mobile* op.187 and Krenek's theories on opera.

   a. "Minutes of a conversation between Will Ogdon and Ernst Krenek." In *Horizons Circled; Reflections on My Music,* by Ernst Krenek. (K864) (Berkeley: University of California Press, 1974): 142-152.

B933. ——. "*Horizon circled* observed." In *Horizons Circled; Reflections on My Music,* by Ernst Krenek. (K864) (Berkeley: University of California Press, 1974): 121-141.

A detailed analysis of the composition op.196.

B934. Ohrmann, Fritz. "Zwei schwarze Tage für die extreme musikalische Moderne in Berlin." *Signale für die musikalische Welt* 86:50 (December 12, 1928): 1521-1525.

Review of the premiere of the three one-act operas *Der Diktator* op.49, *Das geheime Konigreich* op.50 and *Schwergewicht* op.55.

B935. "Old and new music heard in concert." *Los Angeles Times* 76 (October 29, 1957): IV:9.

Review of the first American performance of *Capriccio* op.145.

B936. Olivier, Antje. "Krenek widmete ihr *Die vier Winde.*" *Neue Rhein-Zeitung* (March 14, 1977)

Review of the premiere of *Four Winds* for organ op.223.

B937. Olmstead, Andreas. "Thouvenel String Quartet: Krenek." *High Fidelity/Musical America* 31:3 (March 1981): MA27.

Review of four Krenek/Beethoven concerts in New York, and an announcement of the June 7th premiere of the *Eighth string quartet* op.233.

B938. O'Loughlin, Niall. "*Gottfried von Einem* by Dominik Hartmann. *Ernst Krenek* by Lothar Knessel." *Tempo* no.88 (Spring 1969): 67-68.

Review of the book (B662).

B939. Olsen, William A. "Goodman: *Quintet for winds*. Piston: *Pieces for flute, clarinet and bassoon*. And Krenek: *Pentagram for winds*." *The New Records* 34:9 (November 1966): 9.

Record review of Lyrichord LL 158 and Lyrichord LLST 7158.

B940. Oltner, Hermann. "Krenek, Ernst: *Reisebuch aus den österreichischen Alpen*." *Phono* 7:5 (May/June 1961): 104.

Record review of the song cycle op.62 on Telefunken BLE 14113.

B941. "Onderhoud met Ernst Krenek." *Algemeen Handelsblad* (Amsterdam) (March 15, 1938): 9.

Discussion of the forthcoming premiere of the *Second piano concerto* op.81. Picture.

B942. "Oper." *Musikblätter des Anbruch* 9:1/2 (January-February 1927): 103.

Picture: drawing of a scene from the opera *Zwingburg* op.14.

B943. "Opera." *BMI, the Many Worlds of Music* (November 1970): 18-19.

Review of the premiere of *Das Kommt Davon* op.206.

B944. "Opera and concert: Krenek and Lavery collaborate on an experimental lyric work." *New York Times* 89:29968 (February 11, 1940)

Discusses the new opera, *Tarquin* op.90, being composed by Krenek to a libretto by Emmet Lavery dealing with contemporary problems. It stresses new materials and methods of production; its direction will be more imaginative than elaborate. The whole production is designed to keep expenses down.

B945. Orga, Ates. "Composer's thoughts." *Composer* no.22 (Winter 1966/7): 25-27.

Review of the book of essays *Exploring music* (K817).

B946. Osborne, Charles. "Recent music books." *London Magazine* N.S. 6:11 (February 1967): 109-114.

Includes a review of the book of essays *Exploring music* (K817).

B947. Osborne, Conrad L. "Krenek on campus." *High Fidelity/Musical America* 15:10 (October 1965): 148-149.

The premiere of *Fibonacci Mobile* op.187 at Dartmouth College was preceded by a lecture by the composer. The concert also included performances of the *string quartet* op.96, *Pentagram* op.163, *Sonata for viola and piano* op.117, and *Trio for violin, clarinet and piano* op.108.

B948. Oster, Otto. "Ernst Krenek: *Leben des Orest*." *Schwäbische Thalia, der Stuttgarter Dramaturgischen Blätter* 17:42 (June 15, 1930): 1-11.

A discussion of the opera and its text.

B949. P.B. "Rote Fahnen." *Musikblätter des Anbruch* 6:11 (November-December 1924): 432.

> A response to L. Schmidt, the reviewer from the *Berliner Tageblatt*, who called Krenek's opera *Zwingburg* op.14 a "red flag" (B1149).

B950. P.M. "Neue Proprien." *Musica sacra* 77 (September 1957): 284.

> Review of the publication of *Proprium Missae in Dominica tertia in quadragesima* op.89.

B951. P.W.M. "New music at Forum concert." *San Francisco News* (November 6, 1948)

> Review of the premiere of the *Fourth piano sonata* op.114.

B952. Pahlen, Kurt. "Ernst Krenek." In his *Oper der Welt.* (Zürich: Schweizer Druk- und Verlagshaus, 1963): 183-185.

> General survey of the operas.

B953. Palisca, Claude. "Krenek's Campanile." *Opera News* 21:23 (April 15, 1957): 15.

> Review of the premiere of the chamber opera *The bell tower* op.153. Picture.

B954. Parker, C. Gerald. "Krenek, Ernst. *Horizons circled.*" *Library Journal* 99:8 (April 15, 1974): 1136-1137.

> Review of the book (K864).

B955. Parker, T.H. "New ballet and music premiered." *The Hartford Daily Courant* (May 20, 1939)

> Review of the premiere of the ballet *Eight column line* op.85.

B956. Parmenter, Ross. "Alice Howland sings 5 new Krenek works." *New York Times* 96:32492 (January 9, 1947): 21.

> Review of the first New York performance of songs from *Travelogue from the Austrian Alps* op.62.

B957. ———. "1,100 hear Steber in initial recital." *New York Times* 99:33675 (April 6, 1950): 33.

> Review of the premiere of the *Ballad of the railroads* op.98.

B958. ———. "New Friends hear Philharmonic unit." *New York Times* 102:34631 (November 17, 1952): 21.

> Review of the first American performance of *Symphonic music* op.11 conducted by Dimitri Mitropoulos in Town Hall.

B959. ———. "New Friends give Krenek premieres." *New York Times* 102:34680 (January 5, 1953): 19.

> Review of the premiere of *Two sacred songs* op.132.

B960. ———. "Music: Recital for harp." *New York Times* 107:36529 (January 28, 1958): 31.

> Review of the premiere of the *Harp sonata* op.150.

B961. ———. "Music: Four Fromm commissions." *New York Times* 111:38096 (May 14, 1962): 34.

> Review of the first American performance of *Quaestio temporis* op.170.

B962. Parrott, Ian. "*Tonal counterpoint in the style of the eighteenth century.* By Ernst Krenek." *Musical Times* 100:1400 (October 1959): 530-531.

Review of the text book (K632).

B963. ——. *"Modal counterpoint in the style of the sixteenth century."* *Musical Times* 100:1402 (December 1959): 663.

Review of the text book (K628).

B964. **Pasler, Jann.** "Ernst Krenek - In retrospect." *Perspectives of New Music* 24:1 (Fall-Winter 1985): 424-432.

Report of a three-day festival held at the University of California, San Diego in December 1985 and a review of the concerts and lectures.

B965. **Pasles, Chris.** "Belated tribute: Symphony to perform composition by Krenek." *Los Angeles Times* 105:38 (January 10, 1986): 6:10 & 15.

Information and interview about the forthcoming first American performance of *Fivefold enfoldment* op.205. Picture.

B966. **Patzer, Franz.** "War es ein Fehler, dass er zu arbeiten anfing? Kaum ..." In *Ernst Krenek: Fünf Lieder nach Worten von Franz Kafka.* (Vienna: Wiener Stadt- und Landesbibliothek, 1985): 4-5.

An introduction to the volume briefly tracing Krenek's life.

B967. **Paulsen, Manfred.** "Aus den Berliner Konzertsälen." *Allgemeine Musikzeitung* 49:19 (May 12, 1922): 403-405.

Review of the premiere of the *Second string quartet* op.8.

B968. **Peppering.** *"Jonny strikes up."* *Gramophone* 8:94 (March 1931): 497.

Record review of excerpts from *Jonny spielt auf* op.45 on Parlophone E 11098.

B969. **Perkins, Francis D.** "Ernst Krenek's *Little Symphony* introduced here." *New York Herald Tribune* (November 7, 1930)

Review of the first American performance of op.58.

B970. ——. "Salzburg Guild presents opera of Monteverdi." *New York Herald Tribune* (November 10, 1937)

Review of the first American performance of Krenek's edition (op.80a) of Monteverdi's *Poppea*.

B971. ——. "New Friends of Music." *New York Herald Tribune* (November 17, 1952)

Review of a performance of *Symphonic music* op.11 at a New Friends of Music concert in Town Hall the previous evening with members of the New York Philharmonic-Symphony conducted by Dimitri Mitropoulos.

B972. ——. "Program of Modern music offered at the New School." *New York Herald Tribune* (March 10, 1958)

Review of a concert sponsored by the Fromm Music Foundation on March 9 which included a performance of *Lamentatio Jeremia prophetae* op.93 by Hugh Ross and his Schola Cantorum and the premiere of *Sestina* op.161.

B973. **Perle, George.** "The harmonic problem in twelve-tone music." *Music Review* 15 (November 1954): 257-267.

Discusses the relationship between vertical structures and the twelve-tone row, including a discussion of Milton Babbitt's and Krenek's twelve-tone theories and practices.

B974. Perle, George. "The set as a 'melodic prototype'." In his *Serial Composition and Atonality; An Introduction to the Music of Schoenberg, Berg, and Webern*. (Berkeley: University of California Press, 1962): 65-70. Includes a discussion of the *Cello suite* op.84.

   a. ——. In his *Serial Composition and Atonality; An Introduction to the Music of Schoenberg, Berg, and Webern*. (London: Faber and Faber, 1962): 65-70.

   b. ——. In his *Serial Composition and Atonality; An Introduction to the Music of Schoenberg, Berg, and Webern*. 2d ed., revised and enlarged. (Berkeley: University of California Press, 1968): 64-68.

   c. ——. In his *Serial Composition and Atonality; An Introduction to the Music of Schoenberg, Berg, and Webern*. 3d ed., revised and enlarged. (Berkeley: University of California Press, 1972): 64-68.

   d. ——. In his *Serial Composition and Atonality; An Introduction to the Music of Schoenberg, Berg, and Webern*. 4th ed., revised. (Berkeley: University of California Press, 1977): 64-68.

   e. ——. In his *Serial Composition and Atonality; An Introduction to the Music of Schoenberg, Berg, and Webern*. 5th ed., revised. (Berkeley: University of California Press, 1981): 64-68.

B975. Pernick, Ben. "Krenek: *Four Pieces for oboe and piano*, Op.193. Wuorinen: *Composition for oboe and piano*. Moss: *Unseen leaves*." *Fanfare* 1:5 (May/June 1978): 53-54.
   Record review of Orion ORS 78288.

B976. ——. "Krenek: *Horizon circled*, Op.196; *From three make seven*, Op.171; *Von vorn herein*, Op.219." *Fanfare* 1:5 (May-June 1978): 54-55.
   Record review of Orion ORS 78290.

B977. ——. "Krenek: *Capriccio for cello and orchestra; The Dissembler*. Moss: *Symphonies*." *Fanfare* 3:5 (May-June 1980): 95.
   Record review of Orion ORS 79362.

B978. Persichetti, Vincent. "Krenek: *Piano sonata, no.4*. Antheil: *Second violin sonata*." *Musical Quarterly* 39:1 (January 1953): 141-142.
   Record review of op.114 on Music Library MLR 7014. "Krenek's Fourth is the best of his piano sonatas."

B979. Peterson, Melody. "Los Angeles: ISCM festival mixes wheat and chaff." *High Fidelity/Musical America* 26:11 (November 1976): MA27.
   Review of the American premiere of *Von vorn herein* op.219.

B980. Pethel, Stanley Robert. "Contemporary composition for the trombone: A survey of selected works." (D.M.A. thesis: University of Kentucky, 1981) 135 pp.
   A performance study of twenty-two works written after 1950 with attention to extended techniques, including Krenek's *Five pieces for trombone and piano* op.198.

   a. ——. *Dissertation Abstracts* 42:7 (1982): 2928-A.

B981. Peyser, Herbert. "*Jonny* over there." *Modern Music* 6:2 (January-February 1929): 32-35.
   Examines the opera as a false reflection of American life and wonders what changes the Metropolitan Opera will effect to make it palatable to American tastes.

B982. Pfeifer, Ellen. "Ernst Krenek opera *Jonny* to be revived here." *Boston Herald American* (May 11, 1976): 35.

Discusses the forthcoming New England Conservatory performance of the opera and the honorary doctorate to be conferred on Krenek. Picture.

B983. Phillips, Anne. "A salute to Ernst Krenek." *Palm Springs Life* (March 1975): 141-142,152.

Surveys Krenek's life in celebration of his seventy-fifth birthday. Picture.

B984. "Piano music of the twentieth century." *The New Records* 8:2 (April 1940): 7.

Record review of RCA Victor M-646 containing *Little suite* op.13a.

B985. Pirir, Peter J. "Gesualdo, Carlo, *Illumina nos*... Krenek, Ernst, *20 Miniatures* for piano." *Music and Letters* 39:2 (April 1958): 202-204.

Review of the publication of op.139.

B986. Pisk, Paul A. "Krenek. *Leben des Orest.*" *Der Auftakt* (Prague) 10:3 (1930): 56-57.

Review of the premiere of the opera op.60.

B987. ——. "Neue Bühnenwerke von Krenek und Schönberg." *Schweizerische Musikzeitung und Sängerblatt* 70:4 (February 15, 1930): 141-143.

Discusses Krenek's opera *Leben des Orest* op.60 and Schoenberg's *Von heute auf morgen.*

B988. ——. "Panorama de la musique autrichienne: I. De Bruckner à Krenek." *La revue musicale* 12:113 (March 1931): 205-210.

Surveys and notes Krenek's importance to modern opera.

B989. Pleasants, Henry. "Do modern composers face an insoluble dilemma?" *Musical America* 75:4 (February 15, 1955): 83.

Examines the problem of the composer's relationship to his audience, and quotes extensively from *Selbstdarstellung* to demonstrate that the composer who works in both tonality and atonality confuses his audience. "This is the answer to those who argue that the solution to the problem of modern music is for the contemporary composer to come down out of his ivory tower and write a couple of good tunes."

B990. Pohl, Brigitta. "Arnold Schönberg-Ernst Krenek, *Sämtliche Orgelwerke.*" *Fono Forum* 26:7 (July 1981): 56-57.

Record review of Musica Viva MV 50-1090.

B991. Porter, Andrew. "Krenek: *Jonny spielt auf*, op.45." *Gramophone* 42:504 (May 1965): 540.

Record review of the opera on Philips AL 3498 and Philips SAL 3498.

B992. ——. "Orestes in Oregon." *New Yorker* 54:42 (December 8, 1975): 174-180.

Review of a performance of *Leben des Orest* op.60 by the Portland Opera. "If I had to name two dominant 'influences' on *Orest*, they would be Schubert and Offenbach, the later for the verve of invention and sheer mastery of putting music together, the former, less demonstrably, for a kind of lyric emotion given musical form."

B993. ——. "At the right time, in the right place." *New Yorker* 51:47 (January 12, 1976): 82-87.

Chastises those who applaud during a concert at inappropriate places. Uses as one example the listener who immediately bawled "Bravo!" as Victor Braun finished his aria in Krenek's opera *Leben des Orest* in Portland.

a. ——. In his *Music of Three Seasons, 1974-1977.* (New York: Farrar Straus Giroux, 1978): 269-275.

B994. ——. "Aristocrat." *New Yorker* 54:40 (November 20, 1978): 160-167.

Includes a brief review of the premiere of *They knew what they wanted* op.227.

a. ——. In his *Music of Three More Seasons, 1977-1980.* (New York: Alfred A. Knopf, 1981): 251-255.

B995. ——. "Champions." *New Yorker* 55:7 (April 2, 1979): 112-121.

Briefly reviews the March performance in Bruno Walter Auditorium of *Gesänge des Späten Jahres* op.71 by Michael Ingham and Carolyn Horn and mentions Krenek's protest to the staging of his opera *Karl V.* op.73 in Darmstadt.

a. ——. In his *Music of Three More Seasons, 1977-1980.* (New York: Alfred A. Knopf, 1981): 328-333.

B996. ——. "All-American." *New Yorker* 59:5 (March 21, 1983): 100-106.

Review of *All American music: Composition in the late twentieth century* by John Rockwell (B1086), a survey of modern American music from Ernst Krenek and other revolutionaries of the thirties to the more recent Talking Heads.

B997. Powell, Mel. "*The Musical quarterly.* Special issue: Problems of modern music. Vol.XLVI, no.2, April 1960." *Journal of music theory* 4:2 (November 1960): 259-269.

Extensive review of the issue, concluding that Krenek's "Extents and limits of serial technique" (K740) is "an orderly treatment of topics which are of prime interest to the contemporary mind."

B998. "Premiere of Ernst Krenek's *Orpheus und Eurydice* in Cassel, Germany." *Musical Courier* 94 (February 3, 1927): 16.

Review of op.21. Picture.

B999. "Premiere of Ernst Krenek's *Jonny* in New York." *Musical Courier* 98 (January 31, 1929): 38.

Review of the first American performance of op.45.

B1000. "Premieres." *Musical Courier* 144:6 (November 1, 1951): 29.

Brief announcement of the premiere of the *Double concerto* op.124.

B1001. "Premieres." *BMI, the Many Worlds of Music* (October 1968): 24.

Excerpts from the reviews by Bernard Jacobson (B607) and Roger Dettmer (B241) of the premiere of *Perspectives* op.199. Also discusses the premiere of *Instant remembered* op.201.

B1002. "Premieres." *BMI, the Many Worlds of Music* (Summer 1970): 44.

Announces the premiere of *Six Profiles* op.203.

B1003. "Premieres." *BMI, the Many Worlds of Music* (March 1972): 7.

Review of the premiere of *Orga-Nastro* op.212 at the annual Organ Conference at the University of Michigan. Includes a caricature of Krenek.

B1004. **Preussner, Eberhard.** "Das VI. Donaueschinger Kammermusikfest." *Neues Wiener Tagblatt* (August 3, 1926): 9.
> Review of the premiere of *Drei lustige Märsche* op.44.

B1005. ——. "Das Sechste Donaueschinger Kammermusikfest." *Die Musik* 18:12 (September 1926): 899-903.
> Review of the festival which included the premiere of *Merry marches* op.44. Picture.

B1006. ——. "Ernst Krenek: *Drei Gesänge op.56, Nr.1 bis 3.*" *Die Musik* 21:6 (March 1929): 464-465.
> Review of the publication.

B1007. ——. "Ernst Krenek." *Anbruch* 11:4 (April 1929): 154-159.
> Discusses Krenek's importance as an opera composer. Picture.

B1008. ——. "Ernst Krenek [und] Ernst Krenek und *Die Zwingburg.*" *Der Scheinwerfer* (Essen) 2:18/19 (June 1929): 8-11.
> Discusses the composer and his opera op.14.

B1009. ——. "Ernst Krenek, *Kantate von der Vergänglichkeit des Irdischen.*" *Die Musikpflege* 4:12 (March 1934): 379.
> Review of the publication of the score of the cantata op.72.

B1010. **Pringsheim, Heinz.** "Aus der Berliner Konzertsälen." *Allgemeine Musikzeitung* 48:7 (February 18, 1921): 102-103.
> Review of the premiere of the *Serenade* op.4.

B1011. ——. "Ernst Krenek. *Reisebuch aus den österreichischen Alpen,* op.62." *Allgemeine Musikzeitung* 57:22/23 (June 6, 1930): 639.
> Review of the publication of the song cycle.

B1012. ——. "Die Züricher Tonkünstler-Versammlung des Allgemeinen Deutschen Musikvereins: Die Orchesterkonzerte." *Allgemeine Musikzeitung* 59:26 (July 1, 1932): 377-378.
> Includes a review of a performance of *Theme and 13 variations* op.69.

B1013. **Procter, Leland H.** "*Tonal counterpoint in the style of the eighteenth century.*" *Journal of music theory* 3:2 (November 1959): 313-315.
> Review of the text book (K632).

B1014. **"Program by Kleiber has wide contrasts."** *New York Times* 80:25585 (November 7, 1930): 8:33.
> Review of the first American performance of *Kleine Symphonie* op.58.

B1015. **"A program of choral excerpts."** *The New Records* 20:7 (September 1952): 11.
> Record review of two of the *Gemischte Chöre* op.61 on New Records NRLP 305.

B1016. **"*Proprium Missae.*"** *Choral and Organ Guide* 7:4 (May 1954): 29.
> Review of the publication of op.89 by Affiliated Musicians.

B1017. **Prunières, Henry.** "Le festival de la Sociètè internationale pour la musique contemporaine à Vienne." *La revue musicale* 13:128 (July-August 1932): 137-141.
> Includes a review of the premiere of *Durch die Nacht* op.67a with accompaniment arranged for orchestra.

B1018. "Public should hear new music -- Krenek." *Minneapolis Star Journal* (September 6, 1942)

An interview shortly after Krenek arrived to start teaching at Hamline University. "Everybody reads new books... Everybody wants to see the new plays and goes to the latest movies. But new music, no." Krenek feels the remedy for this attitude is a greater familiarity with the work of contemporary composers.

B1019. Putnam, Thomas. "At Albright-Knox: New music series." *Buffalo Courier Express* (November 6, 1967)

Review of the premiere of *Five pieces for trombone* op.198.

B1020. r. "Ernst Kreneks neues Schaffen." *Schweizerische Musikzeitung* 86:2 (February 1, 1946): 64.

Discusses Krenek's works written since he emigrated to America in 1938.

B1021. R.K. "Kunst und Bühne: Ernst Krenek *Karl V.*" *Deutsche Presse* (June 23, 1938)

Review of the premiere of the opera op.73.

B1022. R.K. "Whittemore and Lowe join Philharmonic in premieres." *Musical America* 73:14 (November 15, 1953): 22.

Review of the premiere of *Concerto for two pianos* op.127. "Krenek achieves his effects the atonal way, hurtling huge boulders of sound around like leaves whipped by a wind."

B1023. R.S. "Notable works in Fromm concert." *Musical America* 79:15 (December 15, 1959): 26.

Review of the American premiere of the *Sixth string quartet* op.78.

B1024. ——. "Düsseldorf doch eine Kunststadt." *Düsseldorfer Nachrichten* (September 11, 1965)

Review of the premiere of *Wechselrahmen* op.189.

B1025. R.W. "Der Hang zum Universalismus." *Wiener Kurier* (May 1956)

Review of performances conducted by the composer at Ravag (Vienna Radio) of *Elf transparente* op.142, *Symphonisches Stück für Streicher* op.86, and *Kantate für die Kriegszeit* op.95 (Klothilde Kastler, soprano, Rundfunkchor, Gottfried Preinfalk, director) and the first European performance of the *Cello concerto* op.133.

B1026. Rabinowitz, Peter J. "Chance vs. Inspiration." *American Record Guide* 42:4 (February 1979): 21-22.

Record review of Orion ORS 78295 which includes the same recording of *Sestina* op.161 that appeared on Epic LC 3509.

B1027. ——. "Krenek: *Gesaenge des Spaeten Jahres*, Op.71." *American Record Guide* 42:11 (Sept.1979): 31-32.

Record review of Orion ORS 78308.

B1028. "Railroad trip inspires composer." *Minneapolis Star Journal* (March 11, 1947)

A discussion of the forthcoming premiere of the *Santa Fe time table* op.102 and *Aegrotavit Ezechias* op.103.

B1029. Rapoport, Paul. "Krenek: *Spätlese*, Op.218. *Drei Gesänge*, Op.56." *American Record Guide* 42:6 (April 1979): 26.

Record review of Orion ORS 78298.

B1030. ——. "Krenek: *Four songs,* Op.112; *Zwei Zeitlieder,* Op.215; *Three songs,* Op.30a. Nordenstrom: *Zeit XXIV."* *American Record Guide* 43:4 (February 1980): 38.

Record review of Orion ORS 79348.

B1031. Rasch, Hugo. "Aus den Berliner Konzertsälen." *Allgemeine Musikzeitung* 48:26 (June 24, 1921): 490-491.

Review of the premiere of the *First violin and piano sonata in F-sharp minor* op.3.

B1032. ——. "Aus dem Berliner Musikleben." *Allgemeine Musikzeitung* 51:5 (February 1, 1924): 51-52.

Includes a review of the premiere of *Zweite Symphonische Musik* op.23.

B1033. ——. "Aus dem Berliner Musikleben." *Allgemeine Musikzeitung* 51:51/52 (December 19, 1924): 942.

Includes a review of the premiere of the *Piano suites* op.26.

B1034. ——. "Aus dem Berliner Musikleben." *Allgemeine Musikzeitung* 52:3 (January 16, 1925): 58-59.

Review of the premiere of the *Violin concerto* op.29.

B1035. Rayment, Malcolm. "Berio: *Sequenza VII.* Castiglioni: *Alef.* Huber: *Noctes intelligibilis lucis.* Lehmann: *Spiele.* Krenek: *Vier Stücke.* Holliger: *Trio."* *Records and Recording* 16:2 (November 1972): 79-80.

Record review of op.193 on Philips 6500 202.

B1036. Reaney, Gilbert. *"Johannes Ockeghem.* By Ernst Krenek." *Musical Times* 95:1335 (May 1954): 252-253.

Review of the book (K616).

B1037. "Record reviews." *Los Angeles Times* 71 (February 5, 1952)

Record review of New Records NRLP 405 containing the *Fiedellieder,* op.64 (called "Minstrels' airs" in the review).

B1038. Redlich, Hans F. *"Das Leben des Orest."* *Anbruch* 12:2 (February 1930): 75-76.

Review of the premiere of the opera op.60.

B1039. ——. "Heimat und Freiheit; zur Ideologie der jüngsten Werke Ernst Krenek." *Anbruch* 12:2 (February 1930): 54-58.

Discusses the stylistic differences of Krenek's compositions following *Jonny spielt auf* op.45 as contrasted with his earlier operas.

B1040. ——. "Lyrik der Wende." *Anbruch* 13:6/7 (September-October 1931): 154-155.

A discussion and comparison of the songs *Reisebuch aus den österreichischen Alpen* op.62, *Fiedellieder* op.64, *Durch die Nacht* op.67, and *Die Nachtigall* op. 68.

B1041. ——. "Ernst Kreneks Liedschaffen." *Der Auftakt* (Prague) 12:5/6 (May/June 1932): 127-131.

Surveys his output of songs through Op.71.

B1042. ——. "Krenek, Ernst." In *Grove's Dictionary of Music and Musicians,* edited by Erik Blom. 5th ed. Vol.4. (New York: St. Martin's Press, 1954): 844-848.

A biographical essay with list of works.

B1043. Redlich, Hans F. *"Zur Sprache gebracht* von Ernst Krenek." *Music Review* 20:3/4 (August-November 1959): 339-340.

Review of the book of essays (K707).

B1044. Reeves, Robert Henry. "The German organ sonata in the 19th and 20th century: A formal analysis of *Sonata on the 94th Psalm*, Julius Reubke; *Sonata I*, Paul Hindemith; *Sonata, Op.92*, Ernst Krenek." (D.Music thesis: Northwestern University, 1973)

Includes a discussion and analysis of Krenek's sonata (pp.69-84.)

B1045. Rehm, W. "Nach 30 Jahren." *Musica* 8:12 (December 1954): 556.

Review of the premiere of *Symphony Pallas Athene* op.137 and a performance in Kassel of *I wonder as I wander* op.94 conducted by the composer.

B1046. Reich, Willi. "Ernst Krenek im eigenen Wort." *Schweizerische Musikzeitung* 72:21 (November 21, 1932): 641-646.

Discusses the themes of Krenek's operas *Jonny spielt auf* op.45 and *Leben des Orest* op.60.

B1047. ———. "Ernst Kreneks neues Bühnenwerk *Karl V*." *Der Auftakt* (Prague) 14:3/4 (1934): 52-54.

Discusses the opera's subjects.

B1048. ———. "Die Biennale der Musik II." *Wiener Zeitung* 231:269 (September 27, 1934): 10.

Review of the operas presented during the Venetian festival which included the premiere of *Cefalo e Procri* op.77.

B1049. ———. "Oesterreichisches Studio." 23 no.17/19 (December 15, 1934): 14-19.

Review of Krenek's first "Abend des Oesterreichischen Studios" concert on October 25, 1934 in the Ehrbar-Saal, Vienna featuring works by Arnold Schönberg, Julius Bittner, and Franz Schmidt. Includes extensive quotes from his pre-concert talk.

B1050. ———. "Ernst Kreneks Arbeit in der Zwölftontechnik." *Schweizerische Musikzeitung* 89:2 (February 1, 1949): 49-53.

Refers to *Selbstdarstellung* (K569) and Krenek's discussion of twelve-tone music. Discusses his use of the technique in the *Sixth string quartet* op.78, *Symphonic piece* op.86, and *Lamentatio Jeremiae prophetae* op.93.

B1051. ———. "Ernst Krenek als Musikschriftsteller." *Schweizerische Musikzeitung* 93:3 (1953): 113-114.

Discusses Krenek's books *Ueber neue Musik* (K397), *Music here and now* (K495), *Studies in counterpoint* (K496), *Musik im goldenen Westen* (K570), and *Selbstdarstellung* (K569).

B1052. ———. "Krenek und Martinu." *Musica* 12:3 (March 1958): 161-162.

Review of the premiere of *Kette, Kreis und Spiegel* op.160.

B1053. ———. "Martinu und Krenek in Basel uraufgeführt." *Melos* 25:3 (March 1958): 103.

Review of the premiere of *Kette, Kreis und Spiegel* op.160.

B1054. ———. "Svizzera." *Musica d'oggi* N.S.1:6 (June 1958): 381.

Review of the premiere of *Kette, Kreis und Spiegel* op.160.

B1055. ——. "Besprechungen: Essays von Ernst Krenek." *Schweizerische Musikzeitung* 98:9 (September 1, 1958): 359.
Review of the book of essays *Zur Sprache gebracht* (K707).

B1056. ——. "Ernst Krenek: *Jonny spielt auf.*" *Phonoprisma* 8:2 (1965): 43.
Record review of Amadeo AVRS 5038. Picture.

B1057. ——. "Krenek im Spiegel der zwanziger Jahre." *Musica* 25:4 (July-August 1971): 402.
Review of Wolfgang Rogge's book *Ernst Kreneks Opern* (B1093).

B1058. Reif, Adelbert. "Auch für die Neue Musik geht die Entwicklung weiter, ein Gespräch mit Ernst Krenek aus Anlass seines achtzigsten Geburtstages." *Musik und Medizin* 6:8 (August 1980): 48-54.
Interview covering his life, the operas *Jonny spielt auf* op.45 and *Karl V.* op.73, politics, and nationalism in music.

B1059. ——. "Die Musik hat ihre eigene Entwicklung." *Neue Musikzeitung* 29:4 (August-September 1980): 3-4.
Interview with Krenek published in the series "Väter der Avantgarde" discussing new music and the operas *Jonny spielt auf* op.45 and *Karl V.* op.73.

B1060. Reif, Thaddäus. "Kreneks *Zwölfton-Kontrapunkt Studien.*" *Melos* 20:4 (April 1953): 110.
Review of the German translation by Heinz Klaus Metzger of the text book *Studies in counterpoint* (K496).

B1061. Reimann, Hans. "Krscheneks neue Oper." *Die Weltbühne* 26:1 (1930): 178-180.
Review of the premiere of *Leben des Orest* op.60 complaining of its four hour duration. Reimann notes that the hatchek on the "r" in Krenek's name is appropriate for a composer of new music because it makes him different.

B1062. Reimers, Lennart. "Samtida musik i Oesterrike." *Musikrevy* 33:5 (1978): 231-235.
Discusses music in Austria and the role Krenek has played in it.

B1063. Reis, Claire R. "Ernst Krenek." In *Composers in America.* rev.ed. (New York: Macmillan, 1947; reprint Da Capo Press, 1977): 214-215.
A brief biographical essay to the mid-1940s with a list of compositions written in America, 1939-46.

B1064. "*Reisebuch aus den österreichischen Alpen.*" *Allgemeine Musikzeitung* 57:3 (January 17, 1930): 70-71.
Announcement of the premiere of the song cycle op.62.

B1065. Reno, Doris. "Modern music delights Miamians." *Miami Herald* (November 30, 1962)
Review of the premiere of the *Suite for clarinet and piano* op.148.

B1066. "[Review]." *Neue Berner Zeitung* (October 28, 1931)
Review of the premiere of the song *Die Nachtigall* op.68a in the version for voice and orchestra.

B1067. Reynolds, H. Robert. "The CBDNA commissions Ernst Krenek." *Instrumentalist* 32:6 (January 1978): 48-49.

An account of the commissioning by the College Band Directors National Association of *Dream sequences* op.224; includes descriptions of visits to Krenek's Palm Springs home, a transcription of the program notes, and a brief report of the premiere. Pictures.

B1068. Rh. "*Prosa, Dramen, Verse.*" *Schweizerische Musikzeitung* 106:1 (January-February 1966): 59-60.

Review of the book of Krenek's collected writings (K804).

B1069. Rich, Alan. "Why Jonny can't swing." *New York Magazine* 9:22 (May 31, 1976): 72.

Review of a concert performance, and the first performance of an English translation by the composer and Gladys Nordenstrom, of the opera by the New England Conservatory.

B1070. ——. "The once and future swing." *California* 11:2 (February 1986): 82.

Discussion of Krenek's music and the Festival held at the University of California, San Diego in December 1985.

B1071. Riedel, Johannes. "Interview with Ernst Krenek." [Unpublished] US-LJ typescript(10 p.)

The transcript of an interview which took place in Minneapolis, MN mostly concerned with Krenek's relationship to Theodor Wiesengrund Adorno.

B1072. ——. "A twelve-tone setting of the mass." *Sacred Music* 103:2 (December 1976): 24-31.

An extensive analysis of *Missa duodecim tonorum* op.165.

B1073. ——. "Krenek's sacred music, I." *Response* 17:2 (Summer 1977): 28-43.

Krenek expressed his political beliefs in his church music, in which he fuses religious faith and political protest, the finite and infinite, and art and liturgy.

B1074. ——. "Echoes of political processes in music during the Weimar Republic." In *Germany in the Twenties: the Artist as Social Critic*, edited by Frank Hirschbach. (Minneapolis: University of Minnesota, 1980): 62-73.

Examines and compares political views apparent in the works of three generations of German and Austrian composers. Their musical works echo certain political trends, including a satirical-intellectual assessment of the German political situation as found in the texts and music of Krenek's cantatas and operas.

B1075. Riehn, Rainer. "Auswahlbibliographie." *Musik-Konzepte* 39/40 (B895) (October 1984): 38-52.

Selective bibliography of books by Krenek and about 70 writings by others about Krenek.

B1076. Riehn, Rainer ; Zenck, Claudia Maurer. "Chronologisches Werkverzeichnis." *Musik-Konzepte* 39/40 (B895) (October 1984): 161-172.

List of works through op.336 indicating first performances.

B1077. Riemer, Otto. "Vom Musikalienmarkt." *Musica* 11:12 (December 1956): 766-768.

Includes a review of the Bärenreiter publication of *Lamentatio Jeremiae prophetae* op.93.

B1078. ——. "Vom Musikalienmarkt." *Musica* 13:6 (June 1959): 413-415.

Includes a brief review of the publication of *Fünf Lieder nach Worten von Franz Kafka* op.82.

B1079. Rihm, Wolfgang. "Bruchstücke zu: Wandlungen neuer Musik." *Musica* 34:2 (March-April 1980): 126.

Comments and reactions to the idea of Krenek as a force in the development of new music.

B1080. Riley, Robert. "Avant garde piano." *Los Angeles Times* 89 (March 15, 1970): Calender:44.

Record review of *Sechs Vermessene* op.168 on Candide CE 31015.

B1081. ——. "Music books: Iconoclasts three." *Performing Arts* 10:4 (April 1976)

Includes a review of the book *Horizons circled* (K864).

B1082. Ringo, James. "Krenek: *Jonny spielt auf.*" *Opera News* 35:23 (April 3, 1971): 32.

Record review of selections from the opera op.45 on Mace MXX 9094.

B1083. ——. "Kmentt on Krenek." *American Record Guide* 40:6 (May 1977): 24.

Record review of *Reisebuch aus dem österreichischen Alpen* op.62 on Preiserrecords SPR 3269.

B1084. Robb, John D. "Albuquerque hears new Krenek symphony." *Musical America* 70:5 (April 1950): 33.

Review of the premiere of the *Fifth symphony* op.119. "The symphony is concise ... and is masterfully orchestrated."

B1085. Rochberg, George. "Egon Wellesz: *Suite for flute solo...* Ernst Krenek: *Suite for flute and string orchestra.* Ernst Krenek: *Suite for clarinet and string orchestra.*" *Notes* 2d ser. 15:2 (March 1958): 253.

Review of the publications of op.147a and op.148a. "Everything is skillful as befits a man of Krenek's experience, but except for the arresting 'overture', the music is charmingly slight."

B1086. Rockwell, John. "The rise of American art music & the impact of the immigrant wave of the late 1930's: Ernst Krenek." In his *All American music; Composition in the late twentieth century.* (New York: Alfred A. Knopf, 1983): 14-24.

A survey of American music in which Krenek and his music are examined as representatives of the Central European immigrant musicians who brought serialism to America and influenced the generation of composers who followed them. Krenek saw serialism as antithetical to Nazism and "he discovered it simultaneously with his new absorption in the doctrines of the Roman Catholic Church ... as a reaffirmation of spiritual order... There was an emotional veracity to expressionist serialism, which so truly captured the torment and black excitement of [the twenties and thirties]." Rockwell concludes that "Krenek is something more than just an individual composer. He is one of the last of a line of European immigrants who enriched our music but also suppressed the nascent evolution of a truly American musical culture." *See:* B996

B1087. Rössler, Ernst Karl. "Zeitgenössische Kirchenmusik und christliche Gemeinde." *Musik und Kirche* 27:1 (January-February 1957): 14-22.

Survey of contemporary church music including *Lamentatio Jeremiae prophetae* op.93.

B1088. Roger, Kurt. "Konzerte." *Neue Freie Presse* (Vienna) (March 15, 1932)
Review of the premiere of the song *Durch die Nacht* op.67a in the version for
voice and orchestra.

B1089. ——. "Neue Musik." *Die Glocke* 3:36/37 (January 1, 1937): 29-30.
Review of the book *Ueber neue Musik* (K397).

B1090. Rogge, Wolfgang. "Krenek aktualisiert den Medea-Mythos." *Melos*
31:6 (June 1964): 183-190.
Krenek first dealt with the Medea theme which is a large part of his opera
Der goldene Bock op.186 in his monologue *Medea* op.129. Rogge extensively
examines the opera, including many musical examples with pictures of the
scenery and costumes from the forthcoming premiere.

B1091. ——. "Musiktheater des Absurden." *Melos* 32:9 (Sept.1965): 291-303.
A discussion of the theater of the absurd and its effect upon music. Includes
a discussion of the opera *Der goldene Bock* op.186 with musical examples.

B1092. ——. "Ernst Krenek zwischen den Stühlen?" *Melos* 36:5 (May 1969):
217.
Review of the book by Lothar Knessl *Ernst Krenek* (B662).

B1093. ——. *Ernst Kreneks Opern; Spiegel der zwanziger Jahre.* (Wolfenbüttel:
Möseler, 1970) 124 pp.
An examination of Krenek and his operas as a reflection of the twenties with
detailed analysis of *Die Zwingburg* op.14, *Der Sprung über den Schatten* op.17,
Orpheus und Eurydike op.21, *Jonny spielt auf* op.45, the three one-act operas
op.49, op.50, and op.55, *Leben des Orest* op.60 and *Karl V.* op.73. Pictures. *See:*
B1057, B1477

B1094. ——. "Die Realität spielt mit." In *Das musikdramatische Werk*, von
Ernst Krenek. Vol.2. (Wien: Oesterreichische Verlagsanstalt, 1977): 7-
40.
A survey of the operas and their reception.

B1095. ——. "Ernst Krenek." In *Neue Musik*. Musik Aktuell, 1. (Kassel:
Bärenreiter, 1979): 35-41.
Discussion and analyses of *Tape and Double* op.207. The book is
accompanied by recording Bärenreiter Musicaphon 30 SL 5100 which is
excerpted from Orion ORS 75204.

B1096. ——. "Ernst Krenek auf Schallplatten." *Musica* 34:2 (March-April
1980): 185-186.
A survey of the compositions recorded on long-playing records.

B1097. ——. "Oper als Quadratur des Kreises; zum Opernschaffen Ernst
Kreneks." *Oesterreichische Musikzeitschrift* 35:9 (September 1980): 453-
457.
Jonny spielt auf op.45 used many cinematic elements which freed
conventional opera. In his later short operas, the elements of satire and social
criticism become stronger.

B1098. Rosenberg, Herbert. "Ernst Krenek: *Kantate von der Vergänglichkeit
des Irdischen*, op.72." *Melos* 13:5/6 (May/June 1934): 193-194.
Review of the publication.

B1099. Rosenwald, Hans. "Johnny strikes up the band -- no longer!" *Music News* 31:4 (February 16, 1939): 8.

Discusses Krenek's change to twelve-tone composition, his plans to write a ballet for the Hartford Festival, and his summer teaching assignment at the University of Michigan.

B1100. ——. "Krenek." In *The Book of Modern Composers,* edited by David Ewen. (New York: Alfred A. Knoff, 1942): 356-362.

Surveys Krenek's development through his operas, and concludes "Krenek remains, in creative respect, the sole powerful leader of the expressionist school."

B1101. ——. "Krenek to Chicago." *Music News* 41:7 (July 1949): 7.

Announcement of Krenek's appointment at the Chicago Musical College.

B1102. ——. "Speaking of music ..." *Music News* 42:6 (June 1950): 6-7.

A general discussion about contemporary music focused on Arnold Schoenberg and Krenek. Discusses Krenek's use of the twelve-tone technique.

B1103. ——. "Speaking of music ..." *Music News* 42:7 (July 1950): 12-13.

Continuation of a general discussion about contemporary music focused on Krenek and his use of the twelve-tone technique and on Igor Stravinsky.

B1104. Rosenzweig, Alfred. "Kammerorchesterkonzert im Grossen Musikvereinssaal." *Der Wiener Tag* (June 22, 1932)

Review of the premiere of the orchestral version of *Durch die Nacht* op.67a.

B1105. Rothmaier, Monika. "Das Bühnenwerk *Karl V.* von Ernst Krenek; Eine musikdramaturgische Untersuchung." (Master's thesis: Albert-Ludwigs-Universität, 1981) 70 pp.

An examination of the dramatic structure of the opera op.73.

B1106. Rothstein, Edward. "Concert: Recent music." *New York Times* 132:45660 (April 26, 1983): C:12.

Review of the first American performance of *Die Nachtigall* op.68.

B1107. Routh, Francos. "Hindemith: *Quartet.* Krenek: *Trio.* Milhaud: *Suite." Records and Recording* 21:9 (June 1978): 71.

Record review of op.108 on Supraphon 111 2147.

B1108. Rubardt, Paul. "Zwei Krenek-Uraufführungen in Leipzig." *Signale für die musikalische Welt* 88:6 (February 5, 1930): 144-146.

Review of the premieres of the opera *Das Leben des Orest* op.60 and the song cycle *Reisebuch aus den österreichischen Alpen* op.62.

B1109. Ruedenauer, M. "Ein Traum vom ewigen Frieden." *Orchester* 33 (January 1985): 22-23.

Review of the Vienna premiere of *Karl V.* op.73 in the Wiener Staatsoper.

B1110. Ruf, Wolfgang. "Kreneks drei Einakter von 1928." In *Ernst Krenek,* hrsg. von Otto Kolleritsch. (B328) Studien zur Wertungsforschung, Bd.15. (Wien: Universal Edition, 1982): 132-143.

An examination of the thematic ideas of the three one-act operas, *Der Diktator* op.49, *Das geheime Königreich* op.50, and *Schwergewicht oder die Ehre der Nation* op.55, and their reception.

B1111. Rufener, Rudolf. "Dir *Reisebücher* von Ernst Krenek." *Du* (Zürich) 30 (September 1970): 674-677.

Review of a privately issued recording of the song cycles *Das Reisebuch aus den österreichischen Alpen* op.62, *Gesänge des späten Jahre* op.71, and *Ballade von den Eisenbahnen* op.98 sung by Rudo Timper and accompanied by the composer.

B1112. Rufer, Josef. "Ernst Krenek." In *Musiker über Musik*, Ausgewählt und kommentiert von Josef Rufer. (Darmstadt: Im Stichnote Verlag, 1956): 218-223.

Discusses Krenek's aesthetic philosophy with excerpts from "Ueber die Bedeutung der Musik" (K588), *Selbstdarstellung* (K569), and "Fünfzig Jahre Komponierhandwerk" (K599).

B1113. ——. "Ernst Krenek." In his *Bekenntnisse und Erkenntnisse* (Frankfurt: Propylaen, 1979): 238-248.

Includes large excerpts from *Selbstdarstellung* (K569) and "Ueber die Bedeutung von Musik" (K588) focused on Krenek's change to, and support of, twelve-tone music. Picture: p.225.

B1114. Ruppel, Karl Heinz. "Krenek: *Jonny spielt auf.*" *Opernwelt* 6:2 (February 1965): 50, 52.

Record review of op.45 on Amadeo AVRS 5038.

B1115. S.T. "Neue Musik in der Kirche." *Hamburger Abendblatt* (October 18, 1971)

Review of the premiere of *Messe Gib uns den Frieden* op.208.

B1116. Saalfeld, Ralf von. "Ernst Krenek: Streichquartett in einem Satz." *Allgemeine Musikzeitung* 48:23/24 (June 10, 1921): 405-407.

Detailed analysis of the *First string quartet* op.6. Picture; Facsimile.

B1117. Saathen, Friedrich. "Apropos Ernst Krenek." *Oesterreichische Musikzeitschrift* 5:9 (Sept.1950): 175-177.

Discusses Krenek's life in celebration of his fiftieth birthday.

B1118. ——. "Eine österreichische Angelegenheit." *Arbeiter Zeitung* (Vienna) (November 9, 1954)

Discusses Krenek's return to Vienna and the acclaim accorded him in the Wiener Konzerthaus and two days later in the Sendesaal of Radio Wien. There was a performance of the *Seventh string quartet* op.96. The composer conducted the Vienna premiere of the *Harp concerto* op.126 by Emmy Hürlimann, *Symphonic Elegy* op.105, and *Symphony Pallas Athene weint* op.137.

B1119. ——. *Ernst Krenek, ein Essay.* Langen-Müllers kleine Geschenkbücher, 90. (München: Albert Langen - Georg Müller, 1959) 78 pp.

A personal reflection about Krenek's life, aesthetics, and musical output. This survey moves discursively and quickly through Krenek's landmark compositions, emphasizing the operas.

B1120. ——. "Ernst Kreneks Botschaft im Wort." *Schweizerische Musikzeitung* 99:2 (February 1, 1959): 45-50.

Surveys Krenek the writer.

B1121. ——. "Im Endlichen nach allen Seiten: Ernst Krenek." In his *Von Kündern, Käuzen und Ketzern.* (Wien: Böhlau Verlag, 1986): 317-380.

Biographical essay, especially important for information about Krenek's early years told the author by Krenek's mother.

B1122. Sabin, Robert. "Admirable University Project." *Musical America* 74:2 (January 15, 1954): 17.

Record review the *Organ sonata* op.92 on University of Oklahoma 2.

B1123. Sablosky, I. "Festival at Urbana." *New York Times* 106:36247 (April 21, 1957): 2:11.

Review of the premiere of the chamber opera *The bell tower* op.153.

B1124. Salzman, Eric. "Technique isn't everything." *Hi Fi Review* 2:4 (April 1959): 100.

Record review of Epic LC 3509. "One of the most interesting aspects of this record comes from the pairing of two dissimilar works by the same composer. They clearly demonstrate how little the twelve-tone maneuvers have to do with the kind of music being written... It is obvious that the basic essentials of style, personality, and communication are to be found elsewhere."

B1125. ——. "Tonal and non-tonal." *New York Times* 108:37059 (July 12, 1959): 2:15.

Record review of the Glenn Gould recording of the *Third piano sonata* op.92, no.4 on Columbia ML 5336.

B1126. ——. "Showcase hears 3 types of Krenek." *New York Times* 109:37362 (May 10, 1960): 2:9.

Review of concert of all-Krenek music at the Composer's Showcase at the Circle in the Square.

B1127. ——. "'Terrific' modern music for wind band." *Stereo Review* 39:1 (July 1977): 132.

Record review of *Merry marches* op.44 and *Kleine Blasmusik* op.70a on Louisville Orchestra LS 756.

B1128. ——. "Boulez: *Second sonata for piano.* Krenek: *Piano sonata no.4.*" *Stereo Review* 43:2 (August 1979): 108.

Record review of op.114 on Musical Heritage Society MHS 3874.

B1129. Samet, Sydney Bruce. "Hearing aggregates." (Ph.D. diss.: Princeton University, 1985) 201 pp.

A study of the functions of aggregates as elements of perceptible surface progression and as compositional tools in "classical" twelve-tone practice. Part I, "Linear Articulation of the Set as Linear Articulator," examines the perceptible function of individual set statements in examples by Krenek which appear to have been composed without concern for, or awareness of, such a resource, in order to establish the premise that discrete twelve-tone collections can be audible contributors to progression.

a. ——. *Dissertation Abstracts* 46:6 (1985): 1438-A.

B1130. Sams, Jeremy. "*Jonny,* the first jazz opera." *Opera* 35:10 (October 1984): 1085-1090.

A discussion of the opera's plot and its characteristics. It is a *Zeitoper* and "properly defined, can have no future; it reflects changing times which themselves must change... If Krenek's *Jonny* was designed to match the modern mood, he scored a bull's eye, the craze spread beyond the opera house to the record industry, to the world of academia ..., culminating in press slurs and Nazi-organized riots outside performances... It also set off a jazz craze amongst German composers." Pictures: scenes from several productions.

B1131. Sanborn, Pitts. "Kleiber's final concert marked by rare quality." *New York World Tribune* (November 8, 1930)

Review of the first American performance of the *Little symphony* op.58.

B1132. ——. "Monteverdi opera given by the Guild." *World-Telegram* (November 10, 1937)

Discusses the forthcoming production in New York of Krenek's edition (op.80a) of *Poppea*.

B1133. ——. "Monteverdi opera given by the Guild." *World-Telegram* (November 18, 1937)

Review of the first New York performance of Krenek's edition (op.80a) of *Poppea*.

B1134. ——. "Ernst Krenek." In *The Metropolitan Book of the Opera.* (Garden City, NY: Garden City Publishing Co., 1942): 117-118.

Discussion of the opera *Jonny spielt auf* op.45.

B1135. "Satire on modern 'Jazz Age' revealed in Krenek opera of Negro bandmaster." *Musical America* 45:21 (March 12, 1927): 29.

Review of the Leipzig premiere of *Jonny spielt auf* op.45. "The reception by the public was warm after the first act and after the second there was a stormy ovation for the composer, who was present, and for the artistic co-workers."

a. ——. *Musical America* 49:20 (March 1, 1929)

B1136. Saunders, Richard D. "Austrian composer heard." *Hollywood Citizen-News* (December 17, 1937)

Review of the premiere of *Twelve variations in three movements* for piano op.79.

B1137. Sch., G. "Krenek unter Krenek in Düsseldorf." *Neue Zeitschrift für Musik* 117:3 (March 1956): 162

Review of the first German performance of *Elf Transparente* op.142.

a. ——. *Das Orchester* 4:3 (March 1956): 84.

Review of the first European performance of the orchestral work *Elf Transparente* op.142.

B1138. Schaub, Fritz. "Zwei Uraufführungen im Musica-Nova-Konzert." *Luzerner Tagblatt* (August 30, 1966)

Review of the premiere of the *Adagio und Fuge für Sterichochester* op.78a.

B1139. Schaub, Hans F. "Allgemeines Deutsches Tonkünstler-Fest in Cassel." *Der Auftakt* (Prague) 3:7 (1923): 163-165.

Review of the festival including a performance of the *Second symphony* op.12.

B1140. ——. "Frankfurter Tonkünstlerfest." *Der Auftakt* (Prague) 4:8 (1924): 220-222.

Review of the festival including a performance of the opera *Der Sprung über den Schatten* op.17.

B1141. Schelp, Arend. "De componist Ernst Krenek als schrijver." *Mens en melodie* 20:2 (February 1965): 40-43.

Discusses Krenek's writings of the texts of his musical works and essays, and surveys the various printed collections. Picture.

B1142. Scherzer, Ernst. "Krenek-Ausstellung in Wien." *Opernwelt* 23:8/9 (1982): 10.

Review of an exhibition by the Wiener Stadt- und Landesbibliothek in honor of the composer's 80th birthday.

B1143. ——. "Geehrt, doch unbegehrt." *Neue Zeitschrift für Musik* 147:2 (February 1986): 26-29.

An interview with Krenek with the general theme of "honored, but unwanted." Includes a discography. Pictures.

B1144. Schlaf, Johannes. "Musik in der Bauhauswoche." *Berliner Tageblatt* (August 25, 1922)

Review of a the premiere of the *First concerto grosso* op.10.

B1145. Schlager, Karlheinz. "Ernst Krenek dirigiert eigene Werke in Bamberg." *Melos* 34:2 (February 1967): 60.

Review of the premiere of *Kleine suite* for clarinet and piano op.28.

B1146. Schleicher, Fritz. "Philharmonischer höhepunkt mit Krenek-Uraufführung in der Meistersingerhalle." *Nürnberger Nachrichten* (June 16, 1975)

Review of the premiere of *Auf- und Ablehnung* op.220.

   a. ——. *Das Orchester* 23:7/8 (July-August 1975): 494-495.

B1147. Schmid, H.K. "Zweites Donaueschinger Kammermusikfest zur Förderung zeitgenössischer Tonkunst." *Zeitschrift für Musikwissenschaft* 4:11/12 (August-September 1922): 624-625.

Includes a review of the premiere of *Symphonische Musik* op.11.

B1148. Schmid, O. "Konzert und Oper: Dresden." *Zeitschrift für Musik* 97:6 (June 1930): 482-483.

Review of the premiere of the song cycle *Fiedellieder* op.64.

B1149. Schmidt, L. "*Zwingburg.*" *Berliner Tageblatt* (October 22, 1924)

Review of the premiere of the opera op.14.

B1150. Schmidt-Dengler, Wendelin. "Wie schlafende Uhren blicken uns des Lebens Bilder an." In *Ernst Krenek,* hrsg. von Otto Kolleritsch. (B328) Studien zur Wertungsforschung, Bd.15. (Wien: Universal Edition, 1982): 69-78.

An examination of the meanings and the influences on the texts of *Reisebuch aus den österreichischen Alpen* op.62 and *Gesänge des späten Jahres* op.71.

B1151. Schmidt-Garre, Helmut. "Als die Oper sachlich wurde." *Neue Zeitschrift für Musik* 122:9 (1961): 340-344.

Discusses Krenek's operas *Jonny spielt auf* op.45 and *Leben des Orest* op.60 along with those of Bertold Brecht and others.

B1152. ——. "Kreneks *Spaetlese.*" *Neue Zeitschrift für Musik* 135:9 (September 1974): 565-566.

Review of the premiere of the song cycle op.218.

B1153. Schmitt, August. "Konzerte mit Jean Françaix und Ernst Krenek." *Das Orchester* 15:2 (February 1967): 66.

Review of the January 7 Bamberg Bläserquintett concert with the composer at the piano of performances of *Kleine suite* op.28; *Pentagramm* op.163; *Alpbach-Quintett* op.180; *Suite for flute and piano* op.147; *Sonatine for oboe* op.156; and the premiere of *Invention* op.127a.

B1154. ——. "Françaix - Krenek." *Musica* 21:2 (March-April 1967): 65.

Review of a concert on January 7 in Bamberg by the Bamberg Bläserquintett with the composer at the piano. Performances included the premieres of *Kleine Suite für Klarinette und Klavier* op.28 and *Invention* for flute and piano op.127a; the first European performance of *Pentagramm* op.163; and performances of *Suite for flute and piano* op.147, and two other sonatas.

B1155. Schmitz, Eugen. "Kunst und Wissenschaft." *Dresdener Nachrichten* (March 12, 1929)

Review of the premiere of *Monolog der Stella* op.57.

B1156. ——. "Kunst und Wissenschaft." *Dresdener Nachrichten* (April 12, 1930)

Review of the premiere of the song cycle *Fiedellieder* op.64.

B1157. ——. "Dresden." *Die Musik* 22:11 (August 1930): 846.

Review of the premiere of *Fiedellieder* op.64.

B1158. ——. "Musikbriefe: Dresden." *Allgemeine Musikzeitung* 59:20 (May 20, 1932): 274.

Review of the premiere of the song cycle *Gesänge des späten Jahres* op.71.

B1159. ——. "Dresden." *Die Musik* 24:9 (June 1932): 702.

Review of the premiere of *Gesänge des späten Jahres* op.71.

B1160. Schmitz, Hans-Peter. "Flötenmusik aus alter und neuer Zeit." *Musica* 15:9 (September 1961): 517-518.

Review of the publication of *Flötenstück neunphasig* op.171.

B1161. Schneider, J.-Marius. "Ernst Krenek." *La revue musicale* 11:107 (August-September 1930): 126-134.

Discusses Krenek at thirty and surveys his considerable output.

B1162. Schnoor, Hans. "Fünfzigmal 'Neue Musik'." *Dresdener Anzeiger* (April 12, 1930)

Review of the premiere of the song cycle *Fiedellieder* op.64.

B1163. Schoenberg, Arnold. "Glosses on the theories of others." In his *Style and Idea*, edited by Leonard Stein; translated by Leo Black. (Berkeley: University of California Press, 1975): 313-316.

Negative reactions to Krenek's comment that "the design of an opera must be like that of a potpourri" published in *Anbruch* (October 1929), as well as comments by others which appeared in the same issue.

B1164. ——. "Krenek's *Sprung über den Schatten*." In his *Style and Idea*, edited by Leonard Stein. Translated by Leo Black. (Berkeley: University of California Press, 1975): 477-481.

Generally positive reactions after having read through the score of op.17; dated December 21, 1923.

B1165. "Schönberg, Strawinskii und Krenek." *Dresdener Neueste Nachrichten* (March 13, 1929)

>Review of the premiere of *Monolog der Stella* op.57.

B1166. Schöny, Heinz. "Ernst Kreneks Vorfahren; Musikgeschichte und Genealogie 25." *Genealogie* 19:10 (October 1970): 257-259.

>A short biography and genealogy of five generations; Krenek's ancestors were all Bohemians (most were Czechs, but some were German).

B1167. Schollum, Robert. "Ernst Krenek." In his *Das Oesterreichische Lied des 20. Jahrhunderts*. Publikationen des Instituts für Oesterreichische Musikdokumentation, 3. (Tutzing: Schneider, 1977): 117-127.

>Discusses the songs, and especially *Reisebuch aus den österreichischen Alpen* op.62, from the standpoint of text and music relationships and their debt to Schubert as the "father" of the contemporary Lied.

B1168. ——. "Anmerkungen zum Liedschaffen Ernst Kreneks." *Oesterreichische Musikzeitschrift* 35:9 (September 1980): 446-452.

>Surveys Krenek's songs from op.9 through op.229. His early songs demonstrate his "inner sound" and show the conflict of atonality versus tonality. All his songs retain a vocal style independent of his musical style; text is always important.

B1169. Schonberg, Harold C. "Piano music of the 20th century." *The American Music Lover* 6:1 (May 1940): 6-8.

>Record review of *Eine kleine Suite* op.13a on RCA Victor M-646.

B1170. ——. "Krenek: *Eleven short piano pieces* (from op.83)." *The American Music Lover* 6:4 (August 1940): 132.

>Record review of Columbia X 171.

B1171. ——. "Records: *Erwartung*." *New York Times* 101:34483 (June 22, 1952): 2:10.

>Record review of *Symphonic elegy* op.105 on Columbia ML 4524.

B1172. ——. "Comment in Brief." *New York Times* 102:34735 (March 1, 1953): 2:9.

>Record review of *The seasons* op.35 and excerpts from *Lamentatio Jeremiae prophetae* op.93 on New Records NRLP 306.

B1173. ——. "Duo-pianists offer 2 world premieres." *New York Times* 103:34974 (October 26, 1953): 26.

>Review of the premiere of the *Two-piano concerto* op.127.

B1174. ——. "Comment in Brief." *New York Times* 103:35092 (February 21, 1954): 2:9.

>Record review of the *Organ sonata* op.92 on University of Oklahoma 2.

B1175. ——. "Three concertos bow at museum." *New York Times* 104:35474 (March 10, 1955): 31.

>Review of the first American performance of the *Double concerto* op.124.

B1176. Schorr, Dieter. "Kunst ist schwer." *Stuttgarter Zeitung* (October 27, 1962)

>Review of the premiere of *Nach wie vor der Reihe nach* op.182.

B1177. Schreiber, Manfred. "Amadeo Austria issues run of new product." *Billboard* (September 12, 1981): 54.

Announces the release of the recording of *Karl V.* on Amadeo AVRS 305. Picture.

B1178. Schreiber, Ulrich. "Entdeckungen." *Neue Musikzeitung* 36:2 (April-May 1988): 34.

Record review of *String quartets* no.1, op.6 and no.2, op.8 on MD + G L 3280 (CD)

B1179. Schrenk, Walter. "Kompositionskonzerte der Hochschule." *Deutsche Allgemeine Zeitung* (Berlin) (June 21, 1921)

Review of the premiere on June 21, 1921, of the *Violin and piano sonata* op.3 and a performance of the *Serenade* op.4 during a concert of Franz Schreker's students at the Staatliche Akademische Hochschule für Musik, Konzertsaale, Berlin; Oskar Schubert, clarinet; Gustav Havemann, violin; Hans Mahlke, viola; Hermann Hopf, cello.

B1180. ——. "Unknown." *Deutsche Allgemeine Zeitung* (Berlin) (March 20, 1922)

Review of the premiere of the *First symphony* op.7.

B1181. ——. "Klavierabend Erdmann." *Deutsche Allgemeine Zeitung* (Berlin) (October 19, 1922)

Review of the premiere of *Toccata und Chaconne* op.13 and *Eine kleine Suite* op.13a.

B1182. ——. "Die Krenek-Uraufführung." *Deutsche Allgemeine Zeitung* (Berlin) 67:213/214 (May 9, 1928): 2.

Review of the premieres of the one-act operas *Der Diktator* op.49, *Das geheime Königreich* op.50, and *Schwergewicht, oder Die Ehre der Nation* op.55.

B1183. ——. "Ernst Krenek. *Kleine Symphonie.*" *Anbruch* 11:2 (February 1929): 92.

Review of the premiere of op.58.

B1184. Schubert, Giselher. "Claudia Maurer-Zenck: *Ernst Krenek - ein Komponist im Exil.*" *Musikforschung* 35:3 (July-September 1982): 318-320.

Review of the book (B1502 & B1509).

B1185. ——. "Hindemith und Krenek." *Die Musikforschung* 35:3 (July-September 1982): 277-282.

Commentary on the correspondence between the two composers after their arrival in the U.S. showing that they had a good relationship, contrary to Claudia Maurer Zenck's contention in her *Ernst Krenek; Ein Komponist im Exil* (B1502).

B1186. ——. "*Ernst Krenek.* Studien zur Wertungsforschung, Bd.15, hrsg. von Otto Kolleritsch. *Dank an Ernst Krenek.*" *Neue Zeitschrift für Musik* 144:7/8 (July-August 1983): 70.

Review of the catalog of Krenek materials (B550) by Ernst Hilmar and the book of essays (B328).

B1187. Schuh, Willi. "Die Tagung des Allgemeinen Deutschen Musikvereins in Zürich (10.--14. Juni." *Die Musik* 24:10 (July 1932): 754-758.

Review of the festival and performance of *Theme und 13 variationen* op.69.

B1188. ——. "Zürich." *Schweizerische Musikzeitung und Sängerblatt* 73:21 (November 1, 1933): 686-687.

Review of the premiere of *Kantate von der Vergänglichkeit des Irdischen* op.72.

B1189. ——. "Zur Zwölftontechnik bei Ernst Krenek." *Schweizerische Musikzeitung und Sängerblatt* 74:7 (April 1, 1934): 217-223.

A detailed twelve-tone analysis of the opera *Karl V.* op.73, Krenek's first full twelve-tone work, relating the use of the row to specific characters. Includes several examples. Also mentions that he used the twelve-tone row in parts of his works starting in 1929 in *Reisebuch aus den österreichischen Alpen* op.62, *Durch die Nacht* op.67, "Liebeslied" and "Ballade vom Fest" in *Gesänge des späten Jahres* op.71, and *Kantate von der Vergänglichkeit des Irdischen* op.72.

B1190. ——. "Kompositionsaufträge: Ernst Krenek." In *Alte und neue Musik* (Zürich: Atlantis Verlag, 1952): 86-91.

Examines Krenek's relationship to Paul Sacher and his commissions; includes excerpts from correspondence and facsimiles of a letter and the first page of the score of *Symphonic piece* op.86.

B1191. ——. "Zu Ernst Kreneks *Invention*." *Schweizerische Musikzeitung* 93:3 (March 1, 1953): 115.

Analysis of *Invention für Flöte und Klarinette* op.127a written for the *Schweizerische Musikzeitung* and printed with the article.

B1192. Schuhmacher, Gerhard. *Geschichte und Möglichkeiten der Vertonung von Dichtungen Friedrich Hölderlins.* Forschungsbeiträge zur Musikwissenschaft, 18. (Regensburg: Gustav Bosse Verlag, 1967)

Includes a brief interview (pp.331-332) dated October 19, 1964 in Saarbrücken, concerning his settings of texts by Friedrich Hölderlin in *Vier kleine Männerchöre* op.32 and *Die Jahreszeiten* op.35. The book also contains extensive commentaries (pp.270-273) on the two works.

B1193. Schultz, Günter. "Festival der Variationen." *Rheinische Post* (March 14, 1977)

Review of the premiere of *Four Winds* op.223.

B1194. Schulz, Reinhard. "Wichtiges -- zu derb." *Neue Musikzeitung* 36:3 (June-July 1988): 34.

Review of the recording of the *String trio* op.118 on Calig 30861.

B1195. Schulze, Otto Friedrich. *"Glauben und Wissen - Ausgerechnet und verspielt.* Zu Ernst Kreneks 'Dialektischen Klang- und Gesangsspiel'." *Musik im Unterricht* 58:5 (May 1967): 174-177.

Discusses Krenek's use of serialism in the works between opus 179 and opus 194, especially focused on text and timbre.

B1196. Schumann, Karl. "Ernst Kreneks *Prosa, Dramen und Verse*." *Melos* 33:2 (February 1966): 51-52.

Review of the book of Krenek's writings (K804).

B1197. Schwab, Heinrich W. *"Jonny spielt auf."* In *Opernstudien; Anna Amalie Abert zum 65. Geburtstag,* hrsg. von Karl Hortschansky. (Tutzing: Hans Schneider, 1975): 175-187.

Examination of the portrayal of the Negro in Krenek's opera op.45 and the reception of the opera in the European press.

B1198. Schwab, Heinrich W. "The violinist on the globe." *RIdIM/RCMI Newsletter* 7:2 (Fall 1983): 10.

Abstract of a paper read at the Ninth International Conference on Musical Inconography. *Jonny spielt auf* op.45 "ends with the black jazz musician Jonny standing on the globe, playing his stolen violin as the multitudes below him dance to his music. The depiction recalls an iconographic tradition extending from the early Middle Ages through the Renaissance and beyond, in which Christ is shown enthroned on top of the world... In the nineteenth century, pictures of two violinists -- Joseph Joachim, as a young prodigy, and Johann Strauss the Younger -- shown them astride the world, symbolizing the extent to which their music had gripped the public imagination. As contemporary sources confirm, Jonny's apotheosis represents the triumph of jazz over the classical tradition."

B1199. Schweizer, Gottfried. "Darmstädter Ferienkurse 1954: Krenek-Uraufführung in Darmstadt." *Zeitschrift für Musik* 115:9 (September 1954): 565-566.

Review of the first German performance of the opera *Dunkle Wasser* op.125.

B1200. Schweizer, Klaus. "Ernst Krenek. *On new music.*" *Literature, Music, Fine Arts* 14:2 (1981): 191-192.

Review of the 1977 reprint of the book *Ueber neue Musik* (K397).

B1201. ——. "Ernst Krenek: *1. Symphonie op.7, 2. Symphonie op.12, 3. Symphonie op.16.*" *Neue Zeitschrift für Musik* 147:6 (June 1986): 67.

Record review of Amadeo 415 825-1.

B1202. Schwers, Paul. "Das 51. Tonkünstlerfest in Nürnberg." *Allgemeine Musikzeitung* 48:27 (July 1, 1921): 503-505.

Includes a review of the premiere of the *First string quartet* op.6.

B1203. ——. "Aus den Berliner Konzertsälen." *Allgemeine Musikzeitung* 49:12 (March 24, 1922): 223-224.

Review of the premiere of the *First symphony* op.7.

B1204. ——. "Ernst Kreneks Symphonie in Berlin." *Musikblätter des Anbruch* 4:9/10 (May 1922): 155.

Review of the premiere of the *First symphony* op.7.

B1205. ——. "Die Casseler Tonkünstler-Versammlung des Allgemeinen Deutschen Musikvereins." *Allgemeine Musikzeitung* 50:24/25 (June 22, 1923): 443-445.

Includes a review of the premiere of the *Second symphony* op.12.

B1206. ——. "Das Frankfurter Tonkünstlerfest des Allgemeinen Deutschen Musikvereins: II:Die Bühnenwerke." *Allgemeine Musikzeitung* 51:27 (July 4, 1924): 526-528.

Review of the premiere of the opera *Der Sprung über den Schatten* op.17.

B1207. ——. "Ernst Kreneks *Zwingburg.*" *Allgemeine Musikzeitung* 51:44 (October 31, 1924): 794.

Review of the premiere of the opera op.14.

B1208. ——. "Ernst Kreneks *Orpheus und Eurydike.*" *Allgemeine Musikzeitung* 53:50 (December 10, 1926): 1038-1039.

Review of the premiere of the opera op.21. Picture: cover.

B1209. ——. *"Jonny spielt auf."* Allgemeine Musikzeitung 54:7 (February 18, 1927): 151-152.
Review of the premiere of the opera op.45.

B1210. ——. "Aus dem Berliner Musikleben." *Allgemeine Musikzeitung* 56:15 (April 12, 1929): 435.
Includes a review of the premiere of the *Second piano sonata* op.59.

B1211. ——. *"Leben des Orest."* Allgemeine Musikzeitung 57:5 (January 31, 1930): 103-104.
Review of the premiere of the opera op.60. Picture: cover.

B1212. Schwertsik, Kurt. "Krenek -- ein österreichischer Komponist." *Der Opernfreund* 2:9 (May 1, 1957): 8.
A poem in honor of Krenek reflecting on his operas.

B1213. Schwinger, Wolfram. "Krenek dirigiert Eigenes." *Musica* 22:3 (May/June 1968): 186.
Review of a concert by the Sinfonieorchester des Südwestfunk in Hans-Rosbaud-Studio, Baden-Baden, in which the composer conducted his *Third symphony* op.16, *Aus drei mach sieben* op.177, and the first European performance of *Horizont umkreist* op.196.

B1214. ——. "Musikprotokoll des Steirischen Herbstes." *Musica* 25:1 (1971): 31-32.
Includes a review of the premiere of *Doppelt beflügeltes Band* op.207.

B1215. Scott-Maddocks, Daniel. "Breakthrough for modern music." *Records and Recording* 4:11 (August 1961): 14-23, 35.
Includes a record review of *Symphonic elegy* op.105 on Philips ABL 3393.

B1216. Segal, Lewis. "Arriaga String Quartet plays at Bing Theater." *Los Angeles Times* 94 (January 23, 1975)
Review of a Monday Evening Concert which included the first American performance of *Aulokithara* op.213a.

B1217. Seidl, Arthur. "Donaueschingen 1925." In his *Neuzeitliche Tondichter und zeitgenössische Tonkünstler*. Vol.2. Deutsche Musikbücherei, Bd.19. (Regensburg: Gustav Bosse, 1926): 285-301.
A review of the festival including the premiere of the chorus *Die Jahreszeiten* op.35.

B1218. ——. "Ein *Violin-Konzert* von Ernst Krenek u.a." In his *Neuzeitliche Tondichter und zeitgenössische Tonkünstler*. Vol.2. Deutsche Musikbücherei, Bd.19. (Regensburg: Gustav Bosse, 1926): 268-276.
Review of the premiere of the *First violin concerto* op.29. Picture.

B1219. Seidt, Arthur. "Dessau." *Allgemeine Musikzeitung* 52:10 (March 6, 1925): 210-211.
Includes a review of the premiere of the *First violin concerto* op.29.

B1220. Seltsan, William H. *Metropolitan Opera Annals.* (New York: H. W. Wilson, 1947)
Documents the first American performances of *Jonny spielt auf* op.45, January 19 - April 4, 1929. Includes a reprint of W. J. Henderson's review (B530).

B1221. Sessions, Roger. "Exposition by Krenek." *Modern Music* 15 (January-February 1938): 123-128.

Review of the book *Ueber Neue Musik* (K397). Praises the book but objects to two points: 1."works seem to be almost of secondary importance in comparison with the theory, ... [and 2.] the intensely abstract nature of [the twelve-tone composer's] thought."

a. ——. In *Roger Sessions On Music*. (Princeton: Princeton University Press, 1979): 249-255.

B1222. ——. "The function of theory." *Modern Music* 15 (May/June 1938): 257-262.

Compares Krenek's book *Ueber neue Musik* (K397) with Paul Hindemith's *Unterweisung im Tonsatz* and Heinrich Schenker's *Der freie Satz*.

a. ——. In *Roger Sessions On Music*. (Princeton: Princeton University Press, 1979): 263-268.

B1223. Sherman, John K. "Krenek premiere at eight symphony." *Minneapolis Star Journal* (December 12, 1942): 12.

Review of the premiere of *I wonder as I wander* op.94.

B1224. ——. "Music: Sinfonietta is led by Krenek at Hamline." *Minneapolis Star Journal* (April 5, 1943): 17.

Review of the first performance of excerpts from *Lamentatio Jeremiae prophetiae* op.93.

B1225. ——. "Mitropoulos hails Krenek as one of the big men in music." *Minneapolis Star Journal* (December 22, 1943): 2.

Comments by Dimitri Mitropoulos about the preparations by the Minneapolis Symphony of the forthcoming premiere of the *Second symphony* op.12.

B1226. ——. "Krenek symphony in American premiere." *Minneapolis Star Journal* (December 24, 1943): 4.

Review of the first American performance of the *Second symphony* op.12.

B1227. ——. "Hamline choir sings with symphony." *Minneapolis Star Journal* (March 25, 1944): 14.

Review of the premiere of the *Cantata for wartime* op.95.

B1228. ——. "Mauricci, Rateau play solos at 16th concert." *Minneapolis Star Journal* (March 23, 1946): 8.

Review of the premiere of *Tricks and trifles* op.101.

B1229. ——. "A piano-playing Dimitri and a gay Shostakovitch." *Minneapolis Star Journal* (November 23, 1946): 4.

Review of the premiere of the *Third piano concerto* op.107.

B1230. ——. "*Santa Fe time table* is lyric travelogue." *Minneapolis Star Journal* (March 13, 1947)

Review of the premieres of op.102 and *Aegrotavit Ezechias* op.103.

B1231. ——. "Composer Krenek to get 'week' as birthday gift." *Minneapolis Star Journal* (April 18, 1965)

An interview in anticipation of the forthcoming four-day festival. Picture.

B1232. ——. "Krenek leads Civic group in program of own works." *Minneapolis Star Journal* (April 23, 1965)

Review of the first American performance of *Stücke* op.31 and the *Fourth piano concerto* op.123.

B1233. Shupp Jr., Enos E. "Chamber music." *The New Records* 46:1 (March 1978): 8.

Record review of the *Pieces for oboe and piano* op.193 on Orion ORS 78288.

B1234. ——. "Complete organ works of Arnold Schönberg and Ernst Krenek." *The New Records* 51:4 (June 1983): 14.

Record review of Musica Viva MV 50-1090.

B1235. Simon, Robert A. "The cradle again." *New Yorker* 23:42 (December 6, 1947): 114-115.

Review of the premiere of the *Fourth symphony* op.113 in New York.

B1236. Singer, Samuel L. "New scores aired by Philadelphians." *Musical Courier* 147:2 (January 15, 1953): 17.

Review of the premiere of the *Harp concerto* op.126.

B1237. ——. "New Krenek score in Philadelphia." *Musical Courier* 147:7 (April 1, 1953): 18.

Review of the premiere of *Medea* op.129.

B1238. Sivers, Gerd. "Kreneks *Pallas Athene.*" *Musica* 8:11 (November 1954): 493-494.

Review of the premiere of the *Symphony Pallas Athene* op.137, on the twenty-fifth radio program in the series "Das neue Werk" on Nordwestdeutscher Rundfunk (NWDR) Hamburg. The concert also included the first European performance of *Kantata* op.95 and a performance of the *Second piano concerto* op.81.

B1239. Slonimsky, Nicolas. "Musical miscellany." *Etude* 68:12 (December 1950): 6-7.

"The only modern composer who can stand on his head ... is Ernst Krenek." Picture.

B1240. ——. *Music since 1900.* (New York: Charles Scribner's Sons, 1971)

A general chronology which includes approximately forty references to Krenek's life and works.

B1241. Smith, Carleton Sprague. "The I.S.C.M. meets at Barcelona." *Modern Music* 13:4 (May/June 1936): 30-34.

A review of the festival and the premiere of *Fragmente aus dem Bühnenwerk Karl V.* op.73a.

B1242. Smith, Cecil. "Ernst Krenek gives recital of own works." *Chicago Tribune* (January 3, 1941)

Review of a concert in which the composer played the *Piano suite* op.26, no.2 and *Twelve variations* op.79, and then repeated them.

B1243. Smith, George Henry Lovett. "Boston news." *Modern Music* 16:2 (January-February 1939): 114-116.

Review of the Boston performance of the *Second piano concerto* op.81.

B1244. Smith, Moses. "American premiere of Concerto by Krenek, Burgin conducting." *Boston Evening Transcript* 109:260 (November 5, 1938): pt.3, p.6.

Review of the first American performance of the *Second piano concerto* op.81.

B1245. ——. "Ballet and the news." *Boston Evening Transcript* (May 22, 1939)

Review of the premiere of the ballet *Eight column line* op.85.

B1246. Smith, Warren Storey. "Composer soloist at Symphony" *Boston Post* (November 5, 1938): 10.

Review of the first American performance of the *Second piano concerto* op.81.

B1247. Smoley, Lewis M. "Krenek: *Horizon Circled*, Op.196; *From Three Make Seven*, Op.171; *Von Vorn Herein*, Op.219." *American Record Guide* 41:8 (June 1978): 36-37.

Record review of Orion ORS 78290.

B1248. Smolich, N. "Spektakl' Ksheneka." *Novaia muzyka* (Leningrad) 1:2 (1927): 23-27.

Discussion in Russian of the Leningrad production of the opera *Der Sprung über den Schatten* op.17.

B1249. Sonenfield, Irwin. "Ernst Krenek's *Jonny spielt auf.*" *Musician* 53:9/10 (September-October 1948): 88-90.

A synopsis of the opera op.45 with an examination of its symbolism. Second in the series "Contemporary operas."

B1250. Sorenson, Sandra Kay. "A profile of selected works by Ernst Krenek for solo piano, choral and instrumental ensembles." (Master's thesis: California State University, Long Beach, 1982) 111 pp.

Includes a discussion of *Eight piano pieces* op.110, *Scenes from the West* op.134, and *Three Lessons and Three sacred pieces* op.210.

B1251. Sosin, Donald. "University organ conference ... A mass of music." *Michigan Daily* (University of Michigan, Ann Arbor) (October 19, 1971)

Review of the premiere of *Orga-nastro* op.212.

B1252. Sparshott, F.E. "Critic and creator." *Times Literary Supplement* no.3843 (November 7, 1975): 1336.

Review of the book *Briefwechsel* (K862) containing writings by Krenek and Theodor Wiesengrund Adorno.

B1253. Specht, Richard. "Ernst Krenek, *Toccata und Chaconne*, op.13." *Musikblätter des Anbruch* 5:4 (April 1923): 128.

Review of the publication for piano.

B1254. "Spielt auf." *Der Spiegel* 24:27 (June 29, 1970): 136.

Review of the premiere of the opera *Das kommt davon* op.206. Picture.

B1255. Spies, Hansjörg. "80 und kein bisschen müde." *Oberösterreichische Nachrichten* (October 29, 1980)

Review of the premiere of *Im Tal der Zeit* op.232.

B1256. Spingel, Hans Otto. "Hamburger Veranstaltungen." *Die Welt* (October 3, 1960)

Review of the premiere of *Quaestio temporis* op.170.

B1257. ——. "Zeit der Fragen, Fragen der Zeit." *Die Welt* (October 4, 1960)
Review of the premiere of *Quaestio temporis* op.170.

B1258. ——. "Cosǐ'20. stoleti." *Hudebni rozhledy* 23:10/11 (1970): 453.
Review of the premiere of the opera *Sardakai, oder Das kommt davon* op.206.

B1259. ——. "Cosǐ im 20. Jahrhundert." *Opernwelt* 11:8 (August 1970): 24-25.
Review of the premiere of the opera *Das kommt davon* op.206. Pictures.

B1260. Spizizen, Louise. "UCSD concert celebrates Krenek anniversary."
La Jolla Light (January 23, 1975)
Review of an all-Krenek concert at the University of California, San Diego, Mandeville Center on January 18 celebrating his seventy-fifth year which included performances of *Exercises of a late hour* op.200 conducted by John Silber, *Marginal sounds* op.162 conducted by Jean-Charles Francois, and the premiere of *Static and ecstatic* op.214 conducted by the composer.

B1261. St. Andrée, O. G. de. "Düsseldorf-Duisburg." *Opera* 10:3 (March 1959): 165-169.
Review of the first German performance of *Der Glockenturm* op.153. Picture.

B1262. Stadlen, Peter. "Krenek: a lifetime of opera." *Opera* 31:9 (September 1980): 876-882.
A survey of Krenek's operas from the scenic cantata *Die Zwingburg* op.14 to *What price confidence* op.111 with mentions of recent performances seen by the reviewer. Picture: scenes from several operas & portrait.

B1263. Šťedron, Milos. "Janacek a modernismus tricatych let: Hába, Cowell, Krenek." *Hudebni rozhledy* 23:2 (1970): 72-76.
Discusses the music of Leoš Janáček and the premiere of the opera *Jonny spielt auf* op.45.

B1264. Stefan, Paul. "Neue Kammermusik in Donaueschingen." *Musikblätter des Anbruch* 3:15-16 (October 1921): 293-294.
A review of the festival which included performances by two of Franz Schreker's students. Krenek's piece was the early tonal *Serenade* op.4.

B1265. ——. "A new triptych is unfolded." *Musical America* 48:9 (June 16, 1928): 5.
Review of the premiere of the three one-act operas *Der Diktator* op.49, *Das geheime Königreich* op.50, and *Schwergewicht, oder Die Ehre der Nation* op.55. Picture.

B1266. ——. "Erste Tage in Barcelona." *Der Wiener Tag* (April 28, 1936)
Review of the festival which included the premiere of *Fragmente aus dem Bühnenwerk Karl V.* op.73a.

B1267. Stege, Fritz. "Wandlungen? Zeitstimmen zum Stilproblem."
Allgemeine Musikzeitung 58:11 (March 13, 1931): 183-184.
Briefly quotes several composers of new music, including Krenek, about changing musical styles.

B1268. Stehla, A. "Theater und Konzerte: Zweites Donaueschinger Kammermusikfest." *Kölnische Volkszeitung* (August 6, 1922)
Review of the premiere of *Symphonische Musik* op.11.

B1269. Steinbauer, Robert Andrus. "A discussion of the *Third piano sonata, opus 92, no.4* (1943) by Ernst Krenek." (Ph.D. diss.: Indiana University, 1960)

B1270. Steinberg, Michael. "Krenek to conduct his intricate work." *Boston Globe* (March 2, 1965)

  Announces the first American performance of *Circle, chain and mirror* op.160, and discusses its construction and creation.

B1271. ——. "An exciting concert: *Groups, Circles* and Beethoven." *Boston Globe* (March 5, 1965)

  Review of the American premiere of *Circle, chain and mirror* op.160.

B1272. ——. "*What price confidence?*" *Boston Sunday Globe* (August 18, 1968)

  Review of the first American performance of the chamber opera op.111.

B1273. ——. "Krenek's *Jonny* after 47 years." *Boston Globe* (May 13, 1976): 33.

  Review of a concert performance of the opera op.45 by the New England Conservatory, and Krenek's receipt of an honorary doctorate.

B1274. Steinecke, Wolfgang. "Hinweis auf Kreneks 6. *Quartett*." *Der Mittag* (Düsseldorf) (January 29, 1953)

  Review of the premiere in Darmstadt of op.78.

B1275. ——. "Uraufführung nach 16 Jahren." *Musica* 7:3 (March 1953): 108.

  Review of the premiere of the *Sixth string quartet* op.78 in Darmstadt.

B1276. ——. "Kreneks *Glockenturm*." *Neue Zeitschrift für Musik* 120:2 (February 1959): 86-87.

  Review of the first German performance of the chamber opera op.153. Picture of scene.

B1277. Steinhard, Erich. "Die Minaturopern von Toch, Hindemith, Krenek." *Auftakt* (Prague) 9 (1929): 309-312.

  Discusses the one-act operas of the three composers comparing Krenek's *Schwergewicht, oder Die Ehre der Nation* op.55 with Hindemith's *Hin und zurich* and Toch's *Prinzessin auf der Erbse*.

B1278. Steinhof-Tallon, Ninon. "*Jonny spielt auf* d'Ernst Krenek." *La revue musicale* 9:4 (February 1928): 76-77.

  Review of the premiere of the opera op.45.

B1279. Stephan, Rudolf. "Theodore W. Adorno und Ernst Krenek: *Briefwechsel*." *Oesterreichische Musikzeitschrift* 30:8 (August 1975): 427-428.

  Review of the book (K862).

B1280. ——. "Theodor W. Adorno und Ernst Krenek: *Briefwechsel*." *Melos/NZ* 2:2 (March-April 1976): 155.

  Review of the book (K862).

B1281. ——. "Stil und Moral." *Oesterreichische Musikzeitschrift* 35:9 (September 1980): 433-437.

  Krenek is a significant writer on music; not only has he analyzed many of his own works, but he also discusses musical life in the twentieth century. He is concerned with the conveyance of meaning in music, and points to freedom and responsibility as the most important elements for creativity.

B1282. Stephan, Rudolf. "Einzelheiten zur Musik des jungen Krenek." In *Ernst Krenek,* hrsg. von Otto Kolleritsch. (B328) Studien zur Wertungsforschung, Bd.15. (Wien: Universal Edition, 1982): 95-118.

A detailed examination of the early works and their reception including the *Serenade* op.4, *First string quartet* op.6, *First symphony* op.7, *Second string quartet* op.8, *Concerto grosso* op.10, *Symphonische Musik* op.11, *Second symphony* op.12, *Toccata und Chaconne über des Choral Ja ich glaub an Jesum Christum* op.13, *Third symphony* op.16, and *Third string quartet* op.20.

a. ——. In his *Vom musikalischen Denken; Gesammelte Vorträge.* (Mainz: Schott, 1985): 258-274.

B1283. Stevens, Denis. *"Johannes Ockeghem* by Ernst Krenek." *Tempo* no.31 (Spring 1954): 38.

Review of the book (K616).

B1284. Stewart, John L. "Preface." In *Horizons Circled; Reflections on My Music,* by Ernst Krenek. (K864) (Berkeley: University of California Press, 1974): vii-viii.

Describes the circumstances surrounding Krenek's residence as Regents Lecturer in John Muir College at the University of California, San Diego in early 1970 and his influence in shaping the founding of its Music Department.

B1285. ——. "The composer views his time." In *Horizons Circled; Reflections on My Music,* by Ernst Krenek. (K864) (Berkeley: University of California Press, 1974): 98-120.

A biographical essay based upon interviews with Krenek during 1971 and 1972.

B1286. ——. "Ernst Krenek at seventy-five." *American Music Teacher* 25:1 (Sept/October 1975): 10-11.

In discussing Krenek there is one group of the man's qualities which are often overlooked "perhaps because Krenek's reputation is in other respects so awesome. I refer to his sense of humor, his wittiness, his relish for the ridiculous in human behavior." These qualities appear in many works including *Ausgerechnet und verspielt* op.179. "Any serious discussion of the music of our century must take large account of him." Yet recordings are not always easy to get and much of his music is difficult to perform, but some pieces "lie within the compass of young performers." Discusses several of those works.

B1287. ——. "Frauen in den Opern Ernst Kreneks." *Musica* 34:2 (March-April 1980): 136-138.

Discusses the characterization of women in Krenek's operas.

B1288. ——. "Ernst Kreneks Masken." *Oesterreichische Musikzeitschrift* 35:9 (September 1980): 437-444.

The artist generally identifies himself with a single voice whom he hides behind as a mask. Two personality types represent Krenek; one loves tradition, stability and order, and the other presents an anarchic nature. The "Dissembler" becomes the most important figure for Krenek.

B1289. ——. "Krenek as an essayist." In *Ernst Krenek,* hrsg. von Otto Kolleritsch. (B328) Studien zur Wertungsforschung, Bd.15. (Wien: Universal Edition, 1982): 56-68.

A survey of Krenek's writings concluding "taking into account Krenek's whole career and all that he has given us, one cannot regret his decision in 1931 to make composing his primary concern. One should be grateful for the essays we have, both for their intrinsic merit and for their enrichment of our pleasure in his music. And as we read and reread them they offer us yet one more eloquent testimony to Krenek's versatility, learning, creative energy, and monumental achievement."

B1290. Stewart, John L. "Ernst Krenek and music education." *American Music Teacher* 34:4 (1985): 41-43.

A lecture given at the annual meeting in Dearborn, MI. Discusses Krenek's career as a teacher and his teaching method. His only teaching experience before coming to American was as a student at the Berlin Staatliche Akademische Hochschule für Musik where he was a choral coach and privately taught harmony. He briefly taught at the Malkin Conservatory in Boston during the Fall of 1938 shortly after emigrating to the United States; he later taught at Vassar College and Hamline University. His teaching method was characterized as helping the student to find his or her own idiom; he did not impose his own ideas on the student. He stressed counterpoint, and his examples were usually drawn from the music of Johannes Ockeghem and Giovanni Palestrina.

B1291. ——. "Krenek, Ernst." In *The New Grove Dictionary of American Music*, edited by H. Wiley Hitchcock and Stanley Sadie. Vol.2. (London: Macmillan, 1986): 661-664.

Biographical essay with list of works. Picture.

B1292. Stöckl, Rudolf. "Nürnberg Internationale Orgelwoche." *Melos/NZ* 42:5 (September-October 1975): 401-402.

Review of the premiere of *Auf- und Ablehnung* op.220.

B1293. Stoieanova, Ivanka. "Subjekt - Objekt/Erläuterungen zur epischen Dramaturgie in *Karl V.* von Ernst Krenek." In *Ernst Krenek*, hrsg. von Otto Kolleritsch. (B328) Studien zur Wertungsforschung, Bd.15. (Wien: Universal Edition, 1982): 125-132.

An examination of the strong Austrian and Catholic themes of the opera op.73, and the public's reaction to the opera.

B1294. Stolz, Arthur B. "Krasner group offers music in pure form." *Saint Paul Pioneer Press* (November 28, 1946)

Review of the premiere of the *Trio* op.108.

B1295. Stravinsky, Igor ; Craft, Robert. "Some composers." *Musical America* 82:6 (June 1962): 6-11.

Stravinsky recalls his associations with Krenek and concludes "Krenek will be honored one day even at home."

B1296. Strobel, Heinrich. "*Jonny spielt auf* in Leipzig." *Melos* 6:3 (March 1927): 130-131.

Review of the Leipzig premiere of the opera op.45 relating it to Krenek's previously composed operas.

B1297. ——. "Strawinsky und Krenek." *Berliner Börsen-Courier* (November 3, 1928)

Review of the premiere of *Kleine Sinfonie* op.58.

a. ——. In *Experiment Krolloper, 1927-1931,* von Hans Curjel. Studien zur Kunst des neunzehnten Jahrhunderts, Bd.7. (Münich: Prestel-Verlag, 1975): 324-325.

B1298. ——. "Kreneks *Orest* in Leipzig." *Melos* 9:2 (February 1930): 98-99.
Review of the premiere of the opera *Leben des Orest* op.60.

B1299. ——. "Vier Jahrzehnte deutsches Musiktheater." *Melos* 30:10 (October 1963): 326-330.
A survey of German opera in the years following World War I including a brief discussion of *Jonny spielt auf* op.45, *Das Leben des Orest* op.60, and *Karl V.* op.73.

B1300. ——. "Vier Jahrzehnte deutsches Musiktheater." *Das Orchester* 11:12 (December 1963): 398-401.
A survey of German opera starting with Franz Schreker and his student, Krenek. Picture of scene 11 from the premiere of *Jonny spielt auf* op.45.

B1301. Strommer, Jean. "John Donne's text and the music of the first movement of Ernst Krenek's *La corona*; A study in relationships." In *Sacra/Profana; Studies in Sacred and Secular Music for Johannes Riedel,* edited by Audrey Ekdahl Davidson and Clifford Davidson. (Minneapolis: Friends of Minnesota Music, 1985): 53-66.
A detailed analysis of the song, examining the twelve-tone row and its relationship to the text. The study concludes that there is a "circularity" to the work both in detail and in its whole. "It is thus obvious that, as one moves his or her attention from local motions to a panoramic view of the larger structural motions, a consistency of intentions is observed. What holds true for the very center of the work is also true at its periphery."

B1302. Struck, Gustav. "Casseler Tonkünstlerschaft." *Kasseler Post* (June 13, 1923)
Review of the premiere of the *Second symphony* op.12.

B1303. ——. "Kassel." *Die Musik* 18:5 (February 1926): 385.
Mentions Krenek's arrangement of a Rameau ballet, *Der vertauschte Cupido* op.38, and its premiere.

B1304. Stuckenschmidt, Hans Heinz. "Ernst Kreneks Opern." *Melos* 5:11/12 (December 1926): 365-368.
Surveys the operas *Der Zwingburg* op.14, *Der Sprung über den Schatten* op.17, and *Orpheus und Eurydike* op.21.

B1305. ——. "Short operas." *Musikblätter des Anbruch* 10:6/7 (June-July 1928): 204-207.
Surveys contemporary brief and one-act operas, and briefly discusses Krenek's *Jonny spielt auf* op.45.

B1306. ——. "Hellenic jazz." *Modern Music* 7:3 (April-May 1930): 22-25.
Reviews the premiere of the opera *Leben des Orest* op.60 and its subsequent Berlin performance. "The score ... is a mixture of inspiration and the dreariest sort of rubbish." Pictures of set designed by Giorgio de Chirico on pages 2 & 25.

B1307. ——. "Krenek's new opera *Karl V.* acclaimed in Prague." *Musical America* 58:13 (August 1938): 11, 30.
Extensive discussion of the opera op.73 and review of the premiere. "The

question has been put; which Krenek ought we to believe, the youth of premature radicalism, the manager of jazz-opera and fake classicism, or the new Krenek of twelve-tone-espressivo-music. Without answering that, one may retort that it is to the honor of any artist when he works back from cheap success to the sphere of pure and intellectually refined art." Pictures.

B1308. ——. "Forbidden opus, Catholic." *Modern Music* 16 (November-December 1938): 41-44.

Review of the premiere of *Karl V*. op.73, regretting that Krenek had been unable to attend the premiere and noting that the second performance was cancelled due to political pressure.

B1309. ——. "New opera house avoids tradition; Krenek work given first performance." *Musical America* 75:14 (November 15, 1955): 12,31.

Discusses the opening of the new Hamburg Opera House and the premiere of *Pallas Athene weint* op.144. "The audience may not have been prepared for a festival production of such aggressive probity of style and showed a distinct reserve towards the music. But the evening ended with an ovation for Krenek and the cast, which had twenty curtain calls."

B1310. ——. "Ernst Kreneks Freiheitsoper *Pallas Athene weint* - Hamburg Uraufführung." *Universitas* 11:2 (1956): 217-218.

Review of the premiere of op.144.

B1311. ——. "Leningrad Philharmonic, Oistrakh appear in Berlin." *Musical America* 76:9 (July 1956): 33.

Includes a review of the third broadcast of electronic music from Cologne which included the premiere of *Spiritus intelligentiae sanctus* op.152. The review contrasts Krenek's work with Stockhausen's *Song of the youths*.

B1312. ——. "Berlin Festival enhanced by variety of programs." *Musical America* 78:12 (November 1, 1958): 8-9.

Includes a review of a concert conducted by the composer beginning with *Five Kafka songs* op.82, and ending with the first European performance of *Sestina* op.161.

B1313. ——. "Schoenberg opera impresses in Berlin Fete." *Musical America* 79:12 (November 1, 1959): 11.

Review of the Berlin Festival which included the premiere of *Six motets after fragments by Kafka* op.169. "He uses whispering, singing, and recitation in a fascinating melange. Were the whistles after the superb performance for the text or the music?"

B1314. ——. "Henzes neueste Werke in Berlin." *Melos* 26:12 (December 1959): 385.

Review of the premiere of *Motetten nach Worten von Franz Kafka* op.169.

B1315. ——. "Europäer aus Oesterreich." *Oesterreichische Musikzeitschrift* 15:9 (September 1960): 409-411.

Appreciation of his life in honor of his sixtieth birthday on August 23, 1960. Picture.

  a. ——. *Frankfurter Allgemeine Zeitung* (August 23, 1960)

B1316. ——. *Twentieth century music.* Translated by Richard Deveson. (New York: McGraw-Hill, 1969) 248 pp.

A general history of twentieth century music. Discusses Krenek's change of style from atonalism in the writing of *Jonny spielt auf* op.45, and his preoccupation at the time between esotericism and a desire to make a public impact. Also includes a discussion of his use of electronic music in *Spiritus intelligentiae sanctus* op.152.

B1317. ——. "Ernst Krenek." In his *Die grossen Komponisten unseres Jahrhunderts: Deutschland - Mitteleuropa.* (München: R. Piper, 1971): 83-90.

A biographical essay with an examination of his works and tendencies. "The conflicting elements which Krenek himself has observed in his emotional make-up have led time and again to dialectical struggles. He is endowed with great mental powers of receptivity and, like Mozart, he has studied and successfully exploited a great variety of different stimuli. As a young man he adopted Schoenberg's atonal musical language. Under the twin influences of French thought and a southern climate he became a neo-classicist, while in 1927 he used contemporary American dance forms, only to return to strict twelve-tone techniques soon afterwards. In his maturity he has remained equally open to influence. He has the enviable capacity of being able to pursue any idea to its inevitable conclusion, even *ad absurdum.*"

   a. ——. In his *Twentieth-Century Composers*, Vol.2: *Germany and Central Europe.* (New York: Holt, Rinehart & Winston, 1971): 89-96.

B1318. ——. "Weberns *Skizzen.*" *Melos* 38:3 (March 1971): 106-107.
Review of the book (K828) which includes a preface by Krenek.

B1319. ——. "Ernst Kreneks *Spätlese.*" *Musica* 28:5 (1974): 444-445.
Review of the premiere of op.218. Picture.

B1320. ——. "Kreneks *Feiertagskantate.*" *Musica* 29:6 (November-December 1975): 498.
Review of the premiere of op.221.

B1321. ——. "Konzerte der Berliner Festwochen; bukolische Trauer aus Geräusch und Ton." *Frankfurter Allgemeine Zeitung* (September 30, 1980)
Review of the first European performance of the monologue *Der Versteller* op.229.

   a. ——. *Das Orchester* 29:1 (January 1981): 44-45.

B1322. **Stumberg, Lucette Anne.** "Ernst Krenek: His four *Piano sonatas* and the twelve-tone technique." (Master's thesis: University of Texas, Austin, 1949) 106 pp.
Examines the differences and similarities among the first four piano sonatas and the effect the twelve-tone technique had on the *Third sonata* op. 92, no.4, and *Fourth sonata* op.114.

B1323. **Sulzer, Peter.** *Zehn Komponisten um Werner Reinhart.* Vol.1. Neujahrsblatt der Stadtbibliothek Winterthur, Bd.309. (Winterthur: Stadtbibliothek, 1979)
Includes an examination of Krenek's relationship with Reinhart and a discussion of Krenek's Switzerland years (1923/24) and his continuing ties with Winterthur. See especially pages 132-142, 158-177, and 215-220.

B1324. ——. "Ernst Krenek in Winterthur, eine langjährige Freundschaft." *Neue Zürcher Zeitung* 195 (August 1980): 66.

Krenek first came to Winterthur in 1922-23 through the offices of Hermann Scherchen, Werner Reinhart, and Friedrich T. Gubler who promoted him. He continues to maintain his ties with the city.

B1325. Sutcliffe, James Helme. "Copenhagen/Hamburg." *Opera News* 35:2 (Sept.19, 1970): 24-25.

Review of the premiere of the opera *Das kommt davon* op.206. Picture.

B1326. Szmolyan, Walter. "Vorausberechnet, aber unvorhersehbar." *Oesterreichische Musikzeitschrift* 20:8 (August 1965): 418-419.

Traces the development of Krenek's four stylistic periods on the occasion of his sixty-fifth birthday: the atonal first period is characterized by the *Second symphony* op.12; the opera *Jonny spielt auf* op.45 and the song cycle *Reisebuch aus den österrreichischen Alpen* op.62 characterize the second tonally Romantic period; the third twelve-tone period begins with the opera *Karl V.* op.73; and *Sestina* op.161 begins the fourth serial period.

B1327. ——. "Zeitgenössische Komponisten aus Wien." *Oesterreichische Musikzeitschrift* 25:5/6 (May/June 1970): 324-329.

Discusses the artistic growth of 43 Viennese composers born since 1885, including Krenek (p.325-326). Also includes a list of the recipients of the Preis der Stadt Wien which Krenek received in 1955.

B1328. ——. "Geburtstagskalendarium: Ernst Krenek." *Oesterreichische Musikzeitschrift* 24:7 (July 1970): 418-419.

Briefly discusses Krenek's life using the five-part classification of Krenek's works presented by Lothar Knessl.

B1329. ——. "Geburtstagskalendarium: Ernst Krenek." *Oesterreichische Musikzeitschrift* 30:8 (August 1975): 416.

Surveys Krenek's life and newest compositions in a birthday greeting for his seventy-fifth birthday.

B1330. ——. "Krenek-Ehrungen in Wien." *Oesterreichische Musikzeitschrift* 30:11 (November 1975): 601.

Report of a celebratory concert for Krenek given by the Oesterreichische Gesellschaft für Musik on September 22 in Vienna. The music spanned 56 years from the op.1a *Doppelfuge* to the *Drei Lieder für Sopran und Klavier* op.216. On October 1, Krenek was made a member of the Oesterreichische Ehrenzeichen für Wissenschaft und Kunst.

B1331. ——. "Ernst Krenek *The Santa Fe Time Table* ..." *Oesterreichische Musikzeitschrift* 33:2 (February 1978): 110-111.

Review of three Krenek recordings: Orion ORS 75204, Orion ORS 76246, and Preiserrecords SPR 3269.

B1332. ——. "Karl Kraus, sein Verhältnis zur Musik im Lichte der *Fackel*." *Oesterreichische Musikzeitschrift* 35:4/5 (April-May 1980): 208-214.

Karl Kraus produced a cycle of Offenbach operettas in Vienna starting in 1929 on the 110th anniversary of Offenbach's birth which were attacked by Paul Aadeus Pisk in the *Arbeiter-Zeitung*. Kraus defended the cycle in his journal *Die Fackel*, as did Krenek (K91) and others.

B1333. ——. "Die Komponistin Gladys Nordenstrom-Krenek." *Oesterreichische Musikzeitschrift* 35:9 (September 1980): 445.

Krenek married his composition student in 1950; through him, she adopted the twelve-tone technique and serial procedures. She has had several compositions performed.

B1334. ——. "Ernst Krenek-Diskographie." *Oesterreichische Musikzeitschrift* 35:9 (September 1980): 510-512.

A brief survey of the recordings issued by Orion, as well as Preiserrecords SPR 10049, and Amadeo AVRS 5038.

B1335. ——. "Krenek-Symposion und -Personale in Graz." *Oesterreichische Musikzeitschrift* 35:12 (December 1980): 660-661.

Review of the performances and lectures given during the Steirische Herbstes festival devoted to Krenek.

B1336. ——. "Aktivitäten zu Ernst Kreneks 85. Geburtstag." *Oesterreichische Musikzeitschrift* 40:12 (December 1985): 670-671.

Report on the many activities in Austria related to Krenek's eighty-fifth birthday, including the establishment of an Ernst Krenek Preis of 100,000 Schillings to be awarded every two years.

B1337. ——. "Ernst Krenek: *Fünf Lieder nach Worten von Franz Kafka*, op.82." *Oesterreichische Musikzeitschrift* 40:12 (December 1985): 694.

Review of the publication of the manuscript facsimile issued in honor of his eighty-fifth birthday.

B1338. ——. "Neue Schallplatten des Oesterreichischen Musikrats." *Oesterreichische Musikzeitschrift* 40:12 (December 1985): 698.

Record reviews including the first three *Symphonies* op.7, op.12, and op.16 on Amadeo 415 825-1.

B1339. T. "Ernst Krenek -- Sonderkonzert." *Darmstädter Echo* (November 28, 1951)

Review of a performance of *Symphonische Elegie* op.105, Fourth piano concerto op.123 played by Miriam Molin, Fifth Symphony op.119, and *I wonder as I wonder* op.94 all conducted by the composer.

B1340. T.F. "Schallplatten mit neuer Musik." *Melos* 19:6/7 (June-July 1952): 202.

Review of the Viola and piano sonata op.117 on Deutsche Grammophon-Gesellschaft 36005.

B1341. Taitte, W. L. "Midland on a string." *Texas Monthly* 11 (June, 1983): 176-180.

The Thouvenel String Quartet is the pride of the Texas Midlands. Members of the quartet are Eugene Purdue, first violin, Sally Chisholm, viola, Jeffrey Levenson, cello and Edward Stein, second violin. The quartet was formed in 1975. In April 1979 they were invited to perform Ernst Krenek's seven string quartets at the University of California, Santa Barbara festival. The Thouvenal performance was highly acclaimed, and they received similar reviews when they performed the Krenek works in New York and Vienna, Austria. They are considering recording their material.

B1342. Talley, Howard. "Krenek, Meyerowitz operas staged in Illinois festival." *Musical America* 77:5 (April 1957): 8.

Review of first performance of *The bell tower* op.153. Picture.

B1343. Taubman, Howard. "Fresh ways must be found for playing new music." *New York Times* 89:29940 (January 14, 1940): 6:3.

Review of the book *Music here and now* (K495).

B1344. Taubman, Howard. "Music: Twelve-tone." *New York Times* 107:36570 (March 10, 1958): 19.

Review of a concert sponsored by the Fromm Music Foundation which included a performance of *Lamentatio Jeremia prophetae* op.93 by Hugh Ross and his Schola Cantorum and the premiere of *Sestina* op.161. Picture.

B1345. ——. "Music: By U.S. moderns." *New York Times* 109:37194 (November 24, 1959): 46.

Review of the first American performance of the Sixth string quartet op.78.

B1346. Taylor, Deems. "*Johnny strikes up,* and what of it?" *Musical Leader* (June 20, 1929): 9.

Review of the first American performance of *Jonny spielt auf* op.45. Reprinted from *McCalls Magazine* (June 1929)

B1347. Taylor, Timothy D. "Krenek: *String quartet, no.5.*" *American Record Guide* 49:2 (March-April 1986): 12.

Record review of Composers Recordings CRI SD 522.

B1348. Teasdale, May Silva. "*Orestes.*" In her *Handbook of 20th Century Opera.* (New York: E.P. Dutton, 1938; reprint: New York, Da Capo Press, 1976): 141-142.

Performance information and synopsis of op.60.

B1349. Thibodeau, Ralph. "Symphony begins concert year." *Corpus Christi Colle* (January 17, 1982)

Review of the American premiere of the First violin concerto performed by Goetz Bernau and the Corpus Christi Symphony conducted by Eleazar de Carvalho in Bayfront Plaza Auditorium.

B1350. Thompson, Oscar. "Historic opera is revived." *New York Sun* (November 10, 1937)

Review of the first American performance of Krenek's edition of Monteverdi's *Poppea.*

B1351. Thomson, Virgil. "*Symphony, no.4.*" *New York Herald Tribune* (November 27, 1947)

Review of the premiere of the Fourth symphony op.113.

B1352. ——. "Music: Eleanor Steber." *New York Herald Tribune* (April 6, 1950)
Review of the premiere of the *Ballad of the railroads* op.98.

B1353. Thomson, William. "The problem of tonality in pre-Baroque and primitive music." *Journal of music theory* 2:1 (April 1958): 36-46.

Includes a discussion of Krenek's definition of tonality as presented in his book *Music here and now* (K495).

B1354. Thornton, H. Frank. "Choral." *The New Records* 43:12 (February 1976): 8.

Record review of the four choral works on Orion ORS 75204.

B1355. ——. "Vocal." *The New Records* 46:9 (November 1978): 12.
Record review of *Spätlese* op.218 and *Drei Gesänge* op.56 on Orion ORS 78298.

B1356. ——. "Krenek: *Gesänge des späten Jahres, op.71. The New Records* 47:4 (June 1979): 13.

Record review of the song cycle on Orion ORS 78308.

B1357. ———. "Krenek: *(4) Songs, op.112 The New Records* 48:2 (April 1980): 12.
Record review of the Orion ORS 79348 album of songs.

B1358. ———. "Krenek vocal compositions." *The New Records* 48:6 (August 1980): 12.
Record review of Orion ORS 80377.

B1359. **Thornton, John.** "Austrian Classical Marches." *Hi Fi Review* 3:3 (September 1959): 68.
Record review of *Merry marches* op.44 on Boston Records BST 1012.

B1360. "Thoughtful mezzo." *Time* 61:12 (March 23, 1953): 46.
Review of the premiere of *Medea* op.129. Picture of Blanche Thebom.

B1361. **Tilmouth, Michael.** "*Exploring music.*" *Music and Letters* 48:1 (January 1967): 75.
Review of the book (K817). "Our age, perhaps unfortunately, is coming to see music as a problem or rather as a series of problems. This book reveals a composer who is alive to them and articulate about them."

B1362. **Timper, Rudo.** "Ernst Krenek zwischen gestern und morgen." *Oesterreichische Musikzeitschrift* 16:6/7 (June-July 1961): 287-290.
Discusses Krenek and Schubert as great Lieder composers; Schubert is the "morning" of Lieder composition while Krenek is the "afternoon."

B1363. **Tischer, Gerhard.** "Ernst Krenek: *Orpheus und Eurydike.*" *Rheinische Musik- und Theaterzeitung* 27:43/44 (December 4, 1926): 437-438.
Review of the premiere of the opera op.21.

B1364. ———. "Ernst Krenek: *Jonny spielt auf.*" *Rheinische Musik- und Theaterzeitung* 28:7/8 (February 19, 1927): 60.
Review of the premiere of the opera op.45.

B1365. ———. "Ernst Krenek: *Der Diktator - Das geheime Königreich - Schwergewicht.*" *Rheinische Musik- und Theaterzeitung* 29:19/20 (May 12, 1928): 229-230.
Review of the premiere of the three one-act operas op.49, op.50, and op.55. Picture: port., scene from *Diktator*, scene from *Schwergewicht*.

B1366. **Tomzig, Sabine.** "Spielregeln, die man nicht ganz verstand." *Hamburger Abendblatt* (December 22, 1966)
Review of the premiere of *Glauben und Wissen* op.194.

B1367. **Tonkli, O.** "Neue Musik beim Carinthischen Sommer." *Oesterreichische Musikzeitschrift* 40:10 (October 1985): 543-544.
Includes a discussion of the week-long festival devoted to Krenek.

B1368. **Torbe, J.** "Ernst Krenek." *Musikblätter des Anbruch* 4:11 (November 1922): 281-282.
Analysis of the First string quartet op.6.

B1369. **Tranchefort, François-René.** "Ernst Krenek." In his *Guide de la musique symphonique.* (Paris: Fayard, 1986): 400-401.
Discussion of the Second symphony op.12 and *Quaestio temporis* op.170 as major examples of Krenek's orchestral works; also briefly discusses the *Symphonic elegy* op.105 and *Kette, Kreis und Spiegel* op.160.

B1370. Tremblay, George. "Ernst Krenek: *Symphonic elegy for string orchestra*." *Notes* 2d ser. 4:4 (September 1947): 484-485.

Review of the publication of op.105. "This music, in spite of its appeal to the mental processes of music appreciation, is fundamentally 'emotional'."

B1371. Treppmann, Egon. "Kafka in Musik gesetzt." *Melos* 24:2 (February 1957): 50-51.

Review of a Mannheim concert by Carla Henius, soprano, and Richard Laugs, piano, of *Lieder nach Worten von Franz Kafka* op.82.

B1372. *"Triptych* by Ernst Krenek in Wiesbaden May 1928." *Musical Courier* 96 (June 14, 1928): 8.

Review of the premiere of the three one-act operas *Der Diktator* op.49, *Das geheime Königreich* op.50, and *Schwergewicht, oder Die Ehre der Nation* op.55.

B1373. *"Triumph der Empfindsamkeit."* *Allgemeine Musikzeitung* 53:21/22 (May 21, 1926): 483.

Review of the premiere of the incidental music op.43.

B1374. *"Triumph der Empfindsamkeit."* *Musikblätter des Anbruch* 9:12 (December 1927): 448.

Announces two premieres in November: *Potpourri* op.54 conducted by Hermann Abendroth in Cologne and the suite from *Der Triumph der Empfindsamkeit* op.43.

B1375. Trumpff, Gustav Adolf. "Ernst Kreneks *Leben des Orest.*" *Neue Zeitschrift für Musik* 122:5 (1961): 197-200.

Discussion of the opera and its performances. Picture of scene.

B1376. ——. "Baden-Baden: Ernst Krenek dirigierte drei eigene Orchesterwerke." *Neue Zeitschrift für Musik* 129:4 (April 1968): 150-151.

Review of a Sinfonieorchester concert conducted by the composer in the Südwestfunk's Hans-Rosbaud Studio which included the premiere of the 1968 edition of *Aus drei mach sieben* op.177, the first European performance of *Horizont umkreist* op.196, and his Third symphony op.16.

B1377. ——. "Mainz: Die Oboe und die Herztöne--Ars Viva-Konzert." *Neue Zeitschrift für Musik* 133:12 (December 1972): 718.

Review of the premiere of *Aulokithara* op.213a.

B1378. Tschulik, Norbert. "Die verhinderte Uraufführung von Kreneks *Karl V.*" *Oesterreichische Musikzeitschrift* 34:3 (March 1979): 121-129.

Discusses the cancellation of the premiere of *Karl V.* op.73 in Vienna due to conservative political forces. Although events leading up to the cancellation can be documented, it cannot be determined who actually made the final decision to cancel the performance.

B1379. ——. "Jubiläum eines wichtigen Musikinstituts." *Wiener Zeitung* (October 21, 1983)

Review of the first European performance of the Organ concerto op.235.

B1380. Turnblad, John. "American's opera given premiere at Darmstadt Festival." *Stars and Stripes* (August 28, 1954)

A review of the first German performance of *Dark waters* op.125.

B1381. Turok, Paul. "An American Sampler." *Music Journal* 34:6 (July 1976): 56-57.

Brief record review of a collection of Krenek's compositions on Orion ORS 75204.

B1382. ——. "Second Thoughts." *Music Journal* 35:8 (October 1977): 27-29.

Record review of *Merry marches* op.44, and *Kleine Blasmusik* op.70a, on Louisville Orchestra LS 756.

B1383. "Two Krenek works bow in U.S.." *MadAminA* 2:1 (Spring 1981): 3-4.

Brief review of the January Los Angeles Philharmonic's Composer's Choice concert which included the String trio op.118, *Durch die Nacht* op.67, and the U.S. premiere of *In the valley of time* op.232 conducted by the composer. Also mentions that his just completed Eighth string quartet op.233 will receive its premiere by the Thouvenel String Quartet in Carnegie Recital Hall in June.

B1384. "Ueber die Aufführung der *Unvollendeten Symphonie* Gustav Mahlers." *Berliner Börsen-Zeitung* (November 9, 1923)

Announcement and discussion of the upcoming premiere of Krenek's edition (W72).

B1385. Uhl, Edm. "Die Mai-Festwoche in Wiesbaden." *Allgemeine Musikzeitung* 55:20/21 (May 18, 1928): 629-631.

Review of the premiere of the three one-act operas *Der Diktator* op.49, *Das geheime Königreich* op.50, and *Schwergewicht, oder Die Ehre der Nation* op.55.

B1386. Uhlendorff, Franz. "Musik für Intellektuelle." *Kasseler Post* (October 25, 1954)

Review of a performance of *I wonder as I wander* op.94 and the premiere of *Symphony Pallas Athene* op.137.

B1387. Ullrich, Hermann. "Zweites internationales Kammermusikfest in Salzburg." *Allgemeine Musikzeitung* 51:33/34 (August 11, 1924): 594-596.

Includes a review of the premiere of the *Third string quartet* op.20.

B1388. "Un interviu amb el compositor vienès Ernst Krenek." *La bambla de Catalunya* (Barcelona) (April 24, 1936)

An interview following the premiere of *Fragmente aus dem Bühnenwerk "Karl V."* op.73a.

B1389. Unger, Hermann. "Köln: *O Lacrymosa* von Krenek." *Musikblätter des Anbruch* 9:3 (March 1927): 139.

Review of the premiere of the songs op.48a in the version accompanied by instruments.

B1390. Ungerer, I.D. "Madness on the Rhine." *Opera News* 23:21 (March 23, 1959): 25.

Review of the first German performance of the chamber opera *The Bell tower* op.153.

B1391. "Uraufführungen." *Musikhandel* 38:4 (1987): 172.

Premiere of the *String trio in Twelve Stations* op.237.

B1392. us. "Ernst Krenek: *Fünf Lieder nach Worten von Franz Kafka, op.82.*" *Melos* 27:7/8 (July-August 1960): 247.

Review of the publication.

B1393. v.H. "Der künstlerische Höhepunkt: Ernst Kreneks *Lamentatio*." *Kasseler Zeitung* (October 7, 1958)

Review of the first complete performance of op.93 during the Kasseler Musiktage.

B1394. V.U. "Ernst Krenek *Ueber neue Musik.*" *Der Auftakt* (Prague) 17:5/6 (1937): 82-83.

Review of the book (K397).

B1395. V.W. "Krenek-Studio, 5. Abend." *Wiener Musikzeitung* (April 6, 1935)

Review of the concert given as one of Krenek's Oesterreichische Studio evenings.

B1396. Vainkop, IU. "Muzyka Ksheneka v Leningrade." *Novaia muzyka* (Leningrad) 1:2 (1927): 28-29.

Brief discussion, in Russian, of compositions by Krenek performed in Leningrad, including his *Der Sprung über den Schatten* op.17.

B1397. Van Hulse, Camil. "Ernst Krenek. *Zur Sprache gebracht.*" *Books abroad* 33:2 (Spring 1959): 157.

Review of the book of essays (K707).

B1398. Varga, Bálint András. "Three questions on music; Extracts from a book of interviews in the making." *New Hungarian Quarterly* 25:93 (Spring 1984): 197-202.

Responses by John Cage, Krenek, Elliott Carter, Milton Babbitt, George Crumb, Lukas Foss, and Steve Reich to the questions: "Has a piece by another composer radically changed [your] way of thinking... [How important are] the sounds of the outside world [n your compositions and] Up to what point can you talk of a personal style and where does self-repetition begin?" Krenek replies 1.that the last movement of Schubert's *Trio in B-flat major* supplied the basis for the second movement of his *Second piano sonata* op.59; "the whole cycle of the *Reisebuch aus den österreichischen Alpen* op.62 is influenced by Schubert... in my orchestral work, *Eleven transparencies* op.142, in No.10 ... I was 'inspired' by Delius' *Upon hearing the first cuckoo in Spring* ... in my choral work *Lamentatio Jeremiae prophetae* op.92, I was influenced by the general character of Johannes Ockeghem's music... 2.I am unable to remember ever having been 'inspired' by outside sounds... 3.I have expressed myself in various styles or manners of writing (which has been held against me), but I think that [there] are subconscious mannerisms that may be traced through all of [them]."

B1399. Vassenhove, L. van. "*Jonny* ou le triomphe du jazz." *Le courrier musical & théâtral* 30:5 (March 1, 1928): 142-143.

German opera, jazz, and Krenek's opera *Jonny spielt auf* op.45.

B1400. Veidl, Theodor. "E. Krenek: *Konzert für Klavier und Orchester (Fis-Dur).*" *Der Auftakt* (Prague) 4:11/12 (1924): 321.

Review of the publication of op.18.

B1401. Vellekoop, Gerrit. "De *Lamentatio Jeremiae Prophetae* van Ernst Krsjenek." *Mens en melodie* 13:11 (November 1958): 326-329.

Discussion and analysis of the work op.93; including examples of the twelve-tone row. Picture of St. Martin's Church in Kassel, the site of its first complete performance.

B1402. Vermeulen, Ernst. "Berio steht im Mittelpunkt des Holland-Festivals." *Melos* 39:6 (1972): 371-374.

Brief review of the festival including the premiere of *Kitharaulos* op.213.

B1403. **Vernon, Grenville.** *"Jonny spielt auf."* *Commonweal* 9 (1929): 450.
Review of the American performance of op.45.

B1404. *Verzeichnis sämtlicher Werke, 1918-1964. Verzeichnis sämtlicher Werke, 1918-1964.* (Kassel: Bärenreiter, 1964)
A catalog of the musical compositions.

B1405. **vk.** "Zum ersten Mal serielle Musik." *Hessische Allgemeine Zeitung* (October 11, 1960)
Review of the premiere of *Sechs Vermessene* op.168.

B1406. **Vlad, Roman.** "Ernst Krenek. *Quartetto VII, op.96."* *La rassegna musicale* 22:2 (April 1952): 175-177.
Review of the publication of the string quartet.

B1407. ——. "Ernst Krenek, *Five Prayers for women's voices over the Pater Noster as cantus firmus."* *La rassegna musicale* 25 (March 1955): 48.
Review of the publication of the choruses op.97.

B1408. ——. *Storia della dodecafonia.* (Milano: Edizioni Suivini Zerboni, 1958)
A general history of the development of the twelve-tone system. Discusses *Five Prayers over Pater noster* op.97 and *Lamentatio Jeremiae prophetae* op.93 (pp.133-137) in his chapter on the diffusion of serialism, and *Spiritus intelligentiae, Sanctus* op.152 (pp.270-271) in his chapter on the integration of serialism and electronic music.

B1409. ——. "Ernst Krenek, *De rebus prius factis."* *La rassegna musicale* 29 (1959): 367-368.
Review of the book (K671).

B1410. **Völckers, Jürgen.** "Kreneks Sonate für Violine." *Musica* 19:3 (May/June 1965): 184.
Review of the publication of op.33.

B1411. **Vötterle, Karl.** "Schallplatte - Wegbereiter Neuer Musik." *Phonoprisma* 9:6 (1966)
Discusses the Preise der deutschen Schallplattenkritik 1966 and the appropriateness of the award to Krenek.

B1412. **Vogel, Johann Peter.** "Eine noble Korrespondenz." *Mitteilungen der Hans Pfitzner-Gesellschaft* N.F. no.37 (February 1977): 49-50.
Transcription with annotations of the brief correspondence between Krenek and Pfitzner extracted from *Reden, Schriften, Briefe* hrsg. von Walter Abendroth (Berlin: H. Luchterhand, 1955).

B1413. **Vogt, Hans.** *Neue Musik seit 1945.* 2. Aufl. (Stuttgart: Philipp Reclan June , 1972): 229-238.
Includes a brief biographical essay and an analysis of *Lamentatio Jeremiae prophetae* op.93 in a general survey of music in the twentieth century.
a. ——. 3. Aufl. (Stuttgart: Philipp Reclan June , 1982): 239-248.

B1414. **Vuataz, Roger ; Martin, Frank.** "Les systèmes musicaux d'après-guerre." *Musica viva* 1:3 (October 1936): 20-26.
Reactions to Krenek's "Die Musikalischen Systeme der Nachkriegszeit" (K384).

B1415. Vujica, Peter. "Avantgarde aus dem Grazer Dom." *Grazer Montag* (October 20, 1980)

Review of the premiere of *Deutschen Messgesänge zum 29. Sonntag im Jahreskreis* (W101) at the beginning of a week-long festival devoted to Krenek at the Graz Steirischer Herbst.

B1416. W. "Zum Schaffen von Ernst Krenek." *Musica* 23:2 (March-April 1969): 159.

Review of the catalog of Krenek's works published by Broadcast Music Inc.

B1417. W.F. "New Friends of Music." *Musical America* 72:15 (December 1, 1952): 27.

Review of a New Friends of Music concert in Town Hall, November 16, 1952, in which *Symphonic music for nine solo instruments* op.11, was performed by members of the New York Philharmonic-Symphony conducted by Dimitri Mitropoulos as "the core of the program."

B1418. ——. "New Friends of Music." *Musical America* 73:2 (January 15, 1953): 28.

Review of the premiere of *Two sacred songs* op.132.

B1419. W.R. "Ernst Krenek: *Proprium für das Dreifaltigkeitsfest.*" *Melos* 36:6 (June 1969): 283.

Review of the publication op.195.

B1420. Wagner, Klaus. "Die Hamburgische Staatsoper im neuen Haus." *Neue Zeitschrift für Musik* 116:12 (December 1955): 139-141.

A performance of the opera *Pallas Athene weint* op.144 was one of six premieres which opened the house. Picture: Scene from the opera.

B1421. ——. "Die Hamburgische Staatsoper im neuen Haus." *Das Orchester* 3:12 (December 1955): 347-349.

Discusses the new opera house and the premiere of Krenek's opera *Pallas Athene weint* op.144 which opened it. Picture: scene.

B1422. ——. "Hausweihe in Hamburg." *Musica* 9:12 (December 1955): 607-610.

Review of the premiere of the opera *Pallas Athene weint* op.144.

B1423. ——. "Zeit des Fragens." *Frankfurter Allgemeine Zeitung* (October 5, 1960)

Review of the premiere of *Quaestio temporis* op.170.

B1424. ——. "Zeit des Fragens, eine Frage der Zeit?" *Melos* 27:11 (November 1960): 346-347.

Review of the premiere of *Quaestio temporis* op.170.

B1425. ——. "Comic strips aus der Argonautensage." *Melos* 31:7/8 (July-August 1964): 233-235.

Review of the premiere of the opera *Der goldene Bock* op.186. Picture.

B1426. ——. "Krenek meditiert über den Komponisten im Zweifelsfall." *Melos* 34:1 (January 1967): 21-22.

Review of the premiere of the sacred chorus *Glauben und Wissen* op.194. Includes mention of the Hamburg Bach Preis awarded to Krenek.

B1427. Wagner, Klaus. "Farce von der Verführbarkeit: Kreneks oper *Das Kommt Davon*... in Hamburg uraufgeführt." *Frankfurter Allgemeine Zeitung* (June 29, 1970).

Review of the premiere of op.206.

a. ——. *Melos* 37:7/8 (July-August 1970): 296-297.

B1428. ——. "Klangwerkstatt und klingende Kirche im Hamburg." *Melos* 38:12 (December 1971): 534-535.

Review of the premiere of the Mass *Gib uns den Frieden* op.208.

B1429. Ward, William R. "Ernst Krenek." In his *Examples for the Study of Musical Style.* (New York: Wm. C. Brown Co., 1970): 428-436.

In-depth analysis of the twelve-tone aspects of "The moon rises" no.4 from *Twelve short piano pieces* op.83 and *Symphonic elegy* op.105.

B1430. Warrack, John. "Contemporary oboe works." *Gramophone* 50:594 (November 1972): 927.

Record review of *Four Pieces for oboe and piano* op.193 on Philips 6500 202.

B1431. Watkins, Glenn. "Anton von Webern: *Sketches.*" *Notes* 26:3 (March 1970): 612.

Review of the book (K828) including an essay by Krenek which "is more than an introduction to the sketches, and in truth is indispensible as a guide to anyone intent upon working his way through the labyrinth of this material."

B1432. Watt, Charles E. "*Jonny spielt auf* at the New York Metropolitan Opera House." *Music News* 21:17 (April 26, 1929): 14.

Review of the first American performance of the opera.

B1433. Webber, David W. "The Empire Trio." *The New Records* 50:9 (November 1982): 4-5.

Record review of Crystal Records S 645 which includes the *Trio for violin, clarinet and piano* op.108.

B1434. Webster, Daniel. "Concert focuses on Krenek of 60s." *Philadelphia Inquirer* (October 21, 1974)

Review of an all-Krenek concert at the Philadelphia Musical Academy and the performance of *Kitharaulos* op.213 by harpist Sarah Dunlap, oboist James Kavanaugh, and ensemble.

B1435. Wehinger, Rainer. "... es klingt, als wärs ein neuer Anfang." In *Ernst Krenek*, hrsg. von Otto Kolleritsch. (B328) Studien zur Wertungsforschung, Bd.15. (Wien: Universal Edition, 1982): 189-201.

An examination of the electronic music composition *Spiritus intelligentiae, sanctus* op.152 and *Quintina* op.191 which includes electronic music.

B1436. Wehle, Gerhard F. "Gegensätzlichkeiten in der Musik." *Allgemeine Musikzeitung* 53:41 (October 8, 1926): 815-817.

Extensively quotes from Krenek's "Musik in der Gegenwart" (K12) in a discussion about Romanticism in music and an attack on Arnold Schoenberg. See Krenek's "Gegensätzlichkeiten in der Musik" (K40) for a response and Wehle's follow-up (B1437).

B1437. ——. "Nochmals: Gegensätzlichkeiten in der Musik." *Allgemeine Musikzeitung* 53:47 (November 19, 1926): 960.

Reaction to Krenek's polemic in "Gegensätzlichkeiten in der Musik" (K40) against Wehle's comments in "Gegensätzlichkeiten in der Musik" (B1436).

B1438. Weil, Irving. "Letting the cat out of the bag at the Metropolitan." *Musical America* 48:27 (October 27, 1928): 7.

Discussion of the forthcoming first American performance of *Jonny spielt auf* op.45.

B1439. ——. *"Jonny spielt auf* - New York." *Musical America* 49:4 (January 26, 1929): 5, 32.

Review of the first American performance of op.45.

B1440. Weissmann, Adolf. "Konzert-Rundschau." *Berliner Zeit am Mittag* (March 25, 1922)

Review of the premiere of the First symphony op.7.

B1441. ——. "A new concerto for violin." *Musical Times* 66:984 (February 1, 1925): 169.

Review of the premiere of the Violin concerto op.29.

B1442. ——. "Music of modern German composers; Problems before young generation." *New York Times* 75:25047 (August 22, 1926): VII:5.

General discussion of music in Germany mentioning Krenek's *Die Zwingburg* op.14 and *The Seasons* op.35.

B1443. ——. "Kreneks neue Oper." *Musikblätter des Anbruch* 8:10 (December 1926): 425-427.

Review of the premiere of the opera *Orpheus und Eurydike* op.21.

B1444. ——. "The first German jazz opera." *Christian Science Monitor* 19:95 (March 19, 1927): 10.

Review of the premiere of the opera *Jonny spielt auf* op.45.

B1445. ——. "Germany's latest music dramas." *Modern Music* 4:4 (May/June 1927): 20-26.

Discusses German experimental operas represented by Krenek's *Orpheus und Eurydike* op.21 and *Jonny spielt auf* op.45; Berg's *Wozzeck*, Weill's *Royal palace,* and Hindemith's *Cardillac.*

B1446. ——. "The new opera in Wiesbaden." *Christian Science Monitor* 20:155 (May 26, 1928): 10.

Review of the premieres of the one-act operas *Der Diktator* op.49, *Das geheime Königreich* op.50, and *Schwergewicht, oder Die Ehre der Nation* op.55.

B1447. ——. "Ernst Krenek." *Modern Music* 6:1 (November-December 1928): 17-23.

Briefly surveys Krenek's early works: *Toccata und Chaconne* op.13, Second symphony op.12, *Die Zwingburg* op.14, Piano concerto op.18, Violin concerto op.29, *Der Sprung über den Schatten* op.17, *Orpheus und Eurydike* op.21, *Jonny spielt auf* op.45, *Der Diktator* op.49. *Das geheime Königreich* op.50, and *Schwergewicht* op.55. Asserts that "Krenek allied himself so openly with revolutionary principles and attracted so much attention by his earliest works that for Germany he became the truest expression of the spirit of our age... Once the advocate of the most radical tendencies of music, at a sudden moment of creative activity he turned toward life and relinquished all that was uncompromising and systematic."

B1448. Weissmann, Adolf. "Einakters." *Berliner Zeit am Mittag* (December 3, 1928)

Review of the premiere of the three one-act operas *Der Diktator* op.49, *Das geheime Königreich* op.50, and *Schwergewicht* op.55.

a. "[Review]." In *Experiment Krolloper, 1927-1931*, von Hans Curjel. Studien zur Kunst des neunzehnten Jahrhunderts, Bd.7. (Münich: Prestel-Verlag, 1975): 249-250.

B1449. ——. "Ernst Krenek." *Der Auftakt* (Prague) 9:11 (1929): 268-273.

A survey of his music, including a discussion of his style change to tonality.

B1450. Wellesz, Egon. "*Hamline studies in musicology.*" *Music Review* 8:1 (February 1947): 58-59.

Review of volume one of the book (K550).

B1451. Wennerstrom, Mary Hannah. "Parametric analysis of contemporary musical form." (Ph.D. diss.: Indiana University, 1967)

Includes a discussion of *Eleven Transparencies* op.142.

B1452. Werner, Th.W. "Neue Musik in Salzburg." *Zeitschrift für Musikwissenschaft* 5:12 (September 1923): 667-671.

Review of the premiere of the Third string quartet op.20.

B1453. Westergaard, Svend. "Ernst Krenek i roverkloer, eller Hvordan det kan gaa en gammel rover." *Dansk Musiktidsskrift* 40:5 (September 1965): 135-140.

Westergaard reacts to Krenek's comments concerning writings about serial music in "Om roversproget i den moderne musiklitteratur" (K795); Krenek responds in "En gammel rovers bekendelser" (K814).

B1454. Westerman, Gerhart von. "Ernst Krenek." In his *Opera Guide*, translated by Anne Ross. (New York: E.P. Dutton, 1964): 493-496.

Discusses Krenek's operas; includes a synopsis of *Jonny spielt auf* op.45.

B1455. Westermeyer, Karl. "Havemann-Quartett, Ernst Krenek." *Signale für die musikalische Welt* 80:18 (May 3, 1922): 557.

Review of the premiere of the Second string quartet op.8.

B1456. ——. "Walter Rummel, Max Pauer, Eduard Erdmann, Joseph Schwarz." *Signale für die musikalische Welt* 80:43 (October 25, 1922): 1205.

Includes a review of the premiere of *Toccata und Chaconne* op.13.

B1457. ——. "Eduard Erdmann." *Signale für die musikalische Welt* 81:15 (April 11, 1923): 554.

Refers to his premiere of the *Toccata und Chaconne* op.13.

B1458. ——. "Melos, Fritz Behrend." *Signale für die musikalische Welt* 81:46/47 (November 21, 1923): 1612.

Includes a discussion of the Third string quartet op.20.

B1459. ——. "Ernst Kreneks *Zwingburg.*" *Signale für die musikalische Welt* 82:44 (October 29, 1924): 1672-1675.

Review of the premiere of the opera op.14.

B1460. Westphal, Kurt. "Ernst Krenek. *Fiedellieder für Gesang und Klavier,* op.64." *Allgemeine Musikzeitung* 58:7 (February 13, 1931): 125.

Review of the publication of the song cycle.

B1461. "When Ernst Krenek heard the gifted young pianist Miriam Molin ..." *Music News* 42:9 (September 1950): 19.

Announces the forthcoming premiere of the *George Washington variations* op.120 and the composition of the Fourth piano concerto op.123. Picture.

B1462. Whittall, Arnold. "Krenek: *Four Songs,* Op.112. *Zwei Zeitlieder,* Op.215. *Trois chansons,* Op.30a. Nordenstrom: *Zeit XXIV.*" *Gramophone* 59:697 (June 1981): 70.

Record review of Orion ORS 79348.

B1463. Whitwell, David. "20th century Austrian composers, their music for winds." *Instrumentalist* 23:6 (January 1969): 42-43.

Brief survey of Krenek's Symphony for winds op.34; *Kleine Blasmusik* op.70a; *Intrada* op.51a; *Merry marches* op.44; Sopnatina for flute and clarinet op.92, no.2b; Little suite for clarinet and piano op.28; and *Pentagramm* op.163.

B1464. "Who said 'Garbage'." *Time* 69:13 (April 1, 1957): 80.

Includes a brief review of the premiere of the chamber opera *The bell tower* op.153.

B1465. Wienke, Gerhard. "Ernst Kreneks *Kitharaulos.*" *Musica* 26:5 (September-October 1972): 450-451.

Review of the premiere of op.213.

B1466. "Wiesbaden hears new Krenek operas." *New York Times* 77:25705 (June 10, 1928): 8:6.

Review of the premieres of the three one-act operas op.49, op.50, and op.55. Picture of Krenek by Walter Edward Blytae.

B1467. Wiesmann, Sigrid. "Neues Musiktheater in Oesterreich." *Oesterreichische Musikzeitschrift* 35:6 (June 1980): 273-277.

A survey of contemporary Austrian composers working in the field of musical theater. Krenek's entry refers to the forthcoming issue honoring him (September 1980).

B1468. Williams, Alexander. "Symphony concert." *The Boston Herald* 184:128 (November 5, 1938): 22.

Review of the first American performance of the Second piano concerto op.81.

B1469. Willis, Thomas. "Krenek gives more than music world returns." *Chicago Tribune* (July 14, 1968): 5:9.

The satirical drawings exhibited for "The World of Kurt Weill" concerts at Ravinia should have honored Krenek who has given us works such as *Jonny spielt auf, Karl V.,* an edition of Monteverdi's *L'Incoronazione di Poppea,* and the recently premiered *Perspectives.*

B1470. Willnauer, Franz. "Musik, zur Sprache gebracht." *Der Opernfreund* 5:45 (April 1960): 9-10.

Review of the book of essays *Zur Sprache gebracht* (K707).

B1471. ——. "*Ausgerechnet und Verspielt,* eine Fernsehoper von Ernst Krenek." *Neue Zeitschrift für Musik* 123:9 (1962): 417-418.

Review of the premiere showing of the television opera op.179. Picture of a scene.

B1472. ——. "Ernst Krenek, Wanderer zwischen den Welten." *Neue Zeitschrift für Musik* 123:6 (1962): 274-275.

B1473. ——. "*Ausgerechnet und Verspielt*, eine Fernsehoper von Ernst Krenek." *Der Opernfreund* 7 (Winter 1962): 9.

Review of the broadcast of the television opera *Ausgerechnet und verspielt* op.179.

B1474. ——. "Der unzeitgemässe Zeitgenosse." *Musica* 24:4 (July-August 1970): 337-339.

Essay in recognition of Krenek's seventieth birthday surveying his life and works. Picture.

B1475. Winchell, Anna Cora. "Symphony reviewed." *Alameda Times Star* (March 27, 1939)

Review of the first U.S. performance of the *Concertino* op.27.

B1476. ——. "New works are introduced by WPA Orchestra." *Berkeley Daily Gazette* (March 29, 1939)

Review of the first U.S. performance of the *Concertino* op.27.

B1477. Wirth, Helmut. "Wolfgang Rogge: *Ernst Kreneks Opern*." *Die Musikforschung* 26:1 (January-March 1973): 128-129.

Review of the book (B1093).

B1478. Wiser, John D. "Gidon Kremer, Lockenhaus 1982." *Fanfare* 7:3 (January-February 1984): 314-315.

Record review of Philips 411 062-1 which includes *Parvula corona musicalis* op.122.

B1479. Wo.Ro. "Ernst Krenek: *Vier Stücke für Oboe und Klavier*." *Melos* 35:12 (December 1968): 494.

Review of the publication op.193.

B1480. Wörner, Karl H. "Ernst Krenek: *VII. Streichquartett*, op.96." *Zeitschrift für Musik* 115:5 (May 1954): 297-298.

Review of the miniature score published as Philharmonia 386.

B1481. ——. "Krenek, Ernst." In *Die Musik in Geschichte und Gegenwart*, hrsg. von Friedrich Blume. Vol.7 (Kassel: Bärenreiter, 1958): 1759-1763.

Biographical essay with list of works. Picture: op.92.

B1482. Wohlfarth, Siegfried. "Zur Meloskritik." *Melos* 7:4 (April 1928): 183-186.

Reaction to the brief joint review of *Jonny spielt auf* op.45 by Hans Mersmann, Hans Schultze-Ritter, Heinrich Strobel, and Lothar Windsperger in *Melos* 7:1 (January 1928): 24-25. Wohlfarth takes them to task for not fulfilling their duties as music critics.

B1483. Wolf, Johannes. "Altniederländische Kunst und Chormusik von Krenek und Hindemith." *Auftakt* (Prague) 8:5/6 (1928): 114-120.

Discusses the music of the middle ages and compares it to the new music, pointing out the search for new forms and techniques in the music of the two composers.

B1484. Wolff, Ernst Georg. "Offener Brief an Ernst Krenek." *Schweizerische Musikzeitung und Sängerblatt* 76:16/17 (September 1, 1936): 466-470.

Comments to Krenek's review (K374 and K382) of his book, and a defense of tonality.

B1485. Wolffers, Jules. "Music in Review." *The Jewish Advocate* (Boston) (November 4, 1938)

A discussion about Krenek and his Second piano concerto op.81 to be given its American premiere next week.

B1486. ——. "Music in Review." *The Jewish Advocate* (Boston) (November 11, 1938)

Review of the American premiere of the Second piano concerto op.81.

B1487. Wollstein, R.H. "Paris hisses Krenek's *Jonny*." *Musical America* (July? 1928)

Review of the unsuccessful Paris performance of op.45.

B1488. Wong, Carey Gordon. "Supergraphing sets and costumes for the *Life of Orestes*." *Theater Crafts* (September 1976): 20-23,71-77.

Discusses the construction of the scenery and costumes used in the Portland Opera production of op.60.

B1489. Wood, Hugh. "Unfamiliar composers." *Musical Times* 102:1416 (February 1961): 102.

Includes a review of the publication of *Symphonie Pallas Athene* op.137.

B1490. Worbs, Hans Christoph. "*Der goldene Bock*." *Musica* 18:4 (July-August 1964): 200-201.

Review of the premiere of the opera op.186. Picture.

B1491. ——. "Komponisten als Zeichner und Maler." *Du* (Zürich) 24 (December 1964): 71-80.

Briefly examines the characters of composers who paint, including Krenek. He concludes that "Krenek cannot dispense with the control afforded by the figurative in his own artistic creations, the amateur nature of which he explicitly stresses." Picture.

B1492. ——. "Ernst Krenek, *Jonny spielt auf*." In his *Welterfolge der modernen Oper*. (Berlin: Rembrandt Verlag, 1967): 38-49.

Discusses the opera and the effect its premiere had. Notes that it reflected the world of the later 1920s. Picture.

B1493. ——. "Ernst Kreneks *Così fan tutte*." *Musica* 24:5 (1970): 461-462. Picture.

Review of the premiere of *Das kommt davon* op.206. Picture.

B1494. ——. "Ernst Kreneks Deutsche Messe." *Musica* 26:1 (January-February 1972): 42-43.

Review of the premiere of *Gib uns den Frieden* mass op.208.

B1495. ——. "Von Komponisten, die malen, und Malern, die komponieren." *Musik und Medizin* 2:5 (1976): 46-52.

A discussion about composers who paint, including Krenek, as well as painters who compose music.

B1496. Wouters, Jos. "Congres over modern muziektheater te Hamburg." *Mens en melodie* 19:9 (Sept.1964): 260-262.

Review of the premiere of the opera *Der goldene Bock* op.186.

B1497. Würz, Anton. "Ernst Krenek ohne Musik." *Musica* 20:3 (May/June 1966): 146-147.

Review of the book *Prosa, Dramen, Verse* (K804).

B1498. Zenck, Claudia Maurer. "Der geschichtliche Ort von Kreneks 2. Symphonie." *Melos/NZ* 3:5 (September-October 1977): 392-400.
Analysis of op.12 and the events surrounding its premiere.

B1499. ———. "Dir Auseinandersetzung Adornos mit Krenek." *Studien zur Wertungsforschung* 12 (1979): 227-239.
Adorno's three discussions of Krenek are marked by his thorough knowledge of music. Krenek's early atonal works caused him to recognize Krenek as an advanced composer, but the music resisted his sociological interpretation.

B1500. ———. "Unbewältigte Vergangenheit: Kreneks *Karl V.* in Wien. Zur nicht bevorstehenden Wiener Erstaufführung." *Die Musikforschung* 32:3 (1979): 273-288.
Surveys the events which led to the cancellation of the Vienna premiere of the opera op.73 in 1934.

B1501. ———. "Lehrstück von der Zerstörung einer Oper; Kreneks *Karl V.* in Darmstadt." *Musica* 33:1 (January-February 1979): 52-53.
Discusses the events surrounding the composition of the opera op 73 and the subsequent cancellation of its premiere in Vienna in the context of a review of the recent Darmstadt production.

B1502. ———. *Ernst Krenek, ein Komponist im Exil.* (Wien: Lafite, 1980) 347 pp.
Discusses the life and works of Krenek with special emphasis on the period following 1938. His change to the twelve-tone technique with the opera *Karl V.* op.73 and the circumstances of its composition and first performance in Prague are examined. Later works are also examined; the Sixth string quartet op.78, *La corona* op.91, *Lamentatio Jeremiae prophetae* op.93, and *Symphonic elegy* op.105 are analyzed in detail. Krenek's adoption of the serial technique in the years following the war is also explored, including an analysis of *Sestina* op.161. Includes a comprehensive catalog of compositions and bibliography of the writings by Krenek. *See:* B229, B515, B688, B1184, B1185, B1509

B1503. ———. "Ernst Krenek, Wandlungen der Neuen Musik." *Musica* 34:2 (March-April 1980): 118-125.
Discusses Krenek's various styles of composition and his relationship to new music.

B1504. ———. "Musikalisches Welttheater: Kreneks *Karl V.*" *Oesterreichische Musikzeitschrift* 35:7/8 (July-August 1980): 370-372.
Discusses the opera and its concert performance at the Salzburg Festival.

B1505. ———. "Zur Vorgeschichte der Uraufführung von Mahlers *Zehnter Symphonie*." *Archiv für Musikwissenschaft* 39:4 (1982): 245-270.
Thorough examination of the events surrounding the creation of the symphony and leading to the premiere of Krenek's edition (W72) of the "Adagio" and "Purgatorio" movements. Discusses the roles played by Helene Berg (Alban's widow), Krenek, and Franz Schalk who conducted its premiere in Vienna. Includes many facsimile examples.

B1506. ———. "Bruch und Summe." In *Ernst Krenek,* hrsg. von Otto Kolleritsch. (B328) Studien zur Wertungsforschung, Bd.15. (Wien: Universal Edition, 1982): 174-188.

An exploration of the relationship between Krenek and Anton Webern surveying their opinions about one another. With a detailed examination of *Augenblick erinnert* op.201 dedicated to Webern's memory.

B1507. Zenck, Claudia Maurer. "Der verletzliche Komponist." In *Ernst Krenek*, hrsg. von Otto Kolleritsch. (B328) Studien zur Wertungsforschung, Bd.15. (Wien: Universal Edition, 1982): 15-28.

The transcript of a four-hour interview held on June 4, 1980 in a Heurige in the Burgenland discussing his stylistic change to the twelve-tone technique, his reactions to the young serialist composers who rejected him and his music during the 1950s, his feelings about chance and minimalist music, and his feelings regarding the misunderstanding of his music.

   a. ——. *Tagesanzeiger* (Zürich) (August 23, 1980): 47-48.
   Abbreviated.

   b. ——. *Süddeutsche Zeitung* no.194 (August 23/24, 1980): 16.
   Brief excerpts.

B1508. ——. "Kreneks Streichquartette mit dem Thouvenel Quartet." *Oesterreichische Musikzeitschrift* 37:5 (July-August 1982): 423-424.

Review of a series of concerts by the Thouvenel String Quartet of Krenek's eight *String quartets* in Vienna.

B1509. ——. "Diskussionen." *Musikforschung* 36:2 (April-June 1983): 107-109.

Reactions to the review of her book and the interpretation of the Krenek-Hindemith correspondence by Giselher Schubert (B1184 & 1185).

B1510. ——. "Schöne und 'scheene' Musik." *Musik-Konzepte* 39/40 (B895) (October 1984): 38-52.

Surveys and discusses the sketches and manuscripts of the opera *Karl V.* op.73.

B1511. ——. "50 Jahre nach; Kreneks *Karl V.* in Wien." *Oesterreichische Musikzeitschrift* 39:11 (November 1984): 594-596.

Review of a performance of the original version of the opera op.73 in its first staged production in Austria fifty years following its commission.

B1512. ——. "Aus dem Briefwechsel Webern - Krenek." *Musik-Konzept* Sonderband: *Anton Webern II* (November 1984): 151-161.

Transcription and annotation of letters from Anton Webern to Krenek during the period June 17, 1930 to April 18, 1940 discussing their music and performances of Krenek's music by Webern.

B1513. ——. "The ship loaded with faith and hope: Krenek's *Karl V.* and the Vienna politics of the Thirties." *Musical Quarterly* 71:2 (1985): 116-134.

Translation by Jeffery A. Bossin of an abridged version of a talk given at the Krenek Festival, University of California, Santa Barbara, April 8-15, 1979. Discusses the political and aesthetic background to *Karl V.* op.73, the first complete and full-length twelve-tone opera. "Krenek intended *Karl V.* as a type of festival play of Austrian regeneration" which aspired to a Christian corporate state. The premiere was canceled "not only as a result of a Nazi-based intrigue but also because of the opportunistic attitude of the man responsible for the production," Clemens Krauss.

B1514. ——. "Die zerbrochene Geschichte." *Melos* 48:1 (1986): 2-30.

Analysis and discussion of the *Eighth string quartet* op.230.

B1515. ——. "Ernst Krenek, Eine Porträtskizze." In *Komponisten des 20. Jahrhunderts in der Paul Sacher Stiftung.* (Basel: Paul Sacher Stiftung, 1986): 215-219.

A collection of personal impressions of her meetings with Krenek. Picture. Facsimile: *Symphonisches Stück* op.86 (p.220).

B1516. Zenck, Martin. "'Avantgarde' ohne Fortschrittsideologie; Bericht über das Krenek-Festival in Santa Barbara (Kalifornien)." *Musica* 33:4 (July-August 1979): 365-367.

Review of the festival held from April 8 to 15th which included performances of 48 Krenek compositions. The review focuses on *Sestina* op.161, *The Dissembler* op.229, *Spätlese* op.218, and *They knew what they wanted* op.227.

B1517. ——. "Zwischen Restitution der Vergangenheit und radikalem Gegenwartsbewusstsein; Bericht ueber das Krenek-Symposion zum Musikprotokoll des Steirischen Herbstes 1980." *Die Musikforschung* 34:3 (July-September 1981): 321-323.

Report on the concerts and lectures given during the Krenek Symposium held in Graz October 24-26, 1980.

B1518. ——. "Krenek als Problem der Avantgarde." In *Ernst Krenek*, hrsg. von Otto Kolleritsch. (B328) Studien zur Wertungsforschung, Bd.15. (Wien: Universal Edition, 1982): 216-237.

An exploration of Krenek's position in the avant garde, including a discussion of the events surrounding his rejection by the serialists at Darmstadt in the early 1950s and a survey of his later music.

B1519. ——. "Die Ungleichzeitigkeit des Neuen." *Musik-Konzepte* 39/40 (B895) (October 1984): 92-113.

Surveys and discusses the eight *String quartets* with many facsimiles of the manuscripts used for examples. Includes a detailed analysis of the first movement of the *Sixth quartet* op.78.

B1520. Zentner, W. "München." *Zeitschrift für Musik* 99:2 (February 1932): 150.

Review of a performance of Krenek's edition of Mahler's *Symphony no.10* (W72) by the Münchener Philharmoniker conducted by Herman Scherchen.

B1521. Zietz, Hermann. "Nordelbische Tage für neue Kirchenmusik." *Musik und Kirche* 42:1 (1972): 43-44.

Review of the premiere of the mass *Gib uns den Frieden* op.208.

B1522. Zimmermann, B.A. "Die Kölner Uraufführung des *Tarquin*." *Das Musikleben* 3:9 (September 1950): 261-262.

Review of the first performance of the chamber opera op.90 in German. Picture: scene.

B1523. ——. "Deutsche Erstaufführung der *Sinfonischen Elegie*." *Das Musikleben* 3:9 (September 1950): 262.

Review of first German performance of op.105 conducted by Jean Meylan in the Brühler Schlosskonzerten.

B1524. Zingel, Hans Joachim. "Kreneks *Harfensonate*." *Musica* 15:8 (August 1961): 463.

Brief review of the publication op.150.

B1525. Zschorlich, Paul. "[Review]." *Deutsche Zeitung* (December 3, 1928)
Review of the premiere of the three one-act operas *Der Diktator* op.49, *Das geheime Königreich* op.50, and *Schwergewicht* op.55.

a. ——. In *Experiment Krolloper, 1927-1931*, von Hans Curjel. Studien zur Kunst des neunzehnten Jahrhunderts, Bd.7. (Münich: Prestel-Verlag, 1975): 250-252.

B1526. Zuckerkandl, Viktor. "Neue Orchesterwerks in Berliner Konzerten." *Neue Freie Presse* (Vienna) (January 28, 1929)
Review of the premiere of *Kleine Symphonie* op.58.

B1527. ——. "*Leben des Orest*." *Neue Freie Presse* (Vienna) (January 27, 1930)
Reactions to Krenek's article "Pro domo" (K106) and the opera op.60.

B1528. ——. "Zeitgenössisches." *Neue Freie Presse* (Vienna) (April 4, 1931)
Reactions to Krenek's "Gesinnungsgenossen unter sich" (K134), a polemic against their reviews of *Leben des Orest* op.60. Krenek responded in "Nochmals: Gesinnungsgenossen unter sich" (K138).

B1529. Zürcher, Johann. "Alte und neue Ergänzungen zu den fragmentarischen Sonatensätzen Schuberts." *Die Musikforschung* 31:4 (October-December 1978): 467-474.
Briefly mentions Krenek's edition of the unfinished Schubert *Piano sonata*, D.840.

B1530. "*II. Klavier Sonate*, op.59." *Anbruch* 11:4 (April 1929): 186.
Announcement of the premiere.

Appendix A
Compositions : Titles and Genera

Compositions by Krenek are cited by opus number or, for works without opus number, by "W" number as appropriate. Titles of compositions appear in *Italics*, the distinctive titles of individual sections of a composition appear in Roman type, and the first lines of songs are quoted. This appendix also provides access to the compositions by their musical form and instrumentation. Genera classification entries appear in SMALL CAPS. Entries are arranged in alphabetical order; however, initial articles are ignored in filing.

The 104th Psalm, op.132
Das 156. Sonett des Petrarca, W36
A-cappella Chöre, op.47
Ab dafür, mit Anmat, op.234
Abend, W16
Abendstimmung, W17
"Aber Diandle," op.77a
"Aber die Winter!," op.48
Aber es gibt ein finster Geschlecht, op.32
Acco-music, op.225
ACCORDION MUSIC, op.183, op.225
Ach, was wird uns hier bereitet?, op.82
"Ach, wie es tönet," op.30
"Ad te levavi oculos meos," op.143
Adagio und Fuge, op.78a
Aegrotavit Ezechias, op.103
Agnus, op.204, op.208
Air, op.28, op.110
Albumblatt, op.228, W54
"Allein in sonniger Herbstlaube," op.71
Alleluja, laudate, op.89
Allelujah, op.15
Allemande, op.13a
"Alone in the sunny autumn foliage," op.71
Alpbach quintet, op.180
"Die Alpen werden von wilden Nomaden bewohnt," op.62
Alpenbewohner, op.62
Alpland dwellers, op.62
"The Alpland shelters mostly wildy behaving nomads," op.62
"Als ich noch Knabe war," op.56

"Always more softly you slip away," op.71
Am Molo in Triest, W3
"Am Tag nach meiner Heimkehr," op.62
Am Traunsee, W23
Amico Sartori, W100
Amor, Claudio Monteverdi, W105
An evening, op.30a
An sich, op.53
"And even if my life were entrenched," op.71
"And it came to pass that God," W89
"And now I know that it is Spring again," op.67
"And now the rapid train carries me homeward," op.62
"And over the mountains lies southland," op.62
"And when the springtime's flowers are slowly fading," op.35
Ein anderes, op.53
"Anima nostra sicut passer erepta est," op.89
Anniversary cantata, op.221
Annunciation, op.91
"Aperis tu manum tuam," op.149
Appassionato, W51
Arabeske, W56
Arc of life, op.234
Argumentum, op.122
Aria, op.80c
"As the day here through the window strays," op.67
Ascension, op.91

Choruses on Jacobean poems, op.87
"Christe Du Lamm Gottes," op.208
Christmas, W94
Christus, W1
Chrysomallos, op.186
"Cibavit illos ex adipe frumenti," op.149
Circle, chain and mirror, symphonic design, op.160
CLARINET MUSIC, op.157
Clausula, op.122
Cleaning out around St. Stephen, op.66
"Cold rain pelts bare fields," op.71
Communio, op.89, op.143
Concertino, op.27
Concerto grosso, op.10, op.25
Concerto; Cello, op.133, op.236; *Harp*, op.126; *Organ*, op.235; *Organ & string orchestra*, op.230; *Piano*, op.18, op.81, op.107, op.123; *2 pianos*, op.127; *Violin*, op.29, op.140
"Confitemini," W94
Conflict, op.234
Contrapuncti varii, op.122
A contrapuntal excursion through the centuries, op.90a
La corona, op.91
Corona, op.122
Corrente, op.80b
Credo, op.204, op.208
Crucifying, op.91
Cyrano de Bergerac, W32

"Da weht mich wieder jene Ahnung an," op.67
Dämmerung, op.30
Dancing toys, op.83
Danksagung, W94
"Dark and narrow are ther streets between the houses," op.62
Dark waters, op.125
Dass Angst uns, op.97
Dass durch Gefahr, op.97
"Dass Liebe Raum noch hat," op.71
Dass Wissen, op.97
Day of rain, op.62
De! Dimmi tu, Francesco Landini, W103
"De profundis," W94
Decision, op.62
Deep Sea, W85
Deigne at my hands this crown of prayer and praise, op.91
The deliverance of Hezekiah, op.103
"Den Geborenen schreckt das Licht der Welt," op.189
"Den Himmel diesseits trüben die Wolken," W57

"Depuis ces temps troublés d'adieux et de retours," op.30a
Des Glaubens beraubt, op.194
Design from darkness, op.142
Deutsche Messe (Ordinarium), op.204
Deutsche Messgesänge zum 29. Sonntag im Jahreskreis, W101
The dictator, op.49
"Dies wär ein Ende," op.30
Der Diktator, op.49
The dissembler, op.229
"Distant ray that shineth near," op.67
Divertimento, op.23
Divertimento, op.158
"Divites egerunt et esurierunt," op.149
Do our thoughts in spite of muteness have any meaning?, op.191
Do you know the moment, op.215
Donna lombarda, op.77b
Doppelfuge, op.1a, W33, W50
Doppelt beflügeltes Band, op.207
Double concerto, op.124
Double fugue, op.1a, W33, W50
Dream sequence, op.224
Der 30-jährige Krieg, W3
Drinking song, op.71
"Du blühst schön, schöner als sonst," op.57
"Du ewig Wandelbare," op.9
Du kannst dich zurückhalten von den Leiden der Welt, op.82
Du schöner Vogel fliegst, op.30
Dunkle Wasser, op.125
Duo, op.209
Durch die Nacht, op.67

"E'en the dead lie at an angle," op.62
Early pieces, W1, W2, W3
The Earth abideth, op.174
"The earth is full of thy riches," op.174
Easter, W94
Easy pieces, op.146
Echoes from Austria, op.166
"Effuderunt sanguinem sanctorum," op.89
Egregii, carissimi, op.155
"Ehre sei Gott in der Höhe und Friede," op.208
Ehrfurcht, op.30
Eight column line, op.85
"Ein einfaches lichtes Kleid," op.19
"Einflüstrerin, Stimme," op.189
"Einmal, einmal in vielen hunderttausend Tagen," op.71
Einsame Rose, W6
"Einziger Augenblick," op.189
ELECTRONIC MUSIC, op.152, op.185, op.190, op.207, op.209, op.212

Orga-nastro, op.212
Organologia, op.180.5
Orpheus und Eurydike, op.21
Ostern, W94
Our wine, op.62
"Out of the depths," W94
Outlook toward the south, op.62

Paesana, op.80c
Pageant in Paso Robles, op.134
Pallas Athene weeps, op.144
Pallas Athene weint, op.144
Parabel, op.196
Parabola, op.196
Pariser Einzugsmarsch, op.1814, W2
Parvula corona musicalis, op.122
Pasiphaë, op.227
"Passer invenit sibi domum," op.143
Patience, op.112
Peace, op.112
Peaceful mood, op.83
Die Peitsche, op.169
Pentagramm, op.163
Perspectives, op.199
Perspektiven, op.199
Pfingst-Oratorium, op.152
Phantasie, op.65
Phantasiestück, op.135
PIANO MUSIC, op.1, op.3, op.13, op.39,
    op.70, op.79, op.80c, 83, op.100,
    op.110, op.120, op.136, op.139, op.166,
    op.168, op.173, op.197, op.207, W1,
    W2, W3, W4, W11, W33, W50, W51,
    W52, W56, W65, W67, W71, W76,
    W87, W88 *See also* Concerto, Piece,
    Sonata, Sonatina, Suite
Piano piece in eleven parts, op.197
Piano pieces, op.110
PIANO WITH 1 STRING, op.3, op.99, op.117,
    op.135, W30, W54, W61, W80
PIANO WITH 1 WIND, op.28, op.85, op.147,
    op.148, op.171, op.193, op.198, W85,
    W96;
Piece for H. H. Stuckenschmidt, W96
Piece, piano, W78, W79
Piece, violin & piano, W80
Pieces, op.193, op.198, W51, W56
"Plötzlich wird es schwarz zwischen den
    weissen Gipfeln," op.62
Politics, op.62
Politik, op.62
Poppea, op.80a
Potpourri, op.54
Praeludium, op.28
Préambule, W56
Predetermined configuration of sound,
    op.191

"Preiset den Herrn," op.195
Prelude, W87
Princeton study, W93
Profiles, op.203
Proprium für das Dreifaltigkeitsfest, op.195
Proprium für Mariae Geburt, op.202
Proprium Missae for Trinity Sunday, op.195
*Proprium missae in domenica tertia in
    quadragesima,* op.143
*Proprium missae in festo SS. Innocentium
    martyrum (die 28 Decembris),* op.89
*Proprium Missae per a le festa de la nativitat
    de la mare de Deu (8 de setembre),* op.202
Psalm 8, op.89
Psalm 33, op.149
Psalm 41, op.149
Psalm 72, W49
Psalm 78, op.89
Psalm 80, op.149
Psalm 93, W49
Psalm 103, op.138, op.149
Psalm 104, op.132
Psalm 105, W94
Psalm 112, op.89, op.149
Psalm 116, op.149
Psalm 118, W94
Psalm 123, op.89
Psalm 126, op.138, W49
Psalm 130, W94
Psalm 136, W94
Psalmenverse zur Kommunion, op.149
Psalmverse, W92

Quaestio temporis, op.170
"Quemadmodum," op.149
A question of time, op.170
"Qui manducat panem meum," op.149
Quintet, flute, clarinet, oboe, bassoon & horn,
    op.130
Quintina über die fünf Vokale, op.191
Quintona, op.190
"Quoniam confirmata est," op.149

Die Rache des verhöhnten Liebhabers, op.41
Das Rad der Welt dreht rätselhafter
    Zufall, op.161
Rätselspiel, op.9
Räume, op.9
Rays of warmth, op.142
Regentag, op.62
Reinigung, W43
Die Reise über den Ozean, W1
Reisebuch aus den österreichischen Alpen,
    op.62
Reiselied, W41

Appendix B
Writings : Titles

The titles of Krenek's writings are arranged in alphabetical order; however, initial articles are ignored in filing. The "K" number following a title refers to the "Writings" chapter. Titles which consist entirely of the name of one of Krenek's compositions are excluded; they are cited under the entry for the work in the "Compositions" chapter. Titles of books by Krenek appear in *Italics*, while all other titles appear in Roman type.

Aber auch dieses, K182
Accordion, K898
Acht Tage Kanada, K462
Das Aergernis der Unsterblichkeit, K551
Aischylos in Breitensee, K378
Alban Berg zum Gedächtnis, K358
Alban Berg's *Lulu*, K444
Alle spalle dei giovani, K646
Alpine Randbemerkungen, K326
Als Nachspeise, K216
Den alsidige komponist, K746
Alt und neu im graphischen Bild der Musik, K792
Alter Mann, junge Frau, K200
Altes und neues China, K212
Am Alpensüdrand bemerkt, K148
Am Grabe, K344
America's influence on its émigré composers, K730
American experiences, K494
American mixed grill, K482
Amerika, K565
Die Amerika Reise, K518
Amerikanische Landschaft, K478
Amerikanische Städtebilder, K470, K473, K479
Amerikanischer Musiksommer, K729
Amerikanisches Barock, K277
Amerikanisches Filmwesen, K474
Amerikas Einfluss auf eingewanderte Komponisten, K730
An exceptional musician: Kurt Frederick, K604

Analyse der *Altenberg-Lieder* Bergs, K415
Announcement of the ISCM concert, K530, K542
Anpassung an Amerika, K558
Ansprache, K878
Ansprache an einem Abend zeitgenössische Musik, K273
Ansprache bei der Trauerfeier für Karl Kraus, K408
Ansprache für die Gedenkstunde in der Wiener Staatsoper am 13. Maerz 1988, K933
Ansprache zum Abend des zeitgenössischer Musik im Oesterreichischen Studios, K302
Ant story, K498
Anton von Webern, a Profile, K737
Anton Webern, K929
Anton Weberns magisches Quadrat, K811
Anton Weberns Skizzenbücher, K840
Antwort an Paul Bekker, K206
Apologie, K346
The appeal to conscience, K544
Appell an das Gewissen, K544
Arbeiterlyrik, K149
Arbeitsprobleme des Komponisten, K124
Arme Musikwissenschaft?, K159
Arnold Schönberg, K268
Arnold Schönberg 75år, K580
Arnold Schoenberg at seventy, K541
Arnold Schoenbergs *Orchestervariationen* op.31, K815
Art and nationalism, K246

General Index

Entries are arranged in alphabetical order. Compositions by Krenek are cited by opus number or, for works without opus number, by "W" number as appropriate. References to citations in the "Writings" chapter are identified by "K" number for writings by Krenek. References to citations in the "Bibliography" chapter are identified by "B" number for writings about Krenek.

About the Compiler

GARRETT H. BOWLES received his Ph.D. in musicology from Stanford University while he was Head Music Cataloger. He is presently Music Librarian and Curator of the Ernst Krenek Archive at the University of California, San Diego, where he is also Adjunct Assistant Professor of Music.